SPOKEN LANGUAGE UNDERSTANDING

SPOKEN LANGUAGE UNDERSTANDING

SYSTEMS FOR EXTRACTING SEMANTIC INFORMATION FROM SPEECH

Gokhan Tur

Microsoft Speech Labs, Microsoft Research, USA

Renato De Mori

McGill University, Montreal, Canada and University of Avignon, France

WILEY

A John Wiley and Sons, Ltd, Publication

This edition first published 2011

Registered office
John Wiley & Sons Ltd, The Atrium, Southern Gate, Chichester, West Sussex, PO19 8SQ, United Kingdom

For details of our global editorial offices, for customer services and for information about how to apply for permission to reuse the copyright material in this book please see our website at www.wiley.com.

Library of Congress Cataloging-in-Publication Data

Spoken language understanding : systems for extracting semantic information from speech / edited by Gokhan Tur, Renato De Mori.
p. cm.
Includes bibliographical references and index.
ISBN 978-0-470-68824-3 (hardback)
1. Speech processing systems. 2. Semantics. 3. Discourse analysis. 4. Corpora (Linguistics)
I. Tur, Gokhan. II. De Mori, Renato. III. Title.
P95.3.S665 2010
006.4′54–dc22

2010051228

A catalogue record for this book is available from the British Library.

Print ISBN: 9780470688243
E-PDF ISBN: 9781119992707
O-book ISBN: 9781119992691
E-Pub ISBN: 9781119993940
Mobi ISBN: 9781119993957

Set in 10/12pt Times Roman by Thomson Digital, Noida, India.

In memory of Fred Jelinek (1932–2010)

Contents

PART 2 SPOKEN LANGUAGE UNDERSTANDING FOR HUMAN/HUMAN CONVERSATIONS

List of Contributors

Alex Acero received the degrees of MS from the Polytechnic University of Madrid, Spain, in 1985, MS from Rice University, Houston, TX, in 1987, and PhD from Carnegie Mellon University, Pittsburgh, PA, in 1990, all in electrical engineering. He worked in Apple Computers Advanced Technology Group from 1990 to 1991. In 1992, he joined Telefonica I+D, Madrid, as Manager of the Speech Technology Group. Since 1994, he has been with Microsoft Research, Redmond, WA, where he is currently a Research Area Manager directing an organization with 70 engineers conducting research in audio, speech, multimedia, communication, natural language, and information retrieval. He is also an affiliate Professor of Electrical Engineering at the University of Washington, Seattle. Dr. Acero is author of the books *Acoustical and Environmental Robustness in Automatic Speech Recognition* (Kluwer, 1993) and *Spoken Language Processing* (Prentice-Hall, 2001), has written invited chapters in four edited books and 200 technical papers. He holds 53 US patents.

Dr. Acero has served the IEEE Signal Processing Society as Vice President Technical Directions (2007–2009), 2006 Distinguished Lecturer, as a member of the Board of Governors (2004–2005), as an Associate Editor for the IEEE Signal Processing Letters (2003–2005) and the IEEE Transactions on Audio, Speech and Language Processing (2005–2007), and as a member of the editorial board of the IEEE Journal of Selected Topics in Signal Processing (2006–2008) and the IEEE Signal Processing Magazine (2008–2010). He also served as member (1996–2000) and Chair (2000–2002) of the Speech Technical Committee of the IEEE Signal Processing Society. He was Publications Chair of ICASSP'98, Sponsorship Chair of the 1999 IEEE Workshop on Automatic Speech Recognition and Understanding, and General Co-chair of the 2001 IEEE Workshop on Automatic Speech Recognition and Understanding. Since 2004, Dr. Acero, along with co-authors Dr. Huang and Dr. Hon, has been using proceeds from their textbook *Spoken Language Processing* to fund the IEEE Spoken Language Processing Student Travel Grant for the best ICASSP student papers in the speech area. Dr. Acero is a member of the editorial board of Computer Speech and Language and he served as a member of Carnegie Mellon University Deans Leadership Council for College of Engineering.

Frédéric Béchet is a researcher in the field of Speech and Natural Language Processing. His research activities are mainly focused on Spoken Language Understanding for both Spoken Dialogue Systems and Speech Mining applications.

After studying Computer Science at the University of Marseille, he obtained his PhD in Computer Science in 1994 from the University of Avignon, France. Since then he worked at the Ludwig Maximilian University in Munich, Germany, as a Professor Assistant at the University of Avignon, France, as an invited professor at AT&T Research Shannon Lab in Florham Park, New Jersey, USA, and he is currently a full Professor of Computer Science at the Aix Marseille Université in France. Frédéric Béchet is the author/co-author of over 60 refereed papers in journals and international conferences.

Ciprian Chelba received his Diploma Engineer degree in 1993 from the Faculty of Electronics and Telecommunications at Politehnica University, Bucuresti, Romania, and the degrees of MS in 1996 and PhD in 2000 from the Electrical and Computer Engineering Department at the Johns Hopkins University. He is a research scientist with Google and has previously worked at Microsoft Research. His research interests are in statistical modeling of natural language and speech, as well as related areas such as machine learning. Recent projects include large scale language modeling for Google Search by Voice, and indexing, ranking and snippeting of speech content. He is a member of the IEEE, and has served one full term on the IEEE Signal Processing Society Speech and Language Technical Committee (2006–2008), among other community activities.

Renato De Mori received a doctorate degree in Electronic Engineering from Politecnico di Torino (Italy). He is a Fellow of the IEEE Computer Society and has been distinguished lecturer of the IEEE Signal Processing Society.

He has been Professor and Chairman at the University of Turin (Italy) and at McGill University, School of Computer Science (Monteral, Canada), professor at the University of Avignon (France). He is now emeritus professor at McGill University and at the University of Avignon. His major contributions have been in Automatic Speech Recognition and Understanding, Signal Processing, Computer Arithmetic, Software Engineering and Human/Machine Interfaces.

He is Associated Editor of the IEEE Transactions on Audio Speech and Language Processing, has been Chief Editor of SPEECH COMMUNICATION (2003–2005), Associate Editor of the IEEE Transactions on Pattern Analysis and Machine Intelligence (1998–1992). He has been a member of the editorial board of Computer Speech and Language since 1988.

Professor De Mori has been a member of the Executive Advisory Board at the IBM Toronto Lab, Scientific Advisor at France Télécom R&D, Chairman of the Computer and Information Systems Committee, Natural Sciences and Engineering Council of Canada, Vice-President R&D, Centre de Recherche en Informatique de Montral.

He has been a member of the IEEE Speech Technical Committee (1984–1987, 2003–2006), the Interdisciplinary Board, Canadian Foundation for Innovation, Interdisciplinary Committee for Canadian chairs. He has been involved in many Canadian and European projects and has been scientific leader of the LUNA European project on spoken language understanding (2006–2009).

Li Deng received his Bachelor degree from the University of Science and Technology of China (with the Guo Mo-Ruo Award), and received the degree of PhD from the University of Wisconsin, Madison (with the Jerzy E. Rose Award). In 1989, he joined the Department of Electrical and Computer Engineering, University of Waterloo, Ontario, Canada as an Assistant Professor, where he became a Full Professor in 1996.

From 1992 to 1993, he conducted sabbatical research at Laboratory for Computer Science, Massachusetts Institute of Technology, Cambridge, Mass, and from 1997 to 1998, at ATR Interpreting Telecommunications Research Laboratories, Kyoto, Japan. In 1999, he joined Microsoft Research, Redmond, WA as a Senior Researcher, where he is currently a Principal Researcher. He is also an Affiliate Professor in the Department of Electrical Engineering at

University of Washington, Seattle. His past and current research activities include automatic speech and speaker recognition, spoken language identification and understanding, speech-to-speech translation, machine translation, statistical methods and machine learning, neural information processing, deep-structured learning, machine intelligence, audio and acoustic signal processing, statistical signal processing and digital communication, human speech production and perception, acoustic phonetics, auditory speech processing, auditory physiology and modeling, noise robust speech processing, speech synthesis and enhancement, multimedia signal processing, and multimodal human–computer interaction. In these areas, he has published over 300 refereed papers in leading international conferences and journals, 12 book chapters, and has given keynotes, tutorials, and lectures worldwide. He has been granted over 30 US or international patents in acoustics, speech/language technology, and signal processing.

He is a Fellow of the Acoustical Society of America, and a Fellow of the IEEE. He has authored or co-authored three books in speech processing and learning. He serves on the Board of Governors of the IEEE Signal Processing Society (2008–2010), and as Editor-in-Chief for the IEEE Signal Processing Magazine (2009–2012), which ranks consistently among the top journals with the highest citation impact. According to the Thomson Reuters Journal Citation Report, released June 2010, the SPM has ranked first among all IEEE publications (125 in total) and among all publications within the Electrical and Electronics Engineering Category (245 in total) in terms of its impact factor.

Olivier Galibert is an engineer in the Information Systems Evaluation group at LNE which he joined in 2009. He recieved his engineering degree in 1994 from the Ecole Nationale des Mines de Nancy, France and his PhD in 2009 from the University Paris – Sud 11, France. Previously to his joining LNE, he participated at NIST in the Smartspace effort to help create a standard infrastructure for pervasive computing in intelligent rooms. He then went to the Spoken Language Processing group at LIMSI where he participated in system development for speech recognition and has been a prime contributor in speech understanding, named entity detection, question answering and dialogue systems.

Now at LNE, he is a co-leader of varied evaluations in the domain of speech recognition, speaker diariation, named entity detection and question answering. His current activities focus on annotation visualization and edition tools, evaluation tools and advanced metrics development. He is the author/co-author of over 30 refereed papers in journals and national and international conferences.

Mazin Gilbert (http://www.research.att.com/~mazin/) is the Executive Director of Speech and Language Technologies at AT&T Labs-Research. He has a Ph.D. in Electrical and Electronic Engineering, and an MBA for Executives from the Wharton Business School. Dr. Gilbert has over 20 years of research experience working in industry at Bell Labs and AT&T Labs and in academia at Rutgers University, Liverpool University, and Princeton University.

Dr. Gilbert is responsible for the advancement of AT&T's technologies in areas of interactive speech and multimodal user interfaces. This includes fundamental and forward looking research in automatic speech recognition, spoken language understanding, mobile voice search, multimodal user interfaces, and speech and web analytics.

He has over 100 publications in speech, language and signal processing and is the author of the book entitled, Artificial Neural Networks for Speech Analysis/Synthesis (Chapman & Hall, 1994). He holds 40 US patents and is a recipient of several national and international awards including the Most Innovative Award from SpeechTek 2003 and the AT&T Science and Technology Award, 2006.

He is a Senior Member of the IEEE; Board Member, LifeBoat Foundation (2010); Member, Editorial Board for Signal Processing Magazine (2009–present); Member, ISCA Advisory Council (2007–present); Chair, IEEE/ACL workshop on Spoken Language Technology (2006); Chair, SPS Speech and Language Technical Committee (2004–2006); Teaching Professor, Rutgers University (1998–2001) and Princeton University (2004–2005); Chair, Rutgers University CAIP Industrial Board (2003–2006); Associate Editor, IEEE Transaction on Speech and Audio Processing (1995–1999); Chair, 1999 Workshop on Automatic Speech Recognition and Understanding; Member, SPS Speech Technical Committee (2000–2004); Technical Chair and Speaker for several international conferences including ICASSP, SpeechTek, AVIOS, and Interspeech.

Dilek Hakkani-Tür is a senior researcher at ICSI speech group. Prior to joining ICSI, she was a senior technical staff member in the Voice Enabled Services Research Department at AT&T Labs – Research at Florham Park, NJ. She received her BSc degree from Middle East Technical University, in 1994, and MSc and PhD degrees from Bilkent University, Department of Computer Engineering, in 1996 and 2000, respectively. Her PhD thesis is on statistical language modeling for agglutinative languages. She worked on machine translation during her visit to Carnegie Mellon University, Language Technologies Institute in 1997, and her visit to Johns Hopkins University, Computer Science Department, in 1998. In 1998 and 1999, she visited SRI International, Speech Technology and Research Labs, and worked on using lexical and prosodic information for information extraction from speech. In 2000, she worked in Natural Sciences and Engineering Faculty of Sabanci University, Turkey.

Her research interests include natural language and speech processing, spoken dialogue systems, and active and unsupervised learning for language processing. She has 10 patents and has co-authored more than 100 papers in natural language and speech processing. She is the receipent of three best paper awards for her work on active learning, from IEEE Signal Processing Society (with Giuseppe Riccardi), ISCA (with Gokhan Tur and Robert Schapire) and EURASIP (with Gokhan Tur and Robert Schapire). She is a member of ISCA, IEEE, Association for Computational Linguistics. She was an associate editor of IEEE Transactions on Audio, Speech and Language Processing between 2005 and 2008 and is an elected member of the IEEE Speech and Language Technical Committee (2009–2012) and a member of the HLT advisory board.

Timothy J. Hazen received the degrees of SB (1991), SM (1993), and PhD (1998) from the Department of Electrical Engineering and Computer Science at the Massachusetts Institute of Technology (MIT). From 1998 until 2007, Dr. Hazen was a Research Scientist in the Spoken Language Systems Group at the MIT Computer Science and Artificial Intelligence Laboratory. Since 2007, he has been a member of the Human Language Technology Group at MIT Lincoln Laboratory.

Dr. Hazen is a Senior Member of the IEEE and has served as an Associate Editor for the IEEE Transactions on Speech and Audio Processing (2004–2009) and as a member of the IEEE Signal Processing Society's Speech and Language Technical Committee (2008–2010). His research interests are in the areas of speech recognition and understanding, audio indexing, speaker identification, language identification, multi-lingual speech processing, and multi-modal speech processing.

Yun-Cheng Ju received a BS in electrical engineering from National Taiwan University in 1984 and a Master's and PhD in computer science from the University of Illinois at Urbana-Champaign in 1990 and 1992, respectively. He joined Microsoft in 1994. His research interests include spoken dialogue systems, natural language processing, language modeling, and voice search. Prior to joining Microsoft, he worked at Bell Labs for two years. He is the author/co-authorof over 30 journal and conference papers and has filed over 40 US and international patents.

Lori Lamel is a senior CNRS research scientist in the Spoken Language Processing group at LIMSI which she joined in October 1991. She received her PhD degree in EECS in May 1988 from the Massachusetts Institute of Technology. Her principal research activities are in speech recognition; lexical and phonological modeling; spoken language systems and speaker and language identification. She has been a prime contributor to the LIMSI participations in DARPA benchmark evaluations and developed the LIMSI American English pronunciation lexicon.

She has been involved in many European projects and is currently leading the speech processing activities in the Quaero program. Dr. Lamel is a member of the Speech Communication Editorial Board and the Interspeech International Advisory Council. She was a member of the IEEE Signal Processing Society's Speech Technical Committee from 1994 to 1998, and the Advisory Committee of the AFCP, the IEEE James L. Flanagan Speech and Audio Processing Award Committee (2006–2009) and the EU-NSF Working Group for Spoken-word Digital Audio Collections. She has over 230 reviewed publications and is co-recipient of the 2004 ISCA Best Paper Award for a paper in the Speech Communication Journal.

Yang Liu received the degrees of BS and MS degrees from Tsinghua University, Beijing, China, in 1997 and 2000, respectively, and the PhD degree in electrical and computer engineering from Purdue University, West Lafayette, IN, in 2004.

She was a Researcher at the International Computer Science Institute, Berkeley, CA, from 2002 to 2005. She has been an Assistant Professor in Computer Science at the University of Texas at Dallas, Richardson, since 2005. Her research interests are in the area of speech and language processing.

I. Dan Melamed is a Principal Member of Technical Staff at AT&T Labs – Research. He holds a PhD in Computer and Information Science from the University of Pennsylvania (1998). He has over 40 publications in the areas of machine learning and natural language processing, including the book *Empirical Methods for Exploiting Parallel Texts* (MIT Press, 2001). Prior to joining AT&T, Dr. Melamed was a member of the computer science faculty at New York University.

Roberto Pieraccini has been at the leading edge of spoken dialogue technology for more than 25 years, both in research as well as in the development of commercial applications. He worked at CSELT, Bell Laboratories, AT&T Labs, SpeechWorks, IBM Research and he is currently the CTO of SpeechCycle. He has authored more than 120 publications in different areas of human–machine communication. Dr. Pieraccini is a Fellow of ISCA and IEEE.

Matthew Purver is a lecturer in Human Interaction in the School of Electronic Engineering and Computer Science at Queen Mary, University of London. His research interests lie in the computational semantics and pragmatics of dialogue, both for human/computer interaction and for the automatic understanding of natural human/human dialogue. From 2004 to 2008 he was a researcher at CSLI, Stanford University, where he worked on various dialogue system projects including the in-car CHAT system and the CALO meeting assistant.

Bhuvana Ramabhadran is the Manager of the Speech Transcription and Synthesis Research Group at the IBM T. J. Watson Center, Yorktown Heights, NY. Upon joining IBM in 1995, she made significant contributions to the ViaVoice line of products focusing on acoustic modeling including acoustics- based baseform determination, factor analysis applied to covariance modeling, and regression models for Gaussian likelihood computation.

She has served as the Principal Investigator of two major international projects: the NSF-sponsored MALACH Project, developing algorithms for transcription of elderly, accented speech from Holocaust survivors, and the EU-sponsored TC-STAR Project, developing algorithms for recognition of EU parliamentary speeches. She was the Publications Chair of the 2000 ICME Conference, organized the HLT-NAACL 2004 Workshop on Interdisciplinary Approaches to Speech Indexing and Retrieval, and a 2007 Special Session on Speech Transcription and Machine Translation at the 2007 ICASSP in Honolulu, HI. Her research interests include speech recognition algorithms, statistical signal processing, pattern recognition, and biomedical engineering.

Giuseppe Riccardi heads the Signal and Interactive Systems Lab at University of Trento, Italy. He received his Laurea degree in Electrical Engineering and Master in Information Technology, in 1991, from the University of Padua and CEFRIEL/Politechnic of Milan (Italy), respectively. From 1990 to 1993 he collaborated with Alcatel-Telettra Research Laboratories (Milan, Italy). In 1995 he received his PhD in Electrical Engineering from the Department of Electrical Engineering at the University of Padua, Italy. From 1993 to 2005, he was at AT&T Bell Laboratories and then AT&T Labs-Research where he worked in the Speech and Language Processing Lab. In 2005 joined the faculty of University of Trento (Italy). He is affiliated with Engineering School, the Department of Information Engineering and Computer Science and Center for Mind/Brain Sciences.

He has co-authored more than 100 papers and 30 patents in the field of speech processing, speech recognition, understanding and machine translation. His current research interests are language modeling and acquisition, language understanding, spoken/multimodal dialogue, affective computing, machine learning and machine translation.

Prof. Riccardi has been on the scientific and organizing committee of Eurospeech, Interspeech, ICASSP, NAACL, EMNLP, ACL an EACL. He has co-organized the IEEE ASRU Workshop in 1993, 1999, 2001 and was its General Chair in 2009. He has been the Guest Editor of the IEEE Special Issue on Speech-to-Speech Machine Translation. He has been a founder and Editorial Board member of the ACM Transactions of Speech and Language Processing. He has been elected member of the IEEE SPS Speech Technical Committee (2005–2008). He is a member of ACL, ISCA, ACM and Fellow of IEEE. He has received many national and international awards and more recently the Marie Curie Excellence Grant by the European Commission, 2009 IEEE SPS Best Paper Award and IBM Faculty Award.

Sophie Rosset is a senior CNRS researcher in the Spoken Language Processing group at LIMSI which she joined in May 1994. She received her PhD degree in Computer Science from the University Paris – Sud 11, France, in 2000. Her research activities focus mainly on interactive and spoken question-answering systems, including dialogue management and named entities detection.

She has been prime contributor to the LIMSI participations in QAST evaluations (QA@CLEF) and she is the leader for the spoken language processing group participation in the Quaero program evaluations for question-answering system on Web data and named entity detection. She is responsible of the Named Entity activities within the Quaero program and the French Edylex project. She has been involved in different European projects, most recently the Chil and Vital projects. She is author/co-author of over 60 refereed papers in journals and international conferences.

Murat Saraclar received his BS in 1994 from the Electrical and Electronics Engineering Department at Bilkent University and the degrees of MS in 1997 and PhD in 2001 from the Electrical and Computer Engineering Department at the Johns Hopkins University. He is an associate professor at the Electrical and Electronic Engineering Department of Bogazici University. From 2000 to 2005, he was with AT&T Labs – Research. His main research interests include all aspects of speech recognition, its applications, as well as related fields such as speech and language processing, human/computer interaction and machine learning. He was a member of the IEEE Signal Processing Society Speech and Language Technical Committee (2007–2009). He is currently serving as an associate editor for IEEE Signal Processing Letters and he is on the editorial boards of Computer Speech and Language, and Language Resources and Evaluation. He is a Member of the IEEE.

David Suendermann has been working on various fields of speech technology research over the last 10 years. He has worked at multiple industrial and academic institutions including Siemens (Munich), Columbia University (New York), USC (Los Angeles), UPC (Barcelona), RWTH (Aachen), and is currently the Principal Speech Scientist of SpeechCycle. He has authored more than 60 publications and patents and holds a PhD from the Bundeswehr University in Munich.

Gokhan Tur was born in Ankara, Turkey in 1972. He received his BS, MS, and PhD degrees from the Department of Computer Science, Bilkent University, Turkey in 1994, 1996, and 2000, respectively. Between 1997 and 1999, he visited the Center for Machine Translation of CMU, then the Department of Computer Science of Johns Hopkins University, and then the Speech Technology and Research Lab of SRI International. He worked at AT&T Labs – Research from 2001 to 2006 and at the Speech Technology and Research (STAR) Lab of SRI International from 2006 to June 2010. He is currently with Microsoft working as a principal scientist. His research interests include spoken language understanding (SLU), speech and language processing, machine learning, and information retrieval and extraction. He has co-authored more than 75 papers published in refereed journals and presented at international conferences.

Dr. Tur is also the recipient of the Speech Communication Journal Best Paper awards by ISCA for 2004–2006 and by EURASIP for 2005–2006. Dr. Tur is the organizer of the HLT-NAACL 2007 Workshop on Spoken Dialog Technologies, and the HLT-NAACL 2004 and

AAAI 2005 Workshops on SLU, and the editor of the Speech Communication Special Issue on SLU in 2006. He is also the Spoken Language Processing Area Chair for IEEE ICASSP 2007, 2008, and 2009 conferences, Spoken Dialog Area Chair for HLT-NAACL 2007 conference, Finance Chair for IEEE/ACL SLT 2006 and SLT 2010 workshops, and SLU Area Chair for IEEE ASRU 2005 workshop. Dr. Tur is a senior member of IEEE, ACL, and ISCA, and is currently an associate editor for the IEEE Transactions on Audio, Speech, and Language Processing journal, and was a member of IEEE Signal Processing Society (SPS), Speech and Language Technical Committee (SLTC) for 2006–2008.

Ye-Yi Wang received a BS in 1985 and an MS in 1988, both in in computer science from Shanghai Jiao Tong University, as well as an MS in computational linguistics in 1992 and a PhD in human language technology in 1998, both from Carnegie Mellon University. He joined Microsoft Research in 1998.

His research interests include spoken dialogue systems, natural language processing, language modeling, statistical machine translation, and machine learning. He served on the editorial board of the Chinese Contemporary Linguistic Theory series. He is a coauthor of Introduction to Computational Linguistics (China Social Sciences Publishing House, 1997), and he has published over 40 journal and conference papers. He is a Senior Member of IEEE.

Dong Yu joined Microsoft Corporation in 1998 and Microsoft Speech Research Group in 2002, where he is a researcher. He holds a PhD degree in computer science from the University of Idaho, an MS degree in computer science from Indiana University at Bloomington, an MS degree in electrical engineering from Chinese Academy of Sciences, and a BS degree (with honors) in electrical engineering from Zhejiang University (China). His current research interests include speech processing, robust speech recognition, discriminative training, spoken dialogue systems, voice search technology, machine learning, and pattern recognition. He has published more than 70 papers in these areas and is the inventor/coinventor of more than 40 granted/pending patents.

Dr. Dong Yu is a senior member of IEEE, a member of ACM, and a member of ISCA. He is currently serving as an associate editor of IEEE signal processing magazine and the lead guest editor of IEEE Transactions on Audio, Speech, and Language Processing – Special Issue on Deep Learning for Speech and Language Processing. He is also serving as a guest professor at the University of Science and Technology of China.

Foreword

Speech processing has been an active field of research and development for more than a half-century. While including technologies such as coding, recognition and synthesis, a long-term dream has been to create machines which are capable of interacting with humans by voice. This implies the capability of not merely recognizing what is said, but of understanding the meaning of spoken language. Many of us believe such a capability would fundamentally change the manner in which people use machines.

The subject of understanding and meaning has received much attention from philosophers over the centuries. When one person speaks with another, how can we know whether the intended message was understood? One approach is via a form of the Turing Test: evaluate whether the communication was correctly understood on the basis of whether the recipient responded in an expected and appropriate manner. For example, if one requested, from a cashier, change of a dollar in quarters, then one evaluates whether the message was understood by examining the returned coins. This has been distinguished as linguistic performance, i.e. the actual use of language in concrete actions.

This new book, compiled and edited by Tur and De Mori, describes and organizes the latest advances in spoken language understanding (SLU). They address SLU for human/machine interaction and for exploiting large databases of spoken human/human conversations.

While there are many textbooks on speech or natural language processing, there are no previous books devoted wholly to SLU. Methods have been described piece meal in other books and in many scientific publications, but never gathered together in one place with this singular focus. This book fills a significant gap, providing the community with a distillation of the wide variety of up-to-date methods and tasks involving SLU. A common theme throughout the book is to attack targeted SLU tasks rather than attempting to devise a universal solution to "understanding and meaning."

Pioneering research in spoken language understanding systems was intensively conducted in the U.S. during the 1970s by Woods and colleagues at BBN (Hear What I Mean-HWIM), Reddy and colleagues at CMU (Hearsay), and Walker and colleagues at SRI. Many of these efforts were sponsored by the DARPA Speech Understanding Research (SUR) program and have been described in a special issue of the IEEE Transactions on ASSP (1975). During the mid-1970s, SLU research was conducted in Japan by Nakatsu and Shikano at NTT Labs on a bullet-train information system, later switched to air travel information.

During the 1980s, SLU systems for tourist travel information were explored by Zue and colleagues at MIT and airline travel by Levinson and colleagues at AT&T Bell Labs and by Furui and colleagues at NTT Labs. The DARPA Air Travel Information System (ATIS) program and the European ESPRIT SUNDIAL project sponsored major efforts in SLU during the 1990s and have been described in a special issue of Speech Communication Journal (1994). Currently, it is worth noting the European CLASSiC research program in spoken dialog systems and the LUNA program in spoken language understanding.

During recent decades, there has been a growth of deployed SLU systems. In the early stages, the systems involved recognition and understanding of single words and phrases, such as AT&T's Voice Response Call Processing (VRCP) and Tellme's directory assistance. Soon thereafter, deployed systems were able to handle constrained digit sequences such as credit cards and account numbers. Today, airline and train reservation systems understand short utterances including place names, dates, times. These deployments are more restrictive than research systems, where fairly complicated utterances were part of ATIS and subsequent systems.

During the early years of this century, building upon the research foundations for SLU and upon initial successful applications, systems were deployed which understood task-constrained spoken natural language, such as AT&T's How May I Help You? and BBN's Call Director.

The understanding in such systems is grounded in machine action. That is, the goal is to understand the user intent and extract named entities (e.g. phone numbers) accurately enough to perform their tasks. While a limited notion of understanding, it has proved highly useful and led to the many task-oriented research efforts described in this book.

Many textbooks have been written on related topics, such as speech recognition, statistical language modeling and natural language understanding. These each address some piece of the SLU puzzle. While it is impossible here to list them all, they include: *Statistical Methods for Speech Recognition* by Jelinek; *Speech and Language Processing* by Jurafsky and Martin; *Theory and Applications of Digital Speech Processing* by Rabiner and Schafer; *Fundamentals of Speech Recognition* by Rabiner and Juang; *Mathematical Models for Speech Technology* by Levinson; *Digital Speech Processing, Synthesis, and Recognition* by Furui; *Speech Processing Handbook* by Benesty *et al.*; *Spoken Language Processing* by Huang, Hon and Acero; *Corpus-based Methods in Language and Speech Processing* by Young and Bloothooft; *Spoken Dialogs with Computers* by De Mori.

The recent explosion of research and development in SLU has led the community to a wide range of tasks and methods not addressed in these traditional texts. Progress has accelerated because, as described by von Moltke: "No battle plan ever survives contact with the enemy." The editors state, "The book attempts to cover most popular tasks in SLU." They succeed admirably, making this a valuable information source.

The authors divide SLU tasks into two main categories. The first is for natural human/machine interaction. The second is for exploiting large volumes of human/human conversations.

In the area of human/machine interaction, they provide a history of methods to extract and represent the meaning of spoken language. The classic method of semantic frames is then described in detail. The notion of SLU as intent determination and utterance classification is then addressed, critical to many call-center applications. Voice search exploits speech to provide capabilities such as directory assistance and stock quotations. Question answering systems go a step beyond spoken document retrieval, with the goal of providing an actual answer to a question. That is, the machine response to "What is the capital of England?" is not merely a document containing the answer, but rather a response of "London is the capital of England."

There is an excellent discussion of how to deal with the data annotation bottleneck. While modern statistical methods prove more robust than rule-based approaches, they depend heavily on learning from data. Annotation proves to be a fundamental obstacle to scalability: application to a wide range of tasks with changing environments. Active and semi-supervised learning methods are described, which make a significant dent in the scalability problem.

In addition to tasks involving human interaction with machines, technology has enabled us to capture large volumes of speech (in customer-care interactions, voice messaging, teleconference calls, etc.), leading to applications such as spoken document retrieval, segmentation and identification of topics within spoken conversations, identification of social roles of the participants, information extraction and summarization. Early efforts in speech mining were described in a special issue of the IEEE Transactions on Audio and Speech (2004).

Tur and De Mori have made a valuable contribution to the field, providing an up-to-date exposition of the emerging methods in SLU as we explore a growing set of applications in the lab and in the real world. They gather in a single source the new methods and wide variety of tasks being developed for spoken language understanding. While not yet a grand unified theory, it provides an important role in gathering the evolving state-of-the-art in one place.

Allen Gorin
Director, Human Language Technology Research
U.S. DoD, Fort Meade, Maryland
October 2010

Preface

There are a number of books and textbooks on speech processing or natural language processing (even some covering speech and language processing), there are no books focusing on spoken language understanding (SLU) approaches and applications. In that respect, living between two worlds, SLU has not received the attention it deserves in spoken language processing in spite of the fact that it is represented in multiple sessions at major prestigious conferences such as the International Conference on Acoustic Speech and Signal Processing (ICASSP) of the Institution of Electrical and Electronic Engineers (IEEE) or the Interspeech Conference of the International Speech Communication Association (ISCA), and at dedicated workshops such as the Spoken Language Technology (SLT) workshop of the IEEE.

SLU applications are no longer limited to form filling or intent determination tasks in human computer interactions using speech, but now cover a broad range of complex tasks from speech summarization to voice search and speech retrieval. Due to a large variety of approaches and application types, it is rather difficult to follow the rapid extension and evolution of the field by consulting all the conference proceedings and journal papers. This book aims at filling a significant gap in that respect with contributions of experts working in a range of related areas.

The focus of the book will be distilling the state-of-the-art approaches (mostly data-driven) for well-investigated as well as emerging SLU tasks. The goal is to have a complete and coherent picture of each of the SLU areas considered so far, after providing the general picture for both human/machine and human/human communications processing. While this book can be considered as a graduate level source of contributions from recognized leaders in the field, we have tried to make sure that it flows naturally by actively editing the individual chapters and writing some of the chapters ourselves or jointly with other experts. We hope this will provide an up-to-date and complete information source for the speech and natural language research community and for those wishing to join it.

Allen Gorin once said that "Science is social event." We consider ourselves as coordinators of a large joint project involving 21 authors from 14 institutions all over the world. We would like to thank all of the contributing authors, namely Alex Acero, Frédéric Béchet, Ciprian Chelba, Li Deng, Olivier Galibert, Mazin Gilbert, Dilek Hakkani-Tür, Timothy J. Hazen, Yun-Cheng Ju, Lori Lamel, Yang Liu, Dan Melamed, Roberto Pieraccini, Matthew Purver, Bhuvana Ramabhadran, Giuseppe Riccardi, Sophie Rosset, Murat Saraclar, David Suendermann, Ye-Yi Wang and Dong Yu (in alphabetical order). Without their contributions, such a book could not have been published.

Finally, we would like to thank the publisher, Wiley, for the successful completion of this project, especially Georgia Pinteau, who initiated this effort, and editors Nicky Skinner, Alex King and Genna Manaog along with freelance copyeditor Don Emerson and project manager Prakash Naorem.

Gokhan Tur
Microsoft Speech Labs, Microsoft Research, USA

Renato De Mori
McGill University, Montreal, Canada and University of Avignon, France

1

Introduction

Gokhan Tur[1] and Renato De Mori[2]
[1] *Microsoft Speech Labs, Microsoft Research, USA*
[2] *McGill University, Canada and University of Avignon, France*

1.1 A Brief History of Spoken Language Understanding

In 1950, Turing published his most cited paper, entitled "Computing Machinery and Intelligence", trying to answer the question "Can machines think?" (Turing, 1950). Then he proposed the famous imitation game, or the Turing test, which tests whether or not a computer can successfully imitate a human in a conversation. He also prophesied that "at the end of the century the use of words and general educated opinion will have altered so much that one will be able to speak of machines thinking without expecting to be contradicted". Yet, now we are well past the year 2000, and we wonder whether he meant the end of 21st century when machines will be able to "understand" us.

Spoken language understanding (SLU) is currently an emerging field in the intersection of speech processing, natural language processing (NLP) by leveraging technologies from machine learning (ML) and artificial intelligence (AI). While speech is the most natural medium people use to interact with each other, when using tools, machines, or computers we use many other modalities such as mouse, keyboard, stylus, but not speech. Similarly, when people talk to each other, there is no record and the words are simply lost. However there is strong interest – both commercial and academic – in understanding such communications. As speech recognition and NLP algorithms mature, these areas become far from unreachable dreams. It is clear that we will see an increase in the number of SLU applications in the future. For example, robots will better understand what we say instead of reacting to a finite number of predefined commands, or we will be able to ask the computer to retrieve a phone call with a certain person about a particular topic.

Simply put, language understanding aims to extract "meaning" from natural language. In the literature on social sciences and artificial intelligence, many great names have worked on formalizing what meaning constitutes. Jackendoff, who has worked for many decades on the

Spoken Language Understanding: Systems for Extracting Semantic Information from Speech, First Edition.
Edited by Gokhan Tur and Renato De Mori.

semantics of natural language and its lexical and syntactic expressions, admits that "meaning" is the "holy grail" for linguistics and philosophy (Jackendoff, 2002).

One favorite quote from Shannon's well-known 1948 paper on information theory says that: *The fundamental problem of communication is that of reproducing at one point either exactly or approximately a message selected at another point. Frequently the messages have meaning.... These semantic aspects of communication are irrelevant to the engineering problem* (Shannon, 1948). It is ironic that information-theory-based approaches now dominate the field of spoken language understanding. Apparently, and interestingly using such data-driven approaches is very well suited for processing spoken language after several decades of over-promised and under-delivered attempts by using only knowledge-based approaches which tried to mimic the human brain for building intelligent agents. As one of the pioneers of statistical spoken language processing, Fred Jelinek, once put it: *The human analogy is misguided because machines do things differently than biological beings. Airplanes don't flap their wings.*

People no longer believe that machines will be able to converse like humans in the near future. On the other hand, a number of systems aimed at understanding have been developed in the last decade. It is possible to categorize these systems into three, based on their high-level approaches. The first category is the ELIZA like systems, where the system does not really understand what is said, but just mimics understanding. ELIZA was built at MIT in the 1960s (Weizenbaum, 1966) and has been the most popular artificial intelligence program, even though there was no intelligence but instead relied on simple pattern matching. A typical interaction may have such excerpts:

User: I need some help
System: Why do you say you need some help?
User: I am depressed
System: Are you depressed often?

Contemporary clones of ELIZA, such as ALICE,[1] are moving towards embedding more sophisticated language processing technologies within the same framework.

The understanding systems in the second category are rooted in artificial intelligence. They are demonstrated to be successful for very limited domains, using deeper semantics. These systems are typically heavily knowledge-based and rely on formal semantic interpretation, defined as mapping sentences into their logical forms. In its simplest form, a logical form is a context-independent representation of a sentence covering its predicates and arguments. For example, if the sentence is "John loves Mary", the logical form would be "(love john mary)".

During the 1970s, the first systems for understanding continuous speech were developed with interesting approaches for mapping language features into semantic representations. For this purpose, *case grammars* were proposed for representing sets of semantic concepts with thematic roles such as agent or instrument. The ICSI FrameNet project, for instance, focused on defining semantic frames for each of the concepts (Lowe and Baker, 1997). For example, in the "commerce" concept, there is a "buyer" and a "seller" and other arguments such as the "cost", "good", and so on. Therefore, two sentences "A sold X to B" and "B bought X from A" are semantically parsed as the same. Following these ideas, some researchers worked towards building universal semantic grammars (or interlingua), which assumes that all languages have a shared set of semantic features (Chomsky, 1965). Such interlingua-based approaches have

[1] http://alicebot.blogspot.com/

also heavily influenced language translation until late 1990s before statistical approaches began to dominate the field. Allen (1995) may be consulted for more information on the artificial-intelligence-based techniques for language understanding.

The last category of understanding systems is the main focus of this book, where understanding is reduced to a (mostly statistical) language processing problem. This corresponds to attacking targeted speech understanding tasks instead of trying to solve the global machine understanding problem. A good example of targeted understanding is detecting the arguments of an intent given a domain, as in the Air Travel Information System (ATIS) (Price, 1990). ATIS was a popular DARPA-sponsored project, focusing on building an understanding system for the airline domain. In this task, the users utter queries on flight information such as *I want to fly to Boston from New York next week*. In this case, understanding was reduced to the problem of extracting task specific arguments in a given frame-based semantic representation involving, for example, *Destination* and *Departure Date*. While the concept of using semantic frames is motivated by the case frames of the artificial intelligence area, the slots are very specific to the target domain, and finding values of properties from automatically recognized spoken utterances may suffer from automatic speech recognition errors and poor modeling of natural language variability in expressing the same concept. For these reasons, the spoken language understanding researchers employed known classification methods for filling frame slots of the application domain using the provided training data set and performed comparative experiments. These approaches used generative models such as hidden Markov models (Pieraccini *et al.*, 1992), discriminative classification methods (Kuhn and Mori, 1995) and probabilistic context free grammars (Seneff, 1992; Ward and Issar, 1994).

While ATIS project coined the term "spoken language understanding" for human/machine conversations, it is not hard to think of other interactive understanding tasks, such as spoken question answering, voice search, or other similar human/human conversation understanding tasks such as named entity extraction or topic classification. Hence, in this book, we take a liberal view of the term spoken language understanding and attempt to cover such popular tasks which can be considered under this umbrella term. Each of these tasks are studied extensively, and the progress is fascinating.

SLU tasks aim at processing either human/human or human/machine communications. Typically the tasks and the approaches are quite different for each case. Regarding human/machine interactive systems, we start from the heavily studied tasks of determination of intent of its arguments and their interaction with the dialog manager within a spoken dialog system. Recently question answering from speech has become a popular task for human/machine interactive systems. Especially with the proliferation of smart phones, voice search is now an emerging field with ties to both NLP and information retrieval. With respect to human/human communication processing, telephone conversations or multi-party meetings are studied in depth. Recently, the established language processing tasks, such as speech summarization and discourse topic segmentation, have been developed to process human/human spoken conversations. The extraction of specific information from speech conversations to be used for mining speech data and speech analytics is also considered in order to ensure quality of a service or monitor important events in application domains.

With advances in machine learning, speech recognition, and natural language processing, SLU, in the middle of all these fields, has improved dramatically during the last two decades. As the amount of available data (annotated or raw) has grown with the explosion of web sources and other information kinds, another exciting area of research area is coping with spoken information overload. Since SLU is not a single technology, unlike speech recognition, it is hard to present a single application. As mentioned before, any speech processing task eventually requires some sort of spoken language processing. Conventional approaches of plugging in the output of a speech recognizer to the natural language processing engine is not a solution in most cases. The SLU application must be robust to speech, speech recognition errors, certain characteristics of uttered sentences, and so on. For example, most utterances are not grammatical and have disfluencies, and hence off-the-shelf syntactic parsers trained with written text sources, such as newspaper articles, fail frequently.

There is also a strong interest from the commercial world about SLU applications. These typically employ knowledge-based approaches, such as building hand-crafted grammars or using a finite set of commands, and are now used in some environments such as cars, call-centers, and robots. This book also aims to fill this chasm in approaches employed between commercial and academic communities.

The focus of the book will be to cover the state-of-the-art approaches (mostly data-driven) for each of the SLU tasks, with chapters written by well-known researchers in the respecive fields. The book attempts to introduce the reader to the most popular tasks in SLU.

This book is proposed for graduate courses in electronics engineering and/or computer science. However it can also be useful to social science graduates with field expertise such as psycholinguists, linguists, and to other technologists. Experts in text processing will notice how certain language processing tasks (such as summarization or named entity extraction) are handled with speech input. The members of the speech processing community will find surveys of tasks beyond speech and speaker recognition with a comprehensive description of spoken language understanding methods.

1.2 Organization of the Book

This book covers the state-of-the-art approaches to key SLU tasks as listed below. These tasks can be grouped into two categories based on their main intended application area, processing human/human or human/machine conversations, though in some cases this distinction is unclear.

For each of these SLU tasks we provide a motivation for the task, a comprehensive literature survey, the main approaches and the state of the art techniques, and some indicative performance figures in established data sets for that task. For example, when template filling is discussed, ATIS data is used since it is already available for the community.

1.2.1 Part I. Spoken Language Understanding for Human/Machine Interactions

This part of the book covers the established tasks of SLU, namely slot filling and intent determination as used in dialog systems, as well as newer understanding tasks which focus on human/machine interactions such as voice search and spoken question answering. Two final chapters, one on describing SLU in the framework of modern dialog systems, and another discussing active learning methods for SLU conclude Part I.

Chapter 2 History of Knowledge and Processes for Spoken Language Understanding

This chapter reviews the evolution of methods for spoken language understanding systems. Automatic systems for spoken language understanding using these methods are then reviewed, building the stage for the rest of Part I.

Chapter 3 Semantic Frame Based Spoken Language Understanding

This chapter provides a comprehensive coverage of semantic frame-based spoken language understanding approaches as used in human/computer interaction. Being the most extensively studied SLU task, we try to distill the established approaches and recent literature to provide the reader with a comparative and comprehensive view of the state of the art in this area.

Chapter 4 Intent Determination and Spoken Utterance Classification

This chapter focuses on the complementary task of semantic template filling tasks, i.e. spoken utterance classification techniques and illustrates their successful applications to intent determination systems which has emerged partly from commercial call-routing applications. We aim to provide details of such systems, the underlying approaches, and integration with speech recognition and template filling.

Chapter 5 Voice Search

This chapter focuses on one of the most actively investigated speech understanding technologies in recent years: querying a database, such as using speech for directory assistance. A variety of applications (including multi-modal) will be reviewed and the proposed algorithms are discussed in detail along with proposed evaluation metrics.

Chapter 6 Spoken Question Answering

This chapter covers question answering from spoken documents, but also beyond this where questions are spoken. Various approaches and systems for question answering, are presented in detail, with a focus on approaches used for spoken language and on the QAst campaigns.

Chapter 7 SLU in Commercial and Research Spoken Dialog Systems

This chapter shows how different SLU techniques are integrated into commercial and research dialog systems. The focus is providing a comparative view based on example projects, architectures, and corpora associated with the application of SLU to spoken dialog systems.

Chapter 8 Active Learning

This chapter reviews active learning methods that deal with the scarcity of labeled data, focusing on spoken language understanding applications. This is a critical area as statistical, data-driven approaches to SLU have become dominant in recent years. We present applications of active learning for various tasks that are described in this book.

1.2.2 *Part II. Spoken Language Understanding for Human/Human Conversations*

This part of the book covers SLU tasks, which mainly focus on processing human/human spoken conversations such as multi-party meetings, broadcast conversations, and so on. The first chapter serves as a preamble to Part II, since the chapter discusses lower-level tasks, and higher-level SLU applications, such as topic segmentation or summarization are discussed in the following chapters.

Chapter 9 Human/Human Conversation Understanding

This chapter introduces human/human conversation understanding approaches, mainly focusing on discourse modeling, speech act modeling, and argument diagramming. This chapter also serves as a bridge to other higher-level tasks and studies towards processing human/human conversations, such as summarization or topic segmentation.

Chapter 10 Named Entity Recognition

This chapter discusses the major issues concerning the task of named entity extraction in spoken documents. After defining the task and its application frameworks in the context of speech processing, a comparison of different entity extraction approaches is presented in detail.

Chapter 11 Topic Segmentation

This chapter discusses the task of automatically dividing single long recordings or transcripts into shorter, topically coherent segments. Both supervised and unsupervised machine learning approaches, rooted in speech processing, information retrieval, and natural language processing are discussed.

Chapter 12 Topic Identification

This chapter builds on the previous chapter and focuses on the task of identifying the underlying topics being discussed in spoken audio recordings. Both supervised topic classification and topic clustering approaches are discussed in detail.

Chapter 13 Speech Summarization

This chapter focuses on approaches towards automatic summarization of spoken documents, such as meeting recordings or voicemail. While summarization is a well-studied area in natural language processing, its application to speech is relatively recent, and this chapter focuses on extending text-based methods and evaluation metrics to handle spoken input.

Chapter 14 Speech Analytics

This chapter attempts to provide a detailed description of techniques towards speech analytics or speech data mining. Since this task is rooted in commercial applications, especially in call-centers, there is very little published work on the established methods, and in this chapter we aim to fill this gap.

Chapter 15 Speech Retrieval

This chapter discusses the retrieval and browsing of spoken audio documents. This is an area lying between the two distinct scientific communities of information retrieval and speech recognition. This chapter aims to provide an overview of the common tasks and data sets, evaluation metrics, and algorithms most commonly used in this growing area of research.

References

Allen J 1995 *Natural Language Understanding* Benjamin/Cummings, Chapter 8.

Chomsky N 1965 *Aspects of the Theory of Syntax*. MIT Press, Cambridge, MA.

Jackendoff R 2002 *Foundations of Language* Oxford University Press, Chapter 9.

Kuhn R and De Mori R 1995 The application of semantic classification trees to natural language understanding. *IEEE Transactions on Pattern Analysis and Machine Intelligence* **17**, 449–460.

Lowe JB and Baker CF 1997 A frame-semantic approach to semantic annotation *Proceedings of the Annual Meeting of the Association for Computational Linguistics (ACL)-SIGLEX Workshop*, Washington, D.C.

Pieraccini R, Tzoukermann E, Gorelov Z, Gauvain JL, Levin E, Lee CH and Wilpon JG 1992 A speech understanding system based on statistical representation of semantics *Proceedings of the International Conference on Acoustics, Speech and Signal Processing (ICASSP)*, San Francisco, CA.

Price PJ 1990 Evaluation of spoken language systems: The ATIS domain *Proceedings of the DARPA Workshop on Speech and Natural Language*, Hidden Valley, PA.

Seneff S 1992 TINA : A natural language system for spoken language applications. *Computational Linguistics* **18**(1), 61–86.

Shannon CE 1948 A mathematical theory of communication. *Bell System Technical Journal* **27**, 379–423, 623–656.

Turing AM 1950 Computing machinery and intelligence. *Mind* **49**(236), 433–460.

Ward W and Issar S 1994 Recent improvements in the CMU spoken language understanding system *Proceedings of the ARPA Human Language Technology Conference (HLT) Workshop*, pp. 213–216.

Weizenbaum J 1966 Eliza – a computer program for the study of natural language communication between man and machine. *Communications of the ACM* **9**(1), 36–45.

Part 1

Spoken Language Understanding for Human/Machine Interactions

2

History of Knowledge and Processes for Spoken Language Understanding

Renato De Mori
McGill University, Canada and University of Avignon, France

This chapter reviews the evolution of methods for spoken language understanding systems. Meaning representation languages are introduced with methods for obtaining meaning representations from natural language. Probabilistic frameworks accounting for knowledge imprecision and limitations of automatic speech recognition systems are introduced. Automatic systems for spoken language understanding using these methods are then briefly reviewed.

2.1 Introduction

Spoken Language Understanding (SLU) is the interpretation of signs conveyed by a speech signal. Epistemology is the science of knowledge used for interpretation. Epistemology considers a datum as the basic unit. A datum can be an object, an action or an event in the world and can have time and space coordinates, multiple aspects and qualities that make it different from others. A datum can be represented by an image or it can be abstract and be represented by a concept. A concept can be empirical, structural, or an *a priori* one. There may be relations among data.

Natural language describes data in the world and their relations. Sentences of a natural language are sequences of words belonging to a word lexicon. Words of a sentence have associated one or more data conceptualizations, also called *meanings*, that can be selected and composed to form the meaning of the sentence. Correct sentences in a language satisfy constraints described by the language syntax. Words are grouped into syntactic structures according to syntactic rules. A sequence of words can have a specific meaning.

Spoken Language Understanding: Systems for Extracting Semantic Information from Speech, First Edition.
Edited by Gokhan Tur and Renato De Mori.

Semantic knowledge is a collection of models and processes for the organization of meanings and their hypothesization from observable signs. Human conceptualization of the world is not well understood. Nevertheless, good semantic models have been proposed assuming that basic *semantic constituents* are organized into *conceptual structures*. In Jackendoff (2002), p. 124, it is suggested that semantics is an independent generative system correlated with syntax through an interface.

The objective of this book is to describe approaches for conceiving SLU systems based on computational semantics. These approaches attempt to perform a conceptualization of the world using computational schemata and processes for obtaining a meaning representation from available sign descriptions of the enunciation of word sequences.

SLU is a difficult task because signs for meaning are coded into a signal together with other information such as speaker identity and acoustic environment. Natural language sentences are often difficult to analyze. Furthermore, spoken messages can be ungrammatical and may contain disfluencies such as interruptions, self-corrections and other events.

The design of an automatic SLU system should be based on a process implementing an interpretation strategy that uses computational models for various types of knowledge. The process should take into account the fact that models are imperfect and the automatic transcription of user utterances performed by the Automatic Speech Recognition (ASR) component of an SLU system is error prone.

Historically, early SLU systems used text-based natural language understanding (NLU) approaches for processing a sequence of word hypotheses generated by an ASR module with non probabilistic methods and models.

Various types of probabilistic models were introduced later to take into account knowledge imperfection and the possible errors in the word sequence to be interpreted. Signs of prosodic and other types of events were also considered.

2.2 Meaning Representation and Sentence Interpretation

2.2.1 Meaning Representation Languages

Basic ideas for meaning representation were applied in early SLU systems. An initial, considerable effort in SLU research was made with an ARPA project started in 1971. The project, reviewed in Klatt (1977), mostly followed an Artificial Intelligence (AI) approach to NLU. Word hypotheses generated by an ASR system were transformed into meaning representations using methods similar if not equal to those used for text interpretation following the scheme shown in Figure 2.1. An ASR system implements a decoding strategy, indicated as *S control*,

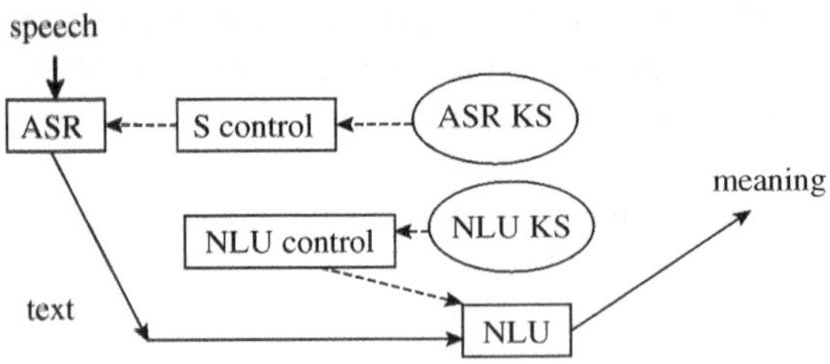

Figure 2.1 Scheme of early SLU system architectures

based on acoustic, lexical and language knowledge sources (KS) indicated as ASR KS. Interpretation is performed by an *NLU control* strategy using syntactic and semantic knowledge sources indicated as *NLU KS* to produce hypotheses about the meaning conveyed by the analyzed speech signal.

Computational models for transforming the samples of a speech signal into an instance of an artificial Meaning Representation Language (MRL) were inspired by knowledge about programming languages and computer processes.

Computer epistemology deals with the representation of semantic knowledge in a computer using an appropriate formalism. Objects are grouped into *classes* by their properties. Classes are organized into *hierarchies* often called *ontologies*. An object is an instance of a class. Judgment is expressed by *predicates* that describe relations between classes. Predicates have arguments represented by variables whose values are instances of specified classes and may have to satisfy other constraints that define the *type* of each variable.

Computer representation of semantic objects and classes is based on well-defined elements of programming languages. Programming languages have their own syntax and semantic. The former defines legal programming statements; the latter specifies the operations a machine performs when a syntactically correct statement is executed. Semantic analysis of a computer program is based on formal methods and is performed for understanding the behavior of a program and its coherence with the design concepts and goals. The use of formal logic methods for computer semantics has also been considered for the automatic interpretation of natural language with the purpose of finding MRL descriptions coherent with the syntactic structure of theit expression in natural language.

Even if some utterances convey meanings that cannot be expressed in formal logics (Jackendoff, 2002), p. 287, methods based on these logics and inspired by program analysis have been considered for representing natural language semantics in many application domains. Early approaches and limitations are discussed (e.g. Jackendoff, 1990; Woods, 1975).

A logic formalism for natural language interpretation should be able to represent, among other things, *intension* (the essence of a concept) and *extension* (the set of possible instances of a given concept). The formalism should also permit, to perform inferences. The semantic knowledge of an application is stored in a *knowledge base* (KB). An observation of the world is described by a logical formula F. Its interpretation is an instance of a fragment of the knowledge represnted in the KB. Such an instance can be found by inference. The purpose of such an inference is to determine whether $KB \models F$, meaning that KB entails F. If KB contains only first order logic formulas, inference can be performed by theorem proving.

Predicates may express relations for composing objects into a prototypical or another semantic structure that has a specific meaning, richer than just the set of meanings of its constituents. Often, composition has to satisfy specific constraints. For example a date is a composition of months and numbers which have to take values in specific relations and intervals.

Semantic relations of a KB can be graphically represented by a semantic network in which relations are assosiated to links between nodes corresponding to entities described by classes. A discussion on what a link can express is presented in Woods (1975). An asserted fact is represented by an instance of a semantic network fragment.

A portion of a semantic network describing the properties of an entity or other composite concepts can be represented by a computational schema called *frame*. A frame has a head identifying a structured entity and a set of *slots*. Each slot corresponds to a predicate describing a relation linking the entity represented by the frame with a property. Slots are filled by fillers that bound the predicate variables to property values. Constraints for slot filling are described in slot *facets*.

Computation methods for filling the slots respecting the constraints expressed by the facets can be attached to the slots.

A slot can be filled by an object which is the instance of another frame whose slots can be filled by other frame instances. In this way, instances of frame structures are obtained by composition. An instance of a frame structure is obtained by filling some or all the slots of the frames in the structure.

Acceptable frame structures for semantic representations in a domain can be obtained by models of frame languages. Theoretical foundations for these languages are presented in Kifer *et al.* (1995).

Frame structures were proposed in Fikes and Nilsson (1971) for representing *chunked* real world knowledge.

The following frame is an example of prototypical knowledge for the semantic structure *ADDRESS* (facets expressing constraints for slot fillers are shown between brackets):

```
{ADDRESS
    loc       [TOWN]
    area          [DEPARTMENT, PROVINCE, STATE]
    country       [NATION]
    street        [STREET_TYPE]
    zip       [NUMBER]
}
```

An instance of the ADDRESS structure is represented as:

```
{a0001
    instance_of ADDRESS
    loc      Avignon
    area         Vaucluse
    country      France
    street       1, avenue Pascal
    zip      84000
}
```

Here *a*0001 is a handle that represents an instance of the class ADDRESS specifying the value of the first slot. The other slots define the property values of this particular instance.

The above frame can be derived (Nilsson, 1980), after skolemization, from the following logic formula:

$$(\exists x). \begin{cases} is\_a(x, ADDRESS) \wedge loc(x, Avignon) \wedge area(x, Vaucluse) \wedge \\ country(x, France) \wedge street(x, 1\_avenue\_Pascal) \wedge zip(x, 84000) \end{cases}$$

Frames describing a class and an instance of it are similar, but their semantics as programming structures are different.

Frames were also used in *lexical* knowlzdge for representing the possible meanings of a word. A frame model for verbs was proposed in Fillmore (1968).

Verbs are fundamental components of natural language sentences. They represent actions for which different entities play different *roles*. A *case* is a particular role that a noun phrase or other syntactic structures take in the state or activity expressed by the verb.

There is a case structure for each main verb. Examples of cases for a verb are *Agent*(*A*), *Object*(*O*), *Location*(*L*).

The possible meanings of a verb are represented by frames as in the following example:

```
{REQUEST
    is_a         VERB
    A        [human...]
    O        [theme...]
    ...
    other roles      [...]
}
```

A frame is associated with a verb in a specific sentence as in the following example:

```
{V003
    instance_of REQUEST
    subject     user
    theme       service_004
    ...
    Other roles      [...]
}
```

In Lowe *et al.* (1997), a lexical semantic *KB* is described based on annotations performed in the FrameNet project. In this approach, a set of frames is associated to each word of a lexicon to represent all the possible meanings the word can have in different contexts.

Discourse actions are instances of illocutory (speech) acts, identified by expressions containing specific verbs. These *speech acts (SA)* may determine sentence types. Various attempts have been made to identify SAs that are domain independent. A possible taxonomy of them is formulated in the Dialogue Act Markup in Several Layers (DAMSL) (Allen and Core, 1997). Dialogue acts (DA) are meaningful discourse units, such as statements and questions. DAs and other dialogue events, such as subjectivity expressions, are related to discourse segments which may contain many sentences. The question: “Does Air Canada fly from Toronto to Dallas?” contains a dialogue act and has the following semantic representation:

```
{Q001
        is_a  QUESTION
                  q_type   Y/N
                  q_theme  CONNECT
                               c_subject  AC
                               c_path     PATH
                                              p_origin      Toronto
                                              p_destination       Dallas
}
```

Different frames may share slots with similarity links. There may be necessary and optional slots. Fillers can be obtained by attachment of methods or detectors of specific syntactic structures (e.g. noun groups) as well as by inheritance or defaults. Descriptions can also be introduced to specify constraints. They may contain connectives, coreference, declarative conditions, quantified expressions.

In KLONE (Brachman and Schmolze, 1985) concept descriptions account for the internal structure with Role–Filler descriptions and for a global Structural Description (SD). Roles have substructures with constraints specifying types and quantities of fillers. SDs are logical expressions indicating relations among role fillers. Role descriptions contain value restrictions. Epistemological relations are defined for composing conceptual structures. They may connect formal objects of compatible types and account for inheritance.

Rich MRLs have been developed based on the just introduced concepts. A noticeable example is the Web Ontology Language (OWL) (Patel-Schneider *et al.*, 2003) that has its origin in the agent markup languages described in Hendler and McGuinness (2000).

2.2.2 *Meaning Extraction from Sentences*

The interpretation of a sentence to obtain an MRL description is a problem solving activity that can be carried out with different methods and models. It is not clear how concepts relate to words. It is argued in Woods (1975) that a specification for natural language semantics is not limited to the transformation of a sentence into a representation, and may require the use of information that is not coded into the sentence but can be inferred from the available context and system knowledge. Furthermore, in Jackendoff (1990) it is argued that each major syntactic constituent of a sentence maps into a conceptual constituent, but the inverse is not true.

Extraction of semantic information from a sentence can be performed by first analyzing the sentence to obtain a full parse of it. Assuming that natural languages are susceptible to the same kind of semantic analysis as programming languages, in Montague (1974), it is suggested that to each syntactic rule of a natural language generative grammar can be attached a semantic building procedure. These procedures translate sentences into first-order logic formulas describing sentence meaning.

The ontology of an application domain is part of system knowledge and can be represented by sets of frame structures. Each structure corresponds to a set of first-order logic formulas. If first-order logics is not adequate for representing certain types of knowledge, higher order or modal logics can be used. Some examples can be found in De Mori (1998).

In Woods (1976), syntactic, semantic and pragmatic knowledge are integrated into procedural semantic context-sensitive Augmented Transition Network Grammars (ATNG). ATNGs are made of states and arcs representing state transitions. ATNGs are an extension of transition network context-free grammars (TNG). In TNGs there are three types of arc, namely, CAT for reading an input word, PUSH for transferring the control of parsing to another TNG and POP for returning the control to the PUSH arc from which the control was transferred. Augmentations consist in associating with certain arcs condition testing and register setting actions. Actions may set the content of registers with linguistic feature values. It is also possible to introduce actions of the type BUILD associated with an arc to compose a parse tree or to generate semantic interpretations. Different ATNGs can be used in cascade for parsing and interpretation. In this case, an arc action TRANSMIT transfers syntactic structures from the

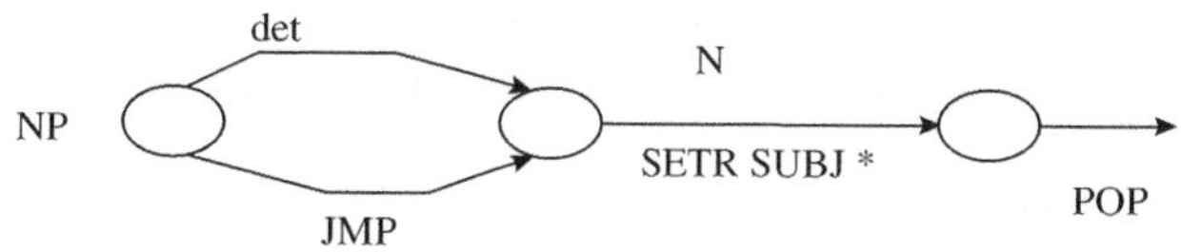

Figure 2.2 Example of Augmented Transition Network Grammars (ATNG)

syntactic to the semantic ATNG. An arc label TEST is introduced to test conditions about the content of some registers or lists. Lists are created and populated with the action LIST. Rules for defining actions, forms and term acts are also introduced.

A simple sub-network ATNG for a noun phrase is shown in Figure 2.2.

An action SETR SUBJ * is associated to the arc labeled with a proper name N. The action sets the register SUBJ to the value of the input word corresponding to the name. The content of this register can be further used by a BUILD action associated to another arc for composing a parse tree of the analyzed sentence or the instance of a semantic structure.

In Walker (1975), semantic knowledge is represented by a partitioned semantic network. The results of a best first parser trigger activations in the partitioned semantic network with which inferences and predictions are performed by spreading node activation through links.

An approach describing a formalization of human knowledge for relating action representations to syntax can be found in Allen (1995), chapter 10.

Semantic relations may use components hypothesized in different sentences and generate structures which may belong to a context-sensitive language. Sequences of conceptual constituents may have to satisfy constraints which are different from the constraints imposed on words expressing each constituent. Semantic constraints can be expressed by template patterns of word sequences and, possibly, other syntactic features.

Formulas describing the meaning of a sentence following the approach proposed in Montague (1974) can be obtained by composition. Combinatory categorical grammars (CCG) have been introduced (Steedman, 1996) for obtaining logical forms for each sentence parsed under the control of a categorical grammar of the type introduced in Ajdukiewicz (1935) and Bar-Hillel (1953). CCGs are mildly context-sensitive lexicalized grammars. Specific categories indicating syntactic constraints are associated with each word of the lexicon together with possible word meanings represented by lambda-expressions. Rules are applied during parsing to perform syntactic analysis and semantic compositions.

An interesting method for inducing a CCG from examples is described in Zettlemoyer and Collins (2005). Recent developments on the use of CCGs for interpreting natural language sentences in dialogues are described in Zettlemoyer and Collins (2009).

In CCGs a word of the application lexicon is described by a category B : g, where B is a syntactic type and g is a semantic type. Syntactic types are composed by primitive types, such as noun phrase (NP), and complex types such as σ/F or $P \setminus \sigma$ where σ/F represents a string σ that needs to be followed by string F to be completed and $P \setminus \sigma$ represents a string σ that needs to be preceded by string P to be completed.

A semantic type can be a lambda-expression which is a function from logical variable values to truth values. Often, lambda-expressions are used for obtaining the argument values of a frame slot by finding the values of variables for which the lambda-expression returns true (Duvert and De Mori, 2010). For example the sentence "a location near Opera" is represented by the lambda-expression $\lambda(x).location(x) \wedge near(x, Opera)$. Lexical items are defined as follows:

location := NP : location
Opera := NP : opera
near := (S/NP)/NP : $\lambda(x).\lambda(y).near(x, y)$

It is possible to parse the sentence and obtain $S : \lambda(x).location(x) \wedge near(x, Opera)$. In this case, $\lambda(x)$ is a function that returns true for certain values of the variable x.

Often a sentence S can be parsed in different ways under the control of a grammar. Each parse tree corresponds to a specific interpretation of S. In order to solve ambiguities and establish priorities among interpretations, probabilistic grammars have been introduced. Each parsing result is scored with the probability of representing the generation and meaning of the sentence.

Probabilities are estimated with a training corpus. Due to the large variety of possibilities and limitations of the available corpora, many probabilities are not well estimated due to *data sparseness*. In order to reduce the effects of this problem, constraints have been applied to the grammar rules and approximations in the model probabilities have been introduced. It has also been found useful to lexicalize the grammars by associating keywords to syntactic components hypothesized during parsing. Important details on the application of these concepts can be found in Zettlemoyer and Collins (2009) and in its references.

Other approaches for sentence interpretation have been proposed. In general, interpretation can be driven by syntactic parsing or by other strategies in which syntactic analysis and semantic composition are interleaved. Furthermore, syntactic analysis can be based on full or partial parsing. Early approaches will be mentioned in the following of this section, while other, more recent approaches will be described in successive sections.

Semantics may drive the parser (Tait, 1985), causing it to make attachments in the syntactic parse tree to resolve ambiguities.

An interesting example of interleaving syntax and semantics in a parser is proposed in Dowding *et al.* (1993).

Other early approaches performed interpretation as a rule-based inference process. Rules may contain parsing features and inference can be performed by a planning system whose goal is to obtain an MRL representation. Rather than incorporating building rules into a grammar, heterarchical architectures were conceived for producing interpretations by triggering the application of production rules (Erman *et al.*, 1980).

Other examples of rule-based systems proposed for generating instances of frame structures expressed by natural language sentences can be found in Norvig (1983).

These approaches essentially use non probabilistic models for translating a sentence into its MRL representation.

Parsing spoken language is particularly difficult, especially in the presence of ASR errors. For this reason, approaches avoiding full parsing have been considered (Woods, 1976). They generate hypotheses of semantic fragments that have to be composed by a successive composition process, a semantic model of which is introduced in the next section.

2.3 Knowledge Fragments and Semantic Composition

Concepts expressed in a sentence are often semantically related. Semantic relations, such as spatial relations, are language independent, while their expression in a sentence is language dependent. An approach is now introduced that generates hypotheses about semantic constituents with shallow parsing in a first step. Constituents are then composed into semantic structures in a second step. This is part of a possible interpretation process motivated by the fact that the syntactic analysis of spoken sentences may produce errors because utterances contain disfluences and ASR systems are error prone. Suitable language and knowledge models can be applied in successive semantic composition steps, depending on the available hypotheses to introduce appropriate constraints and improve overall accuracy.

2.3.1 Concept Tags and Knowledge Fragments

Let V be a vocabulary of words that can be hypothesized by an ASR system. Let $C_1^K = C_1, ..., C_k, ..., C_K$, with $C_k \in V_C$ be a sequence of semantic constituent tags that can be hypothesized from a sequence W of word hypotheses in an initial interpretation step. Let σ_k indicate the word pattern in W supporting the expression of C_k.

Example 1 shows the concept tags and their supporting word sequences for a sentence of the French MEDIA corpus (Bonneau-Maynard *et al.*, 2005).

Example 1
<je souhaite reserver (*I would like to make a reservation*)> [command(reservation)] <un hotel (*for a hotel*)> [object(hotel)] <avec parking (*with parking*)> [hotel_facility(parking)] < à Lyon (*in Lyon*)> [city(Lyon)]

Concept tags are represented by attribute-value pairs between brackets. Word sequences between the < > characters represent the sentence segment, called *concept support*, that expresses the concept.

Hypothesized semantic structures are made of frame instances. For the sake of simplicity, a frame will be indicated with its name. Let F_i be the name of a frame introduced for describing some semantic knowledge of an application domain. The frame has a name and a set of properties. The lth property is represented by a slot $s_{i,l}$. The slot has a name and can be empty or filled with a value. A frame instance is characterized by the association of values with some or all its slots. Some values can be frame instances with slots having frame instances as values. Structures of this type with partially filled slots are *instance fragments*. Some fragments can be further composed into more complex fragments or final semantic structure hypotheses. The semantic interpretation of a sentence, a dialogue turn or a dialogue segment is a collection of semantic structures represented by networks of frame instances.

Definition 1
Let $G_{i,l}$ be the name of the property represented by the lth slot $s_{i,l}$ of frame F_i. Let $\Gamma_{i,a}$ be an instance of frame F_i. Some of the values of $\Gamma_{i,a}$ may be other instance frames and so on. If an instance $\Gamma_{q,b}$ of a frame F_q is the value of slot $s_{i,l}$ and $s_{q,n}$ is a slot of $\Gamma_{q,b}$, then this relation between F_i and $s_{q,n}$ is a *slot chain* indicated as:

$$\delta_n = F_i.G_{i,l}.F_q.s_{q,n}$$

A slot chain can be obtained by chaining slot chains as follows:

$$\delta_r = F_k.G_{k,l}.\delta_x^{\varepsilon}.F_q.s_{q,r}$$

where δ_x^ε is a slot chain ending with an empty slot . The first frame name is the *head* of the chain and the last slot is the chain *tail.*

Definition 2
An *instance fragment* $\Gamma_{i,a}$ is a semantic structure made of a frame name and a slot list represented as:

$$\Gamma_{i,a} = F_i.sl_{i,a}$$

An instance fragment is a set of slot chains.

Definition 3
A *slot list* $sl_{i,a}$ is represented as follows as a set of pairs. Each pair is made of a slot name and its slot value:

$$sl_{i,a} = [G_{i,I}v_{i,a,1}, ..., G_{i,j}v_{i,a,j}, ..., G_{i,J}v_{i,a,J}]$$

$G_{i,j}$ is a slot name and $v_{i,a,j}$ is its value. Each slot $s_{i,j}$ is associated with a *facet* $\Phi_{i,j}$ which is a list of value types. Value types can be names of frames whose instance may be a possible slot value. A facet is represented as follows:

$$\Phi_{i,j} = [\varphi_{i,j,m}]$$

$$\varphi_{i,j,m} = F_y \text{ or } V_y$$

F_y is a frame name while V_y is another type of value.

Frame F_i is the *head* of the instance fragment $\Gamma_{i,a}$. All the unfilled slots of the instance fragment are elements of the *fragment tail list* .

Some slot values can be the results of methods associated with slots. They are executed by an interpretation process with a specific strategy. A method can evaluate a lambda-expression or execute a data base query specified by some values of other slots of the instance.

A concept tag C_k may correspond to one or more fragments of the application ontology, depending on some features of the words of its support and its context. Such a correspondence is established by the designer of the application ontology. The concept tags in V_C are part of the specifications for the annotation of the application corpora.

Example 2 shows a fragment corresponding to a concept tag. The support of a fragment is the support of the corresponding concept tag.

Example 2
Sentence: Un hotel avec parking (*A hotel with parking*)
Concept tag C_k: hotel_facility(parking),
Fragment $\Gamma_{k,a}$: HOTEL.[h_facility FACILITY.[facility_type *parking*]]

Fragment $\Gamma_{k,a}$ is a linear representation of a frame structure in which frame names are in capital letters, the list of slots for a frame is represented between brackets, its elements are separated by a comma and the value of a slot follows the slot name after a blank. When a value is a constant, it is represented in italics. The relation between a frame name and its slot list is represented by a dot.

Instance fragments can be hypothesized by a table look-up procedure. When multiple choices are possible for a concept C_k, a finite set of instance fragments $\mathcal{S}_k$ is associated with it and disambiguation is based on the features of the support σ_k and its context.

In practice, instead of fully parsing a sentence, shallow parsing is performed for extracting syntactic structures. Some syntactic structures are then recognized as supports for hypothesizing instance fragments. A good introduction to models and methods for shallow parsing can be found in a special issue of the Journal of Machine Learning Research (JMLR, 2002).

Some slot methods may use lambda-expressions to perform semantic composition based on an inference involving chunked knowledge, supports and word meanings. Knowledge associated with words can be automatically learned and possible multiple composition hyporheses can be scored using exponential models as described in Zettlemoyer and Collins (2009). Useful inferences can be performed using the powerful definition of frame-slot facets derived from domain ontology.

Concept tags can be associated to sentence segments with manual annotation as in the MEDIA corpus.

Methods for obtaining concept tag hypotheses with different partial and shallow parsing approaches have been compared for the MEDIA corpus as described in the final report of the LUNA project.[1] They will be summarized later on in Section 2.8.

Semantic structures establish n-ary relations between semantic constituents. Each n-ary relation can be composed using binary relations. Supports for binary relations are represented by templates containing features of the constituent supports and their syntactic links that are often represented by local syntactic relations or by simple words such as prepositions.

Some useful composition types are now introduced.

2.3.2 *Composition by Fusion of Fragments*

Let us consider an instance

$$\Gamma_{i,a} = F_i.sl_{i,a} = F_i.[G_{i,1}v_{i,a,1}, \ldots, G_{i,j}F_q.sl_{q,d}, \ldots, G_{i,J}v_{i,a,J}]$$

in which the jth value of the slot list $sl_{i,a}$ is another fragment:

$$v_{i,a,j} = F_q.sl_{q,d}$$

Let assume that this fragment has the same head as another hypothesized fragment $\Gamma_{q,e} = F_q.sl_{q,e}$, i.e.

$$head(v_{i,a,j}) = head(\Gamma_{q,e})$$

A possible composition can be performed by fusing $v_{i,a,j}$ with $\Gamma_{q,e}$ provided that some other conditions, introduced in the following, are verified.

[1] Available at http://www.ist-luna.eu. Annotation examples of the MEDIA corpus can also be found in the chapter *Spoken Language Understanding as Template Filling*.

Let the slot lists of $v_{i,a,j} = F_q.sl_{q,d}$ and $\Gamma_{q,e} = F_q.sl_{q,e}$ be respectively:

$$sl_{q,d} = G_{q,1}v_{q,d,1}, \ldots, G_{q,k}v_{q,d,k}, \ldots, G_{q,K}v_{q,d,K}$$
$$sl_{q,e} = G_{q,1}v_{q,e,1}, \ldots, G_{q,k}v_{q,e,k}, \ldots, G_{q,K}v_{q,e,K}$$

Fusion of $v_{i,a,j}$ with $\Gamma_{q,e}$ is possible if there is a support for it, asserted by the truth of the predicate $supp[fusion(F_q.sl_{q,d}, F_q.sl_{q,e})]$, and only if:

$$\forall k.[(v_{q,d,k} = \varepsilon) \vee (v_{q,e,k} = \varepsilon) \vee (v_{q,d,k} = v_{q,e,k})]$$

where symbol ε represents the fact that the corresponding slot is empty. A more complex condition asserting the possibility of composing two values in a logic formula can also be considered.

The composition action is performed as a consequence of the assertion of the predicate $fusion(F_q.sl_{q,d}, F_q.sl_{q,e})$ made by the following inference rule:

$$[head(v_{i,a,j}) = head(\Gamma_{q,e})] \wedge supp[fusion(F_q.sl_{q,d}, F_q.sl_{q,e})] \wedge$$
$$[\forall k.[(v_{q,d,k} = \varepsilon) \vee (v_{q,e,k} = \varepsilon) \vee (v_{q,d,k} = v_{q,e,k})]] \Rightarrow fusion(F_q.sl_{q,d}, F_q.sl_{q,e})$$

The predicate $supp(x)$ is true when a pattern $\pi_m(x)$, associated with it matches the available hypotheses or data. Different values of m correspond to different template patterns to be matched with the data in order to assert the support.

There may be multiple possible fusions, some of which may not have a support in the data. Possible conflicts in the fusion process are solved by assigning priorities to the fusion candidates based on the posterior probability of the fusion given the data.

In a similar way $\Gamma_{i,a}$ can be composed with another instance as in the following example that shows the result of a fusion action.

Example 3
Sentence: "Un hotel quatre étoiles avec parking" (*A four star hotel with parking*)
Fragments:
HOTEL.[luxury *four_stars*]
HOTEL.[h_facility FACILITY.[facility_type *parking*]]
Head and slot values of fusible fragments:
F_q : HOTEL
$s_{q,d}$: [luxury *four_stars*]
$s_{q,e}$: [h_facility FACILITY.[facility_type *parking*]]

All the other slots of the two instances are empty.
Supports:

fragment supports : σ_1 : four star hotel, σ_2 : parking
$supp[fusion(F_q.sl_{q,d}, F_q.sl_{q,e})] = matches[< \sigma_1 \text{avec}(with)\sigma_2 >, data]$,

where $< \sigma_1 \text{avec}(with)\sigma_2 >$ is a template pattern supporting a fragment fusion involving hotel properties.

Result of composition by fusion:
HOTEL.[luxury *four_stars*, h_facility FACILITY.[facility_type *parking*]]

2.3.3 Composition by Attachment

Given an instance fragment $\Gamma_{i,a}$, let us consider the set Δ_i of all its slot chains having F_i as a head and ending with an unfilled slot. Let $\delta_z^{\varepsilon} \in \Delta_i$ be one of these chains.

Let assume that two instances $\Gamma_{i,a}$ and $\Gamma_{h,b}$ have been hypothesized. Let $head_h$ be the frame name which is the head of $\Gamma_{h,b}$. Let the tail of δ_z^{ε} be an unfilled slot $s_{q,z}$ having name $B_{q,z}$, value $v_{q,z,a}$, and facet $\Phi_{q,z}$. Let $\Phi_{q,z}$ include a frame name which is equal to $head_h$. A binary semantic relation can be asserted between the slot $s_{q,z}$ of $\Gamma_{i,a}$ and $\Gamma_{h,b}$ if there is a support for it in the data from which the instances $\Gamma_{i,a}$ and $\Gamma_{h,b}$ have been hypothesized. The presence of this support is expressed by the truth of the predicate $supp[link(B_{q,z}, \Gamma_{h,b})]$. This triggers a composition action that assigns $\Gamma_{h,b}$ as a value for $B_{q,z}$. The composition action is performed by the assertion of the predicate $link(B_{q,z}, \Gamma_{h,b})$ with the following inference rule:

$$contains(\Phi_{q,z}, head_h) \wedge (v_{q,z,a} = \varepsilon) \wedge supp[link(B_{q,z}, \Gamma_{h,b})] \Rightarrow link(B_{q,z}, \Gamma_{h,b})$$

The predicate $contains(\Phi_{q,z}, head_h)$ is true when the facet $\Phi_{q,z}$ contains $head_h$.

In the MEDIA corpus, semantic entities called *specifiers* have been introduced for annotating some composition links.

Example 4
Sentence: "Un hotel quatre étoiles avec parking à Lyon" (*A four star hotel with a parking in Lyon*)
Fragments:
$\Gamma_{i,a}$: HOTEL. [luxury *four_stars*, h_facility FACILITY.[facility_type *parking*]] (from example 3)
$\Gamma_{h,b}$: ADDRESS.[adr_city *Lyon*]
slot chain in $\Gamma_{i,a}$:
δ_z^{ε} : HOTEL.at_loc ;
tail (δ_z^{ε}) : $B_{q,z}$ = at_loc ;
$\Phi_{q,z}$ = [LOCATION, ADDRESS]
$head_h$ = ADDRESS ;
$head_h \in \Phi_{q,z}$

Supports:

fragment supports : σ_1 [HOTEL], σ_2 : [ADDRESS]
$supp[link(B_{q,z}, \Gamma_{h,b})] = match(< \sigma[HOTEL]\grave{a}(in)\sigma[ADDRESS] >, data)$

Relation support is generalized by considering σ[HOTEL] as an abstraction of all sequences of words expressing a fragment having HOTEL as head and σ[ADDRESS] as an abstraction of all supports for ADDRESS.

Result of composition:
HOTEL. [luxury *four_stars*, h_facility FACILITY.[facility_type *parking*], at_loc ADDRESS.[adr_city *Lyon*]]

Disambiguation is performed, when required, by using posterior probabilities for the supports given the data.

In a similar way, attachment can be defined when a slot is filled with a value that can be composed with another instance fragment using logical operators.

2.3.4 Composition by Attachment and Inference

Let $\Gamma_{i,a}$ be an instance fragment and $\Gamma_{h,b}$ be another fragment that cannot be composed with $\Gamma_{i,a}$ by fusion nor attachment. Let δ_z^ε be a slot chain of $\Gamma_{i,a}$ with head F_i and tail made of an empty slot with name $B_{q,z}$.

Let $\delta_v^\varepsilon = F_c.\delta_x^\varepsilon.F_u.G_{u,v}$ be another slot chain consistent with the application ontology such that:

$$contains(\Phi_{q,z}, F_c) \wedge contains(\Phi_{u,v}, head_h)$$

where $\Phi_{u,v}$ is the facet associated to the slot having name $G_{u,v}$.

An inference rule establishes a link represented by the truth of the predicate $link(B_{q,z}.\delta_z^\varepsilon, \Gamma_{h,b})$ if a suitable support exists. This fact is represented by the truth of the predicate $supp[link(B_{q,z}.\delta_z^\varepsilon, \Gamma_{h,b})]$.

The inference rule is:

$$contains(\Phi_{q,z}, F_c) \wedge contains(\Phi_{u,v}, head_h) \wedge supp[link(B_{q,z}.\delta_z^\varepsilon, \Gamma_{h,b})] \Rightarrow link(B_{q,z}.\delta_z^\varepsilon, \Gamma_{h,b})$$

A similar rule exists for performing the inference of a slot chain before inferring a composition by fusion.

Example 5
Sentence: "J'appelle pour reserver dans un hotel quatre étoiles avec parking à Lyon" (*I call to make a reservation in a four star hotel with a parking in Lyon*)
$\Gamma_{i,a} = \delta_z^\varepsilon$: REQUEST.[request_theme RESERVATION.reserv_obj]
$B_{q,z}$: reserv_obj
$\Phi_{q,z}$=[ROOM, . . .]
$\Gamma_{h,b}$: HOTEL. [luxury *four_stars*, h_facility FACILITY.[facility_type *parking*], at_loc ADDRESS.[adr_city Lyon]]
δ_v^ε : ROOM.lodg_type
$G_{u,v}$ = lodg_type
$\Phi_{u,v}$= [HOTEL, . . .]
$supp[link(B_{q,z}.\delta_z^\varepsilon, \Gamma_{h,b})] = match(< \sigma[RESERVATION]\text{dans(in)}\sigma[HOTEL] >, data)$
Result of composition:
REQUEST.[request_theme RESERVATION .[reserv_obj ROOM.[lodg_type HOTEL. [luxury *four_stars*, h_facility FACILITY.[facility_type *parking*], at_loc ADDRESS.[adr_city *Lyon*]]]]

Different methods have been considered and compared in the LUNA project[2] for performing composition by fusion and by attachment. They use rules obtained with explanation-based learning (EBL) with supports characterized by local syntactic relations, generative models based on dynamic Bayesian networks (DBN) and classification based on conditional random fields (CRF). The use of these models and classifiers will be introduced later. Some results are presented in Section 2.8.

2.4 Probabilistic Interpretation in SLU Systems

In order to obtain useful results in presence of speech disfluencies and error-prone ASR transcriptions, probabilistic models such as stochastic grammars were introduced to be used by parsers capable of generating scored hypotheses in presence of ambiguities and noise.

An early software architecture using relations between syntax and semantics is the Delphi system (Bobrow *et al.*, 1990). It contains different levels, namely, syntactic (using Definite Clause Grammar, DCG), general semantics, domain semantics and action. Different types of representations are composed at various levels to obtain semantic fragments. Probabilities are introduced for different senses of a word and for the application of syntactic rules. These probabilities are estimated from data and used to reduce the parsing effort (Bates *et al.*, 1993). When the unification chart parser could not fully analyze a sentence, the system control executes a robust fallback understanding module (Bates *et al.*, 1994). A directed acyclic graph is introduced whose nodes correspond to meanings of head words. Nodes are connecetd by arcs. Each arc corresponds to a binary semantic relation. One of the parsing actions consists in linking two disconnected graphs with a new arc. If the syntactic parser does not succeed in establishing a connection, a semantic linker attempts to perform composition between lexical nodes with probabilities associated with lexical nodes.

Parsing under the control of stochastic context-free grammars (SCFG) is an activity that involves the application of a finite number of rules. Sequences of rule application can be modeled by a finite-state structure and the history of the rules applied before a given rule can be summarized by finite feature sets. Sequences of rule applications and their probabilities are modeled in history grammars (Black *et al.*, 1993). Let us consider an example in which S is the start symbol of a grammar, r_j is the jth rewriting rule used for parsing a sequence of words W. The probability that the grammar generates a sentence W with a parse tree $\tau_g(W)$ using a sequence g of rewriting rules is computed as follows:

$$P(S \to \tau_g(W)) = \prod_{j=1}^{J} P_g(r_j|R_1^{j-1})$$

where R_1^{j-1} is the history of rule application. R_1^{j-1} can be approximated in various ways.

The possibility of conceiving structured language models (SLM) based on SCFG was investigated in Chelba and Jelinek (2000). The model uses clusters $\Phi(W_1^{i-1})$ of histories of rule

[2] Details can be found in the final report (description of working package WP3) of the LUNA Eurpean project available at http://www.ist-luna.eu

applications found by a parser which computes the following probability:

$$P(w_i|\Phi(W_1^{i-1})) = \sum_{T_i} P(w_i T_i | W_1^{i-1})$$

where the T_i are structures found by the parser.

Parsing actions may have many complex histories causing a data sparseness problem in the estimation of grammar probabilities. A possibility for alleviating this difficulty consists in representing histories with a suitable set of features.

Parsing features to be used for SLU were proposed in Seneff (1989) and other SLU systems (Miller *et al.*, 1994). More details on these approaches can be found in the chapter *Spoken Language Understanding as Template Filling* .

Statistical parsers were proposed for discovering syntactic structures as well as for predicting strings of words (Charniak, 2000; Lease *et al.*, 2005; Roark, 2001). With these parsers a probability that a grammar generates any sequence of words can be computed, thus allowing a complete coverage (but not an always correct parsing result) of every natural language sentence.

At Cambridge University (He and Young, 2003), statistical models of sentence generation were proposed which do not require fully annotated data for training. As a consequence of this, the exact parse state when the reading header is in a specific word position is not known, making the state a hidden variable. More details on this approach can be found in the chapter *Spoken Language Understanding as Template Filling* .

Word lattice rescoring with a statistical parsers is proposed in Roark (2002). Head-driven parsing for word lattices is proposed in Collins *et al.* (2004).

The issue of combining grammar-based and data-driven approaches has been considered in Rayner and Hockey (2003); Wang and Acero (2003).

2.5 Interpretation with Partial Syntactic Analysis

Full parsing may not be possible for many spoken sentences, especially if words are hypothesized by an ASR system. Moreover, the ultimate goal of automatic semantic interpretation is to update the state of the system knowledge about the external world without necessarily performing a complete syntactic analysis.

For some domain applications, semantic and syntactic knowledge can be integrated into a single grammar in which basic semantic constituents are nonterminal symbols. Each of them identifies a sub-network which is a TNG and can be applied just to a segment of a sentence. In the Phoenix system (Ward, 1990; Young *et al.*, 1989), TNGs of this type are proposed and used in procedural attachments to frame slots. Each TNG is activated under the control of the interpretation strategy for hypothesizing semantic fragments.

Simple grammars were also introduced for detecting chunks corresponding to clauses. Classification-based parsing of these clauses was proposed to perform interpretation with inference (Kasper and Hovy, 1990).

Together with partial parsing methods, probabilistic models were proposed for evaluating the plausibility that hypothesized conceptual structures were expressed by the analyzed sentences. Of particular interest are generative models obtained as finite-state approximations of more complex grammars or as conceptual language models. These models are interesting in SLU because they can be directly used in the ASR decoding process.

Some types of pattern matchers were also proposed in semantically driven parsers for detecting supports of semantic hypotheses. Matching may start with lexico-semantic patterns for instantiating initial hypotheses. Interpretations are built by adding nonlexical items inferred by a search algorithm (Stallard and Bobrow, 1993). Different types of matchers can be designed for different purposes. Finite-state pattern matchers, lexical pattern matchers, and sentence level pattern matchers are discussed in Hobbs and Israel (1994).

The Gemini system developed at Stanford Research Institute (SRI) combines a unification grammar and a template matcher (TM) which acts as a fallback (Jackson *et al.*, 1991). The input to the TM is the most likely word sequence hypothesis generated by the ASR module. The TM attempts to detect supports for filling slots of a frame representation. Competing hypotheses are scored, and the template with the best score contributes to the interpretation.

As pattern matching is generally performed using templates of words that can be represented by regular expressions, it appeared interesting to consider generative finite-state statistical models. Models of this type were used in the Air Travel Information System (ATIS) project, carried out in the 1990s and reviewed in De Mori (1998), ch. 14. It was also found useful to estimate probability distribution parameters by a data-driven automatic learning process using manually annotated corpora. With these models, an interpretation process computes the likelihood of a result based on uncertain hypotheses and imprecise knowledge.

For the sake of simplicity, let us assume that a sequence of concept hypotheses $C_1^N = c_1, ..., c_n, ..., c_N$ is expressed by a speaker in a sequence W of words that are hypothesized by an ASR system based on acoustic features Y. This can be represented as follows: $Y \rightarrow_e W \rightarrow_e C_1^N$. Symbol $\rightarrow_e$ indicates an evidential relation meaning that if Y is observed then there is evidence of W and, because of this, there is evidence of C_1^N.

Different concept sequences can be expressed by a sequence W and Y can generate other hypotheses W' which may express C_1^N as well as other sequences of concepts. The presence of C_1^N in a spoken message described by acoustic features Y can only be asserted with a probability that can be computed as follows:

$$
\begin{aligned}
P(C_1^N|Y) &= \frac{1}{P(Y)} \sum_j P(Y|C_1^N W_j) P(C_1^N W_j) \\
&\approx \frac{1}{P(Y)} \sum_j P(Y|W_j) P(C_1^N W_j)
\end{aligned}
$$

A lattice of word hypotheses can be obtained with an ASR system from which a lattice of concept hypotheses, containing concept structures and fillers, can be generated as described in a contribution to a special issue of the *Speech Communication* journal on spoken language understanding (Raymond *et al.*, 2006). Sequences of concept hypotheses for a sentence or a dialogue turn can be extracted from the concept lattice. Let C indicate a sequence of concept hypotheses corresponding to the word sequences W. C can be scored with the following likelihood:

$$
\lambda(C, Y) \approx \arg\max_W P(W|C)P(C)P(Y|W)
$$

$P(Y|W)$ is the acoustic score of W, $P(W|C)$ is obtained with conceptual language models (LM) each of which is a generative model of words expressing concepts in C and $P(C)$ is obtained with a *concept model*. The Chronus system used hidden Markov models (HMMs) for this purpose (Pieraccini *et al.*, 1991). It is reviewed in the chapter *Spoken Language Understanding as Template Filling*.

Other generative models are based on stochastic finite-state transducers (SFST). The topologies of an SFST can be conceived considering approximations of context-free grammars as proposed in Pereira (1990) or approximations of Tree Adjoining Grammars (TAG) as described in Rambow *et al.* (2002). Estimation of probability distributions of SFSTs used for NLU is described, for example, in Prieto *et al.* (1994).

Variable N-gram Stochastic Automata (VNSA) and their use for hypothesizing semantic constituents are proposed in Riccardi *et al.* (1996).

In Nasr *et al.* (1999), SFSTs composed of a variable number of local language models (LM) and a general LM are proposed. Each local model is used for computing the probability of a word sequence knowing a phrase class. Formally, a local model is represented as a tree-structured weighted finite-state automaton (WFSA) whose edges are labelled with words. A path in the WFSA represents a phrase of the class.

Other forms of finite-state conceptual LM for interpretation are discussed in Potamianos *et al.* (2005).

In Camelin *et al.* (2010) improvements are reported for opinion extraction in telephone survey systems when probabilistic conceptual LMs are used in the ASR decoding process.

Generative models based on dynamic Bayesian networks (DBN) have also been proposed. Details of these models, their training and their use can be found in the chapter *Spoken Language Understanding as Template Filling*.

The next section introduces other approaches using discriminatively trained classifiers for generating semantic hypotheses.

2.6 Classification Models for Interpretation

Interpretation can be seen as a classification of groups of signs into classes, each class being identified by a semantic label describing a type of semantic constituents. With the development of discriminative methods for training classifiers from examples, it appeared interesting to learn word patterns useful for distinguishing positive from negative expressions of a concept.

The CHANEL system (Kuhn and De Mori, 1995) generates hypotheses about semantic constituents by means of a forest of specialized decision trees called Semantic Classification Trees (SCTs). Each tree of the forest applies patterns of lexical and syntactic features to a sentence transcription and generates a semantic fragment hypothesis.

A set of template patterns is automatically inferred by discriminative learning from examples of a semantically annotated corpus The required annotation only consists in adding meaning descriptions to the transcription of a sentence.

There is an SCT for every semantic constituent. An SCT is a binary tree with a question associated to each node. A question is about the matching of a specific pattern with the words in a sentence and is automatically constructed in the learning process. One of the node successors is reached if the answer to the node question is positive, otherwise the other successor is reached.

Patterns used in the SCTs can be automatically learned from automatic transcriptions to make the acquired knowledge robust to grammatical and lexical errors. For this purpose, pattern generation tends to minimize the number of words that must be correct to avoid understanding errors. Details on SCT training can be found in (Kuhn and De Mori, 1995). Constituents hypothesized by SCTs are composed into a semantic structure C by rules.

In CHANEL, the interpretation hypotheses are scored by the following probability:

$$P(C|Y) \approx \arg\max_{W} P(C|W)P(W|Y)$$

$P(C|W)$ is obtained using the probabilities of each constitent of C. The probability of a constituent is computed by associating with each leaf of the corresponding tree the number of times the leaf corresponding to the pattern that matched with W is reached.

Other classifiers were developed for detecting non-recursive structures of certain types of natural language phrases such as noun phrases (NP). This type of detection was considered as an operation of shallow parsing that could be integrated in a syntactic parser or in other components for natural language processing. Shallow semantic parsing was mostly applied to written text processing with the purpose of creating a domain independent, predicate/argument representation of meaning (Gildea and Jurafsky, 2002). Most of the approaches to shallow parsing for written text use features for performing classification.

In Hacioglu and Ward (2003), a classification is proposed in which the syntactic tree representation of a sentence is linearized into a sequence of non-terminal syntactic constituents. Each constituent is classified into semantic roles using context features. In another method, features are obtained with a bottom-up process for each word after chunking a sentence into phrases. Assuming that parts of speech (POS) are also available, the words are tagged as inside a phrase (I), outside a phrase (O) or at the beginning of a phrase (B). This is called IOB representation (Ramshaw and Marcus, 1995).

In Pradhan *et al.* (2004), the parsing problem is formulated as a multi-class classification problem using a support vector machine (SVM) classifier whose scores are converted to probabilities with a sigmoid function.

A parser based on tagging actions producing non-overlapping shallow tree structures is described in Hacioglu (2004). A sentence is considered to be a sequence of base phrases at a syntactic level. At a semantic level, predicate arguments have associated sequences of base phrases. The parse strategy is based on tagging actions and consists of three components that are sequentially applied to the input text for a chosen predicate to determine its arguments. These components are POS tagging, base phrase and semantic taggers–chunkers. SVM classifiers are used at all levels. A memory-based approach to learning language patterns useful for shallow parsing is described in Argamon *et al.* (1998).

In Schapire *et al.* (2005), the possibility is considered of using human-crafted knowledge to compensate for the lack of data in building robust classifiers. The AdaBoost algorithm proposed for this task combines many simple and moderately accurate categorization rules that are trained sequentially into a single, highly accurate model. In the proposed approach the loss function combines a measure of fit to the training data with a measure of adequacy to a human-built model.

Exponential models using various types of features are widley used. Features assert, for example, the presence of n-grams, long-distance bigrams, sets of words or the matching of template patterns with the available data.

The results obtained with some of these models applied to SLU are compared in Hahn *et al.* (2008). The evidence of a sequence of concept tag hypotheses is expressed by following probability:

$$P(C|W) = p(c_1^N|w_1^N) = \frac{1}{Z}\prod_{n=1}^{N} exp(\sum_{m=1}^{M} \lambda_m h_m(c_{n-1}, c_n, w_{n-\delta}^{n+\delta}))$$

Z is a normalizing value. It is assumed that a concept hypothesis corresponding to a sequence of words is associated with each word of the sequence. Functions $h_m(c_{n-1}, c_n, w_{n-\delta}^{n+\delta})$ are evaluated for each pair of concept labels and the words in a windows centered at c_n, w_n and spanning 2δ words. The λ_m are the weights associated with each function. They are estimated in the training process.

By defining:

$$H(c_{n-1}, c_n, w_{n-\delta}^{n+\delta}) = exp(\sum_{m=1}^{M} \lambda_m h_m(c_{n-1}, c_n, w_{n-\delta}^{n+\delta}))$$

the posterior probability normalized on positional level (LLPOS) is expressed, for log-linear models, as:

$$p(c_1^N | w_1^N) = \prod_{n=1}^{N} \frac{H(c_{n-1}, c_n, w_{n-\delta}^{n+\delta})}{\sum_{\tilde{c}} H(c_{n-1}, \tilde{c}, w_{n-\delta}^{n+\delta})}$$

while for linear chain conditional random fields (CRF) it is expressed as:

$$p(c_1^N | w_1^N) = \frac{\prod_{n=1}^{N} H(c_{n-1}, c_n, w_{n-\delta}^{n+\delta})}{\sum_{\tilde{c}_1^N} \prod_{n=1}^{N} H(\tilde{c}_{n-1}, \tilde{c}_n, w_{n-\delta}^{n+\delta})}$$

The use of CRFs for semantic role labelling is described in a paper of a special issue of *Computational Linguistics* on semantic role labelling (Toutanova *et al.*, 2008).

Comparisons and experimental results on the use of CRFs for SLU are presented in Raymond and Riccardi (2007). Further details on CRF for SLU can be found in the chapter *Spoken Language Understanding as Template Filling* .

Comparative experiments on the use of generative, classification and exponential models for concept tag hypothesization have been performed in the LUNA project. The results are summarized in Section 2.8.

2.7 Advanced Methods and Resources for Semantic Modeling and Interpretation

In the last decade, based on past and current experience on the difficulty and complexity of SLU, a collection of methods has been proposed. They are briefly reviewed in the following.

In Papieni *et al.* (1998) statistical machine translation (SMT) models are proposed to transform a source sentence W into a target, MRL description C for which the probability $P(C|W)$ is maximum: The central task in training the model is to determine associations between groups of words in one language and MRL descriptions in the other.

Call routing is an important and practical example of spoken message categorization. In applications of this type, a dialogue act expressed by a sentence is classified to generate a semantic primitive action belonging to a well-defined set. A solution to spoken message categorization is proposed in Gorin (1995). A distributed knowledge representation is modeled by a network used for mapping words or phrases into actions. A deployed system for call routing, called How May I Help You (HMIHY) is described in Gorin *et al.* (1997) and a conversational Help Desk natural language call routing application is described in Stewart *et al.* (2006).

LMs based on Latent Semantic Analysis (LSA) capture some semantic relationships between words. LSA maps the words and their histories into a semantic space with reduced dimensions using a Singular Value Decomposition (SVD) technique (Bellegarda, 2000). Word similarities are measured with distance metrics such as the inner product between the corresponding vectors in reduced space. A similar technique was proposed for hypothesizing semantic components in a sentence (Chu-Carroll and Carpenter, 1999). In Zhang and Rudnicky (2002), LSA is proposed for integrating multiple level knowledge. In Li and Chou (2002) latent semantic indexing in call routing is proposed to identify the goal of the utterance.

A knowledge model with which relevant improvements were observed in large corpora experiments is proposed in Wang *et al.* (2002). Super Abstract Role Values (SuperARV) are introduced to encode multiple knowledge sources in a uniform representation that is much more fine-grained than Parts of Speech (POS).

Various techniques have been proposed for DA modeling and detection. Among them, it is worth mentioning semantic classification trees (Mast *et al.*, 1996), decision trees (Ang *et al.*, 2005; Stolcke *et al.*, 1998), hidden Markov models (HMM) (Stolcke *et al.*, 1998), fuzzy fragment-class Markov models (Wu *et al.*, 2002), neural networks (Stolcke *et al.*, 1998), maximum entropy models (Ang *et al.*, 2005; Stolcke *et al.*, 1998).

Methods for relating words and dialogue facts or local semantic labels to query communication goals with belief networks are proposed in Meng *et al.* (1999).

Graphical models and DBNs for DA detection in SLU systems are proposed in Ji and Bilmes (2005).

For joint segmentation and classification of DAs, a technique based on a Hidden-event Language Model (HELM) is described in Zimmermann (2005).

Accurate event detection is obtained if sentence boundaries are identified in spoken messages containing more than one sentence. Approaches to this task have used HMMs (Shriberg *et al.*, 2000) and CRFs (Liu *et al.*, 2005). In Roark *et al.* (2006), a baseline model is used to produce n-best lists of possible segmentations. Disambiguating features are extracted over entire candidate segmentations.

In Thomae *et al.* (2005), a hierarchy of LMs is proposed for interpretation.

The introduction of semantic information in LMs is proposed in Erdogan *et al.* (2005). Finite-state models are used to interpolate scores obtained with a concept LM and a general n-gram LM. In addition to that, semantic parse information is combined with n-gram information using a two-level statistical model. Features are also used for computing the joint probability of a sentence and its parse with a single maximum entropy (ME) model.

Kernel methods and maximum entropy models have been proposed for parsing and interpretation (Moschitti, 2004).

Results in Pradhan *et al.* (2007) with SVM classifiers, have shown that there is a significant drop in performance when training and testing on different corpora.

The concurrent use of SCT, Adaboost and SVM classifiers is proposed in Raymond *et al.* (2007) to increase classification robustness by using the consensus among classifiers as a confidence indicator.

Interpretation can benefit from useful collections of linguistic information. In semantic role labelling, a lexicon is used which lists the possible roles for each syntactic argument of each predicate. A predicate lexicon was developed in the FrameNet project (Lowe *et al.*, 1997), and a verb lexicon was developed in the PropBank project (Palmer *et al.*, 2005). In the VerbNet project (Kipper *et al.*, 2000), a manually developed hierarchical verb lexicon was developed based on the verb classification proposed in Levin (1993). For each verb class, VerbNet specifies the syntactic frames along with the semantic role assigned to each slot of a frame. In the WordNet project (Miller, 1995), a word is represented by a set of synonymous senses belonging to an alphabet of synsets. Word sense disambiguation can be performed using word-nets or various types of context probabilities. In Zechner (1998), a combination is proposed of partial parsing, also called chunking, with the mapping of the verb arguments onto subcategorization frames that can be extracted automatically, for example, from WordNet.

MindNet (Richardson *et al.*, 1998) produces a hierarchical structure of semantic relations (semrels) from a sentence using words in a machine-readable dictionary. These structures are inverted and linked with every word appearing in them, thus allowing one to perform matching and compute similarities by spreading activation.

2.8 Recent Systems

The DARPA Communicator project for spoken dialogues including SLU components was carried out at the beginning of the 21st century in the US. Interesting architectures and paradigms were developed.[3] Evaluations are reported in Walker *et al.* (2002).

In Bangalore and Johnston (2004), a mixture language model for a multi-modal application is described with a component trained with in-domain data and another with data generated by a grammar. Understanding is performed by detecting the sequence C of predicate–argument concept hypotheses that maximizes $P(C|W)$. An approximation is made by considering bigrams and trigrams of concepts.

In Sarikaya *et al.* (2004), a system is proposed that uses a dialogue state dependent trigram LM. Context-free semantic grammars generate word sequences for each cocept and are used for concept spotting.

As a result, semantic hypotheses are generated by filling a number of slots in a frame representation. Decision among these hypotheses is made based on maximum word coverage.

Trigram probabilities are also used for scoring concept hypotheses. The resulting score of a hypothesis is $P(W, C)$.

A second LM, called Maximum Entropy (ME) LM (MELM), computes probabilities of a word, given its history.

Each sentence resulting from ASR hypotheses is scored with the two models to assign a semantic probability to each word. The corresponding semantic features are extracted from each word. A decision tree is built using word features with the purpose of separating the correct and incorrect words. It uses the raw score of the respective features and learns feature combinations for predicting acceptance or rejection. These features are used for computing confidence measures.

A speech understanding framework for Japanese with multiple language models and multiple speech understanding models is proposed in Katsumaru *et al.* (2009).

In the European project LUNA (http://www.ist-luna.eu.), SLU research was conducted using a software architecture scheme shown in Figure 2.3.

[3] http://fofoca.mitre.org/doc.html Galaxy Communicator

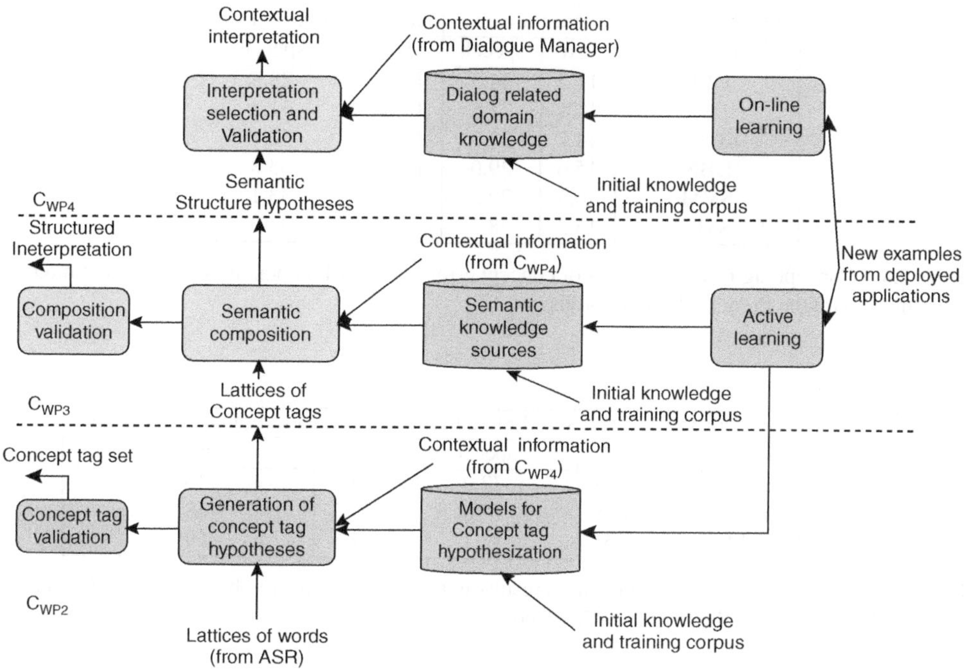

Figure 2.3 Software architecture scheme used in the LUNA project

A lattice of words produced by an ASR system is used for generating concept tag hypotheses in a software layer indicated as C_{WP2}. Concept tags are then used for generating semantic fragments which are composed into frame-based semantic structures in the layer indicated as C_{WP3}. Semantic structure hypotheses are further processed and re-ranked using dialogue history information in a layer indicated as C_{WP4}. At each level, knowledge sources are updated using active learning methods. Scoring and hypothesis validation is performed using suitable confidence indicators.

Different methods and corpora in French, Italian and Polish were compared in different SLU systems.

The results obtained with French MEDIA telephone corpus of a negotiation dialogue application are summarized below. The corpus was used for training and testing methods based on the following models and classifiers:

- Maximum entropy models for statistical machine translation (SMT),
- Finite state transducers (FST),
- Support vector machines (SVM),
- Conditional Random Fields (CRF),
- Dynamic Bayesian Networks (DBN),
- Log-linear models on positional level (LLPos).

CRFs provided the best results in interpreting manual as well as ASR word transcriptions using the same train, development and test sets for all the experiments. The results obtained

MEDIA corpus	concept name		concept name and value	
model	text	speech	text	speech
CRF	11.5	24.3	14.6	28.8
FST	14.1	27.5	16.6	31.3
LLPos	14.7	27.5	17.7	32.1
DBN	15.6	29.0	18.3	33.0
SVM	16.5	29.2	19.2	33.1
SMT	15.2	28.7	23.4	34.9

Figure 2.4 Concept tag results in terms of concept error rates (CER) obtained with different models and methods with the French MEDIA corpus

French MEDIA corpus	F-measure Frame heads		F-measure Frame composition	
model	text	speech	text	speech
rules	85.3	77.0	74.4	66.9
CRF + rules	84.5	77.8	74.2	68.3
DBN-SVM	85	77.1	67.5	59.3

Figure 2.5 Semantic fragment composition results in terms of F-measure obtained with different models and methods with the French MEDIA corpus

on concept tag names and values for the test set are reported in Figure 2.4. The experiments were performed with 74 concept tags. The training and test corpora contain respectively 12908 and 3518 telephone dialogue turns. Results on the transcribed sentences are referred to as text, while results obtained with the best word sequence generated by an ASR system (with a word error rate of 27.4%) are referred to as speech.

Figure 2.5 shows semantic fragment composition results in terms of F-measure obtained with different models and methods with the French MEDIA corpus. In the first approach, compositions by fusion and attachment were performed by rules as described in Section 2.3. In the second approach, specifiers were hypothesized with CRFs and used for composition by rules. In the third approach, frame instances were generated with DBNs and binary compositions were performed with a classification process based on SVMs.

As composition essentially follows a well-characterized logical model, results obtained by rules are similar to those obtained by machine learning methods.

Figure 2.6 shows the architecture of two telephone systems for spoken opinion analysis. The first system, described in detail in Camelin *et al.* (2010), performs surveys of user satisfaction in a customer care center. The second system (Camelin *et al.*, 2008) detects opinions of customers expressing a high degree of dissatisfaction and generates an alarm requiring immediate human intervention.

Opinions are detected by using finite-state conceptual LMs and boostexter classifiers for extracting concept tag hypotheses. Scores computed by classifiers and co-occurrence of hypotheses were used to make a final validation decision on the opinions expressed in a user message. For this application, classification based on boostexter appeared to be more effective in generating correct opinion hypotheses than methods based on CRFs.

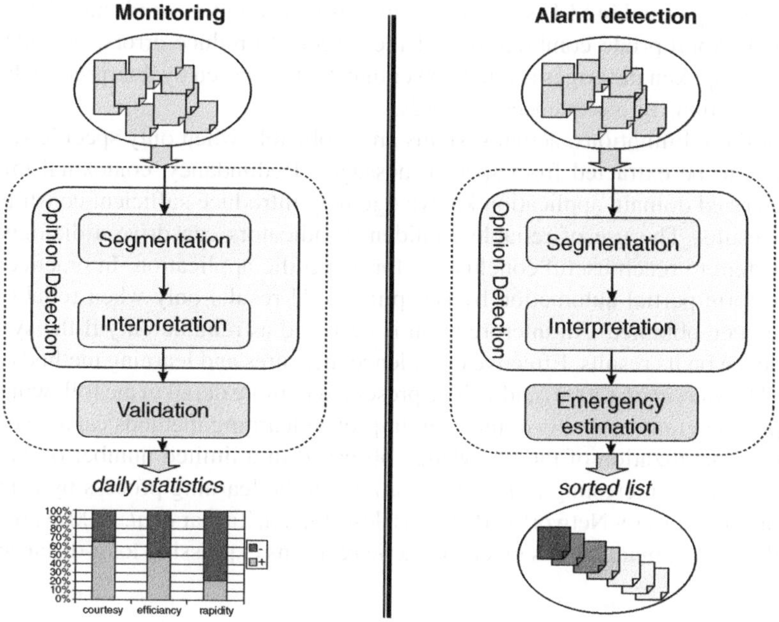

Figure 2.6 Architectures of a system for spoken opinion analysis

2.9 Conclusions

SLU and NLU are performed by processes that use knowledge for transforming signs of a language into meaning representations. As some components of this representation may be implicit in what is observed, interpretation may also involve inference. The result of interpretation may contain complex semantic structures obtained by composing fragments hypothesized with models and relations of observable data. Semantic constituents and semantic structures can be expressed with MRLs that describe logical models and relations. Relations between syntactic sentence structures and their meanings were studied since the beginning of NLU and SLU research resulting in the development of useful hand-crafted knowledge.

Early attempts and experiments showed that there are many ways for expressing the same concept and that the relations between an interpretation hypothesis and its support made of data patterns is often imprecise. Furthermore, especially for SLU, signs used for interpretation are extracted from the speech signal with a process that is not perfect. These problems suggested the use of probabilistic models and machine learning methods for automatically characterizing supports for semantic constituents end their relations. As a consequence, methods were proposed for estimating the parameters of generative models and classification methods. These methods have been reviewed in this chapter and some evaluations have been reported. Evaluation results obtained so far show that interpreting speech transcriptions made by an ASR component is affected by much more errors than interpreting correct transcriptions. Some errors can be avoided by processing n-best lists or lattices of word hypotheses. Training classifiers for correctly interpreting ASR output can be effective if useful lexical and syntactic features are considered, perhaps in the context of available partial semantic hypotheses.

As the knowledge used in SLU systems is imprecise, different methods have been proposed and evaluated. Appropriate combinations of them seem to reduce errors, but interpretation performance on spoken messages is much lower than that observed by interpreting their correct manual transcriptions into sequences of words.

In spite of these limitations, actual systems are applicable when only specific semantic information has to be extracted from speech messages. Redundancy, contextual information, well-characterized domain application knowledge may introduce sufficient constraints to obtain useful results. The use of reliable confidence indicators can drive a dialogue strategy leading a system to reach useful conclusions for a specific application. In practice, it can be useful to perform partial automation by accepting SLU results only when reliable interpretations have been obtained. An interpretation is accepted as reliable only if the system has a large confidence on its results. Effective confidence measures and learning methods are briefly reviewed in De Mori *et al.* (2008) and will be presented in more detail in the following chapters.

Further progress may probably come from improved learning methods capable of performing effective generalization of the knowledge observed in a limited number of examples. In particular, it appears interesting to include relations in the learning process by using, for example, Relational Markov Networks (RMN) as described in Taskar *et al.* (2002) . It is possible to learn in this way semantic links given syntactic relations expressing long-distance syntactic dependences.

References

Ajdukiewicz K 1935 Die syntaktische Konnexität. *Studies in Philosophy* **1**, 1–27.

Allen J 1995 *Natural Language Understanding*. Benjamin Cummings, Menlo Park, CA.

Allen J and Core M 1997 Draft of DAMSL: Dialog act markup in several layers Unpublished manuscript.

Ang J, Liu Y and Shriberg E 2005 Automatic dialog act segmentation and classification in multiparty meetings *in Proc. IEEE Int. Conf. on Acoustics, Speech and Signal Processing*, pp. 1061–1064, Philadelphia, PA, USA.

Argamon S, Dagan I and Krymolowski Y 1998 A memory-based approach to learning shallow natural language patterns *Proc. of the International Conference on Computational linguistics*, pp 67–73, Montreal, Canada.

Bangalore S and Johnston M 2004 Balancing data-driven and rule-based approaches in the context of a multimodal conversational system *in Proc. of the Conference of the North American Chapter of the Association for Computational Linguistics on Human Language Technology*, pp 33–40, Boston, Massachusetts, USA.

Bar-Hillel Y 1953 A quasi-arithmetical notation for syntactic description. *Language* **29**, 47–58.

Bates M, Bobrow R, Fung P, Ingria R, Kubala F, Makhoul J, Nguyen L, Schwartz R and Stallard D 1993 The bbn/harc spoken language understanding system *in Proc. IEEE Int. Conf. on Acoustics, Speech and Signal Processing*, pp 111–114, Minneapolis, Minnesota, USA.

Bates M, Bobrow R, Ingria R, Peters S and Stallard D 1994 Advances in BBN's Spoken Language System *Proceedings of the Spoken Language Technology Workshop*, pp 43–47, Princeton, NJ, USA.

Bellegarda J 2000 Large vocabulary speech recognition with multispan statistical language models. *IEEE Transactions on Speech and Audio Processing* **8**(1), 76 –84.

Black E, Jelinek F, Lafferty J, Magerman DM, Mercer R and Roukos S 1993 Towards history-based grammars: using richer models for probabilistic parsing *Proc. of the International Conference on Computational linguistics*, pp 31–37, Columbus, Ohio, USA.

Bobrow R, Ingria R and Stallard D 1990 Syntactic and semantic knowledge in the delphi unification grammar *in Proc. of the Workshop on Speech and Natural Language*, pp 230–236, Hidden Valley, Pensylvania, USA.

Bonneau-Maynard H, Rosset S, Ayache C, Kuhn A and Mostefa D 2005 Semantic annotation of the french media dialog corpus *in Proc of the INTERSPEECH Conference*, Lisbon, Portugal.

Brachman RJ and Schmolze JG 1985 An overview of the KL-ONE knowledge representation system. *Cognitive Science* **(2)**, 171–216.

Camelin N, Béchet F, Damnati G and De Mori R 2010 Detection and interpretation of opinion expressions in spoken surveys. *IEEE Transactions on Audio, Speech and Language Processing* **18**, 369–381.

Camelin N, De Mori R, Béchet F and Damnati G 2008 Automatic customer feedback processing : alarm detection in open question spoken messages *in Proc. of the INTERSPEECH Conference*, Brisbane, Australia.

Charniak E 2000 A maximum-entropy-inspired parser *Proceedings of the Meeting of the North American Chapter of the Association for Computational Linguistics*, pp 132–139.

Chelba C and Jelinek F 2000 Structured language modeling. *Computer, Speech and Language* **14**(4), 283–332.

Chu-Carroll J and Carpenter B 1999 Vector-based natural language call routing. *Comput. Linguist.* **25**(3), 361–388.

Collins C, Carpenter B and Penn G 2004 Head-driven parsing for word lattices *Proc. of the International Conference on Computational linguistics*, pp 232–239.

De Mori R 1998 *Spoken Dialogues with Computers*. Academic Press.

De Mori R, Béchet F, Hakkani-Tur D, McTear M, Riccardi G and Tur G 2008 Spoken language understanding: a survey. *Signal Processing Magazine, IEEE* **25**(3), 50–58.

Dowding J, Gawron JM, Appelt DE, Bear J, Cherny L, Moore R and Moran DB 1993 GEMINI: A natural language system for spoken-language understanding *Proc. of the International Conference on Computational linguistics*, pp 54–61, Columbus, Ohio, USA.

Duvert F and De Mori R 2010 Conditional models for detecting lambda-functions in a spoken language understanding system *in Proc of the INTERSPEECH Conference*, Tokyo, Japan.

Erdogan H, Sarikaya R, Chen SF, Gao Y and Picheny M 2005 Using semantic analysis to improve speech recognition performance. *Computer Speech and Language* **19**(3), 321–343.

Erman LD, Hayes-Roth F, Lesser VR and Reddy DR 1980 The hearsay-ii speech-understanding system: Integrating knowledge to resolve uncertainty. *ACM Comput. Surv.* **12**(2), 213–253.

Fikes RE and Nilsson NJ 1971 Strips: A new approach to the application of theorem proving to problem solving. *Artificial Intelligence* **2**, 189–208.

Fillmore C 1968 *The Case for Case* Holt, Rinehart, and Winston New York pp 1–88.

Gildea D and Jurafsky D 2002 Automatic labeling of semantic roles. *Computational Linguistics* **28**(3), 245–288.

Gorin A 1995 On automated language acquisition. *Journal of Acoustical Society of America* **97**(6), 3441–3461.

Gorin AL, Riccardi G and Wright JH 1997 How may I help you ?. *Speech Communication* **23**(1–2), 113–127.

Hacioglu K 2004 A lightweight semantic chunker based on tagging *in Proc. of the Conference of the North American Chapter of the Association for Computational Linguistics on Human Language Technology*, pp 145–148, Boston, Massachussetts, USA.

Hacioglu K and Ward W 2003 Target word detection and semantic role chunking using support vector machines *in Proc. of the Conference of the North American Chapter of the Association for Computational Linguistics on Human Language Technology*, pp 25–27, Edmonton, Canada.

Hahn S, Lehnen P, Raymond C and Ney H 2008 A comparison of various methods for concept tagging for spoken language understanding In *in Proc. of the LREC Conference* (ed. (ELRA) ELRA), Marrakesh, Morocco.

He Y and Young S 2003 Hidden vector state model for hierarchical semantic parsing *Proceedings of the IEEE International Conference on Acoustics, Speech and Signal Processing, Hong Kong*, pp 268–271.

Hendler J and McGuinness DL 2000 The DARPA Agent Markup Language. *IEEE Intelligent Systems* **15**(6), 67–73.

Hobbs JR and Israel DJ 1994 Principles of template design *in Proc. of the workshop on Speech and Natural Language*, Princeton, NJ, USA.

Jackendoff R 1990 *Semantic Structures*. MIT Press, Cambridge, MA.

Jackendoff R 2002 *Foundations of Languages*. UK: Oxford Univ. Press.

Jackson E, Appelt DE, Bear J, Moore RC and Podlozny A 1991 A template matcher for robust nl interpretation *in Proc. of the Workshop on Speech and Natural Language*, Pacific Grove, CA,USA.

Ji G and Bilmes J 2005 Dialog act tagging using graphical models *in Proc. IEEE Int. Conf. on Acoustics, Speech and Signal Processing*, Philadelphia, PA, USA.

JMLR 2002 Special issue on shallow parsing. *Journal of Machine Learning Research.*

Kasper RT and Hovy EH 1990 Performing integrated syntactic and semantic parsing using classification *in Proc. of the workshop on Speech and Natural Language*, pp 54–59, Hidden Valley, Pensylvania, USA.

Katsumaru M, Nakano M, Komatani K, Funakoshi K, Ogata T and Okuno HG 2009 A speech understanding framework that uses multiple language models and multiple understanding models *in Proc. of the Conference of the North American Chapter of the Association for Computational Linguistics on Human Language Technology*, vol. 2, pp 133–136, Boulder, Colorado; USA.

Kifer M, Lausen G and Wu J 1995 Logical foundations of object-oriented and frame-based languages. *Journal of the ACM* **42**, 741–843.

Kipper K, Dang HT and Palmer M 2000 Class-based construction of a verb lexicon *Proceedings of the Seventeenth National Conference on Artificial Intelligence and Twelfth Conference on Innovative Applications of Artificial Intelligence*, pp 691–696. AAAI Press / The MIT Press.

Klatt DH 1977 Review of the ARPA speech understanding project. *Journal of the Acoustical Society of America* **62**(6), 1345–1366.

Kuhn R and De Mori R 1995 The application of semantic classification trees to natural language understanding. *IEEE Transactions on Pattern Analysis and Machine Intelligence* **17**(5), 449–460.

Lease M, Charniak E and Johnson M 2005 Parsing and its applications for conversational speech *in Proc. of the International Conference on Acoustics, Speech, and Signal Processing*, pp 451–458, Philadelphia, PA, USA.

Levin B 1993 *English Verb Classes and Alternations*. University of Chicago Press, Chicago and London.

Li L and Chou W 2002 Improving latent semantic indexing based classifier with information gain *in Proc. of the International Conference on Spoken Language Processing*, pp 1141–1144, Denver, CO, USA.

Liu Y, Stolcke A, Shriberg E and Harper M 2005 Using conditional random fields for sentence boundary detection in speech *Proc. of the International Conference on Computational linguistics*, pp 451–458, Ann Arbor, Michigan, USA.

Lowe J, Baker C and Fillmore C 1997 A frame-semantic approach to semantic annotation *Proceedings of the SIGLEX Workshop on Tagging Text with Lexical Semantics: Why, What, and How?*, Washington D.C., USA.

Mast M, Kompe R, Harbeck S, Kießling A, Niemann H, Nöth E, Schukat-Talamazzini EG and Warnke V 1996 Dialog act classification with the help of prosody *in Proc. of the International Conference on Spoken Language Processing*, vol. 3, pp 1732–1735, Philadelphia, PA, USA.

Meng HM, Lam W and Wai C 1999 To believe is to understand *in proc. of the Eurospeech conference*, Budapest, Hungary.

Miller GA 1995 Wordnet: a lexical database for english. *Commun. ACM* **38**(11), 39–41.

Miller S, Bobrow R, Schwartz R and Ingria R 1994 Statistical language processing usign hidden understanding models *Proc. of the International Conference on Computational linguistics*, Las Cruces, NM, USA.

Montague R 1974 *Formal Philosophy: Selected Papers of Richard Montague*. Yale University Press, New Haven, CONN, USA.

Moschitti A 2004 A study on convolution kernels for shallow semantic parsing *in Proc. of the Annual Meeting on Association for Computational Linguistics*, p. 335, Barcelona, Spain.

Nasr A, Estève Y, Béchet F, Spriet T and De Mori R 1999 A language model combining n-grams and stochastic finite state automata *in Proc of the Eurospeech Conference*, vol. 5, pp 2175–2178, Budapest, Hungary.

Nilsson NJ 1980 *Principles of Artificial Intelligence*. Morgan Kaufmann, Los Altos, CA, USA.

Norvig P 1983 Frame activated inferences in a story understanding program *IJCAI'83: Proceedings of the Eighth International Joint Conference on Artificial Intelligence*, pp 624–626. Morgan Kaufmann Publishers Inc., San Francisco, CA, USA.

Palmer M, Gildea D and Kingsbury P 2005 The proposition bank: An annotated corpus of semantic roles. *Comput. Linguist.* **31**(1), 71–106.

Papieni K, Roukos S and Ward R 1998 Maximum likelihood and discriminative training of direct translation models *in Proc. IEEE Int. Conf. on Acoustics, Speech and Signal Processing*, pp 189–192, Seattle, WA, USA.

Patel-Schneider P, Hayes P and Horrocks I 2003 Owl web ontology language semantics and abstract syntax. Technical report, W3C working Draft.

Pereira F 1990 Finite-state approximations of grammars *in Proc. of the workshop on Speech and Natural Language*, pp 20–25, Hidden Valley, Pensylvania, USA.

Pieraccini R, Levin E and Lee CH 1991 Stochastic representation of conceptual structure in the atis task *Speech and Natural Language Workshop*, pp 121–124, Pacific Grove, CA, USA.

Potamianos A, Narayanan S and Riccardi G 2005 Adaptive categorical understanding for spoken dialogue systems. *IEEE Transactions on Speech and Audio Processing* **13**(3), 321–329.

Pradhan S, Ward W and Martin JH 2007 Towards robust semantic role labeling *in Proc. of the Conference of the North American Chapter of the Association for Computational Linguistics on Human Language Technology*, pp 556–563, Rochester, NY, USA.

Pradhan S, Ward W, Hacioglu K, Martin JH and Jurafsky D 2004 Shallow semantic parsing using support vector machines *in Proc. of the Conference of the North American Chapter of the Association for Computational Linguistics on Human Language Technology*, pp 233–240, Boston, Massachusetts, USA.

Prieto N, Sanchis E and Palmero L 1994 Continuous speech understanding based on automatic learning of acoustic and semantic models *International Conference on Spoken Language Processing*, Yokohama, Japan.

Rambow O, Bangalore S, Butt T, Nasr A and Sproat R 2002 Creating a finite-state parser with application semantics *Proc. of the international conference on Computational linguistics*, pp 1–5, Ann Arbor, MI, USA.

Ramshaw LA and Marcus MP 1995 Text chunking using transformation-based learning *Proceedings of the Third Annual Workshop on Very Large Corpora*, pp 82–94, Cambridge, Massachusetts, USA.

Raymond C and Riccardi G 2007 Generative and discriminative algorithms for spoken language understanding *in Proc of the INTERSPEECH Conference*, Antwerp, Belgium.

Raymond C, Béchet F, Camelin N, De Mori R and Damnati G 2007 Sequential decision strategies for machine interpretation of speech. *IEEE Transactions on Audio, Speech and Language Processing* **15**(1), 162–171.

Raymond C, Béchet F, De Mori R and Damnati G 2006 On the use of finite state transducers for semantic interpretation. *Speech Communication* **48**(3–4), 288–304.

Rayner M and Hockey BA 2003 Transparent combination of rule-based and data-driven approaches in a speech understanding architecture *Proceedings of the 10 Conference of the European Chapter of the Association for Computational Linguistics*, pp 299–306, Budapest, Hungary.

Riccardi G, Pieraccini R and Bocchieri E 1996 Stochastic automata for language modeling. *Computer Speech and Language* **4**, 265–293.

Richardson SD, Dolan WB and Vanderwende L 1998 Mindnet: Acquiring and structuring semantic information from text *in Proc. of the Joint COLING-ACL*, pp 1098–1102, Montreal, Canada.

Roark B 2001 Probabilistic top-down parsing and language modeling. *Comput. Linguist.* **27**(2), 249–276.

Roark B 2002 Markov parsing: lattice rescoring with a statistical parser *Proc. of the International Conference on Computational Linguistics*, Philadelphia, PA,USA.

Roark B, Liu Y, Harper M, Stewart R, Lease M, Snover M, Shafran Z, Dorr B, Hale J, Krasnyanskaya A and Young L 2006 Reranking for sentence boundary detection in conversational speech *in Proc. IEEE Int. Conf. on Acoustics, Speech and Signal Processing*, vol. 1, pp 545–548, Toulouse, France.

Sarikaya R, Gao Y and Picheny M 2004 A comparison of rule–based and statistical methods for semantic language modeling and confidence measurement *in Proc. of the Conference of the North American Chapter of the Association for Computational Linguistics on Human Language Technology*, pp 65–68, Boston, Massachusetts, USA.

Schapire RE, Rochery M, Rahim M and Gupta N 2005 Boostingwith prior knowledge for call classification. *IEEE Transactions on Speech and Audio Processing* **SAP-13**, 174–182.

Seneff S 1989 Tina: A probabilistic syntactic parser for speech understanding systems *Proc. of the Speech and Natural Language Workshop*, pp 168–178, Philadelphia, PA, USA.

Shriberg E, Stolcke A, Hakkani-Tur D and Tur G 2000 Prosody-based automatic segmentation of speech into sentences and topics. *Speech Communication* pp 127–154.

Stallard D and Bobrow R 1993 The semantic linker: a new fragment combining method *in Proc. of the Workshop on Speech and Natural Language*, pp 37–42, Princeton, NJ, USA.

Steedman M 1996 *Surface Structure and Interpretation*. MIT Press.

Stewart O, Huerta J, Jan E, Wu C, Li X and Lubensky D 2006 Conversational help desk: Vague callers and context switch *in Proc of the INTERSPEECH Conference*, pp 1910–1913, Pittsburg, Pensylvania, USA.

Stolcke A, Shriberg E, Bates R, Coccaro N, Jurafsky D, Martin R, Meteer M, Ries K, Taylor P and Van Ess-Dykema C 1998 Dialog act modeling for conversational speech In *Applying Machine Learning to Discourse Processing. Papers from the 1998 AAAI Spring Symposium)* (ed. Chu-Carroll J and Green N), pp 98–105. AAAI Press, Stanford, CA.

Tait JI 1985 Semantic parsing and syntactic constraints (mark iv) In *Automatic Natural Language Parsing* (ed. Sparck Jones K and Wilks Y) Ellis Horwood Chichester pp 169–177.

Taskar B, Abbeel P and Koller D 2002 Discriminative probabilistic models for relational data *UAI '02, Proceedings of the 18th Conference on Uncertainty in Artificial Intelligence*, pp 485–492, Edmonton, Alberta, Canada.

Thomae M, Fabian T, Lieb R and Ruske G 2005 Hierarchical language models for one-stage speech interpretation *in Proc of the INTERSPEECH Conference*, pp 1149–1152, Lisbon, Portugal.

Toutanova K, Haghighi A and Manning CD 2008 A global joint model for semantic role labeling. *Computational Linguistics*, **34**(2) 161–191.

Walker D 1975 The sri speech understanding system. *IEEE Transactions on Acoustics, Speech, a Signal Processing* **ASSP-23, NO-5**, 397–416.

Walker MA, Rudnicky A, Prasad R, Aberdeen J, Bratt EO, Garofolo J, Hastie H, Le A, Pellom B, Potamianos A, Passonneau R, Roukos S, Seneff S and Stallard D 2002 Darpa communicator: Cross-system results for the 2001 evaluation *in Proc. of the International Conference on Spoken Language Processing*, pp 269–272.

Wang W, Liu Y and Harper MP 2002 Rescoring effectiveness of language models using different levels of knowledge and their integration *in Proc. IEEE Int. Conf. on Acoustics, Speech and Signal Processing*, pp 785–788, Orlando, FLA, USA.

Wang YY and Acero A 2003 Concept acquisition in example based grammar authoring *in Proc. IEEE Int. Conf. on Acoustics, Speech and Signal Processing*, pp 284–287, Hong Kong.

Ward W 1990 The cmu air travel information service: understanding spontaneous speech *in Proc. of the Workshop on Speech and Natural Language*, pp 127–129, Hidden Valley, Pensylvania, USA.

Woods WA 1975 What's in a link: Foundations for semantic networks In *Representation and Understanding: Studies in Cognitive Science* (ed. Bobrow DG and Collins AM) Academic Press New York pp 35–82.

Woods WA 1976 Speech understanding systems. Technical report, Bolt, Beranek and Newman Inc., Cambridge, MASS.

Wu CH, Yan GL and Lin CL 2002 Speech act modeling in a spoken dialog system using a fuzzy fragment-class markov model. *Speech Commun.* **38**(1), 183–199.

Young SL, Hauptmann AG, Ward WH, Smith ET and Werner P 1989 High level knowledge sources in usable speech recognition systems. *Communications of the Association for Computing Machines* **32**(2), 183–194.

Zechner K 1998 Automatic construction of frame representations for spontaneous speech in unrestricted domains *Proc. of the International Conference on Computational Linguistics*, pp 1448–1452, Montreal, Canada.

Zettlemoyer LS and Collins M 2005 Learning to map sentences to logical form: Structured classification with probabilistic categorial grammars *21st Conference on Uncertainty in Artificial Intelligence (UAI05)*, pp 658–666, Edinburgh, Scotland. UK.

Zettlemoyer LS and Collins M 2009 Learning context-dependent mappings from sentences to logical form *in Proc. of the Joint Conference on Natural Language Processing of ACL and AFNLP*, pp 976–984, Singapore.

Zhang R and Rudnicky EI 2002 Improve latent semantic analysis based language model by integrating multiple level knowledge *in Proc. of the International Conference on Spoken Language Processing*, pp 893–896.

Zimmermann M 2005 Toward joint segmentation and classification of dialog acts in multiparty meetings *Proc. Multimodal Interaction and Related Machine Learning Algorithms Workshop (MLMIâŁ"05*, p. 187. Springer.

3

Semantic Frame-based Spoken Language Understanding*

Ye-Yi Wang, Li Deng and Alex Acero
Microsoft Research, U.S.A.

Semantic frame-based spoken language understanding (frame-based SLU) is one of the most commonly applied and well studied SLU technologies for human-computer interaction. It has been used in many spoken language processing tasks, in particular the transactional dialogue systems, where various pieces of information need to be collected from users. A frame-based SLU system is often limited to a specific domain, which has a well-defined, relatively small semantic space. The structure of the semantic space can be represented by a set of templates represented by *semantic frames* (Fillmore, 1976), whose *slots* (also known as *frame elements*) correspond to the important component variables. The goal of the frame-based SLU is to choose the correct semantic frame for an utterance, and extract from the utterance the values of its component slots.

3.1 Background

3.1.1 History of the Frame-based SLU

In the United States, the study of the frame-based SLU started in the 1970s in the DARPA Speech Understanding Research (SUR) and then the Resource Management (RM) tasks. At this early stage, natural language understanding (NLU) techniques such as finite state machine (FSM) and augmented transition networks (ATNs) were applied for SLU (Woods, 1983). The study of SLU surged in the 1990s, with the DARPA-sponsored Air Travel Information System (ATIS) evaluations (Dahl *et al.*, 1994; Hemphill *et al.*, 1990). Multiple research labs from

* This chapter is based on an article by the same authors published in the IEEE Signal Processing Magazine, Vol 22, No 5., entitled "*Spoken Language Understanding*" (Wang *et al.*, © 2005 IEEE). Substantial revision has been made.

Spoken Language Understanding: Systems for Extracting Semantic Information from Speech, First Edition.
Edited by Gokhan Tur and Renato De Mori.

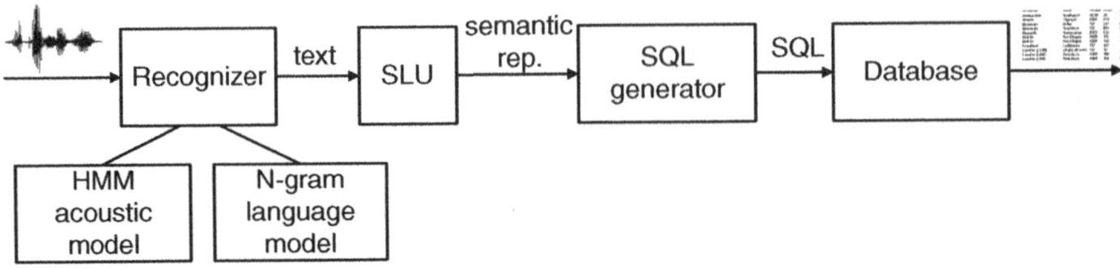

Figure 3.1 Frame-based SLU in a typical ATIS system, which consists of 1) a speech recognizer with both the acoustic model and language model trained with the ATIS specific data; 2) a SLU system that extracts the semantic representation (meaning) from the recognized text; and 3) a SQL generator that automatically creates the database query based on the semantic representation (Wang *et al.*, © 2005 IEEE)

both academia and industry, including AT&T, BBN Technologies (originally Bolt, Beranek and Newman), Carnegie Mellon University, MIT and SRI, developed systems that attempted to understand users' spontaneous spoken queries for air travel information (including flight information, ground transportation information, airport service information, etc.) and then obtain the answers from a standard database. ATIS is an important milestone for the frame-based SLU, largely thanks to its rigorous component-wise and end-to-end evaluation, participated by multiple institutions, with a common test set. Figure 3.1 shows the role of the frame-based SLU component in a typical ATIS system.

While ATIS focused more or less on the understanding of a single-turn utterance, the more recent DARPA Communicator program (Walker *et al.*, 2001) focused on the rapid and cost-effective development of multi-modal speech enabled dialog systems, in which general infrastructures for dialog systems were developed, where different component systems for ASR, SLU, DM and TTS can be plugged in and evaluated. Naturally, many SLU technologies developed in ATIS were used in the SLU component of the Communicator program. Eight systems from AT&T, BBN Technologies, University of Colorado, Carnegie Mellon University, IBM, Lucent Bell Labs, MIT, and SRI participated in the 2001 evaluation (Walker *et al.*, 2002). In the mean time, the AI community had separate effort in building a conversational planning agent, such as the TRAINS system (Allen *et al.*, 1996b).

Parallel efforts were made on the other side of the Atlantic. The French EVALDA/MEDIA project aimed at designing and testing the evaluation methodology to compare and diagnose the context-dependent and independent SLU capability in spoken language dialogues. Participants included both academic organizations (IRIT, LIA, LIMSI, LORIA, VALORIA, CLIPS) and industrial institutions (FRANCE TELECOM R&D, TELIP). Like ATIS, the domain of this study was restricted to database queries for tourist and hotel information.

The more recent LUNA project sponsored by the European Union focused on the problem of real-time understanding of spontaneous speech in the context of advanced telecom services. Its major objective is the development of a robust SLU toolkit for dialogue systems, which enhances users experience by allowing natural human/machine interactions via spontaneous and unconstrained speech. One special characteristic of the project, which is absent in the similar projects in the US, is its emphasis on multilingual portability of the SLU components.

Traditionally, the frame-based SLU has adopted a knowledge-based solution. The problem is tackled by writing context free (CFG) or unification grammars (UG) by hand. The manual grammar authoring process is laborious, expensive and requires a lot of expertise. In the early

1990s, both knowledge-based and data-driven approaches have been applied in different ATIS systems. Currently most commercial applications use the knowledge-based solutions, while most research systems adopt a data-driven, statistical learning approach to SLU. Attempts have also been made to incorporate knowledge in a data-driven system.

3.1.2 Semantic Representation and Semantic Frame

What is the goal for SLU? How can we tell whether a system's understanding is appropriate or not? Ultimately, the appropriateness of the understanding can be measured by the system's responses or by the actions taken by the system after it has "understood" an input utterance. For the frame-based SLU tasks, using the ATIS domain as an example, this can be measured by the accuracy of the air travel related information returned from a system after a spoken query is made by a user. However, generating such information involves more than the SLU component. For better engineering practice and scientific studies, it is desirable to modularize the end-to-end system and isolate the SLU component. For this purpose, an intermediate semantic representation is introduced to serve as the interface between different components. Many spoken language systems adopt their own semantic representations. However, most of them can be abstracted as the semantic frame-based representation, which we introduce now.

The semantic structure of an application domain is defined in terms of the *semantic frames*. Figure 3.2 shows a simplified example of three semantic frames in the ATIS domain. Each frame contains several typed components called "*slots*." The type of a slot specifies what kind of fillers it is expecting. For example, the **topic** slot denotes the specific information that a user is interested in about a flight, such as the general flight information (in this case, the filler of the slot will be the semantic terminal symbol "FLIGHT", which can be expressed by the user with words such as "flight", "flights"), or the fare information (the filler of the slot will be the semantic terminal symbol "FARE", expressed as, for example, "fare", "price" or "cost" in a user's utterance.) In the *Flight* frame, **DCity** stands for "departure city" and **ACity** stands for "arrival city". These two slots require objects with the type "City" as their fillers, which can be, for example, a city name or a city code. This frame has the type "Flight", thereby it can be

<frame name="*ShowFlight*" type="Void">
    <slot name="**topic**" type="Topic">
    <slot name="**flight**" type="Flight">
</frame>
<frame name="*GroundTrans*" type="Void">
    <slot name="**city**" type="City">
    <slot name="**type**" type="TransType">
</frame>
<frame name="*Flight*" type="Flight">
    <slot name="**DCity**" type="City">
    <slot name="**ACity**" type="City">
    <slot name="**DDate**" type="Date">
</frame>

Figure 3.2 A simplified semantic class schema in the ATIS domain. An *italic symbol* represents the name of a semantic frame, a symbol in **bold face** represents the name of a slot. **DCity** stands for "departure city" and **ACity** stands for "arrival city" (Wang *et al.*, © 2005 IEEE)

```
<ShowFlight>
    <topic type="Freeform">FLIGHT</topic>
    <flight frame="Flight" type="Flight">
        <DCity type="City">SEA</DCity>
        <ACity type="City">BOS</ACity>
        <DDate Type="Date">12/24</DDate>
    </flight>
</ShowFlight>
```

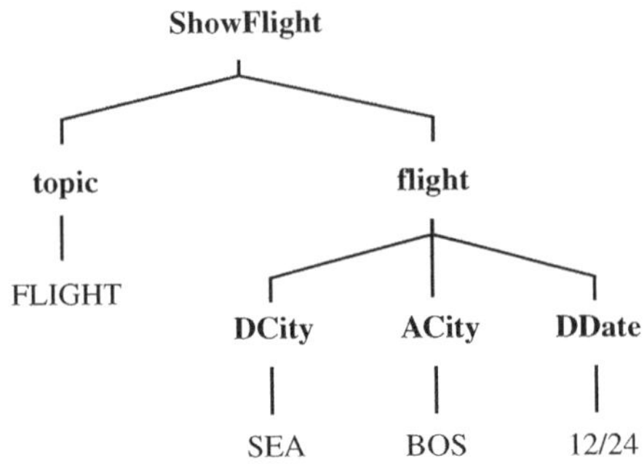

Figure 3.3 The semantic representation for "Show me flights from Seattle to Boston on Christmas Eve" is an instantiation of the semantic frames in Figure 3.2. On the right is its tree representation. The instantiation picks a frame that represents the meaning conveyed in the sentence and fills its slots accordingly. Here an *italic symbol* represents the name of a semantic frame, a symbol in **bold face** denotes the name of a slot, and a word in UPPERCASE stands for a semantic terminal (Wang *et al.*, © 2005 IEEE)

the filler of the "**flight**" slot of the top level frame "*ShowFlight*". Often the semantic frame is related to and derived from the schema of an application database.

The meaning of an input sentence is an instantiation of the semantic frames. Figure 3.3 shows the meaning representation for the sentence "Show me flights from Seattle to Boston on Christmas Eve." Here the frame "*ShowFlight*" contains the sub-frame "*Flight*" as its **flight** slot. Some SLU systems do not allow any sub-structures in a frame. In such a case, the semantic representation is simplified as a list of *attribute-value pairs*, which are also called *keyword-pairs* (Pieraccini and Levin, 1993) or *flat concept* representation (Figure 3.4).

The hierarchical representation is more expressive and allows the sharing of substructures. For example, the *Flight* frame in Figure 3.2 can be shared by both *ShowFlight* and *CancelFlight* (not shown) frames. The flat concept representation is simpler and often results in a simpler model.

The semantic representation in the early French MEDIA project adopts an attribute-value list to represent the hierarchical semantic information (Bonneau-Maynard *et al.*, 2005), as shown in Figure 3.5. This representation, used in the official annotation and evaluation, is ostensibly quite different from the frame-based representation. However, it is possible to construct a hierarchical representation that resembles to the frame-based representation, as described in (Bonneau-Maynard *et al.*, 2005). In Figure 3.5, each segment of the sentence is tagged with a *mode* that takes one of the four possible values: affirmative (+), negative (−), interrogative (?) or optional (@). While most segments are labeled with the "+" mode, the "le" and "tarif" segments are labeled as "?", indicating this ("the rate") is the information that the user is seeking for, which resembles to the **topic** slots in the frame in Figure 3.2. The *attribute names* encode the hierarchical semantic information, and the *normalized values* represent the canonical values

[**topic**: FLIGHT] [**DCity**: SEA] [**ACity**: BOS][**DDate**: 12/24]

Figure 3.4 The attribute-value representation is a special case of the frame representation where no embedded structure is allowed. Here is an attribute-value representation for "Show me the flights from Seattle to Boston on Christmas Eve" (Wang *et al.*, © 2005 IEEE)

words	mode	attribute name	normalized value
donnez-moi	+	`null`	
le	?	`refLink-coRef`	`singular`
tarif	?	`object`	`payment-amount-room`
puisque	+	`connectProp`	`imply`
je voudrais	+	`null`	
une chambre	+	`number-room`	`1`
qui coûte	+	`object`	`payment-amount-room`
pas plus de	+	`comparative-payment`	`less than`
cinquante	+	`payment-amount-integer-room`	`50`
euros	+	`payment-unit`	`euro`

Figure 3.5 Semantic concept (attribute/value) representation for the utterance *"give me the rate for I'd like a room charged not more than fifty euros"* (© 2005 ISCA)

for the attributes, which correspond to the semantic terminals in Figure 3.3. To encode the hierarchical information, an attribute name contains multiple parts separated by hyphens, each part represents an attribute belonging to an attribute class: The *database attributes* class contains the attributes from a database table. For attributes *A* and *B* in this class, *A*-*B* implies that *B* is an attribute in the substructure of *A*. For example, `payment-amount-integer` indicates that `amount` is an attribute in the substructure of `payment`, while `integer` is an attribute in the substructure of `amount`. Similarly, `payment-unit` implies that `unit` is another attribute in the substructure of `payment`. A *modifier attribute M* is linked to a database attribute *A* in the form of *M*-*A*, indicating that *M* modifies *A*. For example, `comparative-payment` states that `comparative` is a modifier of `payment`, hence it is part of the `payment` structure. To fully reconstruct the hierarchical representation, additional information is necessary to specify which components should be grouped together. For that purpose, Bonneau-Maynard *et al.* (2005) introduced the *specifiers* that can be attached to the end of a hierarchical attribute name. For example, the specifier `room` in Figure 3.5 indicates that `number` and `payment` should be grouped together under the `room` specifier.

The attempt of using this flat attribute-value representation for hierarchical semantics makes the meaning representation quite complicated. In the European LUNA project, a different representation was adopted, in which the MEDIA portion of data was re-annotated according to the new annotation protocol (Béchet, 2008). The semantic annotation protocol adopts a multi-level semantic representation, as illustrated by Figure 3.6. Here the concept level represents the concepts that bear important meanings in the input. The semantic composition level represents the utterance level meaning with semantic frames. A FrameNet-based semantic representation (Baker *et al.*, 1998) is adopted as an attempt for better scalability beyond a single application domain. The co-reference level annotation depicts the discourse information between the two related frames, while the fourth level models the dialogue act (e.g. statement, Y/N question, Wh-question, confirmation, etc.)

3.1.3 Technical Challenges

The frame-based SLU is closely related to natural language understanding (NLU), a field that has been studied for more than half a century. NLU focus mainly on the understanding

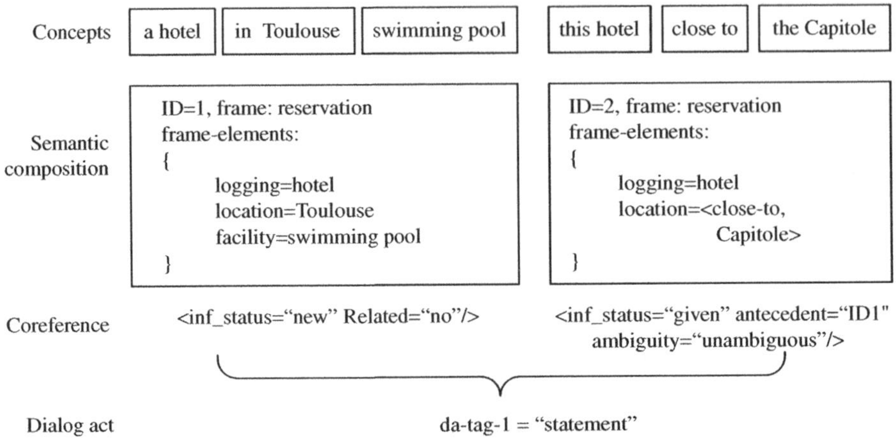

Figure 3.6 The multi-level semantic representation for the utterance "a hotel in Toulouse with a swimming pool hum this hotel must be close to the Capitole" in the European LUNA project (Béchet © 2008 IEEE)

of general domain written texts. Because there is not a specific application domain for the general purpose NLU, the semantics in NLU have to be defined in a broader sense, such as thematic roles (agents, patients, etc.) In contrast, the frame-based SLU has, in the current state of technology, focused only on specific application domains. The semantics are defined very specifically according to the application domain, as illustrated by the above examples of semantic frames. Many domain-specific constraints can be included in the understanding model. Ostensibly, this may make the problem easier to solve. Unfortunately, there are many new challenges for spoken language understanding, including:

- **Extra-grammaticality** – spoken languages are not as well-formed as written languages. People are in general less careful with speech than with writing. They often do not comply with rigid syntactic constraints.
- **Disfluencies** – false starts, repairs, and hesitations are pervasive, especially in conversational speech.
- **Speech recognition errors** – Speech recognition technology is far from perfect. Environment noises, speaker's accent, domain specific terminologies, all make speech recognition errors inevitable. It is common to see that a generic speech recognizer has over 30% word error rates on domain specific data.
- **Out-of-domain utterances** – a dialog system can never restrict a user from saying anything out of a specific domain, even in a system-initiated dialog, where users are prompted for answers to specific questions. Because the frame-based SLU focuses on a specific application domain, out-of-domain utterances are not well modeled and can often be confused as an in-domain utterance. Detecting the out-of-domain utterances is not an easy task – it is complicated by the extra-grammaticality, disfluencies and ASR errors of the in-domain utterances.

In summary, robustness is one of the most important issues in SLU. A system should be able to gracefully handle the unexpected inputs. If an input string is not accepted by a grammar/model, it is still desirable to identify the well-formed concepts in the input that carry important information for a given domain. On the other hand, a robust solution tends to over-generalize and introduce ambiguities, leading to the reduction in understanding accuracy. A major challenge to the frame-based SLU is thus to strike an optimal balance between the robustness and the constraints that prevent the over-generalizations and reduce the ambiguities.

3.1.4 Standard Data Sets

While there are many commercial applications for the frame-based SLU, most of the data used in those applications are proprietary. The ATIS corpus (Dahl *et al.*, 1994; Hemphill *et al.*, 1990) is one of the few data sets available in the public domain that has been broadly used by SLU researchers. The data is more realistic compared with the previous speech corpus – it is the spontaneous spoken language instead of the read speech, therefore it contains disfluencies, corrections, and colloquial pronunciations. It was collected in a normal office setting, with a "Wizard of Oz" interaction between a system and a subject who issued spoken queries for air travel information. Utterances were recorded, manually transcribed, and manually categorized into three different classes: class A for queries that can be interpreted without the context information; class D for queries that can be interpreted with the context information; class X for unanswerable queries (e.g. out-of-domain utterances). The corpus also contains a back-end database of US domestic flights. Each utterance in class A or D is also manually associated with a target SQL query, together with the reference answer, which is obtained by executing the query on the database.

The ATIS data set was designed to advance the state-of-the-art in speech recognition and understanding in the early 1990s. The DARPA Communicator project in the 2000s focused on the rapid and cost-effective development of multi-modal speech-enabled dialog systems with advanced conversational capabilities. The data collected from the project are richly annotated with dialogue-related information, including sessions/turns/operation information, etc.

Both ATIS and Communicator corpus are available through the Linguistic Data Consortium (LDC) (LDC, n.d.). The data collected by the TRAIN project (Allen *et al.*, 1996a) is also available from LDC.

For the European SLU projects, the French corpus MEDIA has been annotated in terms of semantic structures as in Figure 3.5 For the LUNA project that focuses on multilingual SLU and language specific aspects for language modeling and understanding, new corpora with complex human/human dialogues have been acquired in Italian and Polish. They are transcribed and annotated in terms of the syntactic constituents and semantic structures, in the annotation protocol illustrated by Figure 3.6.

The MEDIA data is available via the European Language Resource Association (ELRA) (ELRA, n.d.).

3.1.5 Evaluation Metrics

A variety of metrics are used in the evaluation of the frame-based SLU systems. Some metrics focus on component-wise performance of the SLU sub-system, others emphasize the impact of the SLU component on the performance of the end-to-end system. Here we introduce some commonly used evaluation metrics.

- **Sentence/utterance Level Semantic Accuracy** (SLSA): this metric measures the percentage of the correct semantic representations assigned to the sentences/utterances in a test set. An intermediate reference semantic representation is required with this metric.

$$SLSA = \frac{\text{\# of sentences assigned the correct semantic representation}}{\text{\# of sentences}} \tag{3.1}$$

- **Slot Error Rate** (SER): slot error rate (a.k.a concept error rate (CER)) measures the slot level performance of a frame-based SLU system. It aligns the system-produced semantic representation of a sentence with its reference representation to find the number of slots incorrectly identified by the SLU system. These include the inserted slots (present in the SLU output, absent from the reference representation), deleted slots (absent from the SLU output, present in the reference) and substituted slots (the slots that are aligned to each other between the SLU output and the reference differ in either the slot labels or the sentence segments they cover).

$$SER = \frac{\text{\# of inserted/deleted/substituted slots}}{\text{\# of slots in the reference semantic representations}} \tag{3.2}$$

- **Slot Precision/Recall/F_1 Score**: Precision/Recall is another way to measure the slot level SLU performance. F_1 combines precision and recall into a single score as their harmonic mean:

$$Precision = \frac{\text{\# of reference slots correctly detected by SLU}}{\text{\# of total slots detected by SLU}} \tag{3.3}$$

$$Recall = \frac{\text{\# of reference slots correctly detected by SLU}}{\text{\# of total reference slots}} \tag{3.4}$$

$$F_1 = \frac{2 \times (Precision \times Recall)}{Precision + Recall} \tag{3.5}$$

  Precision and recall can be traded off with the selection of different operating points for different application scenarios. Therefore a recall–precision curve is often reported in SLU evaluations.

- **End-to-end Evaluation**: The above evaluation metrics compare the SLU output with the reference semantic representation. Since different systems may use different intermediate semantic representations, it is difficult to compare different SLU components, even if a common test set is available. In the original DARPA-sponsored ATIS evaluation, the problem is addressed by an end-to-end evaluation metric. Utterances were first recognized and parsed to produce the semantic representations, from which SQL queries were constructed and submitted to the backend database engine. The resulting database outputs were then compared with the target entries obtained by the manually created SQL queries. Here a target entry is a pair of minimum and maximum information, which indicates the columns that have to be returned (minimum information) and the columns that are permitted in the database search results (maximum information). The minimum–maximum restriction penalizes the implementation that always returns the information from all the fields of a database entry without understanding what specific information the user has requested for. The evaluation for SLU can be conducted on both the ASR and the manual transcriptions of the test utterances. The utterance level understanding accuracy is the percentage of the test utterances for which the correct database entries are output with at least the minimum information (database columns) and at most the maximum information.

3.2 Knowledge-based Solutions

3.2.1 Semantically Enhanced Syntactic Grammars

Many advocates of the knowledge-based approach believe that general linguistic knowledge is helpful in modeling domain-specific language. This includes the syntactic constraints as well as some optional rudimentary domain-independent semantic knowledge. However, since the ultimate goal is to extract the domain-dependent semantic information, one major question is how to inject the domain specific semantic constraints into a domain-independent grammar.

MIT's TINA system (Seneff, 1992) aims at the graceful, seamless interface between syntax and semantics. It uses context-free grammar (augmented with a set of features used to enforce several syntactic and semantic constraints via unification). The injection of the domain-dependent semantics is accomplished by replacing the low-level syntactic non-terminals with semantic non-terminals. In doing so, the top level syntactic rules make the grammar capable of modeling the domain-independent linguistic constraints, such as the Wh-movement/trace-management. The feature unifications introduce additional syntactic and semantic constraints such as the person and number agreement and the subject/verb selectional restrictions. On the other hand, the domain-specific semantic content of a sentence is completely encoded by the lower level semantic non-terminals (categories) in the parse tree, thus making it feasible to extract the semantic frame representation directly from a parse tree. Figure 3.7 shows two parse trees – one with the syntactic non terminals only, the other has the low-level syntactic categories replaced by the domain-specific semantic non terminals (in bold face).

The context-free rules are automatically converted to a graph representation of shared transition networks, where the transitions can be associated with probabilities by automatic training when training data is available. It is reported in Seneff (1992) that the introduction of transition probabilities has greatly reduced the perplexity of the grammar – from 368 to 41.4 in the Resource Management domain.

SRI's Gemini system (Dowding *et al.*, 1993) is implemented on top of its Core Language Engine (CLE) (Alshawi, 1992), a general natural language understanding system that parses an

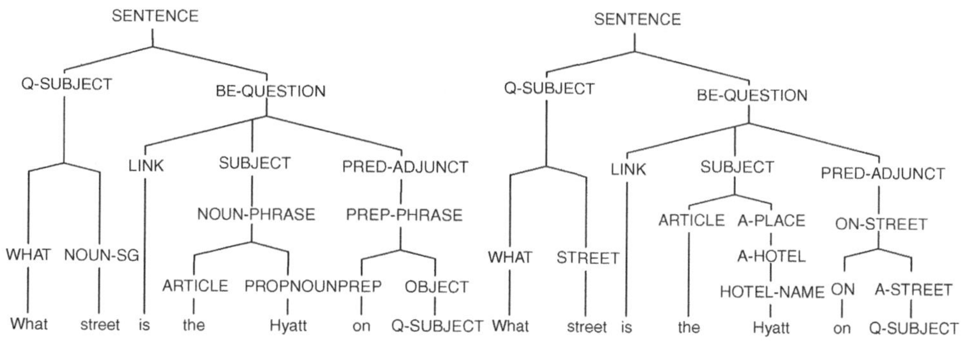

Figure 3.7 TINA parse tree with syntactic rules only (left) and with lower-level syntactic rules replaced by domain-dependent semantic rules (right) (The second tree is reproduced from Seneff (1992) (© 1992 Seneff))

input sentence and generates its semantic representation in the logical forms. Here the unification grammar is also used to model the general syntactic constraints. Unlike TINA that blends syntax and semantics together with the mixed grammar categories in constituent parsing, it clearly separates the domain-independent syntax from the domain-dependent semantics. Another specialty of Gemini is its adoption of the logical forms instead of the frame-like representation for semantics. Logical form in CLE is an extension to the first-order (predicate) logic (Alshawi and van Eijck, 1989). The example below shows the logical form for "a flight to Boston":

```
exists(A, [and, [flight, A], [to, A 'BOSTON']])
```

which can be read as "there is an variable *A*, such that *A* is a flight and *A* is to 'BOSTON'."

In Gemini, the ASR outputs are parsed according to the syntactic rules. Each syntactic node in a parse tree invokes a set of semantic rules to construct a set of logical forms for the node. Both domain-dependent and domain-independent selectional restrictions on logical forms are enforced through *sortal constraints*. Sortal constrains are used by linguists, logicians and philosophers to explain the oddity of sentences such as "the flight to boston is a cat", which cannot be conveniently explained by syntactic theories. Instead, the oddity is explained by sort incompatibility – the semantic interpretation for each constituent in a parse tree is assigned a sort. The sorts of constituents need to be compatible with each other when compositional semantics are constructed with respect to the syntactic rule that combines the constituents. Since the sorts of "flight" and "cat" are incompatible, the reading of the sentence is odd.

Sortal constraints can be used independent of the application domains – they can model the selectional constraints expected by the predicates for their arguments in the logical forms, hence they cut down on structural (e.g. attachment) and word sense ambiguities. In Gemini, sortal constraints are also used to model the semantic restrictions imposed by an application domain, such that the logical forms are restricted by the domain constraints. The following is the logical form with sort assignments for the previous example:

```
exists((A; [flight]),
       [and, [flight, (A; [flight])]; [prop],
             [to, (A; [flight]), ('BOSTON'; [city])]; [prop]
       ];[prop]
      ); [prop]
```

here every expression/sub-expression in the logical form is followed by a sort it has been assigned to, separated by a semicolon. For example, the quantified variable `A` is assigned the sort `[flight]`. The quantifier `exists(A, [P A])` is assigned the sort `[prop]` (proposition), so are the sub-expressions `[flight, (A; [flight])]`, `[to, (A; [flight]), ('BOSTON'; [city])]` and their conjunction (the `and` expression). The literal `'BOSTON'` is assigned the sort `[city]`. The sorts here bear resemblance to the types of the frames in the frame representation illustrated in Figure 3.3.

To construct the logical form in the previous example, a grammar developer needs to introduce the following sortal constraints:

```
sort('BOSTON', [city])
sort(to, [[flight], [city]], [prop])
sort(and, [[prop], [prop]], [prop])
```

Here the first sort rule specifies that the literal `'BOSTON'` can be assigned the sort `[city]`. The second rule indicates that the `to` predicate takes two arguments – one must have been assigned the sort `[flight]`, the other assigned `[city]`. The compositional semantics of the predicate is assigned the sort `[prop]`. The third rule states the conjunction operator takes two arguments assigned with the sort `[prop]` and produces the compositional logical form with the sort `[prop]`.

Gemini adopts a two-stage parser. In the first stage of *constituent parsing*, bottom-up chart parser is used, which applies the syntactic and semantic rules to populate the chart with linguistic constituents that include the syntactic and logical form information. In the second stage of *utterance parsing*, a second set of syntactic and semantic rules is applied. The rules are required to span the entire utterance, such that a complete parse for the utterance can be constructed.

To improve the robustness to spontaneous speech with disfluencies, when no complete parse can be constructed during the stage of utterance parsing due to the violation of either syntactic or sortal constraints, a repair component is invoked to detect and correct the disfluencies. To handle speech recognition errors, Gemini operates on the n-best ASR outputs.

3.2.2 Semantic Grammars

While using the semantically enhanced syntactic grammars saves grammar developers the effort required to model the general language structures, it requires profound knowledge about the general syntactic grammars. In addition, the knowledge-based approach often requires the exact matching of input sentences to the grammar rules, which makes it not robust to ASR errors, extra-grammaticality and disfluencies in spontaneous speech. Often it has to resort to some kind of semantic-based robust parsing as a backup.

The Phoenix spoken language understanding system (Ward, 1991) directly models the domain-dependent semantics with a semantic grammar. It was one of the top-performing SLU systems in the ATIS evaluation. Phoenix used the semantic frames to represent the semantic relations. Slots in a frame were filled by matching the input strings (sentences) against the slot-nets, the recursive transition networks (RTNs) that specified the patterns for the filler strings. RTNs are finite-state transition networks, where the arcs in the networks can be labeled by not only the terminal words, but also the names of other networks. They are the equivalents of the context free grammars in graph representation. During parsing, the system used the slot-nets to match substrings in the input sentence. The matches were passed along for incorporation into the frames in a composition phase. While the slot-nets required the exact matches, the system was robust in the composition phase using a beam search algorithm. When a slot match was found, Phoenix would extend all the active frames that contain the slot, and activate any currently inactive frames that contain the slot. At the end of the search process, the single best parse that covered the most slots discovered by the slot-nets was returned from the beam.

The grammar used by Phoenix for ATIS was very complicated. It consisted of 3.2K non-terminals and 13K grammar rules. Figure 3.8 shows the slot-net for "PriceRange", together with some of the sub-nets that the slot-net calls.

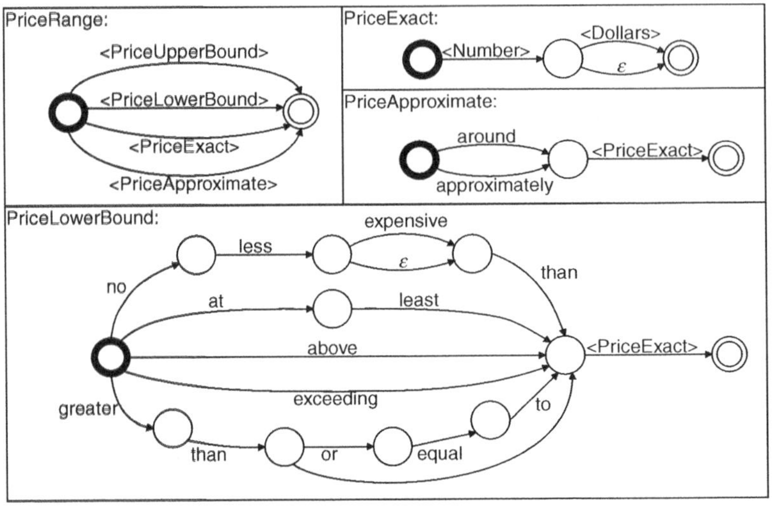

Figure 3.8 Recursive transition network for "PriceRange," together with three sub-nets called by it: "PriceExact", "PriceApproximate" and "PriceLowerBound." The arc labels in angular brackets indicate calls to sub-networks

3.2.3 Knowledge-based Solutions in Commercial Applications

In most commercial spoken dialogue systems, the frame-based SLU is tackled via the knowledge-based approach. Domain dependent semantic context free grammars are developed to provide the powerful domain and linguistic constraints to the ASR component (language model), and to provide a mechanism to construct the target semantic representation from an input utterance. The rules in a grammar define the permissible syntactic/semantic expressions. They are also associated with the semantic interpretation tags, from which the ASR engine can construct the semantic representation from the parse tree.

To ensure the portability of a speech recognition grammar, W3C has standardized the grammar format SRGS (Speech Recognition Grammar Specification) (Hunt and McGlashan, 2004) and the semantic interpretation tags SISR (Semantic Interpretation for Speech Recognition) (Van Tichelen and Burke, 2007). Figure 3.9 shows an exemplar grammar with the semantic interpretation tags defined in the SRGS XML form (the alternative ABNF form is more compact, but less readable). Four rules of the grammar are shown in the figure, which correspond to the RTNs in Figure 3.8. Each rule is associated with a rule variable "`out`", which holds the semantic values of the rule. A rule variable may have a structured value – it can contain hierarchical properties. For example, `out.amount` represents the "`amount`" property of the rule variable. A rule may not be associated with an explicit semantic interpretation tag. In such a case, the semantic structure (value of the rule variable) for the rule is constructed according to the implicit semantic interpretation tags – if there are no rule references (the `<ruleref>` tag) in the parse, the text covered by the rule is assigned to the rule variable. Otherwise, the value of the rule variable of the last referenced rule (nonterminal) in the parse is automatically copied into the rule variable. The semantic of a rule reference can be obtained via the "`rules`" variable. For example, "`rules.PriceExact`" in Figure 3.9 refers to the value of the structured rule

```
<grammar version="1.0" xmlns="http://www.w3.org/2001/06/grammar"
        xml:lang="en-US" tag-format="semantics/1.0-literals"
        root="PriceRange">
  <rule id="PriceRange" scope="public">
    <one-of>
      <item><ruleref uri="#PriceExact"/></item>
      <item><ruleref uri="#PriceApproximate"/></item>
      <item><ruleref uri="#PriceLowerBound"/></item>
      <item><ruleref uri="#PriceUpperBound"/></item>
    </one-of>
    <tag>out.pricerange=rules.latest()</tag>
  </rule>
  <rule id="PriceExact">
    <item><ruleref uri="#Number"/></item>
    <item repeat="0-1"><ruleref uri="#Dollars"/></item>
    <tag>out.amount=rules.Number</tag>
    <tag>out.match="exact"</tag>
  </rule>
  <rule id="PriceApproximate">
    <one-of><item>about</item>
            <item>approximately</item>
    </one-of>
    <item><ruleref uri="#PriceExact"/></item>
    <tag>out.amount=rules.PriceExact.amount</tag>
    <tag>out.match="approximate"</tag>
  </rule>
  <rule id="PriceLowerBound">
    <one-of><item>exceeding</item>
            <item>above</item>
            <item><token>no less</token>
                  <item repeat="0-1">expensive</item>
                  <token>than</token>
            </item>
            <item><token>greater than</token>
                  <item repeat="0-1">or equal to</item>
            </item>
    </one-of>
    <item><ruleref uri="#PriceExact"/></item>
    <tag>out.amount=rules.PriceExact.amount</tag>
    <tag>out.match="lowerbound"</tag>
  </rule>
  ......
</grammar>
```

Figure 3.9 W3C SRGS grammar for "PriceRange" with the SISR semantic interpretation tags

variable (semantic structure) for the rule reference "`PriceExact`" in "`PriceApproximate`" and "`PriceLowerBound`", and "`rules.PriceExact.amount`" represents the value of the "`amount`" attribute in the structured rule variable of "`PriceExact`".

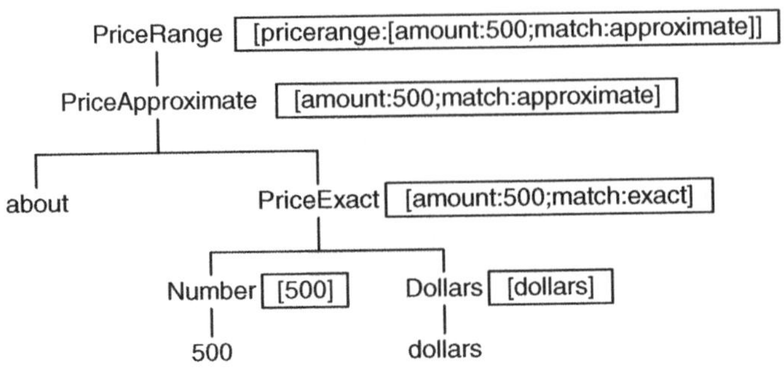

Figure 3.10 The parse tree for the utterance "about 500 dollars" together with the semantic structures for the non-terminal nodes (in boxes), constructed according to the explicit or implicit semantic interpretation tags

Given the grammar in Figure 3.9, the parse tree for the utterance "about 500 dollars," together with the values of the rule variables for the rules referenced in the tree, is illustrated in Figure 3.10. From which the semantic representation for the entire utterance can be constructed as follows:

```
<pricerange>
    <amount>500</amount>
    <match>approximate</match>
</pricerange>
```

Readers can find more detailed information about the SRGS grammar format and the semantic interpretation tags in Hunt and McGlashan (2004) and Van Tichelen and Burke (2007).

3.3 Data-driven Approaches

The knowledge-based solution has the advantage of no or less dependent on labeled data. In addition, almost everyone can start writing a SLU grammar with some basic training. The grammar may be used as both the ASR language model and the SLU model in a single-pass speech understanding system when the rules are associated with the SISR tags. However, a knowledge-based system is difficult and expensive to develop and maintain due to the following reasons:

1. Grammar development is an error-prone process. While it does not take much training for a common developer to learn the syntax for writing a speech understanding grammar, it requires combined linguistic and engineering expertise, plus the deep knowledge about the application domain, to write a *good* grammar. Grammar authoring is a balancing act between simplicity and coverage. People talk differently; therefore a good grammar has to account for the different expressions for the same concept, question, or request. If a grammar is too simple, it is inadequate to model the linguistic diversity. On the other hand, if a grammar is too complicated, it may not only slow down the parser, but also increase the ambiguities, hence confuse the SLU system and degrade its performance. Designing

the structure of a grammar is an act of art. It takes much experience to have a good design where frequently used concepts, for example, are modeled by separate rules to be shared by other rules at a higher level.

2. It takes multiple rounds to fine tune a grammar. Grammar authoring is hardly a one-shot deal – nobody can write a perfect grammar with a single try. Furthermore, grammars need to evolve over time – new features and scenarios may arise in an application after its initial deployment. Ideally, an SLU system should be able to automatically adapt to the real data collected after its deployment. On the contrary, knowledge-based systems require an expert's involvement, sometimes even the involvement of the original system designer, in the adaptation loop.
3. Grammar authoring is difficult to scale up. It is relatively easy to write a grammar to model a single concept as in a system-initiated dialogue system, where the user is prompted to provide a single piece of information (e.g., name, account number, social security number, address, etc.) at each dialogue turn. However, if we allow users to volunteer multiple pieces of information in a single utterance, the ways to put together these pieces are combinational. As we have shown previously, for a very restricted domain like ATIS, the semantic grammar already contains 3.2k non-terminals and 13k grammar rules.

SLU based on data-driven statistical learning approaches directly addresses many of the problems associated with the knowledge-based solution. Statistical SLU systems can automatically learn from example sentences with their corresponding semantics annotated. Compared with manual grammar authoring, the annotations are much easier to create, without the requirement of the specialized knowledge. The statistical approach can adapt to new data, possibly via unsupervised learning. One disadvantage of such an approach, however, is the data-sparseness problem. The requirement of a large amount of labeled training data is not very practical in real-world applications, which are quite different from a few showcase problems studied in research labs. This problem is especially substantial at the early stage of a system development.

In this section, we introduce a general framework for the statistical SLU, and review various types of statistical SLU models in the literature. We assume that most readers have been exposed to HMMs as commonly used in speech recognition and language processing.

3.3.1 Generative Models

In the statistical frame-based SLU, the task is often formalized as a pattern recognition problem. Given the word sequence W, the goal of SLU is to find the semantic representation of its meaning M that has the maximum *a posteriori* probability $P(M \mid W)$. In the generative model framework, the following decision rule is used:

$$\hat{M} = \arg\max_{M} P(M \mid W) = \arg\max_{M} P(W \mid M)P(M) \tag{3.6}$$

The objective function of a generative model is to maximize the joint probability $P(W, M) = P(W \mid M)P(M)$ given a training sample of W and its semantic annotation M.

Two separate models exist in this generative framework. The *semantic prior* model $P(M)$ assigns probability to an underlying semantic structure or meaning M. The *lexicalization* model $P(W \mid M)$, sometimes called *lexical generation* or *realization* model (Miller *et al.*,

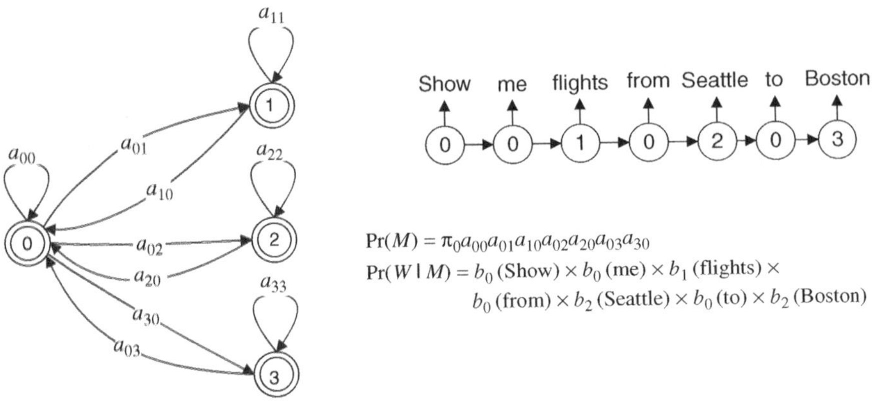

Figure 3.11 An HMM tagging model for SLU. State 0 represents "command", state 1 represents the "topic" slot, state 2 represents the "DCity" slot, and state 3 represents the "ACity" slot. The HMM topology and the transition probabilities a_{ij} form the prior. The meaning of a sentence is represented by its underlying state sequence. The emission distributions b_k of the states form the lexicalization model. On the right is a possible state sequence that aligns to the sentence "Show me flights from Seattle to Boston". Theoretically, the state should encode the semantics of the attribute-value pair like <DCity SEA>. However, since this increases the state space significantly, sometimes infinitely, practical SLU systems often collapse the states corresponding to the same attribute, and extract the value semantics from the observation aligned to the slot state in a post-processing step (Wang *et al.*, © 2005 IEEE)

1994), assigns probability to the surface sentence (i.e. word/lexical sequence) W given the semantic structure. As an example, the HMM tagging model is a simple implementation of Equation (3.6), in which a Markov chain consisting of the states that bear semantic meanings models the semantic prior, and the emissions from the states model the lexicalization process. The alignment between the observations (words) and the states is hidden (Figure 3.11). The tagging model finds the Viterbi alignment between the states and the words, and the meaning associated with a state becomes the semantic tag of the aligned word.

In this simple tagging model, observations (words) depend only on the states without the influence from the other words in the context. This independence assumption does not work well with natural language: according to this assumption, "Show me flights" and "me Show flights" are equally likely. Most statistical SLU systems attempt to overcome this problem by allowing a state to emit one or more "segments" of multiple words at a time. In this case, the generative process for the observations is:

1. Generate a set of segments $S = (s_1, \ldots, s_n)$ according to the semantic structure $M = q_1, \ldots, q_m$ (a state q_i may correspond to multiple segments) .
2. Determine the alignment $A = (a_1, \ldots, a_n)$ that associates each segment s_i with the state q_{a_i} in M.
3. Determine the length $L = (l_1, \ldots, l_n)$ for each segment.
4. Generate l_i words for each segment s_i, for $i = 1, \ldots, n$, assuming the words are correlated and are sensitive to temporal ordering.

Here S, A and L are not observed. They are hidden variables that can be marginalized out according to

$$P(W \mid M) = \sum_{S,A,L} P(W, S, A, L \mid M) \tag{3.7}$$

$$= \sum_{S,A,L} P(S \mid M)\, P(A \mid S, M)\, P(L \mid A, S, M)\, P(W \mid L, A, S, M) \tag{3.8}$$

This type of lexicalization model for correlated word sequences is analogous to the segment model in acoustic modeling for ASR (Ostendorf *et al.*, 1996). One main difference, however, is that in SLU the alignment process is more elaborate than that for ASR. This complexity arises from the syntactic constraints that allow the generation of multiple phrases from a single state and the placement of the phrases in an order that is far more flexible than pronunciations in a dictionary. The latter is largely coded as a left-to-right sequence as defined by the dictionary, which is much less variable than the many different ways a fixed meaning may be expressed as a composite of phrases/words in varying orders. The purpose of the alignment in Step 2 above is to account for this type of variability, which is largely absent in ASR problems.

Equation (3.7) has different implementations in various SLU systems. We will discuss this topic of lexicalization modeling in detail later in this section after surveying semantic-prior modeling first.

Note that in the semantic representation in Figure 3.3 or Figure 3.4, the frame slots have normalized values that may be different from the original text in the utterance (e.g., the original text "Seattle" is normalized as the city code "SEA"). Such a representation relieves the application developers from handling different expressions for the same meaning. However, training a model to produce such a normalized semantic representation requires the training data be labeled in the same way, which adds extra burden to the annotators and makes the model more complicated – we will show one of such models later in a subsection titled "2+1 SLU Model." Instead, a majority of the statistical models just align the segments of an utterance to the slots and produce a semantic representation like the one in Figure 3.12, and employ a separate post-processing step to generate the normalized representation.

<ShowFlight>
    <topic>flights**</topic>**
    <flight>
        <DCity>Seattle**</DCity>**
        <ACity>Boston**</ACity>**
        <DDate>Christmas Eve**</DDate>**
    </flight>
</ShowFlight>

Figure 3.12 A simplified semantic representation – a separate post-processing is necessary for slot value normalization. Nevertheless, the representation is easier to annotate (Wang *et al.*, © 2005 IEEE)

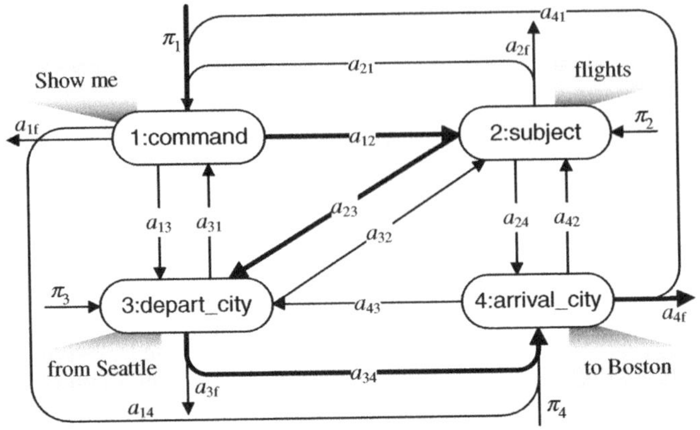

Figure 3.13 The topology of the statistical model that adopts the flat concept semantic representation. Each state represents a concept. States are fully interconnected. The initial state distribution $\pi_i = P(i)$ and the state transition distribution $a_{ij} = P(j \mid i)$ comprise the semantic prior of the model. (The final state f = "</s>" is not shown in the topology.) The thicker lines illustrate the correct state transitions for the sentence "Show me flights from Seattle to Boston." The example sentence segments are also aligned to the states (Wang *et al.*, © 2005 IEEE)

3.3.1.1 Semantic Priors in Understanding Models

In statistical SLU that models the cross-word contextual dependency, each state represents a slot in a semantic frame. For the systems that use the flat concepts for semantic representation, such as AT&T's CHRONUS (Pieraccini and Levin, 1993) and IBM's fertility model (Della Pietra *et al.*, 1997), the topology of the model is a fully connected network as in Figure 3.13. Unlike the topology in Figure 3.11, there is no self loop on a state because it directly models a segment of words with the length information already encoded.

The prior probability of the semantic structure underlying the representation in Figure 3.4, i.e. the flat-concept sequence "Command Topic DCity ACity" can be calculated as the product of the probabilities of the marked transitions in Figure 3.13:

$$\begin{aligned} P(M) = {} & P(\text{Command}|\text{<s>})\, P(\text{Topic}|\text{Command})\, P(\text{ACity}|\text{Topic}) \\ & P(\text{ACity}|\text{DCity})\, P(\text{</s>}|\text{ACity}) = \pi_1 a_{12} a_{23} a_{34} a_{4f} \end{aligned}$$

where <s> represents the start of the semantic concept list and </s> represents the end of the flat-concept list. This model is also used by a MEDIA system that uses attribute-value list to represent the hierarchical semantic information (Lefèvre, 2007).

For models that use hierarchical semantic structures, including BBN Technologies' Hidden Understanding Model (Miller *et al.*, 1994) and Microsoft Research's HMM/CFG composite model (Wang and Acero, 2003a), the semantic prior is a natural extension of Equation (3.9). Figure 3.14 shows the topology of the underlying states for the semantic frames in Figure 3.2. The left-hand side of the diagram shows the top level network topology, and the right-hand side part shows a zoomed-in sub-network for state 2, which represents the embedded "Flight" frame. The initial state probabilities $\pi_1 = P(\text{ShowFlight})$ and $\pi_5 = P(\text{GroundTrans})$ comprise the prior distribution over the top-level semantic frames. The transitional weights a_{12} and a_{13}

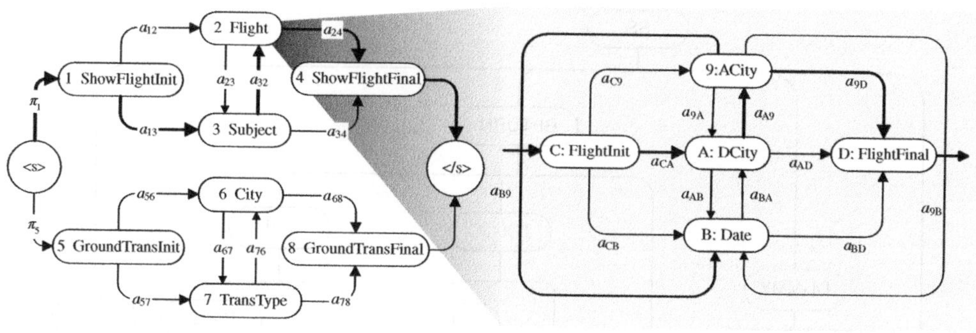

Figure 3.14 Hierarchical model topology for the semantic frames in Figure 3.2. On the left is the top-level network structure. On the right is the sub-network of the semantic frame "Flight." Since the semantic frames are defined in a finite state language, the sub-network can substitute for state 2. Substitutions by the same sub-network may share the parameters of the sub-network. The thicker path shows the correct state sequence for the sentence "Show me the flight from Seattle to Boston on Christmas Eve." (Wang *et al.*, © 2005 IEEE)

comprise the initial slot distribution for the "ShowFlight" frame. The transitional weights a_{56} and a_{57} comprise the initial slot distribution for the "GroundTrans" frame, and the transitional weights a_{C9}, a_{CA} and a_{CB} in the sub-network comprise the initial slot distribution for the Flight frame.

Given this topology, the semantic prior for the semantic structure underlying the meaning representation in Figure 3.3 is the product of the Markov transitional probabilities across the different levels in the semantic hierarchy (the marked path in Figure 3.14):

$$\begin{aligned} P(M) = {} & P(\text{ShowFlight})P(\text{topic}|\text{<s>}; \textit{ShowFlight})P(\text{Flight}|\text{topic}; \textit{ShowFlight}) \\ & P(\text{DCity}|\text{<s>}; \textit{Flight})P(\text{ACity}|\text{DCity}; \textit{Flight})P(\text{</s>}|\text{ACity}; \textit{Flight}) \\ & P(\text{</s>}|\text{Flight}; \textit{ShowFlight}) \\ = {} & \pi_1 a_{13} a_{32} a_{CA} a_{A9} a_{9D} a_{24} a_{4F} \end{aligned} \tag{3.9}$$

In general,

$$P(M) = \prod_{i=1}^{|M|+1} P\left(C_M(i) \mid C_M(i-1)\right) P\left(M(i)\right) \tag{3.10}$$

Here $|M|$ is the number of the instantiated slots in M. $C_M(i)$ is the name of the i-th slot in M, ($C_M(0)$=<s> and $C_M(|M|+1)$=</s> stand for the beginning and the end of a frame, respectively) and $M(i)$ is the sub-structure that fills the ith slot in M. Equation (3.10) recursively calculates the prior probabilities of the sub-structures and includes them in the prior probability of the parent semantic structure.

Cambridge University's Hidden Vector State model (He and Young, 2003) uses another way to model the semantic prior with hierarchical structures. Referred to as the hidden vector states, the states in the Markov chain represent the stack status of the pre-terminal nodes (the nodes immediately above the terminal words) in a semantic tree, as illustrated in Figure 3.15. The hidden vector states encode all the structure information about the tree, so the semantic

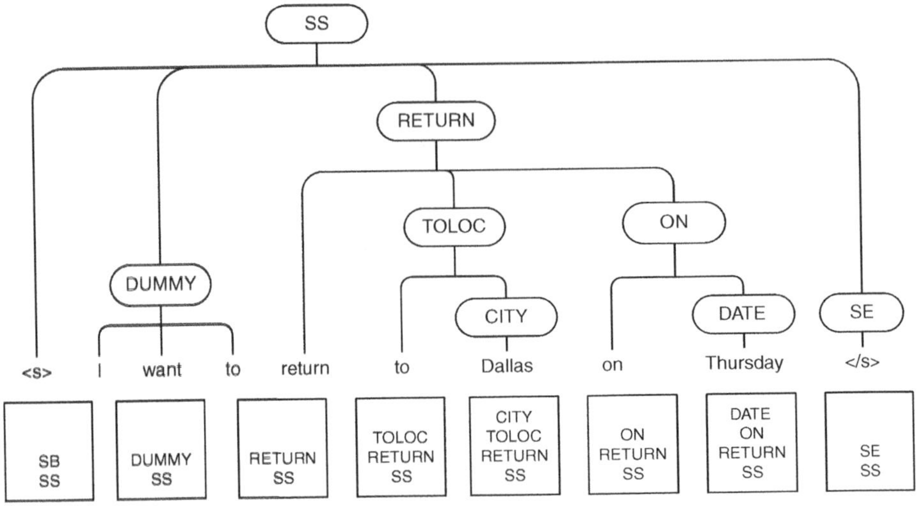

Figure 3.15 In the Hidden Vector State model, the states (illustrated by the blocks) represent the stack status of a pre-terminal nodes (the parent node of the terminal words) in the semantic tree, which is the trace from a pre-terminal (at the top of the stack) to the root of the parse tree (Wang *et al.*, © 2005 IEEE)

tree structure (without the terminal words) can be reconstructed from the hidden vector state sequence. The model imposes a hard limit on the maximum depth of the stack, so the number of the states becomes finite, and the prior model becomes the Markov chain in an HMM. The difference from the earlier examples in Figure 3.13 and Figure 3.14 is that the state transition in this Markov chain is now modeled by the stack operations that transform one stack vector state to another. The stack operations include (1) Pop(n) that pops the top n elements from the stack; and (2) Push(C) that pushes a new concept C into the stack. For example, the transition from the state represented by the fifth block in Figure 3.15 can be made with two operations: Pop(2) and Push(ON). The pop operation depends on the stack contents of the state from which the transition exits, and the push operation depends on the stack contents right before the element is pushed in. Hence the probability of the transition from the fifth block is

$$P_{pop}(2 \mid [\text{CITY TOLOC RETURN SS}])P_{push}(\text{ON} \mid [\text{RETURN SS}]) \tag{3.11}$$

Let $|S|$ denote the depth of the stack S. Given the stack vector states S_{t-1} and S_t, $|S_{t-1}| - |S_t| + 1$ elements have to be popped from S_{t-1} in order to transform S_{t-1} to S_t. Thus the semantic prior is the product of the transition probabilities in the Markov chain:

$$\begin{aligned} P(M) &= \prod_{t=1}^{|M|} P(S_t \mid S_{t-1}) \\ &= \prod_{t=1}^{|M|} P_{pop}(|S_{t-1}| - |S_t| + 1 \mid S_{t-1})P_{push}(\text{TOP}[S_t] \mid \text{POP}[1, S_t]) \\ &\quad \delta(\text{POP}[|S_{t-1}| - |S_t| + 1, S_{t-1}],\ \text{POP}[1, S_t]) \end{aligned} \tag{3.12}$$

Here $|M|$ is the number of stack vector states in M, including the sentence end state $S_{|M|}$. S_0 is the sentence initial state. TOP[S] is the top element of the stack S, and POP[n, S] is the new stack after the top n elements are popped out of the stack S. $\delta(x, y) = 1$ if $x = y$, otherwise $\delta(x, y) = 0$. It guarantees that S_{t-1} to S_t is a legal transition by restricting that all the elements in the two stacks are the same, except for those popped out of S_{t-1} and the one pushed into S_t.

The decomposition of the transition probability into P_{pop} and P_{push} enables different transitions to share the parameters. Therefore, it can potentially reduce the number of parameters in the prior model.

It is important to note that the prior model does not have to be static. It can change depending on the context, for example, at a dialogue state when the system asks users for the departure city information, the probability for the DCity slot can be significantly boosted. The prior model can also be personalized (Yu *et al.*, 2003).

3.3.1.2 Lexicalization Models

In this section we review the lexicalization models under the general framework of Equation (3.7), which captures the dependency and temporal ordering of the observed words within the same state.

N-gram Lexicalization Model

The first lexicalization model, used by both CHRONUS (Pieraccini and Levin, 1993) and the Hidden Understanding Model (Miller *et al.*, 1994), assumes a deterministic one-to-one correspondence between model states and the segments, i.e. there is only one segment per state, and the order of the segments follows that of the states. This effectively gets rid of the hidden variables S and A in Equation (3.7):

$$P(W \mid M) = \sum_{L} P(W, L \mid q_1, \ldots, q_m) = \sum_{\pi=\varphi_1,\ldots,\varphi_m} P(\pi \mid q_1, \ldots, q_m)$$
$$\approx \sum_{\pi=\varphi_1,\ldots,\varphi_m} \prod_{i=1}^{m} P(\varphi_i \mid q_i) \tag{3.13}$$

Here the joint event (W, L) corresponds to a segmentation $\pi = \varphi_1, \ldots, \varphi_m$ of W: φ_1 is the first l_1 words of W, φ_2 is the next l_2 words of W, etc., and the concatenation of the substrings $\varphi_1, \ldots, \varphi_m$ equals W.

Both CHRONUS (Pieraccini and Levin, 1993) and the Hidden Understanding Model (Miller *et al.*, 1994) exploited state specific n-grams to model $P(\varphi \mid q)$. Let's use the flat-concept semantic structure in Figure 3.13 as an example. It illustrates a segmentation π = "show me", "flights", "from Seattle", "to Boston". The probability of the surface sentence under this segmentation is:

$$\begin{aligned}
&P(\pi \mid M = \textbf{command}, \textbf{topic}, \textbf{DCity}, \textbf{ACity}) = \\
&\quad P(\text{Show}|\text{<s>};\ \textbf{command})P(\text{me}|\text{Show};\textbf{command})P(\text{</s>}|\text{me};\textbf{command}) \\
&\quad P(\text{flights}|\text{<s>};\textbf{topic})P(\text{</s>}|\text{flights};\textbf{topic}) \\
&\quad P(\text{from}|\text{<s>};\textbf{DCity})P(\text{Seattle}|\text{from};\ \textbf{DCity})P(\text{</s>}|\text{Seattle};\textbf{DCity}) \\
&\quad P(\text{to}|\text{<s>};\textbf{ACity})P(\text{Boston}|\text{to};\textbf{ACity})P(\text{</s>}|\text{Boston};\textbf{ACity})
\end{aligned} \tag{3.14}$$

In Equation (3.14), the cross-state lexical dependency is not modeled. A word at a state only depends on the history that belongs to the same state (or on the context cue "<s>" if it is the first word emitted from a state). One can opt to model the cross-state lexical dependency too. In this case, instead of depending on "<s>", the initial words from a state may depend on the last few words (The actual number is determined by the n-gram order) from the previous state.

Fertility Lexicalization Model

IBM's *fertility model* (Della Pietra *et al.*, 1997) is another implementation of Equation (3.7). It is based on their statistical machine translation work. Similar idea was adopted in (Macherey *et al.*, 2001). The generative process of the model can be illustrated by the following example: Let the semantic structure be the flat sequence of four states, "DISPLAY FLIGHTS TO ARRIVAL_CITY". The model first picks the number of segments for each state, for example, (2, 1, 1, 1). This results in five segments, which are permutated to form the ordered sequence $S = <\text{SEG}_{\text{DISPLAY}}, \text{SEG}_{\text{FLIGHTS}}, \text{SEG}_{\text{TO}}, \text{SEG}_{\text{ARRIVAL\_CITY}}, \text{SEG}_{\text{DISPLAY}}>$. Each permutation corresponds to an alignment. The permutation in the example corresponds to the alignment $A = (1, 2, 3, 4, 1)$, where each element points to the state that gives rise to a segment. Since there are (5!/2!1!1!1!) different permutations, each possible alignment has the uniform probability 2!/5!. The model then picks the length in each segment, (2, 2, 1, 1, 1), and accordingly generates two words "I want" for the first segment, "to fly" for the second segment, one word "to" for the third segment, "Boston" for the fourth segment, and "please" for the last segment. This produces the final surface sentence "I want to fly to Boston please." As illustrated by this example, a state in this model can emit non-consecutive word sequences (segments).

The fertility model makes the following assumptions in the aforementioned process:

1. $P(S \mid M = q_1, ..., q_m) \approx \prod_{i=1}^{m} f(n_i \mid q_i) = \prod_{i=1}^{m} \frac{e^{-\lambda_{q_i}} \lambda_{q_i}^{n_i}}{n_i!}$, i.e., each state q_i generates n_i segments according to a Poisson distribution called the *fertility model*. Here $m = |M|$ is the number of states in M, $n = \sum_{i=1}^{m} n_i = |S|$ is the total number of segments generated from the m states.
2. The alignment model $P(A = a_1, ..., a_n \mid S = s_1, ..., s_n, M = q_1, ..., q_m)$ follows a uniform distribution. Here a_j is the index of the state in M that the j-th segment is aligned to. In other words, according to A, segment s_j is aligned to the state q_{a_j}.
3. $P(L = l_1, ..., l_n \mid A = a_1, ..., a_n, S = s_1, ..., s_n, M = q_1, ..., q_m) \approx \prod_{j=1}^{n} n(l_j \mid q_{a_j})$, i.e., the length of a segment only depends on the state it is aligned to.
4. $P(W \mid L, A, S, M) \approx \prod_{j=1}^{n} \prod_{k=1}^{l_j} p(w_{jk} \mid q_{a_j})$, i.e., each word in a segment is generated with the dependency on the state which the segment is aligned to; here w_{jk} is the k-th word in segment s_j, which has length l_j.

Given the above assumptions,

$$
\begin{aligned}
&P(W, L, A, S \mid M) \\
&= P(S \mid M)\, P(A \mid S, M)\, P(L \mid A, S, M)\, P(W \mid L, A, S, M) && (3.15) \\
&= \left(\prod_{i=1}^{|M|} \frac{e^{-\lambda_{q_i}} \lambda_{q_i}^{n_i}}{n_i!} \right) \left(\frac{1}{n!} \prod_{i=1}^{|M|} n_i! \right) \left(\prod_{j=1}^{n} n\left(l_j \mid q_{a_j}\right) \prod_{k=1}^{l_j} p\left(w_{jk} \mid q_{a_j}\right) \right) && (3.16) \\
&= \frac{1}{n!} \prod_{i=1}^{|M|} e^{-\lambda_{q_i}} \lambda_{q_i}^{n_i} \prod_{j=1}^{n} n\left(l_j \mid q_{a_j}\right) \prod_{k=1}^{l_j} p\left(w_{jk} \mid q_{a_j}\right) && (3.17)
\end{aligned}
$$

$$= \frac{1}{n!} \prod_{i=1}^{|M|} e^{-\lambda_{q_i}} \prod_{j=1}^{n} \lambda_{q_{a_j}} n\left(l_j \mid q_{a_j}\right) \prod_{k=1}^{l_j} p\left(w_{jk} \mid q_{a_j}\right) \tag{3.18}$$

$$= \frac{1}{n!} \prod_{i=1}^{|M|} e^{-\lambda_{q_i}} \prod_{j=1}^{n} r\left(l_j, s_j | q_{a_j}\right) \tag{3.19}$$

In Equation (3.16), the second factor is the permutation (alignment) probability, which is the inverse of the multinomial coefficient. Equation (3.18) distributes the λ's inside the second product.[1] In Equation (3.19), $r(l, s \mid q) \triangleq \lambda_q n(l \mid q) \prod_{k=1}^{l} p(w_{jk} \mid q)$ is proportional to the probability that a segment $s = w_{j1}, \ldots, w_{jl}$ is generated from the state q. In this form, one can sum over all possible alignments A in polynomial time:

$$P(W, L, S \mid M) = \sum_{A} P(W, L, A, S \mid M)$$

$$= \sum_{A} \frac{1}{n!} \prod_{i=1}^{|M|} e^{-\lambda_{qi}} \prod_{j=1}^{n} r(l_j, s_j \mid q_{a_j}) \tag{3.20}$$

The last step above can be shown by algebraic operations.

The Expectation-Maximization (EM) algorithm is used to estimate the parameters in the model, and a dynamic programming algorithm is applied to search for the meaning according to

$$\hat{M} = \arg\max_{M} P(W \mid M)P(M) = \arg\max_{M} \sum_{S,L} P(W, L, S \mid M)P(M) \tag{3.21}$$

with marginalization over all possible segment sequences S and the length for the segments, L.

2+1 Level SLU Model

In the lexicalization model we have discussed so far, a state (attribute) is assigned to each word in an utterance, such that the utterance can be partitioned into a sequence of segments. From this segmentation, a semantic representation like the one in Figure 3.12 can be constructed, where a segment of the original text specifies the value of a slot in the semantic frame. The text is often not the semantic terminals in the canonical form like the one in Figure 3.3. It often needs a separate rule-based post-processing step to derive the normalized slot values from the text.

Lefèvre (2007) introduced a 2+1 SLU model that integrates the normalization process in the lexicalization model. Here the number "2" stands for the semantic prior model and the concept model, which is the traditional lexicalization model that generates the lexical string from a concept. "1" stands for the additional model that treats the normalized attribute values as hidden variables. Ideally, a decoder can jointly find the concept sequence and the normalized value sequence according to the following decision rule:

$$\hat{C}, \hat{V} = \arg\max_{C,V} P(C, V \mid W) = \arg\max_{C.V} P(W \mid C, V)P(V \mid C)P(C) \tag{3.22}$$

[1] Note that $\sum_{i=1}^{|M|} n_i = n$.

Here the lexicalization model $P(W \mid C, V)$ depends not only on the attribute C, but also on the normalized value of C, V. However, the complexity of this decoding process is too high to allow an efficient algorithm. Hence a two step "2+1" decoding process is adopted instead. In the first step, like the other frame-based SLU models we have reviewed, the semantic prior model and the concept model are applied to obtain the concept segmentation according to

$$\hat{C} = \arg\max_C P(C \mid W) = \arg\max_C P(W \mid C)P(C) \tag{3.23}$$

where $P(C)$ is the flat attribute n-gram semantic prior model, and $P(W \mid C)$ is the attribute dependent n-gram lexicalization model. Both have been reviewed earlier. In the second step, both W and the attribute segment sequences C are observed, and $\hat{V}$ can be found according to

$$\hat{V} = \arg\max_V P(W \mid \hat{C}, V)P(V \mid \hat{C})P(\hat{C}) \tag{3.24}$$

To further simplify the decoding process, the attribute names in C in Equation (3.23) and (3.24) do not include the specifiers in the MEDIA semantic representation (see Section 3.1.2). The specifiers are assigned to the concept sequence in a later stage with a conditional sequential labeling model, which we will review in Section 3.3.4.

Model Training

Maximum likelihood (ML) estimation can be used to estimate the parameters in both the semantic prior model and the lexicalization model. In supervised training, if each word is labeled with the state, as in CHRONUS (Pieraccini and Levin, 1993) and the Hidden Understanding Model in (Miller *et al.*, 1994), then both Markov transition probabilities and the state-conditioned n-gram models can be directly estimated from the data by simply counting the relative frequencies. However, fully annotated training data are expensive to obtain. It is desirable to label only the words that carry the important semantic information, for example, only the slot filler words. In such a case, the state labels for many words are hidden. The Expectation-Maximization (EM) algorithm (Dempster *et al.*, 1977) can be applied to estimate the parameters. Section 3.3.2 presents a case study of the statistical learning with the HMM/CFG composite model, a generative model assisted by the domain/linguistic knowledge.

Implementation of the Generative Models

Many generative models are implemented with the standard toolkits like the stochastic finite-state transducers (SFST) (Raymond and Riccardi, 2007) or the graphic models (Bilmes and Zweig, 2002). For example, each SLU component can be implemented as a SFST, and the SLU system can be built by composing the component SFSTs. Raymond and Riccardi (2007) shows a SFST implementation of a generative model. In this work, the lattice output from an ASR is represented by a stochastic finite state machine (SFSM) λ_W. It uses an n-gram as the lexicalization model for the "concepts", which are the states representing either slots or a null attribute used to model the carrier phrases connecting the slots. N-gram can be represented by a SFSM as well, as described in (Riccardi *et al.*, 1996). An n-gram SFSM for a concept can be turned into a SFST by outputting the accepted words together with the concept's name. The union of all the SFSTs for all concepts forms the lexicalization model λ_{w2c} that maps words to concepts. Finally, a statistical conceptual language model is used as the semantic prior model, which is again represented by a SFST λ_{CLM}. Different λ_{CLM} can be implemented. In

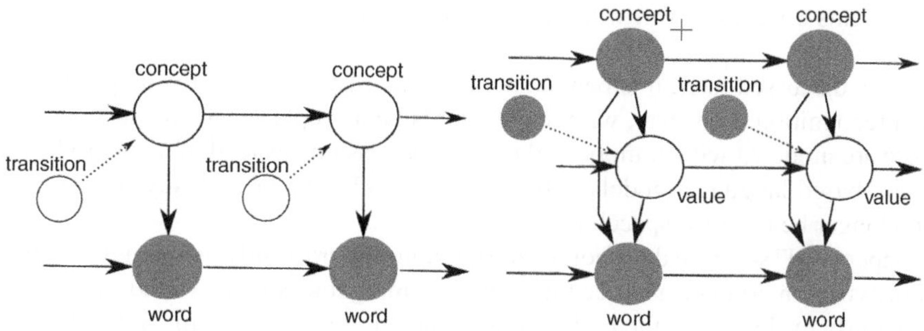

Figure 3.16 The graphic model representation of the DBNs used in the 2+1 level SLU. Left: the DBN used in the first step decoding, in which the words (a shaded node represents a random variable whose value is observed) are aligned to the concepts. Right: the DBN for the second step decoding, in which the concepts and words are observed, and the normalized values for the concepts are identified. (Courtesy of Fabrice Lefèvre, 2007 IEEE)

(Raymond and Riccardi, 2007), the conceptual language model is used to compute the joint probability $P(W, M)$ instead of $P(M)$:

$$P(W, M) = \prod_{i=1}^{k} P(w_i,\ c_i \mid h_i) \tag{3.25}$$

where $M = c_1, c_2, \ldots, c_k$ is a sequence of concepts, $W = w_1, w_2, \ldots, w_k$ is a sequence of words, and $h_i = w_{i-1}c_{i-1}, w_{i-2}c_{i-2}$ is the trigram history of word/concept pairs. The SLU model is thus a SFST composition:

$$\lambda_{SLU} = \lambda_W \circ \lambda_{w2c} \circ \lambda_{CLM} \tag{3.26}$$

The generative models can also be easily implemented with the general purpose graphic model toolkit. For example, researchers from Université d'Avignon used Dynamic Bayesian Networks (DBNs) (Lefèvre, 2007; Meurs *et al.*, 2009) to implement the generative SLU models. The aforementioned "2+1 SLU" model can be represented with the graphic models in Figure 3.16, which is implemented with the generic graphic model toolkit GMTK (Bilmes and Zweig, 2002) and the language model toolkit SRILM (Stolcke, 2002).

3.3.2 *Integrating Knowledge in Statistical Models – A Case Study of the Generative HMM/CFG Composite Model*

One disadvantage of a purely data-driven, statistical SLU approach is the requirement of a large amount of training data. To overcome this problem, many systems utilize a preprocessing step to identify the "superwords" from the input stream with pattern matching. This step includes (a) replacing the words in a semantic class with the class name; e.g. "Seattle" and "Los Angeles" are replaced with the superword "_cityname"; and (b) replacing a word sequence that matches a regular expression with a superword; e.g. "one hundred twenty five" is replaced with the superword "_number".

Two problems arise, however, with this traditional solution:

1. As will be discussed later, it is beneficial to use the SLU model as the language model for speech recognition. However, with actual words being replaced by the superwords, many of these are modeled with complicated regular expressions instead of the word lists used in the class-based language models (Brown *et al.*, 1992; Kneser and Ney, 1993), the model can no longer be used for speech recognition.
2. The "superword" solution does not handle ambiguities gracefully. Although a sophisticated preprocessor can produce a lattice that includes ambiguous tagging of the superwords, they are not fairly evaluated by the understanding model. For example, in "Schedule a meeting tomorrow ten to eleven", the phrase "ten to eleven" may be ambiguously tagged as "_time" as in the interpretation "10:50" or "_time to _time" as in the interpretation "from 10:00 to 11:00". Since the phrase is treated as a single superword in the first interpretation but three words in the second interpretation, only one transition and one emission probability need to be applied for the first interpretation, while multiple transition and emission probabilities have to be applied for the second one. Therefore, the SLU model will be biased toward the first interpretation.

This section presents a case study of the HMM/CFG composite model. The case study serves two purposes. First, it shows an effective way to seamlessly integrate the domain-dependent knowledge in a data-driven, statistical learning framework to improve the SLU performance. Second, it describes the application of the important optimization algorithms for the generative models in SLU, in particular, the EM algorithm, with rigorous mathematic derivations – until now, we have mentioned the EM algorithm several times without detailed descriptions.

3.3.2.1 HMM/CFG Composite Model

Both problems mentioned above can be attributed to the fact that the preprocessing step is not modeled statistically as an integral part of the SLU model. The lack of the information about the preprocessing model makes the statistical SLU model unable to predict the words for speech recognition, and it prohibits the model from properly normalizing the probabilities because the actual length of the segment replaced by the superword is unknown to the SLU model. An HMM/CFG composite lexicalization model has been introduced in (Wang and Acero, 2003a), which we review here, to aim at solving these problems. This model uses the same semantic prior for hierarchical Markov topology as in Equation (3.10). The underlying state corresponding to a slot in the semantic frame is expanded into a preamble–filler–postamble three-state sequence (Figure 3.17). The preamble and postamble serve as the contextual clue for the identity of the slot, while the slot filler decides its value. The lexicalization model follows Equation (3.13), similar to that of CHRONUS and the Hidden Understanding model. The differences here include:

1. The HMM/CFG composite model uses either n-gram models or probabilistic context-free grammars (PCFGs) for $P(\varphi \mid q)$. If q is a state corresponding to a slot filler, a PCFG is used for $p(\varphi \mid q)$. The PCFG embeds the domain-specific and domain-independent knowledge, such as a city-name list and a date grammar. The CFG rules can be populated with database entries or pre-built in a grammar library for domain-independent concepts, for example,

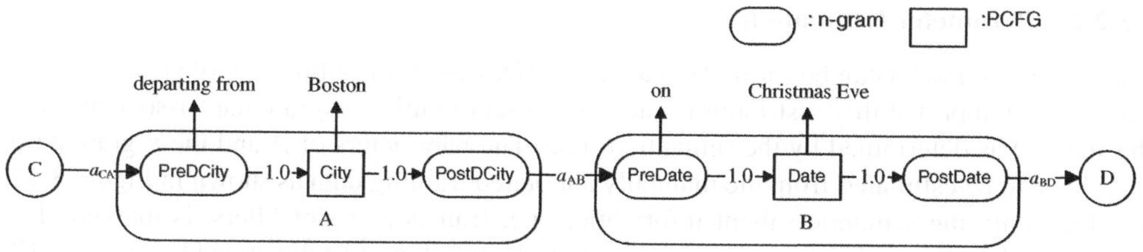

Figure 3.17 The state alignment for the phrase "departing from Boston on Christmas Eve" according to the topology in Figure 3.14. The original states A and B are expanded to three states (Wang *et al.*, © 2005 IEEE).

date and time. The lexicalization of other states is modeled with n-grams. Figure 3.17 shows the state alignment for an example phrase according to the network topology in Figure 3.14. Note the introduction of the preamble and postamble states does not change the semantic prior model, because the transition probabilities from the preambles and to the postambles are always 1.0.

2. The training data for the composite model is not required to be fully annotated – not every word is associated with a state. Instead, only a high-level semantic annotation is required, which labels the slots of semantic frames. For example, the utterance "show flights departing from Seattle flying to Boston on Christmas Eve" is labeled as in Figure 3.12. The words without explicit labels, for example, "on", may be associates with different states in the topology, for instance, either "PostDCity" or "PreDDate" in Figure 3.17. Because the alignments are hidden for those unmarked words, the EM algorithm (Dempster *et al.*, 1977) needs to be applied for model training.

Formally, the lexicalization probability in this composite model is

$$P(W \mid M) = \sum_{\pi=\varphi_1,\ldots,\varphi_m} P(\pi \mid q_1, \ldots, q_m) = \sum_{\pi=\varphi_1,\ldots,\varphi_m} \prod_{i=1}^{m} P_{q_i}(\varphi_i \mid q_i) \tag{3.27}$$

Here P_q is an n-gram model if q is a preamble or a postamble state, or a PCFG if q is a slot filler. It is possible that for some $q \neq r$, $P_q = P_r$. For example, the PCFG for "cityname" are shared by the fillers for both the DCity and the ACity slots.

Modeling slot fillers with PCFG has another advantage – since the slot fillers are the bearers of semantic information, the capability of semantic interpretation of PCFG with the semantic interpretation tags allows compositional construction of normalized semantic representation. For example, both "two fifteen PM" and "quarter past two in the afternoon" may have the same semantic representation like

```
<PreciseTime>
    <TimePoint>2:15</TimePoint>
    <TimeOfDay>PM</TimeOfDay>
</PreciseTime>
```

such that application developers do not have to design an extra post-processing step to specifically process the two literally different phrases.

3.3.2.2 Parameter Estimation

The composite model can be formalized as (S, A, G), where S is a finite set of states, A is the state transition probability distributions, and G is a set of emission grammars associated with the states. S is determined by the semantic frame. The parameters of A and the n-gram parts of G have to be estimated from the manually annotated training data as shown in Figure 3.12, in which only the semantic salient information, i.e. frames and slot fillers, is marked. The annotation determines the state sequence in the model topology,[2] as illustrated by Figure 3.17. Therefore, the counts of state transitions can be collected directly, and the ML estimation is applied for the state transition probabilities. Here a prior count c is used to smooth the transition distributions, which can be optimized with the held-out data. To estimate the lexicalization parameters, one possibility is to extend the Forward-Backward algorithm used in the discrete HMM training (Rabiner and Juang, 1993). Note that in the discrete HMM training, the posterior

$$\gamma_t(q) = P_\phi(q_t = q \mid W) = \frac{\alpha_t(q)\,\beta_t(q)}{\sum_{q'} \alpha_t(q')\,\beta_t(q')} \tag{3.28}$$

can be calculated with the Forward-Backward algorithm. And the emission probability can be then estimated by:

$$b_q(w) = \sum_{t:w_t=w} \gamma_t(q) \bigg/ \sum_{t=1}^{T} \gamma_t(q) \tag{3.29}$$

When a segment of words can be generated from a single state and an n-gram is used to model this generation process, the Forward-Backward algorithm can be extended. Using bigram as an example, the posterior $\xi_t(q, r) = P(q_{t-1} = q, q_t = r \mid W)$ can also be calculated with the Forward-Backward algorithm:

$$\begin{aligned}\xi_t(q, r) &= P(q_{t-1} = q, q_t = r \mid W)\\ &= \frac{\alpha_{t-1}(q)\,t(q, r, w_{t-1})P_r(w_t \mid h(q, r, w_{t-1}))\,\beta_t(r)}{\sum_{q'}\sum_{r'} \alpha_{t-1}(q')\,t(q', r', w_{t-1})P_{r'}(w_t \mid h(q', r', w_{t-1}))\,\beta_t(r')}\end{aligned} \tag{3.30}$$

$$h(q, r, w) = \begin{cases} \text{<s>} & \text{when } q \neq r \\ w & \text{when } q = r \end{cases} \tag{3.31}$$

$$t(q, r, w) = \begin{cases} P_q(\text{</s>} \mid w)a_{qr} & \text{when } q \neq r \\ 1 & \text{when } q = r \end{cases} \tag{3.32}$$

There are several differences from the standard HMM training here. First, the emission probability now depends on $h(q, r, w_{t-1})$, the history of the previous word from the same state or the context cue "<s>" for the initial word in a segment. Second, in the segment model there is no self-loop transition at a state. The generative process stays at the same state unless the end of the segment is predicted by the bigram model for the state. This segment ending probability must be included in the transition probability $t(q, r, w_{t-1})$ when a state transition is made. The computation of the forward and backward probabilities, $\alpha_t(q)$ and $\beta_t(q)$, should be changed

[2] Note that some states may be a dummy state that emits an empty string.

accordingly. With the posterior $\xi_t(q, r)$ defined, the bigram probability can be obtained by

$$P_q(v \mid w) = \frac{\sum_{t:w_{t-1}=w, w_t=v} \xi_t(q, q)}{\sum_{t:w_{t-1}=w} \xi_t(q, q)} \tag{3.33}$$

for $w \neq$ <s>, and

$$P_q(v \mid \text{<s>}) = \frac{\gamma_1(q)\delta(w_1, v) + \sum_{r \neq q} \sum_{t:w_t=v} \xi_t(r, q)}{\gamma_1(q) + \sum_{r \neq q} \sum_t \xi_t(r, q)} \tag{3.34}$$

where $\delta(w, v) = 1$ if $w = v$ and 0 otherwise.

This solution is complicated to implement, given all the boundary conditions in $h(q, r, w_{t-1})$ and $t(q, r, w)$, especially with higher-order n-grams. One simpler solution, given the fact that many standard n-gram training and smoothing implementations are already available, is to obtain all the strings φ that state q can generate, obtain the count $N(q, \varphi)$, i.e. the number of times that q generates φ, and then compute the bigram probability with the standard ML estimation:

$$P_q(w_k \mid w_{k-n+1}, \ldots, w_{k-1}) = \frac{\sum_\varphi N(q, \varphi) C(w_{k-n+1}, \ldots, w_{k;\varphi})}{\sum_\varphi N(q, \varphi) C(w_{k-n+1}, \ldots, w_{k-1;\varphi})} \tag{3.35}$$

Here $C(\omega; \varphi)$ is the number of times that word sequence ω occurs in φ.

When training samples are fully annotated, i.e. every word is marked with its aligned state, $N(q, \varphi)$ can be obtained by a simple counting. When only partial annotation is available, as illustrated by the example in Figure 3.12, $N(q, \varphi)$ can be viewed as the expected fractional count the state q generate the string φ. Notice that the annotation pegs the slot fillers to the slot states, which restricts the alignments of the remaining words and states, so a subsequence of the observation W (e.g. W ="departing from") can only align to a state subsequence Q (e.g., Q ="PostTopic PreFlight PreACity" in Figure 3.12). The counts of these subsequence alignments, $c(Q, W)$, can be empirically collected from all the annotated training examples. Then the state-specific n-gram parameters are estimated with the EM algorithm (Dempster *et al.*, 1977). In the E-step, $N(q, \varphi)$, the fractional count that state q is aligned to the substring φ, is computed with the current model parameters (initially based on the uniform distribution). In the M-step, Equation (3.35) is applied to estimate the n-gram probability (with the proper smoothing such as the deleted interpolation in (Jelinek and Mercer, 1980)]).

To compute $N(q, \varphi)$, the expected count for state q to generate segment φ, note that

$$N(q, \varphi) = \sum_{Q,W} c(Q, W) \sum_\pi P_\phi(\pi \mid Q, W) c(q \uparrow \varphi; \pi, Q, W) \tag{3.36}$$

here $c(Q, W)$ is the number of occurrences that the state sequence $Q = q_1, q_2, \ldots, q_m$ co-occurs with the word sequence $W = w_1, \ldots, w_k$ according to the partially labeled training data. π is a segmentation that breaks W into m non-overlapping segments, each segment corresponds (aligns) to a state in Q. The segment may be an empty string. $c(q \uparrow \varphi; \pi, Q, W)$ is the number of times that state q appears in Q and aligns to the substring φ according to the segmentation π.

The summation over all possible segmentation in Equation (3.36) makes it difficult to compute $N(q, \varphi)$ efficiently. To remove the summation, note that because $P_\phi(\pi, Q, W) =$

$\prod_{q,\varphi} P_\phi(\varphi \mid q)^{c(q\uparrow\varphi;\pi,Q,W)}$,

$$\begin{aligned}\frac{\partial P_\phi(Q,W)}{\partial P_\phi(\varphi \mid q)} &= \frac{\partial \sum_\pi P_\phi(\pi, Q, W)}{\partial P_\phi(\varphi \mid q)} \\ &= \frac{\partial \sum_\pi \prod_{(q,\varphi)\in\pi} P_\phi(\varphi \mid q)^{c(q\uparrow\varphi;\pi,Q,W)}}{\partial P_\phi(\varphi \mid q)} \\ &= \sum_\pi \frac{c(q\uparrow\varphi;\pi,Q,W)\prod_{q',\varphi'} P_\phi(\varphi' | q')^{c(q'\uparrow\varphi';\pi,Q,W)}}{P_\phi(\varphi \mid q)}\end{aligned} \tag{3.37}$$

Rearranging Equation (3.37), we obtain

$$\sum_\pi P_\phi(\pi \mid Q, W) c(q\uparrow\varphi;\pi,Q,W) = \frac{P_\phi(\varphi \mid q)}{P_\phi(Q,W)} \frac{\partial P_\phi(Q,W)}{\partial P_\phi(\varphi \mid q)}. \tag{3.38}$$

On the left of Equation (3.38) is the summation that occurs in the expected count. On the right there is no summation at all. The problem now becomes the efficient computation of $P_\phi(Q, W)$ and $\partial P_\phi(Q, W)/\partial P_\phi(\varphi \mid q)$. For that purpose, define $\alpha_k(i) = \Pr(\pi = \varphi_1, ..., \varphi_m \wedge \varphi_k = ..., w_i; W \mid Q)$ to be the probability of all the segmentations π that align the end of q_k in Q to the i-th word in W, and $\beta_k(i) = P(\pi = \varphi_1, ..., \varphi_m \wedge \varphi_k = w_i...; W \mid Q)$ to be the probability of all the segmentations that align the beginning of q_k to the ith word in W. Then

$$\begin{aligned}P_\phi(Q,W) &= \alpha_m(n) P_\phi(Q) \\ &= P_\phi(Q)\sum_{ij} \alpha_{k-1}(i-1) P_\phi(w_i, ..., w_j \mid q_k)\beta_{k+1}(j+1), \forall k.\end{aligned} \tag{3.39}$$

According to Equation (3.39),

$$\frac{\partial P_\phi(Q,W)}{\partial P_\phi(\varphi \mid q)} = P_\phi(Q) \sum_{\substack{k:\, q_k = q \\ ij:\, \varphi = w_i \ldots w_j}} \alpha_{k-1}(i-1)\beta_{k+1}(j+1) \tag{3.40}$$

Combining Equations (3.38), (3.39) and (3.40), the expected count

$$N(q,\varphi) = P_\phi(\varphi \mid q) \sum_{Q,W} \frac{c(Q,W)}{\alpha_{|Q|}(|W|)} \sum_{\substack{k:\, q_k = q \\ ij:\, \varphi = w_i \ldots w_j}} \alpha_{k-1}(i-1)\beta_{k+1}(j+1) \tag{3.41}$$

$\alpha_k(i)$ and $\beta_k(i)$ can be computed efficiently with dynamic programming according to Equation (3.42):

$$\begin{aligned}\alpha_0(i) &= P_\phi(w_1, ..., w_i \mid q_0); \\ \alpha_k(i) &= \sum_{r\le i} \alpha_{k-1}(r) P_\phi(w_{r+1}, ..., w_i \mid q_k); \\ \beta_m(i) &= P_\phi(w_i, ..., w_n \mid q_m); \\ \beta_k(i) &= \sum_{r\ge i} \beta_{k+1}(r) P_\phi(w_i, ..., w_{r-1} \mid q_k)\end{aligned} \tag{3.42}$$

Here $P_\phi(w_i, ..., w_j \mid q)$ can be obtained according to the n-gram (initially with the uniform distribution) specific to state q. When $r = i$, $P_\phi(w_{r+1}, ..., w_i \mid q) = P_\phi(</s> \mid <s>; q)$ is the probability to generate an empty string from q.

3.3.2.3 The Performance of the HMM/CFG Composite Model

The HMM/CFG composite model balances the trade-off between robustness and the constraints on over-generalizations/ambiguities with the different models for the preambles/postambles and the slot fillers. The CFG model imposes a relatively rigid restriction on the slot fillers, which are more crucial for correct understanding and less subject to the disfluencies because they are semantically coherent units. The fillers are often domain specific and can be obtained from the application database, such as the city names and airport names in the ATIS domain; or they are common domain-independent concepts such as phone number, date, time, which are already modeled in a grammar library; or they can be automatically generated according to some high-level description such as a regular expression for an alphanumeric concept (Wang and Acero, 2006). The non-slot states serve as the "glue" that sticks different slot fillers together. This type of inter-concept language is normally domain dependent, hard to pre-build a model for, and subject to more disfluencies. It varies significantly across different speakers. The n-gram model is more robust and thus suitable for this sub-language. This strategy bears resemblance to the different treatments of slots and frames in the knowledge-based semantic parser of Phoenix, in which the slot fillers were required to exactly match the corresponding slot-net; while the rigid requirement was relaxed when the slots were "assembled" into a frame via the beam search. Furthermore, the knowledge introduced by the CFG sub-model greatly compensates for the data sparseness problem (e.g. it is very unlikely to see all city names occur in all context in the training data).

Figure 3.18 plots the slot error rate of the HMM/CFG composite model with the ATIS 93 category A test set, with respect to the amount of the training data it used. Here the accuracy of the model trained with half of the 1993 ATIS3 training data is close to that of the model trained with all the 1993 data (~1700 sentences). With all the training data, the end-to-end error rate is 5.3%, which is comparable to the best manually developed grammar, and better than the best data-driven statistical model that used all the ATIS2 and ATIS3 training data (over 6000 utterances). The inclusion of domain knowledge in the statistical model reduced the requirement on training data.

3.3.3 Use of Generative Understanding Models in Speech Recognition

3.3.3.1 Sub-optimality of Two-pass SLU

Equation (3.6) assumes that the sentence or word sequence W is the observation. This is only true in a system that takes text at the input. In spoken language understanding, the actual observation is the acoustic feature sequence O. Hence the optimal meaning for a speech utterance O should be

$$\hat{M} = \arg\max_M P(M \mid O) = \arg\max_M P(O \mid M)P(M) \tag{3.43}$$

Equation (3.43) is often implemented with a two-pass approach. In the first pass, a "pseudo" word observation sequence $\hat{W} = \arg\max_W P(W \mid O) = \arg\max_W P(O \mid W)P(W)$ is obtained

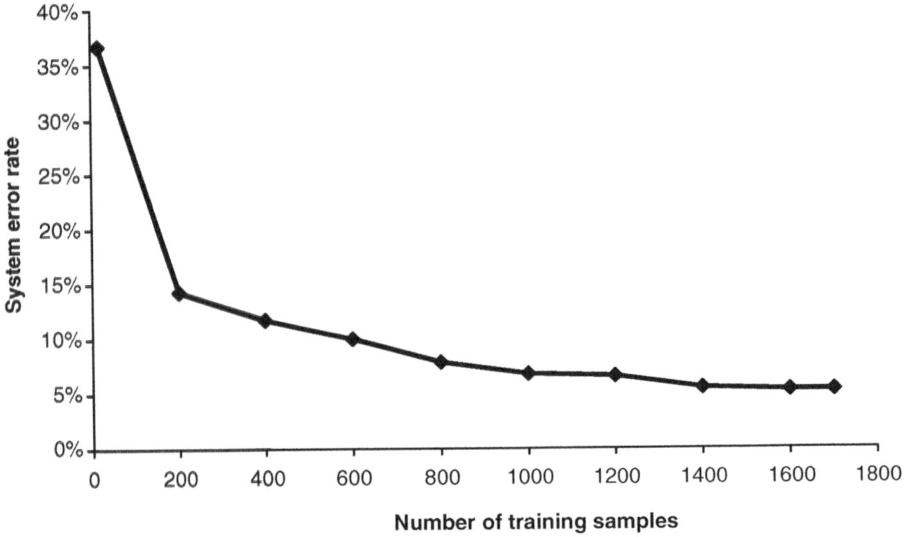

Figure 3.18 ATIS end-to-end system error rate on text input versus training set size for the HMM/CFG composite model (Wang *et al.*, © 2005 IEEE).

with the maximum joint probability $P(O, W)$ probability from a recognizer. In the second pass, the corresponding meaning $\hat{M}$ is extracted from $\hat{W}$ by plugging $\hat{W}$ into Equation (3.6):

$$\begin{aligned}\hat{M} &= \arg\max_{M} P(M \mid \hat{W}) = \arg\max_{M} P\left(M \mid \arg\max_{w}(P(O \mid W)P(W))\right) \\ &= \arg\max_{M} P(M)P\left(\arg\max_{w}(P(O \mid W)P(W))\,|M\right) \end{aligned} \tag{3.44}$$

An alternative to this two-pass solution is shown in Equation (3.45):

$$\begin{aligned}\hat{M} &= \arg\max_{M} \Pr(M \mid O) = \arg\max_{M} P(O \mid M)P(M) \\ &= \arg\max_{M} \sum_{W} P(O, W \mid M)P(M) \\ &= \arg\max_{M} \sum_{W} P(O \mid W, M)P(W \mid M)P(M) \\ &\approx \arg\max_{M} \sum_{W} P(O \mid W)[P(W \mid M)P(M)] \end{aligned} \tag{3.45}$$

Here the understanding model $P(W \mid M)P(M)$, which can be considered as a meaning-specific "language model", is directly used in place of the generic language model in ASR.

The two-pass solution is simpler from the engineering point of view, and it runs faster because there is no need to keep separate search paths with the same prefix strings, but different semantic structures in speech decoding. However, it is a sub-optimal solution because the dependency link between O and M via W is broken. Instead, O is generated via a different language model $P(W)$ and acoustic model $P(O \mid W)$ that have nothing to do with M. In an extreme case we may have $P(W) = 0$ whenever $P(W \mid M) \neq 0$, so no optimal solution can be found at all. In research spoken dialogue systems, this problem has often been heuristically addressed by performing SLU on the n-best outputs from a recognizer. Another disadvantage of the two-pass solution lies in the difficulty to adapt to changes. If new cities are added into a database, or a new type of services is introduced, the language model in a two-pass system has to be retrained unless a class-based language model is used.

3.3.3.2 Using an Understanding Model as the LM for Speech Recognition

For a knowledge-based system that uses the CFG for SLU, it may appear to be easy to use the SLU model for ASR, since many speech recognizers take PCFGs as language models. Even with a non-CFG formalism such as the unification grammar, they can be converted to a CFG for ASR (Moore, 1998; Rayner *et al.*, 2001). However, simplicity remains only at the engineering level. A fundamental problem is that the knowledge-based models are in general not robust to disfluencies in spontaneous speech and recognition errors. They depend on the robust mechanism of the parser in the understanding component to deal with the inputs not covered by the model. This robust mechanism is not available in the speech recognizers.

In statistical SLU, robustness is built into the model itself through proper smoothing. The remaining problems are more of an engineering issue – how can a statistical model like the HMM/CFG composite model be converted into a format that a recognizer can take as a language model. In Wang and Acero (2003b) the HMM/CFG composite model is converted to a CFG as follows: the backbone Markov chain is basically a statistical finite state machine, which is a sub-class of the PCFG. The efficient conversion of the n-gram lexicalization model follows the work in Riccardi *et al.* (1996), and the CFG lexicalization model is used directly. The composite model, in the format of PCFG, was applied under the framework of Equation (3.45), and the results were compared with the two-pass recognition/understanding paradigm under the framework of Equation (3.44), where a domain-specific trigram was used as the language model $P(W)$ in speech recognition and the HMM/CFG composite model was used for the second pass understanding.

Table 3.1 shows the findings with a commercial decoder and a research decoder. For the commercial decoder, even though the composite model's word error rate is over 46% higher than the trigram model, its SLU error rate (again measured as the slot insertion–deletion–substitution rate (SER)) is 17% lower. With the research decoder that is less aggressive in pruning, the word error rate of the HMM/CFG model is about 27% higher than the trigram model. However, the SLU error rate is still marginally lower.

The results clearly demonstrate the sub-optimality of separating the models for ASR and SLU. In this approach, the trigram is trained to optimize the likelihood of the training

Table 3.1 The ASR word error rate and the SLU error rate (slot ins-del-sub) of the trigram model (2-passes) and the HMM/CFG composite mode (1-pass). "Transcription" column shows the SLU error rate on the manual transcriptions. Both automatic and manual transcriptions were sent to the same HMM/CFG model for a second-pass SLU

Decoder		Trigram	HMM/CFG	Transcription
Commercial Decoder	WER	8.2%	12.0%	
	SLUER	11.6%	9.8%	5.1%
Research Decoder	WER	6.0%	7.6%	
	SLUER	9.0%	8.8%	5.1%

Source: © 2008 IEEE

transcriptions. If the test data is drawn from the same distribution, the trigram model assigns higher likelihood to the correct transcriptions and hence reduces the word error rate. On the other hand, the objective of the HMM/CFG composite model training is to maximize the likelihood of the observed semantic representations. Thus the correct semantic representations of the test sentences will be assigned a higher probability. It is important to note that the trigram model in the experiment used all the ATIS2 and ATIS3 training data, while the HMM/CFG composite model only used the 1993 ATIS3 training data. The experiment is seemingly biased toward the trigram model. However, the result is still interesting because unlabeled data for trigram model training is much easier to obtain than the annotated data for HMM/CFG training. When only the 1700 ATIS3 training samples were used for trigram LM training, the two-pass system had 10.4% WER and 13.1% SLUER with the commercial recognizer, and 7.5% WER and 10.2% SLUER with the research recognizer.

The results from other research work also reveal the importance of maintaining the dependency link between the acoustics and the semantics. In Riccardi and Gorin (1998), a language model that interpolated the word n-gram with n-grams containing semantically salient phrases was used for an automatic call-routing (ACR) task. A slight word accuracy improvement from the new language model resulted in a disproportionately substantial improvement in the understanding accuracy. In Chelba *et al.* (2003), a single-pass ASR/ACR system, in which the ACR statistical model was used as the language model for ASR as well, resulted in worse word error rate, but better call classification accuracy. In Estève *et al.* (2003), a concept decoder that adopted a model similar to the HMM/CFG model also yielded better understanding results.

3.3.4 Conditional Models

The statistical models for SLU we have introduced so far are all generative models – the semantic structure M is first generated according to the semantic prior model $P(M)$, from which the observation W is generated according to $P(W \mid M)$, which can be modeled by one of the lexicalization processes we have described.

Conditional models are nongenerative. A conditional model uses a state sequence $\hat{\mathbf{y}}$ to represent the meaning M of an observation sequence $\mathbf{x}$. $\hat{\mathbf{y}}$ is obtained according to the following equation:

$$\hat{\mathbf{y}} = \arg\max_{\mathbf{y}} P(\mathbf{y} \mid \mathbf{x}) \tag{3.46}$$

Here $\mathbf{y}$ is directly conditioned on the observation $\mathbf{x}$. For SLU, Conditional Random Fields (CRFs) or Hidden State Conditional Random Fields (HCRFs) are commonly used conditional models. With CRFs or HCRFs, the conditional probability of the entire state (label) sequence $\mathbf{y}$ given the observation sequence follows an exponential (log-linear) model, with respect to a set of features. A feature $f_k(\mathbf{y}, \mathbf{x})$ in the set is a function of the observation sequence $\mathbf{x}$ and the associated label sequence $\mathbf{y}$:

$$P(\mathbf{y} \mid \mathbf{x}; \Lambda) = \frac{1}{Z(\mathbf{x}; \Lambda)} \exp\left\{\sum_k \lambda_k f_k(\mathbf{y}, \mathbf{x})\right\} \tag{3.47}$$

Here $\Lambda = \{\lambda_k\}$ is a set of parameters. The value of λ_k determines the impact of the feature $f_k(\mathbf{y}, \mathbf{x})$ on the conditional probability. $Z(\mathbf{x}; \Lambda) = \sum_{\mathbf{y}} \exp\left\{\sum_k \lambda_k f_k(\mathbf{y}, \mathbf{x})\right\}$ is a partition function that normalizes the distribution. Given a set of m labeled training examples

$(\mathbf{x}_1, \mathbf{y}_1) \ldots (\mathbf{x}_m, \mathbf{y}_m)$, the model is trained to optimize the following objective function:

$$L(\Lambda) = \frac{1}{m} \sum_{i=1}^{m} \log P(\mathbf{y}_i \mid \mathbf{x}_i; \Lambda) - \frac{1}{2\sigma^2} \|\Lambda\|^2$$
$$= \mathbb{E}_{\hat{P}(\mathbf{x},\mathbf{y})} \log P(\mathbf{y} \mid \mathbf{x}; \Lambda) - \frac{1}{2\sigma^2} \|\Lambda\|^2 \qquad (3.48)$$

where $\hat{P}(\mathbf{x}, \mathbf{y})$ stands for the empirical distribution of the labeled training samples.

The second term in Equation (3.48) regularizes the parameters to keep them from taking extreme values, thus prevents the model from over-fitting the training data. Note that the objective function is a convex function, so a single global optimum exists.

The CRF in Equation (3.47) is unconstrained in the sense that the feature functions are defined on the entire label sequence $\mathbf{y}$. Because the number of all possible label sequences is combinatorial, the model training and inference of an unconstrained CRF is very inefficient. Because of that, it is common to restrict attention to the linear-chain CRFs (Lafferty *et al.*, 2001). The linear chain CRFs impose a Markov constraint on the model topology, and as a consequence, restrict the feature functions to depend only on the labels assigned to the current and the immediately previous states, in the form of $f(y_{t-1}, y_t, \mathbf{x}, t)$. The restrictions enable the application of efficient dynamic programming algorithms in model training and inference – yet still support potentially interdependent features defined on the entire observation sequence $\mathbf{x}$.

Figure 3.19 shows the difference between the HMMs and the linear chain CRFs in graphic model representations. First, since HMMs are generative models, the graph is directed, which points to the direction of the generative process. The state at time t, represented by the random variable $\mathbf{y}_t$, depends on the state at time $t-1$, $\mathbf{y}_{t-1}$. $\mathbf{x}_t$, the observation at time t is generated with the dependency on $\mathbf{y}_t$. CRFs, on the other hand, are represented by undirected graphs since they are direct, non-generative models. Second, observations in HMMs are generated one at a time in a uniformed way, while in CRFs the observation sequence is given, so at each slice of time it can employ features that depends on the entire observation sequence.

When the state sequence $\mathbf{y}$ is not fully observable, as in the previous example in Figure 3.12, where only slot fillers are manually labeled and the remaining word can be aligned to different preamble/postambles, a HCRF can be used. It treats the unknown state assignment as hidden variables, and its features can be defined on these hidden variables. In this case, the following

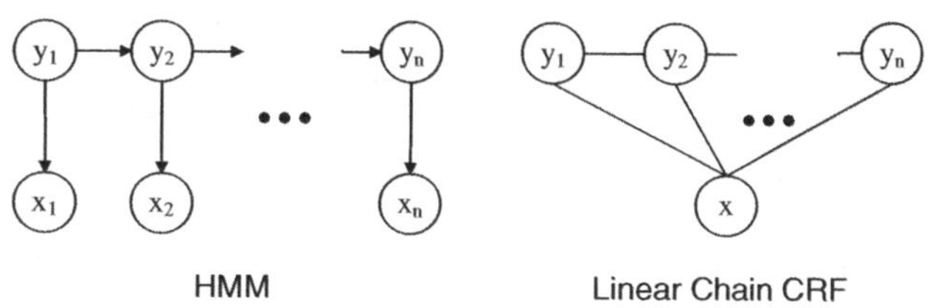

Figure 3.19 The graphic model representations for HMMs (generative model) and CRFs (conditional model). A generative model is a directed graph that points to the direction of the generative process, and observations are generated frame by frame in a uniformed way. Conditional models are represented by undirected models, where the entire observation sequence **o** is observable for every states in the model

conditional probability is used instead in the objective function in Equation (3.48):

$$P(\mathbf{l} \mid \mathbf{x}; \Lambda) = \frac{1}{Z(\mathbf{x}; \Lambda)} \sum_{\mathbf{y}:\mathbf{y} \text{ is consistent with } \mathbf{l}} \exp\left\{\sum_k \lambda_k f_k(\mathbf{y}, \mathbf{x})\right\} \tag{3.49}$$

where $\mathbf{l}$ is the label marked for $\mathbf{x}$ that only partially determines the state sequence for $\mathbf{x}$. The objective function sums over all legal state sequences $\mathbf{y}$ that are consistent with $\mathbf{l}$. Because of this additional summation, the objective function is no longer convex in Λ.

The parameters Λ in CRFs or HCRFs can be optimized according to the objective function in Equation (3.48) with numeric algorithms like stochastic gradient decent or L-BFGS. Both of them use the gradient of the objective function, which can be easily derived as

$$\frac{\partial L(\Lambda)}{\partial \lambda_k} = \mathbb{E}_{\hat{P}(\mathbf{x},\mathbf{y})}\left[f_k(\mathbf{x}, \mathbf{y})\right] - \mathbb{E}_{\hat{P}(\mathbf{x})P(\mathbf{y}|\mathbf{x})}\left[f_k(\mathbf{x}, \mathbf{y})\right] \tag{3.50}$$

for CRFs and

$$\frac{\partial L(\Lambda)}{\partial \lambda_k} = \mathbb{E}_{\hat{P}(\mathbf{x},\mathbf{l})P(\mathbf{y}|\mathbf{x},\mathbf{l})}\left[f_k(\mathbf{x}, \mathbf{y})\right] - \mathbb{E}_{\hat{P}(\mathbf{x})P(\mathbf{y}|\mathbf{x})}\left[f_k(\mathbf{x}, \mathbf{y})\right] \tag{3.51}$$

for HCRFs. In other words, the gradient with respect to a feature weight is the difference between the expected value of the feature given both the observation and the label sequence and the expected value of the feature given only the observation and a model $P(\mathbf{y} \mid \mathbf{x})$ trained so far. The expected value can be collected with the forward-backward algorithm when the linear-chain CRFs or HCRFs are used.

Compared with the generative models, conditional models have the following advantages:

1. A generative model wastes its capacity by modeling the generation of observations, which in practice are always known. Because of that, several discriminative training algorithms such as maximum mutual information (MMI) (Bahl *et al.*, 1986) and minimum classification error (MCE) (Juang *et al.*, 1997) have been proposed. Conditional models, on the other hand, are discriminative in nature – their objective function can only be optimized by maximizing the posterior probability of the correct state sequence while minimizing the posterior of the competing hypotheses.
2. The components of a generative model, such as the transition and emission distributions, need to be a properly normalized probability density function, even though the only probability distribution we care about for a SLU task is $P(\mathbf{y} \mid \mathbf{x})$. This makes the model too restrictive. In contrast, CRFs models the entire state sequence with the exponential model and the only restriction is that $P(\mathbf{y} \mid \mathbf{x})$ forms a proper probabilistic distribution. In the specific case of HMM and CRF, if the same features (transition and emission) are used, then the space of the HMM parameter values is limited to a subset of that of the CRF due to the constraints that is not relevant to the objective function. These extra constraints may limit the model's discriminative capability.
3. A generative model has uniform observation space for each state. It is very expensive to expand the observation context at a state due to the curse of dimensionality – since it needs to model the generative process for all possible such expanded context. In contrast, the observations are random variables with known values in a conditional model, thereby it can

list	**twa**	**flights**	**from**	**washington**	**to**	**philadelphia**
|	|	|	|	|	|	|
null	*AirlineCode*	*null*	*null*	*ACity*	*null*	*DCity*

Figure 3.20 Frame-based SLU as a sequential labeling problem: words are assigned labels representing their meaning

incorporate interdependent, overlapping features only observed in the training data. The features can be defined on the entire observation, as illustrated by Figure 3.19.

In a straightforward application of CRFs for the frame-based SLU, **x** consists of a transcribed utterance, **y** is the semantic label sequence assigned to **x**. Non-slot filler words are assigned a null state, as illustrated by Figure 3.20.

Typical features used by the CRFs for SLU include the transition features, the n-gram features, and the class membership (a.k.a. word list) features. The transition features model the dependency among adjacent states, which capture the influence of context on the label assigned to a given word:

$$f_{i,j}^{TR}(y_{t-1}, y_t, \mathbf{x}, t) = \delta(y_{t-1} = i)\delta(y_t = j) \tag{3.52}$$

where i, j are states (labels) of the model. $\delta(e) = 1$ when $e =$ **true** and $\delta(e) = 0$ when $e =$ **false**.

The n-gram features often include the unigram ($f_{w,j}^{UG}$) and bigram ($f_{w,w',j}^{BG}$) features to capture the relation between the current state and the identity of the current (and previous) words

$$\begin{aligned} f_{w,j}^{UG}(y_{t-1}, y_t, \mathbf{x}, t) &= \delta(x_t = w)\delta(y_t = j) \\ f_{w,w',j}^{BG}(y_{t-1}, y_t, \mathbf{x}, t) &= \delta(x_{t-1} = w)\delta(x_t = w')\delta(y_t = j) \end{aligned} \tag{3.53}$$

where w, w' are words and j is a model state (label).

The class member features check if the current word is part of an entry in the lexicon of a syntactic or semantic class:

$$f_{C,j}^{SC}(y_{t-1}, y_t, \mathbf{x}, t) = \delta(C \triangleright [\mathbf{x}, t])\, \delta(y_t = j) \tag{3.54}$$

where C is a class, $C \triangleright [\mathbf{x}, t]$ indicates that a member of C is a substring of $\mathbf{x}$ that covers x_t. j is a model state. Here the member of C can be defined by a phrase list, a finite state machine (equivalently a regular expression) or a context free grammar. For example, $f_{\mathrm{TIME,DTIME}}^{SC}(y_{t-1}, y_t, \mathbf{x}, t) = 1$ when $\mathbf{x} =$ "I need to fly to Boston three o'clock in the afternoon," "three o'clock in the afternoon" matches the regular expression for TIME, $t \in [7, 11]$ and the model is assigning the state DTIME to position t.

In Raymond and Riccardi (2007), this approach is compared with the SFST generative model, using the same feature set – in this case, the transition feature depends not only on the adjacent states, but also on the words that the states are assigned to. It is found that SFST is more robust when data is sparse and inconsistently labeled; while CRFs surpassed SFST when more labeled data are available. However, directly porting the topology and features of a generative SFST to a conditional model may not be the best practice. Although it takes advantage of the discriminative nature of the model, the model's capability to incorporate interdependent, overlapping features is not leveraged. Jeong and Lee (2008a) shows a good

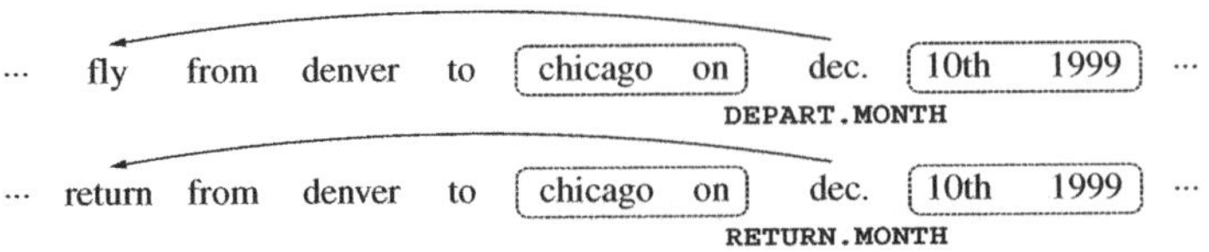

Figure 3.21 Example of long distance dependency in Air Travel data: the interpretation of "dec." depends on the word (pointed to by the arrows) beyond the range covered by the Markov dependency. (Jeong and Lee, © 2008 Elsevier)

example of such features introduced to improve the SLU accuracy. They noticed that long-distance dependency is an important issue in SLU, as illustrated by Figure 3.21.

To overcome this problem, Jeong and Lee (2008a) introduce the trigger features.[3] An element a is a *trigger* for another element b ($a \rightarrow b$) if a is significantly correlated to b, and b is called the *trigged element*. Here an element can be a word, an attribute associated with a word (e.g. the part-of-speech tag of a word), or a model state. a and b form a *trigger pair*. For example, the trigger pair "return $\rightarrow$ dec." indicates that the currently observed word is "dec." and there is a word "return" in the observation that is at least two words (long distance) away before the current word. The trigged element can be null (ϵ) when the identity of the current word is not important. For example, "return $\rightarrow \epsilon$" states that there is a word "return" that is long distance away from the current word.

Given a trigger pair $a \rightarrow b$, a CRF feature function can be defined on the pair:

$$f^{TRI}_{a\rightarrow b,j,k}(y_{t-1}, y_t, \mathbf{x}, t) = \delta(x_t \sim b)\delta(\exists_{t'<t-2} x_{t'} \sim a)\delta(y_{t-1} = j)\delta(y_t = k) \tag{3.55}$$

where $x \sim a$ means that the x is consistent with the element a – if a is a word, it means that $w = a$. If a is a label like a POS tag, it means that w is assigned the part-of-speech a. $x \sim \epsilon$ is always true. For the state variables, $y_i = \epsilon$ is also always true – it means that the feature does not care about the identity of a state.

Note that although by definition a trigger pair can be a pair of model states separated by a long distance, they cannot be incorporated in a linear chain CRF because it breaks the Markov assumption. Since the entire observation is known in a conditional model, this is not a problem when the trigger pair is defined on the observation.

An example can illustrate the power of the trigger features. The feature

$$f^{TRI}_{\text{return}\rightarrow\epsilon,\epsilon,\text{RETURN.MONTH}}(y_{t-1}, y_t, \mathbf{x}, t) \tag{3.56}$$

is activated (has value 1) when t is at the position of the word "dec." in Figure 3.21 and the hypothesized state for the position is "RETURN.MONTH." If this feature has occurred in the training data, namely there is at least one training sample where a word labeled as RETURN.MONTH is preceded by "return" a long distance away, this feature will likely be associated with a positive weight and help generalizing into other cases where the word "return" precedes a month name, as in the example in Figure 3.21.

However, the use of the trigger features introduces another problem. There are too many potential trigger pairs that are observed in the training data – most of them may not satisfy the

[3] Similar idea has been investigated for language modeling (Rosenfeld, 1996).

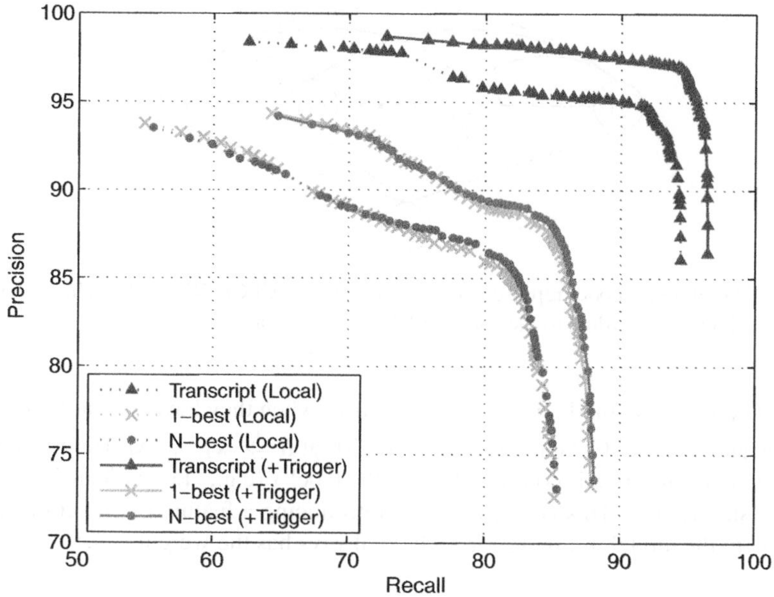

Figure 3.22 The recall-precision curves on Air Travel data used by the Communicator system (Jeong and Lee, © 2008 Elsevier)

requirement of strong correlation. If all those potential pairs are introduced into the model, it will not only slow down the training speed, but also make the model easier to over-fit the training data. Therefore a feature selection mechanism is necessary in this case. Jeong and Lee (2008a) uses a feature selection algorithm adopted and modified from the one in (McCallum, 2003). It is basically a greedy hill-climbing algorithm that iteratively tries each possible individual feature, checks how much gain it brings to the objective function of the CRF when it is added to the model, and selects the one that results in the largest gain. This is, again, a very expensive procedure since it needs to retrain the CRF for each addition of features. However, the procedure can be approximated in several different ways to speed up significantly. Detailed description of the feature selection algorithms is beyond the scope of this introductory book. Interested readers can find the relevant information in McCallum (2003) and Jeong and Lee (2008a).

Figure 3.22 compares the recall-precision curve of the models with or without the long distance features with different types of inputs to the SLU components. It demonstrates significant improvements on both text and speech (one-best ASR and n-best ASR) inputs. The paper also compared the conditional models with the generative Hidden Vector State model introduced in Section 3.3.1.1 and illustrated by Figure 3.15. Both CRFs models with or without the long-distance features outperformed the generative model.

Motivated by the success of the HMM/CFG composite model, Wang *et al.* (2006) investigated the unified CFG/CRF model. To model the long distance dependency, it introduces links between non-adjacent nodes in the graphical model, as illustrated by Figure 3.23.

Note that the nodes are fully connected to each other in Figure 3.23. Exact model inference via dynamic programming will be no longer possible if there is no additional constraint. CFG comes to the rescue by introducing the additional constraint that such a long-distance link is

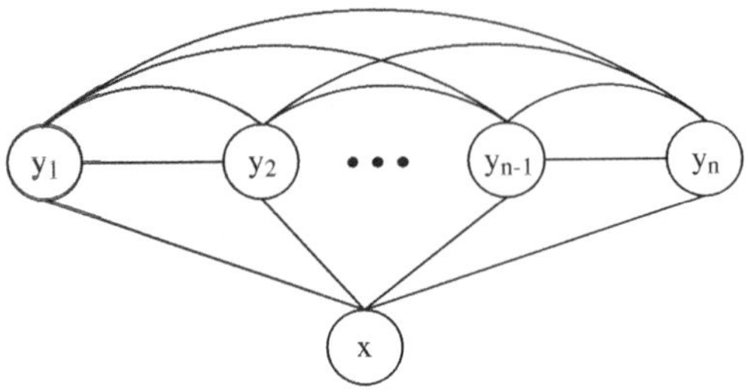

Figure 3.23 The graphic model representation of the unified CFG/CRF model. The nodes are interconnected to each other according to the spans of CFG rule coverage

only allowed between the random variables $\mathbf{y}_j$ and $\mathbf{y}_k$ when they have the values representing the same slot, and there is a CFG rule $R \in R(y)$, such that $R \overset{*}{\Rightarrow} \mathbf{x}_j, \ldots \mathbf{x}_k$. Here $R(y)$ stands for the set of grammar rules that is compatible with the label y (e.g., "PreciseTime" is compatible to the label "StartTime"). This is equivalent to introducing a feature of "no compatible CFG rules (NCR)" to the model in Figure 3.23 which always has the weight $-\infty$:

$$f_{R,j}^{NCR}\left(y, y', \mathbf{x}, j, k\right) = \delta\left(S(y) \neq S(y') \vee \nexists R \in R(y) : R \overset{*}{\Rightarrow} \mathbf{x}_j, \ldots, \mathbf{x}_k\right) \tag{3.57}$$

where $S(y)$ stands for the slot that the label y represents.[4] This constraint of CFG rule matching enables dynamic programming for model training/inference when the observation is chunk parsed into a lattice like the one in Figure 3.24, which consists of not only a word sequence w_1^τ but also a list of CFG non-terminals (NTs) that span different segments of w_1^τ. The task of SLU becomes to select a path from the lattice and assign a semantic label to a segment – the label has to be consistent with a CFG nonterminal covering that segment. To do so, the model must be able to resolve several types of ambiguities:

1. Filler/non-filler ambiguity, e.g. "two" can either fill a Num-of-tickets slot, or be a homophone of "to" that is part of the preamble of an ACity slot.
2. CFG ambiguity, e.g. "Washington" can be either a City or a State.
3. Segmentation ambiguity, e.g. [Washington] [D.C.] versus [Washington D.C.].
4. Semantic label ambiguity, e.g. "Washington D.C." can be either an ACity or a DCity.

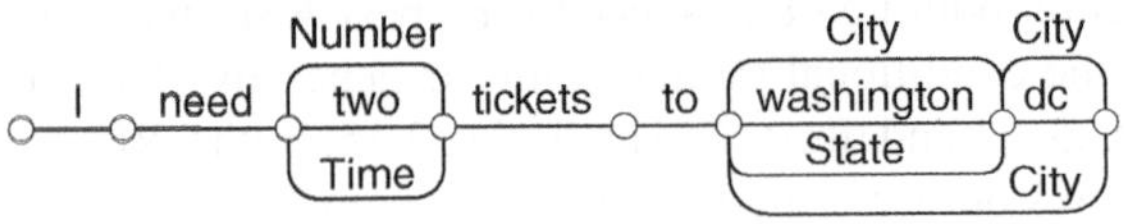

Figure 3.24 The observation includes a word sequence and the subsequences covered by CFG non-terminals (© 2006 Wang *et al.*)

[4] Note that a slot can be represented by multiple labeles, as in the commonly used IOB (inside-outside-begining) labeling scheme.

In one setting, the same model topology and features of the HMM/CFG composite model were directly ported into the CFG/CRF model. Because the state assignment for the non-slot filler words were unknown (e.g. as shown in Figure 3.17, the word "on" could be assigned either the PostDCity state (postamble of the departure city slot) or PreDate state (preamble of the Date slot), HCRF was used for this model.

To model the popularity of different top level semantic frames in the air travel domain such as "ShowFlight,", "GroundTransportation," etc., the model also included the *Frame prior* feature type f^{PR} in addition to the commonly used transition and n-gram features introduced earlier:

$$f_c^{PR}(y_{t-1}, y_{(t)}, \mathbf{x}, t) = \delta(t = 0)\delta(Frame(y_0) = c) \tag{3.58}$$

here $Frame(y)$ stands for the frame of which the state y represents a slot label. The condition $\delta(t = 0)$ ensures that the frame prior feature is only activated once for each utterance.

Figure 3.25 shows the test set slot error rates (SER) at different training iterations. With the flat start initialization that set every parameter to 0 initially (top curve), the error rate never comes close to the 5% baseline of the HMM/CFG model. With the generative model initialization that imported the model parameters of a generative model to initialize the conditional model parameters, the error rate is reduced to 4.8% at the second iteration, but the model quickly gets over-trained afterward.

The failure of the direct porting of the generative model to the conditional model can be attributed to the following reasons:

1. The conditional log-likelihood function is no longer a convex function due to the summation over the values of the hidden variables. This makes the model highly likely to settle on a local optimum. The fact that the flat start initialization failed to achieve the accuracy of the generative model initialization is a clear indication of the problem.
2. In order to account for the words in the test data, the n-grams in the generative model are properly smoothed with back-offs to the uniform distribution over the vocabulary. This results in a huge number of parameters, many of which cannot be estimated reliably in the conditional model, given that model regularization is not as well studied as in n-grams.

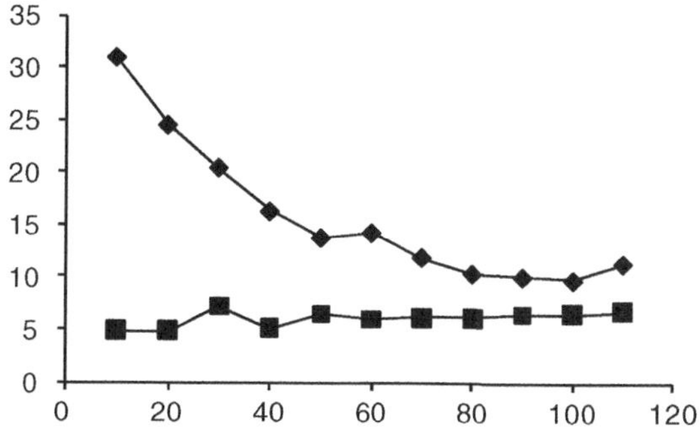

Figure 3.25 Test set slot error rates (in %) at different training iterations. The top curve is for the flat start initialization, the bottom for the generative model initialization (© 2006 Wang *et al.*)

departing	from	boston	on	christmas	eve
|	|	|	|	|	|
PreDCity	*PreDCity*	*DCity*	*PreDate*	*Date*	*Date*

Figure 3.26 The preamble-only labeling scheme: once the slots are marked in the simplified model topology, the state sequence is fully marked, leaving no hidden variables

3. The hidden variables make parameter estimation less reliable, given only a small amount of training data.

An important lesson here is that we should never think generatively when applying the conditional models. While it is important to find cues that help identify the slots, there is no need to exhaustively model the generation of every word from different states in a sentence. Language model smoothing may not be necessary since the task of the model is no longer to assign likelihood to an observation – it is unnecessary to waste the model's capacity to predict unseen observation events. The worst consequence of an unseen test n-gram is the n-gram feature will not be used, while the model may still be able to make the right decision based on the other available features. The distinction of preambles and postambles, which was designed to sharpen the distribution of the generative model to improve the likelihood (perplexity) of the observation, may also be unnecessary. Every word that appears between two slots can be labeled as the preamble state of the second slot, as illustrated by Figure 3.26, or the null state, as illustrated in Figure 3.20. This labeling scheme effectively removes the hidden variables and simplifies the model. It not only expedites model training, but also prevents parameters from settling on a local optimum, because the objective function is convex now.

To fully take advantage of the conditional models' capability in discriminative training and in incorporating interdependent overlapping features, the following types of features are included in the model in addition:

1. The first feature type, *chunk coverage for preamble words*, aims at correcting the confusion between a slot filler state and a slot preamble state – it may be a side effect of not modeling the generation of every word in a sentence. Suppose a preamble state has never occurred in a context that is confusable with a slot state s in the training data, and a word that is part of the string covered by the CFG rule for the filler of s is unseen in the training data. Then, the unigram feature of the word for that preamble state has weight 0, and there is thus no penalty for mislabeling the word as the preamble from either the contextual features or the lexical (unigram) feature. The chunk coverage features detect the potential occurrence of this confusion and informing the model that x_t, which is a potential slot filler according to the knowledge in a grammar, has been labeled as a preamble:

$$f_{NT}^{CC}(y_{t-1}, y_t, \mathbf{x}, t) = \delta(NT \triangleright [\mathbf{x}, t])\delta(\text{IsPreamble}(y_t)) \tag{3.59}$$

2. The *previous-slot context* feature type tries to capture some of the long distance dependency. This is based on the observation that the phrase "*at two PM*" in "*flight from Seattle to Boston at two PM*" and in "*flight departing from Seattle arriving in Boston at two PM.*" has different interpretations, which depends on the identities of the words ("*to*" versus "*arriving at*") in

the preamble of the ACity slots ("*Boston*") preceding the time expression.[5] Since the starting position of the previous slot is unknown given then Markov assumption of the linear chain CRF, its preamble words are approximated by the words in a window preceding the longest segment covered by the CFG rules modeling the filler of the previous slot:

$$f^{PC}_{s_1,s_2,w}(y_{t-1}, y_t, \mathbf{x}, t) = \delta(y_{t-1} = s_1)\delta(y_t = s_2)\delta(w \in x^{\arg\min_i(NT(s_1)\to x_i^{t-1})-1}_{\arg\min_i(NT(s_1)\to x_i^{t-1})-K}) \tag{3.60}$$

here K is a window size, $NT(s)$ stands for the CFG rule name for the filler of the slot represented by the state s, $x_i^j = x_i, \ldots, x_j$, and $\arg\min_i(NT \to x_i^j)$ represents the minimum index (the leftmost position) such that the substring from this position to j is covered by the CFG rule NT. Compared with the trigger features, this feature's capability of modeling long distance dependency is limited to the previous slot's context only. However, since there is only a small set of words for the previous slots' preambles from the training data, there is no need for the expensive feature selection step.

3. The *chunk coverage for slot boundary* feature type is introduced to penalize erroneous segmentations, such as segmenting "*Washington D.C.*" into two separate "City" slots (or a "State" followed by a "City"). It is activated when a slot boundary is covered by a CFG non terminal NT, i.e., when words in two consecutively hypothesized slots ("*Washington*" and "*D.C.*") can also be covered by one single CFG nonterminal:

$$f^{SB}_{NT}(y_{t-1}, y_t, \mathbf{x}, t) = \delta(NT \to \ldots x_{t-1}x_t \ldots)\delta(y_{t-1} \text{ is filler end}) \delta(y_t \text{ is filler start}) \tag{3.61}$$

In Wang *et al.* (2006), this feature type is tired with the *chunk coverage features for preamble words*, and does not introduce any new parameters.

Table 3.2 shows the number of new parameters and the slot error rate (SER) on the test data, after each new feature type has been cumulatively added to the model. The new features improve the prediction of the slot identities and reduce the SER by 21%, relative to the generative HMM/CFG composite model. The additional features, again, are critical in reducing the slot error rate.

While CRF is often characterized as a sequential labeling model, it is important to note that such a model can perform semantic frame classification (picking the correct frame for an utterance) and slot filling simultaneously. In the unified CFG/CRF model, this is achieved by using frame-specific slot labels and the introduction of the frame prior feature in Equation (3.58), which effectively results in the graphic model illustrated by Figure 3.27(a),[6] which can be viewed as a special factorization of the more general model depicted by Figure 3.27(b). Jeong and Lee (2008b) named Figure 3.27(b) the "triangular chain CRF", and introduced a couple of other factorizations of it for the frame-based SLU.

---

[5] Note that the preceding slot is ACity in both cases, hence the transition feature is not able to differentiate these two cases.

[6] For the sake of simplicity, the long-distance dependency introduced by the unified CFG/CRF model is not shown here.

Table 3.2 Number of additional parameters and the slot error rate after each new feature type has been introuced to the model cumulatively

Feature type	Number of parameters	SER(%)
Frame prior	6	
+State transition	+1377	18.68
+Unigrams	+14433	7.29
+Bigrams	+58191	7.23
+Chunk coverage of preamble word	+156	6.87
+Previous-slot context	+290	5.46
+Chunk coverage of slot boundaries	+0	3.94

Source: © 2006 Wang *et al.*

In fact, this type of conditional model for joint classification/sequential labeling is a common practice in many other speech processing applications. For example, Gunawardanaand *et al.* (2005) used HCRF for phone classification, where hidden states are aligned (tagged) to acoustic frames, and a class label is assigned to the entire input in the mean time.

3.3.5 Other Data-driven Approaches to SLU

In the generative and conditional models that we have reviewed so far, only a single decision has to be made according to Equation (3.6) or (3.46). The decision is often made via a dynamic programming or a search algorithm. In this subsection we review some of the data-driven approaches that involve a sequence of decisions. Such an approach is often adopted to take advantage of general purpose natural language processing resources in a divide and conquer style and/or to combine different modules (e.g. knowledge based with a statistical model, or a generative model with a discriminative model) in a solution.

3.3.5.1 FrameNet-Based Semantic Role Labeling

As mentioned in Section 3.1.2, the European LUNA project has adopted the FrameNet representation for semantic annotation, where semantic frames represent prototypical events as

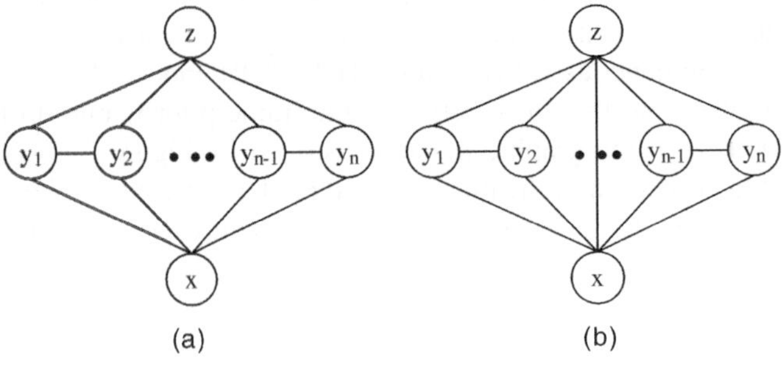

Figure 3.27 Graphical model representation of the joint model for frame classification and slot filling with CRFs. (a) The model used in the unified CFG/CRF model and (b) a general "triangular chain CRF" model

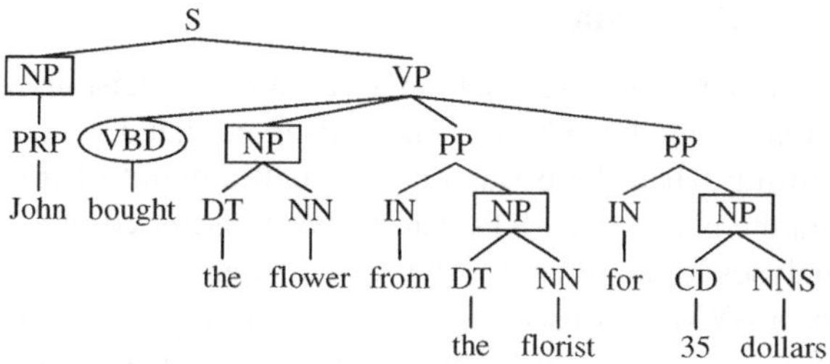

Figure 3.28 The syntactic parse tree for the sentence "John bought the flower from the florist for 35 dollars"

well as the participants (frame elements or semantic roles) of the events. For example, the COMMERCE_SCENARIO frame may include SELLER, BUYER, GOODS, and MONEY as semantic roles, as manifested by the sentence "John bought the flower from the florist for 35 dollars."

Semantic role labeling identifies the frame representing the event described in a sentence and finds its frame elements from the sentence. It often operates on the syntactic parse tree of the sentence to take advantage of the linguistic structural information encoded in the tree (for example, the main verb, the subject, direct object of the verb, etc.) Figure 3.28 shows the syntactic parse tree for the above example sentence.

The following decisions have to be made in the process of semantic role labeling:

1. *Target Word Detection* identifies the *targets* (often verbs) in the parse tree that carry the predicative information of the events. In Figure 3.28, the VBD node "bought" is the single target in the sentence.
2. *Frame Disambiguation* picks the correct frame for the target word in case multiple frames are associated with a target. In the example about, it picks the COMMERCE_SCENARIO frame.
3. *Boundary Detection* finds the nodes in the tree spanning a sequences of words that represent the participating roles of the frame. The four NPs in the blocks are detected as the frame elements of the COMMERCE_SCENARIO frame.
4. *Role Classification* assigns a semantic role to each of the frame element. The four NP's in Figure 3.28 are assigned the BUYER, SELLER, GOODS, and MONEY roles respectively.

Statistical classifiers can be used to make these decisions. Moschitti *et al.* (2008) applied SVMs for the subtasks. Note that many features may contribute to the correct decisions, including linguistic features (e.g. voice of a sentence [active or passive], the head word of an argument (role) phrase, etc). Moschitti *et al.* (2008) used the polynomial kernels for the linguistic features. In additions, it introduced tree kernels to capture the similarity between a parse tree related to a semantic role in a test sentence and those in the training samples. Coppola *et al.* (2009) applied the semantic role labeling to spoken language (on the manually transcribed text) and obtained the F_1 score of the semantic roles around 0.76. It is not clear how robust it is to ASR errors, given its dependency on the well-formed syntactic parse tree.

3.3.5.2 Discriminative Re-ranking

Dinarelli *et al.* (2009) adopted a two step method to re-rank the decisions made by a generative model with a discriminative model (SVMs). They observed that a generative model was less subject to data over-fitting when there was only a small amount of training data available. Therefore they applied the generative FSTs that we have discussed in Section 3.3.1 to obtain the top n semantic analyses for an utterance in the first step.

In the second step, a SVM was used to pairwise rank any two hypotheses in the top n hypotheses. The dominating hypothesis among the n analyses was picked as the meaning for the input. Since the decision made by the SVM was simpler (a binary decision), it is less subject to the over-fitting problem, while it has all the benefit of a discriminative model, for example, the inclusion of many features and the use of the kernel methods. Dinarelli *et al.* (2009) investigated string kernel and tree kernels for the features capturing the difference/similarity of two analyses. The re-ranking has significantly reduced the concept error rate (CER, see Section 3.1.5) on two data set (from 28.6 to 25.0% for a larger data set and from 42.7% to 38.9% for a smaller dataset.) Compared with a single-pass conditional model (CRF), it did not perform as well when training data are in abundance (CRF CER at 24.0% versus SVM re-ranking CER at 25.0%) for the larger data set, while it outperformed CRF on the smaller data set (CRF CER at 41.8% versus SVM re-ranking CER at 38.9%).

3.3.6 Frame-based SLU in Context

Up till now we have only discussed the understanding of an utterance out of its context. In practical spoken dialog systems, however, users seldom specify all the important information in a single utterance. They are often engaged in a dialogue with the system such that important pieces of information (slots) can be accumulated over multiple dialogue turns. The pieces need to be assembled incrementally to form the semantic representation, such that the dialogue system can take appropriate actions according to the information gathered up to the current dialogue turn. Without the capability of understanding in context, a dialogue system cannot interact with users proficiently. In the specific example of the ATIS corpora, there are class D utterances that cannot be correctly interpreted without taking into consideration the context information.

For that purpose, a discourse structure D is used to record the information till the current dialogue turn when the user utters U. D may contain multiple partially instantiated semantic frames. The context-agnostic SLU algorithms/models that we have introduced can be applied to obtain the context-independent meaning M_u of U. From D and M_u, a context-dependent meaning M_D can be constructed.

Constructing M_D from D and M_u is much more than just simply adding together the pieces of information in D and M_u. The information in D often cannot be inherited by M_D. Using ATIS as an example, the mention of a new departure and arrival city often implies that the information in D cannot be carried over to M_D because it signals that the user has switched to another task of finding a different flight. Similarly, if the user mentions a specific flight number, the focus has been reset and all the slot information need to be replaced by the corresponding information of that particular flight. The exemplar dialogue in Figure 3.29 shows the effect of these two constraints. There are many other constraints like these two in the ATIS domain, which were often modeled by hand-crafted rules (Seneff *et al.*, 1991), with an exception of the statistical discourse model introduced in Miller *et al.* (1996), which we discuss now.

USER1:	Show me the flights from Seattle to San Francisco next Wednesday.
SYS1:	<Displays a list of flights, including flight AS 220>
USER2:	I also need a return flight from San Francisco to Seattle.
SYS2:	What's the date for the flight? (Remark: "next Wednesday" is not inherited here)
USER3:	The Monday after.
SYS3:	<Displays a list of flights>
USER4:	Display details of AS 220.
SYS4:	<Displays the detailed information of the outbounding flight AS 220>

Figure 3.29 The effect of constraints on inheriting semantic information from the discourse

The statistical discourse model represents M_D with a vector Y, where each element represents the value of a specific slot. Another vector X of the same dimension as Y is used to represent a combination of M_u and M_p, the latter stands for the latest instantiation of the same frame as M_u in D. The elements in X specify one of the five relations between the fillers of the corresponding slots in M_u and M_p (excerpted from Miller *et al.*, 1996):

INITIAL	Slot filled in M_u but not in M_p
TACIT	Slot filled in M_p but not in M_u
REITERATE	Slot filled in both M_p and M_u, with the same value
CHANGE	Slot filled in both M_p and M_u, with different values
IRRELEVANT	Slot not filled in either M_p or M_u

Then

$$P(M_D \mid D, M_u) \approx P(Y \mid X) = \prod_i P_{slot}(Y_i \mid X; Y_1, \ldots, Y_{i-1}) \tag{3.62}$$

When $X_i \neq$ TACIT, $P_{slot}(Y_i \mid X; Y_1, \ldots, Y_{i-1}) = 1$ if $Y_i = M_{ui}$, the ith slot of M_u. When $X_i =$ TACIT, a binary statistical classifier is trained for each slot to determine if M_{pi} should be copied to M_D. Miller *et al.* (1996) used the decision trees for classification.

Putting it in a broad picture, Equation (3.62) can be embedded in the following decision rule for utterance understanding in context:

$$\begin{aligned}\hat{M} &= \arg\max_{M_D} P(M_D \mid U, D) = \arg\max_{M_D} \sum_{M_u} P(M_D \mid M_u, U, D) P(M_u \mid U, D) \\ &\approx \arg\max_{M_D} \max_{M_u} P(M_D \mid M_u, D) P(M_u \mid U) \\ &= \arg\max_{M_D} \max_{M_u} P(M_D \mid M_u, D) P(U \mid M_u) P(M_u)\end{aligned} \tag{3.63}$$

where D represents the context, $P(M_D \mid M_u, D)$ is the discourse model, $P(U \mid M_u)$ is the lexicalization model, and $P(M_u)$ is the semantic prior model.

3.4 Summary

This chapter has introduced the problem of the semantic frame-based spoken language understanding, a common SLU problem that has been faced in many research and commercial applications. It has covered some important solutions to the problem, ranging from the knowledge-based to the data-driven, statistical learning approaches. In the knowledge-based solutions, manually developed grammars are coupled with robust parsing technologies. There are two major camps in grammar design, one favors the reuse of domain-independent syntactic grammars across different domains and augmenting the grammars with domain-specific semantic information; the other advocates the direct modeling of semantics with a domain-dependent semantic grammar. For the data-driven approaches, both the generative models and the conditional models for the frame-based SLU are reviewed. The generative model framework has two major components, the *semantic prior model* and the *lexicalization model*. Several seminal generative models are reviewed in details in terms of these two component models. The conditional models have the advantages of discriminative learning and the capability of incorporating many interdependent, overlapping features that are difficult to be included in a generative framework. Hence it is powerful in designing specific features to address some difficult problems, such as the long-distance dependency. It has also been shown not a good practice to directly port a generative model's topology and features into a conditional model. Rather the design of a conditional model should focus on taking full advantage of its capabilities.

While it is necessary to have some real usage data for reference in the process of grammar development, the knowledge-based approach in general requires less training data to build a model (grammar), and the data do not have to be labeled. With expert's involvement, it is agile to quickly adapt to the topic/trend shifts that may happen frequently in practical spoken dialogue applications. However, it needs a combination of application and linguistic expertise, and the robustness does not come from the model directly. Instead, it has to depend on a robust parsing mechanism. The statistical models, on the other hand, are robust to noisy, error-prone inputs by design. They do not need linguistic expertise for grammar development. However, their performance is greatly affected by the availability of the labeled training data. In this chapter, we have also shown the advantage of combining statistical models with the knowledge-based solutions, either by integrating CFG rules in both generative and conditional models, or by adopting a multi-step semantic role labeling approach based on the syntactic parse tree produced by a general purpose parser. This can greatly reduce the dependency on a large amount of labeled training data.

References

Allen JF, Miller BW, Ringger EK and Sikorshi T 1996a Robust understanding in a dialogue system. *Proceedings of the 34th Annual Meeting of the Association for Computational Linguistics*, Santa Cruz, CA.

Allen JF, Miller BW, Ringger EK and Sikorski T 1996b A robust system for natural spoken dialogue. *Proceedings of the Annual Meeting of the Association for Computational Linguistics*, pp 62–70.

Alshawi H 1992 *The Core Language Engine.*. MIT Press, Cambridge, MA., USA.

Alshawi H and van Eijck J 1989 Logical forms in the core language engine. *Proceedings of the 27th Annual Meeting of the Association for Computational Linguistics*, pp 25–32. ACL.

Bahl L, Brown P, de Souza P and Mercer R 1986 Maximum mutual information estimation of Hidden Markov Model parameters for speech recognition. *Proceedings of the IEEE International Conference on Acoustics, Speech, and Signal Processing*, pp. 49–52. IEEE, Tokyo, Japan.

Baker CF, Fillmore CJ and Lowe JB 1998 The berkeley framenet project *Proceedings of the 17th International Conference on Computational linguistics*, pp 86–90. Association for Computational Linguistics, Morristown, NJ, USA.

Béchet F 2008 Processing spontaneous speech in deployed spoken language understanding systems: a survey. (lecture on spoken language understanding) *IEEE Workshop on Spoken Language Technology. http://www.ist-luna.eu/pdf/survey_goa_slu_bechet.pdf.* IEEE, Goa, India.

Bilmes J and Zweig G 2002 The graphical models toolkit: An open source software system for speech and time-series processing. *Proceedings of the IEEE International Conference on Acoustics, Speech, and Signal Processing*, pp 3916–3919.

Bonneau-Maynard H, Rosset S, Ayache C, Kuhn A and Mostefa D 2005 Semantic annotation of the French MEDIA dialogue corpus. *Proceedings of INTERSPEECH*, pp 3457–3460.

Brown PF, Della Pietra VJ, deSouza PV, Lai JC and Mercer RL 1992 Class-based n-gram models of natural language. *Computational Linguistics* **18**(4), 467–479.

Chelba C, Mahajan M and Acero A 2003 Speech utterance classification. *Proceedings of the IEEE International Conference on Acoustics, Speech, and Signal Processing*. IEEE.

Coppola B, Moschitti A and Riccardi G 2009 Shallow semantic parsing for spoken language understanding *Proceedings of Human Language Technology/Conference of the North American Chapter of the Association for Computational Linguistics, Companion Volume: Short Papers*, pp 85–88.

Dahl DA, Bates M, Brown M, Fisher W, Hunicke-Smith K, Pallett D, Pao C, Rudnicky A and Shriberg E 1994 Expanding the scope of the ATIS task: the ATIS-3 corpus. *Proceedings of the Human Language Technology Workshop*. Morgan Kaufmann.

Della Pietra S, Epstein M, Roukos S and Ward T 1997 Fertility models for statistical natural language understanding. *Proceedings of the 35th Annual Meeting of the Association for Computational Linguistics*, pp 168–173, Madrid, Spain.

Dempster AP, Laird N and Rubin DB 1977 Maximum likelihood from incomplete data via the EM algorithm. *Journal of the Royal Statistical Society B* **39**, 1–38.

Dinarelli M, Moschitti A and Riccardi G 2009 Re-ranking models based-on small training data for spoken language understanding *Proceedings of the Conference on Empirical Methods in Natural Language Processing*, pp 1076–1085.

Dowding J, Gawron JM, Appelt D, Bear J, Cherny L, Moore R and Moran D 1993 Gemini: A natural language system for spoken-language understanding. *Proceedings of the 31st Annual Meeting of the Association for Computational Linguistics*, pp 54–61, Columbus, Ohio.

ELRA – european language resources association. *http://www.elra.info/*.

Estève Y, Raymond C, Béchét F and de Mori R 2003 Conceptual decoding for spoken dialogue systems. *Proceedings of the Eurospeech Conference*, Geneva, Switzerland.

Fillmore CJ 1976 Frame semantics and the nature of language. *Annals of the New York Academy of Sciences* **280**(1), 20–32.

Gunawardanaand A, Mahajanand M, Acero A and Platt JC 2005 Hidden conditional random fields for phone classification *Proceedings of INTERSPEECH*, pp 1117–1120. ISCA.

He Y and Young S 2003 Hidden vector state model for hierarchical semantic parsing. *Proceedings of the IEEE International Conference on Acoustics, Speech, and Signal Processing*, Hong Kong, China.

Hemphill CT, Godfrey JJ and Doddington GR 1990 The ATIS spoken language systems pilot corpus. *Proceedings of the Workshop on Speech and Natural Language, HLT'90*, pp 96–101. Association for Computational Linguistics, Morristown, NJ, USA.

Hunt A and McGlashan S 2004 Speech recognition grammar specification version 1.0. *http://www.w3.org/TR/speech-grammar/*.

Jelinek F and Mercer EL 1980 Interpolated estimation of Markov source parameters from sparse data. In *Pattern Recognition in Practice* (ed. Gelsema D and Kanal L) North-Holland.

Jeong M and Lee GG 2008a Practical use of non-local features for statistical spoken language understanding. *Computer Speech and Language* **22**(2), 148–170.

Jeong M and Lee G 2008b Triangular-chain conditional random fields. *IEEE Transactions on Audio, Speech, and Language Processing* **16**(7), 1287–1302.

Juang BH, Chou W and Lee CH 1997 Minimum classification error rate methods for speech recognition. *IEEE Transactions on Speech and Audio Processing* **5**(3), 257–265.

Kneser R and Ney H 1993 Improved clustering techniques for class-based statistical language modelling. *Proceedings of the Eurospeech Conference*, pp 973–976, Berlin, Germany.

Lafferty J, McCallum A and Pereira F 2001 Conditional random fields: Probabilistic models for segmenting and labeling sequence data. *Proceedings of ICML*, pp 282–289.

LDC - linguistic data consortium. *http://www.ldc.upenn.edu/*.

Lefèvre F 2007 Dynamic Bayesian networks and discriminative classifiers for multi-stage semantic interpretation. *Proceedings of the IEEE International Conference on Acoustics, Speech, and Signal Processing*, vol. 4, pp 13–16. IEEE.

Macherey K, Och FJ and Ney H 2001 Natural language understanding using statistical machine translation. *Proceedings of the Eurospeech Conference.*

McCallum A 2003 Efficiently inducing features of conditional random fields. *Proceedings of the 19th Conference on Uncertainty in Artificial Intelligence (UAI03)*, Acapulco, Mexico.

Meurs MJ, Lefèvre F and de Mori R 2009 Learning Bayesian networks for semantic frame composition in a spoken dialogue system. *Proceedings of HLT-NAACL*, Boulder, Colorado, USA.

Miller S, Bobrow R, Ingria R and Schwartz R 1994 Hidden understanding models of natural language. *Proceedings of the 31st Annual Meeting of the Association for Computational Linguistics*, New Mexico State University.

Miller S, Stallard D, Bobrow R and Schwartz R 1996 A fully statistical approach to natural language interfaces *Proceedings of the 34th Annual Meeting on Association for Computational Linguistics*, pp 55–61. Association for Computational Linguistics, Morristown, NJ, USA.

Moore R 1998 Using natural language knowledge sources in speech recognition. *NATO Advanced Studies Institute.*

Moschitti A, Pighin D and Basili R 2008 Tree kernels for semantic role labeling. *Computational Linguistics* **34**(2), 193–224.

Ostendorf M, Digalakis V and Kimball O 1996 From HMMs to segment models: A unified view of stochastic modeling for speech recognition. *IEEE Transactions on Speech and Audio Processing* **4**(5), 360–378.

Pieraccini R and Levin E 1993 A learning approach to natural language understanding. *1993 NATO ASI Summer School* New Advances and Trends in Speech Recognition and Coding. Springer-Verlag, Bubion, Spain.

Rabiner L and Juang BH 1993 *Fundamentals of Speech Recognition.* Prentice Hall P T R, Englewood Cliffs, New Jersey.

Raymond C and Riccardi G 2007 Generative and discriminative algorithms for spoken language understanding. *Proceedings of INTERSPEECH*, pp 1605–1608.

Rayner M, Dowding J and Hockey BA 2001 A baseline method for compiling typed unification grammars into context free language models. *Proceedings of the Eurospeech Conference*, Aalborg, Denmark.

Riccardi G and Gorin AL 1998 Stochastic language models for speech recognition and understanding. *Proceedings of the International Conference on Spoken Language Processing*, Sidney, Australia.

Riccardi G, Pieraccini R and Bocchieri E 1996 Stochastic automata for language modeling. *Computer Speech and Language* **10**, 265–293.

Rosenfeld R 1996 A maximum entropy approach to adaptive statistical language modelling. *Computer Speech and Language* **10**, 187–228.

Seneff S 1992 Tina: A natural language system for spoken language applications. *Computational Linguistics* **18**(1), 61–86.

Seneff S, Hirschman L and Zue VW 1991 Interactive problem solving and dialogue in the ATIS domain *Proceedings of the 4th DARPA Speech and Natural Language Workshop*, pp 354–359.

Stolcke A 2002 SRILM - an extensible language modeling toolkit. *Proceedings of the IEEE International Conference on Spoken Language Processing*, Denver, Colorado.

Van Tichelen L and Burke D 2007 Semantic interpretation for speech recognition (SISR) version 1.0. *http://www.w3.org/TR/semantic-interpretation/.*

Walker M, Aberdeen J, Boland J, Bratt E, Garofolo J, Hirschman L, Le A, Lee S, Narayanan S, Papineni K, Pellom B, Polifroni J, Potamianos A, Prabhu P, Rudnicky A and Sanders G 2001 DARPA Communicator dialogue travel planning systems: The June 2000 data collection. *Proceedings of the Eurospeech Conference.*

Walker MA, Rudnicky A, Prasad R, Aberdeen J, Bratt EO, Garofolo J, Hastie H, Le A, Pellom B, Potamianos A, Passonneau R, Roukos S, S G, Seneff S and Stallard D 2002 DARPA Communicator: cross-system results for the 2001 evaluation. *Proceedings of the International Conference on Spoken Language Processing*, pp 269–272.

Wang YY and Acero A 2003a Combination of CFG and *n*-gram modeling in semantic grammar learning. *Proceedings of the Eurospeech Conference*, pp 2809–2812. ISCA.

Wang YY and Acero A 2003b Is word error rate a good indicator for spoken language understanding accuracy. *Proceedings of the IEEE Workshop on Automatic Speech Recognition and Understanding*, pp 577–582.

Wang YY and Acero A 2006 Rapid development of spoken language understanding grammars.. *Speech Communication* **48**(3-4), 390–416.

Wang YY, Lee J, Mahajan M and Acero A 2006 Combining statistical and knowledge-based spoken language understanding in conditional models. *Proceedings of the Annual Meeting of the Association for Computational Linguistics*, pp 882–889. Association for Computational Linguistics.

Ward W 1991 Understanding spontaneous speech: the Phoenix system. *Proceedings of the IEEE International Conference on Acoustics, Speech, and Signal Processing*, pp 365–367, Toronto, Canada.

Woods WA 1983 Language processing for speech understanding. *Computer Speech Processing* Prentice-Hall International Englewood Cliffs, NJ.

Yaman S, Deng L, Yu D, Wang YY and Acero A 2008 An integrative and discriminative technique for spoken utterance classification.. *IEEE Transactions on Audio, Speech, and Language Processing* **16**(6), 1207–1214.

Yu D, Wang K, Mahajan M, Mau P and Acero A 2003 Improved name recognition with user modeling. *Proceedings of the Eurospeech Conference*, Geneva, Switzerland.

4

Intent Determination and Spoken Utterance Classification

Gokhan Tur[1] and Li Deng[2]
[1] *Microsoft Speech Labs, Microsoft Research, USA*
[2] *Microsoft Research, U.S.A.*

As discussed in earlier chapters, one key spoken language understanding (SLU) task is interpreting users' intentions from their speech utterances. This task is closely related to dialogue-based natural language understanding, where the user does not need to know a predefined set of command words in order to use the system successfully. As a special form of SLU, spoken utterance classification (SUC) has found many practical applications, among which call routing or call type classification is a prominent one. In a call-routing system, a critical part of understanding a speech utterance is classification into pre-defined types of intents or call types.

In this chapter, our focus is to review the spoken utterance classification techniques and illustrate their successful applications to intent determination systems, as emerged partly from commercial call-routing applications. We aim to provide details of such systems as they continue to emerge in the tasks ranging from simple keyword detection based approaches to more sophisticated predicate/argument style semantic classification schemes using context that integrates with template filling. We will also aim to link to SLU in human/human communications with similar approaches.

4.1 Background

Almost simulatenously with the semantic template filling based spoken language understanding (SLU) approaches, at the other end of the "meaning" spectrum, a new task had emerged. In this SLU task, "understanding" is reduced to the task of detecting one of the keywords allowed in the users' utterances. A typical example is AT&T's Voice Recognition Call Processing (VRCP) system (Wilpon *et al.*, 1990) used at call centers. A call center (recently renamed as customer

Spoken Language Understanding: Systems for Extracting Semantic Information from Speech, First Edition.
Edited by Gokhan Tur and Renato De Mori.

```
<vxml version="2.0">
<form id= "get_pizza_topping">
<field name= "pizza_topping">
<prompt> What kind of topping would you like to have? </prompt>
<grammar> olive | pepperoni | mushroom </grammar>
<noinput> Please say the topping you wish to have. </noinput>
<nomatch> I didn't understand that. </nomatch>
<filled> Thank you, I added <value expr= "pizza_topping" />
<submit next="next_document.vxml" /> </filled>
</field>
</form>
</vxml>
```

Figure 4.1 A VXML example for getting pizza topping information (from the VXML lecture by François Mairesse)

care center) consists of customer service representatives (CSRs) or associates that handle telephone calls from customers requesting assistance. Among the tasks of such call centers are routing the in coming calls to the proper department, where specific help is provided or where transactions are carried out (Juang and Rabiner, 2005). The number of CSRs in a large call center could reach several thousand. This means a major financial burden for companies and complaint area for customers. The AT&T VRCP system greets the user with this simple prompt: *Please say collect, calling card, or third party*. There has been no interaction with the callers and the system couldn't understand if the user said something other than these three phrases. Even though this system has demonstrated a primitive approach for SLU, it has been a great commercial success and has been deployed nationwide, answered billions of calls per year and been used for many years.

Such *machine-initiative* systems are commonly known as Interactive Voice Response systems (IVR). In IVR systems the interaction is completely controlled by the machines. Machine-initiative systems ask users specific questions and expect the users input to be one of predetermined keywords or phrases. For example a mail delivery system may prompt the user to say *schedule a pick-up, track a package, get rate or order supply* or a pizza delivery system may ask for the possible toppings (see Figure 4.1). Such IVR systems are typically extended to form a machine-initiative directed dialogue in call centers and are now widely implemented using established and standardized platforms such as VoiceXML.

The success of these early IVR systems has triggered more sophisticated versions of this very same idea of *classifying users' utterances into predefined categories* (called as *call-types*). Gorin *et al.* (1997) has published the AT&T *How May I Help You?* system description paper in 1997. HMIHY is essentially a call routing system. The users of the system are greeted by the open-ended prompt *How May I Help You*, encouraging them to talk naturally. This system has also been deployed for AT&T's call center (known as 0300) and used nationwide with great success (Gorin *et al.*, 2002). The system was capable of categorizing an incoming call into one of the six specific call-types (such as *Billing* or *Rates and Plans*) plus an *Other* for the remaining intents along with generic intents such as talking to a human agent or greetings. The calls are then routed to corresponding specialized departments. If the initial utterance of the user is not specific (such as *I have a question*), not informative (such as *Good afternoon*), or

HMIHY: How may I help you?
User: Hi, I have a question about my bill (*Billing*)
HMIHY: OK, what is your question?
User: May I talk to a human please? (*CSR*)
HMIHY: In order to route your call to the most appropriate department can you tell me the specific reason you are calling about?
User: There is an international call I could not recognize (*Unrecognized_Number*)
HMIHY: OK, I am forwarding you to the human agent. Please stay on the line.

Figure 4.2 A conceptual example dialogue between the user and the AT&T HMIHY system

asks for a human agent, the system reprompts the user accordingly to get some specific intent for their call.

Figure 4.2 shows a typical HMIHY dialogue for AT&T call center. The utterance level intents are shown for better understanding.

Following the HMIHY system, a number of similar systems have been built, such as the Lucent call routing system (Chu-Carroll and Carpenter, 1999), the BBN call director (Natarajan *et al.*, 2002), AT&T Helpdesk (Di Fabbrizio *et al.*, 2002), AT&T VoiceTone (Gupta *et al.*, 2006), and the France Telecom 3000 (Damnati *et al.*, 2007) systems.

The biggest difference between the call classification systems and semantic frame filling systems is that, the former does not care much about the arguments provided by the user. The main goal is *routing* the call to the appropriate call center department. The arguments provided by the user are important only in the sense that they help make the right classification. For example, if the user specifies the name of a drug in a system used for medical insurance call center, this can improve the confidence for routing to prescription renewal or refill departments. While this is a totally different perspective for the task of SLU, it is actually complimentary to template filling in two respects:

- First, each call-type can be viewed as a template to be filled. For example, in the case of the DARPA ATIS program, while the majority of the *goals* was *flight reservation*, people have also asked about many other things such as ground transportation or airplane specifications. The program has also defined specialized templates for these less frequent intents. This has led to a seamless integration of call-type classification and template filling based SLU approaches (which was also important for more automation anyways): The users' utterances are first categorized into their *goals* and then the corresponding templates can be filled. Sometimes, two separate systems are used for this purpose. For example, a call-type classification system can be extended by *legs*, which will capture the slot values of the intent, usually using a directed dialogue. Less frequently, a call-type-independent entity extraction is performed, as done in the late HMIHY system, to capture some of the arguments when provided before the legs. In some academic circles, these two systems are modeled *jointly* (as covered in the previous chapter). Also note that, in many practical applications the boundary between a call-type and an argument is not clear. One can ask whether it makes sense to separate the calls about long-distance and short-distance billing or there should be one billing call-type where long distance and short distance are simply arguments.
- Second, while the original HMIHY system has dealt with only several categories, the latter clones of it use tens of categories, which are semantically *atomic* intents (e.g. Gupta *et al.*

(2006). Then a special mapping function can be called to change the *route* of a determined intent. This finer grain categorization of call-types was actually very close to the semantic representation of the template filling tasks. For example, in the AT&T VoiceTone system, when the user says *I am calling to check whether you received my payment*, the intent is *Verify(Payment)*, and for the sentence *I am calling to make a payment*, it is *Make(Payment)*. While in most call centers, these two calls may end up in the Payments department, the goal of the system is not to capture the actions performed by some higher-level system, but instead the intent of the caller only. Such a predicate/argument-type semantic representation is actually very close to the semantic representation of the template filling approaches where the goal is extracting the arguments of user goals.

An interesting link between the call-type classification or intent determination systems and human/human conversation understanding systems is the task of *dialogue act tagging* as covered in Chapter 9. A dialogue act is a primitive abstraction or an approximate representation of the illocutionary force of an utterance and the response, such as *question* or *backchannel*. Dialogue acts are designed to be task-independent. The main goal of dialogue acts is to provide a basis for further discourse analysis and understanding. The two most frequently used dialogue act tagging schema, DAMSL (Dialog Act Markup in Several Layers; Core and Allen, 1997) and MRDA (Meeting Recorder Dialog Act; Shriberg *et al.*, 2004) are structured hierarchically so as to capture finer grain semantic contents. For example, a question can be a rhetorical question or a *yes/no* question, or a statement can be a command or suggestion. Most SLU systems support *generic* intents, such as *Greeting*, which are task-independent by nature. The basic task description of dialogue act tagging is actually very similar to intent determination as the goal is categorizing each of the users' utterances into one of the predefined classes.

4.2 Task Description

The spoken utterance classification (SUC) task aims at classifying a given speech utterance X_r into one of M semantic classes, $\hat{C}_r \in \mathcal{C} = \{C_1, ..., C_M\}$ (where r is the utterance index). Upon the observation of X_r, $\hat{C}_r$ is chosen so that the class-posterior probability given X_r, $P(C_r|X_r)$, is maximized. Formally,

$$\hat{C}_r = \arg\max_{C_r} P(C_r|X_r). \tag{4.1}$$

Semantic classifiers require operation with significant freedom in utterance variations. A user may say *"I want to fly from Boston to New York next week"* and another user may express the same information by saying *"I am looking to fly from JFK to Boston in the coming week"*. In spite of this freedom of expression, utterances in such applications have a clear structure that binds together the specific pieces of information. Not only is there no *a priori* constraint on what the user can say, but it should be able to generalize well from a tractably small amount of training data. For example, the phrase *"Show all flights"* and *"Give me flights"* should be interpreted as variants of a single semantic class "Flight". On the other hand, the command *"Show me fares"* should be interpreted as an instance of another semantic class, "Fare". In doing so, the selection of the feature functions $f_i(C, W)$ aims at capturing the relation between the class C and word sequence W. Typically, binary or weighted n-gram features with $n = 1, 2, 3$

to capture the likelihood of the n-grams are generated to express the user intent for the semantic class C. As an example, binary bigram feature functions are in the form of:

$$f^{BG}_{c,w_x w_y}(C_r, W_r) = \begin{cases} 1, & \text{if } c = C_r \wedge w_x w_y \in W_r, \\ 0, & \text{otherwise.} \end{cases}$$

That is, if two consecutive words, $w_x w_y$, appear in the word sequence W and if the class is one of interest, C_r, then the binary feature function takes on a value of one; it is zero otherwise. Once the features are extracted from the text, the task becomes a text classification problem. Traditional text categorization techniques devise learning methods to maximize the probability of C_r given the text W_r; i.e., the class-posterior probability $P(C_r|W_r)$.

4.3 Technical Challenges

While the template filling based SLU approaches are closer to the field of natural language understanding which is rooted in artificial intelligence, the intent determination based SLU approaches originate from speech processing, which traditionally does not pay enough attention to the underlying message conveyed, and relies heavily on statistical methods.

Such a data-driven approach has fit nicely into spoken language processing as spoken utterances are not typically grammatical and fluent, or prewritten. Even in broadcast conversations where participants are very well trained and prepared, a large percentage of utterances have disfluencies, such as repetitions, false starts, and filler words (such as *uh*) (Stolcke and Shriberg, 1996). Furthermore, speech recognition introduces a great deal of noise due to various reasons, such as background noise, mismatched domain, proper names (such as city or person names), and the need for sub-real-time speech recognition. A typical call routing system operates at around 20–30% word error rate, that is, one out of every three to five words is wrong (Gupta *et al.*, 2006). Furthermore, as the user can say anything, unlike a directed dialogue, it does not make sense to create fine-tuned manual grammars for speech recognition and understanding. Moreover, what the user says is sometimes, actually out of domain. For example, s/he might be talking to his/her spouse and asks a totally irrelevant question. Even with the recent advances in machine learning, it is nontrivial to detect out-of-domain utterances (Lane *et al.*, 2007).

However, natural language call classification has a big advantage over template filling: natural language comes with redundancy. This is very important for being robust to all these challenges. Redundancy, a technical term very closely related to language model perplexity, is exploited by the statistical classifiers. Even when key concepts for some call-type are missing, the secondary surrounding words and entities may help make the correct classification. A typical example is from the ATIS domain: *I wond- I'd like to make uh air- I mean flight reservation from Boston to uh New York tomorrow, uh no the day after*. Note that the main goal of the intent determination system is assigning the class *Flight Reservation*, and not filling the associated semantic template. If such a sentence is recognized as *I wond- I'd like to make uh airy mean flights serve nation from boston to uh new yolk tomorrow, uh no the day after*, the classifier can still handle this case. One important note here is that, similar to template filling, the stopwords are extremely important for call classification. *from* and *to* are discriminative words for flight reservation for example.

However, this does not mean that call classification has no robustness issue. In the VoiceTone corpus, researchers have found that one-third of the intent determination errors are due to speech recognition noise (Gupta *et al.*, 2006). It is still an important challenge for the intent determination systems to be robust to all the challenges coming from spontaneous natural language speech. To this end, researchers have proposed many methods ranging from using n-best lists, word confusion networks to dialogue context to using prior knowledge. We will cover these approaches in the following sections.

4.4 Benchmark Data Sets

Call-type classification systems are categorically different than other SLU tasks. As they are used in call centers, there is no data scarcity; the system developers enjoy sometimes millions of calls, and tens of thousands of them can be quickly transcribed or annotated using semi-automated techniques. Furthermore, the system can be deployed in a very limited fashion to see the effect of different parameterization. For example, different top prompts may be tried in random.

However, such vast amounts of data are strictly confidential, and it is impossible for the researchers to share such sensitive data with the research community. The most commonly used data set for intent determination is the DARPA ATIS corpus. This corpus has 16 different intents, such as flight reservation, or aircraft capacity. However the prior distribution is heavily skewed, and the most frequent intent, flight reservation, takes about 70% of the traffic. Furthermore, since it is very well studied, the error rates are now below 5%, making it uninteresting for many researchers. To this end, a few research sites have initiated intent determination data sets. Three notable examples include the CMU's Let's Go corpus, the DisCoH corpus from ICSI, AT&T, and University of Edinburgh, and finally the European MEDIA corpus as used in the LUNA project.

4.5 Evaluation Metrics

The call classification systems are evaluated using direct and indirect evaluation metrics. Direct metrics are typically used in the research community and heavily borrowed from the machine learning field. The indirect metrics are mostly used for business interests to see the effectiveness of the call routing systems.

4.5.1 *Direct Metrics*

The most commonly used direct metrics are used at the utterance level. They include the utterance intent determination accuracy, F-measure, and false alarm versus miss rates.

The simpler metric accuracy can be computed as:

$$Acc = \frac{\text{\# utterances where the top scoring call-type is amongst the true call-types}}{\text{\# of utterances}}$$

Note that, one utterance can have more than one intent. A typical example is *Can you tell me my balance? I need to make a transfer*. In most cases, where the second intent is a generic one (such as greeting or talk to a human agent), or a vague one it is ignored.

The F-measure is more informative than accuracy, as it also considers the confidence given to the call-types. F-measure is the harmonic mean of recall and precision at a given confidence level, c. In this formulation, the call-types which get some confidence higher than some set confidence level, c, are said to be *accepted*. This is used to compute the number of missed ($FN(c)$) and false alarm ($FP(c)$) call-types at confidence level c:

$$F - Measure(c) = \frac{2 \times R(c) \times P(c)}{R(c) + P(c)}$$
$$R(c) = \frac{TP(c)}{TP(c) + FN(c)}$$
$$P(c) = \frac{TP(c)}{TP(c) + FP(c)}$$

This is a nontraditional way of viewing recall and precision due to resolving multiple label characteristics of intent determination. When $c = 0$, all possible call-types are *accepted* giving very low precision as there will be many false alarms, but 100% recall as there will be no misses. The confidence value, c, optimizing the F-measure can also be used as the *acceptance threshold* in the actual spoken dialogue system. In the AT&T HMHY system, a further complexity due to the *Other* class is also introduced. The sentences where no call-type has reached the set confidence level, c, are also mapped to *Other*, and considered correct if they are indeed *Other*.

Finally, in some limited areas, researchers have checked the dialogue level call classification performance. Since this requires extra annotation effort just for evaluation purposes, they are not popular, but may be better indicators of global performance. One approximation for such annotation is using the first specific user intent. For the example shown above in Figure 4.2, that would be *Unrecognized_Number*.

4.5.2 Indirect Metrics

In addition to these direct evaluation metrics, cost savings and customer satisfaction by using such systems is the most interesting to commercial companies of the call centers. One metric which is easy to gather and very informative is checking the repeat call rates in 24 hour windows. The assumption is that, unsatisfied users will call back, indicating the performance of the system for task completion. Interestingly, compared with existing IVR systems, natural language call routing systems resulted in fewer repeat calls, as users typically get lost in deep IVR menus.

Another good indicator is the hang-up rate, which will indicate a similar performance metric. In some experimental systems, users are also asked about rating the system just before getting routed.

The trend analysis performed on these indirect metrics also indicates the system performance variations. For example, researchers or system developers may have trained new ASR or SLU models or may have been trying alternative opening prompts.

4.6 Technical Approaches

In this section we present the published techniques for call classification or intent determination. We start with a discussion on what constitutes an intent as a semantic representation. Then we briefly review each of the major systems and techniques proposed in the literature. We not only present underlying classification algorithms, but also methods for incorporating prior knowledge, such as manually written rules, for exploiting ASR n-best or word lattice output, and phone-based classification approaches.

4.6.1 *Semantic Representations*

As most call classification systems are naturally tied to some commercial application, the corresponding needs shape what constitutes a semantic representation. In some cases, this results in the classes being the same as possible routes the call can be forwarded. The advantage of this approach lies in the lightweight bootstraping of the computational models for the input–output associations. The disadvantage is the lack of built-in generalization of the model representation (spoken input–action pairs). Should the prompts/actions taken by the dialogue system change over time the semantic representation must also be changed. A more semantically meaningful, and computationally feasible approach would be to use a larger set of atomic semantic classes that can be mapped to routes and/or actions which could be taken by the system. More specifically, the choice of representation language must be made to achieve robustness towards the time-varying nature of the spoken language and the external world (e.g. introduction of a new service), and the annotator disagreement, following a *stable* labeling scheme across various corpora.

This implies a representation where users' utterances are labeled with the intent of the speaker as opposed to the action that the system must take in response. One possible way to capture the intent is using a predicate-argument $v_i(o_j)$ representation scheme as studied extensively in the linguistics and artificial intelligence literature. The predicates v_i are domain-independent verbs reflecting the action the user is trying to perform by the utterance (similar to *dialogue acts*, Austin, 1962). The arguments o_j constitute the domain-related objects, actions or concepts on which these actions are being performed. Having identified the domain-dependent objects and concepts, a list of semantic representation primitives can be generated by joining them with domain-independent predicates. Some examples of the utterances and their labels are given below (Gupta *et al.*, 2006):

- Utterance: "I see charges on my bill that I do not understand"
  Label: Explain(Bill_Charge)
- Utterance: "I am just wanting to tell you that I have made the payment"
  Label: Report(Payment)
- Utterance: "I am calling to check if you received my monthly payment"
  Label: Verify(Payment)

Separating domain dependent aspects from domain independent aspects may provide a systematic method to create a semantic representation for an application. Once labelers understand the semantics of predicates they only need to learn to spot the domain dependent object/concepts in the utterances from different applications. These semantic primitives capture the intents embedded in the utterance, and therefore changes or extensions to an application only require changes to the dialogue manager, and does not require re-labeling of the data. Since the labeling scheme captures the intent that is consistent across applications, it is possible to re-use data labeled for one application for developing other applications. For example, data labeled as "Request(Credit)" can be used for all applications where a caller is likely to ask for credit.

As we mentioned before, in many practical applications the boundary between the object of a call-type o_j and the slot to be filled for that intent is not clear. The rule of thumb can be using the head word of the argument, by leaving the specifics to the slot filling system.

4.6.2 The HMIHY Way: Using Salient Phrases

The pioneering system for call routing is AT&T's How May I Help You system (Gorin *et al.*, 1997). The motivation of this system is building an alternative to traditional menu-driven IVR call center systems, moving the burden from the users to the system. The original system had no intention of automating a call, but simply routing it to the appropriate department (such as Sales or Billing). That understanding task is framed as a classification problem.

HMIHY SLU classifier heavily depends on portions of input utterances, namely *salient phrases*, which are salient to some call-types. For example, in an input utterance such as "*I would like to change oh about long distance service two one charge nine cents a minute*", the salient phrase "*cents a minute*" is strongly related to the call-type *Calling Plans*.

The salient phrases are automatically acquired from a corpus of transcribed and labeled training data. The salience of a word n-gram, f, is computed using the formula:

$$S(f) = \sum_{c_k} P(c_k|f)I(f, c_k)$$

where c_k is a call-type and $I(x, y)$ is the mutual information between x and y:

$$I(x, y) = log\frac{P(x, y)}{P(x)}$$

Note that salient fragments are call-type independent. The phrases such as *I would like* still get high salience scores as these are used to improve the language model used for speech recognition. The salient phrases are then selected based on the following three criteria:

1. The phrases which have low salience scores, i.e. $S(f) < \theta_1$, are filtered out.
2. The phrases which is not an indicator of a call-type, i.e. $maxP(c_k|f) < \theta_2$, are filtered out.
3. The phrases where the mutual information between the final word and the preceding sub-phrase, i.e. $I(f_n^n, f_1^{n-1}) < \theta_3$, are filtered out.

Figure 4.3 presents some salient phrases as extracted from the HMIHY training data from the AT&T call center. The last column shows the call-type for which a peak of the a posteriori probability distribution occurs. If the maximum value for this peak is between 0.5 and 0.9, this is indicated by parentheses. As seen, putting more context, even using stop-words such as *the* and *for*, makes the phrase a more discriminative feature for a call-type.

The remaining salient phrases are then clustered into salient grammar fragments (SGFs) (Gorin *et al.*, 1997; Wright *et al.*, 1997). The rationale for this clustering is better general-

Phrase	$I(f_n^n, f_1^{n-1})$	$maxP(c_k\|f)$	$\text{argmax}_{c_k} P(c_k\|f)$
I would like	7.1	0.24	
made a long distance	7.4	0.93	Billing_Credit
long distance	7.3	0.55	(Billing_Credit)
the area code for	5.6	0.92	Area_Code
area code	6.9	0.65	(Area_Code)

Figure 4.3 Example salient phrases with associated call-types

Fragment	$max P(c_k \mid f)$	$P(f \mid c_k)$
wrong	0.92	0.48
wrong number	0.98	0.41
(a|the|was)wrong(number|call|eos)	0.97	0.42
F(wrong)|F(dialed)	0.95	0.50
SGF(Billing_Credit)	0.95	0.64

Figure 4.4 An example for building a salient grammar fragment (SGF)

ization. Assume two salient phrases *a wrong number* and *the wrong number*, they may be grouped together if they indicate the same call-type. For example Figure 4.4 demonstrates how a grammar is learned using existing salient phrases. When only the word *wrong* is used, $max P(c_k \mid f)$ is 0.92, but the coverage $P(f \mid c_k)$ is low, at 0.48. Then the left and right contexts are incrementally added without sacrificing the discriminative power of this phrase to form a grammar fragment with the kernel *wrong*, $F(wrong)$, reaching $max P(c_k \mid f)$ of 0.97 with coverage 0.42. This process is repeated to build grammar fragments for the other salient phrases for this call-type, such as *dialed* or *disconnected*, reaching $max P(c_k \mid f)$ of 0.95 with coverage 0.64, forming the salient grammar fragment (SGF) for that call-type, $SGF(c_k)$.

Once the SGFs are trained, it is then straightforward to classify an utterance. The salient grammar fragments are first compiled in the format of finite state machines (FSMs). Figure 4.5 shows an example simplified salient grammar fragment. The ASR output or input text, s, is then searched for the occurrences of the SGFs using FSM operations. This is a left-to-right search which searches for the longest matching phrases. This results in a transduction from s to $f_i \in F$. The classification algorithm then chooses the call-type with maximum peak value of the a-posteriori probability distribution, that is:

$$K(s) = \underset{c_k}{\text{argmax}}\ P(c_k \mid f_{i(s)})$$

where

$$i(s) = \underset{i}{\text{argmax}}(\underset{c_k}{\max}\ P(c_k \mid f_i))$$

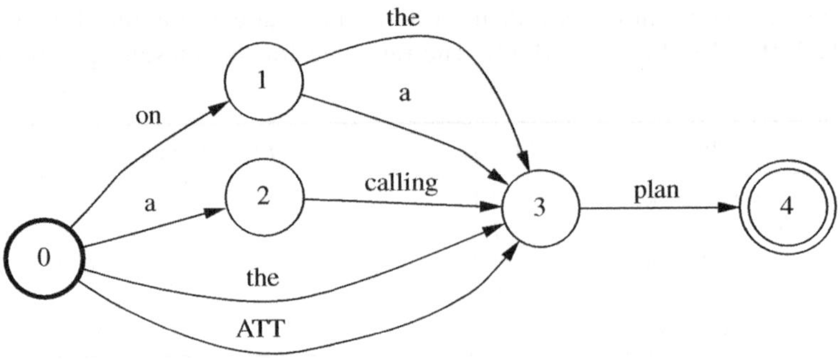

Figure 4.5 An example salient grammar fragment

If this overall peak is less than some threshold, $P(c_k | f_{i(s)}) < \theta$, then the utterance is rejected and classified as *other*.

The raw score given to the call-type is simply $P(c_k | f_{i(s)})$. In order to adjust these individual scores, p, so that they can give the actual probability of being correct, a logistic regression formula using the length, l, and coverage (the percentage of the words occurring inside a salient phrase in an utterance), c, of that utterance is employed:

$$p' = \frac{1}{1 + e^{-(\beta_0 + \beta_1 \times p + \beta_2 \times l + \beta_3 \times c)}}$$

where the β values are learned from the training data, using Newton–Raphson Method (Agresti, 1990). This normalization is needed for a number of reasons. First, it allows the dialogue manager to get reliable confidence scores and use the same threshold for confirmation and rejection for all the call-types. Secondly, it allows a framework to improve the salience-based classification using many other features, not only length. This may include contextual features such as the predicted call-type of the previous turn, or user-related features such as the area code, and so on.

4.6.3 Vector-state Model

One of the earliest yet very successful approaches for call classification, adopted by the Bell Labs, is motivated by the information retrieval (IR)-based vector-state model (Chu-Carroll and Carpenter, 1999). In this approach first stop-words are removed, stemming is performed, following the usual practice in IR. Then a $F \times K$ term-document matrix is created, where a term can be a word or a word phrase and documents are actually the classes or routes the call is routed to. Each term is weighted according to the well-known *tf.idf* (term frequency - inverse document frequency) paradigm. New user requests are then converted and formed as a vector in a similar fashion. The baseline algorithm simply chooses the class where the cosine distance between the user utterance and the route is the minimum as in traditional IR. The original system paper suggests two improvements on top of this baseline system. First, the similarity scores are mapped between 0 and 1 by fitting a non-decreasing sigmoid function using the least-squares method so as to get confidence scores. The second improvement was employing singular value decomposition (SVD) to improve efficiency especially when the training corpus is not small. In SVD, the routing matrix, W is decomposed so as to $W = USV^T$, where U and V are orthonormal matrices and S is a diagonal matrix of eigenvalues.

Later Cox and Shahshahani (2001) proposed extending this approach via latent semantic analysis (LSA). LSA is also based on using SVD to find a compact subspace for the routing matrix. In LSA, after SVD, top R eigenvalues are retained and others are discarded. Then all the processing is done in the reduced subspace.

4.6.4 Using Discriminative Classifiers

With the advances in machine learning, especially in discriminative classification techniques, in the last decade researchers have worked on framing intent determination as a classification task. While the traditional solution to intent determination is the bag-of-words approach used in information retrieval, typically word n-grams are used as features after preprocessing with generic entities, such as dates, locations, or phone numbers. Because of the very large dimensions of the input space, large margin classifiers such as SVMs (Vapnik, 1998) or Adaboost (Schapire and Singer, 2000) were found to be very good candidates. To take into account context when two sentences are compared, the recent trend (Schapire and Singer, 2000) is to match *n-grams* (a substring of n words) rather than words as explained above.

Early work has been done by Schapire and Singer (2000) on the AT&T HMIHY system using the Boostexter tool, an implementation of the AdaBoost.MH multiclass multilabel classification algorithm. Boosting is an iterative algorithm; on each iteration, t, a weak classifier, h_t, is trained on a weighted training set, and at the end, the weak classifiers are combined into a single, combined classifier (Freund and Schapire, 1997). For example, for text categorization, one can use word n-grams as features, and each weak classifier (e.g. decision stump, which is a single-node decision tree) can check the absence or presence of an n-gram. The performance of the classifier closely matched with the salience-based classification approach and beat it especially on high false alarm rates.

Another pioneering work has been from the Bell Labs. Kuo and Lee (2000) have proposed the use of discriminative training on the routing matrix, which significantly improved their vector-based call routing system described earlier (Chu-Carroll and Carpenter, 1999), especially for low rejection rates. Their approach is based on using the minimum classification error (MCE) criterion. To solve the nonlinear optimization problem of achieving MCE, they used the generalized probabilistic descent (GPD) algorithm. The goal is adjusting the routing matrix elements so as to achieve maximum separation of the correct class from competing classes with an iterative approach. In this framework, the dot product of the normalized query and destination vectors is used as the discriminant function. More formally, the routing matrix R is iteratively adjusted as follows:

$$R_{t+1} = R_t + \delta R_t$$

where R_t is the parameter set at tth iteration. The correction term δR_t is solved using the training data, $\vec{x}_t$ with class k:

$$\delta R_t = -\epsilon_t \nabla l_k(\vec{x}_t, R_t)$$

where ϵ_t is the learning step size, and l_k is the class loss function, defined as:

$$l_k(\vec{x}, R) = \frac{1}{1 + e^{-\gamma d_k(\vec{x}, R) + \theta}}$$

where γ and θ are parameters to be tuned and d_k is the misclassification function:

$$d_k(\vec{x}, R) = -g_k(\vec{x}, R) + G_k(\vec{x}, R)$$

where g_k is the discriminant function:

$$g_k(\vec{x}, R) = \vec{r}_j.\vec{x}$$

and G_k is the anti-discriminant function:

$$G_k(\vec{x}, R) = \left(\frac{1}{K-1} \sum_{j \neq k, 1 \leq j \leq K} g_j(\vec{x}, R)^n\right)^{\frac{1}{\rho}}$$

Later they extended this approach so as to cover Boosting and automatic relevance feedback (ARF, Zitouni *et al.*, 2003). They tested these approaches along with MCE, and proposed a novel combination method of Boosting and MCE. While MCE happens to provide the best result amongst these three discriminative classification approaches, they obtain further gain from the combination of MCE with Boosting.

The next category of discriminative call classification systems employed large margin classifiers, such as support vector machines, which were initially demonstrated on binary classification problems. With such classifiers, the definition of the margin is typically unambiguous, and the reasons why this margin leads to good generalization reasonably well understood. Usually, the performance of SVMs can be reduced to a single number: the binary classification accuracy. Unfortunately, generalizing these binary SVM classifiers to multiclass call classification problems is not straightforward. Haffner *et al.* (2003) have proposed a global optimization process based on an optimal channel communication model that allows a combination of *heterogeneous* binary classifiers. As in Markov modeling, computational feasibility is achieved through simplifications and independence assumptions that are easy to interpret. Using this approach, they have managed to decrease the call-type classification error rate for AT&T's HMIHY natural dialogue system significantly, especially on the false rejection rates.

Another study from the same time period (Cox, 2003), proposed using discriminative techniques for call routing. More specifically, Cox proposed the use of generalized probabilistic descent (GPD), corrective training (CT), and linear discriminant analysis (LDA). The GPD study was motivated by the earlier study of Kuo and Lee (2000) described above. LDA relies on a linear transformation of the training and test vectors prior to classification (usually of dimension $N - 1$ when there are N classes.) The transformation matrix A is the matrix of eigenvectors a_i that satisfy the equation:

$$S_W^{-1} S_B a_i = \lambda a_i$$

where S_W is the within-class scatter matrix, S_B is the between-class scatter matrix, and λ an eigenvalue. Then, during classification, instead of conventional cosine distance, they employ the Euclidean distance, since LDA is based on the maximization of this distance. However, they have not seen significant performance improvement on their test set, unlike the tuning set, which is likely due to a lack of training data.

4.6.5 Using Prior Knowledge

While it has been common practice to employ manually written semantic grammars for slot filling tasks, such as the ATIS CMU (Ward and Issar, 1994) and MIT (Seneff, 1992) systems, for intent determination, there is no single published system employing only rules, except some simpler call routing tasks where techniques based on keyword spotting are used. Still, there is some literature on exploiting prior knowledge. The most notable study is by Schapire *et al.* (2005), who extends Boosting with manually written grammars for call-types. To this end, they define two terms in the objective function:

$$sum_i \sum_c [\ln(1 + e^{-y_{ic} h(x_i, c)}) + \eta RE(\pi(c|x_i) || \sigma(h(x_i, c)))]$$

The first term is the standard Adaboost negative log conditional likelihood, which provides a fit to the data. In this term, y_{ic} is $+1$ if the sample x_i has the true class of c, otherwise it is -1, and $h(x_i, c)$ is the classifier output for intent c and input x_i using the weak classifier $h()$. The second term applies a relative entropy measure between the probabilities predicted by the prior knowledge and the model built so far using the training data. Here η is a parameter which is computed empirically to control the relative importance of the two terms. $\pi(c|x_i)$ is the estimate (based on prior knowledge) of the conditional probability that instance x_i belongs to class c, and $\sigma(h(x_i, c))$ is the estimated probability that x_i belongs to c as computed by the constructed logistic Adaboost model.

4.6.6 Beyond ASR 1-Best: Using Word Confusion Networks

In a spoken language understanding system, it is very important for the system to be robust to ASR errors, since all the communication is in natural spoken language. Especially for spontaneous conversational speech, the typical word error rate (WER) is around 20–30%. Consider the example 1-best ASR output, "*I have a few questions about my maybe ill.*" for the utterance "*I have a few questions about my May bill*". Obviously, misrecognizing this salient portion of the sentence may result in misunderstanding the entire utterance, even when all other words are correctly recognized.

To this end, the use of intermediate ASR outputs such as ASR n-best lists, word lattices, and word confusion networks instead of only relying on ASR 1-best has been the usual practice for spoken language processing (e.g. Chelba and Acero, 2005; Hillard *et al.*, 2004), and SLU is no exception (Hakkani-Tür *et al.*, 2006).

Even in speech recognition, these intermediate outputs have usually been used for obtaining better word accuracies, by rescoring them (Mangu *et al.*, 2000). The oracle accuracy, the accuracy of the hypotheses closest to the manual transcriptions, of these intermediate ASR outputs is much higher than for 1-best. For example, it is likely to have the correct phrase "*May bill*" in the ASR intermediate output for the above example.

A lattice is a directed graph of words, which can encode a large number of possible sentences. A special kind of lattice, called word confusion networks (WCNs), or sausages, consist of a concatenation of word sets, one for each word time interval. The general structure of the WCNs and lattices are shown in Figure 4.6. The advantages of the WCNs can be listed as follows:

- Since they force the competing words to be in the same group, they enforce the alignment of the words. This time alignment may be very useful in language processing.
- The words in the WCN come up with their posterior probabilities, which can be used as their confidence scores. This is basically the sum of the probabilities of all paths which contain that word. This confidence score can be used during understanding.
- WCNs are much smaller than lattices. Their sizes are about 1/100 of those of ASR lattices, but they still have comparable oracle accuracies and even lower word error rates using the consensus hypothesis, which is the best path of a WCN (Mangu *et al.*, 2000).

In the literature WCNs have initially been used for decreasing the word error rate or obtaining word confidences (Gretter and Riccardi, 2001; Mangu *et al.*, 2000).

For SLU, they have been first used for the AT&T HMIHY system to better detect the salient phrases in user utterances (Tur *et al.*, 2002). Instead of matching the salient phrases in ASR 1-best, the algorithm extracted all matches in the WCN. Tur *et al.* proposed an efficient method to this end. They form a single finite state transducer (FST) taking the union of the FSTs of the SGFs which can be preceded or followed by any number of words. This FST is then composed

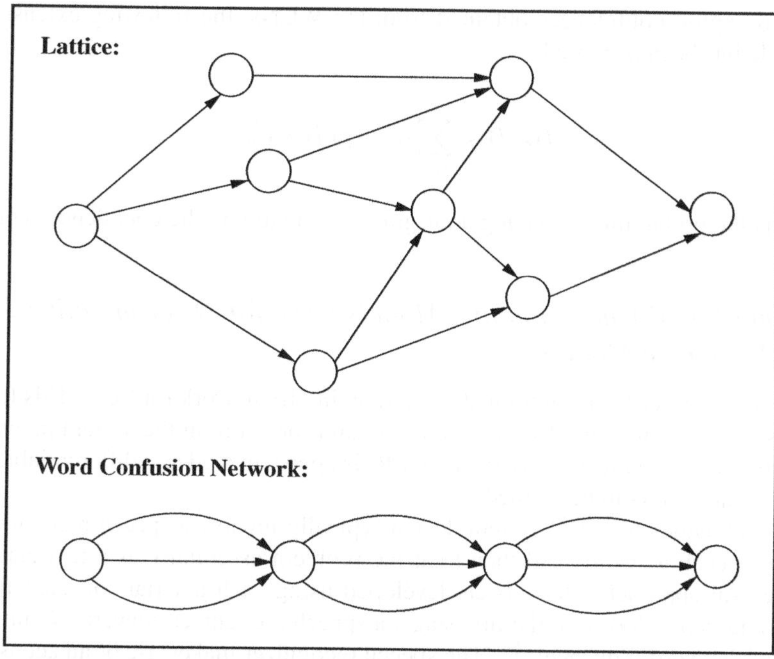

Figure 4.6 Typical structures of lattices and word confusion networks

with the WCN to get the matching phrases. They have used the geometric mean of the word confidences as the confidence of a salient phrase and kept the classification algorithm the same as explained in Section 4.6.2. In the HMIHY data set, while the WER is 31.7%, the oracle WER of the WCN is 9.4%. For a given false rejection rate of 30%, the error rate decreased 38% relative to using WCN with word confidences.

Another approach proposed to intent determination systems is using weighted features for lexical features for classification using SVM (Vapnik, 1998) or Boosting (Freund and Schapire, 1997). For example, if n-grams are used for classification, the features with confidences lower than some threshold may be filtered out, the features may be binned with respect to their confidences, or the weight of that feature can be weighted based on the confidence scores of the words constituting this feature (Hakkani-Tür *et al.*, 2006; Tur *et al.*, 2004). While most classifiers support such weighted features, Hakkani-Tür *et al.* (2006) proposed an algorithm for AdaBoost. Boosting aims to combine "weak" base classifiers to come up with a "strong" classifier. As mentioned before, this is an iterative algorithm, and in each iteration, a weak classifier is learned so as to minimize the training error. For call classification, word n-grams are used as features, and each weak learner checks the presence and absence of an n-gram, j. During runtime, the output of the Boosting classifier for each class for a given utterance, x, is then defined as follows:

$$f(x, l) = \sum_{t=1}^{T} \alpha_t \times c_{jl}^t$$

where c_l^t is the weak learner c_{jl} for iteration t for the class l.

In order to exploit confidences obtained from the WCNs, the following extension to the above formula has been proposed:

$$f(x, l) = \sum_{t=1}^{T} \alpha_t \times p(j) \times c^t_{jl}$$

where $p(j)$ is the probability of having an n-gram, estimated by the confidence scores of the WCN.

4.6.7 *Conditional Understanding Models Used for Discriminative Training of Language Models*

In this section, we describe a conditional understanding framework for SUC. This framework also establishes an architecture for system design and for learning the system parameters. In this framework, the classification error rate (CER) is approximated as a differentiable function of the system parameters to be learned.

Standard techniques for SUC system design typically involve a speech recognizer (ASR) to transform speech to words and then treat the problem essentially as a text classification problem. Several approaches have been developed using such a serial concatenation in the past (e.g. Wang *et al.*, 2005). In the first stage, a speech recognizer converts X_r into the best hypothesis of the word sequence, $\hat{W}_r$. The speech recognizer makes use of an acoustic model (AM) and a language model (LM) to select the most likely sequence of words given the speech signal. In the second stage, the recognized word string $\hat{W}_r$ is passed to a semantic classifier that assigns it a label $\hat{C}$, which ideally captures the user's intent or "meaning". The classifier model and feature functions are two essential components used in the second phase.

Being treated as a two-stage problem, two kinds of errors arise in SUC systems: WER introduced by the speech recognizer in the first stage and CER introduced by the semantic classifier in the second phase. In most conventional SUC approaches, the AM and LM are trained so that the WER in the ASR phase is reduced. Reducing errors in the automatic transcription can improve CER by virtue of providing better transcriptions to the semantic classifier. However, it has been reported that reductions in WER do not necessarily translate into reductions in CER. In many cases, a user's utterance contains multiple salient phrases pointing to a single interpretation of the utterance. Therefore, as long as enough words are recognized to trigger the correct salient phrase, the correct meaning is assigned to the utterance. A similar finding is also recently reported on a speech translation task (He *et. al.*, 2011)

Moreover, the ASR system is not able to fully utilize the more detailed syntactic, semantic and other higher-level knowledge sources for determining the correct words in the signal. As discussed in the previous subsection, performing SLU tasks on the n-best or WCN outputs from a recognizer can overcome some difficulties with using the 1-best speech recognition outputs. Extending this advantage from the SLU operation to the training phase, one can use conditional understanding models to define the objective function to discriminatively training language models (as well as the acoustic models) in the speech recognizer making use of the n-best outputs in the training data.

Multi-pass search techniques can be adopted in which the decoding algorithm is modified to return multiple word sequences with respective scores, which is known as the N-best word sequence list. One integrated technique recently published in the literature (see below) makes use of the N-best list to seamlessly combine the above two phases (Yaman *et al.*, 2008). The

N-best list generated in the first phase were rescored using all available knowledge sources, namely the acoustic model, the language model, and the classifier model. The integrated model is based on a mathematical formulation of a conditional understanding model and is reviewed below.

The integrated approach can be further enhanced by discriminative learning at various levels of the system parameters, from the semantic classifier level to the language model and even to the level of the pronunciation and acoustic models. The classifier learned by distribution estimation often does not lead to optimal performance. This is due to the fact that in most situations the estimated probabilities deviate from the true probabilities. Discriminative training is an alternative technique in which the classification error rate can be directly minimized. The goal of discriminative training is to correctly discriminate the observations for best recognition/classification results rather than to fit the distributions to the data. In Saraclar and Roark (2005), the role of discriminative language modeling in spoken utterance classification is found to be effective, in that it yields reductions in both the ASR word error rate (WER) and the semantic classification error rate (CER). The conditional understanding model, to which discriminative learning has been applied, consists of the acoustic model, the language model, and the classifier model which will be reviewed below.

4.6.7.1 Automatic Speech Recognition

Modern architectures for ASR are mostly based on software systems generating a sequence of word hypotheses from an acoustic signal (Jelinek, 1997). The goal of ASR is to generate the most probable word sequence(s) $\hat{W}_r$ given the acoustic signal X_r:

$$\hat{W}_r = \arg\max_W P(W|X_r). \tag{4.2}$$

Given $P(X_r|W)$ computed by an AM, and $P(W)$ computed by a LM, Equation (4.2) can be rewritten as:

$$\begin{aligned}\hat{W}_r &= \arg\max_W \frac{P(X_r|W)P(W)}{P(X_r)}, \\ &= \arg\max_W P(X_r|W)P(W).\end{aligned} \tag{4.3}$$

An AM incorporates the representation of knowledge about acoustics, phonetics, microphone and environment variables, gender and dialect differences among speakers, etc. On the other hand, an LM represents the system's knowledge of what constitutes a possible word, what words are likely to co-occur, and in what sequence.

There has been significant recent advancement in ASR technology by using all available knowledge sources (KSs) to decide on the spoken word sequence (Baker *et. al.*, 2009). In particular, the use of word graphs and word lattices has become very popular for large-vocabulary continuous speech recognition. The ideal strategy would be to merge all available KS's when finding the best hypotheses. However, it is often difficult or expensive to integrate a very complex KS into the first-pass search. Instead, multi-pass search algorithms are often used in which the decoding algorithm is modified to return multiple paths, and other knowledge sources are used to rescore these paths. A lattice or N-best of word-sequence hypotheses is first produced, where each word has its corresponding score and time boundaries. Then, the set of word-sequence hypotheses are re-ranked using more complex KSs.

The second component in Equation (4.3), $P(W)$, called the LM probability, serves as the prior information. W is a sequence of words w from a specific language, i.e. $W = \{w_1, \ldots, w_D\}$. Let w_0 be a symbol, such as "<s>", chosen appropriately to handle the sequence start. Then, the LM probability of W that contains D words is:

$$p(W) = p(w_1, \ldots, w_D) = \prod_{i=1}^{D} p(w_i | w_0, \ldots, w_{i-1}). \tag{4.4}$$

With the exact factorization, the complexity of the model grows exponentially with D. To remedy this problem, n-gram models make the Markovian assumption that the probability of a word depends only on the $n-1$ proceeding words. With an n-gram model, the probability of a word sequence becomes:

$$P(W) = P(w_1, ..., w_D) = \prod_{i=1}^{D} p(w_i | w_{i-1}, ..., w_{i-(n-1)}). \tag{4.5}$$

One can use a large corpus of text to find the n-gram frequencies, from which the n-gram probabilities $p(w_i | w_{i-1}, .., w_{i-(n-1)})$ can be estimated. A discounting scheme is also employed to account for the unseen events in LM training.

An AM, as represented by HMMs in most SUC systems, is known to underestimate the acoustic probability, due in part to the unrealistic cross-frame independence assumption. Furthermore, since the normalizing factor $P(X_r)$ is typically not computed, AM is not a true probability. Hence, AM and LM scores often have vastly different dynamic ranges. This complication is accounted for empirically by the LM scaling factor, L. Equation (4.3) is then replaced by:

$$\hat{W}_r = \arg\max_W \left[P^{\frac{1}{L}}(X_r | W) P(W) \right]. \tag{4.6}$$

4.6.7.2 Discriminative Learning Algorithm

One interesting aspect of the conditional understanding model discussed above is the way in which the N-best hypotheses generated by the ASR module are used in discriminative training of the system parameters. The technique developed based on this model associates a score to each pair formed by a word sequence in the N-best list and the related semantic class, which represents how likely it is that this word sequence yields classification of the spoken utterance into the associated semantic category. This score provides the information about which sentence in the N-best list is most likely to yield the correct classification, and which are more likely to yield wrong classification. Due to the use of the N-best list in this way, discriminative training is shown to increase the score of the word sequence that is most likely to yield correct classification while reducing the scores of all other word sequences. In the work described in Yaman *et al.* (2008), the authors follow the minimum error classification (MCE) (He *et. al.*, 2008) framework, where the score serves as the class-specific discriminant function in discriminative training.

Suppose that for utterance r, we are given the AM score $P(X_r | W_r)$, the class-posterior probability $P(C_r | W_r)$, the LM scaling factor L, and the LM probability $P(W_r)$. Then, the classification decision rule in Equation (4.3) can be approximated as

$$\begin{aligned}
\hat{C}_r &= \arg\max_{C_r} \left[\sum_{W_r} P(C_r, W_r|X_r) \right] \\
&= \arg\max_{C_r} \left[\sum_{W_r} P(C_r|W_r, X_r) P^{\frac{1}{L}}(X_r|W_r) P(W_r) \right] \\
&\cong \arg\max_{C_r} \left[\sum_{W_r} P(C_r|W_r) P^{\frac{1}{L}}(X_r|W_r) P(W_r) \right] \\
&\cong \arg\max_{C_r} \left[\max_{W_r \in \aleph} P(C_r|W_r) P^{\frac{1}{L}}(X_r|W_r) P(W_r) \right].
\end{aligned} \tag{4.7}$$

In the last line, the summation term is replaced with the selection of the word sequence among the N-best list (denoted by $\aleph$) with the greatest contribution. Upon taking a closer look at Equation (4.7), we see that the decision regarding the most appropriate class $\hat{C}_r$ for X_r involves calculating the *class-discriminant function* $D(C_r, W_r; X_r)$ for each pair W_r and C_r given by:

$$D(C_r, W_r; X_r) = \log[P(C_r|W_r) P^{\frac{1}{L}}(X_r|W_r) P(W_r)]. \tag{4.8}$$

Indeed, the class-discriminant function $D(C_r, W_r; X_r)$ shows how likely it is that the word sequence W_r will yield the semantic class C_r for the spoken utterance X_r. Hence, $D(C_r, W_r; X_r)$ serves as a *integrative score* or joint association score between the semantic class $C_r \in \mathcal{C}$ and the word sequence $W_r \in \aleph$ for the rth spoken utterance, X_r. Additionally, $D(C_r, W_r; X_r)$ is a natural choice to discriminate the word sequence that is most likely to yield the correct class from the rest. Since the computation of D combines the acoustic, language and classifier scores (and hence, integrative score), all available knowledge sources are being used to re-score and re-rank the N-best word sequences in a way that will be most useful for discriminative training.

In the test or the SUC system deployment stage, the decision rule

$$\hat{C}_r = \arg\max_{C_r} \left[\max_{W_r \in \aleph} D(C_r, W_r; X_r) \right]. \tag{4.9}$$

is implemented (for the r-th utterance X_r). The implementation of this decision rule requires re-scoring of the N-best list using the integrative score of $D(C_r, W_r; X_r)$, as indicated by the *max* operation inside the square bracket of Equation (4.9). In the rescoring, M scores $D(C_r, W_r; X_r)$ are first computed for each W_r in the N-best list and for each C_r. Let $T = \min\{M, N\}$, then, a one word sequence W_r is paired with the semantic category C_r^j, for each $j = 1, ..., T$ that gives the highest $D(C_r^j, W_r; X_r)$. This gives T word-sequence and semantic-class pairs (C_r^j, W_r^j). Eventually, for making the classification decision, among the pairs (C_r^j, W_r^j), the category $\hat{C}$ with the highest $D(\hat{C}_r, \hat{W}_r; X_r)$ is selected.

The discriminative training algorithm aims at rescoring the sentences and adjusting LM and classifier parameters so as to ensure that the word sequences in the N-best list are ranked with regard to their strength to yield the correct semantic class.

Throughout this discussion, we reserve the superscript "0" for the correct class and its associated word sequence, whereas the superscript "n" with $n = 1, ..$ is reserved for the wrong classes and their associated word sequences. Hence, W_r^0 is the word sequence that is most likely to yield the correct class, C_r^0. On the other hand, all other sentences in the N-best list, denoted as $W_r^n, n = 1, ..., N$, are more likely than W_r^0 to yield any semantic class, $C_r^n, n = 1, ..., M$, other than the correct one C_r^0. After determining W_r^0, the sentences in the N-best list are paired with the semantic classes. Note that W_r^0 may not be the top-ranking word sequence in the original N-best list, and also may not be the same as the manually transcribed word sequence.

In the training stage, we first extract the word sequence W_r^0 in the N-best list, $\aleph$, according to the definition just described:

$$W_r^0 = \arg\max_{W_r \in \aleph} \left[D(C_r^0, W_r; X_r) \right]. \tag{4.10}$$

The word sequence W_r^0 is extracted among all the word sequences in the N-best list. Therefore, it is the most likely sentence to yield the correct decision independent of whether or not it has the most correct transcription.

For $n = 1, ...T$, let $\mathcal{C}^n$ denote the set of the semantic classes that are not yet paired with any word sequence, i.e., $\mathcal{C}^n = \mathcal{C} \setminus \{C_r^0, ..., C_r^{n-1}\}$. Let also $\aleph^n$ denote the set of the word sequences in the N-best list that are not yet paired with any semantic class, i.e., $\aleph^n = \aleph \setminus \{W_r^0, ..., W_r^{n-1}\}$. Then, the classes in $\mathcal{C}^n$ and the word sequences in $\aleph^n$ are paired according to

$$C_r^n = \arg\max_{C_r \in \mathcal{C}^n} \left[\max_{W_r \in \aleph^n} D(C_r, W_r; X_r) \right]. \tag{4.11}$$

After determining the pairs (C_r^0, W_r^0) and $(C_r^n, W_r^n), n = 1, ..., T$, we now follow the MCE training framework and define the class-specific misclassification function, $d_r(X_r)$, and a class-specific loss function, $\ell_r(d_r(X_r))$, for each speech utterance, X_r, according to

$$d_r(X_r) = -D(C_r^0, W_r^0; X_r) + \log \left[\frac{1}{T-1} \sum_{n=1}^{T} \exp[\eta D(C_r^n, W_r^n; X_r)] \right]^{\frac{1}{\eta}}, \tag{4.12}$$

$$\ell_r(d_r(X_r)) = \frac{1}{1 + \exp(-\alpha d_r(X_r) + \beta)}. \tag{4.13}$$

where η, α, and β are the standard parameters in MCE training.

The total classification loss approximating CER that the LM model, Λ_W, and the semantic classifier model, Λ_λ, induce is then

$$L(\Lambda_W, \Lambda_\lambda) = \sum_r \ell_r(d_r(X_r)). \tag{4.14}$$

The parameters of the LM and the semantic classifier model are trained so that the total loss function is minimized. The details of the update rules are described in Sections 4.6.7.3 and 4.6.7.4, respectively.

4.6.7.3 Optimization of LM Parameters

Let $p_{w_x w_y}$ denote the bigram log-probabilities defined as $p_{w_x w_y} = \log P(w_y|w_x)$, which constitute the major LM parameters, Λ_W, (for all encountered word pairs $w_x w_y$.) These parameters that minimize the total loss function $L(\Lambda_W, \Lambda_\lambda)$ in Equation (4.14) are found by setting the gradient of the total loss function with respect to them to zero, i.e.

$$\frac{\partial L(\Lambda_W, \Lambda_\lambda)}{\partial p_{w_x w_y}} = \frac{\partial}{\partial p_{w_x w_y}} \left[\sum_r \ell_r(d_r(X_r)) \right] = 0. \tag{4.15}$$

Beginning with the log-probabilities $p^{(0)}_{w_x w_y}$ estimated by maximum likelihood, a numerical optimization algorithm generates a set of iterated estimates $\{p_{w_x w_y}\}_{t=0}^{K}$ that terminates when either no more reduction in $L(\Lambda_W, \Lambda_\lambda)$ can be made or when a solution point has been approximated with sufficient accuracy. The goal in deciding how to move from one iterate $p^{(t)}_{w_x w_y}$ to the next $p^{(t+1)}_{w_x w_y}$ is to find the iterate where the total loss $L(\Lambda_W, \Lambda_\lambda)$ is lowered as much as possible. The use of the steepest descent direction $-\nabla L(\Lambda_W, \Lambda_\lambda)$ is intuitive since it is the direction in which the total loss diminishes most rapidly. This gives us the following update rule for the LM probabilities:

$$\begin{aligned} p^{(t+1)}_{w_x w_y} &= p^{(t)}_{w_x w_y} - \varepsilon_{LM} \sum_r \frac{\partial \ell_r(d_r(X_r))}{\partial p_{w_x w_y}} \\ &= p^{(t)}_{w_x w_y} - \varepsilon_{LM} \alpha \sum_r \ell_r(d_r)[1 - \ell_r(d_r)] \frac{\partial d_r(X_r)}{\partial p_{w_x w_y}}. \end{aligned} \tag{4.16}$$

where ε_{LM} is an appropriately chosen step-size. When evaluating the derivative of $d_r(X_r)$ with respect to $p_{w_x w_y}$, we need to compute the derivative of $D(C_r, W_r; X_r)$ with respect to $p_{w_x w_y}$ according to Equation (4.12). Among the terms that constitute $D(C_r, W_r; X_r)$, $P(C_r|W_r)$ and $P(X_r|W_r)$ are not functions of the LM probabilities, and only $P(W_r)$ is. Suppose the bigram $w_{x_i} w_{y_i}$ appears $n(W_r^n, w_{x_i} w_{y_i})$ times in the word sequence W_r^n. Then,

$$\begin{aligned} \log P(W_r^n) &= \log \left[\prod_i [P(w_{y_i}|w_{x_i})]^{n(W_r^n, w_{x_i} w_{y_i})} \right] \\ &= \sum_i n(W_r^n, w_{x_i} w_{y_i}) \log[P(w_{y_i}|w_{x_i})]. \end{aligned}$$

Hence, using Equation (4.12), we have:

$$\frac{\partial d_r(X_r)}{\partial p_{w_x w_y}} = -n(W_r^0, w_x w_y) + \sum_{n=1}^{T} H_r^n n(W_r^n, w_x w_y). \tag{4.17}$$

where the weighting coefficients H_r^n are given by

$$H_r^n = \frac{\exp[\eta D(C_r^n, W_r^n; X_r)]}{\sum_{m=1}^{T} \exp[\eta D(C_r^m, W_r^m; X_r)]}. \tag{4.18}$$

As an example to show the intuition of the gradient in Equation (4.17), when $\eta \rightarrow \infty$, only the correct and the most competitive hypotheses show up. The LM parameters corresponding to the bigrams that are present in W_r^0 but not in W_r^1 (in the example above, *"the transportation"*, *"transportation in"*, *"in atlanta"*) are increased. In contrast, the LM parameters corresponding to the bigrams in W_r^1 but not in W_r^0 (*"the round"*, *"round trip"*, *"trip fare"*, *"fare from"*, *"from Atlanta"*) are decreased. The updates for the bigrams common to both W_r^0 and W_r^1 (*"what is"*, *"is the"*) cancel out and the corresponding LM parameters are left unchanged.

4.6.7.4 Optimization of Classifier Parameters

Let λ_k denote the weight of the kth feature function $f_k(C_r, W_r)$. The weights, called the semantic classifier parameters, which minimize the total loss function $L(\Lambda_W, \Lambda_\lambda)$ in Equation (14) are found by:

$$\frac{\partial L(\Lambda_W, \Lambda_\lambda)}{\partial \lambda_k} = \frac{\partial}{\partial \lambda_k}\left[\sum_r \ell_r(d_r(X_r))\right] = 0. \tag{4.19}$$

Using the steepest gradient method, we obtain the following update rule for the classifier parametersλ_k, $k = 1, ..., K$:

$$\begin{aligned}\lambda_k^{(t+1)} &= \lambda_k^{(t)} - \varepsilon_\lambda \sum_r \frac{\partial \ell_r(d_r(X_r))}{\lambda_k} \\ &= \lambda_k^{(t)} - \varepsilon_\lambda \alpha \sum_r \ell_r(d_r(X_r))[1 - \ell_r(d_r(X_r))]\frac{\partial d_r(X_r)}{\partial \lambda_k}.\end{aligned} \tag{4.20}$$

where ε_λ is an appropriately chosen step-size, and

$$\frac{\partial d_r(X_r)}{\partial \lambda_k} = \frac{\partial D(C_r^0, W_r^0; X_r)}{\partial \lambda_k} + \sum_{j=1}^{T} H_r^j \frac{\partial D(C_r^j, W_r^j; X_r)}{\partial \lambda_k}. \tag{4.21}$$

This learning rule requires some seed classifiers that we assume are available and can use for initializing the parameters $\lambda_k^{(0)}$, i.e. at $t = 0$. Given the classifier parameters λ_i and lexical n-gram feature functions $f_i(C, W)$, the distributions yielding maximal entropy can be shown to be in the form of the following exponential (log-linear) conditional probability distributions:

$$P(C_r|W_r) = \frac{1}{Z_\Lambda(W_r)} \exp\left[\sum_i \lambda_i f_i(C_r, W_r)\right], \tag{4.22}$$

where $Z_\Lambda(W_r)$ is a normalization factor for the word sequence W_r, that is:

$$Z_\Lambda(W_r) = \sum_{C_r} \exp(\lambda_i f_i(C_r, W_r)). \tag{4.23}$$

Again, when evaluating the gradient of $D(C_r, W_r; X_r)$ with respect to λ_k, among the three terms that constitute $D(C_r, W_r; X_r)$, $P(X_r|W_r)$ and $P(W_r)$ do not depend on λ_k, and $P(C_r|W_r)$ is the only term that does. Let $\varphi(C_r^j, W_r^j)$ denote the partial derivative of $P(C_r^j|W_r^j)$ with respect to λ_k. We then have:

$$\begin{aligned}\varphi(C_r^j, W_r^j) &= \frac{\partial \log P(C_r^j|W_r^j)}{\partial \lambda_k} \\ &= f_k(C_r^j, W_r^j) - \sum_{\tilde{C}} \xi(\tilde{C}, W_r^j) f_k(\tilde{C}, W_r^j).\end{aligned} \tag{4.24}$$

where the weighting factors of the feature functions are found with:

$$\xi(\tilde{C}, W_r^j) = \frac{\exp\left[\sum_i \lambda_i f_i(\tilde{C}, W_r^j)\right]}{\sum_{\hat{C}} \exp\left[\sum_i \lambda_i f_i(\hat{C}, W_r^j)\right]} \tag{4.25}$$

Similar to the case with LM parameter updates, when $\eta \to \infty$, the classifier parameters, λ_k, associated with the bigrams that are present in W_r^0 but not in W_r^1 are increased. In contrast, the classifier parameters, λ_k, associated with the bigrams that are present in W_r^1 but not in W_r^0 are decreased. In addition, the updates for the bigrams common to both W_r^0 and W_r^1 cancel out and the corresponding classifier parameters are left unchanged.

This approach is applied to the ATIS domain by Yaman *et al.* (2008). The experiments showed a reduction of the classification error rate from its initial value of 4.92 to 4.04% in the standard ATIS task. More recently, an extension of this approach is reported in Zhang *et. al.* (2011) for a speech translation task with success.

4.6.8 Phone-based Call Classification

Most call classification algorithms employ word and word n-gram level features. However, we must mention two notable studies using phones to provide robustness to the noise introduced by the ASR. The first study is by Huang and Cox (2003). The key idea is assigning a probability of association of segments of the call waveform with routes or classes directly without any requirement to estimate word or phrase identities from the noisy phonetic decoding. Instead of salient phrases as used in the AT&T HMIHY system described below, they identify salient acoustic morphemes and apply linear discriminant analysis to improve the performance. Almost simultaneously Alshawi (2003) suggested a similar idea for the AT&T HMIHY system. A minor difference is that he applied a self-training algorithm for tuning the phone recognizer in an unsupervised fashion.

4.7 Discussion and Conclusions

We have presented state-of-the-art approaches for semantic classification of utterances for intent determination and call routing. While word n-gram-based statistical classification models dominate the field, this is still an unsolved problem, especially for more realistic, naturally spoken utterances from a variety of speakers for more complex tasks.

Tur *et al.* (2010) presented a detailed error analysis for intent determination using the ATIS corpus. Even in this simple task, the classification error hovers around 5% using a word n-gram based Boosting classifier. These errors are then categorized into six clusters:

1. *Prepositional phrases embedded in noun phrases*: These errors involve phrases such as *Capacity of the flight from Boston to Orlando*, where the genitive phrase suggests flight

information, whereas the destination category is mainly determined by the head word of the noun phrase (*capacity* in this case). Since classifier has no syntactic features, such sentences are usually classified erroneously. Using features from a syntactic parser such as the head word can alleviate this problem.

2. *Wrong functional arguments of utterances*: This category is similar to the first category, but the difference is that, instead of a prepositional phrase, the confused phrase is a semantic argument of the utterance. Consider the example utterance *What day of the week does the flight from Boston to Orlando fly?* These are errors that can be solved by using either a syntactic parser that identifies functions of phrases or a semantic role labeler.
3. *Annotation errors*: These are utterances that were assigned the wrong category during manual annotation.
4. *Utterances with multiple sentences*: These are utterances with more than one sentence. In such cases, the intent is usually in the last sentence, whereas the classification output is biased by the other sentences.
5. *Other*: These include several infrequent error types such as ambiguous utterances, ill-formulated queries, and preprocessing/tokenization issues:
    - *Ambiguous utterances*: These errors involve utterances where the destination category is not clear in the utterance. An example from the ATIS test set is *list Los Angeles*. In this utterance, the speaker intent could either be to find cities that have flights *from* Los Angeles or flights *to* Los Angeles.
    - *Ill-formulated queries*: These are utterances which include a phrase that may mislead classification or understanding. An example from the ATIS test set is: *What's the airfare for a taxi to the Denver airport?* In this case, the word *airfare* implies a destination category of *Airfare*, whereas what is meant is *Ground transportation fare*. These type of errors are easier for humans to handle, but it is not presently clear how they can be resolved in automatic processing.
    - *Preprocessing/Tokenization issues*: These are errors that could be resolved by using a domain ontology or special pre-processing or tokenization related to the domain. Some domain-specific abbreviations and restriction codes are examples of this category.
6. *Difficult Cases*: These are utterances that include words or phrases that were previously unseen in the training data. For the example utterance *Are snacks served on Tower Air?*, none of the content words and phrases appear with the *Meal* category in the training data.

Figure 4.7 presents the frequency for each of these error types for three experiments. As seen, error types 1 and 2 constitute a majority of the errors. Both of these error types can be resolved by using a syntactic parser with function tags. However, note that the ATIS corpus is highly artificial and utterances are mostly grammatical and without disfluencies. Furthermore, when working with ASR, utterances may include recognition errors. In more realistic scenarios, one might consider shallow parsing or syntactic and semantic graphs (Hakkani-Tür *et al.*, 2005) for extracting richer and linguistically motivated features that could resolve such cases.

Understanding in context, that is determining the intent of the user in a dialogue, is also another area which is not much studied in the literature. Consider the example from Figure 4.2. Having the first utterance *a question about my bill* may reinforce the *Unrecognized_Number* intent in the third utterance. The ATIS Class D utterances, in a way, provide a test bed to study contextual intent determination, however they are mostly from a directed dialogue, hence not the best data to work with.

Error Type	All Train	25% Train	10-Fold
1	42.5%	33.8%	24.5%
2	22.5%	13.8%	30.0%
3	2.5%	6.1%	18.4%
4	0%	0%	8.0%
5	17.5%	12.5%	7.2%
6	15.0%	33.8%	11.7%

Figure 4.7 The distribution of error categories for intent determination using all and 25% of the training data, and using all the training and the test set with 10-fold cross validation

The task of intent determination has special importance amongst the other SLU tasks since this is where the speech processing community has first met the natural language understanding field and cross-fertilization of ideas and techniques has already resulted in many practical applications beyond simple command-based systems, even though it provides only some shallow understanding of the users' utterances.

References

Agresti A 1990 *Categorical Data Analysis* John Wiley and Sons Chapter 4, pp. 84–117.

Alshawi H 2003 Effective utterance classification with unsupervised phonotactic models *Proceedings of the Human Language Technology Conference (HLT)-NAACL*, Edmonton, Canada.

Austin JL 1962 *How to Do Things with Words*. Harvard University Press.

Baker J, Deng L, Glass J, Khudanpur S, Lee C-H, Morgan N and O'Shgughnessy D 2009 Research Developments and Directions in Speech Recognition and Understanding, *IEEE Signal Processing Magazine*, **26**(3), 75–80.

Chelba C and Acero A 2005 Position specific posterior lattices for indexing speech *Proceedings of the Annual Meeting of the Association for Computational Linguistics (ACL)*, Ann Arbor, MI.

Chu-Carroll J and Carpenter B 1999 Vector-based natural language call routing. *Computational Linguistics* **25**(3), 361–388.

Core M and Allen J 1997 Coding dialogues with the DAMSL annotation scheme *Proceedings of the Working Notes of the Conference of the American Association for Artificial Intelligence (AAAI) Fall Symposium on Communicative Action in Humans and Machines*, Cambridge, MA.

Cox S 2003 Discriminative techniques in call routing *Proceedings of the International Conference on Acoustics, Speech and Signal Processing (ICASSP)*, Hong Kong.

Cox S and Shahshahani B 2001 A comparison of some different techniques for vector based call-routing *Proceedings of the European Conference on Speech Communication and Technology (EUROSPEECH)*, Aalborg, Denmark.

Damnati G, Bechet F and de Mori R 2007 Spoken language understanding strategies on the france telecom 3000 voice agency corpus *Proceedings of the International Conference on Acoustics, Speech and Signal Processing (ICASSP)*, Honolulu, HI.

Di Fabbrizio G, Dutton D, Gupta N, Hollister B, Rahim M, Riccardi G, Schapire R and Schroeter J 2002 AT&T help desk *Proceedings of the International Conference on Spoken Language Processing (ICSLP)*, Denver, CO.

Freund Y and Schapire RE 1997 A decision-theoretic generalization of on-line learning and an application to boosting. *Journal of Computer and System Sciences* **55**(1), 119–139.

Gorin AL, Abella A, Alonso T, Riccardi G and Wright JH 2002 Automated natural spoken dialogue. *IEEE Computer Magazine* **35**(4), 51–56.

Gorin AL, Riccardi G and Wright JH 1997 How May I Help You? . *Speech Communication* **23**, 113–127.

Gretter R and Riccardi G 2001 On-line learning of language models with word error probability distributions *Proceedings of the International Conference on Acoustics, Speech and Signal Processing (ICASSP)*, Salt Lake City, Utah.

Gupta N, Tur G, Hakkani-Tür D, Bangalore S, Riccardi G and Rahim M 2006 The AT&T spoken language understanding system. *IEEE Transactions on Audio, Speech, and Language Processing* **14**(1), 213–222.

Haffner P, Tur G and Wright J 2003 Optimizing SVMs for complex call classification *Proceedings of the International Conference on Acoustics, Speech and Signal Processing (ICASSP)*, Hong Kong.

Hakkani-Tür D, Bechet F, Riccardi G and Tur G 2006 Beyond asr 1-best: Using word confusion networks in spoken language understanding. *Computer Speech and Language* **20**(4), 495–514.

Hakkani-Tür D, Tur G and Chotimongkol A 2005 Using syntactic and semantic graphs for call classification *Proceedings of the Annual Meeting of the Association for Computational Linguistics (ACL) Workshop on Feature Engineering for Machine Learning in Natural Language Processing*, Ann Arbor, MI.

He X, Deng L and Wu C 2008 Discriminative learning in sequential pattern recognition — A unifying review for optimization-oriented speech recognition. *IEEE Signal Processing Magazine*, **25**(5), 14–36.

He X, Deng L, and Acero A 2011 Why word error rate is not a good metric for speech recognizer training for the speech translation task? *Proc. ICASSP*, Prague.

Hillard D, Ostendorf M, Stolcke A, Liu Y and Shriberg E 2004 Improving automatic sentence boundary detection with confusion networks *Proceedings of the Human Language Technology Conference (HLT)-NAACL*, Boston, MA.

Huang Q and Cox S 2003 Automatic call-routing without transcriptions *Proceedings of the European Conference on Speech Communication and Technology (EUROSPEECH)*, Geneva, Switzerland.

Jelinek F 1997 *Statistical Methods for Speech Recognition*. MIT Press, Cambridge, MA.

Juang BH and Rabiner LR 2005 *Automatic Speech Recognition-A Brief History of the Technology*. Elsevier.

Kuo HKJ and Lee CH 2000 Discriminative training in natural language call-routing *Proceedings of International Conference on Spoken Language Processing (ICSLP)*, Beijing, China.

Lane I, Kawahara T, Matsui T and Nakamura S 2007 Out-of-domain utterance detection using classification confidences of multiple topics. *IEEE Transactions on Audio, Speech, and Language Processing* **15**(1), 150–161.

Mangu L, Brill E and Stolcke A 2000 Finding consensus in speech recognition: word error minimization and other applications of confusion networks. *Computer Speech and Language* **14**(4), 373–400.

Natarajan P, Prasad R, Suhm B and McCarthy D 2002 Speech enabled natural language call routing: BBN call director *Proceedings of the International Conference on Spoken Language Processing (ICSLP)*, Denver, CO.

Saraclar M and Roark B 2005 Joint discriminative language modeling and utterance classification *Proceedings of the International Conference on Acoustics, Speech and Signal Processing (ICASSP)*, Philadelphia, PA.

Schapire RE and Singer Y 2000 Boostexter: A boosting-based system for text categorization. *Machine Learning* **39**(2/3), 135–168.

Schapire RE, Rochery M, Rahim M and Gupta N 2005 Boosting with prior knowledge for call classification. *IEEE Transactions on Speech and Audio Processing*.

Seneff S 1992 TINA : A natural language system for spoken language applications. *Computational Linguistics* **18**(1), 61–86.

Shriberg E, Dhillon R, Bhagat S, Ang J and Carvey H 2004 The ICSI Meeting Recorder Dialog Act (MRDA) Corpus *Proceedings of the SigDial Workshop*, Boston, MA.

Stolcke A and Shriberg E 1996 Statistical language modeling for speech disfluencies *Proceedings of the International Conference on Acoustics, Speech and Signal Processing (ICASSP)*, Atlanta, GA.

Tur G, Hakkani-Tür D and Heck L 2010 What is left to be understood in ATIS? *Proceedings of the IEEE Spoken Language Technologies (SLT) Workshop*, Berkeley, CA.

Tur G, Hakkani-Tür D and Riccardi G 2004 Extending boosting for call classification using word confusion networks *Proceedings of the International Conference on Acoustics, Speech and Signal Processing (ICASSP)*, Montreal, Canada.

Tur G, Wright J, Gorin A, Riccardi G and Hakkani-Tür D 2002 Improving spoken language understanding using word confusion networks *Proceedings of the International Conference on Spoken Language Processing (ICSLP)*, Denver, CO.

Vapnik VN 1998 *Statistical Learning Theory*. John Wiley and Sons, New York, NY.

Wang YY, Deng L and Acero A 2005 Spoken language understanding-an introduction to the statistical framework. *IEEE Signal Processing Magazine* **22**(5), 16–31.

Ward W and Issar S 1994 Recent improvements in the CMU spoken language understanding system *Proceedings of the ARPA Human Language Technology Conference (HLT) Workshop*, pp. 213–216.

Wilpon JG, Rabiner LR, Lee CH and Goldman ER 1990 Automatic recognition of keywords in unconstrained speech using hidden markov models. *IEEE Transactions on Speech and Audio Processing* **38**(11), 1870–1878.

Wright J, Gorin A and Riccardi G 1997 Automatic acquisition of salient grammar fragments for call-type classification *Proceedings of the European Conference on Speech Communication and Technology (EUROSPEECH)*, Rhodes, Greece.

Yaman S, Deng L, Yu D, Wang YY and Acero A 2008 An integrative and discriminative technique for spoken utterance classification. *IEEE Transactions on Audio, Speech, and Language Processing* **16**(6), 1207–1214.

Zitouni I, Kuo HKJ and Lee CH 2003 Boosting and combincation of classifiers for natural language call routing systems. *Speech Communication* **41**(4), 647–661.

Zhang Y D, Deng L, He X and Acero A 2011 A novel decision function and the associated decision feedback learning for speech translation, *Proc. ICASSP*, Prague.

5

Voice Search*

Ye-Yi Wang, Dong Yu, Yun-Cheng Ju and Alex Acero
Microsoft Research, U.S.A.

Voice search is one of the most actively investigated speech understanding technologies of recent years. The technology underlies many commercial spoken dialogue systems (SDSs) that provide users with the information they request with a spoken query. The information normally exists in a large database, and the query has to be compared with one or multiple fields in the database to obtain the relevant information. The contents of the fields, such as business or product names, are often unstructured text. For example, directory assistance (DA) (Bacchiani *et al.*, 2008; Yu *et al.*, 2007) is one of the most popular voice search applications, in which users issue a spoken query and an automated system returns the phone number and address information of a business or an individual. The applications include both telephone only services and multi-modal services on mobile devices. Other voice search applications include music/video management (Mann *et al.*, 2007; Song *et al.*, 2009), business and product reviews (Zweig *et al.*, 2007), stock price quotations, and conference information systems (Andreani *et al.*, 2006; Bohus *et al.*, 2007). Recently the task has been extended to using voice queries for Web search from mobile devices, as manifested by the commercial systems from Google, Microsoft and Yahoo!.

5.1 Background

Figure 5.1 shows the typical architecture of a voice search system, where a user's utterance is first recognized with an automatic speech recognizer (ASR) that utilizes an acoustic model (AM), a pronunciation model (PM) and a language model (LM). The m-best results from the ASR are passed to a search component to obtain the n-best semantic interpretations, i.e. a list of up to n entries in the database. The interpretations are passed to a dialogue manager

* This chapter is based on an article by the same authors published in the IEEE Signal Processing Magazine, Vol 25, No 3., entitled "*An Introduction to Voice Search*" (Wang *et al.*, © 2008 IEEE). Substantial revision has been made.

Spoken Language Understanding: Systems for Extracting Semantic Information from Speech, First Edition.
Edited by Gokhan Tur and Renato De Mori.

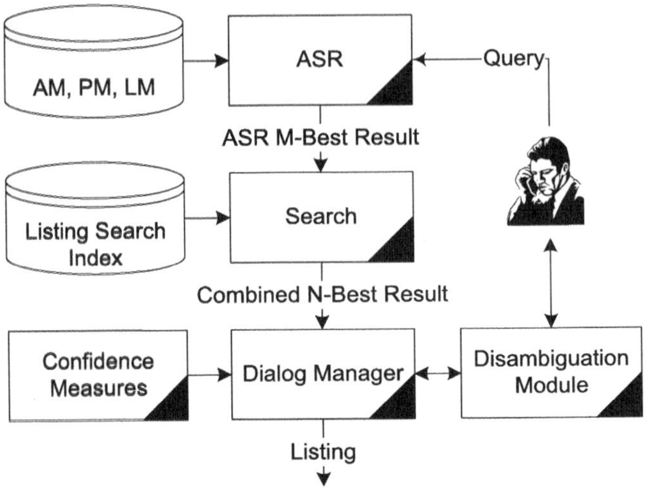

Figure 5.1 Architecture of a typical voice search system (Wang *et al.*, © 2008 IEEE)

(DM) subsequently. The DM utilizes confidence measures, which indicate the certainty of the interpretations, to decide how to present the n-best results. If the system has high confidence on a few entries, it directly presents them to the user. Otherwise, a disambiguation module is exploited to interact with the user to understand his true intent.

5.1.1 Voice Search Compared with the Other Spoken Dialogue Technologies

Compared with other spoken language understanding tasks in automated human/machine interaction, such as the frame-based SLU and call-routing, voice search has its unique characteristics and needs to be addressed differently. The frame-based SLU is used to gather the attribute values of an entity that users are interested in, such as the originating and destination cities of a flight. In such systems, users often have to use canned expressions within a small domain. In a directed dialogue system, a user is limited to providing answers to what the system has prompted for, which often contain a single piece of semantic information; while in a mixed-initiative system, users are allowed to volunteer more semantic information in a single utterance – we call this type of semantic understanding task *high-resolution* in the sense that multiple slots need to be identified. The call-routing applications remove the constraints on what a user can say, so one can speak naturally. This is accomplished at the expense of limiting the target semantic space: the understanding of natural language inputs is often achieved with statistical classifiers, which map a user's input to a destination semantic class (intent) in a predefined set of limited size. The classifiers can hardly perform high-resolution understanding with many slots, or scale up with a huge number (e.g. thousands to millions) of destination classes. Voice search applications differ from the frame-based applications in their lack of detailed, high-resolution semantic analysis. They are similar to the call-routing applications with respect to the naturalness of user inputs and the huge input space. However, they differ from the call-routing applications in the sense that their semantic space, or in the terminology of the call-routing applications, the inventory of the "destination classes," is enormous – sometimes in the range of millions of entries. Data are seldom sufficient to train a statistical classifier.

Table 5.1 Comparison of the frame-based SLU, call-routing and voice search spoken language understanding with respect to the characteristics of the input utterance space and the output semantic space

SLU task	User input utterances		Target semantic representation	
	Naturalness	Input space	Resolution	Semantic space
Frame-based/directed dialogue	Low	Small	Low	Small
Frame-based/mixed-initiative	Low-medium	Small	High	Small
Call routing	High	Large	Low	Small
Voice search	Medium-high	Large	Low	Large

Source: Wang *et al.*, © 2008 IEEE

Instead, information retrieval techniques based on some similarity metrics between a query and a candidate entry are used to select the entry that best matches the query. Hence in general there is no need of labeled training data to train an understanding model. Table 5.1 compares the three types of technologies.

The distinctions here are technological rather than functional. From users' perspective, the differences may not be discernible – they get some responses, either in text or in speech, to their spoken request. Both semantic frame-based understanding or voice search may involve the search of the information that a user is requesting from a database. The underlying technologies, however, are quite different. In a frame-based SLU system such as one in the ATIS domain, a user's input is first mapped to a structured frame representation. From this representation, a structured SQL query is generated to get the exact information from the database. When the target semantic space gets much larger, this front-end SLU approach becomes less practical for the following reasons:

1. Modeling difficulties. The large target space (e.g., millions of business names) implies the need of more training data to properly model the different ways users refer to an entry in the space. In addition, confusability increases as the target semantic space grows – it is more likely that an entry sounds/looks similar to another one in a larger space. Unlike the ATIS domain where entities of interests, for example, city names, dates and times, are expressed quite differently from the general language usage, the entities in voice search may not distributed as differently from the general language usage. For example, song titles in music search can be almost everything that occurs in general language usage, not to mention the spoken queries for general Web search. In other words, the larger space makes the distribution of the terms in the entity of the space flatter and increases the perplexity/ambiguity. Hence the front-end SLU may not be reliable.
2. High level of ambiguity. Having similar contents across different fields in the structured data is another source of ambiguity. For example, "Backstreet Boys" can be the artists, the title of a song or the name of an album in music search. A slot disambiguation decision made by the front-end processing may be premature and result in the absence of the desired target from the search results.
3. Cascading errors. Errors and premature disambiguation decisions may occur in different steps in the ASR/SLU/SQL-generation front-end solution. Furthermore, the formulation of the structured SQL from the frame structure isolates the ASR from the search process. The phonetic confusability in ASR becomes transparent to the backend search process, which

makes it impractical to recover from the recognition errors by finding the desired target that sounds similar to the recognized query.

Therefore, instead of making an upfront decision to generate a structured query from a user's utterance, voice search pushes back the decision into the backend where the transcribed spoken query is compared with the database entries according to some similarity metrics studied in the field of information retrieval (IR). This prevents the premature decisions in the front-end and allows to take into account the phonetic similarities by introducing them into the IR metrics.

Information retrieval has been adopted by other spoken language tasks, including the spoken content retrieval and the speech question answering. The former allows users to search for the occurrences of a term (word or phrase, with text input) from a collection of spoken documents (for example, audio recordings of lectures), and the latter aims at answering the specific questions from a user. While the questions can be asked with speech, a majority of the research in speech QA focuses on questions entered as text. In both of the spoken content retrieval and speech question answering, speech recognition is used to transcribe the audio documents into a text form – a sequence of words or sub-words units. Both need to address the issue of robustness to the ASR errors in the transcriptions of the documents. The spoken content search often does not directly address the need of a user by providing the relevant information – it finds multiple occurrences of a term in the collection within different contexts. Users have to listen to the speech surrounding an occurrence to check if it contains the information they need. Therefore, spoken content retrieval has to be coupled with a visual browsing tool that enables users to quickly and efficiently browse the audio documents. Such a tool may incorporate other spoken language understanding technologies, such as speech summarization. To the contrary, speech question answering can provide the most specific and relevant information to the user (assuming that the system works properly). It achieves this by first retrieving the relevant transcribed documents from the document collection and then extracting and finding the most relevant answers to the user's question – often a single sentence in the relevant document. To perform this difficult task, it often involves domain-independent natural language understating techniques, such as semantic role labeling.

Compared with spoken content retrieval and speech question answering, voice search operates in the opposite direction with respect to the input modality and the media type of the target documents – it uses spoken query to find the text documents. The text documents are often available in the structured form, such as the metadata for audio/video contents, or the business listings containing different fields such as phone number, address and opening hours. The relevance of the search results to user's information need is in between those of the spoken content retrieval and the speech question answering. It provides the user with a small number of search results with sufficient context information, such that the user can quickly scan them to find the one that matches his intent. Table 5.2 summarizes the differences among spoken content retrieval, speech question answering and voice search.

5.1.2 History of Voice Search

Early work on voice search focused on directory assistance (DA). Institutions on both sides of the Atlantic have deployed experimental systems during the mid-late 1990s. The early studies focused mainly on residential DA (Billi *et al.*, 1998; Kamm *et al.*, 1995; Lennig *et al.*, 1994), and speech recognition was the major topic of research – as long as personal names

Table 5.2 Comparison of spoken language technologies related to information retrieval – spoken content retrieval, speech question answering and voice search

Speech IR task	User input		Search target			
	Modality	Unit	Media	Unit	Structured	Relevance
Spoken content IR	Text	Word/phrase	Audio	Term occurence	No	Low
Speech QA	Text/speech	Question	Audio	Sentence	No	High
Voice search	Speech	Query	Text	Document	Often	Medium

were correctly recognized, the search could be a simple database look-up. As a result, the dialogue strategies centered on limiting the scope (hence perplexity) of the target listing space for ASR. The confidence measures mostly relied on features from the ASR. Related work includes enterprise level auto-attendant (a.k.a. name dialing) services from Phonetic Systems (acquired by ScanSoft, then merged with Nuance), AT&T (Buntschuh *et al.*, 1998), IBM (Gao *et al.*, 2001), and Microsoft (Ollason *et al.*, 2004). While automating residential DA is important in reducing the operational cost, it is only a small portion (19%) of the total received calls compared to the 61% of business DA calls (Billi *et al.*, 1998). Therefore there have been increasing interests in business DA, with the commercial deployments from Tellme (acquired by Microsoft), Jingle Networks, AT&T, Google (Bacchiani *et al.*, 2008), Verizon and Cingular (merged with AT&T Wireless now) and Microsoft (Yu *et al.*, 2007). Because the level of linguistic variance is much higher in business DA queries, SLU/search aiming at correctly interpreting user's intent becomes an important research topic. The linguistic variance increases the ambiguity and uncertainty in the interpretation of a user's intent. As a result, dialogue research focuses on the disambiguation strategy, as well as the confidence measures that look into features from different system components to accurately predict the end-to-end performance in interpreting a spoken query.

Other voice search applications include the stock quote system from Tellme and a product/business rating system from Microsoft (Zweig *et al.*, 2007). Separate efforts have been made on conference information systems by Carnegie Mellon University (Bohus *et al.*, 2007) and by the collaboration among AT&T, ICSI, Edinburgh University and Speech Village (Andreani *et al.*, 2006), where users can request information about thousands of papers published in a conference. In the entertainment sector, Daimler has investigated digital music management in automobiles (Mann *et al.*, 2007), and Ford and Microsoft have introduced the commercial dashboard device Ford SYNC that allows in-car music search. Like the business DA applications, many new voice search applications call for research activities in search/SLU and dialogue management in addition to speech recognition.

With the broad adoption of mobile devices and the availability of wireless access to the internet, many companies are actively engaged in the space of voice search on the mobile or in-car devices (Mann *et al.*, 2007). Google has introduced speech recognition for Google Apps on iPhone and Android phones, which allows users to use speech input for business or general Web search. Yahoo! has similar offering with the Yahoo! Search App. Microsoft has also released a voice-enabled Bing Mobile Application that supports dialog in several domains. AT&T is currently working on a voice enabled local search for iPhone (Feng *et al.*, 2009). In addition to the industrial efforts, academia is also studying the problem of voice-enabled general Web search (Vertanen and Kristensson, 2009). New research activities include multi-modal (GUI with touch screen and speech) user interfaces (Acero *et al.*, 2008; Mann *et al.*, 2007) and efficient and scalable client–server architectures.

5.1.3 Technical Challenges

Voice search poses new challenges to the spoken dialogue technology in the following areas:

1. **Speech recognition**: The state-of-the-art ASR systems have high error rates on voice search tasks. A voice search system can have much larger vocabulary size than a typical frame-based or a call routing application and sometimes may contain millions of lexical entries. Many lexical entries in international individual or business names are out of vocabulary and lack the reliable pronunciation information. The audios are often captured under different noisy environments. In addition, the constraints from language models are often weaker than other ASR tasks – the perplexity of a language model is often high (e.g. ~200 bits for business DA) for voice search.
2. **Spoken language understanding**: It is a common misconception that voice search is a simple combination of speech recognition and search, and SLU is not important because an existing search engine is often used as a blackbox in voice search applications. As a matter of fact, many voice search related issues are not in the focus of the information retrieval (IR) research community, which can be addressed by spoken language understanding techniques. We will discuss the challenges related to the backend IR separately below.
3. **Dialog management**: The difficulties in ASR and SLU/IR cause much confusability and uncertainty. The dialogue manager has to effectively narrow down the scope of what a user may say to reduce the confusability and uncertainty. Search results often contain multiple entries. The disambiguation strategy is crucial in order to obtain the sufficient information for the correct understanding of users' intents with as few dialogue turns as possible. Confidence measures are important for the dialogue manager to take the appropriate action with each of the hypothesized interpretations, such that the dialogue can recover gracefully from the ASR and SLU errors.
4. **Feedback loop**: No systems can be perfectly built at the initial deployment. Dialogue system tuning is often performed painstakingly by spoken dialogue experts, starting from error analysis on the logged interaction data to find the flaws in the dialogue and prompt design, language/understanding model development, system implementation, etc. An interesting research topic is the automatic or semi-automatic discovery and remedy of the design/implementation flaws.

Voice search also brings about the following challenges to the backend information retrieval:

1. **Enormous target semantic space**: a DA system can easily contain hundreds of thousands (if not millions) of listings. There is also a high level of linguistic variance in the input space. For example, users may not use the official name of a business in a DA or a business rating system. They would typically say, for instance, "Sears" instead of the listed official name, "Sears Roebuck & Co."
2. **Robustness to speech recognition errors**: Robustness to the ASR errors is particularly important in voice search due to the fact that spoken queries are very short in general. This may cause problems in the following two aspects: (a) the language model can leverage

little context information, hence the word error rate will be high; and (b) there is not much redundant information that the IR component normally relies on. Unlike the spoken content retrieval or speech question answering where multiple occurrences of a term or an answer (note that different sentences may contain the answer to the same question) may exist across a spoken document collection, the effect of a single recognition error in user's query can be catastrophic in voice search. Traditional information retrieval research focuses on text queries and pays little attention to this issue.

3. **Structured data retrieval**: The documents in voice search applications often exist in the structured form that contains multiple fields. A user may describe the document he is interested in with the information about one or many such fields, with different probabilities. Traditional IR approaches that treat query/document as bags of terms cannot take advantage of the structured information. A majority of the limited work on structured data IR treats each field as a separate sub-document, uses the traditional IR approach to compare the content of a field to the query and obtains a similarity score, and then derives the score of a document by combining the scores of its fields. This score combination approach has some intrinsic problems, as discussed in (Robertson *et al.*, 2004).

Like other SLU tasks, the grand challenge in voice search application is robustness. The CSELT's study on Telecom Italia's DA system (Billi *et al.*, 1998) showed that, even though the automation rate was 92% in a laboratory study, the actual field trial automation rate was only 30% due to the unexpected behavior of novice users and the environment noise.

5.1.4 Data Sets

Unlike the research activities in the frame-based SLU, which are sponsored by public funding and participated by multiple institutions from both academia and industry, the activities in voice search are largely conducted by software or telecommunication companies, working with their own proprietary data collected from the services they provide. Out of the concerns about their users' privacy, it is almost impossible for them to share the data with the research community – there were several failed attempts from the researchers in these organizations. Due to this unfortunate situation, there is currently no common data set for voice search research. Researchers from academia have to collect their own data to conduct relevant research (Vertanen and Kristensson, 2009).

5.1.5 Evaluation Metrics

Many evaluation metrics can be found in voice search related publications, some of them are used to assess the performance of a component like speech recognition or language models. Here we focus only on the metrics for the end-to-end evaluation of a voice search system. Many of them, not surprisingly, are commonly used in the information retrieval community. Note that there can be more than one listings that are the "correct" answers to a query (imagine a user search for "Starbucks in Seattle", where you may find two or three Starbucks coffee shops within a block, and also a towing company with the same name). Hence the metrics are designed to reflect a system's capability of finding the correct answers and to reject the incorrect ones. A listing returned from a search engine can be either a true positive (TP, correct answer) or a false positive (FP, incorrect answer); a listing in the database that is not returned by the search engine can be a true negative (*TN*, correct rejection) or a false negative (*FN*, incorrect rejection).

1. **Precision, recall and F$_1$-score:** *Precision* is the percentage of correct answers among all the answers returned from a voice search system:

$$PR = \frac{N(TP)}{N(TP) + N(FP)} \tag{5.1}$$

Precision reflects a system's capability in rejecting incorrect answers. It does not measure its capability in finding as many correct answers as possible. So recall

$$RE = \frac{N(TP)}{N(TP) + N(FN)} \tag{5.2}$$

is introduced for that purpose. *F_1-score* is the harmonic mean of precision and recall:

$$F_1 = \frac{2 * PR * RE}{PR + RE} \tag{5.3}$$

A system may have multiple operating points (often set by different thresholds to accept a hypothesis), at which different precision and recall scores can be observed. A *recall–precision curve* plots the different precision scores in relation to the corresponding recall scores at the same operating point. Similarly, a *receiver operating characteristic (ROC) curve* plots the true positive rates (recall) in relation to the corresponding false positive rates ($N(FP)/\,[N(FP) + N(TN)]$).

2. **Mean reciprocal rank (MRR):** Precision and recall do not reflect the ranking power of a voice search system – if two results are returned, one is correct and the other is not, different placement of the results will not alter the precision/recall/F_1-score. Ideally, placing a relevant answer at a higher rank should be favored by the evaluation metric. The *reciprocal rank* of the search results for a query is the multiplicative inverse of the rank of the first correct answer. The *mean reciprocal rank* is the reciprocal ranks averaged over a set of test queries:

$$MRR = \frac{1}{N}\sum_{i=1}^{N}\frac{1}{r_i} \tag{5.4}$$

where N is the number of test queries, and r_i is the rank of the first correct answer for the ith query.

3. **Mean average precision (MAP):** The mean reciprocal rank metric does not take precision or recall into consideration. The *mean average precision* is proposed to fix this problem. The *average precision* (AP) is the average of precisions computed at different cut-off points in the result list:

$$AP = \frac{\sum_{r=1}^{N(TP)+N(FP)} PR(r) * COR(r)}{N(TP) + N(FN)} \tag{5.5}$$

where r is the rank of a result (smaller number indicates higher rank in a result list), $COR(r)$ is a binary function that has value 1 only when the result at rank r is a correct answer to the query. $PR(r)$ is the precision of the top r search results. *Mean average precision* (MAP) is the mean of the individual precision scores over a test set of queries.

$$MAP = \frac{1}{N}\sum_{i=1}^{N} AP_i \tag{5.6}$$

where AP_i is the average precision of the results for the ith query.

4. **Normalized discounted cumulative gain (NDCG):** The binary judgment of correctness of a search result may not be enough to distinguish the quality of different results. A relevance rating with more grades is more suitable in some cases. For example, the product search results for the query "black iPod player" may include a perfect result of an iPod player that is black, and another result without the color information. It does not make sense to label the second result as incorrect, since it is still more relevant than a result of an MP3 player of a different brand. A 5-grade relevance ranking ("poor", "fair", "good", "excellent" and "perfect") is often used, corresponding to the numeric values 1–5.

   The relevance of a result is discounted by a factor according to its rank in the search results. The discounting factor penalizes presenting a relevant result at a lower rank. The *discounted cumulative gain (DCG) at k* is the sum of the discounted relevance at top k different ranks. A logarithm discounting factor is often used:

$$DCG(k) = \sum_{r=1}^{k} \frac{2^{rel_r} - 1}{\log_2(r+1)} \tag{5.7}$$

   where rel_r is the relevance rating for the rth search result.

   The DCGs of the search results are not directly comparable across different queries, since they may result in different number of results. For each query, an oracle maximum DCG $mDCG(k)$ can be calculated by arranging the k most relevant results according to their relevancy, such that the more relevant results are always presented before the less relevant one. The *normalized discounted cumulative gain (NDCG) at rank k* over a test set of N queries is

$$NDCG(k) = \frac{1}{N}\sum_{i=1}^{N} \frac{DCG_i(k)}{mDCG_i(k)} \tag{5.8}$$

5. **M-best search accuracy**: *M-best Search Accuracy* ACC_M is the percentage of the correct answers among the top M answers:

$$ACC_M = \frac{1}{N*M}\sum_{i=1}^{N}\sum_{r=1}^{M} COR_i(r) \tag{5.9}$$

   where $COR_i(r)$ is a binary function that has value 1 only when the result at rank r is a correct answer to the ith query in the test set.

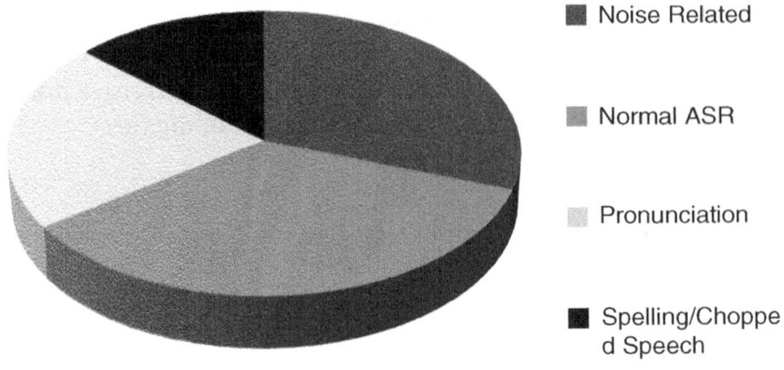

Figure 5.2 Distribution of the different causes of ASR errors, from the error analysis of an auto-attendant system in (Gao *et al.*, 2001; Wang *et al.*, © 2008 IEEE)

When a voice search system has limited capacity to present multiple search results, as in a telephony system, one-best and two-best search accuracy become more important and are popularly used.

5.2 Technology Review

In this section we review the technology that addresses the challenges in the voice search applications, with a focus on the sub-problems of SLU/search and language modeling. Not surprisingly, much of the technology is developed with the DA systems because they are the most popular voice search applications so far. However, the technology is often applicable to other applications as well. For example, the product/business rating systems (Zweig *et al.*, 2007) directly used the technology developed in a DA application (Yu *et al.*, 2007).

5.2.1 Speech Recognition

A detailed error analysis for proper name recognition was reported in an auto-attendant system in (Gao *et al.*, 2001). Figure 5.2 shows the distribution of the different causes of errors – besides 35% of common recognition errors, 31% were noise related and 22% were pronunciation related. Many of the calls were made in a noisy environment over different noise channels. Therefore, noise-robustness is crucial to improve the ASR accuracy. On the other hand, there are many foreign names that are difficult to know the pronunciation in an auto-attendant/DA system. In fact, pronunciation is a pervasive problem that poses challenge in many other voice search applications as well. For example, users may specify a multilingual query "*Petit Bonheur* by *Salvatore Adamo*" in music search. Hence pronunciation modeling is another important topic in ASR for voice search. In addition, better acoustic and language models are always important to reduce the ASR error rate.

5.2.1.1 Acoustic Modeling

IBM's auto-attendant system applied speaker clustering in its acoustic model (Gao *et al.*, 2001). Simple HMMs that have one Gaussian per context-independent phone state were trained first for each speaker. Then the vectors of the means of these models were clustered with the k-means algorithm. For each test utterance, the cluster model that yielded the highest likelihood was selected. In doing so, different channel and noise conditions can be more precisely modeled by the cluster models, so the noise-related problems are alleviated. In addition to speaker clustering, speaker adaptation is effective to bring the performance of a speaker-independent system closer to that of a speaker-dependent system. Unlike the normal speaker adaptation, the adaptation in Gao *et al.* (2001) was *massive* in the sense that the adaptation data was obtained from a pool of recent callers rather than a single speaker. The massive adaptation is helpful due to the fact that a caller often calls the same set of individuals, and that a caller may try a name repeatedly when a recognition error occurs. While massive adaptation is helpful to bring down the error rate for the frequent callers, unsupervised utterance adaptation aims at improving the accuracy from an unknown speaker. In this adaptation scheme, the test utterance itself was used for adaptation with a two-pass decoding. In the first pass, a speaker-independent system or the system after massive adaptation was used to obtain the automatic transcript. Then a forward-backward algorithm was applied to obtain the adaptation statistics. After adapting the acoustic models using the collected statistics, the caller's utterance was decoded in a second pass with the adapted model – this second pass may adversely increase the latency of a voice search system. Overall, with all these acoustic model enhancements and an unsupervised derivation of pronunciations (to be described below), a 28% error reduction was observed.

5.2.1.2 Pronunciation Modeling

One approach to improve the pronunciation model is to augment the dictionary with pronunciation variants. Data-driven algorithms are commonly applied, which typically include four steps: generating phonetic transcriptions with a recognizer; aligning the auto-transcriptions to the manually created canonical pronunciations; deriving rules mapping from the canonical pronunciations to the variants; and pruning the rules. One limitation of this approach is that the canonical reference pronunciations must be available.

The IBM auto-attendant system (Gao *et al.*, 2001) adopted an acoustics-only based pronunciation generation approach (Ramabhadran *et al.*, 1998). The approach has the advantage of not requiring the canonical pronunciation. This makes it more practical in voice search applications since many words do not exist in a pronunciation dictionary. It works as follows: a trellis of sub-phone units was constructed from an utterance. The transition probabilities in the trellis were derived by weighting the transition probabilities of all the context-dependent realizations of the sub-phone units in a HMM acoustic model. A Viterbi search was performed to obtain the best sub-phone sequences from the trellis; and a pronunciation was subsequently derived from the sequence. Experiments in Gao *et al.* (2001) showed a 17% relative error reduction when the test set and training set had overlapping unseen words.

Trade-off often has to be made in adding pronunciation variants to a dictionary. The additional pronunciations, on the one hand, make the word models match the actual acoustic signal more precisely; on the other hand, they give rise to a large number of highly confusable word models. Instead of augmenting an existing pronunciation dictionary with variants, a pronunciation distortion model was introduced in Béchet *et al.* (2002) to rescore the n-best hypotheses generated from a first recognition pass. The distortion model incorporates the "knowledge source" about the common distortions observed in a specific spoken language. For example, only insertions were considered in the distortion model for French in Béchet *et al.* (2002) because it is frequently observed that silence segments are often inserted between certain pairs of consonants like $[m][n]$, and a schwa is often inserted after a consonant at the end of an utterance. Formally, let A and W denote the acoustic signal and the text transcription of a caller's utterance, and τ_w a phone sequence that may be distorted from the canonical pronunciation of W, then a hypothesis $\hat{W}$ can be selected from the first pass n-best recognitions according to the following decision rule:

$$\begin{aligned}\hat{W} &= \arg\max_{W} P(W \mid A) = \arg\max_{W} \sum_{\tau_w} P(W, \tau_w \mid A) \\ &\approx \arg\max_{W} \max_{\tau_w} P(W, \tau_w \mid A) \\ &\approx \arg\max_{W} \max_{\tau_w} P(\tau_w) P(A \mid \tau_w) P(W \mid \tau_w) \end{aligned} \tag{5.10}$$

The last approximation in the equation includes an application of the Bayes rule and an assumption of independence between A and W given τ_w. The prior of a distorted phone sequence, τ_w, can be written in terms of η_w, which is the canonical pronunciation of W; and δ_w, which is the difference between τ_w and η_w:

$$P(\tau_w) = P(\eta_w, \delta_w) = P(\delta_w \mid \eta_w) P(\eta_w) \tag{5.11}$$

In theory, $P(\delta_w \mid \eta_w)$ and $P(\eta_w)$ can be estimated from data. In Béchet *et al.* (2002), a uniform distribution over all plausible insertions was used instead for $P(\delta_w \mid \eta_w)$ due to the lack of data. $P(A \mid \tau_w)$ in the decision rule in Equation (5.10) can be obtained from the acoustic model with all possible alignments between A and τ_w. Since only insertion is considered in Béchet *et al.* (2002), $P(W \mid \tau_w)$ was obtained by multiplying the probabilities of all successful insertions. Experiment results showed that the rescoring had improved the one-best ASR accuracy from 50 to 59.8%.

5.2.1.3 Language Modeling

Early DA systems compiled directory entries into a finite-state grammar as the language model for ASR. This rule-based language model does not scale up well with the directory size due to the increased perplexity. It was observed that the ASR accuracy decreases linearly with the logarithmic increases in the directory size (Kamm *et al.*, 1995). On the other hand, it was noticed that the distribution of the requested listings followed the Zipf's law. 10% (20%) of call volumes were covered by only 245 (870) listings. So (Kamm *et al.*, 1995; Natarajan *et al.*, 2002), a semi-automated DA system was built to cover only the frequently requested listings. The remaining requests were relayed to human operators.

One problem of the rule-based LMs constructed from the database listings is their poor coverage. Callers seldom say a business name exactly as it appears in a database – just consider the earlier example of "Sears Roebuck & Co" versus "Sears." It was mentioned in Béchet *et al.* (2000) that variant expressions for business names could be semi-automatically derived from data. Although it did not report how this was achieved, a straightforward method would compare a caller's utterance (e.g. "Kung-Ho Chinese Restaurant") with the actual listing released to the caller (e.g. "Kung-Ho Cuisine of China") by operators and learn that "Chinese Restaurant" is a synonym of "Cuisine of China." This "synonym" rule-based approach is usually expensive; the rule coverage is highly restricted by the data available; and the rules may be over-generalizing without careful crafting.

The problem was tackled without using the data from the callers in Jan *et al.* (2003). A method was proposed to automatically construct a finite state signature LM from a business directory database alone, which would accept different query variants. Here a *signature* is a sub-sequence of the words in a listing that can uniquely identify the listing. For example, with the listings "3-L Hair World on North 3rd Street" and "Suzie's Hair World on Main Street," "3-L", "Hair 3rd", and "Hair Main" are signatures because they occur in only one listing. On the contrary, the subsequences "Hair World" and "World on" are not signatures because they appear in both listings. Based on the signatures, a finite state transducer can be constructed as follows (the example is taken from Jan *et al.* (2003):

S := 3-L Hair World? On? North? 3rd ? Street? : 1 |
3-L Hair? World? On? North 3rd ? Street? : 1 |
3-L Hair? World on? North? 3rd ? Street? : 1 |
3-L? Hair World? On? North 3rd ? Street? : 1 |
Suzie's? Hair World? On? Main Street? : 2 |
Suzie's Hair World? On? Main? Street? :2 |
Suzie's Hair? World on? Main? Street? :2 |
Suzie's? Hair? World on? Main Street? :2

where each entry in the grammar corresponds to a signature. The terms in a signature are obligatory, whereas the terms in a listing, but not in the signature, are optional (marked by '?'.) The numbers after ':' is the semantic output from the transducer that represents the ID of a listing in the database. In doing so, every utterance matched by a rule can be uniquely associated with a listing. Because the nonessential words are optional, this makes the grammar more robust to utterances that omit these words. As the directory become larger, an entry may bear no signature because each of its sub-sequences can be a sub-sequence of another entry. This problem was handled with the "confusion sets" in Jan *et al.* (2003).

The rationale behind the signature grammar is that any term in an entry is droppable as long as the drop does not cause the confusion with another entry. While this is very practical in reducing the search ambiguity, it may be risky in modeling human language – speakers are very likely to drop terms that would lead to ambiguity. For example, they often say "Calabria" instead of "Calabria Restaurant" even though the former may cause confusions with "Calabria Electric" and "Calabria Jack J Do."

Another approach to improved robustness is via statistical n-gram models (Bacchiani *et al.*, 2008; Natarajan *et al.*, 2002; Yu *et al.*, 2007). An n-gram model is more robust because it does not require a user's utterance to match a rule exactly; in addition, it provides a statistical framework for fair comparison between different hypotheses; and it has well-studied smoothing algorithms to estimate the likelihood of unseen events more accurately. Ideally, a statistical n-gram model should be built from the transcripts of the real calls, which demonstrate not only the different ways callers refer to businesses, but also the probability of each such ways. Unfortunately, it is not realistic to collect enough calls to provide a good coverage for a large listing set, especially during the early stage of development. An interpolated LM was proposed to estimate the n-gram probability in Yu *et al.* (2007):

$$P(w) = \lambda P_t(w) + (1 - \lambda) P_l(w), \tag{5.12}$$

where $P_t(w)$ is the LM built using the transcripts of real calls, $P_l(w)$ is the LM built using a listing database, and λ is the interpolation weight, which is tuned with a cross-validation set collected under the real usage scenario. Here $P_t(w)$ can be constructed from the transcribed data straightforwardly. Building $P_l(w)$, on the other hand, takes more considerations because the database entries may not reflect the actual ways that callers refer to them. A statistical variation model was introduced to account for the common differences between the database listings and the actual callers' queries. The model was based on the rationale similar to that of the signature model, namely callers are more likely to say the words that distinguish one listing from others. However, instead of making the risky binary decisions, it modeled the importance of a word statistically according to its discriminative capability and its positions in a listing (based on the observations that callers are more likely to say the initial words in a listing). Here, the discriminative capability of a word was determined by its inverse document frequency (see Section 5.2.2), and a position importance weight w_l^i, $(0 < w_l^i \leq 1)$ was associated to each word position. A word was droppable with a probability inversely proportional to its importance. In addition, the model took into account the business category information for smoothing – each word had a probability to be followed by the category words (e.g., "restaurant.") This probability correlated to the importance and the category-indication capability (a mutual-information based measure) of a word. Furthermore, an efficient interpolation with a large vocabulary background LM (Yu *et al.*, 2006) had provided additional robustness. The internal investigation in Microsoft has revealed that the statistical language model, together with the vector space model for listing search (see Section 5.2.2), has greatly outperformed the signature-based approach – at the same precision level, the recall has been almost doubled.

Similarly, Bacchiani *et al.* (2008) used a large amount of text from different sources to train an n-gram language model. The data sources include business listings, transcribed voice search queries and the text queries logged by a local search engine. Systematic studies show that the latter two types of queries have significantly improved the search performance, as illustrated by Figure 5.3.

In Li *et al.* (2008), a machine-translation based approach was used to enrich the language model training data in a directory assistance application. It aimed at modeling the linguistic variations – users may refer to a listing in a different way from its original form in the database; and there are often multiple paraphrases for the same listing. For example, the listing *Kung Ho Cuisine of China* can be expressed as *Kung Ho, Kung Ho Chinese Restaurant*, or *Kung Ho Restaurant*. In this case, the LM trained using only the listings in the original form in the database is inadequate to model the actual users' utterances.

Li *et al.* (2008) used transcribed queries to search for the listing database. If the listing of the top search result was close enough to the corresponding query according to some distance measure,[1] the listing/query pair is used as a training example for a machine translation system. The trained translation model is applied to the database listings to obtain a new data set that contains the listings in the original form and up to 3-best translations (paraphrases). The new data set, together with the transcribed queries, forms a set of query and translation augmented listings (QTAL). QTAL was used to train a language model. Its perplexity, measured on a held-out transcribed query set, was compared with that of the language model trained with a set of query augmented listings (QAL) – the QTAL set minus the paraphrases from the machine translation component. Table 5.3 shows significant perplexity reduction by including the translations in the LM training data.

[1] Li *et al.* (2008) used the Tf-Idf weighted vector space model, which we will discuss in Section 5.2.2.

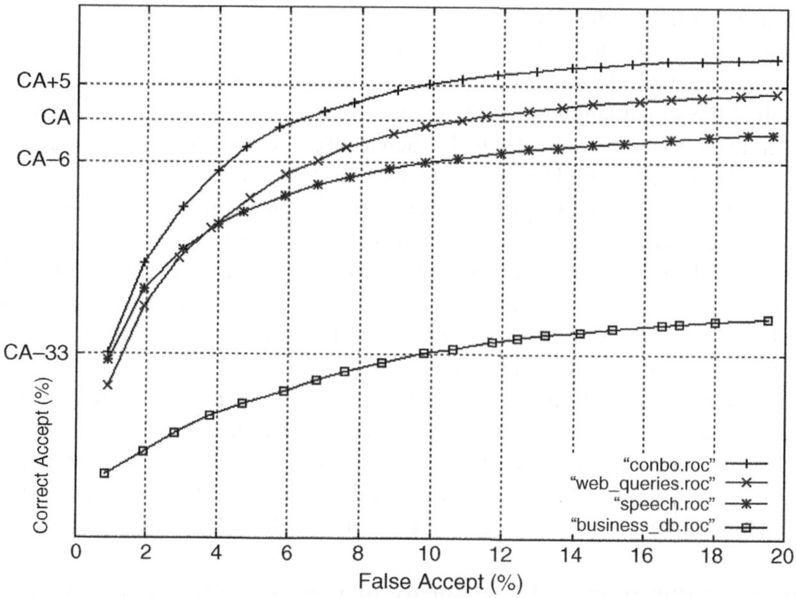

Figure 5.3 ROC curves of the voice search performance for business listings with language models trained with different training materials. The bottom (business_db.roc) is the curve for the language model trained with the listing data alone; the top (combo.roc) is the curve for the language model trained with the listing data and the usage data from transcribed voice queries and logged Web queries. The curves in the middle show the contributions from the transcribed voice search usage data (speech.roc) and the Web search queries (web_queries.roc). The big gaps between the bottom curve and the rest show the style mismatch between the listing data and the actual queries issued by the users (Wang *et al.*, © 2008 IEEE)

5.2.2 Spoken Language Understanding/Search

The task of spoken language understanding is to map a user's utterance to the corresponding semantics. In voice search, the semantics is the intended entry in a database. Hence the SLU becomes a search problem to a large extent.

Traditionally, SLU is only an optional component for voice search. In early voice search applications such as residential DA, SLU was not an issue, since there was not much expression variance in saying a person's name. Search was basically a database look-up, with the careful

Table 5.3 Perplexity comparison between the language models trained with the query augmented listings (QAL) and the query and translation augmented listings (QTAL)

# of queries in training	1k	3k	7k	10k	14k
QAL	1534	1414	1404	1054	888
QTAL	409	314	229	217	190
Relative reduction (%)	73.4	77.8	79.3	80.4	78.5

Source: Wang *et al.*, © 2008 IEEE

considerations of initials, titles and homophones. If a finite-state-based LM is used for ASR, each rule is uniquely associated with a listing or a confusion set, so there is no need of a separate search component either. However, due to the deficiency of the listing data based finite-state LM in modeling the actual language usage in queries, n-gram LMs are often adopted in recent more advanced voice search applications. In such a case, recognitions are no longer associated with a specific database listing. Hence a separate search step is necessary.

A majority of recent commercial products related to mobile local/Web search use a text-based Web search engine as the search component, and ASR is used as an interface to voice-enable the search engine. While this is a practical solution, it is sub-optimal because the search algorithms were developed without the consideration of robustness to the ASR errors, and the voice search application has to adopt the same user interface as text search, which prohibits the system from taking full advantage of a spoken dialogue system.

As voice search applications are getting more popular, SLU in voice search is becoming an important issue. Many applications in a special domain may not have an existing text search engine, such as the task of music/video search on a local device. Some voice search applications based on the existing text search engines also introduced a separate SLU component (Feng *et al.*, 2009). It is important for the SLU component to address the following problems:

1. **Improving the robustness to the linguistic variance of spoken language**. An important difference between a spoken language only directory assistance dialogue system and a speech-enabled local search on a mobile device lies in the characteristics of the input to the systems. In the speech-enabled mobile search, users are directed to speak into a specific search input box, hence their utterances are more likely to be similar to their text counterparts. In the telephony directory assistance, users' speech may be more casual and contain "*carrier phrases*", for example, "*I need the number of* pizza hut in downtown." It is important to treat the carrier phrases differently from the name of a business listing during the search.
2. **Handling the search from structured data**. The backend of many voice search applications has a structured database that contains multiple fields (columns). For example, a product search application may have a backend database with the brand, model, product name, and category fields, etc. Music search may have a database with the artist, composer, title, and genre fields. Users may issue queries that specify information for more than a single field, such as "Yellow Submarine by the Beatles." Local search may have the locality, business name, business category, opening hours, etc. Most existing text search engines adopt a bag-of-words approach that ignores the structural information.
3. **Improving the robustness to recognition errors**. Speech recognition is far from perfect. Directly feeding the 1-best ASR results to a search engine is a suboptimal solution. An SLU component can combine the information from the voice search semantic space (listings) and the information from the recognizer about the competing hypotheses to make a more informed decision, such that the ASR results that make more sense semantically can be chosen to improve the overall voice search performance.

5.2.2.1 Robustness to the Linguistic Variance in Spoken Language

To improve the robustness to the linguistic variance in spoken language, researchers from BBN Technologies (originally Bolt, Beranek and Newman, henceforth BBN) adopted a channel

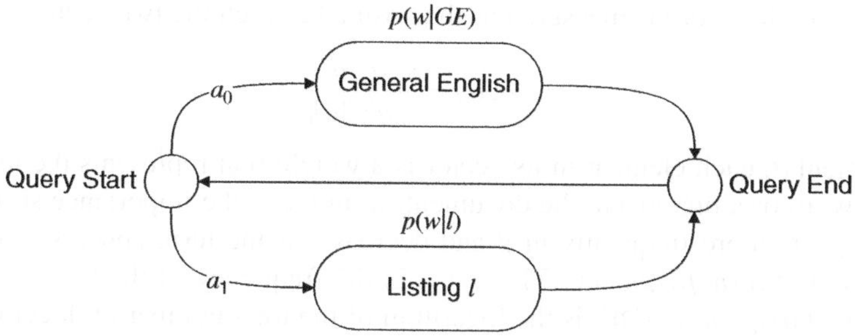

Figure 5.4 An HMM model is used to separate the listing terms from the general English terms (carrier phrases). The model is trained with a combination of users' queries and the listing data (Natarajan *et al.*, © 2002 IEEE)

model (Natarajan *et al.*, 2002). Given a locality[2] C and a query Q recognized from a user's utterance, it looks for the listing $\hat{L}$ according to the following decision rule:

$$\begin{aligned}\hat{L} &= \arg\max_{L} P(L \mid C, Q) = \arg\max_{L} P(C, Q \mid L)\, P(L) \\ &\approx \arg\max_{L} P(C \mid L)\, P(Q \mid L)\, P(L) \end{aligned} \tag{5.13}$$

In Natarajan *et al.* (2002), the prior distribution $P(L)$ and the locality distribution $P(C \mid L)$ were estimated from the training data. The training data were the transcripts of real users' utterances augmented with database listings. The query distributions $P(Q \mid L)$ were modeled with a two-state Hidden Markov Model (HMM) illustrated by Figure 5.4. In this model, a word w in Q is generated from either the General English (GE) state for the carrier phrases or the state corresponding to a listing l, which is a value of the random variable L. With this model,

$$P(Q \mid L) = \prod_{w \in Q} (a_0 P(w \mid GE) + a_1 P(w \mid L)). \tag{5.14}$$

Here the transition weights a_0 and a_1 were tied across the HMMs for all values of L. The transition and emission probabilities were estimated from training data. This model is robust due to the inclusion of the GE state, which captures carrier phrases such as "*I need the number of*" or ASR errors. The combination of the real user data and the database listings facilitates high accuracy on the frequently requested listings and simultaneously enables a broad coverage of the less frequently requested listings.

The HMM-based listing selection requires training data, which is only realistic for a subset of listings that are most popularly sought for. Yu *et al.* (2007) applied the Tf-Idf (term frequency – inversed document frequency) weighted vector space model (VSM) to business listing and product name search. The Tf-Idf weighted vector space model is broadly used in information retrieval (IR). It represents a query (document) with a vector q (d). The relevance (or similarity)

[2] DA dialogues often start by asking users for the city and state information. See Section 5.2.3 for details.

of the document to the query is measured as the cosine between the two vectors:

$$\cos(q, d) = \frac{q \cdot d}{\|q\| \, \|d\|} \tag{5.15}$$

For a document d, each element in its vector is a weight that represents the importance of a term (e.g. a word or a bigram) in the document. Intuitively, the importance should increase as the term appears more frequently in d and decreases if the term appears in many different documents. The *term frequency* (TF) $tf_i(d)$ is the frequency of the term i in d, and the *inverse document frequency* (IDF) is the logarithm of the total number of documents divided by the number of documents containing i:

$$tf_i(d) = \frac{n_i(d)}{\sum_k n_k(d)} \qquad idf_i = \log \frac{|D|}{|\{d : i \in d\}|} \tag{5.16}$$

where $n_i(d)$ is the number of occurrences of term i in d, and D is the entire document collection. The weight for term i in the vector is the product of its TF and IDF scores. The vector for a query can be defined similarly. There are other alternatives to define the TF and IDF scores, but the gist of the metrics are the same – TF measures the relevance of a term to a query/document, while IDF discounts the relevance if the term occurs in too many documents. The vectors for queries may sometimes omit the IDF scores, since they are already taken into consideration by the IDFs in the document vectors. A survey of the vector space model can be found in Greengrass (2001).

In voice search, each listing is treated as a "document" and represented by a vector. The standard VSM has been enhanced for voice search in Yu *et al.* (2007) in the following two aspects:

1. Special treatment of the duplicate words in listings and queries. In the traditional IR, documents and queries are generally long. The term frequency resembles the true distribution underlying a document/query. Listings and queries in voice search, on the other hand, are short in general, so the surface term frequency may not be a reliable estimate of the true underlying distribution. A small noise in the surface form is more likely to bring quite different search results. For example, the query "Big 5," intended for "Big 5 Sporting Goods", results in the listing "5 star 5" – the additional 5 in the listing brings it closer to the query. Since the term frequency is not reliable for search among short listings, each term gets a unit count in voice search. A duplicate word is treated as a different term, e.g. by replacing the second 5 in the example with 5_2nd. This effectively adds another dimension to the vector space. Since the Idf of this new dimension is much higher, it plays a more important role in query matching. A query without duplicate words like "Big 5" will have a larger angle from a listing with the duplicate "5", hence smaller cosine value. The angle will be significantly reduced if the query does contain the 2nd term. So "5 5" will match "5 star 5" better.
2. Inclusion of category information in the listing vectors in addition to the listing names. Callers often voluntarily provide category information (such as restaurant, hospital, etc.) in their queries. These category words can be identified according to the mutual information between them and the categories in a database. If category information is detected in a user's query, the category information about a listing in the database can be appended to the listing's vector so it can be compared with the query's category directly by the vector

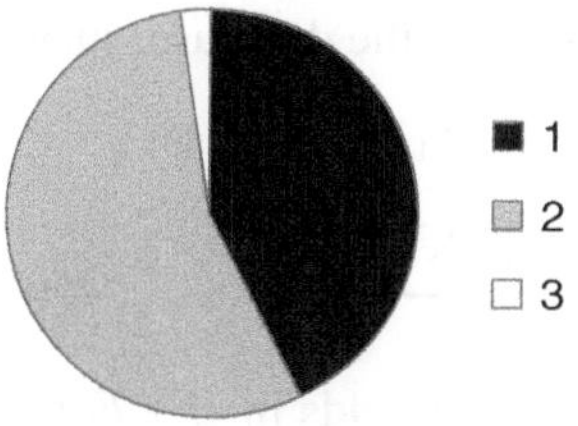

All rise, I guess, from Blues
Sarah, in the arms of an angel
Play legally blonde soundtrack
Glenn Miller, jazz.
Anton Bruckner, 7th Symphony, Leonard Bernstein

Figure 5.5 Left: distribution of queries containing 1, 2, and 3 fields. Right: examples of queries specifying information for multiple fields (Wang *et al.*, © 2008 IEEE)

space model. With this enhancement, the VSM would rank the listing "*Calabria Ristorante Italiano*" higher than "*Calabria Electric*" for the query "*Calabria Restaurant*".

5.2.2.2 Search for Structured Data

In mobile local search, the problem related to the structured data is often alleviated by directly speech enable two separate input boxes, one for the location term[3] and the other for the search term. However, this solution does not fully take advantage of a spoken dialogue system – as shown in Feng *et al.* (2009), the separation of the two terms may add extra burden to the users – the distinction of the two terms is not always clear, as manifested by a user's query such as "restaurants near Manhattan" as the search term and "New York City" as the location term. In addition, the solution may not be sufficient to separate a search **subject** (often business names or categories) from the *constraints*, as in the exemplar query "**night clubs** *open Christmas day.*"

AT&T's Speak4It (Feng *et al.*, 2009) allows users to include both the search term and the location term in a single utterance, and uses the frame-based SLU described in Chapter 3 to separate them from the utterance. More specifically, it uses the n-gram models as the semantic prior model, and the slot-specific n-gram models as the lexicalization model – the same model used by CHRONUS.

To separate the search subjects from the constraints, it assigns a probability $P_{subject}(s)$ to a segment s for being a search subject, based on the observation that the queries with a specific constraints are far fewer than the queries without any constraints (e.g., "night club" is more popular than "night club open Christmas day."). A corpus C of likely subjects is constructed to include the *simple* local search queries and the listing names. Here a simple query is one with no more than five words and containing no constraint indicators like the word "with" or "that." $P_{subject}(s)$ can be estimated from C:

$$P_{subject}(s) = \left(\lambda * \frac{Freq(s \in C)}{|C|} + (1-\lambda) * \frac{1}{|C|}\right)^{\gamma} \tag{5.17}$$

In Song *et al.* (2009), HMM-based models were introduced to handle the search from the structured music metadata, where a query may contain multiple fields. It observed that more than half of users' queries had contained the specification for more than one field (Figure 5.5.) An HMM was proposed to model the field-specific information in a query. Formally, given a

[3] Same as the "locality" in the previously mentioned BBN's HMM model for voice search.

query $Q = w_1, \ldots, w_n$, we need to find the entry $\hat{E}$ from the database, such that

$$\begin{aligned}\hat{E} &= \arg\max_E P(E \mid Q) = \arg\max_E P(Q \mid E)P(E) \\ &\approx \arg\max_E P(Q \mid E) = \arg\max_E \sum_F P(Q, F \mid E)\end{aligned} \tag{5.18}$$

here F is a hidden alignment from the words in Q to the fields in E – F_i represents the field that the word w_i in the query was generated from. While $P(E)$ can be modeled with the music popularity statistics, an uniform distribution was used in Equation (5.18) instead. $P(Q, F \mid E)$ is a distribution that is specific to the entry E, which is modeled by an HMM:

$$P(Q, F \mid E) \approx \prod_{i=1}^{n} P(w_i \mid F_i; E)P(F_i \mid F_{i-1}; E) \tag{5.19}$$

Unlike the HMMs used by BBN for information retrieval, the HMMs here do not need any training data. The emission probabilities for a field are estimated with the database content of the field:

$$P(w \mid F, E) = \lambda_f P_{MLE}(w \mid F, E) + \lambda_e P_{MLE}(w \mid E) + \lambda_c P_{MLE}(w) \tag{5.20}$$

where $\lambda_f + \lambda_e + \lambda_c = 1$. In other words, the emission probability is the linear interpolation of the maximum likelihood estimate of the field-dependent unigram, the entry-dependent unigram and the entry-independent background unigram probability. While the interpolation weights can be set using the held-out data, it is found that the search performance is not very sensitive to these values as long as none of the weights is set too close to 0.

The transition probability is assigned as follows to penalize frequent field jumping:

$$P(F_i \mid F_{i-1}; E) = \begin{cases} \gamma & \text{if } F_i = F_{i-1} \\ (1-\gamma) \times P(F_i \mid E) & \text{otherwise} \end{cases} \tag{5.21}$$

where γ is a parameter related to the likelihood that a query will stay at the same field to continue providing information about the field of a structured entry. A large value for the parameter will effectively avoid frequent field jumping – a tendency to switch to a different field to maximize the emission probability of a query word. Its value can be tuned with a held-out set. $P(F \mid E)$ is the field popularity probability, which is the field prior probability $P(F)$ normalized according to the existence of the fields in the database for the entry E:

$$P(F = x \mid E) = \begin{cases} \frac{P(F=x)}{1.0 - \sum_{\forall y \notin E} P(F=y)} & \text{if } x \in E \\ 0 & \text{otherwise} \end{cases} \tag{5.22}$$

where $P(E)$ can be either a uniform distribution or a distribution determined based on the domain knowledge about the popularity of the fields in users' queries.

In Song *et al.* (2009), it has been shown that the HMM sequential model has reduced the end-to-end search error rate by 28% relatively on the text queries and up to 23% relatively on the spoken queries compared with the baseline system that used a language model IR on the database with the contents of different fields collapsed into a single bag of words. In addition, the paper introduced a phonetic similarity based error model for the HMM emissions to model

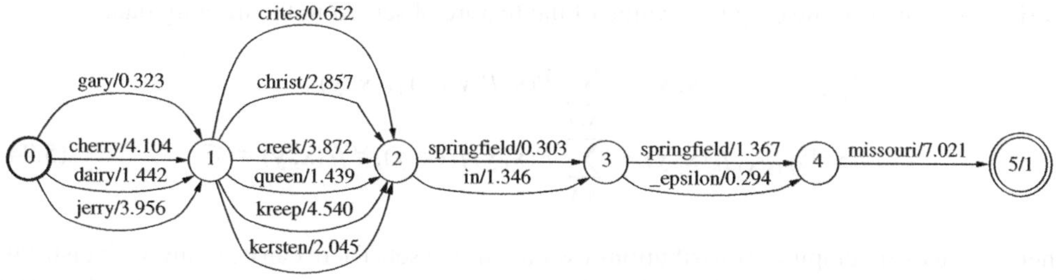

Figure 5.6 A word confusion network is a compact representation of recognition lattice that lists a set of words for each position (Feng and Gilbert, © 2009 ISCA)

the ASR errors, which further improved the end-to-end search accuracy consistently across different levels of speech recognition accuracy.

5.2.2.3 Robustness to Speech Recognition Errors

To improve the robustness to ASR errors, Wang *et al.* (2008) used character n-gram unigrams/bigrams instead of word unigrams/bigrams as terms in the vector space model. The rationale is that the acoustically confusable words may have shared sub-word units orthographically. For example, the listing "Lime Wire" is rewritten as a sequence of character 4-grams – $Lim Lime ime_ me_W e_Wi _Wir Wire ire$, where "$" indicates the start and the end of the listing and "_" indicates separation of words. If a caller's query "Lime Wire" is incorrectly recognized as "Dime Wired". Although there is no word overlapping , there are still many common n-grams between the ASR output and the intended listing.

Feng *et al.* (2009) used the listing information to select an ASR path in the word confusion network, a compact representation of the recognition lattice. Figure 5.6 shows an example of the word confusion network, where each position in an utterance is associated with a set of confusable words along with their negative log posterior probabilities obtained from the speech recognizer. Although the one-best path from the network, "Gary Crites Springfield Missouri," has the listing names "Dairy Queen" misrecognized as "Gary Crites," The correct information is buried in the word confusion network. The knowledge from listing in the semantic space can help unearth the correct recognition – "Dairy Queen" is more like to be a valid listing name than "Gary Crites."

Feng *et al.* (2009) segment the 1-best ASR to find the search term, get the alternative phrases s of the search term in the confusion networks, and rescore them with the subject likelihood:

$$P(s) = P_{WCN}(s)P_{subject}(s)^{\lambda}, \tag{5.23}$$

where $P_{WCN}(s) = \prod_{w \in s} P_{wcn}(w)$ is the posterior probability of the segment s according to the word confusion network, $P_{subject}(s)$ has been introduced earlier for subjects/constraints separation.

Similar idea was investigated with a flat direct model for speech recognition in Heigold *et al.* (2009). It is a Maximum Entropy (MaxEnt) model used to rescore the n-best search results. MaxEnt is a conditional model $P(\mathbf{y} \mid \mathbf{x})$ defined with respect to a set of features $\mathcal{F} = \{f_k(\mathbf{x}, \mathbf{y})\}$, with the constraints that the expected value of a feature predicted according to the conditional distribution equals to the empirical value of the feature observed in the training data:

$$\begin{aligned}\mathbb{E}_{\tilde{P}(\mathbf{x})P(\mathbf{y}\mid\mathbf{x})} f_k(\mathbf{x},\mathbf{y}) &= \sum_{\mathbf{x},\mathbf{y}} \tilde{P}(\mathbf{x})P(\mathbf{y}\mid\mathbf{x}) f_k(\mathbf{x},\mathbf{y}) \\ &= \mathbb{E}_{\tilde{P}(\mathbf{x},\mathbf{y})} f_k(\mathbf{x},\mathbf{y}) = \sum_{\mathbf{x},\mathbf{y}} \tilde{P}(\mathbf{x},\mathbf{y}) f_k(\mathbf{x},\mathbf{y}), \forall f_k(\mathbf{x},\mathbf{y}) \in \mathcal{F}\end{aligned} \tag{5.24}$$

where $\tilde{P}$ stands for empirical distributions over a training set. There can be many such distributions $P(\mathbf{y} \mid \mathbf{x})$ that satisfy Equation (5.24). The maximum entropy principle states that the target distribution should have the maximum entropy subject to the condition of Equation (5.24). In other words, the model should make no assumptions other than the expected feature values according to the empirical distribution from the training data.

It has been proven that the maximum entropy distribution subject to the condition of Equation (5.24) have the following exponential (log-linear) form (Berger *et al.*, 1996):

$$P(\mathbf{y} \mid \mathbf{x}; \Lambda) = \frac{1}{Z(\mathbf{x}; \Lambda)} \exp\left\{\sum_k \lambda_k f_k(\mathbf{y}, \mathbf{x})\right\} \tag{5.25}$$

As in the CRFs, $\Lambda = \{\lambda_k\}$ is a set of parameters. The value of λ_k determines the impact of the feature $f_k(\mathbf{y}, \mathbf{x})$ on the conditional probability, and can be estimated with the numerical algorithms by maximizing the conditional probability of the training data $\sum_{\mathbf{x},\mathbf{y}} P(\mathbf{y} \mid \mathbf{x}; \Lambda)$. $Z(\mathbf{x}; \Lambda) = \sum_{\mathbf{y}} \exp\left\{\sum_k \lambda_k f_k(\mathbf{y}, \mathbf{x})\right\}$ in Equation (5.25) is a partition function that normalizes the distribution. The difference between MaxEnt and the CRFs lies in the form of the label **y**. In the CRFs, **y** is a sequence of random variables that may be interdependent, while in the MaxEnt model, **y** is a single random variable, which makes the model simpler in terms of learning and inference.

Heigold *et al.* (2009) used a rich set of features extracted from the candidate listing **y** and from the speech input **x**, where **x** was consisted of not only the MFCC features but also the n-best results from the recognizer. The feature set included character and/or word n-grams, the posterior probability of word n-grams spotted in **x** with a dynamic time warping (DTW) algorithm, etc. It was found that the direct flat model had reduced the error rate of a HMM recognition baseline from 17.4% to around 13%.

5.2.3 *Dialogue Management*

Figure 5.7 shows the common dialogue strategy in voice search applications. The dialogue starts with prompting a user for the category information about the item they are looking for, in order to narrow down the downstream LM and search spaces. The category can be the locality information in a DA system (Bacchiani *et al.*, 2008; Yu *et al.*, 2007); the business/product separation (national business, local business or product) in a voice rating system (Zweig *et al.*, 2007), or a "search-by" attribute of the music meta-data (e.g. title, album, genre, artist, etc) in a music search dialogue system (Mann *et al.*, 2007). A category-specific LM is subsequently used to recognize the user's query containing the listing information, and the search component looks for the listing in a category-specific database. If multiple listings are found, a disambiguation sub-dialogue is engaged; otherwise the dialogue system either directly sends the user the listing information or asks for user's confirmation if the confidence score is low. As the technology

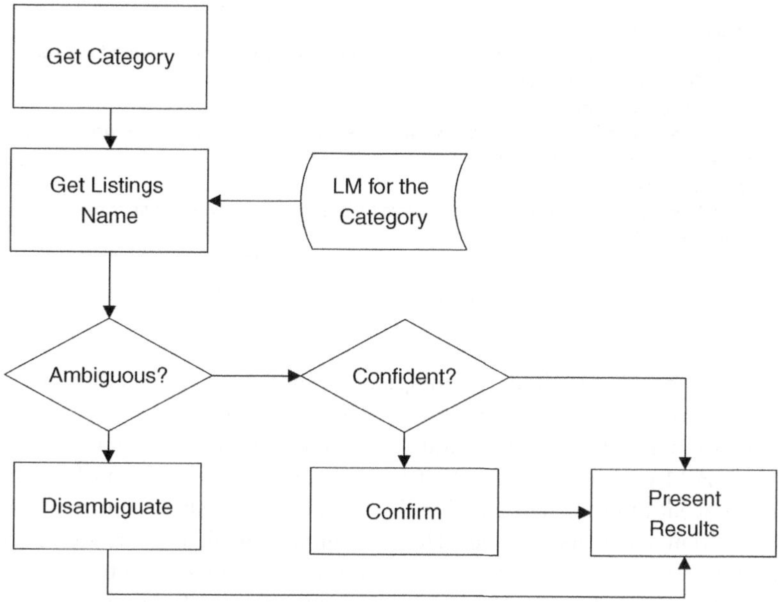

Figure 5.7 A typical dialogue flow of a voice search application (Wang *et al.*, © 2008 IEEE)

advances, it becomes more common for many voice search applications to skip the first "Get Category" step, resulting in a more natural user experience.

Many voice search applications adopt some task-specific dialogue strategies. For example, based on the finding that the accuracy on spelled names is much higher than that on spoken names, the residential DA in Schramm *et al.* (2000) exploited a multi-stage dialogue strategy to improve the accuracy of proper name recognition. A listing was identified by first recognizing its spelling from a caller. The spelling word graph greatly reduced the listing space for the subsequent recognition of names and addresses.

5.2.3.1 Disambiguation

Most voice search dialogue systems adopt an application-specific disambiguation strategy. In residential DA, people with the same name are disambiguated with their addresses (Schramm *et al.*, 2000). In business DA, business categories are used for disambiguation (Yu *et al.*, 2007) – from the set of businesses returned by the search component, a list of possible categories is compiled. For example, the query "*Calabria*" results in multiple search results, "Calabria Ristorante Italiano" in category "**Restaurants**", "*Calabria Jack J Do*" in "**Doctors and Clinics**" and "Calabria Electric" in "**Electric Contractors**." These categories are read to the user for selection. All the matching listing names in the selected category are subsequently read to the user, until one is selected or the list is exhausted. Similar disambiguation strategy is used in a multi-modal voice search application (Mann *et al.*, 2007), where multiple music titles are displayed in a graphical user interface (GUI) for users' selection when they belong to the same category, otherwise a list of different categories is displayed first for disambiguation. The GUI allows users to scan the information visually, which makes the multi-modal interaction more effective.

User: *Tell me about restaurants in London.*
System: *I know of 596 restaurants in London. All price ranges are represented. Some of the cuisine options are Italian, British, European, and French.*
User: *I'm interested in Chinese food.*
System: *I know of 27 restaurants in London that serve Chinese cuisine. All price ranges are represented. Some are near the Leicester square tube station.*
User: *How about a cheap one?*
System: *I know of 14 inexpensive restaurants that serve Chinese cuisine. Some are near the Leicester Square tube station. Some are in Soho.*

Figure 5.8 Search result summarization and disambiguation (Wang *et al.*, © 2008 IEEE)

One problem of the hard-wired disambiguation strategy is its inefficiency with long category/entry lists in a speech only interface. It has been suggested that spoken dialogue strategies such as summaries are a verbal equivalent of the visual scanning behavior that makes GUIs effective (Polifroni and Walker, 2006). Hence, summarization can be applied when the search component returns a large ambiguity set. Figure 5.8 shows an exemplar dialogue taken from (Polifroni and Walker, 2006). Here the ambiguous listings are summarized along common attributes such as price ranges and cuisines, which guide the users to provide the most effective information for disambiguation. In contrast to the hard-wired disambiguation strategy, the attributes were selected automatically by using a decision theoretic user model and using the association rules derived from the database subset in the dialogue focus (Polifroni and Walker, 2006).

Although this summarization/disambiguation strategy was introduced in Polifroni and Walker (2006) for a frame-based spoken dialogue system, it has been adopted by voice search dialogue systems such as the one described in Zweig *et al.* (2007).

5.2.3.2 Confidence Measure

Confidence measures are used to determine what to do with the search results for a spoken query. The results will be presented to callers when the confidences are high, otherwise a confirmation/disambiguation sub-dialogue will be invoked. Confidence measures are also used to determine when to elevate an automated service conversation to a live agent in an early dialogue stage if the confidence on the key information (e.g. an individual's last name in a residential DA system) is too low (Schramm *et al.*, 2000).

ASR-only confidence measures were used in many early residential DA systems because search was not a significant source of uncertainty. A well-studied confidence measure is the word or sentence posterior probability that can be calculated from an ASR lattice, which was shown to be more effective than some other heuristics (Wessel *et al.*, 2001). A sentence posterior probability obtained from an n-best list was used in (Schramm *et al.*, 2000) for DA. Another confidence measure originally proposed for utterance verification (Lee, 1997) was applied in Béchet *et al.* (2000). It was based on hypothesis testing that leads to a measure of likelihood ratio.

In late voice search applications where statistical search is applied for robustness, confidence measures that take into account of uncertainties from different system components are more adequate. BBN's DA system applied a Generalized Linear Model classifier to compute the confidence scores from a set of features extracted from spoken queries and listings Natarajan *et al.* (2002). The feature set included word confidences, ASR n-best frequency, etc. Among them, the two most important features were the required and allowable word sets. Much like the signatures used in IBM's language model for voice search, the required word set for a listing is a set of word tuples, at least one of which must be present in a recognized query in order to associate the listing to the query. The allowable word set is a list of words that are allowable in a query to be associated with the listing.

A confidence model based on a maximum entropy classifier was introduced for the Microsoft Research's experimental business DA system (Wang *et al.*, 2007). Unlike the required and allowable set features in Natarajan *et al.* (2002), it takes into consideration the importance of words in a listing with the features based on the automatically acquired Idf statistics of the words. The classifier takes multiple features drawn from the ASR, the search component and the dialogue-manager, and the combined features extracted from multiple components. For example, the *search-related features* for a hypothesized listing L and a recognized query Q include the VSM similarity between L and Q; the ratio between the maximum Idf value among the words existing in both L and Q and the maximum Idf value among all the words in L. The *combined features* attempt to model the dependency among features across the different components of voice search system. One such feature is the ASR confidence on the word that also exists in L and has the highest Idf value, i.e. the ASR confidence on the word that contributes the most to the search result. The effectiveness of the features were studied with statistical significance tests, which gave rise to several application-independent features for confidence measures in the general voice search framework.

5.2.4 Closing the Feedback Loop

Every spoken dialogue system needs to be tuned, often through multiple iterations, to improve its performance. This involves a painstaking process of error analysis from logged data. An automatic or semi-automatic tuning tool is one of the most wanted items by many dialogue experts. Due to the difficulty of the problem, little work has been done on automatic remedy for design/implementation flaws in the feedback loop. Most research work focused on automatic flaw discovery from the logged data.

In Popovici *et al.* (2002), an unsupervised learning algorithm was proposed to obtain the linguistic variants of listings that were not modeled in Telecom Italia's DA system. A phone-loop model was exploited to obtain the phonetic transcriptions for the utterances that failed the automated service and got routed to the operators. The phonetic transcriptions were clustered with a furthest neighbor hierarchical clustering algorithm, where two clusters with the shortest distance were merged in iterative steps. The distance between any two clusters was defined as the furthest distance between the two instance phonetic transcriptions in the clusters, and the distance between two phonetic transcriptions was obtained with the Viterbi alignment using the log-probability for phone insertion, deletion and substitution, where the probabilities were trained using a set of field data by aligning each decoded phonetic sequence with its corresponding manual transcription. A cluster in the hierarchy was selected according to the following criteria – the number of instances in the cluster must exceed a threshold and the dispersion of the cluster must be smaller than another threshold. The central element of a selected cluster was presented to a spoken dialogue expert as a candidate variant of a business listing.

A similar algorithm was proposed in Li *et al.* (2005) to discover the semantic intents that were not covered by an auto-attendant spoken dialogue system deployed in Microsoft (Ollason *et al.*, 2004). The system was originally designed to connect a caller to a Microsoft employee with name dialing. It was later found that, in addition to name dialing an employee, callers often ask for connections to an office, such as "*security*" or "*shuttle service.*" To discover these uncovered intents, a language-model-based acoustic clustering algorithm was proposed. Unlike the algorithm in Popovici *et al.* (2002) that clusters the 1-best phonetic transcriptions, it treats the *word* transcription and the cluster they belong to as hidden variables, and optimizes the parameters associated with them with respect to an objective function. Specifically, given a fixed number of clusters, it builds a cluster-specific language model $P(w \mid c)$ and a cluster prior model $P(c)$ to maximize $P(x) = \sum_{c,w} P(x, w, c) = \sum_{c,w} P(x \mid w) P(w \mid c) P(c)$, the likelihood of the observed acoustic signal x. In practice, recognition was decoupled from cluster training – a task independent large vocabulary ASR was used to obtain the hypotheses w and their posterior probabilities $P(w \mid x)$. Since w and c are hidden variables, the Expectation-Maximization (EM) algorithm was used to estimate the probability $P(c)$ and $P(w \mid c)$ by maximizing the objective function. Here the EM algorithm took as input the hypotheses w and $P(w \mid x)$ obtained from the task-independent ASR. In Li *et al.* (2005), unigram language models were used for $P(w \mid c)$. With these cluster-specific distributions, a KL-divergence based distance measure was used in hierarchical clustering. The EM algorithm was subsequently applied for several iterations to re-estimate the model parameters after merging two clusters. The cluster priors obtained from the EM algorithm was used to rank the clusters for presentation to spoken dialogue experts.

5.3 Summary

This chapter reviews the problem of voice search, which is one of the most actively investigated technologies underlying many practical applications. We have compared voice search with other spoken language understanding technologies for human/computer interaction, discussed the challenges in developing voice search applications, and reviewed some important research work targeting at these problems. As in other SLU applications, robustness is the central issue in voice search. The technology in acoustic modeling aims at improved the robustness to environment noise, different channel conditions and speaker variance; the pronunciation research addresses the problem of unseen word pronunciation and pronunciation variance; the language model research focuses on linguistic variance; the studies in SLU/search give rise to the improved robustness to linguistic variance and ASR errors; the dialogue management research enables graceful recovery from the confusions and understanding errors; and the learning in the feedback loop speeds up the system tuning for more robust performance.

While tremendous achievements have been accomplished in the past decade on voice search, big challenges remain. Many voice search dialogue systems have automation rates around or below 50% in field trials. This provides a fertile ground and great opportunities for future research.

References

Acero A, Chambers R, Ju YC, Li X, Odell J, Nguyen P, Schölz O and Zweig G 2008 Live search for mobile: Web services by voice on the cellphone. *Proceedings of the IEEE International Conference on Acoustics, Speech, and Signal Processing*. IEEE, Las Vegas, Nevada, USA.

Andreani G, Fabbrizio GD, Gilbert M, Gillick D, Hakkani-Tür D and Lemon O 2006 LetâŁ™s DiSCoH: Collecting an annotated open corpus with dialogue acts and reward signals for natural language helpdesk. *Proceedings of the IEEE/ACL Workshop on Spoken Language Technology*, pp 218–221, Aruba.

Bacchiani M, Beaufays F, Schalkwyk J, Schuster M and Strope B 2008 Deploying GOOG-411: Early lessons in data, measurement, and testing. *Proceedings of the IEEE International Conference on Acoustics, Speech, and Signal Processing*, pp 5260–5263.

Béchet F, de Mori R and Subsol G 2002 Dynamic generation of proper name pronunciations for directory assistance. *Proceedings of the IEEE International Conference on Acoustics, Speech, and Signal Processing*. IEEE.

Béchet F, Os Ed, Boves L and Sienel J 2000 Introduction to the IST-HLT project speech driven multimodal automatic directory assistance (SMADA) . *Proceedings of the 6th International Conference on Spoken Language Processing*, pp 731–734, Beijing, China.

Berger AL, Della Pietra SA and Della Pietra VJ 1996 A maximum entropy approach to natural language processing.. *Computational Linguistics* **22**(1), 39–72.

Billi R, Cainavesio F and Rullent C 1998 Automation of Telecom Italia directory assistance service: fieldtrial results. *Proceedings of the 4th IEEE Workshop on Interactive Voice Technology for Telecommunications Applications*.

Bohus D, Puerto SG, Huggins-Daines D, Keri V, Krishna G, Kumar R, Raux A and Tomko S 2007 ConQuest – an open-source dialogue system for conferences. *Proceedings of the Human Language Technology Conference and the Conference of North American Chapter of the Association for Computational Linguistics*, pp 9–12.

Buntschuh B, Kamm C, Fabbrizio GD, A. Abella MM, Narayanan S, Zeljkovic I, Sharp RD, Wright J, Marcus S, Shaffer J, Duncan R and Wilpon JG 1998 VPQ: A spoken language interface to large scale directory information. *Proceedings of the International Conference on Spoken Language Processing*, pp 2863–2866, Sydney Australia.

Feng J, Banglore S and Gilbert M 2009 Role of natural language understanding in voice local search. *Proceedings of INTERSPEECH*.

Gao Y, Ramabhadran B, Chen J, Erdogan H and Picheny M 2001 Innovative approaches for large vocabulary name recognition. *Proceedings of IEEE International Conference on Acoustics, Speech, and Signal Processing*, vol. 1, pp 53–56.

Greengrass E 2001 *Information Retrieval: A Survey*.

Heigold G, Zweig G, Li X and Nguyen P 2009 A flat direct model for speech recognition. *Proceedings of the IEEE International Conference on Acoustics, Speech, and Signal Processing*, pp 3861–3864, Taipei, Taiwan.

Jan E, Maison B, Mangu L and Zweig G 2003 Automatic construction of unique signatures and confusable sets for natural language directory assistance applications. *Proceedings of the Eurospeech Conference*, pp 1249–1252.

Kamm CA, Shamieh CR and Singhal S 1995 Speech recognition issues for directory assistance applications.. *Speech Communication* **17**(3–4), 303–311.

Lee CH 1997 A unified statistical hypothesis testing approach to speaker verification and verbal information verification. *Proceedings of COST 250*, pp 63–72, Rhodes, Greece.

Lennig M, Bielby G and Massicotte J 1994 Directory assistance automation in Bell Canada: trial results. *Proceedings of the 2nd IEEE Workshop on Interactive Voice Technology for Telecommunications Applications (IVTTA94)*, pp 9–13. IEEE.

Li X, Gunawardana A and Acero A 2005 Unsupervised semantic intent discovery from call log acoustics. *Proceedings of the IEEE International Conference on Acoustics, Speech, and Signal Processing*, pp 45–48, Philadelphia, PA, USA.

Li X, Ju YC, Zweig G and Acero A 2008 Language modeling for voice search: a machine translation approach. *Proceedings of the IEEE International Conference on Acoustics, Speech, and Signal Processing*, Las Vegas, Nevada, USA.

Mann S, Berton A and Ehrlich U 2007 How to access audio files of large data bases using in-car speech dialogue systems. *Proceedings of INTERSPEECH*, pp 138–141, Antwerp, Belgium.

Natarajan P, Prasad R, Schwartz RM and Makhoul J 2002 A scalable architecture for directory assistance automation. *Proceedings of the IEEE International Conference on Acoustics, Speech, and Signal Processing*, vol. 1, pp I–21– I–24.

Ollason D, Ju YC, Bhatia S, Herron D and Liu J 2004 MS Connect: A fully featured auto-attendant: System design, implementation and performance . *Proceedings of the International Conference on Spoken Language Processing*, pp 2845–2848, Jeju, Korea.

Polifroni J and Walker M 2006 An analysis of automatic content selection algorithms for spoken dialogue system summaries. *Proceedings of the IEEE/ACL Workshop on Spoken Language Technology*, Aruba.

Popovici C, Andorno M, Laface P, Fissore L, Nigra M and Vair C 2002 Learning new user formulations in automatic directory assistance. *Proceedings of the IEEE International Conference on Acoustics, Speech, and Signal Processing*, vol. 1, pp I–17– I–20.

Ramabhadran B, Bahl LR, deSouza P and Padmanabhan M 1998 Acoustics-only based automatic phonetic baseform generation. *Proceedings of the IEEE International Conference on Acoustics, Speech, and Signal Processing*, vol. 1, pp 309–312.

Robertson S, Zaragoza H and Taylor M 2004 Simple bm25 extension to multiple weighted fields *Proceedings of the 13th ACM International Conference on Information and Knowledge Management*, pp 42–49. ACM, New York, NY, USA.

Schramm H, Rueber B and Kellner A 2000 Strategies for name recognition in automatic directory assistance systems.. *Speech Communication* **31**(4), 329–338.

Song YI, Wang YY, Ju YC, Seltzer M, Tashev I and Acero A 2009 Voice search of structured media data. *Proceedings of the IEEE International Conference on Acoustics, Speech, and Signal Processing*, Taipei, Taiwan.

Vertanen K and Kristensson PO 2009 Recognition and correction of voice web search queries. *Proceedings of INTERSPEECH*, pp 1863–1866.

Wang YY, Yu D, Ju YC and Acero A 2008 An introduction to voice search.. *IEEE Signal Processing Magazine* **25**(3), 29–38.

Wang YY, Yu D, Ju YC, Zweig G and Acero A 2007 Confidence measures for voice search applications. *Proceedings of INTERSPEECH*, pp 2721–2724, Antwerp, Belgium.

Wessel F, Schlüter R, Macherey K and Ney H 2001 Confidence measures for large vocabulary continuous speech recognition.. *IEEE Transaction on Speech and Audio Processing*.

Yu D, Ju YC, Wang YY and Acero A 2006 N-gram based filler model for robust grammar authoring. *Proceedings of the IEEE International Conference on Acoustics, Speech, and Signal Processing*, pp 1565–1568, Toulouse, France.

Yu D, Ju YC, Wang YY, Zweig G and Acero A 2007 Automated directory assistance system - from theory to practice. *Proceedings of INTERSPEECH*, pp 2709–2712, Antwerp, Belgium.

Zweig G, Ju YC, Nguyen P, Yu D, Wang YY and Acero A 2007 Voice-rate: a dialogue system for consumer ratings. *Proceedings of NAACL/HLT (Demonstration)*, pp 31–32. Association for Computational Linguistics, Rochester, New York, USA.

6

Spoken Question Answering

Sophie Rosset[1], Olivier Galibert[1,2] and Lori Lamel[1]
[1] *CNRS-LIMSI, France*
[2] *LNE, France*

This chapter covers Question-Answering (QA) from spoken documents (referred to as QAst), but also beyond, where questions are also spoken. After a general introduction, Section 6.2 presents some specific aspects that must be considered when handling speech data for question answering. Then, Section 6.3 presents the main evaluation campaigns that have been carried out in the question-answering domain, the majority of which have addressed only written language. To the best of our knowledge, to date there has only been one evaluation for spoken QA. However, since the general problematics are the same, we believe it important to also present the larger view including written QA. The important considerations of QA evaluations are presented, followed by a detailed presentation of the QAst campaigns. Section 6.4 describes and compares different approaches and systems for QA, with a focus on approaches used for spoken language. This is followed by a review of recent projects or work addressing spoken QA. The chapter concludes with a discussion and some perspectives.

6.1 Introduction

Question-Answering systems can be seen as an extension of the Information Retrieval (IR) engines 15 which allow a user to search for information using a set of keywords. The result of the search is a set of documents, or links to documents, which the user needs to peruse to find the precise information wanted. In contrast, the question answering (QA) task consists of providing short, relevant answers to natural language questions which can be textual or spoken. Optionally the task can require the system to also return a document or document snippet supporting or even justifying the answer. Figure 6.1 illustrates the difference between IR and QA, which can be summarize by the following two points: First, the input is a natural-language question rather a keyword query; and second, the answer provides the desired information content and not simply a potentially large set of documents or URLs that the user must plow through. Progress

Spoken Language Understanding: Systems for Extracting Semantic Information from Speech, First Edition.
Edited by Gokhan Tur and Renato De Mori.

Information Retrieval
User query: building Eiffel Tower
System answers:
  Document link: Building of the Eiffel Tower
  Document snippet: Every metallic part of the Eiffel Tower is riveted...

  Document link: Eiffel Tower - Wikipedia
  Document snippet: Go to the *Tower building* (link to another page)
  ...

Question Answering
User query: When was the Eiffel Tower built?
System answer: 1887 - 1889
Document snippet: Built between 1887 and 1889 and followed by its inauguration at the universal exposition of 1889 in Paris, the Eiffel Tower nowadays symbolizes...

Figure 6.1 Looking to know the period when the Eiffel Tower was constructed

in the QA domain can be observed via evaluation campaigns held since 1999 (Dang *et al.*, 2007; Forner *et al.*, 2008; Mitamura *et al.*, 2008; Voorhees and Tice, 1999).

Spoken question-answering is a new challenge for question-answering systems which generally deal with (well-formed) textual data and well-formed written questions. Spoken question-answering implies doing the search in spoken data and/or from spoken questions. This is a departure from much of the QA research carried out by natural-language groups, who have typically developed techniques for written texts that are assumed to have a correct syntactic and semantic structure. The structure of spoken language is different from that of written language, and some of the anchor points used in processing such as punctuation must be inferred and are therefore error-prone. It is also necessary to deal with spoken-language phenomena including disfluencies, repetitions, restarts, and corrections. If automatic processing is used to create the speech transcripts, an additional challenge is dealing with the recognition errors. When dealing with speech data the response can be a short string, as is the case for text-based QA, or a brief audio segment containing the response.

A specific track – Question-Answering on Speech Transcripts (QAst) – has been proposed for now three years (2007, 2008 and 2009) in the Cross Language Evaluation Forum (CLEF) campaigns (Turmo *et al.*, 2007a, 2008, 2009).

Question-answering in *spoken data* collections means that the answer has to be found in the audio data. These data can be of various types: broadcast news, meetings, seminars, etc. The difficulty is quite dependent on the kind of data: broadcast news data are principally comprised of prepared speech and are quite similar to news texts; meetings and seminars contain spontaneous, interactive speech with a number of oral phenomena such as speech repairs, hesitations, etc, typical of this speaking style. Moreover, in real-use cases, spoken data are only accessible after having been processed by automatic speech recognizer (ASR) which means that the input to the QA engine is almost always an imperfect transcription of what was said. It is also well known that ASR performance is dependent on the task. These factors increase the difficulty of the QA task.

Question-answering is not only a matter of the kind of data in which the answer has to be found, but also of the way the question is formulated. The input to spoken question-answering can be a written or a *spoken question* (which may or may not be interactive). Spoken questions are not necessary well formed, at least not in the sense of written questions, with the syntax of oral language being quite different, in particular for questions, from that of written language. Of course, if the input is spoken, then there is also the need for automatic speech recognition, and the possibility that errors are introduced in the question (either by the user or the system).

A important question when working on (spoken) question-answering concerns the need of an understanding process. Why is understanding needed for question-answering? First of all, to find a precise answer to a precise question requires understanding the question. This means that the system has to understand what kind of answer is expected, which in turn means understanding the important elements of the question. Moreover, it is also necessary to understand the documents in which the answer has to be found (answer extraction). An important consideration is that the same information can be formulated in many different ways, which must be taken into account when searching for an answer. In conclusion, question-answering requires working with a semantic level representation of both documents and questions.

6.2 Specific Aspects of Handling Speech in QA Systems

In this section, we present and illustrate the specific aspects of handling speech in QA systems, which entails working on two levels. The first level is developing or adapting methods, algorithms and tools to be efficient on transcribed speech. The second level is enhancing these approaches to handle, or at least be robust to, errors produced by automatic speech recognition systems.

Multiple aspects differ when working with spoken rather than with written language. First, transcribed speech is structurally different from written texts. At the surface level one can notice the lack of punctuation and of clearly delimited frontiers between chunks, in particular numbers which are typically written out as words. For instance in *by trial two thousand five hundred twenty tests had failed* is the topic 20 tests, 120 tests, 520 tests, 2520 tests, or even a date followed by a number of tests? A human transcriber could add a comma to disambiguate this text or reconstruct the numbers in digits, but even humans can make an incorrect interpretation. Prosody may help in disambiguating such sentences, but current automatic speech recognition systems do not provide information at that level. Studies, for example Liu *et al.* (2006), have addressed the use of prosodic information for the annotation (and handling) of disfluencies and sentence boundaries. Although widely acknowledged to be useful for a human reader (Jones *et al.*, 2003) and often required for downstream processing (Lee *et al.*, 2006), one of the reasons that ASR systems do not usually produce a punctuated output is that attempts to evaluate automatic punctuation have been inconclusive (Gauvain, 2006). Another example illustrating the importance of punctuation is *the release of Christian Chesnot and Georges Malbrunot the prime minister nevertheless condemned ....* In this example, without the structural clues that would usually be present in a written text, it is hard to decide without world knowledge whether *Georges Malbrunot* should be attached with *Christian Chesnot* to *release*, or whether he should be associated with *prime minister*.

Manual transcript: one of the captives is from the Philippines one is from Kosovo and one Annetta Flanigan is from my constituency of Northern Ireland .

ASR A: one of the captives from the Philippines from possible on one another fun against from my constituency of Northern Ireland
ASR B: one of the capitals from the for the previous ones from possible and one another for elegance from my constituency of Northern Ireland
ASR C: ONE OF THE CAPTIVES FROM_THE FROM_THE PLAINS WARMS FROM POSSIBLE ON ONE ANOTHER FUN AGAIN THIS FROM MY CONSTITUENCY OF NORTHERN IRELAND

Figure 6.2 Examples of specificities of spoken language and automatic speech recognition outputs

Lack of punctuation can also be problematic when extracting passages, since a large number of QA systems rely on the concept of a sentence and define passages as individual sentences. Without specific tokens delimiting sentences, such approaches are no longer viable. Another aspect is the deep structure of the word sequence. The syntax of speech is different than for written text, even if there are many commonalities. In particular the structuration is more local and dependencies generally link chunks which are closer in speech than in text (Miller and Weinert, 1998).

Finally, the last aspect, and one not to be neglected, is that handling speech usually means handling the output of automatic speech recognition systems, along with their errors. When using the word error rate (WER) [1] to evaluate an ASR system, a mistake on a proper noun is considered as important as an incorrect pronoun-reference agreement. However, when using the ASR output as the input to another task such as QA, some errors are critical and others not important.

Figure 6.2 presents some example problems that can be encountered in ASR system outputs. We first notice that the system *ASR_C* does not provide true casing, which may complicate the task of Named Entity recognition. Comparing all ASR transcripts to the reference, it can be seen that the named entity *Kosovo* is not recognized by any of the systems, which makes it difficult – if not impossible – to answer the question *Which country are the prisoners from?*. The system *ASR_B* did not recognize the word *captives*, selecting the word *capitals* instead. Without that key element which matches the word *prisoners* part of the question, it is unlikely to find an answer in this passage.

As will be seen further in Section 6.4 these problems have been studied and taken into account by the participants to the QAst evaluation campaigns (Turmo *et al.*, 2007a, 2008, 2009).

6.3 QA Evaluation Campaigns

This section gives an overview of the main question-answering evaluation campaigns, most of which were part of the TREC or CLEF benchmarks, and for the most part have focused on written language.

[1] It has been reported that the overall word error rate is closely correlated with the error rate of named entities (Kubala *et al.*, 1998), and the WER has remained the metric used to assess ASR system performance.

6.3.1 General Presentation

Evaluations in the field of Question-Answering started with the Text REtrieval Conference (TREC) benchmarks, organized by the National Institute of Standards and Technology (NIST). The first QA task was introduced in 1999 (Voorhees and Tice, 1999) and were subsequently organized annually until 2008 when TREC became TAC (Text Analysis Conference) with different objectives. In Europe, the Cross-Language Evaluation Forum (CLEF) was created in 2000 and introduced QA as one of the tasks in 2003 (Magnini *et al.*, 2003). On the Asian front, NII Test Collection for IR systems (NTCIR) was created in 1999 with QA making a first appearance there in 2002 (Fukumoto *et al.*, 2002). These three evaluation frameworks can be considered the most influential in the field. Of these evaluation campaigns, only one addressed the issue of QA and speech. QAst, one of the QA-related tracks of CLEF, proposed an evaluation with spoken documents and written questions from 2007 to 2009, adding spoken questions in 2009.

Table 6.1 shows some of the characteristics which have an impact on what needs to be done to answer questions. The top block of this table focuses on question type; the second block concerns the data collection and the last one concerns miscellaneous aspects.

Some of these characteristics are common between QAst and other QA evaluations, and are the focus of the following discussion. The characteristics that are specific to the QAst evaluation are fully described in Section 6.3.1.3.

6.3.1.1 Question Types

When working on question-answering, the first question to answer is *what kind of questions should the system be able to answer?* For different question types, different algorithms are often used.

The simplest and most frequent question type is a factual question. These questions are questions for which the answer can be a single word or a multi-word expression, often is a named entity. An example question is: *Who is the French president?* These kinds of questions are present in all QA evaluation campaigns.

There have been attempts to move from factual questions to so-called 'list' questions. These are factual questions for which the answer is a list of elements. In this category, two kinds of questions can be distinguished. Closed-list questions give the number of expected elements (*which are the three press companies that were subject to judgment by the Supreme Court?*. Open-list questions give no information about how many elements are expected (*what are the ingredients of Creme Anglaise?*. List questions have never been part of the QAst evaluation campaigns.

The second type of questions are "definition" ones for which two categories can be distinguished. For a general definition question, any kind of answer (named entity or not, simple word, phrase, complete sentence, etc.) is possible. The second category is one in which only simplified definition questions have been proposed, as in Vallin *et al.* (2005). These include questions of the type *who is Barack Obama?* and the answer can be a simple word, a multi-word expression or a named entity. This last category was present in TREC 2000 and 2001, in QA@CLEF 2004-2008 and in all QAst evaluation campaigns.

More complex question types also exist, such as *how*, *why* and *yes/no* questions. These questions are considered *complex* because the answer is not a word or a simple expression. For

Table 6.1 Table summarizing the main characteristics of the principal QA evaluations

	TREC									QA@Clef Main Track							QAst			NTCIR				
	1999	2000	2001	2002	2003	2004	2005	2006	2007	2003	2004	2005	2006	2007	2008	2009	2007	2008	2009	2002	2004	2005	2007	2008
Factual	•	•	•	•	•	•	•	•	•	•	•	•	•	•	•	•	•	•	•	•	•	•	•	•
Simple definition		•	•								•	•	•	•	•							•		
Definitions					•													•					•	•
Why																							•	
How											•											•		
Yes/no																								
Open lists					•	•	•	•	•				•	•	•					•		•	•	•
Closed lists			◇	◇									•	•	•					•		•	•	
Follow-up			◇				•	•	•					•	•					•	◇	•		
Topics						•	•	•	•															
Information						•	•	•	•															
Spoken questions																			•					
Newspapers	•	•	•	•	•	•	•	•	•	•	•	•	•	•	•					•	•	•	•	•
Speech																	•	•	•					
Law																•								
Wikipedia														•	•									
Blogs									•															
Question class given					•	•	•	•	•											•	•			
Multiple answers	•	•	•							•			•				•	•	•	•	•	•	•	•
Long answers	•	•	•							•	•													
Justification												•	•	•	•									
Translingual										•	•	•	•	•	•	•						◇	◇	•
Parallel docs.																•								
Temporal restriction												•	•	•	•									
Timecodes																		•	•					

◇: external task Sources:

- TREC: (Dang *et al.* 2006, 2007; Voorhees 2000, 2002, 2003, 2004; Voorhees and Dang 2005; Voorhees and Tice 1999, 2001).
- QA@Clef Main Track: (Forner *et al.* 2008; Giampiccolo *et al.* 2007; Magnini *et al.* 2003, 2004, 2006; Peas *et al.* 2008; Vallin *et al.* 2005).
- QA@Clef QAst: (Turmo *et al.* 2007a, 2008, 2009).
- NTCIR: (Fukumoto *et al.* 2002, 2004, 2007; Kato *et al.* 2004, 2005; Mitamura *et al.* 2008; Sasaki *et al.* 2005, 2007).

example, an answer to the question *How do dolphins get caught in driftnets?* could be *though intended to catch fish, the nets indiscriminately catch virtually all aquatic life including fish, whales, dolphins, sea turtles, and sea birds*. The *why* question *Why do college students eat poorly?* could answered by the following excerpt: *Stress, irregular schedules, parties, and the freedom to eat French fries smothered in cheese sauce*. In a similar vein, while yes–no questions can be answered with a simple word (yes or no), this is usually not considered satisfactory. For instance, a better answer to the question *Was Rosa Parks an African American?* would be a wikipedia citation such as *Rosa Louise McCauley Parks was an African American civil rights activist ...* rather than a simple *yes*.

In order to mimic interactivity, follow-up questions have been experimented with some evaluations (cf. Giampiccolo *et al.*, 2007; Kato *et al.*, 2005; Voorhees and Dang, 2005). The idea was to measure how well systems could handle anaphora resolution. An alternative, proposed by (Voorhees, 2004), introduced a set of questions linked to a topic. None of these complex questions were used in the QAst evaluation campaigns.

The 2009 QAst evaluation proposed natural, spontaneously spoken questions. It is the only evaluation which proposed such question types in an open domain. A more detailed discussion of these questions is presented in the Section 6.3.1.3.

6.3.1.2 Document Types

Another important aspect of the question-answering evaluation is the collection of data in which the search has to be carried out. Of the different campaigns, only the QAst evaluation explicitly worked with spoken data. Most of the QA evaluation campaigns use data collections of newspaper documents. The corresponding spoken data are broadcast news documents which were used in some QAst evaluations. These documents have various advantages in the QA sense: first, they are relatively well formatted and clearly written (for broadcast news these contain primarily prepared speech); there is a lot of factual information and a fair amount of redundancy. Some evaluation campaigns included Wikipedia data in their data collections. The quantity of information is much bigger in Wikipedia than in typical two-year collections of newspaper documents, but the redundancy is a lot less. Other specific domain data collections have occasionally been used, for example, the JRC-Acquis in the QA@CLEF 2009 (see Peas *et al.*, 2008).

The QAst evaluations have been organized with the objective of specifically working with spoken documents as further described next.

6.3.1.3 Spoken Documents and Spoken Questions

Two different aspects have been investigated in the QAst evaluation campaigns: question-answering in spoken data and question-answering from spoken questions (in spoken data). The data collections used in the different editions of this evaluation campaign are described in Section 6.3.2, along with the different kinds of questions that have been proposed.

6.3.1.4 Metrics

There are several metrics typically used to evaluate question-answering systems. The simplest one is the *accuracy*, that is the ratio between the number of correct answers and the number of questions. When systems are allowed to return multiple answers, only the first one is taken into account when determining the accuracy. Letting CA_i be the rank of the first correct answer for the question i, defaulting to $+\infty$ if no answer was found:

$$\text{accuracy} = \frac{\#\text{CA}_i = 1}{\#\text{questions}} \tag{6.1}$$

Stopping at the first answer is somewhat limiting. A direct extension is the *top-n* accuracy, which takes into account correct answers between ranks 1 and n:

$$\textit{top-n} = \frac{\#\text{CA}_i \leq n}{\#\text{questions}} \tag{6.2}$$

In practice, in addition to $n = 1$ which is also referred to as the "raw" accuracy, *top-n* tends to be used with n equal to the maximum number of answers the systems are allowed to return. This use turns the *top-n* measure into a kind of *recall*.

The system is required to put the most probable answers at the top of the list. To measure the quality of that classification, the *Mean Reciprocal Rank* (MRR) is often used. The first correct answer gives a score for the question equal to the inverse of its rank. The lack of a correct answer is equivalent to an infinite rank and hence a score equal to zero. The final score is the arithmetic mean of the individual question scores:

$$\text{MRR} = \frac{\sum \frac{1}{\text{CA}_i}}{\#\text{questions}} \tag{6.3}$$

Accuracy, MRR and *top-n* taken together are a triplet of values which give an idea of the quality of a system and its evolution potential. They are also useful to compare results between multiple versions of the same system. These three metrics were used in the QAst campaigns. Other metrics exist to handle other question types such as lists or extra information such as confidence levels, but they were not pertinent for the QAst campaigns.

6.3.2 Question Answering on Speech Transcripts: Evaluation Campaigns

The Question-Answering on Speech Transcripts evaluation campaign (QAst) was created in 2007 to investigate the problem of question-answering on speech data (Turmo *et al.*, 2007b).

The data for the QAst evaluation campaigns was derived from five different resources listed below, covering spontaneous speech, semi-spontaneous speech and prepared speech. Data from the first two corpora (CHIL, AMI) were used in the 2007 and 2008 editions (Turmo *et al.*, 2007a, 2008). Data from the other corpora were used in the 2008 and 2009 editions (Turmo *et al.*, 2009).

- The **CHIL corpus**:[2] The corpus contains about 25 hours of speech, mostly spoken by non-native speakers of English, with an estimated ASR WER of 20%.
- The **AMI corpus**:[3] This corpus contains about 100 hours of speech, with an ASR WER of about 38%.
- French broadcast news: The test portion of the **ESTER corpus** (Galliano *et al.*, 2006) contains 10 hours of broadcast news in French, recorded from different sources (France Inter, Radio France International, Radio Classique, France Culture, Radio Television du Maroc). There are three different automatic speech recognition outputs with different error rates (WER = 11.0, 23.9 and 35.4%). The manual reference transcriptions were produced by the Evaluations and Language resources Distribution Agency (ELDA).
- Spanish parliament: The **TC-STAR05 EPPS Spanish corpus** (TC-Star, 2004-2008) is comprised of three hours of recordings from the European Parliament in Spanish. The data was used to evaluate recognition systems developed in the TC-STAR project. There are three different automatic speech recognition outputs with different word error rates (11.5, 12.7 and 13.7%). The manual reference transcriptions were produced by ELDA.

[2] http://chil.server.de
[3] http://www.amiproject.org

- English parliament: The **TC-STAR05 EPPS English corpus** (TC-Star, 2004-2008) contains three hours of recordings from the European Parliament in English. The data was used to evaluate speech recognizers in the TC-STAR project. There are three different automatic speech recognition outputs with different word error rates (10.6, 14 and 24.1%). The manual reference transcriptions were produced by ELDA.

The spoken data cover a broad range of types, both in terms of content and in speaking style. The Broadcast News and European Parliament data are less spontaneous and less interactive than the lecture and meeting speech, typically being prepared in advance, and as such are closer in structure to written texts. While meetings and lectures are representative of *spontaneous speech*, Broadcast News and European Parliament sessions are usually referred to as *prepared speech*. Although they typically have few interruptions and turn-taking problems when compared with meeting data, many of the characteristics of spoken language are still present (hesitations, breath noises, speech errors, false starts, mispronunciations and corrections). One of the reasons for including the prepared speech data was to be closer to the textual data used to assess written QA, and to benefit from the availability of multiple speech recognizers that had been developed for these languages and tasks in the context of European or national projects (Galliano *et al.*, 2006; TC-Star, 2004-2008).

6.3.2.1 Questions and Answer Types

Two kinds of questions were considered: *factual questions* and *definition questions*. To the first question type, the expected answer of the search is a Named Entity. The definition questions are questions such as *What is the Vlaams Blok?* and the answer can be anything. In this example, given the data collection (see Figure 6.3), the answer could be *a criminal organization*. The definition questions can be further subdivided into the following types:

- **Person:** question about someone
  Q: *Who is George Bush?*
  R: *The President of the United States of America.*
- **Organization:** question about an organization
  Q: *What is Cortes?*
  R: *Parliament of Spain.*
- **Object:** question about any kind of objects
  Q: *What is F-15?*
  R: *Combat aircraft.*
- **Other:** questions about technology, natural phenomena, etc.
  Q: *What is the name of the system created by AT&T?*
  R: *The How can I help you system.*

An answer was given as an `(answer string, document id)` pair, where the answer string contains nothing more than the full and exact answer, and the document id is a unique identifier of the document supporting the answer.

For the tasks using automatic speech transcripts, the answer string specified the `<start-time>` and the `<end-time>` of the answer in the signal. Figure 6.3 illustrates this point comparing the expected answer to the question *What is the Vlaams Blok?* in a manual transcript

Question: *What is the Vlaams Blok?*

Manual transcript: *the Belgian Supreme Court has upheld a previous ruling that declares the Vlaams Blok a criminal organization and effectively bans it .*
Answer: *criminal organization*

Extracted portion of an **automatic transcript (CTM file format):**
(...)
20041115_1705_1735_EN_SAT 1 1018.408 0.440 Vlaams 0.9779
20041115_1705_1735_EN_SAT 1 1018.848 0.300 Blok 0.8305
20041115_1705_1735_EN_SAT 1 1019.168 0.060 a 0.4176
20041115_1705_1735_EN_SAT 1 **1019.228** 0.470 criminal 0.9131
20041115_1705_1735_EN_SAT 1 **1019.858 0.840** organization 0.5847
20041115_1705_1735_EN_SAT 1 1020.938 0.100 and 0.9747
(...)
Answer: 1019.228 1020.698

Figure 6.3 Example query *What is the Vlaams Blok?* and response from manual (top) and automatic (bottom) transcripts. The CTM file format is *document id, channel number, temporal position, duration, word* and *confidence score*

(the text *criminal organization*) and in an automatic transcript (the time segment *1019.228 1020.698*).

6.4 Question-answering systems

6.4.1 General Overview

Question-answering systems are generally organized as shown in Figure 6.4. They usually start by preprocessing documents prior to indexing them. This preprocessing stage can be separated into two parts. The first part, which does not always exist, is a form of language analysis which attempts to extract some structured information from the documents. This analysis can be relatively simple, for example determining only the levels of Parts-of-Speech and Named Entities (e.g. Comas *et al.*, 2007; Molla *et al.*, 2006, 2007). These relatively simple levels of analysis are particularly relevant for the Question-Answering on Speech Transcripts task, as reported in (Turmo *et al.*, 2007a, 2008), probably because of the difficulty of adapting more complex analyses, such as syntactic analysis, to speech. In the case of processing clean texts, the analysis may try to reach deeper levels through syntactic and even semantic analysis (Hickl *et al.*, 2006; Laurent *et al.*, 2006; Neumann and Wang, 2007).

The second part of the document preprocessing concerns reformatting prior to indexation. Systems designers often do not want to work with whole, raw documents as the indexation unit, so it is common to split the documents into smaller units. Sentences can be a preferred unit, or small blocks of them (Laurent *et al.*, 2006). In the speech case, sentence-like blocks can be built (Krsten *et al.*, 2008).

Indexation for subsequent retrieval is then done by a search engine. A very popular choice is LUCENE (Apache, 2007), an open-source search engine currently developed by the Apache

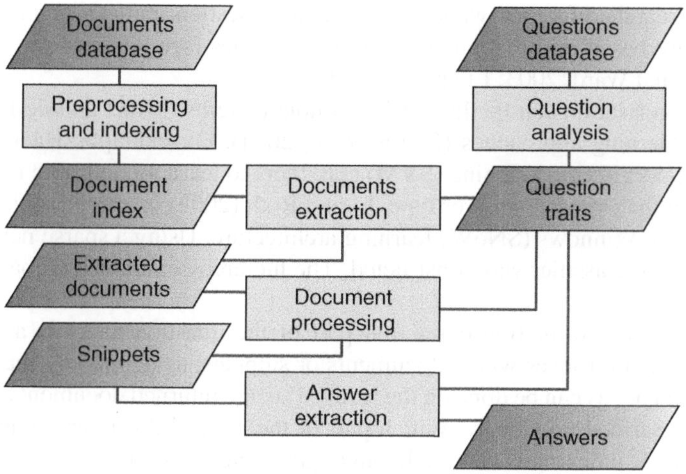

Figure 6.4 Overview of typical QA system architecture (Inspired by Ligozat, 2006)

foundation (Comas *et al.*, 2007; Neumann and Wang, 2007). Managing Gigabytes (MG) is also used, for instance by (Grau *et al.*, 2005), but since development has stopped its popularity has been declining. A number of systems use their own indexation and retrieval engines (Rosset *et al.*, 2008), in particular those who do linguistic analysis in the preprocessing and want to be able to search in the results; (Laurent *et al.*, 2006) with its deep analysis and associated specialized indexing is a good example.

In the specific case of speech, where the speech recognition engine may generates a transcription with errors, two systems (Turmo *et al.*, 2008, 2009) tried to use a phonemic based search. The underlying assumption is that the speech recognition engine errors can derail the question answering process if they occur on critical keywords (proper names for instance) but that the phonetic transcription of the erroneous words is not far from the true content of the audio signal. This approach was promoted by Clements *et al.* (2001) to locate information in audio archives. For Q&A Comas and Turmo (2008a) used a specific retrieval engine, PHAST (PHonetic Alignment Search Tool), to retrieve near sequences of phones built for the question keywords in the documents using a similarity measure. This approach called *Keyword Spotting* in the speech retrieval domain.

Once retrieval is ready to run, the work turns towards the questions. The question analysis aims at handling two problems: the first is to detect which information in the question has to be found in the documents. This information often takes the form of keywords and named entities, but sometimes is a syntactic or semantic relation. This first analysis is usually very close to what is done for document analysis, in order to be able to compare the information found in questions and documents, a necessity for the following extraction steps. The second problem is to predict what type of answer to the question is expected (Pardio *et al.*, 2008). The answer type is usually a named entity category (person, location...), but can be more specific or have a broader coverage when more advanced taxonomies are used. This process is often called *question classification* or *expected answer type detection*. Question classification is an important task, allowing unrelated documents to be filtered out or applying specific handling for snippet or answer extraction. Question classification allow predicting what kind of precise answer is to be searched for, and what constraints the question imposes on possible answers. Most systems are based on predefined question categories (see for example, Amaral *et al.*, 2005; Hacioglu and Ward, 2003; Li and Roth, 2002).

Question categorization can be done using simple patterns (Monz and de Rijke, 2001) or using machine learning approaches (Ferres *et al.*, 2004). For example, Hacioglu and Ward (2003) used Support Vector Machine (SVM) classifiers to learn models able to classify questions and predict the expected answer type. Li and Roth (2002) used a classifier based on the Sparse Network of Winnows (SNoW) learning architecture. Using a sparse network of linear units, a hierarchical classifier was constructed. The hierarchy contained 6 coarse classes and 50 fine-grained classes.

The results of the information extraction part of the question analysis are given to the search engine which retrieves whole documents or snippets, as defined by the indexation. A complementary analysis can be done on the results (i.e. the returned documents), similar to the preprocessing described previously. Which part of the general document analysis should be done before or after indexing is essentially an engineering question, balancing preprocessing time, response time, indexing complexities and scaling issues. In any case, the final step is to extract candidate answers from these analyzed snippets and rank them. In most of the cases, candidates answers are chosen as words or phrases annotated with the expected type for the answers. A score is given to each of them which can be based on answer-keyword distance (Pardio *et al.*, 2008), density (Comas and Turmo, 2008a; Gillard *et al.*, 2006), or even syntactic similarities and dependency relations (Bouma *et al.*, 2005). The system then ranks the answers according to the scores.

This very general structure covers most of the linguistically motivated approaches to question answering. Some alternative methodologies exist, which rely on a minimal or even no linguistic knowledge. Berger *et al.* (2000) for instance uses statistical models based on co-occurrence measurements. Ittycheriah and Roukos (2002) added two enhancements to this approach. First, a snippet selection method based on IBM Model1 translation models, considering pertinent justification snippets as "translations" of the question and using the estimated translation probability as a snippet sentence pertinence score. Second, a set of automatically extracted answer patterns is proposed to improve over the co-occurrence measurements. Whittaker *et al.* (2007) applied similar approaches in the QAst 2007 evaluation.

The evaluation campaigns show that the best performing systems are usually based on a deep linguistic analysis. The LCC system (Moldovan *et al.*, 2002) is a good example of such a system. In the 2005 TREC evaluation, this system obtained the best results with 71% correct answers on factual questions. In comparison, the fully stochastic Tokyo Institute system (Whittaker *et al.*, 2005), obtained only 21% correct answers in the same evaluation (Voorhees and Dang, 2005).

6.4.2 *Approaches Used in the QAst Campaigns*

Most of the systems participating in the QAst evaluations used a standard architecture. The main differences concern the way speech data (transcriptions) was dealt with. There are several aspects where question answering can be adapted to spoken language.

The difficulties of transcribed speech can be handled at two different steps in the system: when analyzing the documents or when matching documents and questions. In other words, specific treatment can be carried out at indexation time or at information retrieval time. In the first case, the aim is to take into account the structural specificities of speech. In the second, the issue is more about handling and compensating for speech recognition errors.

In the following sections we describe the adaptation for handling speech that has been done at the different stages of question-answering systems in the QAst evaluations: question and document processing, and information retrieval. The answer extraction and ranking did not require specific adaptation. Three participants proposed adaptations to deal with speech: the Universitat Politecnica de Catalunya (UPC), the Instituto Nacional de Astrofisica, Optica y Electronica (INAOE) and the Laboratoire d'Informatique pour la Mécanique et les Sciences de l'Ingénieur (LIMSI).

6.4.2.1 Question and Document Processing

Working on spoken data does not fundamentally change the way systems work, although some adaptations are required. First, not all text analysis approaches are robust on transcriptions of speech, and in particular on automatic speech recognition outputs. Second, alternative approaches can try to mitigate the impact of speech recognition errors.

Document processing can be adapted in different ways, from enrichment of the document representation to an adapted analysis. Analysis can concern both document and question processing, and usually takes the form of simple POS tagging and Named Entity detection. Most QAst systems only apply such an analysis to the documents and not to the questions. The LIMSI systems (Bernard *et al.*, 2009; Rosset *et al.*, 2007, 2008) and (Neumann and Wang, 2007) system are exceptions. All other systems try to classify the question in order to extract the answer type and to extract the keywords used for information retrieval (see for example, Comas *et al.*, 2007; Krsten *et al.*, 2008).

Neumann and Wang (2007) carried out a complete question analysis leveraging from the fact that the QAst 2007 questions were provided in a written form. Their question parser computes for each question a syntactic dependency tree which also contains the recognized named entities. This parser is the same one that is used for text-based question-answering. Based on this analysis, their system produces a list of expected answer types.

It can be observed that Named Entity detection plays a central role in question-answering systems, and in particular in the QAst systems. The task limits the acceptable answers to named entities of a fixed type set, making detection of these entities in the documents particularly valuable. Neumann and Wang (2007) explored the use of different existing Named Entity and POS taggers, POS tagging often being the first step for a NE tagger, and concluded that the models trained for written language are not very efficient on spoken language, and that linguistic annotated spoken data is needed.

To address this problem, the UPC team (Comas and Turmo, 2008a, 2009) used development data to train a specialized model for English. This approach gave good results (F-measure of 75) on a set-aside test portion of the AMI meeting development data but not for the CHIL lecture data with a F-measure of 33. For the latter, the outputs of different systems (the one trained on the development data, a model trained on ConLL English corpus[4] and a rule-based system) were merged. This combination did not improve the precision, but obtained better recall. The features used by the system and applied on manually transcribed documents are words, lem-

[4] http://cnts.ua.ac.be/conll2002/ner

mas, POS tags, word affixes, flags indicating the presence of numerals and capitalization, and n-grams of these features. Gazetteers were also applied to provide an additional set features.

These features are relatively standard in the community. UPC also developed specific models to deal with ASR outputs, by expanding the features used by the classifiers to include with phonetic attributes. The basic arguement for this is that with ASR the phonemic structure tends to be maintained, even if the word sequence is incorrect. For example, *Sun* can be misrecognized as *some* which while obviously an error is still phonemically similar. An unsupervised hierarchical clustering algorithm was used to group tokens based on the similarity of their phonetic features. The cluster of each token is added as a feature during training of the Named Entity recognition model. For the Spanish data, in 2008, a system was trained on the ConLL Spanish corpus. This system is not well suited to the QAst task because the corpus covers only three different types of named entities: *person, location* and *organization*). For the 2009 edition, the same strategy of system combination and specific models trained for ASR outputs was applied to develop a model for Spanish.

LIMSI (Bernard *et al.*, 2009; Rosset *et al.*, 2007, 2008; Toney *et al.*, 2008; van Schooten *et al.*, 2007) considers that the same analysis needs to be performed on questions and documents. Moreover, the team argues that because the speech transcriptions are the output of automatic speech recognizers they can benefit from some of the work already done when training ASR language models: words are clearly delimited, abbreviations are expanded which removes some of their inherent ambiguity, and uppercase, when present, is limited to proper nouns and acronyms. Ideally, the text at the entry of an analysis step would combine the advantages of both spoken and written text: words separated from the punctuation and from each other, uppercase only on proper nouns and acronyms, the presence of punctuation to allow splitting of sentences, etc. Therefore, a *normalized* form was defined which is the produced by the first stage of any of their systems, whether they apply to speech transcripts or to texts. This normalization stage includes the following processing steps:

1. Separating words and numbers from punctuation.
2. Reconstructing correct case for the words.
3. Adding punctuation.
4. Splitting document into sentences at period marks.

The first step relies on a series of algorithmic and regular-expression based transformations. Steps 2 and 3 are done simultaneously using a 4-gram language model trained on (reasonably) close written texts with punctuation and appropriate casing (on proper nouns and acronyms only) (Dchelotte *et al.*, 2007). A word graph containing all possible punctuation and casing hypotheses is generated and the most probable one is selected via the language model. The result of the normalization is passed to the analyzer, which uses a multi-level approach to detect and type phrases according to a hierarchical taxonomy. For the French language, the analyzer detects approximatively 300 different types, spanning not only classic named entities and several extensions, but also morphosyntaxic chunks and dialogue acts. The analyzers for English and Spanish are partial adaptations of the French one.

To specifically handle the automatic speech recognition errors, INAOE (Reyes-Barragan *et al.*, 2009), has proposed to enrich the request with a phonetic representation of the words in addition to traditional lemmas and other lexical derivatives. They used the Soundex (Odell and Russell, 1918) code to derive phonetic forms. Since this representation having is used for information retrieval, more details are provided in the the next section.

To summarize, the three approaches have been proposed to better handle spoken language. These can be used alone or in combination. The first one aims to adapt models designed for written text to speech transcripts. The second approach is to develop a common representation for documents independent of whether their origin is speech or text, and to build an appropriate analysis. The third one is to enrich the representation with a phonetic layer.

Document processing can involve another operations, for instance, often the documents are split in shorter units. Sentences can be the preferred unit or small blocks of sentences. In the speech case, sentence-like blocks can be automatically identified. (Krsten *et al.*, 2008) uses punctuation marks present in the manually transcribed documents. Neumann and Wang (2007) used the sentence splitter of the OpenNLP tool, based on maximum entropy modeling, to identify sentence boundaries using a standard language model optimized for written documents.

6.4.2.2 Information Retrieval

This step is one of the most important in a question-answering system. In the case of question-answering on speech transcripts, two original approaches have been proposed. The first one based on a phonetic codification was investigated by (Reyes-Barragan *et al.*, 2009). The second one was explored by (Comas *et al.*, 2007; Comas and Turmo, 2008a, 2009) who proposed and developed a specialized Information Retrieval engine relying on phone similarity.

6.4.2.3 Phonetic Codification

INAOE made use of the Soundex (Odell and Russell, 1918) system. Designed only for the English language, the algorithm is based on a *it place of articulation* phonetic classification of human speech sounds (bilabial, labiodental, dental, alveolar, velar and glottal). Every word is transformed into a code composed of a initial letter, the first of the word, followed by a series of digits representing classes of sounds. A complete description of the algorithm is available in Reyes-Barragan *et al.* (2009). The following example illustrates its use:

ASR output: I am starting to work I do not know what <NOM> Frank Sinatra </NOM> must have felt like as his fellow appearances decided on in the seventies

After elimination of stopwords: starting work <NOM> Frank Sinatra </NOM> felt like fellow appearances decided seventies

Phonetic codification: S36352 W62000 F65200 S53600 F43000 L20000 F40000 A16522 D23300 S15320

Enriched representation: starting work <NOM> Frank Sinatra </NOM> felt like fellow appearances decided seventies S36352 W62000 F65200 S53600 F43000 L20000 F40000 A16522 D23300 S15320

6.4.2.4 Phonetic Similarity

Alternatively, UPC (Comas and Turmo, 2008a, 2009; Comas *et al.*, 2007) proposed to handle the speech recognition errors in the information retrieval model. The authors built the *PHAST* IR engine which has the capability to handling errors using phone similarity measures. PHAST uses pattern-matching to find short phone sequences (the keywords in the requests) in large phone sequences (the documents), and sorts them using a similarity measure. This is

Table 6.2 Best and worst accuracy and MRR on spontaneous speech data for 2007 and 2008 evaluation campaign

	2007				2008			
	Acc.		MRR		Acc.		MRR	
	best	worst	best	worst	best	worst	best	worst
CHIL man.	51.0%	5.0%	0.53	0.09	41.0%	16.0%	0.45	0.16
CHIL ASR	36.0%	2.0%	0.37	0.05	31.0%	27.0%	0.34	0.30
AMI man.	25.0%	16.0%	0.21	0.06	33.0%	26.0%	0.40	0.29
AMI ASR	21.0%	6.0%	0.22	0.10	18.0%	14.0%	0.20	0.18

reminiscent of a traditional *word spotting* technique. The passage selection algorithm is then applied using the words found in that way by PHAST (Comas and Turmo, 2008b).

6.4.3 QAst Campaign Results

This section highlights the results of the QAst evaluation campaigns held from 2007-2009. As described in Section 6.3.2, two different kinds of speech data have been used in QAst evaluation campaigns: prepared speech and spontaneous speech. Moreover, in the 2009 QAst evaluation campaign, spoken questions have been introduced.

6.4.3.1 Speech Style

The spontaneous speech data used in the QAst 2007 and 2008 campaigns were:

- The **CHIL**[5] **corpus** with about 25 hours of speech, mostly from non-native speakers of English, with an estimated ASR Word Error Rate (WER) of 20%.
- The **AMI**[6] **corpus** containing about 100 hours of speech, with an ASR WER of about 38%.

Table 6.2 gives an overview of the results obtained by the participating systems in 2007 and 2008 on spontaneous speech. For each condition, the performance of the best and worst system are shown.

Three data sets comprised of (primarily) prepared speech were used in QAst 2008 and 2009 evaluations:

- **French broadcast news data:** containing about 10 hours of broadcast news in French.
- **Spanish EPPS data** comprised of three hours of recordings from the European Parliament in Spanish.
- **English EPPS data** consisting of 3 hours of recordings from the European Parliament in English.

For each data set automatic transcriptions from three different automatic speech recognition systems with different error rates were used.

[5] http://chil.server.de

[6] http://www.amiproject.org

Table 6.3 Best and worst accuracy and MRR on prepared speech data for 2008 and 2009 QAst evaluation campaigns

	2008				2009			
	Acc.		MRR		Acc.		MRR	
	best	worst	best	worst	best	worst	best	worst
EPPS-E man	34.0%	20.0%	0.42	0.21	28.0%	5.0%	0.36	0.08
EPPS-E asr_1	30.0%	7.0%	0.33	0.10	26.0%	3.0%	0.31	0.07
EPPS-E asr_2	20.0%	10.0%	0.24	0.12	21.0%	3.0%	0.25	0.06
EPPS-E asr_3	19.0%	10.0%	0.23	0.12	25.0%	5.0%	0.28	0.11
EPPS-S man	31.0%	7.0%	0.35	0.09	36.0%	14.0%	0.45	0.20
EPPS-S asr_1	24.0%	3.0%	0.26	0.04	27.0%	6.0%	0.32	0.07
EPPS-S asr_2	19.0%	4.0%	0.22	0.05	25.0%	7.0%	0.29	0.10
EPPS-S asr_3	23.0%	2.0%	0.25	0.02	23.0%	9.0%	0.28	0.11
BN-fr man	45.0%	42.0%	0.49	0.47	28.0%	27.0%	0.39	0.38
BN-fr asr_1	41.0%	-	0.45	-	29.0%	-	0.37	-
BN-fr asr_2	25.0%	-	0.30	-	27.0%	-	0.32	-
BN-fr asr_3	21.0%	-	0.24	-	23.0%	-	0.28	-

Table 6.3 gives an overview of the results obtained in the 2008 and 2009 evaluations on prepared speech, showing the best and worst results among the participating systems.

These two tables give an overview of the results obtained by multiple systems on a reasonably standard QA task which required searching in transcribed speech data. They also show the difference in performance when searching in error-free data (manual transcripts) and in data with ASR errors. Globally, the results are inferior to what the best systems obtain in clean textual data such as newswire and newspapers, for instance in the TREC (Voorhees, 2002; Voorhees and Tice, 2001) and QA@CLEF (Magnini *et al.*, 2006; Vallin *et al.*, 2005) evaluations. Although there is a clear loss of performance when switching from manual to automatic transcriptions, the speech type does not seem to be a significant factor in that loss. The results on the CHIL and AMI data are similar to those for the English European Parliament data.

6.4.3.2 Question Style

One of the aims of the 2009 QAst evaluation was to compare using spoken and written questions. Table 6.4 shows the results obtained on spoken *vs* written question on the manually transcribed data collections.

Table 6.4 Best and worst accuracy and MRR given the question style during the 2009 evaluation campaign

Data	Question types	Acc.		MRR	
		best	worst	best	worst
EPPS-E	written q.	28.0%	5.0%	0.36	0.08
EPPS-E	spoken q.	26.0%	3.0%	0.34	0.06
EPPS-S	written q.	36.0%	14.0%	0.45	0.20
EPPS-S	spoken q.	36.0%	17.0%	0.45	0.22
BN-fr	written q.	28.0%	27.0%	0.39	0.38
BN-fr	spoken q.	28.0%	28.0%	0.39	0.39

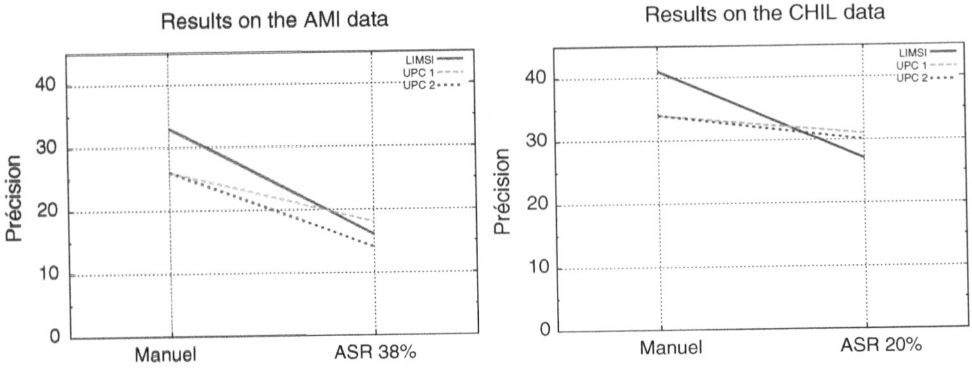

Figure 6.5 Results of the UPC and LIMSI systems on the CHIL and AMI tasks in 2008

It can be seen that there is almost no difference in the results with written or human transcripts of spoken questions. Looking more closely at all of individual system results and not only the best and worst ones (see Turmo *et al.*, 2009 for more information), five of the seven systems participating in the English task had a small loss of 2–5% when using transcripts of the spoken questions instead of written ones. The other two systems had a larger losses of 13 and 16%.

6.4.3.3 Discussion of Results and Approaches

Figures 6.5–6.7 show the results obtained by the INAOE, LIMSI, UPC systems in the QAst 2008 and 2009 evaluations. As previously described, these three systems are the ones which proposed specific approaches to handle question answering in speech data. Moreover, the best result was always obtained by one of the three in each task of these evaluations.

For the CHIL and AMI tasks (Figure 6.5) featuring spontaneous speech, the LIMSI system obtained the best results on manual transcriptions while UPC in the best on automatic transcriptions. For the EPPS and BN tasks which feature prepared speech, the INAOE English system achieved the highest precision level on the manual transcriptions with an identical *MRR* as the LIMSI system. When it comes to automatic transcriptions, the LIMSI gets the best results for

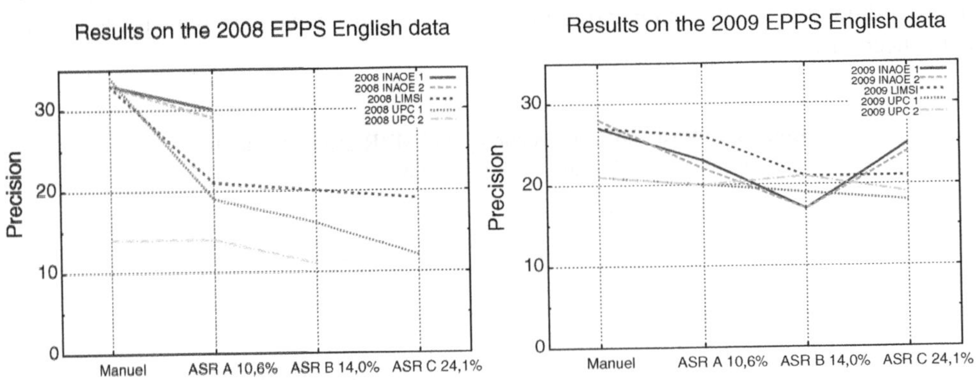

Figure 6.6 Results of the INAOE, LIMSI and UPC systems on the EPPS English task in 2008 and 2009

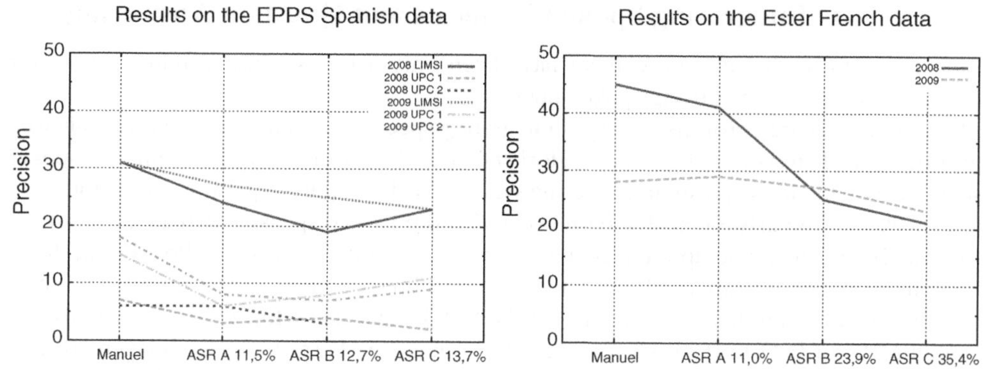

Figure 6.7 Results of the LIMSI and UPC systems on the EPPS Spanish and Ester French tasks in 2008 and 2009

transcripts with the lowest two error rates (10.6 and 14.0%). INAOE proposed an alternative, *multi-ASR* approach for the third error rate, using information extracted with their Named Entity Recogniser from all of the ASR outputs, while still considering the third ASR output as the primary one. While that method is realistic in applicative setup when multiple ASR systems are available, it precludes measuring the impact of ASR errors. For Spanish LIMSI achieves the best results on both manual and automatic transcriptions.

LIMSI was the only participant for the French Ester BN task, so it is difficult to conclude much about the results. The performance on this task is globally among the best for all tasks, but it is difficult to ascertain if the is due to the approaches, to better processing and analysis for the French language, experience with the task or simply the task difficulty.

What can we learn from these results? First, we see that normalizing the documents of different origins to a unique surface representation seems to be beneficial. The system using that approach obtains close to or the best results on the manual transcriptions, and seems to be somewhat robust on the automatic transcriptions given that nothing specific is done. We can see that doing something specific at the analysis level, such as training a named entity extractor on ASR outputs as UPC did, gives an undeniable advantage on lectures and meetings where speech recognition errors are numerous.

Enhancing the requests or the documents with phonetic-level information does not seem to result in better performance. INAOE, which experimented with such an approach using the Soundex code to add phonetic class attributes to documents and requests, did not measure any improvement using it (Reyes-Barragan *et al.*, 2009). Similarly, no matter the task or the language, the UPC system which did not use phonetic proximities for information retrieval ended up with better results than the one which did (Comas and Turmo, 2008a, 2009). Nevertheless, it is intuitive that explicitly handling speech recognition errors one way or another should improve the robustness of the QA systems when the answer needs to be found in automatically transcribed documents. The main issue is determining how. Unfortunately most of the methods tried thus far, especially the phonetically motivated ones, do not seem to enhance the results and even sometimes add noise, reducing performance.

6.5 Projects Integrating Spoken Requests and Question Answering

Compared with text-based Q&A, there have been only a few studies searching in spoken documents and even fewer using spoken queries.

Most of the research projects aiming at integrating speech recognition and question answering systems made use of read questions. Hori *et al.* (2003), for instance, developing on spoken and interactive Japanese question-answering system, used as input 69 questions read aloud by 7 male speakers. Similarly, Gonzalez-Ferreras *et al.* (2008) asked speakers to read the questions of CLEF 2005. Such a setup reduces the intrinsic variability of speech, allowing the focus to be on the difficulties arising from automatic speech recognition (ASR) errors. And these difficulties can be significant: the results of the SPIQA system ((Hori *et al.*, 2003)) dropped from an MRR of 0.43 to 0.25 when using ASR. (Gonzalez-Ferreras *et al.*, 2008) reported a similar effect with their results dropping from 30.5 to 23.0% when using an ASR systems with a WER of 15.2%.

Harabagiu *et al.* (2002) went further in their experiments. When they used read TREC-8 questions (30% WER for the ASR system) for their evaluations, the MRR dropped from 0.76 to 0.07. They then worked on the integration between Q&A and ASR and increased the MRR to 0.41 through a combination of filtering and language model selection, directed by knowledge dynamically extracted by the Q&A system. An additional gain of 0.07 was obtained if the system was allowed to ask the user for additional precisions and clarifications. This was the first step towards an interactive Q&A system.

van Schooten *et al.* (2007) went still further by being first an interactive spoken system and second a Q&A service. The system was built around a dialogue core with real-time ASR allowing spontaneous exchanges between a human and the computer. The system had to extract pertinent information to build a request, information which was often spread across multiple utterances. The request was then communicated to an open-domain Q&A system. One aim of the approach was to compensate for speech recognition errors via interaction by using an implicit confirmation request while running the Q&A system in parallel.

Although not strictly a QAst task, the distillation task, introduced in the GALE program (http://www.darpa.mil/ipto/programs/gale/gale_approach.asp) aims to use automated language technolgoies to extract relevant information in foreign language audio or text documents, and present it to users in English. Queries are specified in English and systems are to report relatant and non-redundant information, along with supporting documents (in English and in the source language). Different template types for queries were defined (in Phase 2 there were 17 different templates), and human references consist of nuggets of information extracted from snippets (Babko-Malaya, 2008; Babko-Malaya *et al.*, 2010). Performance is measured in terms of information content and document support.

Recently the Deep Q&A research project at IBM has received a lot of media attention, with the Watson system Jeopardy challenge, in which the computer will compete against some of the world's best Jeopardy! quiz show contestants. The game requires contestants to quickly respond to questions or clues, making fine distinctions of meaning and inferences about relationship between words and information content. While Watson can make use of massively parallel hardware and huge stores of information, it will not be connected to the Internet, thus needing to rely only on its memory and pre-coded logic. Although human contestants will respond to spoken questions, Watson will have typed ones, both to save time and avoid any potential ASR errors.

6.6 Conclusions

Spoken language question-answering is a newly emerging field, covering at the same time searching for answers in spoken documents and asking questions vocally. It builds upon over 20 years of research in speech recognition and spoken language processing, and a decade of in text-based Q&A. To date most research has addressed the first aspect, that is locating information in spoken documents, with less effort having been directed to using spoken queries. This latter aspect has been extensively addressed in spoken language understanding systems, typically for limited domains (travel or tourist information, for example). There are many potential applications of spoken Q&A technology for any tasks involving audio data mining or speech analytics. Speech recognition errors remain a problem, in particular if an error is made on an important word. Since the goal is to give a precise answer to a precise query, ASR errors may be more problematic for Q&A system than for IR ones, where a document may contain multiple instance of the information, one of which may be located. As speech recognition and search technologies improve, so will the potential for open-domain, interactive spoken Q&A systems. In additional to refining the search, natural interaction with a Q&A system can help improve speech recognition for voice queries by allowing the user to reformulate or clarify their questions.

References

Amaral C, Figueira H, Martins A, Mendes A, Mendes P and Pinto C 2005 Priberam's question answering system for Portuguese *Working Notes for the CLEF 2005 Workshop*, Vienna. Austria.

Apache 2007 Apache lucene, an overview http://lucene.apache.org/java/docs/.

Babko-Malaya O 2008 Annotation of nuggets and relevance in gale distillation evaluation In *Proceedings of the Sixth International Language Resources and Evaluation (LREC'08)* (ed. (ELRA) ELRA), Marrakech, Morocco.

Babko-Malaya O, Hunter D, Fournelle C and White J 2010 Evaluation of document citations in phase 2 gale distillation *Proceedings of the Seventh conference on International Language Resources and Evaluation (LREC'10)*. European Language Resources Association (ELRA), Valletta, Malta.

Berger A, Caruana R, Cohn D, Freitag D and Mittal V 2000 Bridging the lexical chasm: statistical approaches to answer-finding *Proceedings of the 23rd Annual Internation ACM SIGIR Conference on Research and Develomment in Information Retrieval*, Athens, Greece.

Bernard G, Rosset S, Galibert O, Bilinski E and Adda G 2009 The limsi participation to the qast 2009 track *Working Notes of CLEF 2009 Workshop*, Corfu, Greece.

Bouma G, Mur J, van Noord G, van der Plas L and Tiedemann J 2005 Question answering for dutch using dependency relations *Working Notes for the CLEF 2005 Workshop*, Vienna, Austria.

Clements M, Cardillo P and Miller M 2001 Phonetic searching vs large vocabulary continuous speech recognition: How to find what you really want in audio archives *Proceedings, Conference of Applied Voice Input/Output Society*, San Jose, CA.

Comas P, Turmo J and Surdeanu M 2007 Robust question answering for speech transcripts using minimal syntactic analysis *Working Notes for the CLEF 2007 Workshop*, Budapest, Hungary.

Comas P and Turmo J 2008a Robust question answering for speech transcripts: Upc experience in qast 2008 *Working Notes of CLEF 2008 Workshop*, Aarhus, Denmark.

Comas PR and Turmo J 2008b Spoken document retrieval based on approximated sequence alignment *TSD '08: Proceedings of the 11th International Conference on Text,Speech and Dialogue*, pp 285–292. Springer-Verlag.

Comas P and Turmo J 2009 Robust question answering for speech transcripts: Upc experience in qast 2009 *Working Notes of CLEF 2009 Workshop*, Corfu, Greece.

Dang HT, Lin J and Kelly D 2006 Overview of the trec 2006 question answering track *Text Retrieval Conference TREC-15*, pp. 99–116, Gaithersburg, MD, USA.

Dang HT, Lin J and Kelly D 2007 Overview of the trec 2007 question answering track *Text Retrieval Conference TREC-15*, Gaithersburg, MD, USA.

Dchelotte D, Schwenk H, Adda G and Gauvain JL 2007 Improved machine translation of speech-to-text outputs *Interspeech'07*, Antwerp, Belgium.

Ferres D, Kanaan S, Gonzales E, Ageno A, Rodriguez H, Surdeanu M and turmo J 2004 Talp-qa system at trec 2004: Structural and hierarchical relaxing of semantic constraints *Text Retrieval Conference TREC-13*, Gaithersburg, MD, USA.

Forner P, Peñas A, Alegria I, Forascu C, Moreau N, Osenova P, Prokopidis P, Rocha P, Sacaleanu B, Sutcliffe R and Sang ETK 2008 Overview of the clef 2008 multilingual question answering track *Working Notes for the CLEF 2008 Workshop*, Aarhus, Denmark.

Fukumoto J, Kato T and Masui F 2002 Question answering challenge (qac-1): Question answering evaluation at ntcir workshop 3 *Proceedings of the Third NTCIR Workshop on Research in Information Retrieval, Automatic Text Summarization and Question Answering*, Tokyo, Japan.

Fukumoto J, Kato T and Masui F 2004 Question answering challenge for five ranked answers and list answers - overview of ntcir4 qac2 subtask 1 and 2 *Proceedings of the Fourth NTCIR Workshop on Research in Information Access Technologies Information Retrieval, Question Answering and Summarization*, Tokyo, Japan.

Fukumoto J, Kato T, Masui F and Mori T 2007 An overview of the 4th question answering challenge (qac-4) at ntcir workshop 6 *Proceedings of the Sixth NTCIR Workshop Meeting on Evaluation of Information Access Technologies: Information Retrieval, Question Answering, and Cross-Lingual Information Access*, Tokyo, Japan.

Galliano S, Geoffrois E, Gravier G, Bonastre J, Mostefa D and Choukri K 2006 Corpus description of the ester evaluation campaign for the rich transcription of french broadcast news *Proceedings of LREC'06*, Genoa.

Gauvain J 2006 Overview of the ASR Evaluation *TC-STAR Workshop on Speech-to-Speech Translation*, Barcelona, Spain.

Giampiccolo D, Forner P, Peñas A, Ayache C, Cristea D, Jijkoun V, Osenova P, Rocha P, Sacaleanu B and Sutcliffe R 2007 Overview of the clef 2007 multilingual question answering track *Working Notes for the CLEF 2007 Workshop*, Budapest, Hungary.

Gillard L, Sitbon L, Blaudez E, Bellot P and El-Bèze M 2006 The lia at qa@clef-2006 *Working Notes for the CLEF 2006 Workshop*, Alicante, Spain.

Gonzalez-Ferreras C, Cardenoso-Payo V and Arnal ES 2008 Experiments in speech driven question-answering *Spoken Language Technology*.

Grau B, Ligozat AL, Robba I, Sialeu M and Vilnat A 2005 Term translation validation by retrieving bi-terms *Working Notes for the CLEF 2005 Workshop*, Vienna, Austria.

Hacioglu K and Ward W 2003 Question classification with support vector machines and error correcting codes *NAACL '03: Proceedings of the 2003 Conference of the North American Chapter of the Association for Computational Linguistics on Human Language Technology*, pp. 28–30. Association for Computational Linguistics, Morristown, NJ, USA.

Harabagiu SM, Moldovan DI and Picone J 2002 Open-domain voice-activated question answering *COLING*.

Hickl A, Williams J, Bensley J, Roberts K, Shi Y and Rink B 2006 Question answering with lcc's Chaucer at trec 2006 *The 15th TREC Conference (TREC 2006)*.

Hori C, Hori T, Tsukada H, Isozaki H, Sasaki Y and Maeda E 2003 Spoken interactive odqa system: Spiqa *The Companion Volume to the Proceedings of 41st Annual Meeting of the Association for Computational Linguistics*, pp. 153–156. Association for Computational Linguistics, Sapporo, Japan.

Ittycheriah A and Roukos S 2002 Ibm's statistical question-answering system - trec-11 *Proceedings of the TREC 2002 Conference*.

Jones D, Wolf F, Gibson E, Williams E, Fedorenko E, Reynolds D and Zissman M 2003 Measuring the Readability of Automatic Speech-to-Text Transcripts *Proceedings of Eurospeech'03*, pp. 1586–1588, Geneva, Switzerland.

Kato T, Fukumoto J and Masui F 2004 Question answering challenge for information access dialogue - overview of ntcir4 qac2 subtask 3 *Proceedings of the Fourth NTCIR Workshop on Research in Information Access Technologies Information Retrieval, Question Answering and Summarization*, Tokyo, Japan.

Kato T, Fukumoto J and Masui F 2005 An overview of ntcir-5 qac3 *Proceedings of the Fifth NTCIR Workshop Meeting on Evaluation of Information Access Technologies: Information Retrieval, Question Answering and Cross-Lingual Information Access*, Tokyo, Japan.

Krsten J, Kundisch H and Eibl M 2008 Qa extension for xtrieval: Contribution to the qast track *Working Notes of CLEF 2008 Workshop*, Aarhus, Denmark.

Kubala F, Schwartz R, Stone R and Weischedel R 1998 Named Entity Extraction from Speech *Proceedings of the DARPA Broadcast News Transcription and Understanding Workshop*, Lansdowne, Va.

Laurent D, Séguéla P and Nègre S 2006 Cross lingual question answering using qristal for clef 2006 *Working Notes for the CLEF 2006 Workshop*, Alicante, Spain.

Lee Y, Al-Onaizan Y, Papineni K and Roukos S 2006 IBM Spoken Language Translation System *TC-STAR Workshop on Speech-to-Speech Translation*, pp. 13–18, Barcelona, Spain.

Li X and Roth D 2002 Learning question classifiers *Proceedings of the 19th international conference on Computational linguistics*, pp. 1–7. Association for Computational Linguistics, Morristown, NJ, USA.

Ligozat AL 2006 *Exploitation et fusion de connaissances locales pour la recherche d'informations précises* PhD Thesis Université Paris-Sud 11 Orsay, France.

Liu Y, Shriberg E, Stolcke A, Hillard D, Ostendorf M and Harper M 2006 Enriching speech recognition with automatic detection of sentence boundaries and disfluencies. *IEEE Transactions on Audio, Speech, and Language Processing* **14**, 1526–1540.

Magnini B, Giampiccolo D, Forner P, Ayache C, Osenova P, Peñas A, Jijkoun V, Sacaleanu B, Rocha P and Sutcliffe R 2006 Overview of the clef 2006 multilingual question answering track *Working Notes for the CLEF 2006 Workshop*, Alicante, Spain.

Magnini B, Romagnoli S, Vallin A, Herrera J, Peñas A, Peinado V, Verdejo F and de Rijke M 2003 The multiple language question answering track at clef 2003 *Working Notes for the CLEF 2003 Workshop*, Trondheim, Norway.

Magnini B, Vallin A, Ayache C, Erbach G, Peñas A, de Rijke M, Rocha P, Simov K and Sutcliffe R 2004 Overview of the clef 2004 multilingual question answering track *Working Notes for the CLEF 2004 Workshop*, Bath, UK.

Miller J and Weinert R 1998 *Spontaneous Spoken Language. Syntax and Discourse.*

Mitamura T, Nyberg E, Shima H, Kato T, Mori T, Lin CY, Song R, Lin CJ, Sakai T, Ji D and Kando N 2008 Overview of the ntcir-7 aclia tasks: Advanced cross-lingual information access *Proceedings of the Seventh NTCIR Workshop Meeting on Evaluation of Information Access Technologies: Information Retrieval, Question Answering, and Cross-Lingual Information Access*, Tokyo, Japan.

Moldovan D, Harabagiu A, Girju R, Morarescu P, Lacatusu F, Novischi A, Badulescu A and Bolohan O 2002 Lcc tools for question answering *Proceedings of the 2002 Text Retrieval Conference.*

Molla D, Cassidy S and van Zaanen M 2007 Answerfinder at qast 2007: Named entity recognition for qa on speech transcripts *Working Notes for the CLEF 2007 Workshop*, Budapest, Hungary.

Molla D, van Zaanen M and Pizzato L 2006 Answerfinder at trec 2006 *The 15th TREC Conference (TREC 2006) Proceedings.*

Monz C and de Rijke M 2001 The university of amsterdam's textual question answering system *Text Retrieval Conference TREC-10*, Gaithersburg, MD, USA.

Neumann G and Wang R 2007 Dfki-lt at qast 2007: Adapting qa components to mine answers in speech transcripts *Working Notes for the CLEF 2007 Workshop*, Budapest, Hungary.

Odell M and Russell R 1918 Us patent numbers 1261167 (1918) and 1435663 (1922) U.S. Patent Office.

Pardio M, Gómez J, Llorens H, Muñoz-Terol R, Navarro-Colorado B, Saquete E, Martínez-Barco P, Moreda P and Palomar M 2008 Adapting ibqas to work with text transcriptions in qast task: Ibqast *Working Notes of CLEF 2008 Workshop*, Aarhus, Denmark.

Peas A, Forner P, Sutcliffe R, Rodrigo A, Forascu C, Alegria I, Giampiccolo D, Moreau N and Osenova P 2008 Overview of the respubliqa 2009: Question-answering evaluation over European legislation *Working Notes for the CLEF 2008 Workshop*, Aarhus, Denmark.

Reyes-Barragan A, Villasenor-Pineda L and y Gomez MM 2009 Inaoe at qast 2009: Evaluating the usefulness of a phonetic codification of transcriptions *Working Notes of CLEF 2009 Workshop*, Corfu, Greece.

Rosset S, Galibert O, Adda G and Bilinski E 2007 The limsi participation to the qast track *Working Notes for the CLEF 2007 Workshop*, Budapest, Hungary.

Rosset S, Galibert O, Bernard G, Bilinski E and Adda G 2008 The limsi participation to the qast track *Working Notes of CLEF 2008 Workshop*, Aarhus, Denmark.

Sasaki Y, Chen HH, hua Chen K and Lin CJ 2005 Overview of the ntcir-5 cross-lingual question answering task (clqa1) *Proceedings of the Fifth NTCIR Workshop Meeting on Evaluation of Information Access Technologies: Information Retrieval, Question Answering and Cross-Lingual Information Access*, Tokyo, Japan.

Sasaki Y, Lin CJ, hua Chen K and Chen HH 2007 Overview of the ntcir-6 cross-lingual question answering (clqa) task *Proceedings of the Sixth NTCIR Workshop Meeting on Evaluation of Information Access Technologies: Information Retrieval, Question Answering, and Cross-Lingual Information Access*, Tokyo, Japan.

TC-Star 2004-2008 http://www.tc-star.org.

Toney D, Rosset S, Max A, Galibert O and Bilinski E 2008 An evaluation of spoken and textual interaction in the ritel interactive question answering system In *Proceedings of the Sixth International Language Resources and Evaluation (LREC'08)* (ed. (ELRA) ELRA), Marrakech, Morocco.

Turmo J, Comas P, Ayache C, Mostefa D, Rosset S and Lamel L 2007a Overview of the qast 2007 *Working Notes for the CLEF 2007 Workshop*, Budapest, Hungary.

Turmo J, Comas P, Ayache C, Mostefa D, Rosset S and Lamel L 2007b Overview of the QAST 2007 *Working Notes for the CLEF 2007 Workshop*, Budapest, Hungary.

Turmo J, Comas P, Rosset S, Galibert O, Moreau N, Mostefa D, Rosso P and Buscaldi D 2009 Overview of qast 2009 *Working Notes for the CLEF 2009 Workshop*, Corfu, Greece.

Turmo J, Comas P, Rosset S, Lamel L, Moreau N and Mostefa D 2008 Overview of qast 2008 *Working Notes for the CLEF 2008 Workshop*, Aarhus, Denmark.

Vallin A, Giampiccolo D, Aunimo L, Ayache C, Osenova P, Peñas A, de Rijke M, Sacaleanu B, Santos D and Sutcliffe R 2005 Overview of the clef 2005 multilingual question answering track *Working Notes for the CLEF 2005 Workshop*, Vienna, Austria.

van Schooten B, Rosset S, Galibert O, Max A, op den Akker R and Illouz G 2007 Handling speech input in the ritel qa dialogue system *in InterSpeech'07*, Anvers, Belgique.

Voorhees EM 2000 Overview of the trec-9 question answering track *Text Retrieval Conference TREC-9*, pp. 71–80, Gaithersburg, MD, USA.

Voorhees EM 2002 Overview of the trec 2002 question answering track *Text Retrieval Conference TREC-11*, Gaithersburg, MD, USA.

Voorhees EM 2003 Overview of the trec 2003 question answering track *Text Retrieval Conference TREC-12*, pp. 54–68, Gaithersburg, MD, USA.

Voorhees EM 2004 Overview of the trec 2004 question answering track *Text Retrieval Conference TREC-13*, Gaithersburg, MD, USA.

Voorhees EM and Dang HT 2005 Overview of the trec 2005 question answering track *Text Retrieval Conference TREC-14*, Gaithersburg, MD, USA.

Voorhees EM and Tice DM 1999 The trec-8 question answering track report *Text Retrieval Conference TREC-8*, pp. 77–82, Gaithersburg, MD, USA.

Voorhees EM and Tice DM 2001 Overview of the trec 2001 question answering track *Text Retrieval Conference TREC-10*, pp. 42–51, Gaithersburg, MD, USA.

Whittaker E, Chatain P, Furui S and Klakow D 2005 Trec2005 question answering experiments at tokyo institute of technology *Proceedings of the 14th Text Retrieval Conference*.

Whittaker E, Novak J, Heie M and Furui S 2007 Clef2007 question answering experiments at tokyo institute of technology *Working Notes for the CLEF 2007 Workshop*, Budapest, Hungary.

7

SLU in Commercial and Research Spoken Dialogue Systems

David Suendermann and Roberto Pieraccini
Speechcycle, U.S.A.

Spoken language understanding plays a key role in every spoken dialogue system. This chapter shows how different SLU techniques are integrated into dialogue systems, focusing on the significant differences between research and commercial implementations. After speaking about how to make this integration robust against speech recognition glitches, we review example projects, architectures, and corpora associated with the application of SLU to spoken dialogue systems.

7.1 Why Spoken Dialogue Systems do not have to Understand

Spoken dialogue systems are probably among the most widely adopted applications of spoken language understanding. A spoken dialogue system is defined as an application where a machine communicates with humans using speech (De Mori, 1998; Minker and Bennacef, 2004). In its simplest form, a spoken dialogue system can be described by the functional diagram of Figure 7.1. The dialogue manager, based on a set of rules, upon receiving the interpretation of the user's speech from a speech recognition and understanding module, directs a speech generation module on what information or request will be spoken next which in turn operates with a speech synthesizer (or prompt player) to produce the acoustic output. It also interacts with external backend knowledge repositories in order to extract additional information necessary to complete the interaction.

Now, the question is why a spoken dialogue system has to understand, i.e. why is it that the dialogue manager cannot accept direct input from speech recognition and act upon that? Similarly, you may ask why the dialogue manager cannot directly produce the word string to be processed by the speech synthesizer, but makes use of a language generation component.

Spoken Language Understanding: Systems for Extracting Semantic Information from Speech, First Edition.
Edited by Gokhan Tur and Renato De Mori.

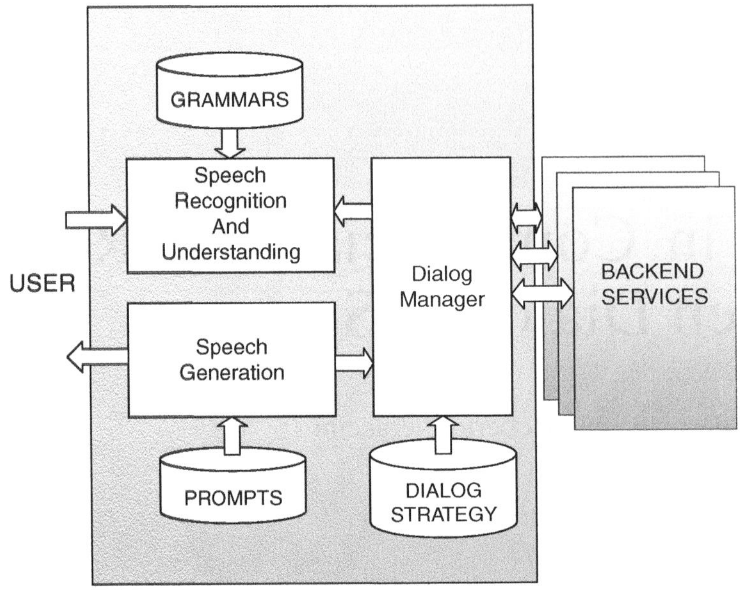

Figure 7.1 A high-level functional diagram of a spoken dialogue system

You may even go one step further and ask why the dialogue manager does not accept speech as input and produce speech as output.

While these questions seem to be purely philosophical and a matter of definition, in fact, the coupling of individual components of spoken language processing systems has a long-standing history. Let us look into the annals of speech recognition where the original approach was to describe recognition by a step-wise process where, after feature extraction, a phoneme recognizer converted features into a phoneme sequence and, thereafter, the phoneme sequence was converted into graphemes by yet another module. Each of the modules (in particular feature-to-phoneme and phoneme-to-grapheme conversion) was optimized independently and finally plugged together. Soon, it became clear that the (optimal) hard decision made by the first module in conjunction with a hard decision of the second results in a worse performance than optimizing both modules together, i.e. making a hard decision only at the very end of the process (Klatt, 1977). In spoken language processing, there are other examples showing similar outcomes such as the coupling of speech recognition with language translation (Matusov *et al.*, 2005), speech recognition with semantic classification (Kuhn and De Mori, 1995; Nöth *et al.*, 1996), or, last but not least, spoken language understanding and dialogue management (Young, 2002).

In face of the performance gain that could be shown in all of the aforementioned examples, very few of them found their way into large-scale applications: speech translation is still performed in two steps, and semantic classification is likewise applied to the speech recognizer's n-best hypotheses (most often first-best). The reasons of the absence of integrated systems in practice are:

- Integrated systems may become unwieldy and hard to maintain and improve. For example, when you consider an integrated speech translation system which takes speech of a source

language as input and returns text translated to a target language, and the output is wrong, you would probably like to know whether the recognition or the translation is the cause of that. However, there is no intermediate level anymore, everything is tied together in an overly complex structure of interconnected statistical models, resulting in a huge tree which is completely unmanageable without several levels of pruning and suboptimal decisions.
- The systems' complexity has also impact on the computational load. Hard decisions as usually made in modular systems strongly reduce memory and computation time requirements and make systems more appropriate for real-world applications as in the telecommunications industry.
- Knowledge and expertise about the individual components of integrated systems are most often distributed among different institutions. The most powerful speech recognizer may be provided by party *A* while the best translation system may be built by *B*. It may be very hard if not impossible to bring *A* and *B* together and produce an integrated speech translation system. Furthermore, industrial trends are heading the opposite direction by standardizing the interfaces between speech and language processing components (such as VoiceXML, MRCP, SSML, SRGS, ECMAScript, etc.). While regarded major milestones in the development of commercial speech systems by promoting a plug-and-play architecture, they draw clear lines between individual modules: Dialog managers communicate by means of VoiceXML (McGlashan *et al.*, 2004) with a platform called *voice browser* which in turn engages with a speech recognizer via MRCP (Media Resource Control Protocol, Burke, 2007) defining language models using SRGS (Speech Recognition Grammar Specification, Hunt and McGlashan, 2004) and language understanding, i.e. the reconition hypotheses' semantic interpretation, using ECMAScript (ECMA, 1999), and with a speech synthesizer via SSML (Speech Synthesis Markup Language, Burnett *et al.*, 2004).

To conclude: Although performance improvement as the result of integrating components of speech and language processing systems has been shown, the current trend (and presumably that of the next couple of years) is that of creating modular architectures together with a strong effort to standardize the interfaces between the modules. For the architecture of a spoken dialogue system, this implies that speech recognition and understanding are kept separate from dialogue management. So, while a semantic layer is required to reduce the complexity of the spoken dialogue task (spoken dialogue systems have to understand), most often, understanding is decoupled from dialogue management and viewed as a black box (spoken dialogue systems do not have to understand).

This chapter is to give an overview about both research and commercial aspects of spoken language understanding in dialogue systems. We will review approaches, deal with deficiencies regarding speech input, talk about example datasets and applications, show how to measure performance, and finally draw the conclusion that research and commercial worlds, despite of major differences in their approaches to SLU and dialogue management, are slowly growing together.

7.2 Approaches to SLU for Dialogue Systems

Section 7.1 has already indicated that there are certain constraints put upon spoken dialogue systems in general and the involved language understanding in particular imposed by commercial requirements (such as standardized interfaces, restrictions of computational load, manageability of complex systems). As a result, SLU techniques used in commercial dialogue systems essentially differ from those used in research. The present section is to give an overview about techniques from both worlds.

7.2.1 Rule-based Semantic Grammars

While speech recognizers became more and more powerful over the last decades (reducing error rates by about 10% every year, Gray, 2003), speech recognition is still not on a par with humans in most cases. Like humans, machines are able to manage very large vocabularies (sometimes hundreds of thousands of words). Acoustic and language models are often trained on more data than a human being will ever be able to hear and read in a lifetime (Evermann *et al.*, 2005), but, as soon as tasks become a little more complex (as in broadcast news or conversational speech), even the best speech recognizers disastrously fail. The main reason for the performance difference is the recognizer's lack of situational awareness (Hura *et al.*, 2009). In fact, although the *a priori* human language model may be worse than that of a state-of-the-art recognizer, it is situation-adaptive. The human understands stuff well which makes sense in the current context and fails understanding out-of-scope input:

> Roberto: *What did you have for lunch today?*
> David: *Wreck a nice beach.*
> Roberto: *?!*

In order to commercialize speech recognition technology, this obstacle had to be overcome, and, in the mid-1990s, technology providers went a step back and reasoned

> *Roberto pretty much knows that David has potato soup for lunch every other day, so why should he try to recognize all these hundreds of thousands of fancy phrases when there is only a handful of well-known dishes he possibly enjoyed.*

It was at this time when the concept of *speech recognition grammar* was developed (Hunt and McGlashan, 2004; Sun Microsystems, 1998): A grammar is a specification of "the words and patterns of words to be listened for by a speech recognizer". Let us give an example. Suppose, apart from potato soup, David usually eates meat balls or rollmops, a list of expected responses to Roberto's question might look like

> *guess what*
> *potato soup like always*
> *soup*
> *meat balls*
> *balls*
> *rollmops*
> *herring*
> *fish*

So, that is all. The speech recognizer has to distinguish between no more than eight items in the list as opposed to a virtually unlimited set of possible phrases. Naturally, speech recognition accuracy gains significantly for responses falling into this list. Moreover, semantic interpretation of these responses is trivial. If the business logic of the dialogue application calls for distinguishing among types of meals, and not among all the possible varieties, we simply have to assign one of the semantic categories (*soup/meat/fish*) to each list item. As motivated in Section 7.1, these semantic categories are the output of the black box and processed as input for the dialogue manager. Our list enriched by semantic categories looks like this:

guess what ⟶ **soup**
potato soup like always ⟶ **soup**
soup ⟶ **soup**
meat balls ⟶ **meat**
balls ⟶ **meat**
rollmops ⟶ **fish**
herring ⟶ **fish**
fish ⟶ **fish**

Recognition accuracy can be further improved by *directing* the conversation partner by offering choices such as

Roberto: *What did you have for lunch today? Potato soup, meat balls, or roll mops?*

This so-called *directed dialog* (Cohen *et al.*, 2004) is common practice in the vast majority of commercial spoken dialogue systems resulting in robust recognition performance, even on noisy telephone speech in very complex problem-solving dialogue systems (Acomb *et al.*, 2007).

7.2.2 Statistical SLU

Now consider, *David* asks *Roberto* about his lunch choice. There appears to be a sheer endless diversity of cuisines in his very neighborhood that Roberto greedily avails himself of. So, a directed dialogue may not be the preferable way to go:

David: *What did you have for lunch today? Grilled vegetable lasagna; rack of lamb with Dijon and pistachio crumb; marinated flank steak stuffed with roasted red peppers, basil and prosciutto; . . . ; or Cajun grilled salmon served with a pineapple salsa?*

Apparently, prompting all choices is not advisable in a situation where there is an extremely long list of possible responses. Here, the only feasible approach is an open prompt as used in Section 7.2.1 together with a grammar listing all responses and their corresponding semantic categories. There may be very frequent phrases such as *pasta*, as well as very unlikely ones as *roast pork loin stuffed with apples and prunes accompanied by a cider gravy and cranberry wild rice*. To make sure that phrases are treated by the speech recognizer according to their probability of occurrence, the grammar would have to associate frequency-dependent weights to the different responses. While this is still possible, there is a high chance that many of the responses to an open-ended prompt in a dialogue system are not among the expected items and, hence, are not listed in the grammar and are likely to be misclassified. Even when the list of responses is populated based on a training collection of a number of caller utterances (tokens) in a production system as suggested by Gorin *et al.* (1997) and even when this number

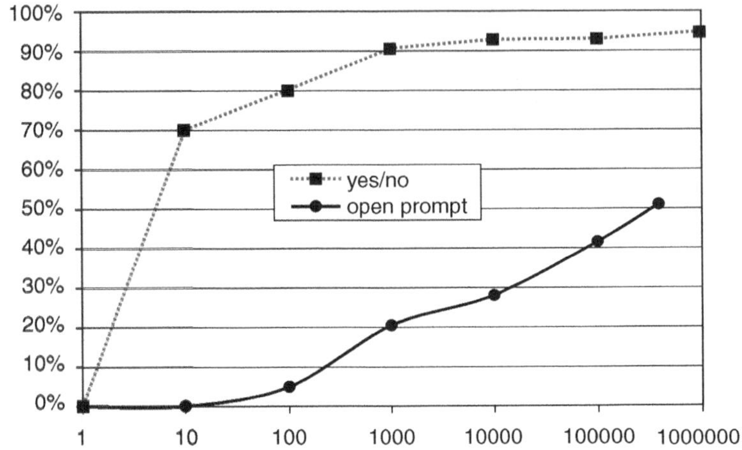

Figure 7.2 Dependency between number of collected utterances and grammar coverage percentage for a directed dialogue (yes/no) and an open prompt

is very large (one million or the like), there is still a significant number of expected utterances not covered by this grammar. Figure 7.2 demonstrates how coverage depends on the number of collected utterances in two typical contexts (directed dialogue versus open prompt) of a commercial troubleshooting dialogue system.

Facing coverages of as low as 50% in open prompt contexts, it is obvious that regular rule-based grammars will hardly be able to achieve reasonable performance. This is because there is little one can do to increase coverage apart from adding prefix and suffix rules and some other rules based on experience. A different approach is the *statistical* treatment of the problem by means of statistical language models and classifiers. As opposed to rule-based grammars, language models are able to match any word sequence composed of word types encountered in the training data. The same applies to the statistical classifier which generally determines the most likely semantic category based on occurrence and co-occurence probabilities of word types in association with this category; for details, see Evanini *et al.* (2007).

Figure 7.2 suggests that there can be a huge coverage difference between directed dialogue and open prompt – so, for the former, a conventional rule-based grammar may be applicable whereas, for the latter, statistical language model and classifier is the only reasonable choice. As a result of this, one may ask where the boundary between these paradigms is to be drawn? How directed or open may a dialogue context be in order to qualify for the one or the other paradigm?

The suprising answer to this question is that, in fact, statistical language models and classifiers *always* outperform even the most carefully designed rule-based grammars throughout the diversity of contexts as long as enough data is available for them to be trained properly. In Suendermann *et al.* (2009b), more than two million utterances from over 2000 recognition contexts of a large-scale triple-play troubleshooting and call-routing application were collected, and statistical language models and classifiers were trained for all these contexts. While the baseline system that almost exclusively used rule-based grammars performed at a rather low 78.0% average True Total (see Suendermann *et al.* (2009a) for the definition of this metric), the system completely based on statistical grammars improved to 90.5% True Total including a challenging open call-routing prompt with 250 different semantic categories (Suendermann *et al.*, 2008).

7.2.3 *Dealing with Deficiencies of Speech Recognition and SLU in Dialogue Systems*

In the last section we talked about SLU performances of 80 or 90% True Total, implying 10 or 20% of all acoustic events being wrongly interpreted. This means if we would blindly rely on the SLU hypothesis, even a system using a single dialogue turn would fail to accomplish its goal in a good number of cases. Considering complex systems with dozens or even hundreds of dialogue turns, the likelihood of successfully completing the call would exponentially appoach zero. This simple consideration demonstrates that one needs robust strategies to assure the correctness of SLU hypotheses. In the following, a collection of techniques are described that aim to overcome the challenges using speech input.

7.2.4 *Robust Interaction Design and Multiple Levels of Confidence Thresholds*

The output of the SLU black box introduced in Section 7.1 usually does not only consist of just the semantic hypothesis, but also includes a confidence score, a numeric value indicating how likely the response is correct. Since speech recognizers and many approaches to SLU are designed to *always* return a hypothesis, it becomes essential to learn how trustworthy it is. For example when a caller's response is out-of-scope of a rule-based grammar, it will still return the most likely semantic category. An utterance such as *I had no money today* may acoustically best fit the in-scope utterance *potato soup like always* and would therefore return the category *soup* as in the example of Section 7.2.1. However, the confidence score would be rather low, indicating that we should be careful about this hypothesis.

A common approach to dealing with confidence scores is to split the score space into three intervals limited by confidence thresholds as follows:

1 **Low confidence–reject.** The hypothesis is likely wrong and gets rejected:

> Roberto: *What did you have for lunch today?*
> David: *Wreck a nice beach.*
> Roberto: *Sorry? I was asking about your lunch today. What did you have?*

2 **Medium confidence–confirm.** The hypothesis may be correct or wrong and gets confirmed:

> Roberto: *What did you have for lunch today?*
> David: *Like always.*
> Roberto: *Potato soup, right?*

3 **High confidence–accept.** The hypothesis is most likely correct and gets accepted:

> Roberto: *What did you have for lunch today?*
> David: *Potato soup.*
> Roberto: *Did I ever tell you about my potato soup experience at Eurospeech'93?*

These confidence thresholds are often established by voice application designers according to their anecdotal experience. More precise thresholds can be trained in offline experiments using recorded utterance data from the respective recognition contexts and an objective error criterion such as the maximization of True Total. Alternatively, one can apply reinforcement learning or similar techniques to train thresholds in production systems optimizing overall task completion or the like (Walker, 2000).

7.2.5 N-best Lists

Speech recognizers and, likewise, statistical classifiers can populate ranked lists of recognition (or classification) hypotheses and associated confidence scores, the so-called n-best lists. As we said in Section 7.1, recognition and semantic classification are rarely coupled, so classification is applied to every single item of the recognizer's n-best list. Now, as the classifier itself can populate an n-best list (or let us call it m-best list for easier distinction), for every input hypothesis, we can have $n \cdot m$ different hypotheses with their associated confidence scores which may simply be the products of recognition and classification confidences. Since we said that, most often, spoken language understanding, i.e. recognition and classification in the present case, is regarded as a black box with respect to dialogue management, the system has to care only about the semantic hypotheses which can be derived from the $n \cdot m$ matrix by summing up the scores for identical classes and re-ordering the resulting list into a final m-best list to be processed by the dialogue manager.

A simple example (yes/no classifier) for this approach is given in Table 7.1. Here, the recognizer returns a 3-best list with the hypotheses (*rec hyp*) and their respective confidence scores (*rec conf*). The semantic classifier returns a 2-best list for every recognition hypothesis consisting of all possible classification hypotheses (*class hyp*: *Y* and *N*) and their confidence scores (*class conf*). After multiplication and summation, the final semantic 2-best list is derived with the final confidence scores (*sum conf*).

Table 7.1 Example for tying recognizer and classifier n-best lists

		class hyp/conf	
rec hyp	rec conf	Y	N
yo	0.5	0.5	0.5
no yes	0.3	0.7	0.3
no	0.2	0.1	0.9
	sum conf	0.48	0.52

Thus, the dialogue manager makes use of a semantic n-best list from the spoken language understanding module regarded as a black box. The unarguably simplest and trivial approach (and the most frequently used one in nowaday's spoken dialogue systems) is *to ignore all hypotheses but the first best*. This is what we earlier called *hard decision*, and some of the reasons for sticking with it were explained before. Another rather simple approach (also adopted by commercial spoken dialogue systems) is to use second- and third-best hypotheses as backup candidates. A typical dialogue reads:

Roberto: *What did you have for lunch today?*
David: *Quark*[1].
Roberto: *This was* pork, *is that right?*
David: *No.*
Roberto: *Sorry, my mistake. You said* shark, *right?*
David: *No.*
Roberto: *Sorry for having so much trouble understanding you. Was it* quark*?*
David: *Yes.*

7.2.6 One-step Correction and Mixed Initiative

Consider the following variation of the above dialogue

Roberto: *What did you have for lunch today?*
David: *Quark.*
Roberto: *This was* pork, *is that right?*
David: *I said* quark.
Roberto: *Sorry, I could not tell if this was* yes *or* no.
David: *No.*
Roberto: ...

Although this behavior seems to be rather strange and unpleasant, it is the usual way commercial dialogue systems work. This is because in the *confirmation context*, that is when we verify a recognition result with the caller, most often a simple yes/no grammar is being used that does not cover utterances such as *I said quark*.

A little more sophisticated technique consists in the so-called *one-step correction* (Schalkwyk *et al.*, 2003) that, in addition to *yes* and *no*, provides the same semantic categories in the confirmation contexts as those being used in the *collection context* (the main question context). The above response *I said quark* would have led to a replacement of the first hypothesis (pork) by its correction (quark).

One-step correction is an example of a general user input methodology referred to as *mixed initiative* where the system supports user input that does not directly respond to the preceding system question prompt. Typical examples include global commands such as *operator, hold on, repeat, go back*, etc. which most commercial systems allow users to request at any time in a dialogue. Research systems such as the one described by Pieraccini *et al.* (1997), allow for mixed initiative to a much larger degree:

Roberto: *What did you have for lunch today?*
David: *Quark. But what about you?*
Roberto: *I had Parmesan breaded eggplant topped with grilled tilapia and salsa cruda.*
David: *Oh.*

[1] http://en.wikipedia.org/wiki/Quark_(cheese)

7.2.7 Belief Systems

Dealing with confidence levels introduced in the confirmation context is one of the problems with one-step correction. Assuming the three levels in Section 7.2.4, you can straight-forwardly reject (low level) or accept (high level) the correction, but how do you want to deal with corrections of medium confidence level? Should you confirm the correction? Or should you rather confirm the collection's second best? Should you compare their confidences to make a decision? What if collection hypothesis and correction are the same? Should you lower the rejection threshold in this case? How do confidence thresholds of different grammars compare? Is there a generic way to combine hypotheses of collection and correction?

A positive answer to these questions is given by the *belief system* approach, often used in research dialogue systems (Bohus and Rudnicky, 2005; Williams, 2008; Young *et al.*, 2007). This approach tries to model the user's true (but hidden) actions and goals by means of a tuple of likelihoods established using all possible input channels available to the spoken dialogue system.

In the case of the aforementioned example, David's true hidden goal is to convey the dish he had for lunch. Now, the response to Roberto's first question results in an n-best list where each of the possible answers gets a certain confidence score creating the distribution of likelihoods of the system's beliefs for what David's true lunch was up to this point. For example, *pork* may get $p_p = p_p^1 = 0.5$, *shark* $p_s = p_s^1 = 0.3$, and *quark* $p_q = p_q^1 = 0.1$. Based on the likelihood of the first best response (*pork*), the system may decide to confirm it getting another distribution such as $p_p^2 = 0.1$, $p_s^2 = 0.1$, and $p_q^2 = 0.7$. Combining all evidence gathered up to here would result in (for this example, we simply average over the collection and confirmation likelihoods): $p_p = 0.3$, $p_s = 0.2$, and $p_q = 0.4$. So, after the confirmation, *quark* has a higher likelihood than the others. Depending on the following actions performed by the dialogue system, a hard decision may not be necessary at this point of the conversation, so the system could keep the likelihood distribution and try to collect more evidence further down the dialogue to update the belief distribution.

Even more interestingly, the belief system approach allows for combining speech input with a multitude of other resources available to the system. In the above example, one could think of background knowledge about the conversation partners such as whether David prefers vegetarian or kosher food (both clearly lowering the *a priori* likelihood of *pork*) or the geographical location where the conversation is made (e.g. in America, quark is expensive and hard to find whereas, in Germany, it is available everywhere for pennies).

7.3 From Call Flow to POMDP: How Dialogue Management Integrates with SLU

While, so far, we have repeatedly treated SLU as a black box whose output is processed by the dialogue manager, we have equally treated the dialogue manager as black box. In Section 7.1, we said the dialogue manager is "based on a set of rules". In Section 7.2.5, we concluded "it is up to the dialogue manager to make use of [the n-best list's] power". And in the last section, we introduced belief systems and stated that the dialogue manager "could keep the likelihood distribution and try to collect more evidence further down the dialogue to update the belief distribution". In this section, we want to briefly introduce the major dialogue management strategies to understand their relationship with the SLU approaches discussed previously.

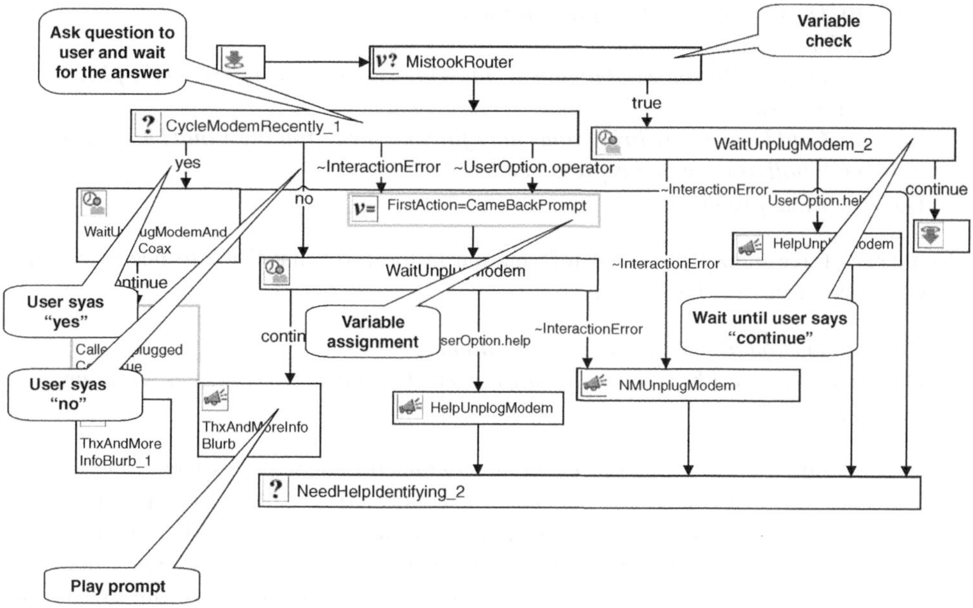

Figure 7.3 Example of a call flow specification

7.3.1 *Rule-based Approaches: Call Flow, Form-filling, Agenda, Call-routing, Inference*

In a typical industrial implementation of a spoken dialogue system, the dialogue strategy is expressed as a *call flow* (Pieraccini *et al.*, 2001). The call flow is a finite-state machine, often structured in a hierarchical fashion, with nodes representing dialogue activities and arcs corresponding to conditions. A typical activity can instruct the speech generation module to play a specific recorded prompt, or synthesize it using a text-to-speech synthesizer, and activate the speech recognition module with a specific grammar. Other activities can query external backend knowledge repositories, set and access variables, perform any type of computation, or invoke another call flow as a subroutine. Call flows are often built using drag-and-drop WYSIWYG tools that allow to specify and visualize all the details of the interaction flow. Figure 7.3 is an example of a graphical call flow specification.

Call flows most often use directed dialogues as introduced in Section 7.2.1 and open prompts (see Section 7.2.2) to some extend. There is very limited support for more sophisticated techniques such as mixed initiative or belief systems because of the unmanageable complexity of the graphs which, even without these techniques, extend over hundreds of pages in said visualization tools.

Many tasks in the scope of spoken dialogue are about gathering a certain set of information items. These items can very well be thought of as a form whose fields have to be filled. Mostly, call flows gather information pieces from the user in a linear fashion, i.e. one form item after the other:

Roberto: *Do you already have plans for dinner?*
David: *Not yet.*
Roberto: *Perfect. Do you want to join me tonight? I am having a party at my place.*
David: *Yes, great!*
Roberto: *Could you please bring some juice for your own? You know that I normally only serve Italian wine and espresso coffee.*
David: *OK, no problem.*

So, there is three binary pieces of information in the form that Roberto needs to gather. Imagine, David takes over the initiative:

Roberto: *Do you already have plans for dinner?*
David: *Not yet, but I bet you are having a party. Can I come over – I will bring my own juice?*

Here, the required information pieces are all contained in a single response, and the form could be completed at once. While call flows generally do not allow for inputting several information items at a time, the *form-filling* (aka *slot-filling*) approach (Potamianos *et al.*, 2000; Souvignier *et al.*, 2000), particularly intended to tackle mixed initiative, does. The whole dialogue system or parts of it are represented as a form whose items are dynamically filled with user and backend system input. The dialogue manager determines the next question to ask (or action to take) by estimating priorities of all still empty form items and choosing the highest one.

Obviously, it is hard to represent complex systems by means of a single form. For example, the CMU Communicator (Rudnicky *et al.*, 1999) handling a complex travel planning task consisting of air travel, hotels, and car reservations could hardly have been built based on either call flow or form-filling or a combination thereof. Instead, a dynamic hierarchy of trees to be able to spontaneously switch between the tasks while consistently keeping and managing information gathered in the course of the dialogue was established, the so-called *agenda-based* approach (Rudnicky and Xu, 1999).

Related to the form-filling approach is that of natural language call-routing (Gorin *et al.*, 1997). Here, the intent is to route a caller to the right destination (either a specific type of call center agent or another spoken dialogue application) based on free-form speech input in response to an open system prompt. Depending on how detailed the speech input is and how confident the SLU is in the recognition result, the call router has to follow up with the caller requesting confirmation or clarification:

Roberto: *What's up?*
David: *Not much, but when was the last time you had Nuremberg <cough>?*
Roberto: *Do you mean Nuremberg sausages or ginger bread?*
David: *Sausages.*
Roberto: *I don't remember. But did I tell you the story about my father when he returned from the war in 1945 and he came to Nuremberg...?*

Yet another dialogue management paradigm is based on *inference*. Applying formalisms established in communication theory (Lésperance *et al.*, 1995), an inference dialogue manager implements a set of logical axioms covering priciples of rational behavior, communication, and cooperation. The main goal is to provide a pleasant user experience by avoiding redudancy, asking cooperative, suggestive, or even corrective questions, modelling the states of caller and system (their attitudes, beliefs, desires, intentions, mutual belief, joint intention, obligation, etc.) and, in doing so, help the user as best as possible through the unavoidable human/machine interaction. Practical implementations of this approach include France Telecom's ARTIMIS (Sadek *et al.*, 1997) and other research projects in Europe (Egges *et al.*, 2001) and the USA (Allen *et al.*, 2001).

7.3.2 *Statistical Dialogue Management: Reinforcement Learning, MDP, POMDP*

Earlier in this section, we compared rule-based (Section 7.2.1) with statistical approaches (Section 7.2.2) to SLU under the umbrella of spoken dialogue systems. There are clear pros for the former (easy to build; predictable output; cheap since no data required) as well as for the latter (higher performance; highly automatable). In the late 1990s, only a few years after the first large-scale spoken dialogue systems where built, the community started to investigate the applicability of statistical approaches to dialogue management in expectation of the pros that such techniques had shown in SLU and other human language processing fields.

Levin and Pieraccini (1997) used the aforementioned *reinforcement learning* paradigm (see Section 7.2.4) in a much larger scope than just for optimizing confidence thresholds. They formalized the generic model of a dialogue system by means of a finite set of dialogue states, system actions, and a system strategy defining a mapping between states and actions. This formalization allowed for the mathematical description of a dialogue system as a Markov decision process (MDP) (Kaelbling *et al.*, 1996) that enabled automatic learning and adaptation of the dialogue strategy in a production dialogue system (also known as exploration). Single requirement for this to work is the establishing of an objective cost function that can be a combination of multiple terms representing measureable dimensions such as the ones that will be discussed in Section 7.5. Based on the global cost of a number of dialogues, the system can establish and update state- and action-dependent local costs in an attempt to minimize the overall expected dialogue cost. At every state, that action is performed which results in the minimum local cost until the dialogue is completed, and yet another data point is gathered to update the dialogue strategy, i.e. the local costs.

MDPs are a sound statistical framework for dialogue strategy optimization. However, they suppose that dialogue system states are *observable*. This is, they do not account for any uncertainty in the user state or dialogue history. In contrast, the application of *partially observable* Markov decision processes (POMDP) (Sondik, 1971) to the statistical modeling of dialogue systems (Young, 2002) combines the MDP approach with what we referred to as *belief systems* in Section 7.2.7. It takes the user's objective (that is unknown to the system) into account by estimating its probability distribution after every interaction turn. Now, the estimation of the local cost is based not only on the current action performed (observable) but also on the belief probability distribution over user actions and goals as well as dialogue history (nonobservable). Figure 7.4 shows a high-level comparison of MDP and POMDP dialogue systems according to Young *et al.* (2009).

Since POMDPs are currently the most popular framework for statistical dialogue management, we give a concise representation of the underlying theory at this point. Formally, a

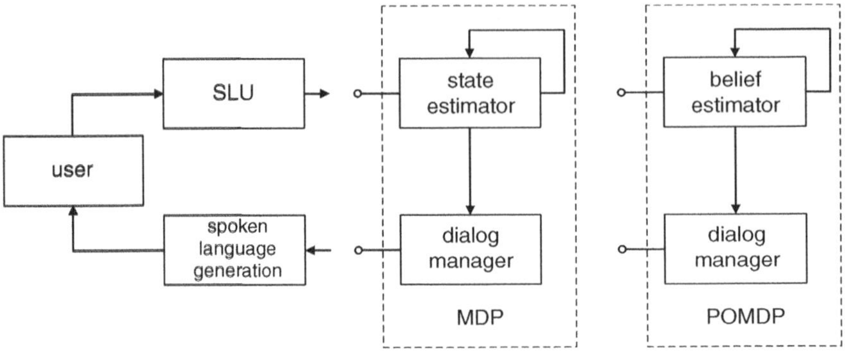

Figure 7.4 A high-level comparison of MDP and POMDP dialogue systems

POMDP can be defined as a tuple essentially consisting of a number of variables (Young, 2006):

- a set of machine states S,
- a set of machine actions A,
- a set of observations O,
- a reward function $r(s, a)$,
- a number of probability distributions such as the transition probability $P(s'|s, a)$ or the observation probability $P(o'|s', a)$.

Given this definition, a POMDP cycles through the following steps until the call is either completed, needs to be escalated, or the caller hangs up:

1. The dialogue system is in some state s that, in fact, is *unobserved* as it contains the user's input act, the user goal, as well as a record of the dialogue history. As s is not known, a probability distribution over all possible $s \in S$ is maintained. This distribution b is called *belief state*, a term indicating that it is subject to an update in every cycle making it state-dependent.
2. Using the current belief state b, the dialogue system performs an action a resulting in a reward $r(s, a)$ and moves to the next state s'.
3. Next, the caller responds, and the dialogue system receives observation o'.
4. Finally, the belief state is updated to b' based on s', o', a, and b as described in Kaelbling *et al.* (1998). This belief update is also called *belief monitoring*.

While both approaches, MDP as well as POMDP, are mathematically sound and well understood, they have found no adoption in the commercial world so far. A major drawback is the lack of data to train the dialogue strategy. To build a real-world dialogue system, one needs to have a baseline system in place, based on which the local cost functions can be initialized. A pure random initialization would result in a completely useless system taking arbitrary actions until, after gathering thousands and thousands of data points (i.e. thousands and thousands of dissatisfied callers), it starts acting more reasonably. A partial solution to this problem is the application of a *simulated user* (Scheffler and Young, 2002) that is trained on data from a prototype system. This user model would then be engaged in as many dialogues as necessary to produce a reasonable system that can be released to production.

Another disadvantage is the huge computational complexity of the involved algorithms (particularly associated with POMDP). Young (2002) states that "all current exact algorithms are effectively computationally intractable for all but very small state sets". This is due to the dimensionality of state variables in conjunction with the size of the belief space that maintains the probability distribution over all possible outputs of the SLU. In real-world scenarios, the variable space is so large that it is very hard, if not impossible, to train the policy maximizing the total reward due to training data sparseness. Obviously, another severe problem is the computational complexity to maintain the state distribution at system runtime.

To overcome these drawbacks, in practice, the state space resolution is decreased by subdividing the space into *partitions* treated as homogenious entities. An example is the hidden information state framework where a single belief is maintained for every partition each of which can bundle several thousand individual dialogue states (Young *et al.*, 2007). Partitions can be incrementally split into smaller partitions to maintain competing hypotheses coming up during the course of a call. This process is called *belief refinement* as it distributes the probability mass across multiple sub-partitions. Since the repeated refinement again produces more and more competing partitions ultimately leading to tractability issues, very recently, Williams (2010) proposed to incrementally *recombine* partitions whose belief is considered too low.

Although it is not an absolute requirement, statistical dialogue management most often comes along with statistical SLU. This is most preferable as the probability distributions used to perform belief updates, compute the accumulative reward and, during training, optimize the policy, include conditional probabilities of the SLU's semantic hypotheses.

To this end, semantic classifiers as discussed in Section 7.2.2 can be straight-forwardly applied. Obviously, there are limitations to classifiers since they are not able to easily capture multiple pieces of information from a single user input. A solution to overcome this lack is to use a *tagger* instead of a classifier since it is able to assign semantic tags to individual words or word sub-sequences in user utterances. An early example is the semantic tagger based on a finite state machine implemented by Pieraccini and Levin (1991). This approach consists of an HMM where the hidden states are the semantic tags and the state outputs are the (observed) word tokens.

Although the tagging approach goes a significant step farther than the semantic classifier, it still lacks a hierarchical representation of semantic concepts essential to capture long-distance dependencies and to disambiguate occurrences of entities of similar types in user utterances (consider the example "Manhattan is where I come from Brooklyn is where I want to go to" for which a non-hierarchical tagger would most probably assign the *point-of-departure* tag to the token *Brooklyn* although the correct tag is *point-of-arrival*). While full semantic parsers such as the hidden understanding model (Schwartz *et al.*, 1997) or hierarchical HMMs (Fine *et al.*, 1998) provide solutions to this problem, they require large amounts of fully annotated treebank data to train their statistical models. An approach that aims at combining the advantages of the flat semantic tagger with that of hierarchical parsers is the hidden vector state technique (He and Young, 2005). Instead of a simple one-dimensional tag, it assignes a *vector state* to each word where this vector state consists of an agglomeration of all hierarchy levels applying to the current token. A simple push-down automaton logic in conjunction with a strictly right-branching generation model is applied to strongly constrain the complexity of the involved algorithm. This allows a hidden vector state parser to be trained on relatively little and relatively superficially annotated data and also goes along with positive computational properties.

As we will see in the next section, the availability of training data is the major bottle neck when statistical SLU and dialogue management is concerned. Consequently, approaches that achieve reasonable performance with little data, noisy data, or quickly hand-crafted data are preferable. This is also to allow for a fast turn-around of dialogue system generations especially important in industrial implementations. The hidden vector state approach has shown to behave nicely with regard to all these prerequisites as was demonstrated in (He and Young, 2006).

7.4 Benchmark Projects and Data Sets

Beginning in the early 1990s, the coupling of SLU and dialogue management was the subject of a number of large-scale research projects. These projects were not only testbed and evaluation framework for state-of-the-art technology in the field, but very often released train and test corpora and sometimes even entire reference systems for open use by the research community. This section will briefly report about some of these research projects and corpora and finally discuss how things are treated differently in commercial applications.

7.4.1 ATIS

The Air Travel Information System (ATIS) project (Hemphill *et al.*, 1990) sponsored by the DARPA (Defense Advanced Research Projects Agency) between 1989 and 1995 was the first of a series of projects dedicated to SLU coupled with a dialogue engine. Specifically, ATIS aimed at answering questions in the flight scheduling domain including departure and arrival times, airports, fares, etc. Data collected in the course of the project were released in several rounds via the Linguistic Data Consortium (LDC) and include speech utterances, transcriptions, annotations as well as the relational database containing the flight scheduling reference information (Dahl *et al.*, 1994).

7.4.2 Communicator

The DARPA Communicator project (1999–2002) can be seen as the sequel to ATIS by extending its domain to multiple-leg flights, hotel and car reservation, and moving from pure question answering to full dialogue management. Participants were asked to make their systems compliant to the well-defined API of the Galaxy architecture originating from the Massachusetts Institute of Technology (Seneff *et al.*, 1998). This requirement was to make sure that system components be compatible with each other across project participants. Consequently, research groups could participate in certain sub-disciplines only. According to the Galaxy infrastructure, all components of a dialogue system communicate with a *hub* using a particular protocol (see Figure 7.5). Galaxy-compliant components of the same type (say SLU, or dialogue manager) are exchangeable. This plug-and-play concept allowed participants to focus on their specialty by using other participants' modules. Similarly to the ATIS project, corpora produced in the scope of the Communicator project were released to the community by the LDC (Walker *et al.*, 2003). The data contains speech utterances, transcriptions, annotations, as well as dialogue act tags and named-entity tags.

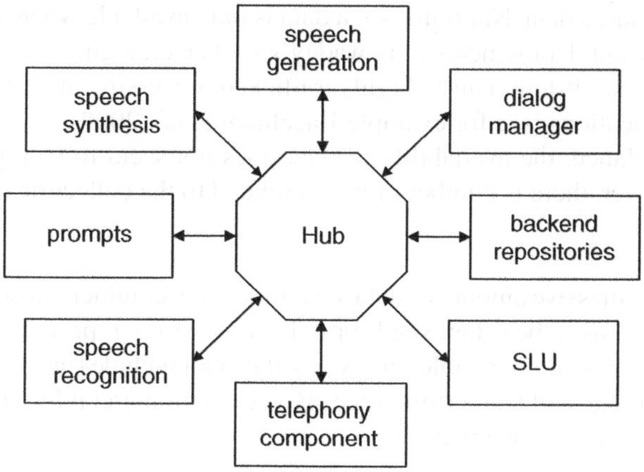

Figure 7.5 The Galaxy Communicator architecture

7.4.3 *Let's Go!*

Let's Go: Improved Speech Interfaces For The General Public was a project conducted at the Carnegie Mellon University between 2002 and 2008 (Raux *et al.*, 2003). The task was travel scheduling, much like ATIS and Communicator, however, in the case of Let's Go, the specific focus was on bus information for the Pittsburgh metropolitan area, including schedules and route details. An important goal of the Let's Go project was the creation of a real-world system deployed to the phone lines of the Pittsburgh Port Authority Transport.

Being conducted at a single research facility, the Language Technologies Institute at CMU, this unilateral project broadened its scope by releasing the entire data collected throughout the lifetime of the bus information system (since March 2005, a total of over 1 TB of accumulated audio and log data from more than 90 000 recorded dialogues have been collected (Raux *et al.*, 2005)). Even further, the entire dialogue system has been released to the public as open source. It includes components such as the speech recognizer Sphinx (Seymore *et al.*, 1998), the SLU module Phoenix (Ward, 1991), the dialogue manager Agenda (Rudnicky and Xu, 1999), the spoken language generation module Rosetta (Oh and Rudnicki, 2000), and the speech synthesizer Festival (Taylor *et al.*, 1998).

Most recently, the Spoken Dialogue Challenge, a competition bringing together multiple research institutions from industry and academia, saw the light of day (Black and Eskenazi, 2009). The first round is based on the Let's Go domain, so, participants are requested to build spoken dialogue systems competing with the above described baseline system for providing bus information. The Spoken Dialogue Challenge is also to compare performance evaluation systems and methods (see Section 7.5) as well as simulated users (Section 7.3).

7.4.4 *Datasets in Commercial Dialogue Systems*

The Let's Go project differs from the previously discussed ATIS and Communicator in that it is deployed to a real-world application, accumulating a good number of live calls. All these calls were carefully recorded and analyzed, since the most difficult part of many of today's research activities into SLU for spoken dialogue systems is to collect enough and properly transcribed and annotated data. Naturally, such data is only available when a system is actually deployed. All significant deployments of nowaday's spoken dialogue systems are commercial implementations. These systems can be highly trafficked processing millions of calls per week for some major applications (see for example Bacchiani *et al.*, 2008).

Hence, at a first glance, the availability of data does not seem to be a problem in a commercial setup. However, there is number of issues related to the collection of data in industrial deployments:

- **Storage.** Given the massive amount of data accumulated in commercial deployments, a powerful infrastructure has to be established for collecting, storing, processing, managing, and querying all this data. Items available for every single call include (in parenthesis the storage required for an average call taken from SpeechCycle's commercial Internet troubleshooting application of one sample customer)
  - a full-duplex call recording [mono, 8 kHz, 8 bit] (2355 kB)
  - individual speech utterances [mono, 8 kHz, 8 bit] (277 kB)
  - speech recognition logs (76 kB)
  - voice browser logs (351 kB)
  - application logs (106 kB)

  This makes some 3165 kB per call. For the above mentioned sample customer, the application handled 482,101 calls in January 2010 resulting in a required storage of more than 1.4 TB. Considering the accumulation of years worth of data across multiple applications and customers, commercial infrastructures would have to store data in the range of petabytes unless portions of the data get compressed or purged.
- **Data management.** The massive size of data does not only produce storage problems, but there are also issues in terms of accessibility. To compute simple call statistics by scanning millions of log files is an extremely time-consuming endeavor. Log files are not rendered to store data efficiently and require complex parsing to extract useful facts. This is why they are often post-processed and stored in form of normalized tables in huge databases. Even though normalized and indexed databases may allow for a significant speed gain, the search in database tables with billions of rows is not trivial and requires a server cluster with extremely powerful hardware.
- **Legal infrastructure.** Data handled in commercial environments very often contains confidential and sensitive information, such as social security numbers, e-mail addresses, or credit card numbers. Legal policies may require the data to stay on certain servers or in the hands of a certain department within a company. Particularly in large companies, it may be difficult or even impossible for research and development people to access data processed in operation departments due to legal, political, or burocratic constraints. Even less likely is the release of data portions to any party outside of the company as for instance academic research institutions.
- **Data understanding.** One of the main goals of accessing the data for research purposes is the tuning of speech recognition and understanding. This envolves heavy manual transcription and annotation, potentially covering millions of caller utterances per month (Suendermann *et al.*, 2009b). While recognition and understanding tuning is relatively straightforward, there are attempts to use the massive amounts of available log data to learn

optimal strategies for commercial dialogue systems. Examples include controlled call escalation (Levin and Pieraccini, 2006) or optimal call flow generation (Suendermann *et al.*, 2010a). These attempts, however, are still far from a global optimal framework like the one provided by POMDPs as introduced in Section 7.3. The main reason is that commercial systems hardly allow for experimentations on live systems due to the requirements of predictability and reliability. Hence, most often analyses have to be carried out based on past calls which all the aforementioned projects do. To "understand" the logs by extracting all possible information to optimize spoken dialogue systems offline is the ultimate goal.

7.5 Time is Money: The Relationship between SLU and Overall Dialogue System Performance

The performance of SLU is mostly measured on data sets providing reference annotations for all test samples, minimal and maximal answers accepted, and the decision whether the underlying query is ambiguous or answerable. This is true for all the corpora discussed in Section 7.4. SLU is applied to every sample speech utterance, returning a semantic interpretation of the utterance. This interpretation is then compared with the reference truth using one of a multitude of possible performance metrics. Even though the exact definition of these metrics varies from case to case and is subject to lengthy discussions and compromises, the underlying principle of an utterance-wise one-to-one comparsion holds true for all of them.

When it comes to measuring the performance of an entire dialogue system not only comprising SLU and dialogue manager, but also natural language generation, text-to-speech synthesis and backend logic, the notion of performance becomes fuzzy. The reason is that one-to-one comparison is not possible anymore because of the interactive nature of a dialogue. An SLU error at time t can cause the system to go down an entirely unexpected interaction path for which no reference annotation is available. Consequently, complete dialogue systems are often evaluated using *observable* metrics. Here, observable refers to facts that the system knows (such as whether a message was delivered, the SLU produced a no-match, the caller hung up, etc.) as opposed to facts hidden to the system such as how often a user's speech failed to trigger the speech recognizer or how often the SLU returned a wrong first-best hypothesis. A detailed discussion about dialogue system performance evaluation can be found in Suendermann *et al.* (2010b).

7.5.1 Automation Rate

The main objective of a spoken dialogue system is to replace human agents by computers. At this time, it is fair to claim that no computer whatsoever is able to replace arbitrary human tasks, so, the question arises, *to which extend* the machine is able to replace a human. Out of n sessions, how many could be automated? Dividing this number by n results in the *automation rate* aka *completion rate* or *containment rate*.

Depending on the system's specific purpose, automated calls include for instance:

- calls to a troubleshooting application that ended with the problem being resolved
- calls to a call router that ended up with the right type of agent or IVR
- calls to a bus scheduling application that provided the requested information

7.5.2 Average Handling Time

The primary reason why spoken dialogue systems are used to replace human agents is to save costs. Some companies' customer service hotlines process millions of calls per week, a volume that would require an immense number of agents to be handled manually. Furthermore, human agents are not scalable to unpredictable events of enlarged call traffic as in cases of outages or recall campaigns. One can quantify an automated call in terms of the minutes of human agent time it saved. In doing so, one has to consider that the amount of minutes saved depends on the performed task. If the system was used to pay an outstanding bill, one has to consider the average time a human agent would have needed to perform this task in order to estimate the savings resulting from this automation. Likewise with successfully troubleshooting bad cable, Internet, or telephone connections. Likewise with banking transactions, ordering tickets, routing calls, answering questions, etc.

While spoken dialogue systems save costs by replacing humans, they *produce* costs as well. Every minute of hosting a spoken dialogue system produces telephony costs, software license fees, energy, hardware, and maintenance fees, and so on. Optimizing savings must therefore include both, the automation rate (if possible per call type) on the one hand, and the handling time for this call on the other hand. The former should be maximum, the later minimum. Formally, one can estimate the savings a call produced by

$$S = W_A A - W_T T$$

where W_A is the average cost of a human agent handling this call type, $A \in \{0, 1\}$ indicates whether the call was automated or not, W_T is the per-minute hosting costs for the spoken dialogue system, and T is the call's handling time.

7.5.3 Retry Rate and Speech Errors

As stated before, the application of standard metrics to measure SLU performance in spoken dialogue systems is difficult due to the unpredictability of the interaction performed by the system and an actual caller. This means that standard corpora cannot be applied to evaluate system end-to-end performance. SLU can only by rigorously evaluated by transcribing and semantically annotating a set of system–caller dialogues handled by the spoken dialogue system. When the system changes, the whole procedure has to be repeated since previously transcribed and annotated data cannot be applied for measuring the performance of new transactions.

Without the capacity to evaluate the actual SLU performance, a spoken dialogue system is often assessed by means of the *retry rate*. This metric is the average number of turns it takes to gather a piece of information from the caller minus one. The inclusion of minus one in the metric is due to the fact that an optimal exchange of information takes only one turn, and, thus, has zero retries. This metric is somewhat related to the SLU performance as events associated with poor SLU performance (rejections due to low confidence, recognition hypotheses being out-of-scope, or dis-confirmation by the caller) result in retries and, consequently, in an increase of the retry rate.

Another class of events supposed to indicate SLU problems often used in commercial dialogue system implementations are the so-called *speech errors*. They include the above listed retry events as well as other undesired events such as time-outs or speech overflows. In many cases, they are not actual errors as, for instance, when a caller's coughing is rejected or when the caller remains silent and that results in a time-out.

7.6 Conclusion

This chapter has discussed how SLU intergrates with spoken dialogue systems, drawing a line between the two worlds of research and commercial applications. This distinction is important since techniques strongly differ between these worlds in both domains, SLU and dialogue management. Statistical, data-driven approaches such as hidden-vector-state-based SLU or POMDP dialogue management predominate in academic research, whereas rule-based techniques such as SRGS-compliant grammars and call flows are being used by most commercial applications.

Paradoxically, we have seen that, in academia, relatively small data sets are available due to a lack of deployed systems to collect live data. One of the major themes in academic research has therefore been how to overcome data sparseness. On the other hand, tremendous amounts of data are available in commercial applications, often exceeding storage and network capacity and making data management, search, and evaluation major topics in the spoken dialogue industry. However, the successful statistical exploitation of this data is in its infancy for a number of reasons:

- Most commercial applications are required to be deterministic; i.e. at every stage of a dialogue, given a caller input, the system reaction must be predictable for business stakeholders. This prerequisite is called *VUI completeness* (Pieraccini and Huerta, 2005).
- Statistical SLU requires manually transcribed and annotated training data for which a well-designed infrastructure is necessary to ensure continuous content updates and performance improvement. This process may include millions of utterances per month, i.e. dedicated teams with full-time transcribers and annotators.
- The evaluation of data collected in live dialogues without interfering with the course of the dialogue can be useful, for instance to tune speech recognition and understanding performance, perform escalation optimization (Levin and Pieraccini, 2006) or minimize the average handling time by re-ordering activities (Suendermann *et al.*, 2010a). However, there are numerous optimizations which can only be tested by trial-and-error, an approach forbidden in almost all commercial applications.

Slowly relaxing this paradox, over the past few years, both worlds, academia and industry, have been moving closer together by sharing corpora and technology, publishing results in major journals and proceedings, making statistical approaches more robust and applicable to the real world, and, last but not least, major progress in telephony-based speech recognition.

References

Acomb K, Bloom J, Dayanidhi K, Hunter P, Krogh P, Levin E and Pieraccini R 2007 Technical Support Dialog Systems: Issues, Problems, and Solutions *Proc. of the HLT-NAACL*, Rochester, USA.

Allen J, Ferguson G and Stent A 2001 An Architecture for More Realistic Conversational Systems *Proc. of the IUI*, Santa Fe, USA.

Bacchiani M, Beaufays F, Schalkwyk J, Schuster M and Strope B 2008 Deploying GOOG-411: Early Lessons in Data, Measurement, and Testing *Proc. of the ICASSP*, Las Vegas, USA.

Black A and Eskenazi M 2009 The Spoken Dialogue Challenge *Proc. of the SIGdial Workshop on Discourse and Dialogue*, London, UK.

Bohus D and Rudnicky A 2005 Constructing Accurate Beliefs in Spoken Dialog Systems *Proc. of the ASRU*, San Juan, Puerto Rico.

Burke D 2007 *Speech Processing for IP Networks: Media Resource Control Protocol (MRCP)*. Wiley, New York, USA.

Burnett D, Walker M and Hunt A 2004 Speech Synthesis Markup Language (SSML) Version 1.0. W3C Recommendation. http://www.w3.org/TR/2004/REC-speech-synthesis-20040907/.

Cohen M, Giangola J and Balogh J 2004 *Voice User Interface Design*. Addison Wesley, Redwood City, USA.

Dahl D, Bates M, Brown M, Fisher W, Hunicke-Smith K, Pallett D, Pao C, Rudnicky A, Shriberg E, Garofolo J, Fiscus J, Danielson D, Bocchieri E, Buntschuh B, Schwartz B, Peters S, Ingria R, Weide R, Chang Y, Thayer E, Hirschman L, Polifroni J, Lund B, Kawai G, Kuhn T and Norton L 1994 *ATIS3 Training Data*. Linguistic Data Consortium, Philadelphia, USA.

De Mori R 1998 *Spoken Dialogue With Computers*. Academic Press, San Diego, USA.

ECMA 1999 Standard ECMA-262 ECMAScript Language Specification. http://www.ecma-international.org/publications/standards/Ecma-262.htm.

Egges A, Nijholt A and op den Akker H 2001 Dialogs with BDP Agents in Virtual Environments *Proc. of the IJCAI*, Seattle, USA.

Evanini K, Suendermann D and Pieraccini R 2007 Call Classification for Automated Troubleshooting on Large Corpora *Proc. of the ASRU*, Kyoto, Japan.

Evermann G, Chan H, Gales M, Jia B, Mrva D, Woodland P and Yu K 2005 Training LVCSR Systems on Thousands of Hours of Data *Proc. of the ICASSP*, Philadelphia, USA.

Fine S, Singer Y and Tishby N 1998 The Hierarchical Hidden Markov Model: Analysis and Applications. *Machine Learning*.

Gorin A, Riccardi G and Wright J 1997 How May I Help You? *Speech Communication*.

Gray J 2003 What Next?: A Dozen Information-Technology Research Goals. *Journal of the ACM*.

He Y and Young S 2005 Semantic Processing Using the Hidden Vector State Model. *Computer Speech and Language*.

He Y and Young S 2006 Spoken Language Understanding Using the Hidden Vector State Model. *Speech Communication*.

Hemphill C, Godfrey J and Doddington G 1990 The ATIS Spoken Language Systems Pilot Corpus *Proc. of the Workshop on Speech and Natural Language*, Hidden Valley, USA.

Hunt A and McGlashan S 2004 Speech Recognition Grammar Specification Version 1.0. W3C Recommendation. http://www.w3.org/TR/2004/REC-speech-grammar-20040316.

Hura S, Bloom J, Hunter P, Leathem C, McKienzie J, O'Sullivan D, Suendermann D and Tucker D 2009 Let's Not Get Personal! IVR Customization via Situational Awareness *Proc. of the AVIxD*, New York, USA.

Kaelbling L, Littman M and Cassandra A 1998 Planning and Acting in Partially Observable Stochastic Domains. *Journal of Artificial Intelligence Research*.

Kaelbling L, Littman M and Moore A 1996 Reinforcement Learning: A Survey. *Journal of Articial Intelligence Research*.

Klatt D 1977 Review of the DARPA Speech Understanding Project. *Journal of the Acoustical Society of America*.

Kuhn R and De Mori R 1995 The Application of Semantic Classification Trees to Natural Language Understanding. *IEEE Trans. on Pattern Analysis and Machine Intelligence*.

Lésperance Y, Levesque H, Lin F, Marcu D, Reiter R and Scherl R 1995 Foundations of a Logical Approach to Agent Programming *Proc. of the IJCAI*, Montréal, Canada.

Levin E and Pieraccini R 1997 A Stochastic Model of Computer-Human Interaction for Learning Dialogue Strategies *Proc. of the Eurospeech*, Rhodes, Greece.

Levin E and Pieraccini R 2006 Value-Based Optimal Decision for Dialog Systems *Proc. of the SLT*, Palm Beach, Aruba.

Matusov E, Kanthak S and Ney H 2005 On the Integration of Speech Recognition and Statistical Machine Translation *Proc. of the Interspeech*, Lisbon, Portugal.

McGlashan S, Burnett D, Carter J, Danielsen P, Ferrans J, Hunt A, Lucas B, Porter B, Rehor K and Tryphonas S 2004 VoiceXML 2.0. W3C Recommendation. `http://www.w3.org/TR/2004/REC-voicexml20-20040316`.

Minker W and Bennacef S 2004 *Speech and Human-Machine Dialog*. Springer, New York, USA.

Nöth E, De Mori R, Fischer J, Gebhard A, Harbeck S, Kompe R, Kuhn R, Niemann H and Mast M 1996 An Integrated Model of Acoustics and Language Using Semantic Classification Trees *Proc. of the ICASSP*, Atlanta, USA.

Oh A and Rudnicki A 2000 Stochastic Language Generation for Spoken Dialogue Systems *Proc. of the ANLP/NAACL Workshop on Conversational Systems*, Seattle, USA.

Pieraccini R and Huerta J 2005 Where Do We Go from Here? Research and Commercial Spoken Dialog Systems *Proc. of the SIGdial Workshop on Discourse and Dialogue*, Lisbon, Portugal.

Pieraccini R and Levin E 1991 Stochastic Representation of Semantic Structure for Speech Understanding *Proc. of the Eurospeech*, Genova, Italy.

Pieraccini R, Caskey S, Dayanidhi K, Carpenter B and Phillips M 2001 ETUDE, a Recursive Dialog Manager with Embedded User Interface Patterns *Proc. of the ASRU*, Madonna di Campiglio, Italy.

Pieraccini R, Levin E and Eckert W 1997 AMICA: The AT&T Mixed Initiative Conversational Architecture *Proc. of the Eurospeech*, Rhodes, Greece.

Potamianos A, Ammicht E and Kuo J 2000 Dialogue Management in the Bell Labs Communicator System *Proc. of the ICSLP*, Beijing, China.

Raux A, Langner B, Black A and Eskenazi M 2003 LET'S GO: Improving Spoken Dialog Systems for the Elderly and Non-Native *Proc. of the Eurospeech*, Geneva, Switzerland.

Raux A, Langner B, Bohus D, Black A and Eskenazi M 2005 Let's Go Public! Taking a Spoken Dialog System to the Real World *Proc. of the Interspeech*, Lisbon, Portugal.

Rudnicky A and Xu W 1999 An Agenda-Based Dialog Management Architecture for Spoken Language Systems *Proc. of the ASRU*, Keystone, USA.

Rudnicky A, Thayer E, Constantinides F, Tchou C, Shern R, Lenzo K, Xu W and Oh A 1999 Creating Natural Dialog in the Carnegie Mellon Communicator System *Proc. of the Eurospeech*, Budapest, Hungary.

Sadek M, Bretier P and Panaget F 1997 ARTIMIS: Natural Dialogue Meets Rational Agency *Proc. of the IJCAI*, Nagoya, Japan.

Schalkwyk J, Hetherington L and Story E 2003 Speech Recognition with Dynamic Grammars Using Finite-State Transducers *Proc. of the Eurospeech*, Geneva, Switzerland.

Scheffler K and Young S 2002 Automatic Learning of Dialogue Strategy Using Dialogue Simulation and Reinforcement Learning *Proc. of the HLT*, San Diego, USA.

Schwartz R, Miller S, Stallard D and Makhoul J 1997 Hidden Understanding Models for Statistical Sentence Understanding *Proc. of the ICASSP*, Munich, Germany.

Seneff S, Hurley E, Lau R, Pao C, Schmid P and Zue V 1998 Galaxy-II: A Reference Architecture for Conversational System Development *Proc. of the ICSLP*, Sydney, Australia.

Seymore K, Chen S, Doh S, Eskenazi M, Gouvea E, Raj B, Ravishankar M, Rosenfeld R, Siegler M, Stern R and Thayer E 1998 The 1997 CMU Sphinx-3 English Broadcast News Transcription System *Proc. of the DARPA Broadcast News Transcription and Understanding Workshop*, Lansdowne, USA.

Sondik E 1971 *The Optimal Control of Partially Observable Markov Decision Processes* PhD thesis Stanford University Standford, USA.

Souvignier B, Kellner A, Rueber B, Schramm H and Seide F 2000 The Thoughtful Elephant: Strategies for Spoken Dialog Systems *IEEE Trans. on Speech and Audio Processing*.

Suendermann D, Hunter P and Pieraccini R 2008 Call Classification with Hundreds of Classes and Hundred Thousands of Training Utterances ... and No Target Domain Data *Proc. of the PIT*, Kloster Irsee, Germany.

Suendermann D, Liscombe J and Pieraccini R 2010a Optimize the Obvious: Automatic Call Flow Generation *Proc. of the ICASSP*, Dallas, USA.

Suendermann D, Liscombe J, Dayanidhi K and Pieraccini R 2009a A Handsome Set of Metrics to Measure Utterance Classification Performance in Spoken Dialog Systems *Proc. of the SIGdial Workshop on Discourse and Dialogue*, London, UK.

Suendermann D, Liscombe J, Evanini K, Dayanidhi K and Pieraccini R 2009b From Rule-Based to Statistical Grammars: Continuous Improvement of Large-Scale Spoken Dialog Systems *Proc. of the ICASSP*, Taipei, Taiwan.

Suendermann D, Liscombe J, Pieraccini R and Evanini K 2010b 'How am I Doing?' A New Framework to Effectively Measure the Performance of Automated Customer Care Contact Centers In *Advances in Speech Recognition: Mobile Environments, Call Centers and Clinics* (ed. Neustein A) Springer New York, USA.

Sun Microsystems 1998 Java Speech Grammar Format Specification Version 1.0. http://java.sun.com/products/java-media/speech/forDevelopers/JSGF/.

Taylor P, Black A and Caley R 1998 The Architecture of the Festival Speech Synthesis System *Proc. of the ESCA Workshop on Speech Synthesis*, Jenolan Caves, Australia.

Walker M 2000 An Application of Reinforcement Learning to Dialogue Strategy Selection in a Spoken Dialogue System for Email. *Journal of Artificial Intelligence Research*.

Walker M, Aberdeen J and Sanders G 2003 *2001 Communicator Evaluation*. Linguistic Data Consortium, Philadelphia, USA.

Ward W 1991 Understanding Spontaneous Speech: The Phoenix System *Proc. of the ICASSP*, Toronto, Canada.

Williams J 2008 Exploiting the ASR *N*-Best by Tracking Multiple Dialogue State Hypotheses *Proc. of the Interspeech*, Brisbane, Australia.

Williams J 2010 Incremental Partition Recombination for Efficient Tracking of Multiple Dialogue States *Proc. of the ICASSP*, Dallas, USA.

Young S 2002 Talking to Machines (Statistically Speaking) *Proc. of the ICSLP*, Denver, USA.

Young S 2006 Using POMDPs for Dialog Management *Proc. of the SLT*, Palm Beach, Aruba.

Young S, Gašića M, Keizer S, Mairesse F, Schatzmann J, Thomson B and Yu K 2009 The Hidden Information State Model: A Practical Framework for POMDP-Based Spoken Dialogue Management . *Computer Speech and Language*.

Young S, Schatzmann J, Weilhammer K and Ye H 2007 The Hidden Information State Approach to Dialogue Management *Proc. of the ICASSP*, Hawaii, USA.

8

Active Learning

Dilek Hakkani-Tür[1] and Giuseppe Riccardi[2]
[1] *Microsoft Speech Labs, Microsoft Research, U.S.A.*
[2] *University of Trento, Italy*

Statistical, data-driven approaches to spoken language processing have become dominant in recent years, giving rise to viable spoken language understanding (SLU) technologies, such as intent determination, slot filling, question answering and information extraction as presented in earlier chapters. The driving force behind this success has been the creation and exploitation of large collections of carefully transcribed and annotated training data. The creation of such large annotated data sets is time consuming, error-prone, and expensive. As a result, accurate language processing is only available for a few domains or genre for some high-resource languages such as English. Even when large annotated corpora are available, the performance of language processing systems degrade on inputs with distributions different from the training data, due to nonstationarities or noisy conditions (e.g. ASR errors). For these reasons, examples have to be selected to maximize the performance and robustness of SLU components. In this chapter, we review machine learning algorithms for example selections, so-called active learning methods, and describe relevant spoken language processing applications.

8.1 Introduction

In spoken language understanding, the knowledge for mapping words into meaning constructs is often encoded by grammar rules that are constructed by analyzing examples x from human/machine interactions. These examples can be either experimentally acquired or artificially generated. When such mapping is encoded in statistical models, their parameters are estimated during a training phase using examples x and their associated labels y. In both cases of knowledge-based and statistical-based models, the resulting inference model may contain errors due to models' limitations, ambiguous interpretations or noisy input/output x, y associations. Models' errors usually originate from the limitations in the coverage of grammars or poor estimation of probability distributions. Ambiguous interpretations usually originate

Spoken Language Understanding: Systems for Extracting Semantic Information from Speech, First Edition.
Edited by Gokhan Tur and Renato De Mori.

from the lack of contextual information or world knowledge in the representation or models. Noisy input is usually generated by pattern variability, ranging from the phone to the word and phrase level. The goal of a machine that understands spoken language is the ability to improve its performance as it *observes* new examples x with minimal or no human supervision. Thus three fundamental questions arise:

Q1 How much data, generated from the distribution $P(x)$, will be needed to achieve optimal performance?
Q2 How to select the examples for annotation that will optimize machine's performance?
Q3 How to acquire examples, not necessarily from $P(x)$, to achieve optimal performance?

The first question, **Q1**, relates to the long-standing problem associated with the adoption of statistical approaches to decode speech and language structures. Statistical models have generally relied on strong assumptions on the nature of the distribution $P(x)$. These models are trained and evaluated on training and test sets that are assumed to be identically and independently distributed. The generation of the training samples are restricted to subsets which are defined *ad hoc* in terms of *task, domain, speaking style*, etc. The second question,**Q2**, relates to the quest for a methodology and machine learning algorithms that allow for sampling of x from a distribution $P(x)$ *actively*, to improve the performance of a given (formal or statistical) model of spoken language understanding, and to adapt its parameters or rules. Such selection may be followed by a request for human supervision and recover the label y for the example x. The third question,**Q3**, relates to the observability of the label y from the distribution $P(x)$ only. This occurs when the information content of the source x with distribution $P(x)$ does not fully *explain* the label y. For example, understanding the meaning of a spoken conversation in a face-to-face meeting will require a multidimensional distribution $P(\mathbf{x})$ associated with the modalities involved in the communicative acts (i.e. speech, gesture, visual cues) and to the scene analysis.

In this chapter, we address the class of machine learning algorithms that cover these fundamental questions, and focus especially on **Q2**. In the next section we cover the motivation for employing active learning approaches. Then, we discuss the theoretical point of view on active learning and present active learning approaches proposed in the literature, independent of specific application areas. In Section 8.6, we discuss the salient case studies of active learning applications to spoken language understanding systems. Finally, we present a higher level architecture for an active approach for building SLU systems.

8.2 Motivation

In this section, we will focus on key issues towards employing active learning while building SLU applications. These mainly cover variability coming with natural language, noise introduced during annotation, abundance of candidate data for annotation, and the unbalanced distribution of semantic concepts.

8.2.1 Language Variability

The **Q1** problem originates from the complexity of acquiring semantic constructs and their lexical realizations with sufficient coverage to support spoken conversation on a large variety of domains and interactive experiences. In the past, this problem has been overlooked by

```
question about my bill
question on my bill
calling about my bill
talk to somebody about my bill
talk about my bill
problem with my phone bill
question about the bill
problem with my billing
calling concerning my bill
calling regarding my statement
```

Figure 8.1 Excerpt from the list of 1,083 unique phrase variations associated to the *questions-on-bill* semantic category in the "How May I Help You?" corpus

computer scientists, and machine understanding of language has been seriously hampered. Such complexity has to be imputed to the many sources of variabilities and their alignments to language features. Let us examine the most important source of variabilities.

For example, one of the subtasks of spoken language understanding is the ability to classify a spoken utterance into categories such as speech acts or coarse semantic categories. The latter case has been thoroughly investigated and applied to call routing and email classification. In this classification task, features are extracted from the utterance transcription and mapped into the semantic categories, as described in Chapter 4. Utterance classification had been first proposed as part of call-routing dialogue task in (Gorin *et al.*, 1997, 2002). In Figure 8.1, we show an excerpt from the list of 1, 083 unique phrase variations associated to the *questions-on-bill* semantic category in the "How May I Help You?" corpus. From this example, it is evident that machines need to have the ability to capture lexical variations corresponding to *base* concepts which have been predefined. Robust mapping of such variations requires machines to detect *novel* examples in the course of the user/machine interactions over time.

Another source of the variability is due to the differences in human/machine and human/human spoken communicative experiences. The human expectation and preconceptions on machine skills play an important role in defining the attitude and ultimately human behavior (e.g. cooperative versus non cooperative) and the language s/he uses. Table 8.1 shows the ten most frequent dialogue act bigrams for human/machine and human/human dialogue corpora for the same application domain (Dinarelli *et al.*, 2009). In this study the machine role is enacted by a Wizard of Oz which is not simulating any misrecognition or misunderstanding errors. It is evident that the cooperativeness aspect of the human/human interaction is supported by the statistics of the *acknowledgment* dialogue act in contrast to the *mostly* interrogative (*info-req*) dialogue. Such dialogue act differences also have an impact on the linguistic realization and on the scope of the interaction.

The **Q3** problem arises when analyzing the language acquisition skills of humans. Language acquisition in humans is a multisensorial experience, where speech input is processed along with visual and gesture stimuli. Psycholinguists have thoroughly studied word vocabulary learning rates in infants and toddlers, and found that since the early age of language development, children exploit multimodal stimuli that enable them to recognize, understand and interact. Fenson *et al.* (1994) report a detailed quantitative analysis of infant and toddler's

Table 8.1 The 10 most frequent dialogue act bigrams for human/machine and human-human dialogues in the LUNA corpora

Human/machine (HM)	Human/human (HH)
info-req answer	ack info
answer info-req	info ack
info info-req	info info
info-req y-answer	ack ack
sentence_beginning greet	info-req answer
greet info	info info-req
info quit	info-req y-answer
offer info	ack info-req
thank info	answer ack
y-answer thank	quit *sentence_end*

ability to learn words over the first years of their cognitive developments. In Figure 8.2 we report an excerpt of their studies, in particular the median values of the number of words acquired in the 18 *months*, from age 12 months to 30 months. The time interval corresponds to an estimated 12 600 hours of spoken, visual and sensorial stimuli. The learning rate of the first months is remarkable, however the learning rate slows down in the adolescence period with an estimated active vocabulary of $60K$ words (Aitchinson, 1994). In Roy (2009) they acquire audio and video recordings of child-caregiver interactions throughout their daily lives and search the large amount of data for language acquisition mechanisms. These studies indicate that in language understanding the modeling problem is as relevant as the example selection problem and they should be a part of the same incremental learning framework.

8.2.2 *The Domain Concept Variability*

The mapping from words into concepts requires a conceptual lexicon and more generally a conceptual system. Models for such a system or relations amongst concepts, have been proposed since the early days by philosophers, and coded as an *ontology*. In the design of spoken language systems the segmentation and mapping of words, chunks and structures into concep-

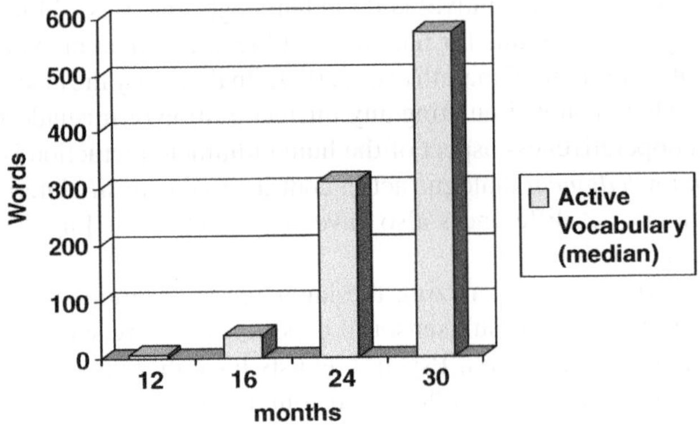

Figure 8.2 Language acquisition in children 12-30 months (adapted from Fenson *et al.* 1994)

tual constructs has received little attention. In the early SLU systems for information-seeking tasks (Miller *et al.*, 1994; Pieraccini and Levin, 1993), semantic parsing resembled the structure of knowledge bases (e.g. databases) and lacked generalization. In utterance classification, the list of semantic categories is usually flat and grows over time with application requirements. While such an engineering approach can work in limited applications for limited time, it can lead to poor system interoperability and suffer from concept scalability and classification performance in the long run. Figures 8.3 and 8.4 show part of the ontologies that were designed for an information-seeking task and HW/SW problem solving task (Quarteroni *et al.*, 2009).

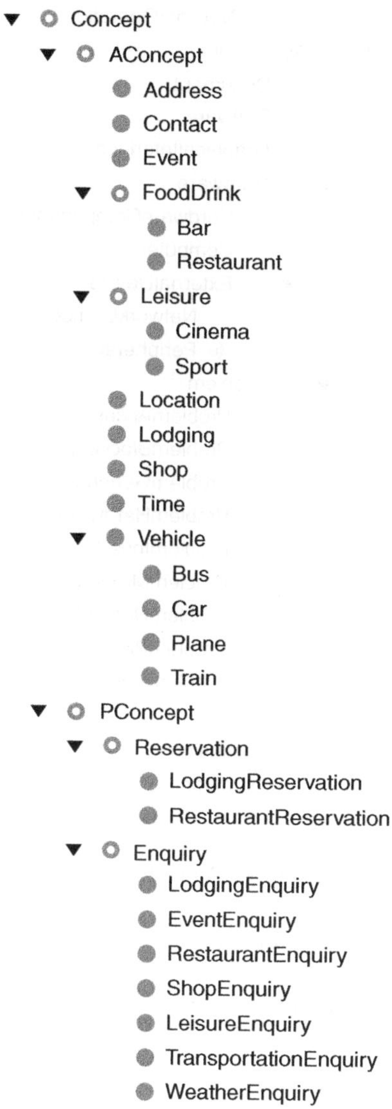

Figure 8.3 Excerpt from the domain concept ontology for a tourist information-seeking task

- Concept
  - PConcept
    - GenericAction
    - Operation
      - GenericOperation
      - DocumentOperation
      - SoftwareOperation
      - HardwareOperation
      - HardSoftOperation
      - NetworkOperation
  - AConcept
    - Document
    - Software
    - GraphicalInterface
    - Hardware
      - HardwareComponent
      - Computer
      - ExternalDevice
        - NetworkComponent
        - Peripheral
    - Problem
      - ProblemAccess
      - ProblemBlocking
      - ProblemGeneral
      - ProblemHardware
      - ProblemInsert
      - ProblemMissing
      - ProblemNetwork
      - ProblemProtocol
      - ProblemSoftware
    - User
    - Institution
    - Number
    - Time

Figure 8.4 Excerpt from the domain concept ontology for a HW/SW problem solving task

The design of such ontologies is based on a set of *canonical* relations and can be used both by humans for annotation and by machines to structure the learning space. Another important advantage of ontologies is that they can be used as part of the utterance interpretation model (Quarteroni *et al.*, 2009).

8.2.3 Noisy Annotation

Machine learning algorithms learn from training examples x to predict labels y which can be coarse semantic categories (e.g. utterance class) or complex syntactic and semantic structures.

In the canonical definition of y, such a label is assumed to be the ground truth with no label *noise*. Human annotation of language features such as syntactic and semantic structures are prone to human errors that need to be taken into account in the model learning (Artstein and Poesio, 2008; Hakkani-Tür *et al.*, 2006). In addition, a large amount of data can be annotated with an off-the-shelf parser to bootstrap the labels y with their approximation $\hat{y}$. The training of spoken language understanding models needs to take into account the uncertainty in the example target label y by using the most robust algorithm to label noise.

8.2.4 The Data Overflow

While the amount of data is limited in most research projects on spoken language understanding (e.g. ARPA, 1993; Bonneau-Maynard *et al.*, 2005; Dinarelli *et al.*, 2009) , speech service companies benefit from very large amounts of corpora that are partially annotated (Alberti *et al.*, 2009; Fabbrizio *et al.*, 2004; Suendermann *et al.*, 2009). Moreover, the availability of mixed sources such as web documents, email and chat logs, tagged images and videos pose the problem of how to exploit such language data diversified by speaking, and writing styles (Seltzer and Zhang, 2009). The availability of audio, video and text data streams makes it possible to track language variations and to learn spoken language models from multiple streams. Such abundance and diversity is an opportunity to augment the speech signal features with evidence from other resources whose size is virtually unbounded. To complement such data deluge, machine learning models that select salient data streams or patterns are crucial to improve the performance of the systems.

8.3 Learning Architectures

8.3.1 Passive Learning

The basic supervised learning architecture for training learners $\lambda : x \rightarrow y$ includes a passive consumption of the training examples. For this reason such schemes are also known as supervised passive learning. For instance, when the maximum likelihood parameter estimation is used, the parameters are estimated so that the training data likelihood is maximized (Jelinek, 1997):

$$\hat{\theta} = \arg\max_{\theta} P(D|\theta)$$

where $D = \{x_1, x_2, ..., x_n\}$ is the available training set, x_i $(i = 1, ..., n, n = |D|)$ is the ith labeled example and $P(D|\theta)$ is the probability of observing the set of training examples in D, for a given model parameter set θ. Data is usually randomly collected, transcribed, and split into a training and a test set. In the maximum likelihood formulation, D is fixed and the identical-and-independent-distribution (i.i.d) assumption is made. The set of training examples, $x_i \in D$, are drawn at random from the set $\mathcal{D}$, which has been selected *a priori* and fixed in time.[1]

In Figure 8.5 we give the architecture of the learning process in the case of passive supervised learning. In this learning scheme there is no relation between the expected error rate and the set

[1] Similar arguments can be applied to training algorithms directly minimizing the error rate, such as in discriminative classifiers (e.g., Boosting, Schapire and Singer, 2000). These algorithms are not designed to adaptively select the training examples.

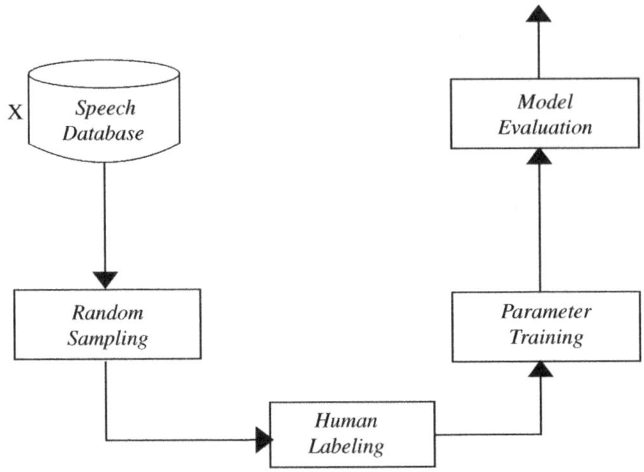

Figure 8.5 Supervised passive learning (Riccardi and Hakkani-Tür © 2005 IEEE)

of training examples D. In other words, if a new set of training examples, D', is provided, it is not possible to predict if this set would decrease or increase the error rate estimated on D. Since the training and test sets are sampled randomly from x, *all* examples are considered equally *informative* for the purpose of learning. The test set sample distribution matches the training set, hence the historical motto "There is no data like more data"[2] holds for any statistical learning algorithm with no guarantee of performance improvement. No example is disregarded or generated automatically. In a passive supervised approach, no unlabeled data is exploited. The data is assumed to be stationary, and all the examples are assumed to be obtained and labeled at the same time. In this approach, evaluations are made for comparing different models obtained with different methods but trained on the same given training set.

8.3.2 Active Learning

A passive approach delegates the estimation of learner's parameters to the selected algorithms (e.g. Maximum Likelihood, Maximum Entropy, etc.). In contrast, Active Learning (AL) emphasizes the role of the data selection algorithm for the purpose of improving the expected error rate over time, hence adapting to the changes in the incoming data stream, in the most general case. The training and test sets are not fixed *a priori*. We also do not assume that they are stationary. This means that the training set is not given, instead formed dynamically from a stream of incoming data using a buffering mechanism. The distribution of this data is also allowed to vary in time. The training set is not sampled randomly from x. *Active learning* aims for the selection of the most informative examples. The test set is randomly selected to track the dynamic system performance, and to compare re-trained models with the already trained model. The models are updated regularly and automatically.

[2] This motto has been attributed to Bob Mercer of then IBM T. J. Watson Research Center, Speech Group, dating back to 1985 in an Arden House ARPA ASR Workshop.

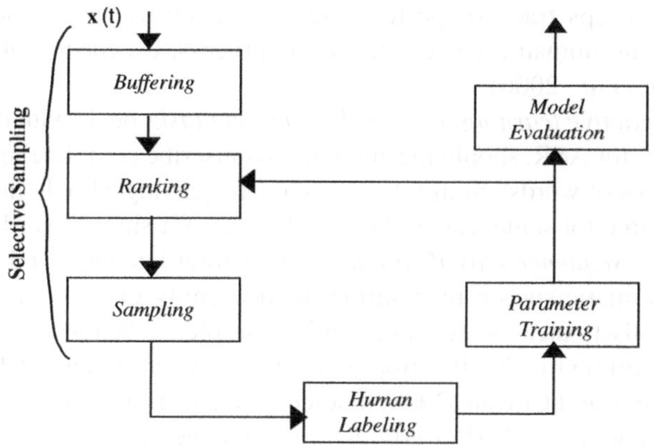

Figure 8.6 The active learning approach (Riccardi and Hakkani-Tür © 2005 IEEE)

In Figure 8.6, we show the architecture for active learning in the general case of X being a continuous stream of data samples. In such a general case, the data memory *buffer* also plays an important role in the system performance (Riccardi and Hakkani-Tür, 2005).

8.3.2.1 Issues and Challenges in Active Learning

- *Example selection criteria:* Example selection deals with finding the examples that would result in the largest improvement in the performance of the learning algorithm if labeled. In the next section, we will review previous work on example selection.
- *Stopping criteria:* Stopping criteria is used to determine when to stop selecting examples for manual annotation. The optimum stopping point is when none of the unlabeled examples would improve performance, if manually labeled and added to the training set. The optimum stopping point is usually reached when no more unlabeled examples are available with passive learning. Several methods have been proposed for automatically detecting the optimum stopping point, some of which will be reviewed in the next section.
- *Manual annotation quality:* Manual annotation refers to the assignment of correct categories to training examples by one or more human annotators. For any machine learning problem, including active learning, the quality of manual annotation is critical. For complex annotation tasks, inter-annotation agreement measures, such as Cohen's Kappa (Cohen, 1960), aim to estimate the annotatation task difficulty and annotation quality.
- *Biased prior disribution:* As described in the previous sections most learning algorithms assume that the data is identically and independently distributed (i.i.d.). However, non-random selection of the training data may result in divergence from the prior distribution of the data. Such divergence usually hurts classification performance as the i.i.d. assumption is no longer valid. Previous work (Hakkani-Tür *et al.*, 2006) integrated the divergence between the prior model and the constructed model, and aimed to minimize this divergence when selecting new examples.
- *Exploiting unlabeled data:* When reaching the optimum stopping criteria is not feasible (i.e., no more manual annotation is possible), the unlabaled examples may be used with unsupervised or semi-supervised learning methods to improve classification performance.

- *Active evaluation* keeps track of performance and controls active and semi-supervised learning. There is no human involvement in this process, except for labeling the selected data (Hakkani-Tür *et al.*, 2006).
- *The granularity of active learning for complex labeling tasks* deals with the unit to be annotated. For example, for ASR, should the annotators transcribe complete sentences/utterances or shorter sequences of words? Similarly, for syntactic parsing, should the annotators annotate the full parse tree for sentences or the sub-structure for shorter word sequences?
- *Active learning for sequence classification:* Most natural language and speech processing tasks, such as automatic speech recognition, named entity extraction, and part-of-speech tagging, are typically treated as sequence labeling problems. While there have been several studies in active learning for classification, active learning for sequence labeling has received less attention. Settles and Craven (2008) studied active learning for sequence classification with conditional random fields (Lafferty *et al.*, 2001) and proposed new measures such as sequence entropy.
- *Outlier detection:* Outliers in the data are examples that differ numerically from the rest of the data, and are expected to occur by chance. Manually labeling the outliers may not help in the estimation of the class of previously unseen examples, as similar examples are not likely to be observed.

8.4 Active Learning Methods

Earlier work on active learning considered examples that create the most confusion for the current classifier(s) as the most informative ones. For finding these examples, previous work concentrated on two approaches: certainty-based methods and committee-based methods, however later work investigated density-based approaches to active learning. We will cover these approaches after providing a theoretical foundation for active learning. Then, we will discuss various methods proposed for determining stopping criteria and exploiting unselected samples for better performance.

8.4.1 The Statistical Framework

Let $D = x_1, ..., x_N$ be the initial training set of examples with manually assigned labels $Y = y_1, ..., y_N$ from the set of the categories L, that is $y_i \in L = \{l_1, ..., l_{|L|}\}$, for $i = 1, ..., N$, and $Z = z_1, ..., z_m$ be the set of unlabeled examples. The aim in active learning is selecting the subset of examples from Z that would result in highest performance improvement, for manual labeling.

The problem of selecting the optimal data set to train a learner, $f(x)$, has been widely studied in statistics in the context of optimal experimental design. In this case the source of errors are defined in terms of the statistical properties of the learner. The characterization of such errors is conveniently carried when we adopt the squared error cost function:

$$\sum_{i=1}^{N}(y_i - f(x_i)^2)$$

over the N examples x_i in the training set $\mathcal{D}$. The expected mean-squared-error (MSE) can then be decomposed as follows (Geman *et al.*, 1992):

$$E[(y - f(x))^2|x]) = E[(y - E[y|x])^2|x] + (f(x) - E[y|x])^2 \quad (8.1)$$
$$\geq E[(y - E[y|x])^2|x] \quad (8.2)$$

The first contribution to the MSE in 8.1 is independent of the data set $\mathcal{D}$. From Equation 8.2, the MSE is minimized when $f(x) = E[y|x]$. We remark the dependence of $f(x)$ on $\mathcal{D}$ by rewriting as $f(x; \mathcal{D})$ and compute the goodness of f as an estimator of $E[y|x]$ in the MSE sense (Geman *et al.*, 1992):

$$E_{\mathcal{D}}[(f(x) - E[y|x])^2] = (E_{\mathcal{D}}[f(x; \mathcal{D})] - E[y|x])^2 \quad \mathit{Bias} \quad (8.3)$$
$$+ E_{\mathcal{D}}[(f(x; \mathcal{D} - E_{\mathcal{D}}[f(x; \mathcal{D}])^2] \quad \mathit{Variance} \quad (8.4)$$

Equation 8.4 explicitly defines the trade-offs available in designing a learner when the dataset $\mathcal{D}$ is given. The MSE of the estimator $f(x; \mathcal{D})$ is decomposed into *Bias* and *Variance* terms. Such trade-offs could lead to an unbiased estimator f and still have large MSE due to the high variance term and vice versa. In this analysis the dataset has been fixed. The goal of active learning is then to select the best ensemble of examples to optimize a cost function. In Cohn *et al.* (1996) variance minimization techniques are discussed for estimators such as feedforward neural networks, locally weighted regression, and Gaussians mixture.

8.4.2 Certainty-based Active Learning Methods

In the *certainty-based methods*, an initial system is trained using a small set of annotated examples (Lewis and Catlett, 1994). Then, the system examines and labels the unannotated examples, $z_i \in S_p, i = 1, \ldots, m$ and determines the certainties, $C(z_i)$, or uncertainties, $U(z_i)$, of its predictions of the labels. The examples with the lowest certainties (or highest uncertainties), S_k, are then presented to human labelers for annotation, hence at each iteration, the example z with:

$$z = \arg\min_{z_i} C(z_i)$$

or

$$z = \arg\max_{z_i} U(z_i)$$

is selected for labeling. The certainty-based active learning algorithm is described in Figure 8.7 and depicted in Figure 8.8.

The probability of the label, y_i, assigned to the example, can be used as the certainty of the classifier:

$$C(z_i) = \max_{y_i} P(y_i|z_i)$$

Since the classifier assigns the class with the highest posterior probability to the example, this approach is also called *minmax* (Laws and Schütze, 2008).

A widely used uncertainty measurement in active learning is entropy (Zhang and Chen, 2002):

$$U(z_i) = -\sum_{j=1}^{|Y|} P(y_j|z_i) \log P(y_j|z_i)$$

```
1. Given some amount of training data S_t, and a larger amount
   of unlabeled data in the pool S_p = {z_1, ..., z_n}
2. While (labelers/utterances are available) do
  (a) Train a classifier using the current training data S_t
  (b) Classify the utterances in S_p using this classifier com-
      puting the corresponding confidence scores C(z_i),   i =
      1, ..., n
  (c) Manually label the set S_k = {z_i : C(z_i) < th}
  (d) S_t = S_t ∪ S_k
  (e) S_p = S_p − S_k
```

Figure 8.7 The certainty-based active learning algorithm

For automatic speech recognition, the examples are utterances formed from a sequence of words, hence the posterior probability of the utterance given the acoustic signal can be used as the confidence score of the utterance (Kamm and Meyer, 2001), or the individual word posterior probabilities can be combined. For example, Hakkani-Tür *et al.* (2002a) and Chen *et al.* (2008) used word confidence scores obtained from word confusion networks to score the

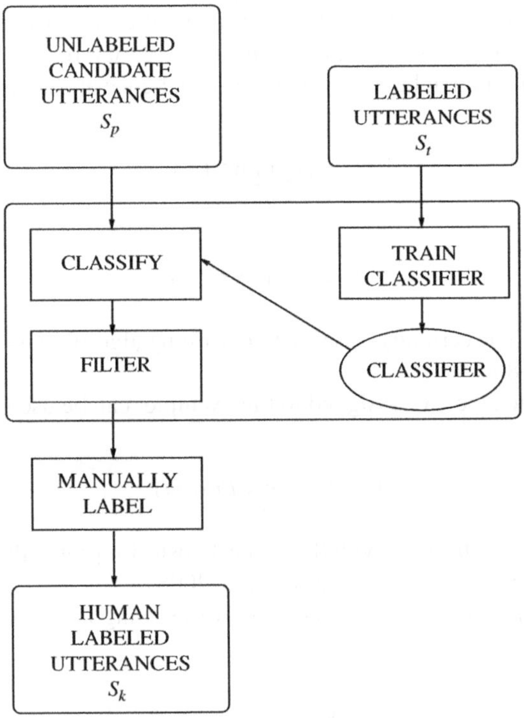

Figure 8.8 The certainty-based active learning algorithm (Tur *et al.* © 2005 Elsevier)

utterances. Another measure that has been used as the certainty of a classifier is *margin* (Tong and Koller, 2001a), $C_M(z)$, the difference between the posterior probabilities assigned to the most probable two categories, y_i and y_i^2, for example z_i:

$$C_M(z_i) = |P(y_i|z_i) - P(y_i^2|z_i)|$$

Dredze and Crammer (2008) proposed using both margin and minmax criterion together, since they do not necessarily select the same examples at each iteration.

Farris *et al.* (2008) have proposed an example selection criteria that is based on the relative likelihood for language identification tasks that use Gaussian Mixture Models:

$$RL(x_i) = \log p(x|UBM) - max_l(\log P(x|l)$$

where $P(x|UBM)$ is the likelihood according to a universal background model (UBM), and l is the language. This measure was shown to perform better than random sampling, and very similar to entropy. However, the examples chosen by relative likelihood and entropy were different.

An advantage of the certainty-based active learning method is that it is independent of the classifier used. The confidence score threshold θ for selecting examples is mainly determined by the capacity of the manual labeling effort or by the performance of the current classifier. However confidence scores may be low due to factors not related to the usefulness of an example for training, such as background noise for automatic speech recognition. Varadarajan *et al.* (2009) proposed a new confidence-based approach, the global entropy reduction maximization (GERM) algorithm, which aims to select examples that would result in the largest lattice entropy reduction over the whole data set, for adding to acoustic model (AM) training set. Assume $A_1, A_2, ..., A_r$ are the lattices output by the speech recognizer for example utterances $a_1, a_2, ..., a_r$, θ denotes the original AM, and θ^s denotes the new AM, trained after the selected utterances $z_1, ...z_k$ are added to the training set, then:

$$E[\Delta H(A_1, ..., A_r|z_1, ..., z_k)] =$$

$$E[H(A_1, ..., A_m|\theta) - H(A_1, ..., A_m|\theta^s)] =$$

$$E[H(A_1, ..., A_m|\theta)] - E[H(A_1, ..., A_m|\theta^s)] =$$

$$H(A_1, ..., A_m|\theta) - E[H(A_1, ..., A_m|\theta^s)]$$

is maximized. Since $H(A_1, ..., A_m)$ is fixed, this is equivalent to minimizing the expected entropy with the new model, $E[H(A_1, ..., A_m)]$. As the selection of an utterance for inclusion in the training set would affect the selection of another, this is an NP-hard optimization problem. Hence a greedy algorithm that makes two assumptions is proposed. The first assumption is that the expected entropy reduction on A_i is proportional to its original entropy:

$$E[\Delta H(A_i|a_j)] \cong \alpha H(A_i|\theta)$$

where α is a parameter related to the training algorithm used and the number of examples in the original training set. The second assumption is that the impact of an example utterance a_i on another example utterance a_j is a function of the distance $d(a_i, a_j)$ between the examples a_i and a_j. Hence, the approximate expected entropy reduction over A_i, when a_j is selected for transcription, is approximated by:

$$E[\Delta G(A_i|a_j)] \cong \alpha H(A_j|\theta)e^{-\beta d(a_i,a_j)}$$

where α and β can be estimated from the initial training set. Varadarajan *et al.* (2009) used a fixed value for these two parameters, and set them to 1. For measuring the distance between two example utterances a_i and a_j, they used the Kullback–Leibler divergence between the lattices A_i and A_j of the two examples. They showed superior active learning results in comparison to random sampling and speech recognizer confidence scores. Furthermore, they obtained better performance when they weighted each example a_i with weight w_i, computed by counting the utterances very close to it, according to the distance measure used:

$$w_i \propto \sum_{j \in R(i)} e^{-\beta d(a_i,a_j)}$$

where $j \in R(i)$ if and only if a_j is not selected for transcription and is closer to a_i than all utterances selected.

Certainty-based active learning methods have been studied in the context of many speech and natural language processing (NLP) tasks, including natural language parsing (Hwa, 2000; Thompson *et al.*, 1999), automatic speech recognition (Riccardi and Hakkani-Tür, 2005) and spoken utterance classification (Tur *et al.*, 2005). Compared with simpler statistical classification tasks, statistical parsers have a larger parameter space and instead of a fixed set of class labels, they recursively build parse trees as output. For example, Thompson *et al.* (1999) used certainty-based sample selection for active learning for semantic parsing, combining the certainty for each decision made during the parsing of an example. Hwa (2000) used sentence length and tree entropy as selection criteria in certainty-based methods for parsing and showed that using the latter for sample selection allowed one to achieve higher parsing accuracy with less data.

8.4.3 Committee-based Active Learning

In the *committee-based methods*, a distinct set of classifiers is created using the small set of annotated examples (Cohn *et al.*, 1994; Dagan and Engelson, 1995). The unannotated instances, whose annotations differ the most when presented to different classifiers, are considered as examples with highest uncertainty, and these are presented to labelers for annotation. Seung *et al.* (1992) introduced this approach calling it *query by committee*. The committee of classifiers can be formed by training each committee member using a random subset of the labeled training examples (Nomoto and Matsumoto, 1999) or using a different classification method. For example, Osborne (2002) used ensemble models trained with randomly sampled examples for active learning for Head-driven Phrase Structure Grammar (HPSG) parse selection.

The committee-based active learning algorithm is described in Figure 8.9 and depicted in Figure 8.10. In this algorithm, one proposed method to compute the annotation agreement between the different classifiers is the vote entropy (Dagan and Engelson, 1995), $V(z_i)$:

$$V(z_i) = -\frac{1}{\log m} \sum_{j=1}^{|L|} \frac{v(l_j, z_i)}{m} \log \frac{v(l_j, z_i)}{m}$$

where m is the number of classifiers in the committee, and $v(l_j, z_i)$ is the number of classifiers that assigned class l_j to the example z_i. Kappa statistics (Cohen, 1960), or other similar mea-

```
1. Given some amount of training data S_t, and a larger amount
   of unlabeled data in the pool S_p = {z_1, ..., z_n} where
2. While (labelers/utterances are available) do
   (a) Train the m classifiers, C_1, ..., C_m, using the current
       training data S_t
   (b) Classify the utterances in S_p using these classi-
       fiers computing the corresponding confidence scores
       C_1(z_i), ..., C_m(z_i),   i = 1, ..., n
   (c) Manually label the set S_k = {z_i : agg(C_1, ..., C_m) < θ}, where
       agg(C_1, ..., C_m) is the agreement between m different classi-
       fiers and θ is a threshold
   (d) S_t = S_t ⋃ S_k
   (e) S_p = S_p − S_k
```

Figure 8.9 The committee-based active learning algorithm

sures used for computing inter-annotator agreement can also be used to compute agreement of classifiers (Nomoto and Matsumoto, 1999).

Freund *et al.* (1997) provided an extensive analysis of the committee-based active learning approach, especially for learning of perceptrons. Liere and Tadepalli (1997) employed committee-based active learning for text categorization and obtained 2- to 30-fold reductions in the amount of human labeled data required, depending on the size of labeled dataset.

One drawback with the certainty-based methods is that it is hard to distinguish an informative example from an outlier. On the other hand, in order to train multiple classifiers required by committee-based active learning, one may need to divide the training data or feature set into multiple parts, and this may result in many weak classifiers instead of a single strong one.

8.4.4 Density-based Active Learning

Certainty- and committee-based active learning methods use the labeled data to train classification models, which are then used to automatically estimate labels for the unlabeled examples. One issue with these methods is that they do not consider the representativeness of the selected examples, and while selecting informative examples, they disregard any interaction between similar samples. However, when there are two unlabeled examples that have similar

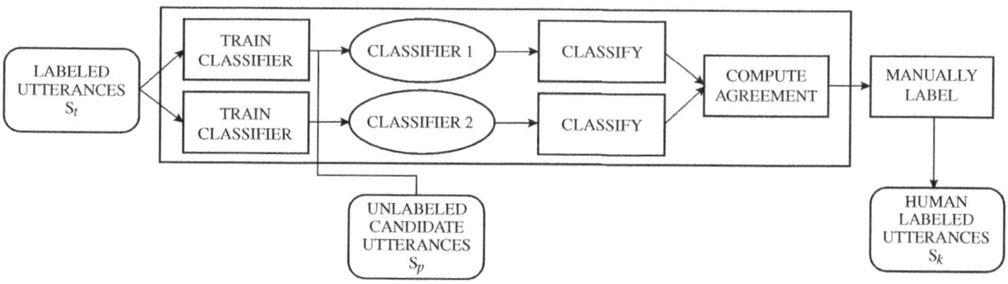

Figure 8.10 The committee-based active learning algorithm with two views

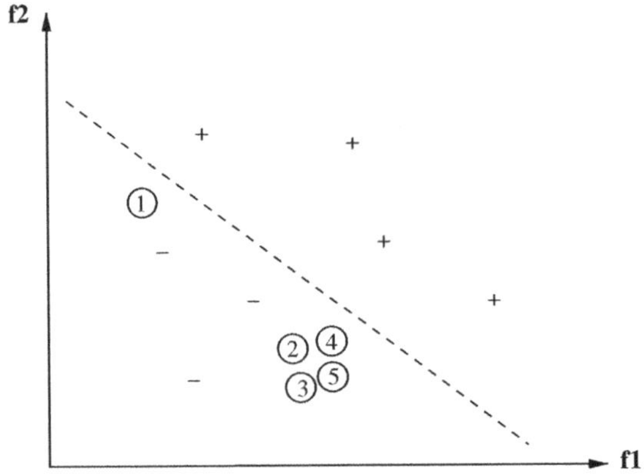

Figure 8.11 Example demonstrating the utility of density based active learning methods (adapted from Kuo and Goel, 2005)

low confidence scores, intuitively the one that has several similar examples in the unlabeled dataset is expected to be beneficial for a larger set of examples. The examples that have low certainties may also be outliers or rare examples, such that manual labeling may not improve classification performance. For example, Figure 8.11, shows a classification example, where the axes show feature values f1 and f2, and positive and negative examples are marked with "+" and "-" signs, unlabeled examples are shown with circles (with numbers for identification of specific examples). Examples 1 and 4 would be assigned a class label by the classifier with a low certainty, but manual labeling of example 4 may provide more information than example 1, in that its label may affect decisions for examples 2,3, and 5.

Density-based active learning methods aim to deal with the issue of representativeness of examples. They prefer examples to label from high density unlabeled regions. These approaches refine the models to effect a larger number of the unlabeled examples, and weigh certainty versus density (Nguyen and Smeulders, 2004; Xu *et al.*, 2003).

Xu *et al.* (2003) proposed a heuristics-based representative sampling approach that trains an initial support vector machine (SVM) classifier from labeled examples, then uses this to classify all unlabeled examples. Then, the examples that lie in the margin of the newly trained SVM are clustered into k groups by k-means clustering and k examples that are closest to the center of each cluster are presented to human experts for labeling.

Similarly, Tang *et al.* (2002) used k-means clustering to cluster the examples, using the similarity of their estimated parse trees (which can be erroneous), and then calculated the density of an example inside its cluster, and compared this method with several certainty-based sample selection measures for a semantic parsing task.

Simplifying a computationally expensive method that selects examples that result in minimum expected error proposed by Zhu *et al.* (2003), Kuo and Goel (2005) select examples that maximize the following value:

$$c(x)Q(\lambda(x))$$

where $c(x)$ is the count of example x, $\lambda(x)$ is the learned labeling rule, and $Q(\lambda(x))$ is the probability that the estimated class $\lambda(x)$ is in error, that is $Q(\lambda(x)) = 1 - P(\lambda(x)|x)$. They compared this method with a certainty-based baseline for natural language call-routing tasks and showed significant gains, especially when fewer unlabeled examples were annotated.

Donmez *et al.* (2007) empirically showed that density estimation methods perform well when the amount of labeled data is small, whereas certainty-based methods are better later in the learning curves. They proposed a context-sensitive, dual strategy for active learning, which switches the sample selection strategy based on an estimated future residual error criteria.

8.4.5 Stopping Criteria for Active Learning

Most of the previous work on active learning focused on example selection methods, and used the convergence of the error rate on a held-out data set as the stopping criterion (Farris *et al.*, 2008). However, creating an additional annotated held-out data set for estimating stopping point is against the purpose of active learning, as the goal is to minimize the annotation effort. Furthermore, there is no guarantee that a held-out data set will be representative of future examples, as this set is usually kept small to reduce annotation costs. To estimate a stopping point without using any extra annotation data, Hakkani-Tür *et al.* (2006) proposed using the convergence of error rate on the training data. Similarly, Kamm and Meyer (2004) proposed stopping when the likelihood of the training set increases, as the likelihood of the training data decreases when new data is introduced, hence there is potential to further improve the model with this new data.

Vlachos (2008) proposed using the confidence score of the classifier on an unlabeled data set, as this is expected to increase as we add labeled examples to the training data, since the classifier obtains more information about the task. However, when examples are added to the training data that contradict the information already in the model, the confidence is expected to drop, since existing features become weaker cues for classification. Hence, after each round of uncertainty-based sampling, they run the classifier over a separate, large dataset and estimate its confidence. When the confidence of the classifier drops, the annotation is stopped. Laws and Schütze (2008) also experimented with the confidence-based stopping criterion, and showed that the confidence can fluctuate and be noisy, hence estimating the peak performance can be difficult. They instead identify the point of convergence by computing gradients on the curve of estimated performance or confidence and stop when it approaches zero, as the rise of the performance estimation slows to an almost horizontal slope at about the time when true performance reaches its peak. They experiment with this approach using three selection functions: entropy, margin and minmax, and show that gradient based stopping reliably stops active learning for a named entity recognition task.

8.5 Combining Active Learning with Semi-supervised Learning

While building spoken language processing systems, the complementary problem of active learning is also very important: how can we exploit the remaining set of utterances which are not labeled by a human? This is a crucial component towards training statistical models with higher performance in a shorter time frame. The idea is to exploit the unlabeled examples by adding them to the smaller set of labeled data optionally in a weighted manner in order to improve performance of the classifier.

Semi-supervised learning algorithms have been extensively studied in the areas of machine learning, natural and spoken language processing, and artificial intelligence. Two very popular semi-supervised learning approaches include self-training and co-training. For self-training, the given model estimates the classes for the unlabeled portion of the data. Then the examples

1. Given some amount of human-labeled training data S_t, and a larger amount of unlabeled data in the pool $S_p = \{s_1, ..., s_n\}$
2. $S_u = \emptyset$
3. While (labelers/utterances are available) do
   (a) Train a classifier using the current training data S_t
   (b) Classify the utterances in S_p using this classifier
   (c) Selective sample the set S_k and manually annotate it
   (d) $S_t = S_t \bigcup S_k$
   (e) $S_p = S_p \backslash S_k$
   (f) $S_u = S_u \bigcup S_p$
   (g) Employ semi-supervised learning using S_u

Figure 8.12 Conceptual algorithm for combining active and semi-supervised learning

that are classified automatically are added to the training set, the model is retrained, and the whole process is iterated (Nigam and Ghani, 2000). In co-training, contrary to the traditional single view machine learning concept, the set of features in a multiview approach consists of two or more different feature subsets (views), each of which is distinguishable and sufficient for learning from itself individually (Blum and Mitchell, 1998). The main difference between these two approaches is that in the multiview concept the views are bootstrapped from each other, while in the single view self-training approach the algorithm trains itself.

Noting the parallellisms covering self-training and co-training versus certainty-based and committee-based active learning methods, the idea of combining active and semi-supervised learning was first introduced by McCallum and Nigam (1998). The conceptual algorithm is shown in Figure 8.12 and depicted in Figure 8.13. For speech processing, Riccardi and Hakkani-

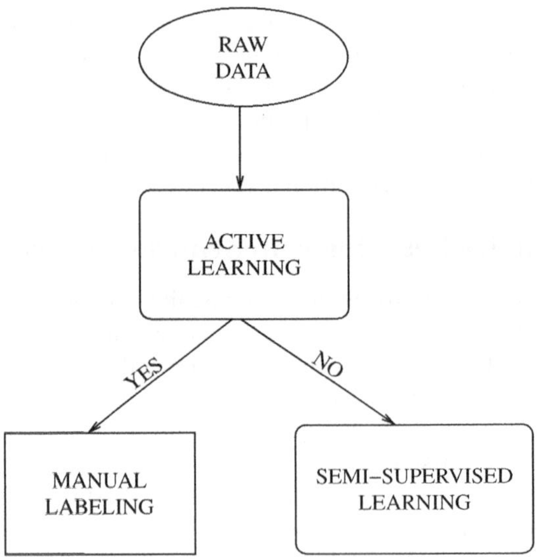

Figure 8.13 Combining active and semi-supervised learning (Tur *et al.* © 2005 Elsevier)

Tür (2003a) used a combination of active and semi-supervised learning for automatic speech recognition and have shown improvements for statistical language modeling. In that work, they mainly exploited confidence scores for words and utterances computed from ASR word lattices. Similarly, Tur *et al.* (2005) proposed similar methods for intent determination. They reported significant gains over active learning, especially when the in-domain data is limited.

8.6 Applications

While active learning approaches originated from machine learning, and its effectivess was first demonstrated in natural language processing related tasks such as parsing, text classification, web page categorization, and information extraction (Hwa, 2000; Liere and Tadepalli, 1997; McCallum and Nigam, 1998; Thompson *et al.*, 1999; Tong and Koller, 2001b), applications to spoken language processing immediately followed, beginning with speech recognition and then spoken language understanding. In this section we describe applications of active learning to selected automatic speech recognition and understanding tasks.

8.6.1 Automatic Speech Recognition

Two notable pioneering studies for employing active learning for speech recognition include (Hakkani-Tür *et al.*, 2002b) and (Kamm and Meyer, 2002). They both employed certainty-based active learning methods using the posterior probabilities (i.e., confidence scores) of the utterances, $c_{w_1^n}$, where w_1^n is an utterance with n words.

There are two leading methods in the literature, for confidence score estimation. The first one is based on acoustic measurements (Rose *et al.*, 1995) and the other one is based on word lattices (Falavigna *et al.*, 2002; Mangu *et al.*, 2000). The latter one has the advantage that the probability computation does not require training of an error estimator. There are also hybrid approaches, which use features from the two types of methods (Zhang and Rudnicky, 2001).

In the case of Hakkani-Tür *et al.* (2002b), utterance scores are estimated using the word confidence scores from the lattice output of ASR. This algorithm is based on word confusion networks and a detailed explanation and comparison of its performance with other approaches is presented in Hakkani-Tür and Riccardi (2003). A summary of the algorithm is as follows:

1. Compute the posterior probabilities for all transitions in the lattice.
2. Extract a path from the lattice (which can be the best, longest or a random path), and call this as the *pivot* of the alignment.
3. Traverse the lattice, and align all the transitions with the pivot, merging the transitions that correspond to the same word (or label) and occur in the same interval (by summing their posterior probabilities) to populate the word confusion network.

Hakkani-Tür *et al.* (2002b) use the state times or approximate state locations on the lattice, to align transitions that have occurred at or around the same time interval. Then they use the word posterior probability estimates on the best path of the confusion networks as word confidence scores, c_{w_i}, where w_i denotes a word.

To compute utterance level scores, various approaches were tried, and it was found out that two of them resulted in a better performance. One approach is to compute the confidence score of an utterance as the arithmetic mean of the confidence scores of all the words that the utterance contains:

$$c_{w_1^n} = \frac{1}{n}\sum_{i=1}^{n} c_{w_i} \tag{8.5}$$

The second approach is using a voting scheme with a threshold. The words with a score less than the threshold do not have any contribution to the utterance score. The words with a confidence score greater than the threshold contribute to the utterance score by 1. The final utterance score is normalized by the utterance length.

$$c_{w_1^n} = \frac{1}{n}\sum_{i=1}^{n} tr(c_{w_i}) \tag{8.6}$$

where

$$tr(c_{w_i}) = \left\{ \begin{array}{l} 1 \text{ if } c_{w_i} > \text{threshold} \\ 0 \text{ otherwise} \end{array} \right\} \tag{8.7}$$

These methods have been experimented using 26 963 utterances from the AT&T *How May I Help You?*^{SM} (HMIHY) human-machine speech dialogue database (Gorin *et al.*, 1997). The language models used in the experiments were trigram models based on Variable Ngram Stochastic Automata (VNSA), (Riccardi *et al.*, 1996). The acoustic models were based on subword units, with triphone context modeling.

Figure 8.14 shows the receiver operating characteristic (ROC) curve of correct classification versus false rejection rates of the words, by varying the confidence threshold value.

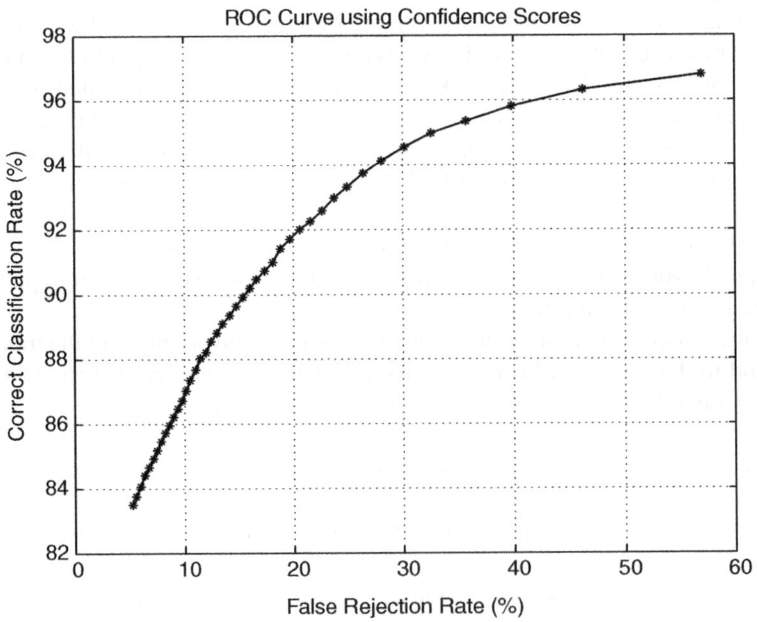

Figure 8.14 ROC curves (Riccardi and Hakkani-Tür © 2005 IEEE)

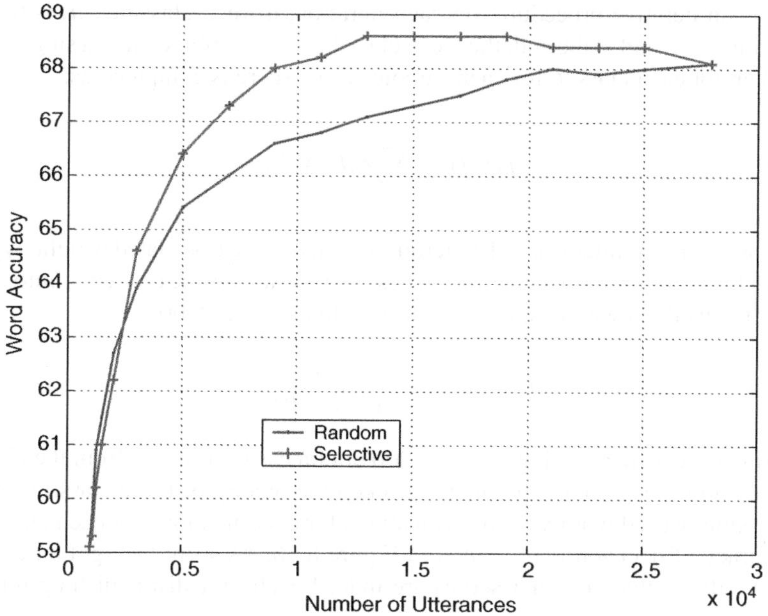

Figure 8.15 Learning curves for novel domain language using fixed acoustic model (Riccardi and Hakkani-Tür © 2005 IEEE)

The random and selective sampling learning curves are plotted in Figure 8.15.

As expected, the best performance with random sampling was achieved using all of the training data (27 963 utterances). Active learning achieved the same word accuracy (68.1%) with selective sampling and using 64% less data (around 10 000 utterances). Furthermore, the best accuracy with active learning (68.6%) was significantly better when 13,000 utterances (less than half of all the data) were used.

Later this work was extended to exploit unselected samples in a semi-supervised learning framework (Hakkani-Tür *et al.*, 2004; Riccardi and Hakkani-Tür, 2003b).

Kamm and Meyer, on the other hand, employed active learning using 46 730 sentences (a series of 6 alphadigits) from the OGI Alphadigit Corpus and focused only on the acoustic model. They have also observed that using about 25% of the training data, they achieve the same performance as using all of the data. Furthermore, when 65% of the data is used, a significantly better recognition performance can be obtained.

8.6.2 Intent Determination

As discussed in Chapter 4, intent determination aims at classifying the user's utterance into one of the predefined categories. This task can be framed as a statistical classification problem for goal-oriented call routing systems (Kuo *et al.*, 2002; Natarajan *et al.*, 2002; Tur *et al.*, 2002). For intent determination, Tur *et al.* (2004) have proposed certainty-based approaches and performed experiments using the AT&T HMIHY system. In this study, they used a Boosting-style classification algorithm for call classification (Schapire, 2001).

Boosting is an iterative procedure; on each iteration, a weak classifier, h, is trained on a weighted training set, and at the end, the weak classifiers are combined into a single, combined classifier. Then for each class, l, for each sample, x, the score is computed as:

$$f(x, l) = \sum_{t=1}^{T} \alpha_t h_t(x, l).$$

where h_t is the weak classifier learned at iteration t and α is the associated weight, typically associated with the accuracy of that classifier. These scores can then be converted into confidence scores using the well known logistic function (Friedman *et al.*, 2000):

$$Conf(l|x) = \frac{1}{1 + e^{-2f(x,l)}}$$

They performed experiments using about 40 000 utterances for training from the HMIHY call classification corpus. The first experiment checked the quality of these classifier confidence scores. They simply used word n-grams as features for classification. For each classifier score bin, the accuracy of decision is presented in Figure 8.16. As seen, they got an almost diagonal curve, verifying that classifier scores are indeed useful for distinguishing misclassified utterances.

Figure 8.17 shows the results of active learning. It is evident that selective sampling significantly reduces the need for labeled data. For instance, achieving a test error of 26% requires 40 000 examples if they are randomly chosen, but only around 11 000 selected examples, a saving of 72.5%.

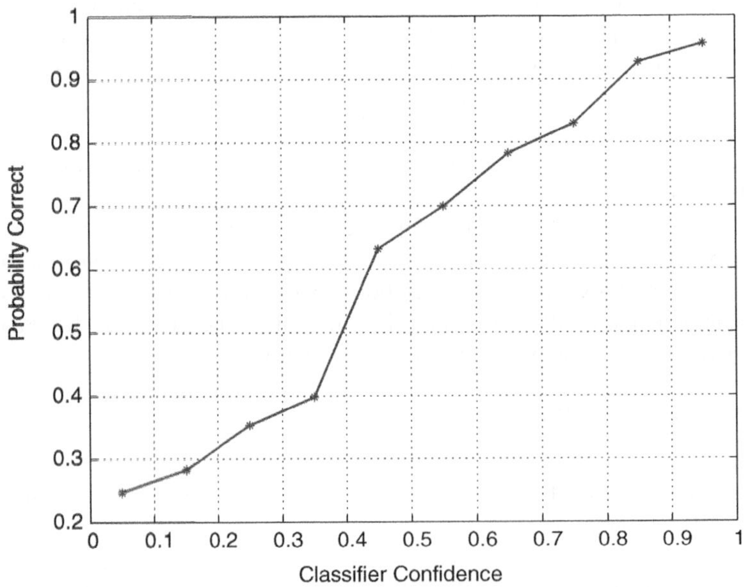

Figure 8.16 Classification accuracy with respect to the classifier score (Tur *et al.* © 2005 Elsevier)

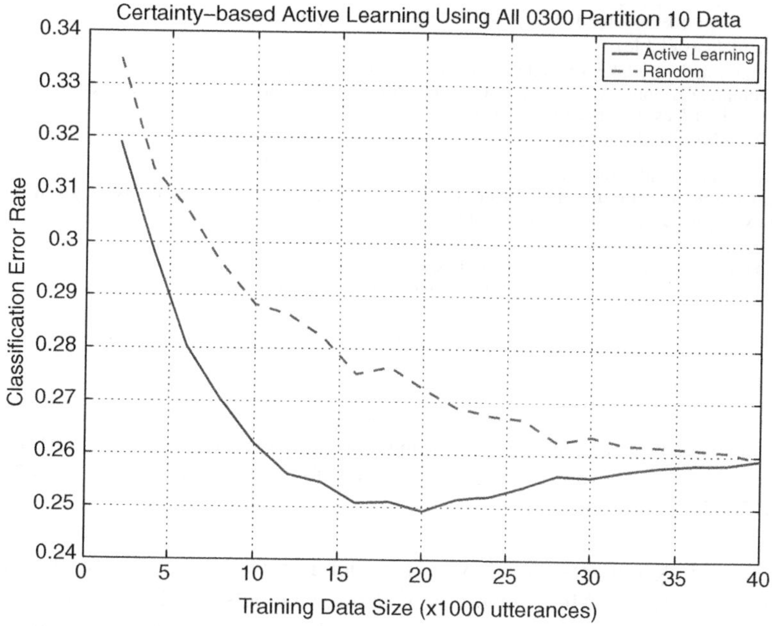

Figure 8.17 The error rates achieved using active learning and random selection of examples for labeling. At each iteration, utterances are selected from a fixed pool containing all the unlabeled utterances (Tur *et al.* © 2005 Elsevier)

8.6.3 Concept Segmentation/Labeling

As seen in Chapter 3, conversational systems require the SLU component to extract domain-specific concepts (and its values) such as those shown in Figure 8.3 and 8.4. An example of such segmentation from the ATIS corpus is shown in Figure 8.18.

The concept labels identify relevant concepts for the task, such as the departure city (*fromlog.city*) and the *null* tag is for the empty concept. Such segmentation is performed by a chunk parser where the semantic labels are domain specific and their values are extracted from the surface forms. Such values are generally disambiguated and normalized according to the domain knowledge base (e.g. flight relational database).

Identifying the correct concepts and their values is critical to enable the dialogue manager to formulate the most appropriate strategies such as resolving concept ambiguities (e.g. unknown departure city), formulating additional task constraints (e.g. requesting time of departure) etc.. As mentioned in the previous chapter, the two approaches available for such shallow parsing tasks are either based on grammars or statistical models. In the first case grammar development is a human-intensive, time-consuming process. For this reason, grammar-based approaches are

Figure 8.18 Example of domain concept segmentation

1. Train a model μ using small amount of N labeled data randomly selected (S_L)
2. while (labeler/data available)
   (a) Use μ to automatically label the unlabeled part of the corpus (S_U)
   (b) Rank automatically annotated examples (S_U) according to the confidence measure given by μ
   (c) Select a batch of k examples with the lowest score (S_k)
   (d) Ask for human labeling on S_k

   (e) **Use μ to automatically label S_L**
   (f) **Rank automatically annotated examples (S_L) according to the confidence measure given by μ**
   (g) **select I examples under a given threshold (S_I)**

   (g).1. STRATEGY 1: **remove (S_I) from the train data ($S_L = S_L - S_I$)**
   (g).2. STRATEGY 2: **Manually check/correct S_I to obtain S'_I then ($S_L = S_L - S_I + S'_I$)**

   (h) $S_L = S_L + S_k$
   (i) Train a new model μ with S_L

Figure 8.19 The label-noise robust active learning algorithm: the uncertainty based AL follows the steps 1,2(a,b,c,d,h,i), the noise-label robust AL algorithms follow the baseline + the steps 2(e,f,g) in bold (© IEEE 2005)

appropriate for simple conversational systems which require few (one or two) concepts to be parsed for each utterance. More generally, statistical models can handle the complexity of spoken natural language by learning from annotated examples such as in Figure 8.6.3. The annotation of training examples is costly and time-consuming and such costs can be minimized by making active learning a key component of SLU model learning. Semantic annotation by humans can also be noisy due to language ambiguity or lack of contextual information, as available in conversational systems.

In Figure 8.19 we outlined the algorithm for active learning that combines the certainty-based approach with noise-robustness strategies proposed in (Raymond and Riccardi, 2008). The algorithm is an extension of the committee-based AL algorithm and augmented with heuristic strategies to control the quality of semantic labels. The two strategies highlighted in bold are either *data intensive* (strategy 1) or *supervision intensive* (strategy 2). In the first strategy, annotated examples falling below a given confidence threshold are removed from the selected training set, while in the second strategy, further supervision is requested for the selected example x and a new label is provided.

In Figure 8.20 the performance of the algorithm is presented on the ATIS corpus. The performance of the uncertainty based algorithm (B in Figure 8.20) are improved in the region of the learning curve where asymptotic performances are reached or affected by outliers (rightmost part of the curve). The superior performance of the *supervision intensive* strategy supports the general claim of the active learning approach, *the less the better*, in contrast to the original claim of passive approaches, *the more the better*.

8.6.4 Dialogue Act Tagging

Venkataraman *et al.* (2005) have employed active learning for dialogue act tagging. Dialogue act tagging will be covered in Chapter 9. Basically, it is the task of categorizing each of the spoken utterances into one of the task-independent semantic categories, such as *Suggestion*, or *Agreement*. They have used hidden Markov model (HMM) and Maximum Entropy (MaxEnt) based classification algorithms for this task. They performed experiments using

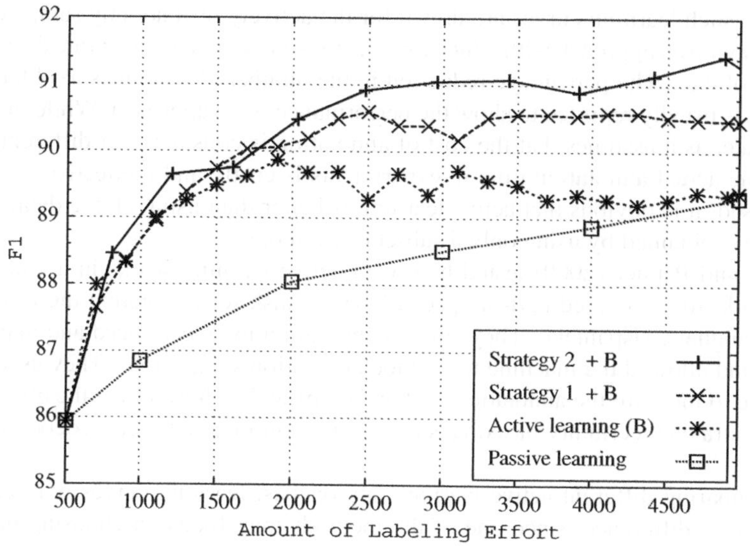

Figure 8.20 Performance (F1 measure) of the label-noise robust active learning algorithm on the ATIS semantic chunk parsing task (© IEEE 2005)

the ICSI meeting corpus (Shriberg *et al.*, 2004) which has 75 naturally occurring meetings, each about an hour long. The higher level dialogue act tags are used in this study, which are backchannels, questions, statements, disruptions, and floor mechanisms.

They basically employed certainty-based active learning and computed the entropy of the distribution over all dialogue act tags:

$$H(DA|x) = \sum_{DA_i} -P(DA_i|x) \log P(DA_i|x)$$

where DA_i is one of the five dialogue act tags. The samples which have highest entropy are selected for manual annotation. While the paper does not provide any learning curves, they computed the performance at one point when 10 000 samples were selectively or randomly sampled. They observed that while for HMM there is no performance improvement, MaxEnt performance improves significantly. Furthermore, they attempted to exploit the unselected data in a semi-supervised fashion using hypothesized tags, but with no success. One thing to note is that, they did not used any sophisticated contextual cues. Their features consisted of first and last two words, utterance length, speaker change, and first word of the next utterance. The active learning framework did not help the classification of the frequent and highly ambiguous utterances such as *yeah* or *right* with this feature set. In that sense, this study showed an interesting problem of the dependency of the active learning approaches on the feature set employed for the classification task.

8.7 Evaluation of Active Learning Methods

A common way of comparing and evaluating active learning methods is plotting accuracy or error rate learning curves of the task performance with differing amounts of annotated training data. Usually such learning curves are drawn for the actively or randomly sampled data sets. The goal is having an approach with which the accuracy increases (or error rate decreases) with less amount of data. The percentage reduction in the number of examples to obtain the same performance is usually reported to show the performance of an approach. While this approach is approximate, as it assumes that the cost of annotation is constant over different examples, measuring the actual annotation time in experiments is costly and ineffective. If a complete data set is used, it is obvious that active learning is better than using all the data, if the same performance is obtained by using only a subset of examples.

Baldridge and Palmer (2009) tested how well active learning works in a real data labeling framework, for a detailed part-of-speech labeling task for annotating the morphemes of the Mayan language Uspanteko. They studied annotation by experienced and unexperienced annotators, and allowed the machine to provide annotation suggestions. They used actual annotation time to measure the annotation cost and empirically showed that the effectiveness of the selection strategy (certainty-based versus random sampling in this case) depends on labeler expertise.

When comparing different active learning approaches, learning curves only approximate the performance difference, since one of the methods may focus on choosing hard-to-label examples, which may be costly in terms of annotation time. This may not be critical for tasks such as automatic speech recognition, where there is probably not much variation in the transcription of words. However, annotation time is important for tasks such as parsing, where the cost of annotating a longer sentence with a rare grammatical form may be significantly different from a very simple sentence. If a data set with approximate annotation times, possibly averaged over multiple annotators, for each example is collected, it would provide a better framework for measuring the performance of active learning methods for tasks such as parsing.

8.8 Discussion and Conclusions

We have presented various studies employing active learning techniques for building better SLU systems in shorter time frames. Given that, state-of-the-art SLU systems are based on statistical modeling approaches, the need for in-domain annotated data will persist for some time. We believe that the methods presented in this chapter will guide readers to pursue new directions to alleviate the need for more and better quality data. This is also important to ease the pre-processing headache of all the available data, and to cope with the information overload due to the ever increasing quantity of natural and spoken language data.

Two noteworthy directions to this end include crowdsourcing and light or implicit supervision. Crowdsourcing refers to outsourcing annotation tasks, traditionally performed by professional annotators. While the quality of these annotations depend on the task and the clarity of the annotation guidelines, the number of studies employing such approaches are increasing. Services such as Amazon Mechanical Turk allows for access to labelers, however reliability of the annotation may be unknown. In the case of multiple labelers/oracles with different reliabilities, Donmez *et al.* (2009) estimate confidence intervals of individual labelers. Regarding SLU systems, Paek *et al.* (2007) used a web-based computer game to collect data for producing alternatives of business listings to build a directory assistance system. A recent study analyzing the applicability of crowdsourcing for spoken language understanding is presented by Liu *et al.* (2010). They used Amazon Turk to collect data for a spoken dialogue system. In just 3 days, they collected thousands of useful sentences, proving the feasibility of the approach.

The other direction waiting to be explored is the tighter coupling of advances in unsupervised learning techniques with very small amounts of selectively sampled annotated in-domain data. This requires employing data mining and clustering techniques considering the already annotated data despite relatively small quantities. Given that it is almost always possible to produce "some" amount of representative in-domain data, the main idea is using this as a seed for unsupervised learning from the "found" data, such as from the web. There are some studies which have worked in this direction. Kamangar *et al.* (2008) presented a template-based question answering system, where, based on the question, the models are re-trained on-the-fly. This is similar to dynamic adaptation of language models for speech recognition as presented by Bulyko *et al.* (2007). The adaptation data is collected from the web or a news corpus using retrieval or classification techniques.

References

Aitchinson J 1994 *Words in the mind: An introduction to the mental lexicon.* Oxford:Blackwell.

Alberti C, Bacchiani M, Bezman A, Chelba C, Drofa A, Liao H, Moreno P, Power T, t AS, Shugrina M and Siohan O 2009 An audio indexing system for election video material *Acoustics, Speech and Signal Processing, 2009. ICASSP 2009. IEEE International Conference*, pp 4873–4876.

ARPA 1993 Arpa spoken language systems technology workshop.

Artstein R and Poesio M 2008 Inter-coder agreement for computational linguistics. *Computational Linguistics* **34**(4), 555–596.

Baldridge J and Palmer A 2009 How well does active learning actually work? time-based evaluation of cost-reduction strategies for language documentation *Proceedings of the 2009 Conference on Empirical Methods in Natural Language Processing*.

Blum A and Mitchell T 1998 Combining labeled and unlabeled data with co-training *Proceedings of the Workshop on Computational Learning Theory (COLT)*, Madison, WI.

Bonneau-Maynard H, Rosset S, Ayache C, Kuhn A and Mostefa D 2005 Semantic annotation of the french media dialogue corpus *Proceedings INTERSPEECH 2005*.

Bulyko I, Ostendorf M, Siu M, Ng T, Stolcke A and Cetin O 2007 Web resources for language modeling in conversational speech recognition. *ACM Transactions on Speech and Language Processing* **5**(1), 1–25.

Chen W, Liu G and Guo J 2008 A confusion network based confusion measure for active learning in speech recognition *Proceedings of the International Conference on Natural Language Processing and Knowledge Engineering (NLP-KE)*, Beijing.

Cohen J 1960 A coefficient of agreement for nominal scale. *Educational and Psychological Measurement* **20**(1), 37–46.

Cohn D, Atlas L and Ladner R 1994 Improving generalization with active learning. *Machine Learning* **15**, 201–221.

Cohn D, Ghaharamani Z and Jordan M 1996 Active learning with statistical models. *Journal of Artificial Intelligence Research* (4), 129–145.

Dagan I and Engelson S 1995 Committee-based sampling for training probabilistic classifier s *Proc. of the 12th International Conference on Machine Lea rning*, pp 150–157.

Dinarelli M, Quarteroni S, Tonelli S, Moschitti A and Riccardi G 2009 Annotating spoken dialogues: from speech segments to dialogue acts and frame semantics *Proceedings of SRSL 2009 Workshop of EACL, Athens, Greece*.

Donmez P, Carbonell JG and Bennett PN 2007 Dual strategy active learning *Proceedings of the 18th European Conference on Machine Learning*.

Donmez P, Carbonell JG and Schneider J 2009 Efficiently learning the accuracy of labeling sources for selective sampling *Proceedings of the International Conference on Knowledge Discovery and Data Mining (KDD)*.

Dredze M and Crammer K 2008 Active learning with confidence *Proceedings of ACL-08: HLT*, pp 233–236, Columbus, Ohio.

Fabbrizio GD, Tur G and Hakkani-Tür D 2004 Bootstrapping spoken dialogue systems with data reuse *Proceedings of the 5th SIGdial Workshop on Discourse and Dialogue*.

Falavigna D, Gretter R and Riccardi G 2002 Acoustic and word lattice based algorithms for confidence scores *Proceedings of the International Conference on Spoken Language Processing (ICSLP)*, Denver, CO.

Farris D, White C and Khudanpur S 2008 Sample selection for automatic language identification *Proceedings of the 2008 IEEE International Conference on Acoustics, Speech and Signal Processing*, pp 4225–4228.

Fenson, L. D, Reznick P, J.S. B, E., Thal D and Pethick S 1994 *Variability in early communicative development*. Monographs of the Society for Research in Child Development.

Freund Y, Seung HS, Shamir E and Tishby N 1997 Selective sampling using the query by committee algorithm. *Machine Learning* **28**, 133–168.

Friedman J, Hastie T and Tibshirani R 2000 Additive logistic regression: A statistical view of boosting. *The Annals of Statistics* **38**(2), 337–374.

Geman S, Bienenstock E and Doursat R 1992 Neural networks and the bias/variance dilemma. *Neural Computation* (4), 4–58.

Gorin AL, Abella A, Alonso T, Riccardi G and Wright JH 2002 Automated natural spoken dialogue. *IEEE Computer Magazine* **35**(4), 51–56.

Gorin AL, Riccardi G and Wright JH 1997 How May I Help You? . *Speech Communication* **23**, 113–127.

Hakkani-Tür D and Riccardi G 2003 A general algorithm for word graph matrix decomposition *Proceedings of the International Conference on Acoustics, Speech and Signal Processing (ICASSP)*, Hong Kong.

Hakkani-Tür D, Riccardi G and Gorin A 2002a Active learning for automatic speech recognition *IEEE INTERNATIONAL CONFERENCE ON ACOUSTICS SPEECH AND SIGNAL PROCESSING*, vol. 4, pp 3904–3907.

Hakkani-Tür D, Riccardi G and Gorin A 2002b Active learning for automatic speech recognition *Proceedings of the International Conference on Acoustics, Speech and Signal Processing (ICASSP)*, Orlando, FL.

Hakkani-Tür D, Riccardi G and Tur G 2006 An active approach to spoken language processing. *ACM Transactions on Speech and Language Processing (TSLP)* **3**(3), 1â31.

Hakkani-Tür D, Tur G, Rahim M and Riccardi G 2004 Unsupervised and active learning in automatic speech recognition for call classification *Proceedings of the International Conference on Acoustics, Speech and Signal Processing (ICASSP)*, Montreal, Canada.

Hwa R 2000 Sample selection for statistical grammar induction *Proceedings of the Joint SIGDAT Conference on Empirical Methods in Natural Language Processing and Very Large Corpora*.

Jelinek F 1997 *Statistical Methods for Speech Recognition*. MIT Press, Cambridge, MA.

Kamangar K, Hakkani-Tür D, Tur G and Levit M 2008 An iterative unsupervised learning method for information distillation *Proceedings of ICASSP*.

Kamm T and Meyer G 2001 Automatic selection of transcribed training material *Proceedings of IEEE Workshop on Automatic Speech Recognition and Understanding*, pp 417–420.

Kamm T and Meyer G 2002 Selective sampling of training data for speech recognition *Proceedings of Human Language Technology Conference*, San Diego.

Kamm TM and Meyer GGL 2004 Robustness aspects of active learning for acoustic modeling *Proceedings of ICSLP*, Jeju Island, Korea.

Kuo HKJ and Goel V 2005 Active learning with minimum expected error for spoken language understanding *Proceedings of Interspeech*, pp 437–440.

Kuo HKJ, Lee C, Zitouni I, Fosler-Lusser E and Ammicht E 2002 Discriminative training for call classification and routing *Proceedings of the International Conference on Spoken Language Processing (ICSLP)*, Denver, CO.

Lafferty J, McCallum A and Pereira F 2001 Conditional random fields: Probabilistic models for segmenting and labeling sequence data *Proc. 18th International Conf. on Machine Learning*, San Francisco, CA.

Laws F and Schütze H 2008 Stopping criteria for active learning of named entity recognition *Proceedings of the 22nd International Conference on Computational Linguistics (Coling 2008)*.

Lewis D and Catlett J 1994 Heterogeneous uncertainty sampling for supervised learning *Proc. of the 11th International Conference on Machine Learning*, pp 148–156.

Liere R and Tadepalli P 1997 Active learning with committees for text categorization *Proceedings of the Conference of the American Association for Artificial Intelligence (AAAI)*, Providence, RI.

Liu S, Seneff S and Glass J 2010 A collective data generation method for speech language models *Proceedings of the IEEE Spoken Language Technologies (SLT) Workshop*, Berkeley, CA.

Mangu L, Brill E and Stolcke A 2000 Finding consensus in speech recognition: word error minimization and other applications of confusion networks. *Computer Speech and Language* **14**(4), 373–400.

McCallum AK and Nigam K 1998 Employing EM and pool-based active learning for text classification *Proceedings of the International Conference on Machine Learning (ICML)*, Madison, WI.

Miller S, Schwartz R, Bobrow R and Ingria R 1994 Statistical language processing using hidden understanding models *Spoken Language Systems Technology Workshop*, Princeton, N.J.

Natarajan P, Prasad R, Suhm B and McCarthy D 2002 Speech enabled natural language call routing: BBN call director *Proceedings of the International Conference on Spoken Language Processing (ICSLP)*, Denver, CO.

Nguyen HT and Smeulders A 2004 Active learning using pre-clustering *Proceedings of the 21th International Conference on Machine Learning (ICML)*.

Nigam K and Ghani R 2000 Understanding the behaviour of co-training *Proceedings of the Workshop on Text Mining at the 6th ACM SIGKDD at the KDD*.

Nomoto T and Matsumoto F 1999 Learning discourse relations with active data selection *Proceedings of EMNLP*, College Park, MD.

Osborne M 2002 Shallow parsing using noisy and non-stationary training material. *The Journal of Machine Learning Research* **2**, 695–719.

Paek T, Ju Y and Meek C 2007 People watcher: A game for eliciting human-transcribed data for automated directory assistance *Proceedings of the Interspeech*, Antwerp, Belgium.

Pieraccini R and Levin E 1993 A learning approach to natural language understanding *NATO-ASI, New Advances and Trends in Speech Recognition and Coding*, vol. 1, pp 261–279, Bubion (Granada), Spain.

Quarteroni S, Riccardi G and Dinarelli M 2009 What's in an ontology for spoken language understanding.

Raymond C and Riccardi G 2008 Learning with noisy supervision for spoken language understanding *Proceedings of International Conference on Spoken Language Processing (Interspeech)*, vol. 16, pp 4989–4992, Brighton, UK.

Riccardi G and Hakkani-Tür D 2003a Active and unsupervised learning for automatic speech recognition *Proceedings of the European Conference on Speech Communication and Technology (EUROSPEECH)*, Geneva, Switzerland.

Riccardi G and Hakkani-Tür D 2003b Active and unsupervised learning for automatic speech recognition *Proceedings of the European Conference on Speech Communication and Technology (EUROSPEECH)*, Geneva, Switzerland.

Riccardi G and Hakkani-Tür D 2005 Active learning: Theory and applications to automatic speech recognition. *IEEE Transactions on Speech and Audio Processing* **13**(4), 504–511.

Riccardi G, Pieraccini R and Bocchieri E 1996 Stochastic automata for language modeling. *Computer Speech and Language* **10**, 265–293.

Rose R, B.H.Juang and Lee C 1995 A training procedure for verifying string hypotheses in continuous speech recognition *Proceedings of the International Conference on Acoustics, Speech and Signal Processing (ICASSP)*, Detroit, MI.

Roy D 2009 New horizons in the study of child language acquisition *Proceedings of the INTERSPEECH*.

Schapire RE 2001 The boosting approach to machine learning: An overview *Proceedings of the MSRI Workshop on Nonlinear Estimation and Classification*, Berkeley, CA.

Schapire RE and Singer Y 2000 BoosTexter: A boosting-based system for text categorization. *Machine Learning* **39**(2/3), 135–168.

Seltzer ML and Zhang L 2009 The data deluge: Challenges and opportunities of unlimited data in statistical signal processing *Proceedings of the 2009 IEEE International Conference on Acoustics, Speech and Signal Processing*, pp 3701–3704.

Settles B and Craven M 2008 An analysis of active learning strategies for sequence labeling tasks *Proceedings of the 2008 Conference on Empirical Methods in Natural Language Processing*, Honolulu, HI.

Seung HS, Opper M and Sompolinsky H 1992 Query by committee *Proceedings of the Workshop on Computational Learning Theory (COLT)*, Pittsburgh, PA.

Shriberg E, Dhillon R, Bhagat S, Ang J and Carvey H 2004 The ICSI Meeting Recorder Dialogue Act (MRDA) corpus *Proceedings of the 5th SIGdial Workshop on Discourse and Dialogue at Human Language Technology Conference (HLT)-Conference of the North American Chapter of the Association for Computational Linguistics (NAACL) 2004*, pp 97–100.

Suendermann D, Evanini K, Liscombe J, Hunter P, Dayanidhi K and Pieraccini R 2009 From rule-based to statistical grammars: Continuous improvement of large-scale spoken dialogue systems *Proc. of the ICASSP*.

Tang M, Luo X and Roukos S 2002 Active learning for statistical natural language parsing *Proceedings of the 40th Annual Meeting of the Association for Computational Linguistics (ACL)*.

Thompson CA, Califf ME and Mooney RJ 1999 Active learning for natural language parsing and information extraction *Proceedings of the 16th International Conference on Machine Learning Conference (ICML)*.

Tong S and Koller D 2001a Active learning for structure in bayesian networks *Seventeenth International Joint Conference on Artificial Intelligence*, pp 863–869, Seattle, WA.

Tong S and Koller D 2001b Support vector machine active learning with applications to text classification. *Journal of Machine Learning Research* **2**, 45–66.
Tur G, Hakkani-Tür D and Schapire RE 2005 Combining active and semi-supervised learning for spoken language understanding. *Speech Communication* **45**(2), 171–186.
Tur G, Schapire RE and Hakkani-Tür D 2004 Active learning for spoken language understanding *Proceedings of the ICASSP*.
Tur G, Wright J, Gorin A, Riccardi G and Hakkani-Tür D 2002 Improving spoken language understanding using word confusion networks *Proceedings of the International Conference on Spoken Language Processing (ICSLP)*, Denver, CO.
Varadarajan D, Yu D, Deng L and Acero A 2009 Maximizing global entropy reduction for active learning in speech recognition *Proceedings of ICASSP*, Taipei, Taiwan.
Venkataraman A, Liu Y, Shriberg E and Stolcke A 2005 Does active learning help automatic dialogue act tagging in meeting data? *Proceedings of the Interspeech*, Lisbon, Portugal.
Vlachos A 2008 A stopping criterion for active learning. *Computer, Speech and Language* **22**(3), 295–312.
Xu Z, Yu K, Tresp V, Xu X and Wang J 2003 Representative sampling for text classification using support vector machines *Proceedings of the 25th European Conf. on Information Retrieval Research (ECIR)*.
Zhang C and Chen T 2002 An active learning framework for content-based information retrieval. *IEEE Transactions on Multimedia* **4**(2), 260–268.
Zhang R and Rudnicky A 2001 Word level confidence annotation using combinations of features *Proceedings of the European Conference on Speech Communication and Technology (EUROSPEECH)*, Aalborg, Denmark.
Zhu X, Lafferty J and Ghahramani Z 2003 Combining active learning and semi-supervised learning using gaussian fields and harmonic functions *Proceedings of ICML Workshop on the Continuum from Labeled to Unlabeled Data in Machine Learning and Data Mining*, pp 58–65.

Part 2

Spoken Language Understanding for Human/Human Conversations

9

Human/Human Conversation Understanding

Gokhan Tur and Dilek Hakkani-Tür
Microsoft Speech Labs, Microsoft Research, U.S.A.

While the term spoken language understanding mostly refers to the understanding of spoken utterances directed at machines, as they are more constrained, recent progress in recognition and understanding of human/human conversations and multiparty meetings is not negligible. On the other hand, even though there is significant amount of previous work on discourse processing, particularly in social sciences (such as in the field of conversation analysis), automatic processing of human/human conversations is a relatively newer area for spoken language processing.

In this chapter, we discuss on two-party and multiparty human/human conversation understanding, mainly focusing on discourse modeling, speech act modeling, and argument diagramming. We also try to bridge the gap between studies in human/human conversations and human/machine systems in order to either build better human/machine conversational systems or to better understand human/human conversations.

9.1 Background

While speech is the most natural medium of human/human communication, little spoken data is available for research purposes due to privacy or copyright issues or issues relating to signal quality such as non-ideal recording conditions. Unlike textual communication, such as email or instant messaging, almost all spoken interactions are lost because they remain unrecorded and unprocessed.

Switchboard (Godfrey *et al.*, 1992), collected in the early 1990s in an effort sponsored by the U.S. Defense Advanced Research Projects Agency (DARPA), is arguably the most famous human/human conversations corpus. It is a large multi-speaker corpus with 2,430 telephone conversations lasting from 3 to 10 minutes duration (averaging 6 minutes) each, spoken by about 500 paid volunteers on predetermined topics. The corpus totals 240 hours of speech

Spoken Language Understanding: Systems for Extracting Semantic Information from Speech, First Edition.
Edited by Gokhan Tur and Renato De Mori.

- ...
- 172.16 175.05 A: because anytime you can walk through a door make ten dollars an hour. laugh
- 175.20 176.87 B: %oh, that's, that's very good.
- 175.47 176.92 A: i, i don't, i don't see any
- 176.92 179.25 A: ((well)) yes it is very good, you know?
- 178.02 179.31 B: mhm, that's ((really)) good.
- 179.80 182.61 B: i know a friend of mine also, he worked at the post office
- 182.63 186.70 B: and, i worked at the post office a long time ago, ((and)) it was very powerful.
- 182.87 183.35 A: mhm.
- 185.64 186.63 A: ((y)) so did i.
- 187.03 188.97 B: oh you did? laugh okay laugh.
- 187.07 187.48 A: mhm.
- 187.84 188.88 A: yes i did.
- 189.03 189.75 B: {breath} and
- 189.42 192.41 A: as a matter of fact, i worked at the ~DC office, north ^ Capital street.
- 192.46 193.38 B: %oh okay.
- 193.46 194.01 A: yeah.
- 193.91 195.49 B: and when, remember when
- 195.55 198.07 B: well, y- i don't know how old you are, but i'm telling my age.
- 198.09 201.89 B: (( )) when the post off- when the postal workers, when they went on strike
- 198.59 198.99 A: {laugh}
- ...

Figure 9.1 An excerpt transcription from the Switchboard corpus with disfluency (%), lower human transcriber confidence (double parentheses) nonspeech (e.g. "breath"), and named entity (~) annotations

and about 3 million words of transcription. This corpus was first designed to complement the TIMIT corpus (Zue *et al.*, 1990), which was read speech transcribed in terms of words and phonemes and the ATIS corpus (Price, 1990), which consists of human/machine interactions. Figure 9.1 shows an excerpt from the Switchboard corpus. The original targeted research areas focused on speech and speaker recognition rather than speech understanding. This corpus has indeed been extensively used in these areas and is still being used. After the success of this study, a follow-up corpus, named Switchboard-II, was collected.

The need for more natural and multilingual/accented conversational speech corpora has led to collections named as Call-Home and Call-Friend, which contain a smaller number of speakers making relatively longer telephone conversations to people they already know.

Furthermore, goal-oriented human/human dialogues have been collected, which is a mix of ATIS and Switchboard corpora. Some notable studies include the TRAINS (Allen *et al.*, 1995) corpus for transportation planning, the Monroe (Stent, 2000) corpus for disaster handling, and the MapTask (Anderson *et al.*, 1991) corpus for giving directions on a map. TRAINS is a collection of task-oriented human/human dialogues for the transportation domain. The speaker tries to ship boxcars to some location. The other human, playing an assistant system which has access to extra information tries to help the speaker.

With the start of another large scale DARPA program, named EARS (Effective, Affordable, Reusable Speech-to-Text), a larger corpus, named Fisher, has been collected with 16,454 English conversations, totaling 2,742 hours of speech. This data has been transcribed using LDC "quick transcription" specifications, that include a single pass with some automated preprocessing.

The speech processing community has then studied extensions of two-party human/human conversations in few directions: multiparty human/human conversations (or meetings), lectures, and broadcast conversations (such as talkshows, broadcast discussions, etc.).

Projects initiated at Carnegie Mellon University (CMU) (Burger *et al.*, 2002) and International Computer Science Institute (ICSI) (Janin *et al.*, 2004) in the late 1990s and early 2000s collected substantial meeting corpora and investigated many of the standard speech processing tasks on this genre. Subsequently, several large, interdisciplinary, and multi-site government-funded research projects have investigated processing of multiparty meetings of various kinds. The AMI[1] (Augmented Multiparty Interaction) Consortium and DARPA-funded CALO[2] (Cognitive Assistant that Learns and Organizes) projects concentrate on conference-room meetings with small numbers of participants. The CHIL[3] (Computers in the Human Interaction Loop) project collected a series of lectures dominated by a single presenter with shorter question/answer portions, as well as some "interactive" lectures involving smaller groups. AMI and CHIL also produced corpora of time-synchronized media, generally including close-talking and far-field microphones, microphone arrays, individual and room-view video cameras, and output from slide projectors and electronic whiteboards.

Starting in 2002, the annual NIST (U.S. National Institute of Standards and Technology) Rich Transcription (RT) Evaluations have become a driving force for research in conversational speech processing technology, with substantial performance improvements in recent years. In order to promote robustness and domain-independence, the NIST evaluations cover several genres and topics, ranging from largely open-ended, interactive chit-chat, to topic-focused project meetings and technical seminars dominated by lecture-style presentations. NIST evaluates only the speech recognition and speaker diarization systems, with a focus on recognition from multiple distant table-top microphones.

However, technology has advanced such that many other types of information can be detected and evaluated – not least including dialogue acts, topics, and action items. In the next sections, we will try to cover the basic understanding tasks studied in the literature.

9.2 Human/Human Conversation Understanding Tasks

Conversations between humans is the most natural and efficient way of communication. Various types of conversational setups such as two-party conversations, multiparty meetings, and lectures exist in everyday human life. For example, within organizations, people meet for various reasons, such as discussing issues, task assignments, and planning. While such conversational interactions are common, there is still no globally adopted automated or semi-automated mechanism for tracking conversations, saving the conversation content for later use by participants or non participants, or automatically annotating certain content related features such as topics discussed or argued, and decisions made.

The growth in the availability of conversational speech corpora, as discussed earlier, and shared task evaluations such as the ones performed by NIST, has facilitated research on automatic processing of conversational speech. Furthermore, in general, such human/human communication in stored audio form has rapidly grown in providing ample source material for later use. In particular, the increased prominence of searching as a basic user activity has

[1] http://www.amiproject.org.

[2] http://www.ai.sri.com/project/CALO.

[3] http://chil.server.de.

meant that the ability to automatically extract information useful for specific purposes, browse, summarize, and graphically visualize various aspects of the spoken content has become far more important.

However, there are still open questions: What information from these interactions would be useful for later use? Does this information depend on user/purpose? How could the transcripts of these conversations be used? Our goal in this chapter is not to answer these questions, but to provide an overview of some of the research done in the last decade for processing and accessing the content of human/human conversational speech. The reviewed research activities are grouped in the following areas:

- *Dialogue act tagging*: aims to annotate speech acts such as suggestions, questions, jointly with conversational linguistic acts such as acknowledgment, agreement, and so on. This task is heavily influenced by annotated corpora from human/human and multiparty meetings such as Switchboard and ICSI/AMI data sets. This is mainly treated as an enabling technology for further conversation processing, such as extracting action items or discussions. Dialogue act tagging is generally framed as an utterance classification problem (Stolcke *et al.*, 2000; Tur *et al.*, 2006, among others), following the dialogue act segmentation.
- *Dialogue act segmentation*: aims to chop spoken utterances into dialogue act units as defined by the dialogue act tagging schema. While this task is very close to sentence segmentation, there are certain nuances due to the nature of spontaneous conversational speech. Dialogue act segmentation is treated as a binary boundary classification problem using lexical, prosodic, and acoustic features (Kolar *et al.*, 2006; Shriberg *et al.*, 2000, among others). There are also few studies performing joint dialogue act segmentation and tagging (Warnke *et al.*, 1997; Zimmermann *et al.*, 2005). We will cover both dialogue act tagging and segmentation in Section 9.3 after providing detailed information on various dialogue act tagging schema.
- *Discourse and topic segmentation*: aims to chop a conversation into topically coherent units. While topic segmentation of text or prewritten speech is a well established area, there are relatively fewer studies on processing human/human conversations and multiparty meetings. We cover this area in Chapter 12 of this book.
- *Summarization*: aims to generate a compact, summary version of meeting discussions. The summaries can be formed by extracting original speaker utterances (extractive summarization) or by formulating new sentences for the summary (abstractive summarization). Speech summarization is covered in detail in Chapter 13.
- *Action item and decision detection*: aims to detect task assignments to people and associated deadlines and decision making subdialogues during a meeting. These can be used to enter such information into the person's calendar, or to track the status and progress of these action items or decisions in the following meetings. The decisions made in meetings can be used for indexing meetings, and one can go back and access the content of the meeting where a specific decision was made. They can also be used to track the progress and efficiency of meetings. We will cover some preliminary work towards detecting action items and decisions in formal multiparty meetings in Section 9.4.
- *Agreement/disagreement detection*: aims to mark agreements and/or disagreements between meeting participants with the goal of supporting meeting summarization, and decision and action item detection. While this task can be seen under dialogue act modeling, depending on the following application it will be used for, it can be treated as a special sub-task. We will cover this task under dialogue act tagging, action item and decision detection sections.

- *Subjectivity and opinion detection*: aims to mark subjective content in meetings, such as opinions, sentiments and arguing. While there is much literature on text processing in these areas, speech-based opinion processing is relatively newer but growing very quickly. This topic will be analyzed in Section 9.7.
- *Modeling Dominance*: aims to detect dominant speakers in spoken conversations using acoustic and lexical cues. Dominant speakers are defined as trying to assert authority by manipulating the group or certain individuals in the group. Other nonverbal features, such as speaking time, and verbal cues, such as number of words spoken have also been found to be useful. This new area is briefly covered in Section 9.9.
- *Speaker role detection*: aims to classify each of the speakers with respect to their institutional roles. While this is an area deeply rooted in the social sciences, most systems have taken a simplistic view and instead focused on professional roles, such as professor versus student, boss versus employee, or project manager versus software engineer. This topic will be covered in Section 9.8.
- *Hot spot detection*: aims to mark regions in which participants are highly involved in the discussion (e.g. heated arguments, points of excitement, and so on). This relatively newer area in processing conversations will be covered in Section 9.6.
- *Addressee detection*: An important enabling task in processing conversations is determining who the speaker is referring to. This is useful in downstream understanding of conversations in that it provides essential semantic grounding for the analyzed dialogue. This task also covers resolving references (especially pronominal references) in utterances. More detailed information is provided in Section 9.5.
- *Argument diagramming*: aims to display the flow and structure of reasoning in conversations, especially in discussions and arguments. For example, one meeting utterance may open a new issue and another utterance may elaborate on it in response. While deeply rooted in the social sciences, there is an emerging interest to this task and some preliminary studies exist. Argument diagramming is described in more detail in Section 9.10.

9.3 Dialogue Act Segmentation and Tagging

A speech act is a primitive abstraction or an approximate representation of the (typically) illocutionary (rather than locutionary or perlocutionary) force of an utterance, such as asking, answering, promising, suggesting, warning, or requesting. Communicative speech act theory goes back to the 1960s, when Austin (1962) defined an utterance in a conversation as a kind of action being performed by the speaker. Later Searle modified the taxonomy of Austin into five major classes (Jurafsky and Martin, 2008):

- Assertives (or representatives) for committing the speaker to something is being the case such as suggesting, concluding
- Directives for attempts by the speaker to do something such as ordering or advising
- Commissives for committing the speaker to some future action such as planning or betting
- Expressives for expressing the psychological state of the speaker such as thanking or apologizing
- Declarations for bringing about a different state of the world such as "I name this ship the Titanic"

While this taxomony covers many of the actions conveyed in speech, it ignores the *conversational* aspect of the spoken interactions such as grounding and contributions such as acknowledgments or backchannels. According to Clark and Schaefer (1989), a conversation is a series of presentations and acceptances. In the first phase, a speaker performs a kind of speech act, as explained above. The difference is in the second phase where the hearer acts upon this speech act. In this acceptance phase, the hearer *grounds* the previous utterance in a variety of methods such as acknowledging, repeating or paraphrasing the previous utterance, utters on the next relevant contribution, or simply shows continued attention:

A: I worked at the DC office as the branch manager

- B1: Oh, okay (acknowledgment)
- B2: And that was in 2000, right? (next contribution)
- B3: Oh, you were the manager there (paraphrasing)

This more complex framework of joint linguistic acts with two phases is studied under the name of *dialogue act tagging*. The main goal of dialogue acts is to provide a basis for further discourse analysis and understanding. For example, it has been shown that dialogue acts can be used to extract the action items or question/answer pairs in conversations as is discussed later. Furthermore, as dialogue acts are designed to be task-independent, it is easier to reuse them or use them as a starting point when processing new genres.

9.3.1 Annotation Schema

There are a number of dialogue act tagging schema proposed in the literature. Two popular contemporary dialogue act sets for conversational speech in the literature are DAMSL (Dialogue Act Markup in Several Layers (Core and Allen, 1997) and MRDA (Meeting Recorder Dialogue Act) (Shriberg *et al.*, 2004b). In this section, we cover these two schema and a few others in more detail.

DAMSL focuses on providing multiple layers of dialogue act markup. Each layer allows multiple communicative functions of an utterance to be labeled. For example an utterance can simultaneously perform actions such as responding to a question, confirming understanding, promising to perform an action, and informing. DAMSL is organized into three main categories, one for each of the speech acts, another for the acceptance phase, and a third set for covering extra dimensions of communication:

- The Forward Communicative Functions consist of a taxonomy in a similar style as the actions of traditional speech act theory, namely representatives (or statements), directives, commissives, and performatives (or declaratives). Since it has been designed for task-oriented dialogues, they added one more category, called Open-Option, where a speaker gives a potential course of action but does not show preference toward it (hence different than a suggestion) such as in "how about this?".
- The Backward Communicative Functions indicate how the current utterance relates to the previous dialogue, corresponding to the acceptance phase above, such as accepting a proposal confirming understanding or answering a question. It consists of four categories: Agreement classes, namely Accept, Reject, Maybe, Hold, Partial-Accept and Partial-Reject; understanding classes, namely Acknowledgment, Repeat/Paraphrase, Completion, Correct

Forward Communicative Functions (Speech act phase)

- Statements (Assertives or Representatives)
- Directives and Open-Option
- Commitments
- Performatives
- Other

Backward Communicative Functions (Acceptance phase)

- Agreements
- Understandings
- Answers
- Information-Relation

Utterance Features

- Information Level
- Communicative Status
- Syntactic Features

Figure 9.2 The DAMSL annotation categories

misspeaking, answering. They also added one class for signaling nonunderstanding, such as "huh?" or "you mean, to Dansville?", and another class for covering utterances with an information relation to the previous one, such as providing examples, elaborating on it, etc.

- The Utterance Features include information about an utterance's form and content such as whether an utterance concerns the communication process itself or deals with the subject at hand. It has three subcategories: The information level identifies whether an utterance is about a task, task management (such as "What times are available"), or else (communication management) utterances. The communicative status level is for the abandoned and uninterpretable utterances. The syntactic features level (a misnomer) cover generic communicative utterances such as "hello", and exclamations such as emotional utterances.

Figure 9.2 provides a summary of the three main categories for annotation. Some popular corpora annotated with DAMSL tags are the TRAINS (Allen *et al.*, 1995) corpus for transportation planning, the Monroe (Stent, 2000) corpus for disaster handling, the MapTask (Anderson *et al.*, 1991) corpus for giving directions on a map, and the Switchboard (Godfrey *et al.*, 1992) corpus.

Jurafsky *et al.* (1997) have adopted the DAMSL schema for the Switchboard corpus. They managed to exploit about 80% of the DAMSL tags, but for certain cases they made some changes. For example, they added non-verbal (such as breath) and third-party talk to communicative status, formed subcategories for answers (such as yes/no answers, descriptive answers, etc.), and similarly for the information request set (such as yes/no questions, open-ended questions, etc.), merged assert and reassert, and marked hedge. They ended up with about 60 tags, which can be clustered into 40 categories.

Note that, not all dialogue act tagging schema creation efforts have been motivated by existing social theories. A notable example is the Verbmobil dialogue act tagging schema, which is used for planning schedules (Susanne *et al.*, 1995). The designers have come up with a tagset motivated by the existing corpus instead of the other way around. They have generic tags such as thanks, greet, introduce, a subset of traditional speech acts such as request or suggest, and a subset of acceptance tags such as reject, accept, confirm, clarify, and a number of task related tags such as backchannel, garbage, give-reason (e.g. "because I have meetings all afternoon"), and initial-request (e.g. "I want to make an appointment for tomorrow"). At this point, also note the relationship between the dialogue act tagging and the intent determination task studied for human/machine interactions covered in Chapter 4.

A different view for conversation act tagging has been proposed by Traum and Hinkelman (1992). Their schema consists of four layers, depending on the unit to be tagged:

- Turn taking tags for sub-utterance units. These are mainly floor mechanisms for keeping or releasing the turn.
- Speech acts for discourse units. These include traditional speech acts such as suggest, request, questions, etc. But instead of tagging one utterance, a set of utterances called discourse units are tagged. A discourse unit consists of an initial presentation and subsequent utterances until an act is mutually understood (or grounded). Hence, the shortest discourse unit is an initial presentation and an agreement or acknowledgment.
- Grounding tags for utterance units. These correspond to single utterances or sentential units for the acceptance phase, such as for acknowledgment, continue, or repair.
- Argumentation acts for one or more discourse units. In the most basic form, a question/answer pair is an argumentation act with one discourse unit. However, argumentation acts can be built up hierarchically. For example, a typical conversation from the TRAINS corpus can start with goal specification, followed by planning and then verification of the plan. These tags are also very closely related to the argument diagramming of the conversations which we will cover later.

The other popular dialogue act tag annotation scheme, MRDA, focuses on multiparty meetings. This schema has been used to annotate the ICSI meeting corpus, a collection of 75 multiparty dialogues. Each dialogue consists of naturally occurring speech in an academic setting and is about one hour in length. While the corpus is similar to SWBD-DAMSL, one big difference is that it includes a set of labels for floor management mechanisms, such as *floor grabbing* and *holding*, which are common in meetings. Furthermore additional tags were used for topic changes and humorous material such as jokes. Interrupted sentences were also assigned their dedicated tags, differed from abandoned sentences. Statements and subjective statements are combined as well. The tag sets for MRDA and DAMSL extended for the Switchboard corpus (SWBD-DAMSL) schema are presented in Figure 9.3. A sample meeting (actually about the ICSI meetings processing project itself) is also presented in Figure 9.4.

Clark and Popescu-Belis (2004) also proposed a more shallow tagging schema called MALTUS, which is easier to tag automatically. MALTUS basically clustered some of the MRDA

Tag	DAMSL	MRDA	Tag	DAMSL	MRDA
Indecipherable	%	%	Conventional Opening	fp	
Abandoned	%-	%–	Conventional Closing	fc	
Interruption		%-	Topic Change		tc
Nonspeech	x	x	Explicit-Performative	fx	
Self-Talk	t1	t1	Exclamation	fe	fe
3rd-Party Talk	t3	t3	Other Forward Function	fo	
Task Management	t	t	Thanks	ft	ft
Communication Management	c		Welcome	fw	fw
Statement	sd	s	Apology	fa	fa
Subjective Statement	sv	s	Floor Holder		fh
Wh- Question	qw	qw	Floor Grabber		fg
Y/N Question	qy	qy	Accept, Yes	ny, aa	aa
Open Ended Question	qo	qo	Partial Accept	aap	aap
Or Question	qr	qr	Partial Reject	arp	arp
Or Clause After Y/N Question	qrr	qrr	Maybe	am	am
Rhetorical Question	qh	qh	Reject, No	nn, ar	ar
Declarative Question	d	d	Hold	h	h
Tag Question	g	g	Collaborative Completion	2	2
Open Option	oo		Backchannel	b	b
Command	ad	co	Acknowledgment	bk	bk
Suggestion	co	cs	Mimic	m	m
Commit	cc	cc	Repeat		r
Reformulation	bf	bs	Appreciateion	ba	ba
Sympathy	by	by	Downplayer	bd	bd
Misspeak Correction	bc	bc	Nonlabeled		z
Rhetorical-Question Backchannel	bh	bh	Signal Non-understanding	br	br
Understanding Check		bu	Defending/Explanation		df
Misspeak Self-Correction		bsc	"Follow me"		f
Expansion/Supporting Addition	e	e	Narrative-Affirmative Answers	na	na
Narrative-Negative Answers	ng	ng	No-Knowledge Answers	no	no
Dispreferred Answersnd	nd	nd	Quoted Material	q	
Humorous Material		j	Continued From Previous Line	+	
Hedge	h				

Figure 9.3 SWBD-DAMSL and MRDA tag sets

tags and dropped others. An utterance is then tagged with one of the four high-level tags: statement, question, backchannel, and floor mechanism, followed by one of the eight subcategories, such as attention, action, correction/repetition, politeness, and positive/negative/undecided responses. More detailed information about various dialogue act schema and comparisons can be found in Popescu-Belis (2005).

Time	Speaker	DA Tag	Transcript
2804-2810	c3	s ^df ^e.%-	I mean you can't just print the values in ascii ==
2810-2811	c6	fg	well ===
2810-2811	c5	s ^arp ^j	not unless you had a lot of time
2811-2812	c5	%-	and ==
2811-2814	c6	s ^bu	uh and also they're not - I mean as I understand it you - you don't have a way to optimize the features
2814-2817	c6	qy ^d ^g ^rt	right?
2818-2818	c2	s ^aa	right

Figure 9.4 A sample excerpt from the ICSI meeting corpus annotated with MRDA tags. ^ is used for multiple labels for the same dialogue act unit and is used for consecutive dialogue act tags (from Shriberg *et al.*, 2004b)

9.3.2 Modeling Dialogue Act Tagging

Dialogue act tagging is generally framed as an utterance classification problem (Mast *et al.*, 1996; Stolcke *et al.*, 2000; Tur *et al.*, 2006, among others). Previous studies differ in the features and classification algorithms they have employed and the dialogue act set (as presented above) used. The range of features include lexical (such as word n-grams), prosodic (such as pitch and energy), syntactic, contextual (such as the previous and next estimated dialogue act tags), and other features, such as number of words and duration. Continuous valued features are optionally normalized by the speaker or the conversation.

The basic approach as taken by Tur *et al.* (2006) is to treat each sentence independently and to employ lexical features, that is word n-grams and number of words in the sentence, for classification. They used the ICSI meeting corpus with high-level MRDA tags: *question*, *statement*, *backchannel*, *disruptions*, and *floor grabbers/holders* with a Boosting classifier.

Mast *et al.* (1996) used semantic classification trees, similar to the approach taken by Kuhn and Mori (1995). They are basically decision trees where the nodes query about existence of phrases. Following the decision tree training literature of the early 1990s, they used the Gini criterion to decide on convergence. They showed performance results using 19 dialogue act tags on the German VerbMobil spontaneous speech corpus.

The first study using prosodic information for dialogue act tagging was presented in (Shriberg *et al.*, 1998). They used decision trees to query prosodic features such as pitch, duration, pause, energy, and speaking rate. They demonstrated that prosody contributed significantly to improving dialogue act tagging performance both when using manual and automatic speech transcriptions of the Switchboard corpus, following the SWBD-DAMSL schema, as explained above.

Stolcke *et al.* (2000) presented a more comprehensive system for classifying dialogue acts based on lexical, collocational, and prosodic cues, as well as on the discourse coherence of the dialogue act sequence. The dialogue model is based on treating the discourse structure of a conversation as an HMM and the individual dialogue acts as observations emanating from the model states. Constraints on the likely sequence of dialogue acts are modeled via dialogue act n-grams. The statistical dialogue act grammar is combined with word n-grams, decision trees, and neural networks modeling the idiosyncratic lexical and prosodic manifestations of each dialogue act. They also reported performance figures using the Switchboard spontaneous speech corpus.

Following these studies, Venkataraman *et al.* (2002, 2005) tried employing active learning and lightly supervised learning for reducing the amount of labeled data needed for dialogue act tagging with HMMs. They concluded that while active learning does not help significantly for this task, exploiting unlabeled data by using minimal supervision is effective when the dialogue act tag sequence is also modeled.

Tur *et al.* (2006) proposed model adaptation methods for dialogue act tagging. They used the ICSI meeting corpus with five high-level meeting recognition dialogue act tags, and performed controlled adaptation experiments using the Switchboard (SWBD) corpus with SWBD-DAMSL tags as the out-of-domain corpus. They obtained significantly better performance by automatically selecting a subset of the Switchboard corpus and combining the confidences obtained by both in-domain and out-of-domain models via logistic regression.

Margolis *et al.* (2010) presented an extension of this study recently, focusing on cross-lingual adaptation using nonlexical features and using machine translation output in the other language. They performed experiments using MRDA and SWBD, similar to Tur *et al.* (2006) for English and the Spanish Call-Home corpus for cross-lingual adaptation. They mainly explored the use of structural correspondence learning (SCL) for domain adaptation, which relies on feature transformation of learned pivot features, which are informative for both domains.

More recently, Rangarajan *et al.* (2007) proposed exploiting prosodic and syntactic features in a Maximum Entropy classification framework. Their contribution was to use a syntax-based categorical prosody prediction. They reported improved results using the Switchboard corpus over the baseline using only lexical features.

9.3.3 Dialogue Act Segmentation

Dialogue act segmentation is a crucial first step in processing conversational speech such as meetings or broadcast conversations since most of the follow-up processing such as summarization or argument diagramming rely on sentential units. Dialogue act segmentation is generally framed as a word boundary classification problem. More formally, the goal is to find the most likely boundary tag sequence, T given the features, F, in a sentence:.

$$argmax_T P(T|F)$$

To this end, generative, discriminative, or hybrid models are mostly used. The most well-known generative model is the hidden event language model (HELM), as introduced by (Stolcke and Shriberg, 1996). In this approach, sentence boundaries are treated as hidden events and the above optimization is simply done by the Viterbi algorithm using only lexical features, i.e. the language model.

For example, Figure 9.5 shows the model for the two-class problem: *nonboundary* (NB) and *sentence boundary* (SB) for sentence segmentation. Figure 9.6 shows an example sequence of words emitted. This method was extended by using confusion networks in Hillard *et al.* (2004).

Note that this is no different from using an HMM as is typically done in similar tagging tasks, such as part of speech (POS) tagging (Church, 1988) or named entity extraction (Bikel *et al.*, 1999). However, it has been shown that the conventional HMM approach has certain weaknesses. For example, it is not possible to use any information beyond words, such as POS tags of the words or prosodic cues for speech segmentation.

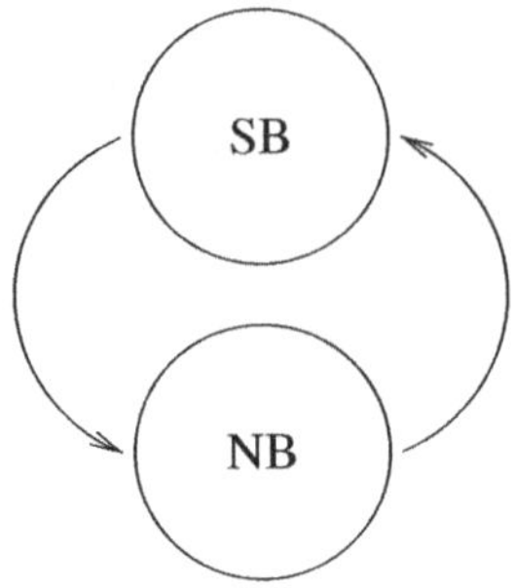

Figure 9.5 Conceptual hidden Markov model for segmentation with two states: one for segment boundaries, one for others

Emitted Words	...	people	are	dead	few	pictures	...
State Sequence	...	NB	NB	SB	NB	NB	...

Figure 9.6 Sentence segmentation with simple two-state Markov model

To this end, two simple extensions have been proposed: Shriberg *et al.* (2000) suggested using explicit states to emit the boundary tokens, hence incorporating nonlexical information via a combination of other models. This approach is used for sentence segmentation and was originally designed for speech disfluencies. The approach was to treat such events as extra meta-tokens. In this model, one state is reserved for each boundary token, *SB* and *NB*, and the rest of the states are for generating words. To ease computation, an imaginary token is inserted between all consecutive words in case the word preceding the boundary is not part of a disfluency. The following example is a conceptual representation of a sequence with boundary tokens:

...people NB are NB dead SB few NB pictures ...

The most probable boundary token sequence is again obtained simply by Viterbi decoding. The conceptual HELM for segmentation is depicted in Figure 9.7.

These extra boundary tokens are then used to capture other meta-information. The most commonly used meta-information is the feedback obtained from other classifiers, such as decision trees. Typically, the posterior probability of being in that boundary state is used as

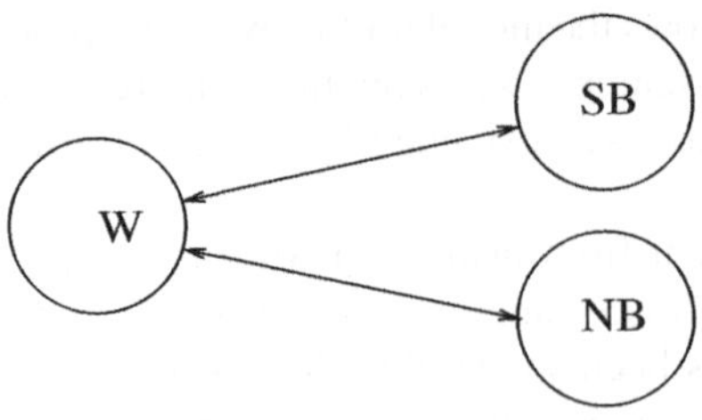

Figure 9.7 Conceptual hidden event language model for segmentation

a state observation likelihood after being divided by prior probabilities following the Bayes' rule. These other classifiers may also be trained with other feature sets, such as using prosodic or syntactic information, to get hybrid models (Shriberg *et al.*, 2000).

The second extension is inspired by factored language models (fLMs) (Bilmes and Kirchhoff, 2003), which capture not only words, but also morphological and syntactic information. Guz *et al.* (2009) proposed using factored HELM (fHELM) for sentence segmentation using POS tags in addition to words for incorporating morphological information, which is especially important for tagging inflectional languages.

With the advances in discriminative classification algorithms, researchers tried using Conditional Random Fields (Liu *et al.*, 2005), Boosting (Cuendet *et al.*, 2006), multi-layer perceptrons (Mast *et al.*, 1996), and hybrid approaches using Boosting and Maximum Entropy classification algorithms (Zimmerman *et al.*, 2006). Features can be the presence of specific word n-grams around the candidate boundary, an indicator of being inside a quotation in text, an indicator of presence of the preceding word tokens in an abbreviation list, or duration of pause, pitch, energy, and other duration-related features in speech.

Zimmerman *et al.* (2006) provides an overview of different classification algorithms (Boosting, hidden-event language model, maximum entropy and decision trees) applied to the dialogue act segmentation for multilingual broadcast news. They concluded that hybrid approaches are always superior and (Guz *et al.*, 2009) concluded that this is also true with CRF, although to a lesser degree.

So far, most approaches to sentence segmentation have focused on recognizing boundaries rather than sentences in themselves. This has occurred because of the quadratic number of sentence hypotheses that must be assessed in comparison to the number of boundaries. To tackle that problem, Roark *et al.* (2006) segment the input according to likely sentence boundaries established by a local model, and then train a reranker on the n-best lists of segmentations. This approach allows leveraging of sentence-level features such as scores from a syntactic parser or from global prosodic features. Favre *et al.* (2008b) proposed to extend this concept to a pruned sentence lattice, which allows combining of local scores with sentence-level scores in a more efficient manner.

Recent research has focused on model adaptation methods for improving dialogue act segmentation for meetings using spontaneous telephone conversations, and for improving speaker-specific prosodic (Kolar *et al.*, 2007) and lexical modeling (Cuendet *et al.*, 2006). Guz *et al.* (2010) studied the effect of model adaptation of segmentation and tagging jointly applied in a cascaded manner. There are also a number of studies studying the impact of segmentation on follow-up tasks such as summarization (Liu and Xie, 2008), information extraction (Favre *et al.*, 2008a), and translation, (Matusov *et al.*, 2007).

9.3.4 Joint Modeling of Dialogue Act Segmentation and Tagging

While most systems first segment input speech utterances into dialogue act units and then assign dialogue act tags (e.g. Ang *et al.*, 2005; Mast *et al.*, 1996; Tur *et al.*, 2010, among others) there are a number of studies proposing joint segmentation and tagging. Two notable ones include the following: Warnke *et al.* (1997) proposed to use the A* algorithm to search for optimal segmentation and classification of dialogue acts. The candidates for boundaries are determined using a multi-layer perceptron classifier and the dialogue act candidate tags are determined using statistical language models. Then the task of the integration is choosing the optimal joint segmentation and tagging. Zimmermann *et al.* (2005), on the other hand, proposed a completely joint modeling approach, without any underlying segmentation and tagging components. Their approach is based on generative approaches for segmentation, and instead of using only two boundary classes (e.g. SB and NB in the above example), they reserved one boundary class per dialogue act tag. Note that, using hidden event models, this approach may be used to build hybrid joint classification models trained with prosodic or other features.

9.4 Action Item and Decision Detection

A practical high-level task for understanding human/human conversations is extracting key information related to action items and decisions. These tasks are also among the most commonly requested outputs from meetings according to user studies (Banerjee *et al.*, 2005; Lisowska, 2003).

However, it is not clear what constitutes a decision or an action item. For example, one would argue that an action item consists of an assertion, command, or suggestion (e.g. "do this until tomorrow") which optionally has an assignee and a due date, followed by an agreement. However it is not hard to think of cases where such a simplistic view fails to cover what is intended in this task (e.g. "open the window now"), as natural language is riddled with grey areas when it comes to semantic processing.

While some researchers have treated this task as a subtask of argument diagramming (Section 9.10), putting it in a larger scope (e.g. Verbree *et al.*, 2006), a number of studies have directly attacked these tasks after carefully limiting the scope of the task and the conversation style to minimize these grey areas (more formally, to increase the interannotator agreement). For example, consider the excerpt in Figure 9.8 from the CALO corpus, where there is a clear task that needs to be done and an assignee.

More specifically, both tasks are defined as marking dialogue act units which have information about action items (typically the task itself together with the due date and responsible party) and decisions (the issue involved and the resolved course of action).

There is some related work in the text processing domain, focusing on the emails under the DARPA PAL program, using Enron email corpus.[4] This is a binary classification task, trying to detect whether an email (or a sentence in an email) has any content related to any action item (Bennett and Carbonell, 2005, 2007; Corston-Oliver *et al.*, 2004). F-scores around 80% are achieved on the task of classifying emails as containing action items, and 60–70% when classifying individual sentences. They used word n-grams with SVM classifiers.

To process spoken multiparty conversations, similar approaches were employed, but with mixed results. Some success has been shown in detecting decision-making utterances in meetings in a constrained domain. For example, Hsueh and Moore (2007) achieve F-scores of 60–70% for the task of detecting decision-making utterances as identified from within a manually selected summary set using the AMI corpus. They employed a Maximum Entropy classifier using lexical (words and phrases), prosodic (pitch and intensity), semantic (dialogue act tags, temporal expressions) and contextual (relative position within the meeting) features. This study assumed that they have the manual transcriptions and annotation of dialogue act tags, topic boundaries and topics.

[4] http://www.cs.cmu.edu/~enron/

- *John Smith*: so we need to arrange an office for joe browning (statement/all)
- *Kathy Brown*: are there special requirements (question/John)
- *Cindy Green*: when is he co- (disruption/John)
- *John Smith*: yes (affirmation/Kathy) // there are (statement/Kathy)
- *John Smith*: we want him to be close to you (statement/Kathy)
- *Kathy Brown*: okay (agreement/John) // I'll talk to the secretary (commitment/John)
- *Cindy Green*: hold on (floor grabber/all) // wh- when is he coming (question/John)
- *John Smith*: next monday (statement/Cindy)
- *Cindy Green*: uh-huh (backchannel/all)

Action Item: Arrangement of Joe's office location
Owner: Kathy

Decision: Location of Joe's office to be close to Kathy

Summary:

- *John Smith*: so we need to arrange an office for joe browning (statement/all)
- *John Smith*: we want him to be close to you (statement/Kathy)

Figure 9.8 An excerpt from the CALO meeting corpus. Dialogue act tags and addressed persons are shown in parentheses. This meeting data has one action item and one decision. A brief extractive summary corresponding to this meeting data follows

On the other hand, when the task is to detect utterances from within an entire meeting, and when the domain is less constrained, accuracy seems to suffer significantly: Morgan *et al.* (2006) achieved F-scores of only around 30% when detecting action item utterances over the ICSI Meeting Corpus using similar features.

This result demonstrates the importance of the meeting style for this task: structured and artificial project meetings of the AMI corpus versus unstructured, naturally occurring meetings of the ICSI corpus. In naturally occurring speech, tasks are defined incrementally, and commitment to them is established through interaction between the people concerned; cues to their detection can therefore lie as much in the discourse structure itself as in the content of its constituent sentences.

To this end, for the DARPA CALO project, Purver *et al.* (2007) and Fernández *et al.* (2008) took a structural approach to action item and decision detection: utterances are first classified according to their role in the commitment process (namely, task definition, agreement, acceptance of responsibility, issue under discussion, decision made) using one binary SVM classifier for each possible utterance role. Then action items or decision discussions are detected from patterns of these roles using a binary classifier or a probabilistic graphical model. Four types of action-item-related utterances are identified: task description, responsible party identification, deadline assignment, and agreement/disagreement of the responsible party. For decisions, they used three categories: utterances which initiate a discussion by raising an issue, utterances which propose a resolution for the raised issue (such as proposals considered or restatements), and utterances which express agreement for a proposed resolution

On manual transcripts of the AMI meeting corpus, the detectors achieve F-scores of around 45% for action items (Purver *et al.*, 2007) and 60% for decisions (Fernández *et al.*, 2008). This is a significant improvement over the baseline results obtained with non-structured detectors trained on the same data, which achieve 37 and 50% F-scores, respectively. When ASR output is used, there is a drop in the detection performance, but this is still above the chance baseline.

They also studied towards building a real-time detector, where the detector runs at regular and frequent intervals during the meeting. It reprocesses recent utterances in case a decision discussion straddles these and brand new utterances, and it merges overlapping hypothesized decision discussions, and removes duplicates. The real-time decision detector does not perform significantly worse than the offline version (Frampton *et al.*, 2009b).

Yang *et al.* (2008) have explored the use of prosodic cues for improving action item agreement detection. The motivation is that, most agreement phrases are also used for backchanneling (e.g. "yeah"), acknowledgment (e.g. "okay"), or even questions (e.g. "right?"). While the dialogue context is critical to disambiguate the correct dialogue act tag for them, prosodic features are shown to be helpful, improving the baseline by around 25% for single-word utterances.

Other studies on detecting agreement and disagreements have demonstrated the feasibility of this task, using textual, durational, contextual and acoustic features, from the annotations of the conversational corpora. For example, Hillard *et al.* (2003) built an agreement/disagreement classifier using decision trees with lexical and prosodic features from the ICSI meeting corpus. Prosodic features do not improve the performance. However, when only prosodic features are used, performance degradation due to ASR output was much less, as expected. One thing to note is that, this is a four-way classification task, with positive, negative, neutral utterances and backchannels. Frequent single-word utterances, such as "yeah" or "right" are not considered to be agreements but instead backchannels as they usually reflect encouragement for the speaker to continue more than actual agreement, an assumption which may not be the case all the time.

Galley *et al.* (2004) exploited adjacency pair information as obtained from addressee detection tasks as an additional feature while identifying agreement and disagreements. They reported better performance than Hillard *et al.* using the same corpus with a Maximum Entropy classifier using manual transcriptions. However, most of the improvement comes from the classification algorithm (3% of 4% improvement in accuracy). Their approach can be considered as a preliminary task for argument diagramming-based studies (Section 9.10) for detecting agreement/disagreements.

9.5 Addressee Detection and Co-reference Resolution

In spoken interactions, one particular key task is going beyond automatic transcription and dialogue act tagging for each of the utterances and determining the speaker this utterance is addressed to or the entities and individuals referred in the utterance. This is a critical enabling task for downstream conversation understanding tasks such as action item or decision detection or argument diagramming. For example, in order to fully understand the owner of an action item, the system must resolve who this action item is addressed to.

While this task resembles the well-known coreference resolution and mention detection tasks in information extraction, spoken conversations are done jointly between the participants. Speakers and addressees (and overhearers too) are continually trying to establish common ground with each other, using a number of means in different modalities. Eye gaze, physical orientation, backchanneling ("uh-huh", "mm-hmm"), and contextual reference are core components to this process. In contrast to two-party human/computer or human/human dialogues, however, the multiparty nature of meetings presents novel challenges to the analysis of these features. The potential referents and addressees are more numerous, and the complexity of physical interaction increases.

Consider the example in Figure 9.8. Even in this short excerpt there are a number of pronominal references, and the resolution of "you" is especially critical. In a command such as "I want you to do this until this time", it is not necessarily the next speaker who is referred by "you".

The most useful feature for detecting the addressee found in the literature is not the lexical, visual, or contextual cues, but a smart fusion of multimodal features, such as head pose estimation from omnidirectional table-top video, prosodic speech waveform analysis, context, lexical cues, named entities, and higher-level linguistic analysis such as parsing. Stiefelhagen *et al.* (2002) focused on using visual cues and estimated visual focus of attention at each frame of three 4-person meetings. Using automatically estimated head poses as input to neural networks, they obtained an 8% error reduction (from 74% to 76% accuracy) by adding speaker information.

Research in automatic addressee detection has produced similar results. The task is typically approached as an utterance-level classification where some subset of the participants in the meeting are identified as addressees. Jovanovic *et al.* (2006) used a combination of lexical features of the utterance (e.g. personal, possessive, and indefinite pronouns, and participant names) and gaze features from each participant to detect addressee in 4-person meetings using Bayesian networks. Multimodality again emerged as a key, with utterance features alone achieving 53% accuracy, speaker gaze 62%, everyone's gaze 66%, and their combination 71%.

In the DARPA CALO meeting assistant project (Tur *et al.*, 2010), without using video, Gupta *et al.* (2007) automatically detected addressee with 47% accuracy over a 37% baseline by exploring a number of structural, durational, and lexical features taken from the speech transcript only. To leverage dialogue context as well, they used a conditional random field (CRF) as a classifier, looking both forward and backward into the dialogue. For the same project, they employed deeper linguistic analysis for processing pronominal references. As a pre-processor to a downstream reference resolution system, Müller (2006) used a rule induction classifier to determine whether "it" was referential in meetings from the ICSI corpus. This is important since "it" has also non-referential senses as in "it's raining". Note that, this is also the case for "you" as in "you know" or "this is how you do that". Furthermore, "you" has singular and plural senses, which makes the addressee detection task much harder. Using several automatically extracted syntactic, lexical, and word distance input features, he achieved an F-score of 62%. Gupta *et al.* (2007) performed a similar experiment to automatically resolve the referentiality of second-person pronouns, achieving a 63% accuracy over a 58% baseline. Müller (2007) and Gupta *et al.* (2007) also describe classifiers for resolving these pronouns, if they are indeed classified as referential.

The details of the addressee approach of CSLI used for CALO is presented in (Frampton *et al.*, 2009a; Purver *et al.*, 2009). After distinguishing between generic versus referential *you* and referential singular versus plurals, they identify the individual addressee for the referential singulars. They used Bayesian Networks, using linguistic and visual features, with the AMI meeting corpus. Using a test set composed of around 1000 utterances which contain the word *you*, they computed visual features to indicate at which target each participant's gaze was directed the longest during different periods of time. A further feature indicated with whom the speaker spent most time sharing a mutual gaze over the utterance as a whole. Other features include structural, durational, lexical and shallow syntactic patterns of the *you*-utterance. They also used Backward Looking (BL)/Forward Looking (FL) features, which express the similarity or distance (e.g. ratio of common words, time separation) between the *you*-utterance and the previous/next utterance by each nonspeaker. The BL/FL speaker order and the number of speakers in the previous/next five utterances are addded as contextual features. Finally, for the manual systems, they also used the AMI dialogue acts of the *you*-utterances, and of the BL/FL utterances. They found out that after visual cues, contextual cues are the most informative.

9.6 Hot Spot Detection

Recent interest in the automatic processing of meetings is motivated by a desire to summarize, browse, and retrieve important information from lengthy archives of spoken data. One of the most useful capabilities such a technology could provide is a way for users to locate "hot spots", or regions in which participants are highly involved in the discussion (e.g. heated arguments, points of excitement, and so on). While this task is inherently subjective, Wrede and Shriberg (2003) found that after training, human raters show good agreement in labeling utterances for involvement. Such hot spot regions are likely to contain important information for users who are browsing a meeting for applications of information retrieval.

To enable research, the dialogue-act-labeled ICSI meeting corpus (Dhillon *et al.*, 2004; Shriberg *et al.*, 2004a) is annotated for hot spots as described in Wrede *et al.* (2005). Each hot spot consists of a sequence of one or more dialogue acts, by one or more speakers. Hot spots have an internal structure, and are also labeled for type. Structural points, such as the hot spot "trigger" or "closure" are determined based on semantics, with reference to hot spot "peaks" in normalized speaker involvement occurring within the hot spot. Type (e.g. disagreement, amusement) are marked, as is the level of "hotness," or perceived speaker affect.

Research has found correlations between types of hot spots and specific dialogue acts, as well as between factors such as utterance length and utterance perplexity (Wrede and Shriberg, 2003). Certain hot spot types, namely jokes, are associated with higher rates of out-of-vocabulary words for an automatic speech recognizer. Contextual factors such as the individual speaker and meeting type also correlate with overall hot spot production. As one might expect, increased speaker involvement tends to occur in regions of speaker overlap; however, this association is of only moderate degree. A large-scale study of speaker overlap (Cetin and Shriberg, 2006), found that hot spots are about 50% more probable during overlapped speech than overall, but that a 16% overall overlap rate for the meeting corpus increases to only 25% when conditioned on hot spots. Thus, while there is an association between hot spots and overlap, they appear to reflect distinct phenomena.

Automatic detection of hot spots can make use of a multitude of cues. In addition to the factors mentioned above, hot spots show marked acoustic-prosodic features such as pitch and energy. One advantage of such features is that they do not require the output of a speech recognizer. Early work reported in Wrede and Shriberg (2003) found significant cues to hot spots from speaker-normalized prosodic features, particularly from maximum and mean normalized pitch features, however this is clearly an area for further research.

9.7 Subjectivity, Sentiment, and Opinion Detection

Opinion detection is a very well studied area in natural language processing, especially for processing reviews of certain entities (such as restaurants) or events (such as presidential

Agreement (Kappa)	Raw Text Only	Raw Text + Speech
Positive Sentiment	0.57	0.69
Negative Sentiment	0.41	0.61

Figure 9.9 Inter-annotator agreement for sentiment annotation using speech and text (© 2006 Somasundaran *et al.*)

elections), (Pang and Lee, 2008). Application of this field to speech is more recent. Note that opinion or sentiment detection is different than emotion detection, though they are closely related. Typically they are modeled using very different techniques, for example, while emotion detection is typically modeled using mostly audio features, opinion detection mostly relies on lexical features. In this section we focus on opinion detection. For a more comprehensive survey of emotion detection, one may refer to Schuller *et al.* (2010).

When talking about opinion detection from speech, it is useful to separate monologues used for reviews from interactive conversations. While the first one may seem like a natural extension of review processing, there is only one study, to the best of our knowledge, that uses ASR output instead of text for such a system : Polifroni *et al.* (2010) reported performance figures from a preliminary experiment in processing audio restaurant reviews using an existing multi-aspect opinion processing framework. Note that this is different from a directed dialogue to enter your review, but instead focusing on classifying the spoken review according to various aspects related to the restaurant domain, such as food, price, ambiance, etc.

The literature is richer regarding processing interactive conversations and multiparty meetings. For example, Somasundaran *et al.* (2006) studied manual annotation of sentiment and arguing using the AMI meeting corpus, using textual and audio information, and showed that human annotators achieve higher annotation agreement when using both textual and audio information, especially for negative sentiment, as shown in Figure 9.9. This suggests that automatic systems should also benefit from access to acoustic and prosodic features. In a follow-up study, Wilson (2008) showed similar figures using the same corpus for subjectivity. She proposed having the dimension of subjective versus objective for positive and negative sentiments. For the sentence "this camera is really bad", this is subjectively negative, but for the sentence "this camera broke one week after I bought it" is an objective negative sentiment.

Later, Somasundaran *et al.* (2007) proposed a system for detecting arguing and sentiments in meetings. They used not only word n-grams but also existing sentiment lexicons, dialogue act tags, and adjacency pairs. The sentiment lexicons, which include positive and negative words, subjectivity indicator phrases, valence shifters, and intensifiers, helped the most on top of the baseline trained using only word n-grams. Camelin *et al.* (2006) presented an automatic opinion analysis system in the survey of telephone services. Word n-grams as well as sentiment lexicons are employed as in the previous study for modeling customer satisfaction.

9.8 Speaker Role Detection

Social scientists have long understood that the link between the identity of the speakers and the interaction is fundamental, and have established different approaches to explain how participants' embodiment of different identities is relevant for actions in interactions. The most well-known study is about institutional roles by Drew and Heritage (1992). It represents one approach to examine task-oriented conduct, distinct from ordinary conversation, in an attempt to locate and ground the identification of relevant roles. A range of conversational practices for (1) managing agreement/disagreement, (2) managing epistemic authority and subordination, and (3) designing questions and responses to them can be very precisely linked to social roles and culturally variable identities in specific interactions.

Previous work on speaker role detection has mainly concentrated on identifying roles in formal multiparty meetings, broadcast news and broadcast conversations (such as talk shows). Note that most of these conversations have clearly defined roles, such as anchor versus guest, or professor versus student. In other words, the roles of the speakers do not change throughout the interaction. This is in contrast to discourse-specific roles, where each person may be classified with multiple roles in a conversation. Some typical examples include attacker versus supporter in a discussion or presenter and listener in a meeting. While there is some work on detecting these discourse specific roles, (e.g. Banerjee and Rudnicky, 2004), in this section, our focus is on institutional roles.

The earliest work in this area is only a decade old. Barzilay *et al.* (2000) focused on identifying three roles in radio broadcast news: the anchor, a journalist, and a guest. Only textual features such as word *n*-grams, explicit speaker introductions, duration features, and features from surrounding context were used. They observed significant gains using the content, but the assumption is that the system knows who is talking when. Later, Liu (2006) studied these three roles in Mandarin broadcast news shows, using a maximum entropy classifier with similar features. She also used contextual speaker role information as a feature.

A study on detecting discourse specific roles worthy of discussion is Banerjee and Rudnicky (2004). They defined three main meeting states (discourse): presentation, discussion, briefing, and other (for capturing smalltalk, etc.). For each meeting state they defined the social roles, such as, presenter and listener for the presentation state. They performed experiments using a small in-house meeting data collection. The features they used include turn-taking patterns, the number of persons speaking at or around the same time, and overlap patterns, however no lexical information is exploited.

Vinciarelli (2007) used interaction patterns and information from social network analysis to detect six roles in Swiss radio broadcast news. In this work, information from interaction patterns was captured by centrality measures and relative interactions between speakers, computed using duration-related features, ignoring the content. Later, Garg *et al.* (2008) combined lexical features in the form of word *n*-grams, interaction patterns, and centrality features for identifying speaker roles in multiparty meetings. One interesting observation is that lexical features performed significantly better than only speech-based social network analysis features. They experimentally showed that the combination obtained better results than either type of feature alone using the AMI meeting corpus.

More recently, Yaman *et al.* (2010) presented a dynamic Bayesian network-based approach for detecting roles in broadcast shows. The main advantage of this work is to capture the sequential patterns of roles between host, guest, journalist, and the audience participants. The features used in the states include the duration of linguistic phenomena in a given turn, and the ratio of the linguistic phenomena to the entire turn, where the linguistic phenomena includes person addresses and mentions, disfluencies, and prefaces (e.g. "Well...")

Hutchinson *et al.* (2010) presented an approach for unsupervised speaker role labeling in broadcast talk shows. They used both turn taking features and lexical features to cluster speaker roles. They aim to find signature phrases (such as "welcome back") which are uttered in all shows, but by a very small number of people, and conversational phrases (such as "but" or "you know") which are frequent in broadcast conversations, but infrequent in broadcast news. They performed experiments using both English and Mandarin data sets. Results demonstrated that spectral clustering beat k-means or GMM and turn-taking features outperform lexical features in English and vice versa in Mandarin.

9.9 Modeling Dominance

An area on which automatic social relation detection research has focused is detecting dominant speakers. These are the people who dominate the meeting by controlling the flow of the discussion and conversation, by intervening, cutting off others, and raising new points, and furthermore are obeyed by others. In a typical broadcast talk show, the host may be considered as the dominant person as he has the role of moderating the conversation. Note that, this is different from the person who has the most authority, which often comes with expertise in an area. Following the broadcast talk show example, an expert scientist guest on some technical area is the authority in the conversation, but not necessarily dominating it. Similarly, while it is known that dominant speakers behave more actively and talk and move more, in certain interactions this may not be the case. Furthermore, the dominant person in a conversation or a multiparty meeting may change throughout the duration of the interaction and this may well align with the topics discussed.

While, modeling dominance has been extensively studied in the social sciences literature, recently a few practical studies have been presented towards automatically tagging the most dominant person in meetings using audio (Rienks and Heylen, 2006) and visual cues (Jayagopi *et al.*, 2009), but these studies ignored lexical content. According to Rienks and Heylen (2006), dominant speakers try to assert authority by manipulating the group or certain individuals in the group. This research categorized speakers' dominance level as high, medium, and low, using nonverbal features, such as speaking time, and verbal cues, such as number of words spoken.

Jayagopi *et al.* (2009) presented a multi-modal processing system using audio (speaking length, energy) and video (motion activity) features, and simply classified speakers with the highest feature values as dominant. They also checked the spoken and visual interruptions such as patterns of who is interrupting whom using speech and video features. They built statistical models using SVMs for the AMI meeting corpus. Using the baseline of tagging the most talkative person as dominant achieved an accuracy of 82%. Using the remaining features this increased to 91%, mostly with the help of speech energy and turn-taking patterns.

Future work on dominance modeling involves exploiting content in addition to audio and visual cues, such as checking topic patterns and even some simple key phrases as proven to be useful in the speaker role detection research presented above.

9.10 Argument Diagramming

Argument diagramming aims to display a visual representation of the flow and structure of reasoning in conversations, especially in discussions and arguments (Rienks *et al.*, 2005). The utterances and their relationships are tagged with predefined classes representing the characteristics of discussion and argumentation. For example, one utterance may open a new issue and another utterance may elaborate on it in response. Typically in argument diagrams, utterances are represented via typed nodes, and relationships between pairs of utterances via

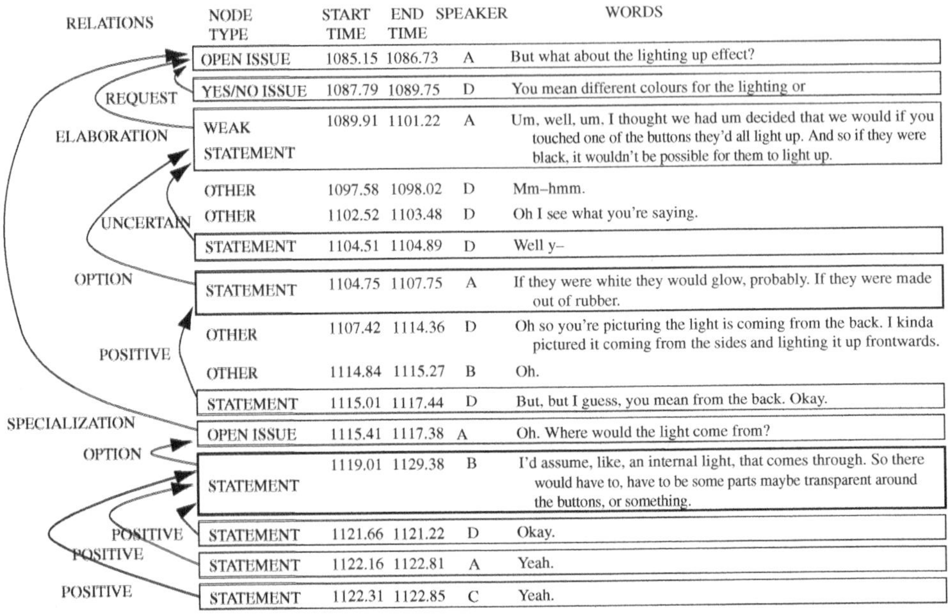

Figure 9.10 Example meeting transcript with argument nodes and relation annotations. The start and end time (in seconds), speaker identity (A,B,C, or D), as well as the words of every speaker turn is shown

typed edges connecting two nodes, forming a tree structure for the topics discussed. Figure 9.10 shows the transcription of an excerpt from the AMI corpus with argument diagram annotations, where the participants are discussing the design of a remote control device. The rectangles mark the nodes, and the arcs mark the relations of the argument diagram.

Argument diagrams extracted from meetings can be useful for meeting participants, to help them follow discussions and catch up with arguments, if the maps can be extracted during the meeting.

There also is a wide body of work on annotating and finding discourse structure, mainly focused on text and dialogues. For example, the Penn Discourse Treebank (PDTB, Miltsakaki *et al.*, 2004) includes manual annotations of explicit (such as a result) and implicit discourse connectives, as well as their host and anaphoric arguments in the Wall Street Journal articles. The host argument is the argument in which the discourse connective occurs, while the anaphoric argument is the argument related to the host argument by the discourse connective. While automatically finding anaphoric arguments of discourse connectives is similar to argument diagramming, the PDTB annotation mainly includes annotation of discourse connectives, rather than abstract relations as in argument diagrams. Baldridge and Lascarides (2005) aimed at annotating dialogues with rhetorical relations that conform to Segmented Discourse Representation Theory (Lascarides and Asher, 2007), using probabilistic context-free grammars to extract the discourse structure of these dialogues. Carlson *et al.* (2003) presented another study on forming a discourse-tagged corpus, and also described measures for quality assurance and consistency, found by mapping hierarchical structures into sets of units and measuring annotator agreement.

There is a wide body of work that focuses on visualization of argument maps, as entered by the conversation participants (Fujita *et al.*, 1998, among others). Argument diagrams can also help users in browsing past meetings, tracking progress across several meetings and can be useful in meeting summarization. Rienks and Verbree (2006) have performed experiments with human subjects, and their results indicated that argumentation information from meetings can be useful in question answering. Argument diagrams can also help the related tasks of action item extraction and decision detection in meetings (see above). Note that argument diagramming is different from decision detection in several ways, the most important one is that not all discussions are required to include a decision.

For the multiparty meetings domain, two studies proposed argumentative models of meeting discussion. Combining their experience from two meeting processing projects, DARPA CALO and the Swiss National Research project IM2, Pallotta *et al.* (2005) discussed four perspectives (persuasion, decision making, episodes, and conversations), and a theoretical model for each perspective.

Similarly, Rienks *et al.* (2005) proposed the Twente Argumentation Schema (TAS), and annotated the AMI meeting corpus according to TAS. In this representation, there are six node types, and nine relation types. The relations apply to specific node type pairs. Below we cover TAS in more detail.

TAS was created at University of Twente, where argument diagrams for parts of meeting transcripts that contain discussions around a specific topic, were also formed. In TAS, argument diagrams are tree-structured; the nodes of the tree contain speech act units (usually parts of or complete speaker turns) and the edges show the relations between the nodes, the edges emanate from parents and end at children nodes, where the children nodes follow parent nodes in time. At a high level, there are two types of nodes: *issues and statements*. The *issue* nodes mainly open up an issue and request a response and are further categorized into three-depending on the form of the response they expect: *open issue* (OIS), *A/B issue* (AIS) and Yes/No issue (YIS). The *open issues* are utterances that allow for various possible responses, that are not included in the utterances themselves. In contrast, *A/B issues* are utterances that request possible responses that are specified in the utterance. The *Yes/No issues* directly request the other participants' opinion as a "Yes" or "No". The *statements* are utterances that convey the position of the speaker on a subject/topic. To be able to represent the statements for which the speaker is not highly certain about what they say, the *statements* are split into two: *statements* (STA) and *weak statements* (WST). The *weak statements* represent the cases where the speaker is not very confident. The rest of the utterances that are not involved in reasoning or backchannelling utterances are represented with an additional (OTHER) category. Figure 9.11 shows example utterances for each node type.

The relations between a pair of utterances are categorized into nine types: *Elaboration*, *Specialization*, *Request*, *Positive*, *Negative*, *Uncertain*, *Option*, *Option Exclusion*, and *Subject To*. As its name implies, the *Elaboration* relation applies to a pair of utterances (both which can be statements or issues), where the child node utterance elaborates on the parent node utterance. Similarly, the *Specialization* relation applies to pairs (statements and statements or issues and issues), where the child node is a specialization of the parent node. The *Request* relation relates two utterances (statements to issues), where the child utterance asks for more information about the parent. The *Positive* and *Negative* relations apply to utterances, where the child utterance supports or refutes the parent utterance, respectively. The *Uncertain* relation applies to pairs, where it is not clear if the child supports or refutes the parent node. The *Option*

TYPE	EXAMPLE
STA	And you keep losing them.
WST	We should probably just use conventional batteries.
OIS	What's the functionality of that?
AIS	So, double or triple?
YIS	Do we need an LCD display?
OTHER	Mm-hmm.

Figure 9.11 Examples of utterances that belong to statement (STA), weak statement (WST), open issue (OIS), A/B issue (AIS), Yes/No issue (YIS), and OTHER node types

relation relates pairs of utterances (statements to issues or other statements), where the where the child is a possible answer, option or solution to the parent utterance. The *Option Exclusion* relates pairs (statements or issues to issues), where the child node eliminates one or more of the possible answers, options or solutions to the parent utterance. The *Subject To* relation applies to pairs (statements and Yes/No or A/B issues or statements), where the child provides criteria that need to be fulfilled before the parent node can be supported or denied. More information about the relation types and example utterance pairs and annotated tree structures can be found in Rienks *et al.* (2005).

Following the TAS schema, Hakkani-Tür (2009) tackled the problem of assigning node types to user utterances, and studied the use of several lexical and prosodic features for this task. More specifically, she has employed a cascaded approach relying on two classifiers, using lexical and prosodic features for tagging the argumentation types of the utterances. Prosodic information is shown to be very helpful in distinguishing the backchannels and questions raising issues, as expected. One important thing to note about relations is that they usually relate pairs of utterances of specific node types. Therefore, the detection of node types before determining the relations is intuitively the processing sequence for extracting argument diagrams from conversations, while joint modeling techniques should also be investigated in the future.

Murray *et al.* (2006) investigated the use of prosodic features to detect rhetorical relations, which aim to describe conversations in terms of coherence. Rienks and Verbree (2006) used decision trees with features extracted from manual annotations, such as the presence of a question mark, utterance length, label of the preceding segment, and automatically computed features, such as part of speech tags to investigate the learnability of argument diagram node types. While their work resulted in promising improvements over a fairly simple baseline, most of the features used in that work are extracted from manual annotations. Also, the automatic annotation of relations was not considered.

9.11 Discussion and Conclusions

As speech and language processing technologies become more mature and robust, we are in that phase where exploring automatic methods for processing human/human conversational understanding tasks are now feasible. Progress in these tasks, from low-level transcription to higher-level shallow understanding functions, such as action item extraction and summarization, potentially has enormous impact on human productivity in many professional settings. However, these tasks are still very shallow and focused on targeted understanding of certain phenomena. Most higher level semantic understanding tasks are only vaguely defined and annotator agreement is still very low. One potential solution is studying limited domain and maybe goal-oriented conversations instead of unstructured chit-chat for better inter-annotator agreement and therefore potentially deeper understanding.

Promising future work includes integration of these tasks and features from multiple modalities, such as from video, or digital pen and paper. Furthermore, personalization of these tasks and exploiting meta information such as project related documentation or email may bring these technologies to individual users. Another interesting research direction would be processing the aggregate of conversations and meetings, tracking the topics, participants, and action items, similar to emails.

References

Allen JF, Schubert LK, Ferguson G, Heeman P, Hwang T, Kato T, Light M, Martin NG, Miller BW, Poesio DR and Traum DR 1995 The TRAINS project: a case study in building a conversational planning agent. *Journal of Experimental and Theoretical AI (JETAI)* **2**(2), 119–129.

Anderson A, Bader M, Bard E, Boyle E, Doherty GM, Garrod S, Isard S, Kowtko J, McAllister J, Miller J, Sotillo C, Thompson H and Weinert R 1991 The HCRC maptask corpus. *Language and Speech* **34**, 351–366.

Ang J, Liu Y and Shriberg E 2005 Automatic dialogue act segmentation and classification in multiparty meetings *Proceedings of the International Conference on Acoustics, Speech and Signal Processing (ICASSP)*, Philadelphia, PA.

Austin JL 1962 *How to do things with words*. Harvard University Press.

Baldridge J and Lascarides A 2005 Probabilistic head-driven parsing for discourse structure *Proceedings of the CONLL*.

Banerjee S and Rudnicky A 2004 Using simple speech based features to detect the state of a meeting and the roles of the meeting participants *Proceedings of the International Conference on Spoken Language Processing (ICSLP)*, Jeju-Island, Korea.

Banerjee S, Rosé C and Rudnicky A 2005 The necessity of a meeting recording and playback system, and the benefit of topic-level annotations to meeting browsing *Proceedings of the 10th International Conference on Human-Computer Interaction (CHI)*.

Barzilay R, Collins M, Hirschberg J and Whittaker S 2000 The rules behind roles: Identifying speaker role in radio broadcasts *Proceedings of the Conference of the American Association for Artificial Intelligence (AAAI)*.

Bennett PN and Carbonell J 2005 Detecting action-items in e-mail *Proceedings of the ACM Annual International ACM SIGIR Conference on Research and Development in Information Retrieval*, Salvador, Brazil.

Bennett PN and Carbonell JG 2007 Combining probability-based rankers for action-item detection *Proceedings of the HLT/NAACL*, pp 324–331. Association for Computational Linguistics, Rochester, NY.

Bikel DM, Schwartz R and Weischedel RM 1999 An algorithm that learns what's in a name. *Machine Learning Journal Special Issue on Natural Language Learning* **34**(1-3), 211–231.

Bilmes JA and Kirchhoff K 2003 Factored language models and generalized parallel backoff *Proceedings of the Human Language Technology Conference (HLT)-Conference of the North American Chapter of the Association for Computational Linguistics (NAACL)*, Edmonton, Canada.

Burger S, MacLaren V and Yu H 2002 The ISL Meeting Corpus : The impact of meeting type on speech style *Proceedings of the International Conference on Spoken Language Processing (ICSLP)*, Denver, Colorado.

Carlson L, Marcu D and Okurowski ME 2003 Current directions in discourse and dialogue *Building a Discourse-Tagged Corpus in the Framework of Rhetorical Structure Theory*. Kluwer Academic Publishers.

Camelin N, Damnati G, Bechet F, and De Mori R. 2006 Opinion mining in a telephone survey corpus *Proceedings of the International Conference on Spoken Language Processing (ICSLP)*, Pittsburgh, PA.

Cetin O and Shriberg E 2006 Analysis of overlaps in meetings by dialogue factors, hot spots, speakers, and collection site: Insights for automatic speech recognition *Proceedings of the International Conference on Spoken Language Processing (ICSLP)*, pp 293–296.

Church KW 1988 A stochastic parts program and noun phrase parser for unrestricted text *Proceedings of the Conference on Applied Natural Language Processing (ANLP)*, pp 136–143, Austin, Texas.

Clark A and Popescu-Belis A 2004 Multi-level dialogue act tags *Proceedings of the SigDial Workshop*, Boston, MA.

Clark HH and Schaefer EF 1989 Contributing to discourse *Cognitive Science*, vol. 13, pp 259–294.

Core M and Allen J 1997 Coding dialogues with the DAMSL annotation scheme *Proceedings of the Working Notes of the Conference of the American Association for Artificial Intelligence (AAAI) Fall Symposium on Communicative Action in Humans and Machines*, Cambridge, MA.

Corston-Oliver S, Ringger E, Gamon M and Campbell R 2004 Task-focused summarization of email *Proceedings of the ACL Workshop Text Summarization Branches Out.*

Cuendet S, Hakkani-Tür D and Tur G 2006 Model adaptation for sentence segmentation from speech *Proceedings of the IEEE Spoken Language Technologies (SLT) Workshop*, Aruba.

Dhillon R, Bhagat S, Carvey H and Shriberg E 2004 Meeting recorder project: Dialogue act labeling guide. Technical Report TR-04-002, International Computer Science Institute, Berkeley, CA.

Drew P and Heritage J 1992 *Talk at Work*. Cambridge University Press.

Favre B, Grishman R, Hillard D, Ji H and Hakkani-Tür D 2008a Punctuating speech for information extraction *Proceedings of the International Conference on Acoustics, Speech and Signal Processing (ICASSP)*, Las Vegas, NV.

Favre B, Hakkani-Tür D, Petrov S and Klein D 2008b Efficient sentence segmentation using syntactic features *Proceedings of the IEEE Spoken Language Technologies (SLT) Workshop*, Goa, India.

Fernández R, Frampton M, Ehlen P, Purver M and Peters S 2008 Modelling and detecting decisions in multiparty dialogue *Proceedings of the 9th SIGdial Workshop on Discourse and Dialogue*, pp 156–163. Association for Computational Linguistics, Columbus, OH.

Frampton M, Fernández R, Ehlen P, Christoudias M, Darrell T and Peters S 2009a Who is "you "? combining linguistic and gaze features to resolve second-person references in dialogue *Proceedings of the Conference of the European Chapter of the Association for Computational Linguistics (EACL).*

Frampton M, Huang J, Bui TH and Peters S 2009b Real-time decision detection in multiparty dialogue *Proceedings of the Conference on Empirical Methods in Natural Language Processing (EMNLP)*, Singapore.

Fujita K, Nishimoto K, Sumi Y, Kunifuji S and Mase K 1998 Meeting support by visualizing discussion structure and semantics *Proceedings of the Second International Conference on Knowledge-Based Intelligent Electronic Systems*, Adelaide, Australia.

Galley M, McKeown K, Hirschberg J and Shriberg E 2004 Identifying agreement and disagreement in conversational speech: Use of B ayesian networks to model pragmatic dependencies *Proceedings of the Annual Meeting of the Association for Computational Linguistics (ACL).*

Garg N, Favre S, Salamin H, Hakkani-Tür D and Vinciarelli A 2008 Role recognition for meeting participants: an approach based on lexical information and social network analysis *Proceedings of the ACM Multimedia Conference*.

Godfrey JJ, Holliman EC and McDaniel J 1992 Switchboard: Telephone speech corpus for research and development *Proceedings of the International Conference on Acoustics, Speech and Signal Processing (ICASSP)*, vol. 1, pp 517–520, San Francisco, USA.

Gupta S, Niekrasz J, Purver M and Jurafsky D 2007 Resolving "you" in multiparty dialogue *Proceedings of the 8th SIGdial Workshop on Discourse and Dialogue*, Antwerp, Belgium.

Guz U, Favre B, Tur G and Hakkani-Tür D 2009 Generative and discriminative methods using morphological information for sentence segmentation of Turkish . *IEEE Transactions on Audio, Speech, and Language Processing* **17**(5), 895–903.

Guz U, Tur G, Hakkani-Tür D and Cuendet S 2010 Cascaded model adaptation for dialogue act segmentation and tagging. *Computer Speech and Language* **18**(2), 289–306.

Hakkani-Tür D 2009 Towards automatic argument diagramming of multiparty meetings *Proceedings of the International Conference on Acoustics, Speech and Signal Processing (ICASSP)*, Taipei, Taiwan.

Hillard D, Ostendorf M and Shriberg E 2003 Detection of agreement vs. disagreement in meetings: Training with unlabeled data *Companion Volume of the Proceedings of the HLT-NAACL -Short Papers*, Edmonton, Alberta.

Hillard D, Ostendorf M, Stolcke A, Liu Y and Shriberg E 2004 Improving automatic sentence boundary detection with confusion networks *Proceedings of the Human Language Technology Conference (HLT)-NAACL*, Boston, MA.

Hsueh PY and Moore J 2007 What decisions have you made?: Automatic decision detection in meeting conversations *Proceedings of NAACL/HLT*, Rochester, New York.

Hutchinson B, Zhang B and Ostendorf M 2010 Unsupervised broadcast conversation speaker role labeling *Proceedings of the International Conference on Acoustics, Speech and Signal Processing (ICASSP).*

Janin A, Ang J, Bhagat S, Dhillon R, Edwards J, Macias-Guarasa J, Morgan N, Peskin B, Shriberg E, Stolcke A, Wooters C and Wrede B 2004 The ICSI meeting project: Resources and research *Proceedings of the International Conference on Acoustics, Speech and Signal Processing (ICASSP)*, Montreal.

Jayagopi DB, Hung H, Yeo C and Gatica-perez D 2009 Modeling dominance in group conversations using non-verbal activity cues. *IEEE Transactions on Audio, Speech, and Language Processing* **17**(3), 501–513.

Jovanovic N, op den Akker R and Nijholt A 2006 Addressee identification in face-to-face meetings *Proceedings of the Conference of the European Chapter of the Association for Computational Linguistics (EACL)*, pp 169–176, Trento, Italy.

Jurafsky D and Martin JH 2008 *Speech and Language Processing* second edition edn. Prentice Hall, NJ.

Jurafsky D, Shriberg E and Biasca D 1997 Switchboard SWBD-DAMSL labeling project coder's manual. Technical Report 97-02, University of Colorado Institute of Cognitive Science.

Kolar J, Liu Y and Shriberg E 2007 Speaker adaptation of language models for automatic dialogue act segmentation of meetings *Proceedings of the International Conference on Spoken Language Processing (Interspeech)*, Antwerp, Belgium.

Kolar J, Shriberg E and Liu Y 2006 Using prosody for automatic sentence segmentation of multiparty meetings *Proceedings of the International Conference on Text, Speech, and Dialogue (TSD)* , Czech Republic.

Kuhn R and Mori RD 1995 The application of semantic classification trees to natural language understanding. *IEEE Transactions on Pattern Analysis and Machine Intelligence* **17**, 449–460.

Lascarides A and Asher N 2007 Segmented discourse representation theory: Dynamic semantics with discourse structure In *Computing Meaning* (ed. Bunt H and Muskens R). Kluwer Academic Publishers.

Lisowska A 2003 Multimodal interface design for the multimodal meeting domain: Preliminary indications from a query analysis study. Technical Report IM2.MDM-11 , ISSCO , University of Geneva.

Liu Y 2006 Initial study in automatic identification of speaker role in broadcast news speech *Proceedings of the Human Language Technology Conference (HLT) / Conference of the North American Chapter of the Association for Computational Linguistics (NAACL)*, New York City, USA.

Liu Y and Xie S 2008 Impact of automatic sentence segmentation on meeting summarization *Proceedings of the International Conference on Acoustics, Speech and Signal Processing (ICASSP)*, Las Vegas, NV.

Liu Y, Stolcke A, Shriberg E and Harper M 2005 Using conditional random fields for sentence boundary detection in speech *Proceedings of the Annual Meeting of the Association for Computational Linguistics (ACL)*, Ann Arbor, MI.

Margolis A, Livescu K and Ostendorf M 2010 Domain adaptation with unlabeled data for dialogue act tagging *Proceedings of the Annual Meeting of the Association for Computational Linguistics (ACL)*, Uppsala, Sweden.

Mast M, Kompe R, Harbeck S, Kiessling A, Niemann H, Nöth E, Schukat-Talamazzini EG and Warnke V 1996 Dialogue act classification with the help of prosody *Proceedings of the International Conference on Spoken Language Processing (ICSLP)*, Philadelphia.

Matusov E, Hillard D, Magimai-Doss M, Hakkani-Tür D, Ostendorf M and Ney H 2007 Improving speech translation with automatic boundary prediction *Proceedings of the International Conference on Spoken Language Processing (Interspeech)*, Antwerp, Belgium.

Miltsakaki E, Prasad R, Joshi A, and Webber B 2004 The penn discourse treebank *Proceedings of the International Conference on Language Resources and Evaluation (LREC)*.

Morgan W, Chang PC, Gupta S and Brenier JM 2006 Automatically detecting action items in audio meeting recordings *Proceedings of the 7th SIGdial Workshop on Discourse and Dialogue*, pp 96–103. Association for Computational Linguistics, Sydney, Australia.

Müller C 2006 Automatic detection of nonreferential *It* in spoken multiparty dialogue *Proceedings of the Conference of the European Chapter of the Association for Computational Linguistics (EACL)*, pp 49–56, Trento, Italy.

Müller C 2007 Resolving it, this, and that in unrestricted multiparty dialogue *Proceedings of the Annual Meeting of the Association for Computational Linguistics (ACL)*, pp 816–823.

Murray G, Renals S and Taboada M 2006 Prosodic correlates of rhetorical relations *Proceedings of Human Language Technology Conference (HLT)-NAACL Workshop on Analyzing Conversations in Text and Speech (ACTS)*, New York City, NY, USA.

Pallotta V, Niekrasz J and Purver M 2005 Collaborative and argumentative models of meeting discussions *Proceedings of the 5th Workshop on Computational Models of Natural Argument (CMNA)*, Edinburgh, Scotland.

Pang B and Lee L 2008 *Opinion mining and sentiment analysis*. Now publishers.

Polifroni J, Seneff S, Branavan SRK, Wang C and Barzilay R 2010 Good grief, I can speak it! preliminary experiments in audio restaurant reviews *Proceedings of the IEEE Spoken Language Technologies (SLT) Workshop*, Berkeley, CA.

Popescu-Belis A 2005 Dialogue acts: One or more dimensions. ISSCO Working Paper no. 62, University of Geneva.

Price PJ 1990 Evaluation of spoken language systems: The ATIS domain *Proceedings of the DARPA Workshop on Speech and Natural Language*, Hidden Valley, PA.

Purver M, Dowding J, Niekrasz J, Ehlen P, Noorbaloochi S and Peters S 2007 Detecting and summarizing action items in multiparty dialogue *Proceedings of the 8th SIGdial Workshop on Discourse and Dialogue*, Antwerp, Belgium.

Purver M, Fernández R, Frampton M and Peters S 2009 Cascaded lexicalised classifiers for second-person reference resolution *Proceedings of the SIGDIAL Meeting on Discourse and Dialogue,*, London, UK.

Rangarajan V, Bangalore S and Narayanan S 2007 Exploiting prosodic features for dialogue act tagging in a discriminative modeling framework *Proceedings of the International Conference on Spoken Language Processing (Interspeech)*, Antwerp, Belgium.

Rienks R and Heylen D 2006 Automatic dominance detection in meetings using easily obtainable features In *MLMI, Revised Selected Papers* (ed. Renals S and Bengio S) vol. 3869 of *Lecture Notes in Computer Science* Springer pp 76–86.

Rienks R and Verbree D 2006 About the usefulness and learnability of argument-diagrams from real discussions *3rd Joint Workshop on Multimodal Interaction and Related Machine Learning Algorithms*, Washington D.C., USA.

Rienks R, Heylen D and van der Weijden E 2005 Argument diagramming of meeting conversations *Multimodal Multiparty Meeting Processing, Workshop at the International Conference on Multimodal Interaction (ICMI)*, Trento, Italy.

Roark B, Liu Y, Harper M, Stewart R, Lease M, Snover M, Shafran I, Dorr B, Hale J, Krasnyanskaya A and Yung L 2006 Reranking for sentence boundary detection in conversational speech *Proceedings of the International Conference on Acoustics, Speech and Signal Processing (ICASSP)*, Toulouse, France.

Schuller B, Wöllmer M, Eyben F and Rigoll G 2010 Retrieval of paralinguistic information in broadcasts In *Multimedia Information Extraction* (ed. Maybury M). MIT Press, Cambridge, MA.

Shriberg E, Bates R, Stolcke A, Taylor P, Jurafsky D, Ries K, Coccaro N, Martin R, Meteer M and Ess-Dykema CV 1998 Can prosody aid the automatic classification of dialogue acts in conversational speech. *Language and Speech* 41(3–4), 439–487.

Shriberg E, Dhillon R, Bhagat S, Ang J and Carvey H 2004a The ICSI Meeting Recorder Dialogue Act (MRDA) corpus *Proceedings of the 5th SIGdial Workshop on Discourse and Dialogue at Human Language Technology Conference (HLT)-NAACL 2004*, pp 97–100.

Shriberg E, Dhillon R, Bhagat S, Ang J and Carvey H 2004b The ICSI Meeting Recorder Dialogue Act (MRDA) Corpus *Proceedings of the SigDial Workshop*, Boston, MA.

Shriberg E, Stolcke A, Hakkani-Tür D and Tur G 2000 Prosody-based automatic segmentation of speech into sentences and topics. *Speech Communication* **32**(1-2), 127–154.

Somasundaran S, Ruppenhofer J and Wiebe J 2007 Detecting arguing and sentiment in meetings *Proceedings of the 8th SIGdial Workshop on Discourse and Dialogue*, Antwerp, Belgium.

Somasundaran S, Wiebe J, Hoffmann P and Litman D 2006 Manual annotation of opinion categories in meetings *Proceedings of the ACL/COLING Workshop: Frontiers in Linguistically Annotated Corpora*, Sydney, Australia.

Stent A 2000 The monroe corpus. TR728 and TN99-2, University of Rochester.

Stiefelhagen R, Yang J and Waibel A 2002 Modeling focus of attention for meeting indexing based on multiple cues. *IEEE Transactions on Neural Networks* **13**(3), 928–938.

Stolcke A and Shriberg E 1996 Statistical language modeling for speech disfluencies *Proceedings of the International Conference on Acoustics, Speech and Signal Processing (ICASSP)*, Atlanta, GA.

Stolcke A, Ries K, Coccaro N, Shriberg E, Bates R, Jurafsky D, Taylor P, Martin R, van Ess-Dykema C and Meteer M 2000 Dialogue act modeling for automatic tagging and recognition of conversational speech. *Computational Linguistics* **26**(3), 339–373.

Susanne J, Klein A, Maier E, Maleck I, Mast M and Quantz J 1995 Dialogue acts in VERBMOBIL . Report 65, University of Hamburg, DFKI GmbH, University of Erlangen, and TU Berlin.

Traum DR and Hinkelman EA 1992 Conversation acts in task-oriented spoken dialogue. *Computational Intelligence* **8**(3), 575–599.

Tur G, Guz U and Hakkani-Tür D 2006 Model adaptation for dialogue act tagging *Proceedings of the IEEE Spoken Language Technologies (SLT) Workshop.*

Tur G, Stolcke A, Voss L, Peters S, Hakkani-Tür D, Dowding J, Favre B, Fernandez R, Frampton M, Frandsen M, Frederickson C, Graciarena M, Kintzing D, Leveque K, Mason S, Niekrasz J, Purver M, Riedhammer K, Shriberg E, Tien J, Vergyri D and Yang F 2010 The CALO meeting assistant system. *IEEE Transactions on Audio, Speech, and Audio Processing* **18**(6), 1601–1611.

Venkataraman A, Liu Y, Shriberg E and Stolcke A 2005 Does active learning help automatic dialogue act tagging in meeting data? *Proceedings of the International Conference on Spoken Language Processing (Interspeech)*, Lisbon, Portugal.

Venkataraman A, Stolcke A and Shriberg EE 2002 Automatic dialogue act tagging with minimal supervision *Proceedings of the Australian International Conference on Speech Science and Technology*, Melbourne, Australia.

Verbree A, Rienks R and Heylen D 2006 First steps towards the automatic construction of argument-diagrams from real discussions *Proceedings of the 1st International Conference on Computational Models of Argument, September 11 2006, Frontiers in Artificial Intelligence and Applications*, vol. 144, pp 183–194. IOS press.

Vinciarelli A 2007 Speakers role recognition in multiparty audio recordings using social network analysis and duration distribution modeling. *IEEE Transactions on Multimedia Processing.*

Warnke V, Kompe R, Niemann H and Nöth E 1997 Integrated dialogue act segmentation and classification using prosodic features and language models *Proceedings of the European Conference on Speech Communication and Technology (EUROSPEECH)*, Rhodes, Greece.

Wilson T 2008 Annotating subjective content in meetings *Proceedings of the International Conference on Language Resources and Evaluation (LREC)*, Marrakech, Morocco.

Wrede B and Shriberg E 2003 The relationship between dialogue acts and hot spots in meetings *Proceedings of the IEEE Automatic Speech Recognition and Understanding (ASRU) Workshop*.

Wrede B, Bhagat S, Dhillon R and Shriberg E 2005 Meeting recorder project: Hot spot labeling guide. Technical Report TR-05-004, International Computer Science Institute, Berkeley, CA.

Yaman S, Hakkani-Tür D and Tur G 2010 Social role discovery from spoken language using dynamic bayesian networks *Proceedings of the International Conference on Spoken Language Processing (Interspeech)*, Makuhari, Japan.

Yang F, Tur G and Shriberg E 2008 Exploiting dialogue act tagging and prosodic information for action item identification *Proceedings of the International Conference on Acoustics, Speech and Signal Processing (ICASSP)*, Las Vegas, NV.

Zimmerman M, Hakkani-Tür D, Fung J, Mirghafori N, Gottlieb L, Shriberg E and Liu Y 2006 The ICSI+ multilingual sentence segmentation system *Proceedings of the International Conference on Spoken Language Processing (ICSLP)*, Pittsburg, PA.

Zimmermann M, Liu Y, Shriberg E and Stolcke A 2005 Toward joint segmentation and classification of dialogue acts in multiparty meetings *Proceedings of the Workshop on Multimodal Interaction and Related Machine Learning Algorithms (MLMI)*, Edinburgh, U.K.

Zue V, Seneff S and Glass J 1990 Speech database development at MIT : Timit and beyond. *Speech Communication* **9**(4), 351–356.

10

Named Entity Recognition

Frédéric Béchet
Aix Marseille Université, France

Named Entity Recognition (NER) can be defined as follows: a task consisting of detecting segments of a document (text or speech) expressing a direct reference to a unique identifier. For example the sequence of words corresponding to a specific person name is a Named Entity. NER is a crucial process preliminary to any further processes aimed at extracting a deeper semantic or syntactic representation of a document. Therefore NER has been a task in a lot of evaluation programs for the last 20 years, starting with the Message Understanding Conferences (MUC) (Chinchor and Robinson, 1998; Sundheim, 1996). These evaluation programs have produced corpora for several languages (English, Chinese, Spanish, Japanese, ...) allowing researchers to use this core task for developing and evaluating various parsing, tagging and classification methods based on handcrafted knowledge or supervised learning with or without linguistic resources.

The application of NER to speech has been studied in parallel to NER from text since the DARPA HUB-4 program in 1998 (Przybocki *et al.*, 1999) where the main goal was to evaluate the impact of Automatic Speech Recognition (ASR) errors on an Information Extraction task. The NER performance can be seen as an evaluation measure for an ASR system in conjunction with Word Error Rate (WER). The link between these two measures has been widely studied. Applying an NER technique developed for written text to ASR transcriptions is useful to assess the robustness of the technique in presence of noise. In general, noise in written text may depend on unreliable capitalization or punctuation as well as on erroneous words in messages gathered through the WEB (emails, blogs) or obtained with an automatic process performing ASR, Optical Character Recognition, Machine Translation. More recently NER has been seen as a specific SLU task where the decoding strategy does not just consist of applying an NER system developed on written texts to the output of an ASR system, but rather to adapt and combine more closely both processes.

After defining more precisely the NER task and its applicative frameworks in the context of speech processing in Section 10.1, this chapter reviews all the major issues linked to NER

Spoken Language Understanding: Systems for Extracting Semantic Information from Speech, First Edition.
Edited by Gokhan Tur and Renato De Mori.

from speech in Section 10.2, presents the corpora and benchmarks available to the scientific community in Section 10.3, discusses the evaluation metrics used for the evaluation of NER systems in Section 10.4 and compares the different approaches that have been proposed in Sections 10.5 and 10.6.

10.1 Task Description

10.1.1 What is a Named Entity?

There is no formal definition of what is a *Named Entity* from a linguistic point of view. The term was introduced at the MUC-6 evaluation program (Sundheim and Grishman, 1996) as one of the *shallow* understanding tasks. The basic idea was to detect in a text the names of people, organizations and geographic locations. To these "*named*" categories were also added time, currency and percentage expressions. The goal was to extract from a text all the word strings corresponding to these kinds of entities and from which a unique identifier can be obtained without resolving any reference resolution process. For example the word strings "*New York city*" or "*the big apple*", if tagged as *location* entities, refer without any ambiguity to the city of New York and will be considered as Named Entities. On the contrary the word string "*the city*", even if it also refers to New York City in a given document, won't be marked as a NE since a further linguistic process is needed for solving the reference. In a similar manner in the string "*the US president declared ...*" only the string "*US*" can be marked as a NE (either *location* or *organisation*). The string "*US president*" won't be marked as a *person* NE because it is not possible to identify which US president is referred to without a deeper analysis of the document.

In MUC seven categories of entities were grouped in three classes:

1. ENAMEX
   - ORGANIZATION: named corporate, governmental, or other organizational entity
   - PERSON: named person or family
   - LOCATION: name of politically or geographically defined location (cities, provinces, countries, international regions, bodies of water, mountains, etc.)
2. TIMEX
   - DATE: complete or partial date expression
   - TIME: complete or partial expression of time of day
3. NUMEX
   - MONEY: monetary expression
   - PERCENT: percentage

An example of text with MUC-6 annotations taken from Sundheim and Grishman (1996) is presented in Figure 10.1.

Most of the studies that have followed the MUC-6 and MUC-7 evaluation programs have used the MUC categories and guidelines as a starting point. The main differences that can be found compared with these original guidelines is the set of NE categories considered and the way the context of use of an entity is taken into account.

10.1.1.1 NE Tagset

The number of NE categories is very limited in MUC. In addition to the seven original categories, several other types of NEs have been proposed like FACILITY (Airport, Building-

```
Mr. <ENAMEX TYPE="PERSON">Dooner</ENAMEX> met with <ENAMEX:TYPE=
"PERSON">Martin Puris</ENAMEX>, president and chief executive
officer of <ENAMEX TYPE="ORGANIZATION">Ammirati & Puris</ENAMEX>,
about <ENAMEX TYPE="ORGANIZATION">McCann</ENAMEX>'s acquiring the
agency with billings of <NUMEX TYPE="MONEY">$400 million</NUMEX>,
but nothing has materialized.
```

Figure 10.1 Example of MUC-6 NE annotations (Sundheim and Grishman, 1996)

Grounds, Path, Plant, etc.) in the ACE program and ARTEFACT (human products, prizes, ...) in the IREX and ESTER programs. In addition to these *general purpose* entities, some restricted domains have defined their own set of Named Entities relevant to their particular context. This is the case, for example, in the biology domain (Kim *et al.*, 2004). In NER from speech, the SLU module of Spoken Dialogue Systems (SDS) often relies on the detection and extraction of application-specific entities such as telephone numbers or customers' names. They represent a specific kind of NEs that will be presented in Section 10.1.3.

Even with these additions, the set of categories usually considered in NER is limited. For IE tasks that require a precise semantic representation of a document, such as the Question Answering (QA) task, hierarchical NE categories have been proposed in order to refine the basic NEs usually considered. Sekine *et al.* (2002) proposed about 200 different categories that would be necessary for a QA application. However, like for any semantic model, there is no consensus about what should be the ideal set of categories to use in a NER task. Adding new categories leads to a more precise annotation, but also increases the annotation ambiguities and therefore makes the manual annotation process more difficult.

10.1.1.2 Defining NEs According to Their Context of Use

In MUC the definition of some NEs is ambiguous. For example all the country or town names are considered as *LOCATION* entities. However they are often used as organisation names rather than geographic locations in sentences such as: "*In the following year, the USA and France decided to negotiate directly with...*". Similarly an organisation name can be used to refer to a specific building and therefore becomes a locative expression: "*We will meet at The Louvre*".

To deal with these ambiguities some studies have chosen to create new ad-hoc categories grouping together entities that can belong to several NE types:

- *GPE* (Geo-Political Entity) in ACE (Doddington *et al.*, 2004), grouping together location names that can also be considered as an political organisation (Continent, County-or-District, Nation, Population-Center, State-or-Province);
- *GOE* (Geographical and Organizational Entity) in Sekine *et al.* (2002) grouping entities that can be either an organisation or a facility (museum, hospital, airport, ...).

Another way to deal with this issue is to label each entity according to its context of occurrence. In this case the entity "*France*" will be labelled as an organization in the sentence

"*France decided...*" and as a location in "*The mountains of France*". This annotation scheme was used in the French ESTER corpus (Galliano *et al.*, 2009).

10.1.2 What are the Main Issues in the NER Task?

NER can be split into two sub-tasks: a **segmentation task** in charge of finding the start and the end of the sequence of words expressing an entity in a document and a **classification task** that labels the entity with a category according to the NE tagset used. An additional **value extraction task** can also be added, especially in some speech applicative frameworks such as Spoken Dialogue Systems or Directory Assistance, where a canonical value has to be extracted for each entity detected (for example translating "*July 4th*" and "*fourth of July*" into "*04/07*" or translating "*UC Berkeley*" and "*Berkeley University of California*" into a single identifier such as "*UCB*").

The two main sources of ambiguities in NER are:

- *segmentation ambiguity*: should we split "*Berkeley University of California*" into two entities or consider it as a whole;
- *classification ambiguity*: the same surface form can refer to different entities. For example the string "*Charles de Gaulle*" can refer to the man (PERSON), to an airport (FACILITY), or to a ship (ARTEFACT).

The level of ambiguity in the NER task varies greatly according to the NE tagset used and the applicative domain targeted. However independently of any specific tagset and corpus, there are two main issues that make the NER task particularly challenging, especially when dealing with speech:

1. Most of the NE expressions contain proper names.
2. Non-local models (models taking into account several occurrences of a NE in a document) and prior knowledge are often necessary in order to remove the segmentation and classification ambiguities.

Proper names are an issue for any NLP process using a lexicon of a fixed size as it is impossible to have a full coverage of all the proper names that can occur in a document: they represent most of the out-of-vocabulary words found in the processing of any documents. This can be explained by the fact that proper names have generally a very low frequency and are very sensitive to time: they appear and disappear as new events occur and are often singletons even on very large corpora. For example it was shown (Favre *et al.*, 2005) on a news corpus collected on a daily basis that 72% of the NEs occur only one day in the corpus. Therefore it is difficult to maintain a lexicon with a good coverage on proper names. This problem is crucial in NER from speech, as we will discuss in Section 10.2, because the ASR lexicon *must* contain all the proper names that are going to be uttered in the spoken document to be processed. Any missing item will lead to a missed NE detection regardless of the quality of the NER system used.

Having all the words in the ASR lexicon that can occur in the NEs of a corpus to be processed is crucial. It is also important to collect prior knowledge about these words since surface form and local context are not always sufficient in order to remove the NER ambiguities. This issue

```
BLINKER BAN LIFTED.
Dutch forward Reggie Blinker had his indefinite suspension lifted
by FIFA on Friday and was set to make his Sheffield Wednesday
comeback on Saturday .
Blinker missed his club's last two games after FIFA slapped a
worldwide ban on him for appearing to sign contracts for both
Wednesday and Udinese while he was playing for Feyenoord.


PERSON = { "BLINKER" , "Reggie Blinker" , "Blinker" }
ORGANISATION = { "FIFA" , "Sheffield Wednesday" , "Wednesday" ,
                 "Udinese" , "Feyenoord" }
```

Figure 10.2 Example illustrating the need for non-local and prior knowledge in the NER task (Ratinov and Roth, 2009)

is illustrated by the example given in Figure 10.2 and taken from the Lev Ratinov and Dan Roth paper in CoNNL 2009 (Ratinov and Roth, 2009).

As we can see in this example the local context of the first sentence ("*BLINKER BAN LIFTED*") does not contain enough information to decide that "*BLINKER*" is a person. This can be disambiguated thanks to the beginning of the second sentence: "*Dutch forward Reggie Blinker*". And even with the whole document it is very hard without prior knowledge to guess that "*Sheffield Wednesday*" and "*Wednesday*" should be tagged as organisations since they refer to an English football team.

10.1.3 Applicative Frameworks of NER in Speech

Extracting NEs from speech has been studied in two applicative frameworks: Spoken Dialogue Systems (SDS) where NEs represent the first level in the Spoken Language Understanding (SLU) process of a dialogue turn and Spoken Information Extraction where NEs are extracted from spoken documents such as TV shows, news or interviews and debates. These two applicative frameworks contain different challenges for the NER task however they are both faced with similar issues such as speech disfluencies, ASR errors and the lack (or the unreliability) of punctuation and capital letters.

10.1.3.1 Spoken Information Extraction

This applicative framework consists of building systems that can describe an audio document by a set of descriptors, both at the acoustic and linguistic level, allowing users to perform complex search queries on large audio archives. Such a system is described in the IEEE Makhoul *et al.* paper (Makhoul *et al.*, 2000) with the following architecture:

- the continuous audio input stream is segmented by speaker turns;
- all the audio segments are clustered by speaker;
- the speaker corresponding to each cluster is identified if known by the system;
- all the segments are automatically transcribed;
- a NER system is applied to the transcriptions as well as a thematic classification;
- all these features are stored in a database and can be used to build search queries for retrieving specific content from large audio archives.

NER is a crucial component of such systems since many queries that can be addressed to an audio web search engine contain proper names belonging to the standard set of NEs (*PERSON, LOCATION, ORGANISATION, ARTEFACT, FACILITIES*).

10.1.3.2 Spoken Dialogue Systems

Most of the Spoken Dialogue Systems (SDS) deployed so far can be considered as an interface between a user and a database. The goal of the SLU module of such SDS is to find what kind of query the users are making to the database. In this framework NEs can be some of the *parameters* of such queries. For example in a flight booking application such as the one used to build the ATIS (Pallett *et al.*, 1992) corpus, city and airport names are both *standard* NEs and the parameters of the SQL queries that represent the users requests.

Temporal and numerical NEs such as dates and identification numbers are also widely used in SDS. For example in the AT&T *How May I Help You?* (HMIHY) customer care corpus (Gorin *et al.*, 1997), if a user wants his account balance and provides his identification number, the query will be *accessing the account balance field of the database* with the customer identification number as a parameter. Such parameters can be considered as NEs, even if in SDS their classification is more application-dependent. As an example the only NEs which are manually tagged in the HMIHY corpus are those which can be useful to the Dialogue Manager and their definitions contain additional semantic information compared with standard NEs. This additional semantic annotation level corresponds to the *interpretations* of the roles of the NEs within the dialogue. For example, the tag `Which_Bill` refers to an expression that identifies a customer's bill, such as: `my January bill`, `my previous statement` or `my bill issued on the second of January`. As can be seen, a NE date can represent a `Which_Bill` entity, but at the same time a date can be an `Item_Date` which corresponds to the date of a phone call.

Examples of HMIY and standard NE tags with their corresponding normalized values are given in Table 10.1.

Table 10.1 Examples of tags used in the How May I Help You? corpus with the corresponding NE tags and the normalized values

NE tag	HMIHY tag	Context	Value
Amount	Item_Amount	this 22 dollar charge	22.00
Adress	Phone	386 5715 area code 201	2013865715
Date	Item_Date	June tenth	????/06/10
Date	Which_Bill	my bill issued on the second of January	????/01/02
none	Which_Bill	most recent statement	latest
Location	Item_Place	calling Clementon New Jersey	Clementon, NJ

Source: Béchet *et al.*, 2004

Similarly in a booking application such as ATIS (Pallett *et al.*, 1992, flight booking) or MEDIA (Bonneau-Maynard *et al.*, 2005, hotel booking) the standard NEs dates and locations need to be enriched with a semantic specifier label such as *departure* and *arrival*. This additional level of information distinguishes the NER task presented in this chapter from the slot filling task presented in the chapter *Spoken Language Understanding as Template Filling*. NEs are more general than the concepts used in form filling applications.

10.2 Challenges Using Speech Input

The first challenge we face when dealing with speech, and more specifically with spontaneous speech, is the fact that speech represents a different language register from text, although most of the corpora containing NEs available to the scientific community are text corpora. In addition to this lack of spoken resources, the most obvious phenomenon that will have an impact on the NER process is speech disfluencies: hesitations, filled pauses, false starts,.... They can be inserted inside an entity, such as: *University of* ***hmm*** *California*, University of **Cal-** California or even *University of* ***you know*** *California*. These disfluencies represent an issue for NER detection as they break the continuity of the expression of an entity. The two ways of dealing with them is either to remove them prior to NER or to modify the NER models in order to integrate such disfluencies.

The second challenge of using speech input is to deal with ASR errors: the speech transcriptions produced by an ASR process contain errors: words can be replaced, deleted and false detection can insert erroneous words.

The NIST Topic Detection and Tracking (Fiscus and Doddington, 2002) and TREC document retrieval evaluation programs have studied the impact of recognition errors in the overall performance of Information Extraction systems for tasks such as story segmentation or topic detection and retrieval. The results obtained by Fiscus and Doddington (2002) have shown that this impact was very limited, compared with those obtained on *clean* text corpora. Similar results were obtained during the TREC program for a document retrieval task (Barnett *et al.*, 1997).

The main explanation for this phenomenon is the *redundancy effect*: themes, topics are very likely to be represented in texts by many occurrences of salient words characterizing them. Therefore, even if some of these words are missing, numerical Information Extraction methods can use the remaining salient words and discard the noise generated by ASR errors.

However, this phenomenon is not true for tasks related to the extraction of fine grained entities, such as Named Entities. Indeed, several studies have shown that F-measure[1] and WER are strongly correlated : 0.7 points of F-measure lost for each additional 1% of WER according to Miller *et al.* (2000) on the experiments of 1998 NIST Hub-4 evaluations (Przybocki *et al.*, 1999). Similar results were reported, also on the Hub-4 evaluations in Palmer *et al.* (1999), they are presented in Table 10.2.

Even topic-related tasks can be affected when NEs, that proved to be efficient features, are used. For example the results obtained during the 8 Text Retrieval Conference (TREC 8) clearly showed that there was a linear correlation between Named Entity recognition and document retrieval performance (Garofolo *et al.*, 1999).

[1] The F-measure is one of the evaluation metrics that are used to measure NER performance. It will be presented in Section 10.3.

Table 10.2 F-measure versus Word Error Rate for the NER task of DARPA Hub-4

Word error rate (%)	F-measure
28.3	71.1
21.1	78.1
14.5	82.2
13.5	81.6
0	88.2

Source: Palmer *et al.*, 1999

Despite the continuous improvement of ASR techniques, high WER transcriptions are inevitable in difficult conditions such as those found in large spoken archives. Moreover, Named Entities extraction performance is greatly affected by a mismatch between training and testing data. This mismatch is inevitable when dealing with archives spreading over a long period of time and containing multiple domain information.

Besides the intrinsic difficulties of ASR (robustness to noise, speaker variation, lack of coverage of the Language Models used, ...), there is a source of errors which is particularly important in IE from speech input: the out-of-vocabulary (OOV) word phenomenon. Indeed, ASR models are built on huge textual corpus and only contain the most frequent words to limit computation and memory usage. If this is the right approach to WER reduction, it is certainly not valid for information extraction where unlikely events are considered as important. For instance, many document retrieval models use inverse document frequency (rareness) as a word weighting parameter. So, unlikely proper names are not in reach of the ASR transcription system and hence cannot be spotted by a Named Entity extraction module.

This is illustrated by Table 10.3 reporting an experiment conducted at BBN on the Hub-4 evaluation corpus. They built lexicons extracted from the 1998 Hub-4 Language Model corpus by ordering the words according to frequency, and truncating the list at various lengths. Then they measured the percentage of in-vocabulary words in the NE expressions of the Hub-4 evaluation corpus for each lexicon produced. These results are given according to each NE type in Table 10.3. As expected the numeric NE types are well covered even with small lexicon sizes. Broadcast News ASR lexicons contain usually around 80K words. With this value,

Table 10.3 Percentage of in-vocabulary words of each NE type as a function of lexicon size on the 1998 Hub-4 evaluation test corpus

Name category	Lexicon size							
	5K	10K	20K	40K	60K	80K	100K	120K
PERSON	34.7	52.7	69.9	85.1	89.4	91.1	91.9	93.9
ORGANIZATION	73.2	90.2	94.2	97.5	98.2	98.5	98.7	98.8
LOCATION	76.6	87.1	92.2	96.2	97.5	98.0	98.8	99.1
TIME	97.0	97.0	99.0	100	100	100	100	100
MONEY	94.4	98.2	98.8	100	100	100	100	100
DATE	96.1	99.3	99.8	100	100	100	100	100
PERCENT	98.9	99.3	100	100	100	100	100	100

Source: Palmer *et al.*, 1999

reasonable coverage can be obtained for the *LOCATION* and *ORGANIZATION* entities however the out-of-vocabulary rate for the *PERSON* name category is still very high (9%). Increasing the lexicon size helps increase the coverage however the relation between these two quantities is far from being linear: when the lexicon size is doubled from 60K to 120K, the lexicon coverage of the *PERSON* entities only increases by 5%.

This is a very important issue for NER from speech as increasing the ASR lexicon size has a direct impact on the ASR process: each new word added to the lexicon results in additional features in the Language Model and therefore increases the need for a larger training corpus. The size of the ASR search space is also directly linked to the lexicon size: by increasing the search space we increase decoding time. This can lead also to an increase in the ASR pruning factors in order to keep an acceptable search space, with a potential negative impact on the ASR performance. The OOV phenomenon is certainly one of the biggest issues of NER from speech.

In addition to OOV words, the insertion of erroneous proper names that automatically trigger the insertion of an entity also has a strong impact on NER performance. Short and frequent proper names can be easily inserted in an ASR transcription. If they are usually unambiguously associated with a NE, they are likely to foul the NER process, even if their context of occurrence is incoherent. This issue stresses the need for including ASR confidence scores in the NER process and more generally integrating the two ASR and NER processes, as will be discussed in Section 10.6.

10.3 Benchmark Data Sets, Applications

10.3.1 NER as an IE Task

As mentioned in Section 10.1, NER from text has been widely studied in the NLP community through several evaluation programs. Table 10.4 summarizes some of the main NER evaluation programs that have been organised both on text and speech data. Most of the annotated corpora obtained through these programs contain newspaper data. For NER from speech, the choice is more limited. Several studies have used existing speech corpora to which they have added their own NE annotations. For example in Zhai *et al.* (2004) a Chinese corpus of Broadcast News from the Xinhua News Agency was annotated. In Surdeanu *et al.* (2005) a portion of the Switchboard corpus was annotated following the CoNNL guidelines. Another example is an NTT corpus (Hori and Nakamura, 2006) containing spoken queries to an open domain Question Answering system.

Table 10.4 Examples of NER evaluation programs

Program	Language	NE tagset size	Nature
MUC	English	7	Text
HUB-4	English	7	Speech
ACE	Arabic, English, Chinese	8	Speech
CoNNL	Dutch, Spanish, English, German	4	Text
IREX	Japanese	8	Text
ESTER	French	7	Speech

The first benchmark speech corpus annotated with Named Entities available to the scientific community is the HUB-4 corpus containing English Broadcast News transcriptions. This corpus has been widely used in numerous studies. In the ACE 2007 evaluation, Broadcast News transcriptions for Arabic and Chinese were added to the original HUB4 corpus. These annotation guidelines in HUB-4 are based on the Message Understanding Conference (MUC) Named Entity task which involved the tagging of person, organization, location names and other numerical entities in newswire text. Named-Entity-based scoring is used in HUB-4 as an alternative to traditional Word-Error-Rate(WER)-based scoring in evaluating continuous speech recognition performance.

In France, the French ESTER 2 program (Galliano *et al.*, 2009) contained three categories of tasks, namely segmentation, transcription and information extraction from speech. The NE tag set consists of seven main categories: persons, locations, organizations, human products, amounts, time and functions. Although not used in this evaluation, 38 sub-categories have been also defined and annotated in the corpus. Each NE is labelled according to its context of use. For example the NE "*University of Avignon*" can be considered either as an organization in the sentence: "*The University of Avignon is delivering a new diploma.*" or as a location in the sentence "*Let's meet near the University of Avignon.*" Most of the data contains Broadcast News however talk shows with a lot of spontaneous speech are also in the corpus.

10.3.2 NER as an SLU Task in a Spoken Dialogue Context

As mentioned in Section 10.1.3, another applicative framework for NER is in the development of Spoken Dialogue Systems (SDS). Most of the spoken dialogue corpora containing NE annotations are not available to the scientific community as they have been recorded through deployed SDS and therefore contain private customer data. For example the AT&T HMIHY corpus (Gorin *et al.*, 1997) and the France Telecom FT3000 corpus (Damnati *et al.*, 2007) contain dialogues between the deployed service and real customers and cannot be distributed because of privacy issues.

Therefore the only spoken dialogue corpora available are those collected through academic programs, often with a simulated system (Wizard Of Oz, Kelley (1984)) and *fake* customers. This is the case of the French MEDIA corpus. The evaluation program MEDIA (Bonneau-Maynard *et al.*, 2005) was dedicated to evaluating different conceptual decoding systems within the framework of a spoken dialogue system dedicated to providing tourist information and hotel booking service. A 1250 dialogue corpus was recorded by ELDA following a Wizard of Oz protocol: 250 speakers followed 5 hotel reservation scenarios. This corpus has been manually transcribed, then conceptually annotated according to a semantic representation defined within the project. The semantic dictionary MEDIA contains 83 concept labels. Among them we can find some *traditional* NEs such as location, organization (restaurant and hotel names), date and monetary value.

10.4 Evaluation Metrics

Evaluating NER from speech raises two issues: aligning an annotation sequence hypothesis with the reference annotation (*gold standard*) and measuring the quality of this hypothesis with respect to the reference.

10.4.1 Aligning the Reference and Hypothesis NE Annotations

The first issue is specific to speech processing: for NER from text, the reference and hypothesis annotations are simply aligned at the word level as both of them are based on the same sequence of words. When the hypothesis word sequence is produced by an ASR system the recognition errors can affect this direct alignment. In ASR evaluation this issue is solved by performing a dynamic programming alignment between the two word sequences with a scoring tool such as NIST SCLITE (Fiscus *et al.*, 2006). After this alignment the numbers of insertions, deletions and substitutions between the reference word sequence and the hypothesis word sequence are calculated in order to estimate the Word Error Rate between the two strings. The effect of this word alignment process on NER evaluation has been studied (Burger *et al.*, 1998). In addition to the NE insertion and deletion errors, three kinds of substitution are defined: *type*, *extent* and *content*.

By considering a reference annotation sequence such as `<p> A B C D </p>`, we can illustrate these three kinds of errors:

- *type*: `<o> A B C D </o>`
  This is the simplest error, where the substitution is only on the NE type.
- *extent*: `<p> A B C </p> D`
  In this case the boundaries of the entity are erroneous.
- *content*:
  The boundaries and the type of the entity are correct however there are ASR errors in the words describing the entity.

Of course these errors can occur simultaneously, for example *type+extent* or *type+content*, or a reference entity can be split in several entities with *extent* and possibly *type* and *content* errors. These errors are grouped together into several kinds of *multiple* errors to avoid counting them several times during the evaluation process.

An example of such an alignment is shown in Table 10.5 between the MUC reference annotation given in Figure 10.1 and a simulated hypothesis annotation performed on a word sequence containing ASR errors:

```
Mr.<ENAMEX TYPE="PERSON">Dooner</ENAMEX> met with<ENAMEX:TYPE=
"PERSON">Martin</ENAMEX> for is president and chief executive
officer of and  <ENAMEX TYPE="LOCATION"> Paris </ENAMEX>,
about <ENAMEX TYPE="ORGANIZATION">McCann</ENAMEX> acquiring
```

In this example only the first NE is correct, all the other NE hypotheses contain several substitution error types.

10.4.2 Scoring

The most commonly used measures for evaluating NE extraction performance are *Precision*, *Recall*, *F-measure* and *Slot Error Rate* (SER). They can be defined by the following notations (Makhoul *et al.*, 1999):

Table 10.5 Example of an alignment between a reference NE annotation and a hypothesis one produced by an ASR system

Ref. word	*Hyp. word*	*Ref. NE tag*	*Hyp. NE tag*	*Eval.*
Mr	Mr	none	none	
Dooner	Dooner	PERS	PERS	[*correct*]
met	met	none	none	
with	with	none	none	
Martin	Martin	PERS	PERS	[extent
Puris	*for*	PERS	none	*]
*	*is*	none	none	
president	president	none	none	
and	and	none	none	
chief	chief	none	none	
executive	executive	none	none	
officer	officer	none	none	
of	of	none	none	
Ammirati	*	ORG	none	[*
and	and	ORG	none	*
Puris	*Paris*	ORG	LOC	type+extent]
about	*about*	none	none	
McCann	*McCain*	ORG	ORG	[content]
's	*	none	none	
acquiring	acquiring	none	none	

- N = total number of slots in the reference
- M = total number of slots in the hypothesis
- C = number of correct slots: slots in the hypothesis that align with slots in the reference and are scored as correct
- S = number of substitutions as defined in the previous section (*extent*, *type*, *content* and *multiple* errors)
- D = number of deletions (missing slots or false rejections): slots in the reference that do not align with any slot in the hypothesis
- I = number of insertions (spurious slots or false acceptances): slots in the hypothesis that do not align with any slot in the reference

With these notations we have: $N = C + S + D$ and $M = C + S + I$.

Precision and Recall are defined by:

$$Precision: P = \frac{C}{M} = \frac{C}{C+S+I} \quad Recall: R = \frac{C}{N} = \frac{C}{C+S+D}$$

In order to have a single measure for comparing the performance of different systems, the *F-measure* has been introduced as the harmonic mean of the precision P and recall R measures:

$$F_\beta = \frac{(1+\beta^2)RP}{R+\beta^2 P}$$

The measure F_1 is usually chosen.

As explained in Makhoul *et al.* (1999), the weight of the deletion and insertion errors is underestimated in the calculation of the F-measure, that is why another measure is commonly used in NER: the *Slot Error Rate* (SER). This measure is very similar to the Word Error Rate used to evaluate ASR systems: all the errors are cumulated and divided by the number of slots in the reference. A different weight can be given to each type of error. SER can be defined by:

$$SER = 100 \times \frac{\alpha_d D + \alpha_i I + \sum_{s \in \mathcal{S}} \alpha_s s}{N}$$

with $s \in \mathcal{S}$ being an error substitution type (type, extent, type+extent, multiple, ...) and α_i its weight. For example in the French ESTER evaluation, the following weights were chosen: $\alpha_i = 1$, $\alpha_d = 1$, $\alpha_{type} = 0.5$, $\alpha_{extent} = 0.5$, $\alpha_{type+extent} = 0.8$, $\alpha_{multiple} = 1.5$.

Whereas lower means better for SER, higher means better for F-measure. Notice that F-measure is bounded between 0 and 1 even though SER can be more than 100 (if $I + D + S > N$).

10.5 Main Approaches for Extracting NEs from Text

As mentioned in the introduction of this chapter, NER was first studied on written documents rather than speech. Therefore NER from speech is usually seen as a sequential process where an ASR system produces an automatic transcription from a speech signal; this transcription is then segmented into sentences and sent as a *text* to a NER system originally developed for processing written text. With this kind of architecture there is no cooperation between the speech and NLP processes, and speech is just seen as a *noisy* form of a written document. This approach is clearly sub-optimal as ASR systems don't output structured text, but rather a stream of words with no punctuation and unreliable capital letters, both crucial features in NER from text. That is why alternative approaches to this sequential process have been proposed by developing specific NER systems for processing speech and adapting ASR processes to the NER task.

This section reviews the main approaches that have been proposed for extracting NE from text, the adaptation of these methods to speech is presented in Section 10.6.

10.5.1 Rules and Grammars

Most of the early work done on NEs followed a rule-based approach. When dealing with text input, hand-written rule-based systems have proven to give the best performance on the NE extraction task of MUC-7 (Bikel *et al.*, 1999a). NER from text is a well suited task for such approaches as NEs often occur in contexts that directly characterize their categories. For example if a proper name "*X*" immediately follows the word "*Mrs*", it is very likely that the sequence "*Mrs X*" will be a *PERSON* name entity. A lot of these very discriminant features can be obtained through an analysis of a text corpus. These features can be related to the format of the text (punctuation, capitalization), some morphological and syntactic information or to semantic categories obtained through the use of large lexicon of proper names (also called *gazetteer*). All these features can be used to build contextual rules such as the example given in Table 10.6 and taken from Mikheev *et al.* (1999).

Instead of using contextual rules, this hand-crafted knowledge can also be encoded as a cascade of Finite State Transducers (Appelt and Martin, 1999). In this case the words from the

Table 10.6 Examples of rules for extracting NE. `Xxxx+` is a sequence of capitalized words; `DD` is a digit; `PROF` is a profession; `REL` is a relative; `JJ*` is a sequence of zero or more adjectives; `LOC` is a known location

Context rule	Assign	Example
`Xxxx+ is? a? JJ* PROF`	PERS	*Yuri Gromov, a former director*
`Xxxx+ is? a? JJ* REL`	PERS	*John White is beloved brother*
`Xxxx+ himself`	PERS	*White himself*
`Xxxx+, DD+,`	PERS	*White, 33,*
`shares in Xxxx+`	ORG	*shares in Trinity Motors*
`PROF of/at/with Xxxx+`	ORG	*director of Trinity Motors*
`Xxxx+ area`	LOC	*Beribidjan area*

Source: Mikheev *et al.*, 1999

input text are generalized thanks to a set of transducers translating them into features related to their categories. These categories can be obtained according to large proper name lexicon (town names, company names, ...) or from the format of the word in the text (contains digit, with a capital letter, ...). Then regular grammars representing the different NE expressions which can be built from these words and categories are applied in order to detect every NE occurrence.

Following the most popular rule-based approach proposed for POS tagging by Brill (1992), the same rule induction strategy was applied to the NER task by Kim and Woodland (2000). In this method the rules are automatically derived from a corpus and a set of features before being pruned in order to increase the detection score on an annotated development corpus.

10.5.2 NER as a Word Tagging Problem

As presented in Section 10.1.2, NER is made of two sub-tasks: a segmentation task consisting of finding the span of each entity occurring in a text; a classification task labeling each entity detected with its correct category (*PERSON*, *LOCATION*, etc). These two tasks can be merged if we apply the classification process at the word level: each word occurring in a NE receives a label corresponding to the category of the NE, and possibly its position inside it. All the words occurring outside the NEs of a text are labelled with the same *outside* label. It is this kind of model that was used by Ramshaw and Marcus (1995) for the text chunking task. They used three position labels: *B* indicating the beginning of a chunk; *I* indicating that the word is inside a chunk but not the first word of it; and *O* for all the words outside any entities. This *BIO* models, applied to the sentence in Figure 10.1, is presented in Figure 10.3.

This very simple position model can be enriched, for example in the *BILOU* model by adding two more tags: one to the last word of an entity (last unit: *L*); the other one to entities made of only one word (unit-length entities: *U*). Adding more position tags increases the precision of the model, but adds new features that have to be learnt, and therefore stresses the need for a large training corpus. In Ratinov and Roth (2009), on the CoNNL shared task, the *BILOU* model outperforms the *BIO* one.

By considering NER as a tagging task thanks to these position models, all the statistical methods originally developed for the part-of-speech tagging task have been applied to NER from text: Hidden Markov Models, MaxEnt classifiers and Conditional Random Fields. We briefly review these methods in the following sections.

```
Mr.(O) Dooner(PERSON_B) met(O) with(O) Martin(PERSON_B) Puris(PERSON_I)
,(O) president(O) and(O) chief(O) executive(O) officer(O) of(O)
Ammirati(ORG_B) &(ORG_I) Puris(ORG_I) ,(O) about(O) McCann(ORG_B)
's(O) acquiring(O) the(O) agency(O) with(O) billings(O) of(O)
$400(MONEY_B) million(MONEY_I) ,(O) but(O) nothing(O) has(O)
materialized(O) .(O)
```

Figure 10.3 Example of MUC-6 NE annotations annotated with the BIO model. After each word is indicated between bracket the tag representing the NE category and its position

10.5.3 Hidden Markov Model

Following the formal presentation of tagging models in (Charniak *et al.*, 1993), we can define NE detection as finding the best sequence of tags $t_{1,n}$ over a string of n words $w_{1,n}$. Let's denote this sequence as $\tau(w_{1,n})$. Each tag to predict corresponds to the *BIO* or *BILOU* labels as presented in Figure 10.3. $\tau(w_{1,n})$ is calculated by Equation (10.1).

$$\tau(w_{1,n}) = arg \max_{t_{1,n}} P(t_{1,n}, w_{1,n}) \tag{10.1}$$

By suitably defining terms like $t_{1,0}$ and their probabilities, we obtain Equation (10.2).

$$P(t_{1,n}, w_{1,n}) \approx \prod_{i=1}^{n} P(t_i|t_{1,i-1}, w_{1,i-1})P(w_i|t_{1,i}, w_{1,i-1}) \tag{10.2}$$

In POS tagging the following Markov assumptions are usually made (for a 3-gram model): $P(t_i|t_{1,i-1}, w_{1,i-1}) = P(t_i|t_{i-2,i-1})$ and $P(w_i|t_{1,i}, w_{1,i-1}) = P(w_i|t_i)$ leading to the general POS tagging equation:

$$\tau(w_{1,n}) = arg \max_{t_{1,n}} \prod_{i=1}^{n} P(t_i|t_{i-2,i-1})P(w_i|t_i) \tag{10.3}$$

For NER these assumptions are too strong as the transitions between labels are not very informative and have to be linked to the words or at least to some characteristics of the words.

For example, in the sentence from Figure 10.3: `chief(O) executive(O) officer(O) of(O) Ammirati(ORG_B) &(ORG_I) Puris(ORG_I)`
if we apply the POS model we will consider only the following probabilities (with a 3-gram model):

$$\ldots P(\mathtt{O}|\mathtt{O},\mathtt{O})P(\mathtt{officer}|\mathtt{O}) \times P(\mathtt{O}|\mathtt{O},\mathtt{O})P(\mathtt{of}|\mathtt{O}) \times P(\mathtt{ORG\_B}|\mathtt{O},\mathtt{O})P(\mathtt{Ammirati}|\mathtt{ORG\_B})\ldots$$

As we can see a term such as $P(\mathtt{ORG\_B}|\mathtt{O},\mathtt{O})P(\mathtt{Ammirati}|\mathtt{ORG\_B})$ is not very informative. We would rather condition the occurrence of ORG_B not only on the previous labels, but also on the previous words, such as: $P(\mathtt{ORG\_B}|\mathtt{O},\mathtt{O},\mathtt{of},\mathtt{officer})P(\mathtt{Ammirati}|\mathtt{ORG\_B})$. This is done by changing the Markov assumptions in order to keep some lexical context in the transition probability between labels.

A lot of variations on this kind of HMM approach have been proposed (Kubala *et al.*, 1998; Palmer *et al.*, 1999; Renals *et al.*, 1999), most of them inspired by the BBN system *IdentiFinder* (Bikel *et al.*, 1999b). These models differ not only in the Markov assumptions chosen, but also in their back-off strategy. Back-off is crucial in such models as most of NEs are made with proper names which are likely to be unknown or at least to have a very low frequency in the training corpus on which the models are trained.

For example in *IdentiFinder*, the formal HMM model is as follows:

$$P(t_i|t_{1,i-1}, w_{1,i-1}) = P(t_i|t_{i-1}, w_{i-1})$$

$$P(w_i|t_{1,i}, w_{1,i-1}) = P(< w_i, f_i >_{first} |t_{i-1,i})$$

for the first word of a NE of class t_i and

$$P(w_i|t_{1,i}, w_{1,i-1}) = P(< w_i, f_i > | < w_{i-1}, f_{i-1} >, t_i)$$

for all the words inside a NE class.

The estimation of these probabilities is straightforward: the maximum likelihood criterion is used by counting on a training corpus the occurrences of each n-gram. If $C(x)$ is a function returning the number of occurrences of the event x in a training corpus, we have:

$$P(t_i|t_{i-1}, w_{i-1}) = \frac{C(t_{i-1,i}, w_{i-1})}{C(t_{i-1}, w_{i-1})}$$

$$P(< w_i, f_i >_{first} |t_{i-1,i}) = \frac{C(< w_i, f_i >_{first}, t_{i-1,i})}{C(t_{i-1,i})}$$

$$P(< w_i, f_i > | < w_{i-1}, f_{i-1} >, t_i) = \frac{C(< w_{i-1,i}, f_{i-1,i} >, t_i)}{C(< w_{i-1}, f_{i-1} >, t_i)}$$

Standard language model back-off strategies are added to deal with n-grams not seen in the training corpus. The term $< w, f >$ is a way to introduce in the model a feature f attached to a word w. These word features correspond to properties that can be directly extracted from the word occurrence. For example the feature `initCap` is for words starting with a capital letter; `allCaps` corresponds to words all in capital letters, etc. These features are a way to smooth the probabilities of the model. For example even if a proper name X starting with a capital letter has not been seen in the training corpus, if it appears in a context such as "*Mrs X*", it can be labelled as a *PERSON* thanks to the very frequent context "*Mrs* `initCap`" even if the bigram "*Mrs X*" is unknown.

When processing text, this method is an efficient way of dealing with out-of-vocabulary words. However the tagging performance is still strongly linked to the amount of training data available and the more a word is seen in different contexts, the better it will be handled by the model. This is illustrated by Table 10.7 where the performance of the BBN NE tagging model is given according to the number of occurrence of each word in the training corpus. As we can

Table 10.7 NE tagging error at the word level according to the number of occurrence of each word in the training corpus

# occurrence	# errors	% error rate
0	313/710	44
1–63	38/817	5
63–1023	7/520	1

Source: Kubala *et al.*, 1998

see the tagging error rate is over 40% for out-of-vocabulary words. It drops to about 1% for words which have been seen over 60 times in the training corpus.

10.5.4 Maximum Entropy

HMM being a generative approach, the main issue is the necessity of modeling every input distribution of the parameters in the model, independently of their relevance to the task targeted. As an alternative to HMM, discriminant models such as Maximum Entropy (ME) approaches have been proposed as a very efficient way to easily integrate a very large set of arbitrary features in a model. Maximum Entropy has been successfully used in NLP tasks such as part-of-speech tagging (Ratnaparkhi *et al.*, 1996) or information extraction (McCallum *et al.*, 2000). Following the work done at New York University (Borthwick *et al.*, 1998), ME has been successfully applied to NER, alone or in conjunction with reranking models (Collins, 2002).

As for HMM, ME applied to NER is also a tagging process where each word inside a NE receives a tag corresponding to its category and position inside it, or an *outside* tag for words that do not belong to any NE. The ME model consists of estimating the probability $P(t_i|h_i)$ for every word w_i of a sentence with t_i belonging to the space of possible tags T and h_i being the set of information relative to the word w_i that can be derived from its context of occurrence. The main advantage of the ME approach is the flexibility in the definition of contexts h_i. They are usually defined as a set of binary functions $f(t, h)$ including a very large range of linguistic levels and dependencies.

For example, in Collins (2002) the following features are considered:

- The word being tagged, the previous word, and the next word.
- The previous tag, and the previous two tags (bigram and trigram features).
- A compound feature of three fields: Is the word at the start of a sentence?; does the word occur in a list of words which occur more frequently as lower-case rather than upper-case words in a large corpus of text?; the type of the first letter of the word (capital or lower case letter, digit,...).
- The word with each character mapped to its type.
- The word with each character mapped to its type, but repeated consecutive character types are not repeated in the mapped string.

A set of m binary function $f(t, h)$ is built from this set of features, such as:

$$f(t,h) = \begin{cases} 1 \text{ capitalized(h) = true and f=location\_start} \\ 0 \text{ else} \end{cases}$$

Given this set of features f and a training corpus, the ME estimation process is in charge of estimating the weight α_j of every feature function f_j. The estimation of $P(t|h)$ is defined as follows:

$$P(t|h) = \frac{e^{\sum_{j=1}^{m} \alpha_j . f_j(t,h)}}{Z(h)}$$

with $Z(h)$ being a normalization factor such as:

$$Z(h) = \sum_{t'=1}^{T} e^{\sum_{j=1}^{m} \alpha_j . f_j(t',h)}$$

The parameters α_j of the model are trained using Generalized Iterative Scaling. In decoding, a beam or a Viterbi search can be used in order to find the best sequence of coherent tags over the sequence of words.

The main advantage in the ME approach is the freedom in the generation of the feature functions, knowing that it is the ME estimation process which is in charge of assigning the relative weights to each of them.

10.5.5 Conditional Random Field

Conditional Random Fields (CRFs, Lafferty *et al.* (2001)) are based on the same exponential form as Maximum Entropy models. The main difference is that they represent undirected graphical models corresponding to conditionally-trained Finite State Machines (FSM). These FSMs are made of two kinds of nodes: input nodes corresponding to all the features describing the data to process and output nodes corresponding to the labels to predict. Any kind of dependences can be represented between all these nodes in the model. The conditional probability of a sequence of output labels is based on the total probability over the state sequences.

CRFs are a particular case of Markov Random Fields. They combine the advantages of discriminative approaches such as ME models and generative approaches such as HMM. They directly compute the probability of a label, given a context without modelling the distributions of the input observations. Unlike ME models they are not affected by the *label bias problem* as described in Lafferty *et al.* (2001). This problem arises when a state has a single outgoing transition (or more generally a low-entropy next state distribution): since the observations a are not generated by the states, a will be ignored in the probability estimation of $P(t_n|t_{n-1}, a)$ if there is no alternative transition from t_{n-1} to t_n. CRFs, by estimating probabilities on the whole sequence of states, prevent this *label bias problem* and have had better results than HMM and other discriminant models for tasks such as POS tagging (Lafferty *et al.*, 2001), noun phrase segmentation (Sha and Pereira, 2003) or concept tagging (Raymond and Riccardi, 2007).

Following (McCallum and Li, 2003) for notation, CRFs can be defined as follows:

Let $w_{1,n} = \langle w_1, w_2, \ldots w_n \rangle$ be an input observation sequence such as a word sequence. Let S be a set of FSM states with a label $t \in T$ associated to each state and corresponding to one of the NE+position tag to predict (such as *PERSON_B*). Let $s_{1,n} = \langle s_1, s_2, \ldots s_n \rangle$ be a sequence of such states that has to be predicted on the observations $w_{1,n}$.

The conditional probability of $s_{1,n}$ given $w_{1,n}$ is:

$$P(s_{1,n}|w_{1,n}) = \frac{1}{Z_0} \exp\left(\sum_{i=1}^{n}\sum_{k} \lambda_k f_k(s_{i-1}, s_i, w_{1,n}, i)\right)$$

where Z_0 is a normalization factor over all state sequences:

$$Z_0 = \sum_{s \in S^n} \exp\left(\sum_{i=1}^{n}\sum_{k} \lambda_k f_k(s_{i-1}, s_i, w_{1,n}, i)\right)$$

The weights λ_k can be estimated on a training corpus. The feature functions are similar to those that can be found in a ME model: functions returning 0 or 1 according to the features chosen to represent a context and the dependencies between the input and output nodes defined in the model. The dependencies on the output states can also integrate the previous and next output states.

CRFs define the conditional probability of a tag sequence $t_{1,n}$ based on total probability over the state sequences s:

$$P(t_{1,n}|w_{1,n}) = \sum_{s_{1,n}:t(s_{1,n})=t_{1,n}} P(s_{1,n}|w_{1,n})$$

with $t(s_{1,n})$ being the sequence of labels associated to the output states $s_{1,n}$.

If there is no constraint on the dependency model, the calculation of the normalization factor is intractable since the number of possible label sequences s is exponential on the size of the observation sequence $w_{1,n}$. However when the output nodes of the graphical model are linked by edges and represent a linear chain, as in a tagging problem such as the NER task, the probability of each transition between two output states at a defined position in the input sequence can be calculated efficiently by dynamic programming.

10.5.6 Sample Classification Methods

The HMM, ME and CRF models presented in the previous sections are all probabilistic tagging models estimating the probability $P(t_{1,n}|w_{1,n})$. The alternative to this probabilistic framework is to consider the tagging problem as a classification task. The goal of classification methods is to find a function that minimizes the misclassification risk. Among them we can find decision trees, perceptron, logistic regression, or k-nearest neighbour algorithm. Large-margin classification methods such as *Support Vector Machine* (SVM) (Vapnik, 2000) and *Boosting* methods such as *Adaboost* (Schapire and Singer, 2000) are considered as state-of-the-art methods and have been used for the NER task.

Most of the classifiers consider only the binary classification problem. When applying such models to a multi-class problem like NER, two methods have been proposed:

- One class *versus* all others. If we consider a k-class problem $(c_1, c_2, \ldots, c_k)$, we build k binary classifiers, each of them in charge of separating the examples of class c_i from the examples of all the other classes $c_{j\in[1\ldots k], j\neq i}$.

- Pairwise classification. $K \times (K-1)/2$ classifiers are built to separate examples for each pair (c_i, c_j) of class (with $i \neq j$). The final decision is given by a weighted vote of all the classifiers.

Like ME and CRF methods, the observations are not generated by the classification models and a very large number of features can be easily integrated, usually represented by a feature vector. The output of a classification function is a score that can be projected into a probability by means of a regression function whose parameters are tuned on a corpus of labeled examples.

The application of classification methods such as SVM to NER follows the work done by Kudo and Matsumoto (2001) on chunking with SVM: each word of a sentence is labelled with a tag related to the chunk category and its position within the chunk following the BIO or BILOU models. A dynamic programming algorithm (Viterbi or Beam search) is then used to find the most likely sequence of categories.

In Isozaki and Kazawa (2002), a set of k SVM (for k possible NE+position labels) is trained with a *one class versus all others* scheme using three kinds of features: the word itself, its part-of-speech tag and its character type. The context is represented by the two previous and two following words, leading to a set of 15 features for describing a sample to classify. Each sample is represented by a binary vector whose length depends on the size of the vocabulary, POS tagset and character types. For example, in the sentence "*... President Obama declared...*", the sample $w =$ "*Obama*" is represented by a vector $X = (x[1], x[2], \ldots, x[D])$ where only 15 elements are set to 1, all the others being false and set to 0:

```
; feature = current word
w!='Alice'      => x[1]=0
w!='Bush'       => x[2]=0
....
w='Obama'       => x[6864]=1
....
; feature = previous word
w-1!='Alice'    => X[12034]=0
....
; feature = current POS
POS(w)=NP       => x[42042]=1
....
```

At decoding time, once each word has received a score for every possible category thanks to the k SVM classifiers, a Viterbi search is performed in order to find the best sequence of labels over the sequence of words.

10.5.7 Conclusions on the Methods for NER from Text

All the methods presented in the previous sections have been evaluated on the NER task of several research programs, as presented in Section 10.3, however it is very difficult to declare a clear winner among them. For example in the last CoNLL shared task on NER (CoNLL 2003), the best results for English were obtained by a combination of different methods (Florian *et al.*, 2003): robust linear classifier, Maximum Entropy, transformation-based learning, and HMM.

In the 2009 ESTER Broadcast News NER task the best results on French were obtained by a rule-based system on the reference transcriptions and by a CRF tagging system on the ASR transcriptions (more details on this evaluation are given in the next section).

Therefore, as for many NLP tasks, only general comments can be made:

- Better features and more data are more important than better algorithms.
- Corpus-based methods are more robust than rule-based methods when processing *noisy* inputs, such as ASR transcriptions.
- System combination is always a good way of improving the performance of each individual system.

10.6 Comparative Methods for NER from Speech

Most of the early work done on NER from speech used the *sequential* approach already mentioned consisting of performing ASR first then applying a NER system developed for text on the ASR transcriptions. In order to increase the performance of NER from speech, two alternative approaches to the sequential approach have been proposed: the first one consists of adapting NER systems by adding acoustic and ASR features to the tagging models; the second one consists of integrating the ASR and NER processes together, resulting in a bias of the ASR system toward optimizing NE detection rather than word accuracy. Examples of both approaches are given in the next sections.

10.6.1 Adapting NER Systems to ASR Output

10.6.1.1 Feature Robustness

The first adaptation of a NER system is to check the robustness of its features to ASR output. A lot of these features include graphical information such as capitalization, punctuation and page layout. In ASR transcriptions all this information is likely to be either erroneous or missing as in the SNOR (Speech Normalized Orthographic Representation) format that normalizes text by removing punctuation and turning all words into upper case letters.

Rule-based systems can achieve a very good level of performance on text by carefully designing rules integrating graphical features with other contextual features and knowledge resources. However these rules will not work with SNOR transcriptions or are likely to be misled by any punctuation or upper-case mistakes. Statistical systems on the other hand can be trained on SNOR transcriptions, or on ASR transcriptions, and can be more easily adapted to processing speech.

This is illustrated by the results obtained at the 2009 French ESTER 2 NER task using several systems, some implementing a rule-based approach, some implementing a statistical approach. The ESTER 2 corpus contains broadcast speech and conversations from news and talk shows. The test corpus manually annotated with NEs contains 5123 NE occurrences.

The official results of the ESTER evaluation program for the two best systems are given in Table 10.8 (see Galliano *et al.*, 2009, for a complete overview of the evaluation for all tasks). This table reports results in terms of Slot Error Rate (SER) for two of the seven systems that participated in the evaluation: the best statistical system and the best rule-based system.

Table 10.8 Official results of the ESTER evaluation program on NE. Slot Error Rate (SER) measures according to the WER for the best statistical and the best rule-based systems

System/WER	WER=0	WER=12.1	WER=17.8	WER=26.1
Best statistical system	23.9	43.4	51.6	56.8
Best rule-based system	9.9	44.9	60.7	66.2

Source: Galliano *et al.*, 2009

Different conditions were evaluated according to the WER of the transcriptions to process: from 0% WER for the reference transcriptions to 26.1% WER.

As we can see the best rule-based system outperforms the best statistical system (based on a combination of HMM and CRF models, Béchet and Charton, 2010) on the reference transcriptions (WER=0%): less than 10% SER instead of 23.9%. This can be explained by the very large number of carefully designed rules incorporating graphical, contextual and linguistic features such as syntactic (this system includes a dependency parser) and semantic features (very large dictionaries of entities and proper names).

Although these carefully hand-crafted knowledge models give excellent performance on the reference transcriptions, there is a clear lack of robustness of these models when applied to speech transcriptions where it is the statistical approach which achieves the best results. In addition to high WER, the last two corpora with WER=17.8 and WER=26.1 have no capitalization and no punctuation. This explains the very bad results obtained by the rule-based systems on these corpora.

By retraining all the statistical models on the training corpus with a SNOR format, the HMM+CRF system remains particularly robust to high WER conditions. This is illustrated by Figure 10.4: the SER/WER histogram presents the results of the statistical system with two conditions: *standard* where the capitalization produced by the ASR module is kept[2] and *normalize* when the corpora has been processed by the *normalize* tool which removes all punctuation and capitalization to obtain a SNOR format. For the *standard* condition the models are trained on a corpus with capitalization and punctuation; for the *normalize* condition another version of the tagger is used, trained on corpora processed by the *normalize* tool. As we can see, removing punctuation and normalization to the reference transcription has a strong negative impact on the performance of the system. However, for both the ASR transcriptions with capitalization, this system performs better if we remove the capital letters predicted by the ASR module. This gain increases with higher WER. This means that ASR n-gram language models are not very good predictors of word capitalization. Therefore it is better to let models with a richer linguistic representation such as NE models decide whether or not a word is a proper name and needs to start with a capital letter.

10.6.1.2 Modeling ASR Errors

Increasing the robustness of extraction information systems to ASR errors is one of the current important issues of Spoken Language processing. Even if statistical models are much more robust to ASR errors than rule-based systems, the models are usually trained on manually transcribed speech and the ASR errors are not taken into account explicitly. This strategy

[2] Except for the WER=12.1 and WER=17.8 conditions where no capitalized output were given.

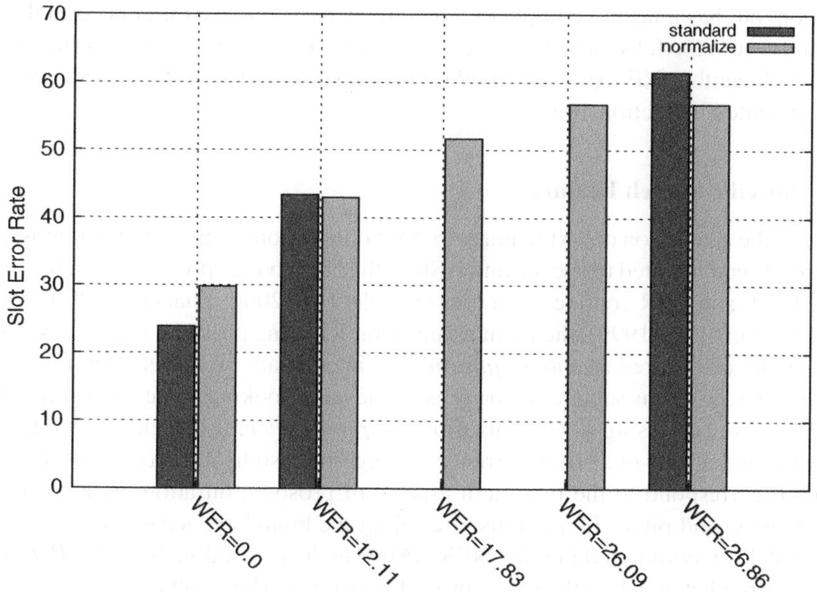

Figure 10.4 Slot Error Rate (SER) as a function of the Word Error Rate (WER) for the best statistical system of the ESTER evaluation program. Two conditions are examined: with capitalization (*standard*) and without capitalization (*normalize*) (Béchet and Charton © 2010 IEEE)

certainly emphasizes the precision of the detection, but a great loss in recall can occur by not modeling the ASR behaviour. For example, a word can be considered as very salient information for detecting a particular NE tag. But if this word is, for any reason, very often badly recognized by the ASR system, its salience will not be useful in processing ASR output.

Several studies have tried to increase the robustness of their models to ASR errors, first by randomly generating errors in order to introduce noise into the training data (Grishman, 1998; Palmer *et al.*, 1999), then by using errors made by an ASR system Palmer (2001). The latter approach can be considered as one of the first successful attempts to model ASR errors in automatic speech transcription processing. One very interesting result shown in (Palmer, 2001) is that it is crucial to train the models with *real* errors made by the same system as the one which will be used for the tests. Generating errors, randomly or based on speech science consideration, does not bring any improvement.

In Béchet *et al.* (2004), the whole training corpus is processed by the ASR system in order to learn automatically the confusions and the mistakes that are likely to occur in the deployed system. This ASR output corpus is then aligned, at the word level, with the transcription corpus. A symbol NULL is added to the ASR transcript for every deletion and each insertion is attached to the previous word with the symbol +. By this means, both manual transcriptions and ASR outputs contain the same number of tokens. The last process consists of transferring the NE tags attached to each word of the reference transcription to the corresponding token in the ASR output. Such a method balances the inconvenience of training a model directly on a very noisy channel (ASR output) by structuring the noisy data according to constraints obtained on the clean channel (reference transcriptions). This method increases the recall measure in the

NE detection, but has a negative impact on the precision: the noise introduced in the tagging model will increase the false detection rate. That is why in Béchet *et al.* (2004) this method is combined with another NE extraction method in charge of rejecting these false detections as it will be presented in Section 10.6.2.

10.6.1.3 Specific Speech Features

In addition to the adaptation of text features to ASR output, some studies have proposed adding new features directly related to speech and ASR to the NE models: prosodic features (Hakkani-Tur *et al.*, 1999) and ASR confidence scores (Sudoh *et al.*, 2006; Zhai *et al.*, 2004).

In Hakkani-Tur *et al.* (1999), the main assumption for using prosodic features is the following: NEs can be considered as *salient information* in a stream of words; therefore we would expect to find a trace of this salience at the prosodic level by looking at the pitch accent and time duration of words expressing a NE. This prosodic *prominence*, if detected, can help NER by increasing the probability of a NE occurrence in a region prosodically prominent. The prosodic features used correspond to the two main aspects of prosody: duration (pauses, final vowel and final rhymes) and pitch (F0 patterns, preceding the boundary, across the boundary). The prosodic model is incorporated into the NER HMM models by adding the term $P(F|T)$ where T is the tag to predict and F is the set of prosodic features. This probability is estimated on a training corpus by a CART decision tree approach. Even if no significative gain was observed in the NER performance when adding prosody to the HMM models, this study proposes an interesting framework toward the handling of the NER process as a multi-view problem with the acoustic channel in addition to the linguistic channel.

In addition to acoustic features, ASR scores can also be considered as specific speech features because of the uncertainty of each word produced by an ASR system. As mentioned before, any word deletion can prevent the detection of a NE and a word confusion (or an insertion) can lead to the false detection of an erroneous NE. ASR confidence scores can help prevent this false detection phenomenon: for example a proper name such as a city name, which normally would automatically trigger the detection of a location NE, can be dismissed if it appears in an unusual context for the expression of a location with a low ASR confidence score. In Sudoh *et al.* (2006) the authors proposed adding confidence scores as a new feature in their SVM-based NE classifier. A confidence score is attached to each word as a binary value equal to 1 if the confidence is above a given threshold or 0 if the confidence is below the same threshold. These confidence scores are obtained by another SVM taking as input several features: word, part-of-speech tag and ASR posterior probability of a word and its context of occurrence (two preceding and following words).

The main constraint with the use of confidence features in NER models is the necessity to have a speech training corpus (labelled with NEs) different from the one used to train the ASR acoustic and language models. This issue is similar for the methods presented in the previous section that tried to model ASR errors: in order to have realistic features (both for confidence scores and ASR errors) the ASR models cannot be trained on the same corpus used to train the NER models. This is an issue because speech transcription corpora with NE annotations are a limited resource and it is crucial to train the ASR language model on a corpus containing as many NEs as possible in order to collect enough n-grams representing NEs. A solution to this problem is often to use an n-fold training strategy: the NE speech training corpus is split in n partitions $p_1, p_2, \ldots, p_n$; for each partition i the ASR language model is trained on the

$n-1$ partitions j with $j \neq i$ and used to transcribe partition i on which the confidence features are extracted. At the end of this process we obtain realistic confidence measures on the whole training corpus.

10.6.2 Integrating ASR and NER Processes

One way to integrate the ASR and NER processes is to exploit a search space bigger than the 1-best hypothesis alone, either by taking into account an n-best list (Zhai *et al.*, 2004) or the whole word lattice (Béchet *et al.*, 2004; Favre *et al.*, 2005; Horlock and King, 2003; Saraclar and Sproat, 2004). This can be done by either modifying the ASR search criterion in order to obtain a new word transcription guided by the NER process; or by looking directly into the search space for the best NEs without necessarily producing an automatic transcription. These two methods are illustrated by the next examples.

10.6.2.1 Modifying the ASR Search Function

In ASR, the best sequence of n words $w\hat{1}_{,n}$ for a sequence of acoustic features A is obtained by:

$$w\hat{1}_{,n} = \underset{w_{1,n}}{argmax} P(w_{1,n}|A)$$

with

$$P(w_{1,n}|A) = \frac{P(A|w_{1,n}) \times P(w_{1,n})}{P(A)} \approx P(A|w_{1,n}) \times P(w_{1,n})$$

Integrating the search for the best sequence of words $w_{1,n}$ and the best sequence of NE tags $t_{1,n}$ leads to an adaptation of Equation (10.1):

$$\tau(w\hat{1}_{,n}) = \underset{w_{1,n},t_{1,n}}{argmax} P(t_{1,n}, w_{1,n}|A) \approx \underset{w_{1,n},t_{1,n}}{argmax} P(A|w_{1,n}) \times P(t_{1,n}, w_{1,n}) \tag{10.4}$$

The term $P(t_{1,n}, w_{1,n})$ is now not only a tagging model, but also a language model responsible for finding the best sequence of words as well as the best sequence of tags from an ASR search space. This is usually done on a word lattice produced by a first ASR system based on standard word n-grams. All the paths in such lattices are rescored according to the joint model $P(t_{1,n}, w_{1,n})$. Different approximations can be made for estimating this probability. For example in Favre *et al.* (2005), this probability is estimated by a trigram on the word/tag pairs:

$$P_{t_{1,n},w_{1,n}} \approx \prod_{i=1}^{n} P(w_i, t_i|w_{i-1}, t_{i-1}, w_{i-2}, t_{i-2})$$

In Horlock and King (2003), the transition probabilities between the words and the tags are modeled separately:

$$P_{t_{1,n},w_{1,n}} \approx \prod_{i=1}^{n} P(w_i|w_{i-1}, w_{i-2}, t_i) \times P(t_i|t_{i-1})$$

These studies show that a slight improvement can be observed in NER performance by using such models, although the global WER is not improved (Horlock and King, 2003). However the main advantage of such approaches is the projection from a word lattice to a NE lattice where different decision strategies can be used to extract the final NE hypotheses. The potential of having a NE lattice is illustrated by the *Oracle* NER performance on the lattice. This measure is the recall measure upper bound that can be obtained by extracting all the possible entities from an NE lattice, and simulating a perfect strategy that always take the right decision in choosing among all the possible entities.

In Favre *et al.* (2005), on the ESTER1 test corpus, the NER F-measure on the ASR transcriptions is 63.0% (with WER=26.4) and the Oracle measure on the entity lattices is 76.9%. This means that nearly 80% of the NEs to be detected are in the entity lattice produced. A decision strategy can be applied to all these NE candidates involving other levels of information on the document to process, like the date or the theme, for example.

10.6.2.2 Extracting NE Directly from Multiple ASR Outputs

As seen in the previous section it is possible to bias the ASR process in order to maximize the NER performance rather than the WER. Pushing along this line it is also possible to directly extract NEs from an ASR search space such as a word lattice or an n-best list of hypothesis without necessarily producing a word transcription.

For example in Zhai *et al.* (2004) an n-best list of word transcription hypotheses is first processed by a NER system based on a Maximum Entropy approach. Then a vote (weighted by different confidence scores) is made among all the entities detected in the n-best transcriptions: those having enough votes are kept, even if they don't occur in the 1-best word string produced.

The main issue when processing n-best list of ASR transcriptions is that most of them will differ only by some short non-content words that won't have any effect on the NER performance. In order to prevent tagging each word transcription produced as an n-best list, other studies have proposed directly parsing the word lattice.

Several methods have been proposed to apply parsing techniques to word lattices. Some of these methods (Chappelier *et al.*, 1999; Kieffer *et al.*, 2000) aim to efficiently produce parse trees with chart-based parsing algorithms, without rescoring the arcs of the graphs. Other methods use grammars in order to calculate the best path in the graph, by mean of a A$*$ algorithm (Chelba and Jelinek, 2000) or a Markov parsing technique (Roark, 2002). In the case of NER, because NEs are usually short, they can be represented by regular grammars that can easily be represented by Finite State Machines (FSM). Applying such FSMs to word lattices is a straightforward operation if the graphs are also represented by FSMs (see Mohri *et al.* (2000, 2002) for more details about regular grammars and FSM).

In Saraclar and Sproat (2004) the authors present a Spoken Utterance Retrieval method that consists of looking directly into a word or a phone lattice for a given utterance represented as an FSM. NER can also be seen as a Spoken Utterance Retrieval task when NEs are represented by regular grammars lexicalized with the ASR lexicon. For example in Favre *et al.* (2005), each NE category is attached to a set of regular grammars, extracted from a training corpus and generalized by the annotation guidelines and web-gathered word lists. These grammars are represented by Finite State Machines (FSMs) thanks to the AT&T GRM/FSM toolkit (Allauzen *et al.*, 2003). These FSMs are transducers that accept word sequences on the input symbols and output NE labels on the output symbols. They are all grouped together in a single transducer, with a filler model that accepts any string of words. During the NER process, the first step is to compose the FSM representing the NE transducer and the word lattice produced by the ASR module.

In Béchet *et al.* (2004) an approach is proposed based on a two-step process, which tries to take advantage of the different methods previously presented: firstly, the NEs are detected on the 1-best word hypothesis by means of an NE tagger trained on ASR output, as presented in Section 10.6.1; secondly, once areas in the speech input which are likely to contain NEs are detected, we verify that we can find a match for each of them in the word lattice with regular grammars representing NEs. These grammars are applied *only* on the areas selected by the NE tagger.

The reason behind is, when processing an utterance, to use the tagger in order to have a general idea of its content, then to go back to the word-lattice and refine the transcription with very constrained models (the regular grammars) applied locally to the areas detected by the tagger. By doing so the understanding and transcribing processes are linked together and the final transcription output is a product of the Spoken Language Understanding module instead of the ASR module.

This hybrid method presents several advantages compared to each method taken separately:

- The Language Model used by the tagger can afford to be trained on a small training corpus. Indeed, because the second step of the process checks the occurrence of the NEs that are detected, the tagger can over generate NE tags.
- Using nonstochastic grammars is not a problem here because the aim of these grammars is not to help find the best path in the graph, but to check the existence of a parse hypothesis, representative of a given NE, in an area detected by the tagger.

Table 10.9 shows the results obtained by this approach on the HMIHY corpus. As we can see, training the tagger on ASR transcriptions has a small negative impact on the precision but produces a big improvement on the recall measure.

Table 10.9 NE detection results on the HMIHY corpus with the hybrid tagger+FSM approach according to the kind of corpus used to train the tagger: training on the reference transcriptions of the training corpus; training on the ASR output of the training corpus

	Date Training on ref. trans.	Training on ASR trans.
P	87.2	85.9
R	57.1	65.7
F	69.0	74.5

	Phone Training on ref. trans.	Training on ASR trans.
P	96.3	94.8
R	71.8	80.9
F	82.3	87.3

Source: Béchet *et al.*, 2004

10.7 New Trends in NER from Speech

Most of the current work done on NER from speech is linked to the collection and the use of meta-data information on the data to process. As mentioned earlier in this chapter, the main difference between extracting NEs from speech rather than text is the *closed-vocabulary* phenomenon due to the ASR systems used to produce the transcriptions: there is no *generic* ASR system as the vocabulary and the language model must be carefully designed for each applicative framework and by consequence there is no *generic* NER system from speech.

This situation has led to a change in the design of NER systems: rather than developing their capacity to handle unknown words as is done on NER from text, NER designers must collect as much information as possible on the data to process then adapt the ASR lexicon and the NER models using this knowledge. In this section we report several studies following this principle, first to adapt the ASR lexicon and second to specialize a NER system to a given ASR lexicon.

Lastly we present some work carried out in an attempt to eliminate the closed-vocabulary constraint of ASR systems and this could be applied to NER from speech.

10.7.1 Adapting the ASR Lexicon

When designing an ASR system for a new applicative framework, one of the first tasks is to select an ASR lexicon and train a Language Model. Several methods have been proposed in order to select the best ASR lexicon possible, given a lexicon size and a set of text documents on which the LM will be trained. Adapting ASR lexicon for NER raises several issues since the collection of new words to add does not necessarily bring textual data containing them and on which the ASR LM can be adapted, such as a list of proper names for example. One way to deal with this problem is to consider not only words in the LM, but also *classes* of words which will receive the new words collected. For example in Allauzen and Gauvain (2005) the authors are processing broadcast news data and for each show they have a short description that is too short to adapt the LM, but which might contain very relevant words for transcribing it (such as proper names). By adding these words to the lexica l classes of the ASR lexicon (such as POS classes), the authors combine the advantage of having a dynamic lexicon and a static LM.

This collection of meta-data information is not always possible before the processing of a speech document for which no contextual information is available. One possibility is to try to adapt the ASR lexicon *dynamically* by exploiting the context of the utterances already transcribed in order to collect matching data, for example on the WEB, which might contain relevant OOV words that should be added to the ASR lexicon. Of course the main problem with this approach is to decide whether or not a given OOV word should be added, as adding all the words collected would add too much noise in the transcription process. In Oger *et al.* (2008), a method is proposed for collecting dynamically new words once an area susceptible to containing an OOV occurrence is detected. This method performs a WEB request with the immediate word-context of the area detected, and then a local search is performed with the ASR lexicon augmented with the words obtained from the textual data gathered on the WEB.

These two lexicon adaptation processes are not specific to NER, even if the new words added are principally proper names likely to trigger the occurrence of a NE. Another study has pushed the lexicon adaptation process one step further by considering that *each* NE likely to occur in the speech document to process should be an entry in the ASR lexicon (Hori and Nakamura, 2006). This leads to a huge increase in the size of the ASR lexicon, but simplifies the NER detection.

10.7.2 Collecting Data on the ASR Lexicon

Once the ASR lexicon is chosen, we know all the words that the NER system is able to process. Being in a *closed lexicon* environment, the NER system can afford to be overtrained on these words by collecting information about them such as the set of entities they can belong to or a distribution of their occurrences over the set of NE categories. For example the word "*De_Gaulle*" can be seen in a PERSON entity (*General De Gaulle*), in a FACILITY entity (*the Roissy Charles de Gaulle airport*) or in a PRODUCT entity (*the Charles de Gaulle aircraft carrier*).

This kind of information can be easily added as features in the NE tagging approaches, for example in the estimation $P(w|t)$ of an HMM tagger, or as binary feature functions in a Maximum Entropy or a CRF approach. These features can be collected through large lexicons of proper names (locations, companies, business listings, ...) or directly on corpora containing NE annotations. These corpora can be obtained by several means:

- manual annotation: these are the training corpora used to train the NER models;
- through the automatic annotation of large collection of text thanks to robust pattern matching methods (Collins and Singer, 1999; Etzioni *et al.*, 2005);
- by using semi-structured semantic resources such as the *Wikipedia* database.

This latter method, based on the exploitation of *Wikipedia*, recently received a lot of attention (Kazama and Torisawa, 2007; Richman and Schone, 2008) as the coverage of this resource is increasing every day, the data is freely available and although the *Wikipedia* database has not been designed for automatic processing, a lot of valuable semantic relations can be extracted from the internal links of the WEB pages.

For example in Béchet and Charton (2010), a method that extracts semantic data from *Wikipedia* for training a NER system is presented. By assuming that each page correspond to an entity, all the internal links of *Wikipedia* (titles, redirect pages, disambiguation pages) are used to generate entity graphs that can be used as features in an NER system. A *Wikipedia* document can include links to related documents contained in other linguistic editions of Wikipedia. Such links are called *interwiki*, a redirection in *Wikipedia*, linking an encyclopaedic entry to equivalent documents in other languages. These *interwiki* relations are used to aggregate in one graph all the possible writing forms collected from the five linguistic editions of *Wikipedia* (English, German, Italian, Spanish and French). As an example, the graph set for the name *Paris* contains 39 surface forms, (e.g. *Ville Lumiere*, *Ville de Paris*, *Paname*, *Capitale de la France*, *Departement de Paris*).

Each graph corresponds to one entity. In order to use these graphs in an NER system, each entity must be labelled with a NE category such as: person, location, organization or product. This can be done using rules developed for parsing the first sentence of each entity description (Kazama and Torisawa, 2007) or by means of a classification process trained on a manually annotated bootstrap training corpus.

Table 10.10 Coverage of the entities obtained from *Wikipedia* on the entities occurring in the ESTER evaluation test corpus

NE	From test set	Equ in meta-data	Coverage (%)
PERSON	1096	483	44
ORGANISATION	1204	764	63
LOCATION	1218	1017	83

Source: Béchet and Charton, 2010

Once the association *entity/NE label* is done, we obtain a NE corpus, without any supervision, directly from the *Wikipedia* resource. For example, the 39 surface forms of the entity *Paris* are associated with the NE label LOCATION. Such a corpus can be used at various steps in the development of a NER system.

In Béchet and Charton (2010) such a corpus was used to estimate the counts (w_i, t_j) for all the words w_i belonging to an entity of label t_j and to update the model $P(w_i|t_i)$ of the NER HMM tagger. The coverage of the entities obtained on *Wikipedia* with this method on the main entities (PERSON, ORGANISATION, LOCATION) of the test set of the French ESTER Broadcast News NER evaluation is given in Table 10.10. As we can see almost half of the person names can be found as an entry in *Wikipedia*. In the 2009 ESTER evaluation, this unsupervised knowledge extraction method brought an absolute 2% improvement in the Slot Error Rate measure of the system.

10.7.3 Toward an Open-vocabulary ASR System for NER from Speech

In addition to limiting the risk of finding OOV words when processing a spoken document, ASR systems could also be designed to be more dynamic: they should be able to detect when an OOV word has been uttered, propose a spelling for the word and add it to the ASR lexicon and language model.

Several studies have partly addressed this challenge by using sub-word units for the ASR lexicon in replacement of or in addition to words. The first application framework of such methods was the *utterance classification* task consisting of classifying a spoken utterance according to a set of predefined classes, such as *call-types* in spoken dialogue systems such as *How May I Help You?* (Gorin *et al.*, 1997). By using sub-word units, utterance classification systems have proven to be much less dependent on a fixed lexicon and a text training corpus, while providing satisfying classification accuracy (Alshawi, 2003). Sub-word units have also been used for *spoken term detection* systems (Vergyri *et al.*, 2007) when the terms of a query are not in the ASR lexicon. In both these application frameworks, sub-word units are a way to open the ASR lexicon but no new words are acquired by these methods.

Other studies use sub-words at the same time as words during the ASR process in order to reduce the recognition errors of in-vocabulary words placed next to OOVs. For example, it is shown in Bisani and Ney (2005) that each OOV word is responsible for two word errors on average. By allowing the ASR decoder to choose sub-words to decode OOV words rather than choosing a phonetically close erroneous word, a reduction of WER can be achieved, especially for morphologically rich languages (Creutz *et al.*, 2007). However, the acquisition of new words, thanks to these methods, remains very limited as the projection from a sequence of sub-word units to a valid word or sequence of words is not straightforward.

The only examples of real acquisition of new words, particularly proper names, was proposed in the context of spoken dialogue systems (Choueiter *et al.*, 2007; Filisko and Seneff, 2005) where an interactive process proposes a set of alternative spellings for a new word uttered by a speaker who can validate the correct one.

A dynamic NER system from speech should follow these research directions, although none of them provide a satisfying answer to the open issue of automatically acquiring new words expressing a new NE unknown to all the ASR and NER models.

10.8 Conclusions

NER is now a standard task for many NLP applications. Numerous methods, from rule-based to tagging approaches have been proposed, each of them having pros and cons, depending on the size of the tagset or the availability of an annotated corpus. Whatever method is used, NER from speech is usually seen as an application of a NER system developed for text on the automatic transcriptions produced by an ASR system. We have seen in this chapter that this approach is clearly sub-optimal and that the limitations of ASR systems, particularly at the lexicon level, will greatly affect the performance of a NER system originally built for processing text.

The integration of the ASR and NER processes, as described in Section 10.6.2, is a promising research direction as it is a way of dealing with the characteristics of speech, such as speech disfluencies or transcription ambiguities, by jointly optimizing the ASR and NER models.

Despite the different integrated approaches proposed so far and described in this chapter, there is not yet a satisfying answer to the main issue we face in NER from speech: because of the dynamic behavior of proper names, NER systems are built to process *new* entities, containing *new* words (mainly proper names and acronyms) never before seen in any training corpus. However, ASR systems only perform well on in-vocabulary words, seen in a training corpus, on which lexical and language models can be trained.

One way to deal with this issue, as presented in Section 10.7, is to collect information on the spoken documents to process in order to increase the size of the ASR and NER lexicon and reduce the risk of processing an OOV word. Another way to deal with OOV words is to make NER/ASR systems more dynamic by the automatic acquisition of new words when occurring in a spoken document. Humans perform well at this task, even if the spelling of a new proper name is sometimes unsure. For automatic systems, this is still an open issue.

References

Allauzen A and Gauvain J 2005 Open vocabulary ASR for audiovisual document indexation *IEEE International Conference on Acoustics, Speech and Signal Processing, ICASSP*, pp 1013–1016.

Allauzen C, Mohri M and Roark B 2003 Generalized algorithms for constructing statistical language models *41st Annual Meeting of the Association for Computational Linguistics (ACL'03), Sapporo, Japan*.

Alshawi H 2003 Effective utterance classification with unsupervised phonotactic models *Proceedings of the 2003 Conference of the North American Chapter of the Association for Computational Linguistics on Human Language Technology-Volume 1*, p. 7 Association for Computational Linguistics.

Appelt D and Martin D 1999 Named entity extraction from speech: Approach and results using the TextPro system *Proceedings Darpa Broadcast News Workshop*.

Barnett J, Anderson S, Broglio J, Singh M, Hudson R and Kuo S 1997 Experiments in spoken queries for document retrieval *ISCA Eurospeech*, pp 1323–1326.

Béchet F and Charton E 2010 Unsupervised knowledge acquisition for extracting named entities from speech *2010 IEEE International Conference on Acoustics, Speech and Signal Processing, 2010. ICASSP 2010 Proceedings.*

Béchet F, Gorin A, Wright J and Hakkani-Tur D 2004 Detecting and extracting named entities from spontaneous speech in a mixed initiative spoken dialogue context: How May I Help Y. *Speech Communication* **42**, 207–225.

Bikel DM, Schwartz R and Weischedel R 1999a An algorithm that learns what's in a name. *Machine Learning : Special Issue on Natural Language learning* **34**(1-3), 211–231.

Bikel DM, Schwartz RL and Weischedel RM 1999b An algorithm that learns what's in a name. *Machine Learning* **24**(1-3), 211–231.

Bisani M and Ney H 2005 Open vocabulary speech recognition with flat hybrid models *9th European Conference on Speech Communication and Technology.*

Bonneau-Maynard H, Rosset S, Ayache C, Kuhn A and Mostefa D 2005 Semantic annotation of the french media dialogue corpus *Interspeech*, Lisboa, Portugal.

Borthwick A, Sterling J, Agichtein E and Grishman R 1998 Nyu: Description of the mene named entity system as used in MUC *Proceedings of the Seventh Message Understanding Conference (MUC-7).*

Brill E 1992 A simple rule-based part of speech tagger *Proceedings of the workshop on Speech and Natural Language*, p. 116 Association for Computational Linguistics.

Burger J, Palmer D and Hirschman L 1998 Named entity scoring for speech input *Proceedings of the 36th Annual Meeting of the Association for Computational Linguistics and 17th International Conference on Computational Linguistics-Volume 1*, pp 201–205 Association for Computational Linguistics Morristown, NJ, USA.

Chappelier J, Rajman M, Aragues R and Rozenknop A 1999 Lattice parsing for speech recognition *ATALA TALN.*

Charniak E, Hendrickson C, Jacobson N and Perkowitz M 1993 Equations for part-of-speech tagging *11th National Conference on Artificial Intelligence*, pp 784–789.

Chelba C and Jelinek F 2000 Structured language modeling. *Computer Speech and Language* **14(4)**, 283–332.

Chinchor N and Robinson P 1998 Muc-7 named entity task definition *Proceedings of the Seventh Message Understanding Conference.*

Choueiter G, Seneff S and Glass J 2007 New word acquisition using subword modeling *Proceedings of Interspeech*, vol. 2007.

Collins M 2002 Ranking algorithms for named-entity extraction: Boosting and the voted perceptron *Proceedings of the 40th Annual Meeting on Association for Computational Linguistics, July*, pp 07–12.

Collins M and Singer Y 1999 Unsupervised models for named entity classification *Proceedings of the Joint SIGDAT Conference on Empirical Methods in Natural Language Processing and Very Large Corpora*, pp 189–196.

Creutz M, Hirsimaki T, Kurimo M, Puurula A, Pylkkonen J, Siivola V, Varjokallio M, Arisoy E, Saraclar M and Stolcke A 2007 Morph-based speech recognition and modeling of out-of-vocabulary words across languages. *ACM Transactions on Speech and Language Processing (TSLP)* **5**(1), 1–29.

Damnati G, Béchet F and De Mori R 2007 Spoken language understanding strategies on the France Telecom 3000 Voice Agency corpus *IEEE International Conference on Acoustics, Speech and Signal Processing, ICASSP*, Honolulu, HI.

Doddington G, Mitchell A, Przybocki M, Ramshaw L, Strassel S and Weischedel R 2004 The automatic content extraction (ACE) program–tasks, data, and evaluation *Proceedings of Language Resources and Evaluation (LREC)*, vol. 4, pp 837–840.

Etzioni O, Cafarella M, Downey D, Popescu A, Shaked T, Soderland S, Weld D and Yates A 2005 Unsupervised named-entity extraction from the web: An experimental study. *Artificial Intelligence* **165**(1), 91–134.

Favre B, Béchet F and Nocéra P 2005 Robust named entity extraction from large spoken archives *Conference on Human Language Technology (HLT) and Empirical Methods in Natural Language Processing (EMNLP)*, pp 491–498. Association for Computational Linguistics Morristown, NJ, USA.

Filisko E and Seneff S 2005 Developing city name acquisition strategies in spoken dialogue systems via user simulation *6th SIGdial Workshop on Discourse and Dialogue.*

Fiscus J, Ajot J, Radde N and Laprun C 2006 Multiple Dimension Levenshtein Edit Distance Calculations for Evaluating Automatic Speech Recognition Systems During Simultaneous Speech *Proceedings of Language Resources and Evaluation (LREC).*

Fiscus JG and Doddington GR 2002 Topic detection and tracking evaluation overview. *Topic detection and tracking: event-based information organization* pp 17–31.

Florian R, Ittycheriah A, Jing H and Zhang T 2003 Named entity recognition through classifier combination *Proceedings of CoNLL-2003*, vol. 58.

Galliano S, Gravier G and Chaubard L 2009 The Ester 2 Evaluation Campaign for the Rich Transcription of French Radio Broadcasts *Interspeech 2009.*

Garofolo JS, Auzanne CGP and Voorhees EM 1999 The TREC spoken document retrieval track: A success story *in Text Retrieval Conference (TREC) 8, E. Voorhees, Ed., Gaithersburg.*

Gorin AL, Riccardi G and Wright J 1997 How May I Help You ? *Speech Communication*, vol. 23, pp 113–127.

Grishman R 1998 Information extraction and speech recognition *Proceedings of the DARPA Broadcast News Transcription and Understanding Workshop.*

Hakkani-Tur D, Tur G, Stolcke A and Shriberg E 1999 Combining words and prosody for information extraction from speech *Sixth European Conference on Speech Communication and Technology.*

Hori T and Nakamura A 2006 An Extremely Large Vocabulary Approach to Named Entity Extraction from Speech *2006 IEEE International Conference on Acoustics, Speech and Signal Processing, 2006. ICASSP 2006 Proceedings*, vol. 1.

Horlock J and King S 2003 Named Entity extraction from word lattices *ISCA Eurospeech.*

Isozaki H and Kazawa H 2002 Efficient support vector classifiers for named entity recognition *Proceedings of COLING*, pp 390–396.

Kazama J and Torisawa K 2007 Exploiting Wikipedia as External Knowledge for Named Entity Recognition *Proceedings of the 2007 Joint Conference on Empirical Methods in Natural Language Processing and Computational Natural Language Learning (EMNLP-CoNLL)*, pp 698–707 Association for Computational Linguistics.

Kelley JF 1984 An iterative design methodology for user-friendly natural language office information applications. *ACM Trans. Inf. Syst.* **2**(1), 26–41.

Kieffer B, Krieger HU and Nederhof MJ 2000 Efficient and robust parsing of word graphs. *W. Wahlster, editor, Verbmobil: Foundations of Speech-to-Speech Translation* pp 280–295.

Kim J and Woodland P 2000 A rule-based named entity recognition system for speech input *ICSLP.*

Kim J, Ohta T, Tsuruoka Y, Tateisi Y and Collier N 2004 Introduction to the bio-entity recognition task at JNLPBA *Proceedings of the International Joint Workshop on Natural Language Processing in Biomedicine and its Applications*, pp 70–75 Association for Computational Linguistics.

Kubala F, Schwartz R, Stone R and Weischedel R 1998 Named entity extraction from speech *Proceedings of the DARPA Broadcast News Workshop.*

Kudo T and Matsumoto Y 2001 Chunking with support vector machines *Second meeting of the North American Chapter of the Association for Computational Linguistics on Language technologies*, pp 1–8.

Lafferty J, McCallum A and Pereira F 2001 Conditional random fields: Probabilistic models for segmenting and labeling sequence data *Proc. 18th International Conf. on Machine Learning*, pp 282–289. Morgan Kaufmann, San Francisco, CA.

Makhoul J, Kubala F, Leek T, Liu D, Nguyen L, Schwartz R and Srivastava A 2000 Speech and language technologies for audio indexing and retrieval. *Proc. IEEE* **88**(8), 1338–1353.

Makhoul J, Kubala F, Schwartz R and Weischedel R 1999 Performance measures for information extraction *Broadcast News Workshop'99 Proceedings*, p. 249 Morgan Kaufmann.

McCallum A and Li W 2003 Early results for named entity recognition with conditional random fields, feature induction and web-enhanced lexicons *Seventh Conference on Natural Language Learning (CoNLL).*

McCallum A, Freitag D and Pereira F 2000 Maximum entropy Markov models for information extraction and segmentation *Proc. 17th International Conf. on Machine Learning*, pp 591–598.

Mikheev A, Moens M and Grover C 1999 Named entity recognition without gazetteers *Proceedings of the ninth conference on European chapter of the Association for Computational Linguistics*, pp 1–8 Association for Computational Linguistics Morristown, NJ, USA.

Miller D, Boisen S, Schwartz R, Stone R and Weischedel R 2000 Named entity extraction from noisy input: Speech and OCR *Proceedings of ANLP-NAACL 2000*, pp 316–324.

Mohri M, Pereira F and Riley M 2000 The design principles of a weighted finite-state transducer library. *Theoretical Computer Science* **231**, 17–32.

Mohri M, Pereira F and Riley M 2002 Weighted finite-state transducers in speech recognition. *Computer, Speech and Language* **16**(1), 69–88.

Oger S, Linarès G, Béchet F and Nocéra P 2008 On-demand new word learning using world wide web *IEEE International Conference on Acoustics, Speech and Signal Processing, ICASSP*, vol. 4.

Pallett D, Dahlgren N, Fiscus J, Fisher W, Garofolo J and Tjaden B 1992 DARPA February 1992 ATIS benchmark test results *Workshop on Speech and Natural Language*, pp 15–27. Association for Computational Linguistics Morristown, NJ, USA.

Palmer DD 2001 Modeling uncertainty for information extraction from speech data. *PhD Thesis, University of Washington*.

Palmer DD, Ostendorf M and Burger JD 1999 Robust information extraction from spoken language data *ISCA Eurospeech*.

Przybocki MA, Fiscus JG, Garofolo JS and Pallett DS 1999 1998 Hub-4 Information Extraction Evaluation *Proceedings Of The DARPA Broadcast News Workshop*, pp 13–18. Morgan Kaufmann Publishers.

Ramshaw L and Marcus M 1995 Text chunking using transformation-based learning *Third ACL Workshop on Very Large Corpora*, pp 82–94. Cambridge MA, USA.

Ratinov L and Roth D 2009 Design challenges and misconceptions in named entity recognition *Proceedings of the Thirteenth Conference on Computational Natural Language Learning*, pp 147–155 Association for Computational Linguistics.

Ratnaparkhi A *et al.* 1996 A maximum entropy model for part-of-speech tagging *Conference on Empirical Methods in Natural Language Processing EMNLP*, pp 133–142. Association for Computational Linguistics.

Raymond C and Riccardi G 2007 Generative and discriminative algorithms for spoken language understanding *ISCA Interspeech*, vol. 2.

Renals S, Gotoh Y, Gaizauskas R and Stevenson M 1999 Baseline IE-NE experiments using the SPRACH/LaSIE system *Proceedings of the DARPA Broadcast News Workshop*, pp 47–50.

Richman A and Schone P 2008 Mining wiki resources for multilingual named entity recognition. *Association for Computational Linguistics (ACL-08: HLT)* pp 1–9.

Roark B 2002 Markov parsing: lattice rescoring with a statistical parser *Proceedings of the 40th ACL meeting, Philadelphia*.

Saraclar M and Sproat R 2004 Lattice-based search for spoken utterance retrieval *HLT-NAACL 2004: Main Proceedings*, pp 129–136. Association for Computational Linguistics, Boston, Massachusetts, USA.

Schapire RE and Singer Y 2000 BoosTexter: A boosting-based system for text categorization. *Machine Learning* **39**, 135–168.

Sekine S, Sudo K and Nobata C 2002 Extended Named Entity Hierarchy *Proceedings of Language Resources and Evaluation (LREC)*, pp 1818–1824.

Sha F and Pereira F 2003 Shallow parsing with conditional random fields *Proceedings of HLT-NAACL*, pp 213–220.

Sudoh K, Tsukada H and Isozaki H 2006 Incorporating speech recognition confidence into discriminative named entity recognition of speech data *44th Annual Meeting of the Association for Computational Linguistics*, pp 617–624 Association for Computational Linguistics Morristown, NJ, USA.

Sundheim B 1996 Overview of results of the MUC-6 evaluation *Proceedings of a workshop on held at Vienna, Virginia: May 6-8, 1996*, p. 442 Association for Computational Linguistics.

Sundheim R and Grishman R 1996 Message understanding conference-6: A brief history *Proc. 16th Int'l Conf. on Computational Linguistics (COLING 96), Copenhagen*.

Surdeanu M, Turmo J and Comelles E 2005 Named entity recognition from spontaneous open-domain speech *Ninth European Conference on Speech Communication and Technology*.

Vapnik V 2000 *The Nature of Statistical Learning Theory*. Springer.

Vergyri D, Shafran I, Stolcke A, Gadde R, Akbacak M, Roark B and Wang W 2007 The SRI/OGI 2006 spoken term detection system *Proc. Interspeech*, pp 2393–2396.

Zhai L, Fung P, Schwartz R, Carpuat M and Wu D 2004 Using n-best lists for named entity recognition from chinese speech *HLT-NAACL 2004: Short Papers*, pp 37–40. Association for Computational Linguistics, Boston, Massachusetts, USA.

11

Topic Segmentation

Matthew Purver
Queen Mary University of London, U.K.

This chapter discusses the task of *topic segmentation*: automatically dividing single long recordings or transcripts into shorter, topically coherent segments. First, we look at the task itself, the applications which require it, and some ways to evaluate accuracy. We then explain the most influential approaches – generative and discriminative, supervised and unsupervised – and discuss their application in particular domains.

11.1 Task Description

11.1.1 Introduction

So far, we have mainly looked at techniques for understanding on a fine-grained, bottom-up level: identifying fundamental units of meaning or interactional structure, such as sentences, named entities and dialogue acts. In this chapter, we look at the problem from a more coarse-grained, top-down perspective: given a complete recording or transcript (which may be quite long, and include talk on all sorts of different subjects) can we divide it into shorter, more useful, topically coherent segments?

There are many reasons why we might want to do this, but perhaps the most obvious is that it makes it much easier for a user to browse or search the results. Imagine being faced with a long uninterrupted transcript of a news broadcast or a business meeting. If you want to find a particular news story, or the discussion of a particular subject, you're faced with a problem–particularly if you don't want to read or listen to the whole thing. You could search for relevant keywords, of course: but finding them doesn't tell you where the part you're interested in starts (or ends). There's no guarantee that you'll find the keywords you've chosen either, of course–particularly if ASR word error rates are high. But if you're given the same transcript divided up into segments, with each corresponding to a different topic (or news story, or agenda item), the task becomes much easier. If you can find the keywords you're looking for in a particular segment, you just have to go to the beginning of that segment and start listening (or reading). In

Spoken Language Understanding: Systems for Extracting Semantic Information from Speech, First Edition.
Edited by Gokhan Tur and Renato De Mori.

the worst case, you could examine the start of each segment until you find what you're looking for: still much easier than reading the whole thing.

We can go much further than this, of course: we might want to analyse or classify the contents of each segment, so that we can relate topics from one meeting to another, or track the progress of news stories across different broadcasts. We might want to produce a condensed summary, with the highlights of each topic (the main headlines of a news story, or the final decision and action items of a meeting agenda item). We'll look at some of these more advanced tasks in later chapters. But the first pre-requisite for each of them is to understand the topic structure: when does the conversation move from one topic to another? When does one topic end, and another one start?

11.1.2 What is a Topic?

The answer to that question, of course, depends to a large extent on what exactly we mean by a *topic* – and this can be hard to define. In particular applications, it may seem obvious: if we're interested in segmenting a news broadcast, our notion of a topic probably corresponds to an individual news story or report. If we want to segment a court transcript, we might be more concerned with the segments in which different arguments are being presented, or different pieces of evidence are being discussed. We might want to divide a business meeting according to the items on the agenda.

However, sometimes it's not so clear. We can imagine a discussion of a single agenda item in a meeting, but which consists of several distinct phases: perhaps a round-table discussion of the problem in hand, then a couple of presentations from individuals on their proposed solutions, and then a concluding decision-making section. While the subject matter might be broadly topically coherent, we can see the segments as representing separate *activities* (discussion versus presentation), or in the terms of Passonneau and Litman (1997), different *intentions* (question-raising versus information-giving versus decision-making). Whether we want to include all of these in one segment, or treat them all separately, really depends on our intentions as users: our interests and desired application (see, e.g. Niekrasz and Moore, 2009, for discussion in more depth).

This means that in some domains, segmentation can be a hard task, even for humans, particularly where subject matter and discourse structure is less constrained. Gruenstein *et al.* (2008) asked annotators to mark topic shifts in the ICSI Meeting Corpus (Janin *et al.*, 2003) – a collection of open-domain, mostly loosely structured meetings on subjects which the annotators themselves were not familiar with – and found that they did not agree with each other at all well, especially as the notion of topic became more fine-grained. If people have a clear idea of what they are looking for, though, agreement gets much better: Banerjee and Rudnicky (2007) found that agreement improved significantly if annotators were given more information (an agenda list from which to choose topics). Galley *et al.* (2003) also found that annotators could achieve reasonable agreement if they stuck to coarse-grained topics – although even then some meetings were problematic.

11.1.3 Linear versus Hierarchical Segmentation

One of the reasons that it can be hard to define exactly what a topic consists of, and where it starts and ends, is that topics (and discourse itself) often display a *hierarchical* structure (see, e.g. Grosz and Sidner, 1986; Mann and Thompson, 1988; Marcu, 2000; Polanyi, 1988). Just as stretches of dialogue can be analysed as being composed of smaller sub-episodes, we can often think of topics and their discussion as being composed of sub-topics and sub-discussions. It might be that an ideal approach to assigning topic structure would be one which assigned not only a linear segmentation, as we've discussed so far, but a hierarchical structure. Retrieval and browsing would then benefit even more, as a user could refine the level of granularity as desired.

However, producing a fine-grained segmentation turns out to be an extremely difficult task. For one thing, as we zoom in to ever-finer distinctions, the information we need to segment the discourse becomes harder to produce. While distinguishing between broad-brush topics might be achievable just from looking at the words people use, or the way people behave (as we'll see below), distinguishing between the discussion of distinct but related issues really requires us to understand something about the semantics of individual contributions and how they inter-relate: the questions people ask, the way they get answered, whether proposals are accepted or not. This is hard: while there are formal models of dialogue which do deal with these matters (see, e.g. Asher and Lascarides, 2003; Ginzburg, 2011; Larsson, 2002, amongst others), applying them to open-domain speech isn't yet achievable.

And secondly, it seems that fine sub-topic distinctions are hard for even humans to make. Both Galley *et al.* (2003) and Gruenstein *et al.* (2008) found that annotators asked to mark topic shifts over the open-domain ICSI Meeting Corpus often didn't agree with each other at all well; and while they might agree on coarser-grained top-level topics, their agreement became worse on lower-level sub-topics. It may be that these lower-level distinctions really depend on our intentions and requirements; the ideal segmentation may not be definable *a priori*, but may depend on the view we take on the data and the use we're going to put our segmentation to.

Here, then, we restrict ourselves to the task of linear, coarse-grained segmentation: a well-studied task with several alternative approaches, many of which show very encouraging performance.

11.2 Basic Approaches, and the Challenge of Speech

The task has been approached in many different ways, and we'll discuss a few of them in more detail below. Here, we take a quick look at the two basic insights that most of them use; while some algorithms are based on one more than another, many combine the two.

11.2.1 Changes in Content

The first one is that people talk about different topics in different ways: they use different words, and refer to different things. If we are discussing a particular set of concepts, we will use words relevant to those concepts; and discussion of particular people, objects or places will involve a relevant set of names and related referring expressions. Repeated mention of the same objects or concepts will therefore be associated with repeated reference, whether by using the same words or phrases or by using co-referent or anaphoric terms (Morris and Hirst, 1991). Conversely, a change in topic will be associated with the introduction of new vocabulary (Youmans, 1991).

If we look at a discussion containing different topical segments, then, we should see that the vocabulary (and/or the set of referring expressions) being used remains relatively constant during the discussion of each topic, but changes markedly when we move between them.

Regions with relatively small changes should then correspond to topic segments, with large changes at the segment boundaries. The same may be true for features of the nonlinguistic content, depending on the domain: in multiparty dialogue we may find that different speakers are more active during the discussion of different topics, or that people are more likely to look at particular relevant objects or make characteristic gestures (see, e.g. Eisenstein *et al.*, 2008).

There are various ways we might be able to exploit this. We can use a discriminative approach: use a suitable similarity metric to measure the difference between neighbouring sections of the discourse directly, and hypothesize boundaries where this indicates large (enough) differences (Hearst, 1997). We could use clustering: group together neighbouring sentences which appear very similar to each other until we build up a set of topic clusters which cover the whole discourse (Reynar, 1994). We can use a generative approach: estimate language models for topics, and hypothesize boundaries by finding the most likely sequence of topic states to generate the observed discourse (Yamron *et al.*, 1998). But all use the same basic insight: that topics are associated with content and therefore characterized by a particular set of words, concepts and referents.

11.2.2 Distinctive Boundary Features

The second basic insight is that boundaries between topics have their own characteristic features, independent of the subject matter. When switching from one topic to another, we tend to signal this to our audience in various ways. Firstly, there are various cue words and phrases (*discourse markers*) that directly provide clues about discourse structure (Grosz and Sidner, 1986; Hirschberg and Litman, 1993), and we can signal the end of one topic, or the beginning of another, by words like *Okay*, *Anyway*, *So* or *Now*. In certain domains there can be more specific cues: formal meeting proceedings often see mention of *the next item on the agenda*, and news broadcasts see reporters sign off at the end of their reports with their name and network identifier (Beeferman *et al.*, 1999).

There can also be cues in the prosodic features of the speech (Hirschberg and Nakatani, 1996, 1998; Passonneau and Litman, 1997). Just before moving to a new segment, it's common to pause for longer than usual. When starting a new segment, speakers then tend to speed up, speak louder and pause less. Non-linguistic features can be useful here too: topic changes may correspond to changes in physical posture of speaker or audience (Cassell *et al.*, 2001), or perhaps the introduction of new documents onto a meeting table.

The features that are most indicative of topic change will often depend on the nature of the data: the domain, broadcast medium and the number of participants. But once these features have been identified (using manual or standard automatic feature extraction methods), they can be used to help segment the dialogue, either by inclusion in a discriminative classifier (e.g. Galley *et al.*, 2003) or as observed variables in a generative model associated with a change in topic state (e.g. Dowman *et al.*, 2008).

11.2.3 Monologue

Automatic topic segmentation is less important in written language: text documents have their own structure, marked more or less explicitly (Power *et al.*, 2003), and we are as likely to want to segment a document on the basis of its existing sections or chapters, or a news story by its existing paragraphs, as we are to try to find our own independent segmentation. There are certainly uses for automatic text segmentation – Hearst (1997) argues that breaking up long unstructured paragraphs can aid retrieval and summarization, and Barzilay and Lee (2004) use segmentation as the basis for automatic text generation – but it is really when we look at transcripts of spoken language that segmentation becomes important.

The first serious efforts at topic segmentation were made on monologue, for example stories told by individuals (Passonneau and Litman, 1997) or transcripts of news broadcasts (Allan *et al.*, 1998). Before substantial collections of audio transcripts were available, some work used simulated corpora, built by concatenating written texts without their structure (e.g. Reynar, 1994, with Wall Street Journal articles) – but the intention was to simulate a particular kind of monologue in both content and structure.

Moving to spoken language must introduce speech recognition errors, of course; and given the heavily lexical nature of the basic approaches outlined above, we can see that high error rates might have quite serious effects. Being able to exploit non-lexical features such as prosody, or even non-audio features such as video scene changes or interactional changes can therefore be important. However, monologue data does have the major advantage of being (usually) well-structured: we might expect the breaks between news stories, for example, to be fairly clear.

11.2.4 Dialogue

Dialogue (between two or many people),[1] though, can be a trickier problem. Face-to-face human dialogue can be much harder to segment accurately than monologue data, even for humans – dialogue in informal settings, in particular, typically flows much more smoothly, with discussion often moving naturally from one subject to another without a clear break, and is much less well-structured, with topics being revisited or interleaved. As a result of this, and of the less controlled physical and audio environment that dialogues often occur in, speech recognition error rates also tend to be significantly higher.

Some genres of dialogue lend themselves better to analysis than others, though, so it is the more formal genres such as business meetings that have received most attention. Here, the structure of the discussion tends to be more constrained: a meeting may have an agenda item list at the start which drives the topic sequence. Information independent from the audio stream may also be available, too: agenda-related documents to initialise language models, observable topic-related behaviour such as note-taking, and perhaps even a set of minutes at the end.

11.3 Applications and Benchmark Datasets

Clearly, this is only a useful task when applied to recordings of some length – short segments of speech such as an utterance in a typical spoken dialogue system tend already to be topically homogeneous and thus not to require segmentation. As a result, it only started to receive attention once long recordings became available.

[1] It's a common misconception that the word *dialogue* refers only to interaction between two people, and terms like *multilogue* have been proposed to cover cases with more than two. In fact, the prefix in *dialogue* is not *di*-(meaning *two*), but *dia*-(meaning *between*). While the distinction between two-party and multiparty dialogue can be very useful in some contexts, we intend the term *dialogue* to cover both here.

11.3.1 Monologue

11.3.1.1 Broadcast News

The DARPA Topic Detection and Tracking (TDT) project (Allan *et al.*, 1998; Doddington, 1998, etc.) started much of the work in topic segmentation which forms the basis of methods still used today, both for the task itself and its evaluation. The project focussed on radio and TV news broadcasts, as well as text news stories from newswire and web sources. The project involved much more than just segmentation: the overarching idea was to produce methods to identify, cluster, track and link topics, thus enabling and improving access to news stories via improved browsing and search. For the spoken rather than written part of the data (i.e. the TV and radio broadcasts), though, segmentation becomes a necessary first step before topic identification and other deeper annotation become possible.

The datasets produced are large, include manual topic segment annotations, and are available via the Linguistic Data Consortium.[2] Both the TDT2 and TDT3 collections include audio recordings of over 600 hours, in English and Chinese – see the next chapter for more details.

11.3.1.2 Lectures and Testimonies

Other monologue domains are also good candidates for automatic segmentation: one is university lectures, which usually consist of long recordings with a distinct topical structure. There is interest in making lectures available to students for real-time transcription or offline browsing: segmentation would aid search and improve the ease of access. MIT has set up a Lecture Browser project to work towards this, which has produced a large dataset and investigated methods for segmentation (Glass *et al.*, 2007).[3] The European CHIL and LECTRA projects have also produced lecture sets and systems for segmentation (Fügen *et al.*, 2006; Trancoso *et al.*, 2006).[4]

The Shoah Foundation Institute have also built up a large dataset of 120 000 hours of largely monologue spoken testimonies from Holocaust survivors.[5] Such a large data set requires segmentation and topic identification to make search practical, but carries its own challenges (Franz *et al.*, 2003; Oard and Leuski, 2003).

11.3.2 Dialogue

11.3.2.1 Meeting Understanding

While two-person dialogue systems have been the subject of a huge amount of research (not to mention commercial interest), the dialogue they usually involve does not immediately lend itself to segmentation of this kind. Utterances are usually short, and topics are often coherent throughout dialogues and limited to a particular task (call routing, ticket booking and so on). However, in multiparty dialogue the situation becomes very different, and one case in point is business meetings: they can be long, involve several topics, and require indexing by topic

[2] See http://projects.ldc.upenn.edu/TDT/.

[3] See http://web.sls.csail.mit.edu/lectures/.

[4] See http://chil.server.de/ and http://www.l2f.inesc-id.pt/.

[5] See http://college.usc.edu/vhi/.

segment to allow a record to be usefully browsed or searched afterwards. User studies show that people would like a meeting browser to help with general questions like *"What was discussed at the meeting?"*, as well as more specific ones such as *"What did X say about topic Y?"* (Banerjee *et al.*, 2005; Lisowska, 2003).

Two major collections of meeting data have been produced in recent years. The ICSI Meeting Corpus (Janin *et al.*, 2003) includes 75 recorded and transcribed meetings – all real research group meetings – and is available via the LDC; topic segmentation annotations are available separately (Galley *et al.*, 2003; Gruenstein *et al.*, 2008).[6] The AMI Corpus (McCowan *et al.*, 2005) contains 100 hours of recorded and transcribed meetings, including video as well as audio; most of the meetings involve actors playing a given scenario resembling a product design process. This includes topic segmentation annotations as part of the general release (Hsueh and Moore, 2006).[7]

11.3.2.2 Tutorial Dialogues

There has been less work in topic segmentation for two-person dialogue, as discussed above; but some domains involve longer and more varied conversations. One such is tutorial dialogue, which can involve two-way dialogue which progresses between related topics; some small data sets have been produced and investigated (see, e.g. Olney and Cai, 2005).

11.4 Evaluation Metrics

The nature of segmentation as a task means that the standard evaluation metrics one might use in classification tasks aren't always suitable. In this section, we see why that is, and examine some alternatives that have been proposed.

11.4.1 Classification-based

In the majority of classification tasks, evaluation metrics generally start by comparing each instance in the classifier output with a gold standard to determine whether it is correct or incorrect, and counting up the scores. From this we can determine a raw accuracy figure, or more advanced measures such as precision, recall or F-score. We could apply the same approach here simply by considering each potential boundary placement as an instance.

As potential boundaries, we can take sentence (or dialogue act) ends, and assume that whatever classifier we use tells us for each candidate whether it is a boundary (a transition from one topic segment to another) or a nonboundary (just a transition between sentences within the same segment). A hypothesized boundary in the same place as a true boundary scores a hit; as does a hypothesized nonboundary in the same place as a true nonboundary. Hypothesized boundaries where there is no true boundary are false positives; hypothesized nonboundaries where there is a true boundary are false negatives. This way, we can calculate the standard error metrics. (Automatic sentence segmentation errors may mean that we need to align the output transcript with a true gold-standard transcript first, but we'll ignore that complication here). Figure 11.1 shows an example, representing boundaries by 1 and nonboundaries by -:

[6] See http://www.icsi.berkeley.edu/Speech/mr/.

[7] See http://corpus.amiproject.org/.

sentences	S_1	S_2	S_3	S_4	S_5	S_6	S_7	S_8	S_9	S_{10}	S_{11}	S_{12}	S_{13}
actual	-	1	-	-	-	1	-	-	-	-	1	-	1
predicted	1	-	-	-	1	1	-	-	1	-	-	1	1
correct?	N	N	Y	Y	N	Y	Y	Y	N	Y	N	N	Y

Figure 11.1 An example of a binary classification evaluation

sentences	S_1	S_2	S_3	S_4	S_5	S_6	S_7	S_8	S_9	S_{10}	S_{11}	S_{12}	S_{13}
actual	-	-	-	1	-	-	-	-	-	-	1	-	-
system 1	1	-	-	-	-	-	1	-	-	-	-	-	-
system 2	-	-	1	-	-	-	-	-	-	1	-	-	-

Figure 11.2 Evaluating two very different systems

Early work in topic segmentation used exactly this approach; Reynar (1994), for example, evaluates his approach in terms of recall and precision. But we can see a problem (see e.g. Beeferman *et al.*, 1999; Passonneau and Litman, 1996) if we compare the outputs of two imaginary systems, one which is pretty terrible, and one which always gets quite close (see Figure 11.2).

An evaluation on this basis will score both of them the same: both have 0% accuracy, as neither get any hits. In a sentence segmentation task, this might not matter: the segments are quite short, and a hypothesized sentence with "close" boundaries might be just as useless to a parser as one whose boundaries are completely wrong. But with topic segmentation, we'd really like to score system 2 higher than system 1: each of its boundaries is only 1 sentence away from a true boundary, and its output would be quite helpful. As Beeferman *et al.* (1999) put it:

> In almost any conceivable application, a segmenting tool that consistently comes close—off by a sentence, say—is preferable to one that places boundaries willy-nilly. [. . .] It is natural to expect that in a segmenter, close should count for something.

One simple way round this problem might be to allow hypothesized boundaries to score a hit if they are "close to" true boundaries, rather than requiring that they be in exactly the same place. Reynar (1994) does exactly this, giving an alternative evaluation figures which allow matches within a three-sentence window. The choice of window is arbitrary, of course, and might depend on the data and application of interest; but more seriously, this essentially still suffers from exactly the same problem – a hypothesized boundary just outside the "close" window will score just as badly as one further away. It also fails to distinguish between a perfect segmenter and one which always gets close. In general, then, we need a different approach.

11.4.2 Segmentation-based

11.4.2.1 P_k (Beeferman *et al.*, 1999)

To combat this problem, Beeferman *et al.* (1999) propose an alternative measure, P_k, which expresses a *probability of segmentation error*: the average probability, given two points in the dataset, that the segmenter is incorrect as to whether they are separated by a boundary or not.

(Note that as P_k scores are probabilities, they range between 0 and 1, but a higher score means a *less* accurate segmenter: a higher probability of error).

To calculate P_k, we take a window of fixed width k and move it across the data set, at each step examining whether the hypothesized segmentation is correct about the separation (or not) of the two ends of the window. For a single window position with start i and end j, we can express this separation via the indicator function $\delta_S(i, j)$:

$$\delta_S(i, j) = \begin{cases} 1 \text{ if segmentation } S \text{ assigns } i \text{ and } j \text{ to the same segment} \\ 0 \text{ otherwise} \end{cases}$$

For a single window (i, j), the correctness of a hypothesized segmentation H relative to a reference segmentation R can then be calculated as:

$$\delta_H(i, j) \overline{\oplus} \delta_R(i, j)$$

where $\overline{\oplus}$ is the XNOR "both or neither" operator. This evaluates to 1 only if both sides equal 0 or both equal 1, and thus only if segmentations H and R agree about the separation of i and j. The inverse of this gives us our basic error function, giving 1 only if H and R *dis*agree:

$$1 - \delta_H(i, j) \overline{\oplus} \delta_R(i, j)$$

or equivalently:

$$\delta_H(i, j) \oplus \delta_R(i, j)$$

where $\oplus$ is the XOR operator. We can then obtain P_k by moving the window across the entire dataset, summing this score, and dividing by the number of windows:

$$P_k = \frac{\sum_{i=1}^{N-k} \delta_H(i, i+k) \oplus \delta_R(i, i+k)}{(N-k)}$$

The choice of k is, in principle, arbitrary; but is generally set to be half the average segment length in the reference segmentation R. This value ensures (under some assumptions) that the four obvious baseline algorithms (hypothesizing no boundaries, boundaries everywhere, evenly spaced boundaries or randomly spaced boundaries) all have $P_k = 0.5$. A perfect segmenter will score 0, of course; a score of 1.0 will only be achieved by a truly terrible segmenter which manages to hypothesize boundaries in all and only the wrong places.

It is helpful to look at the calculation of P_k in a slightly different way, which helps us see how it relates to other possible measures, and when it might leave something to be desired. Figure 11.3 shows examples of the four possible situations when comparing segmentations in a fixed-width window.

Windows (a) and (d) are both "correct": the hypothesized and reference segmentations either both show a boundary in the window or both show none. Window (b) shows a *false negative* or *miss* – the hypothesized output has failed to spot a reference boundary; window (c) shows a *false positive* or *false alarm* – the segmenter has hypothesized a boundary where none really exists. Distinguishing these two situations can be helpful in evaluating the suitability of a segmenter for a particular application (as with precision and recall for standard classification tasks). We can do this by decomposing the calculation of P_k into two parts, one expressing the

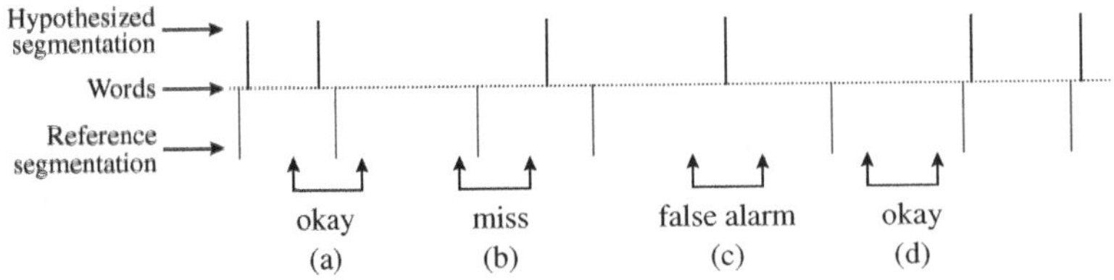

Figure 11.3 Evaluating a hypothesized segmentation against a reference segmentation (Beeferman *et al.*, © 1999 Springer)

probability of misses, and the probability of false alarms, using the general framework used in the description of the evaluation in the original TDT program (Allan *et al.*, 1998):

$$P_k = P_{Miss} + P_{FalseAlarm}$$

where

$$P_{Miss} = \frac{\sum_{i=1}^{N-k} \delta_H(i, i+k) \cdot (1 - \delta_R(i, i+k))}{\sum_{i=1}^{N-k} (1 - \delta_R(i, i+k))}$$

$$P_{FalseAlarm} = \frac{\sum_{i=1}^{N-k} (1 - \delta_H(i, i+k)) \cdot \delta_R(i, i+k)}{\sum_{i=1}^{N-k} \delta_R(i, i+k)}$$

11.4.2.2 *WD* (Pevzner and Hearst, 2002)

P_k clearly gives us a more suitable measure than a simple accuracy or F-score, and is still perhaps the most widely-used metric for segmentation evaluation. However, Pevzner and Hearst (2002) point out that it has several shortcomings, all of which essentially stem from the fact that the underlying question it poses of the segmentations being compared is whether they agree on *whether two points are separated or not*, rather on *how many boundaries lie between them*. As Figure 11.4 shows, this can lead to situations where P_k fails to penalize false alarms: Here, the false hypothesized boundary falls within the window width k of a true reference boundary, and the P_k evaluation will rate all the windows shown as "correct" in that both segmentations agree that the two ends of the windows fall into different segments. Misses

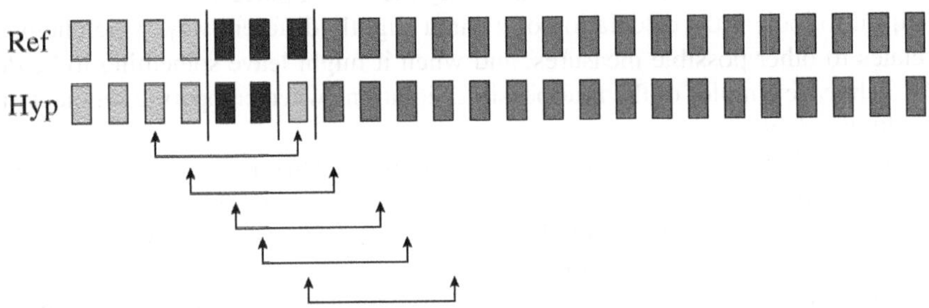

Figure 11.4 P_k can fail to penalize false alarms that fall within a window width k of a true boundary (Pevzner and Hearst, 2002)

(false negatives) don't suffer from the same problem, though, with the result that P_k can effectively penalize them more than false alarms.

Instead, they propose a measure called WindowDiff (WD), which works in a similar way by moving a fixed-width window across the data; this time, though, windows are scored as "correct" if they assign the same number of segment boundaries between their start and end. If $b_S(i, j)$ is the number of boundaries between i and j according to segmentation S, the basic error function for a window becomes:

$$|b_H(i, j) - b_R(i, j)| > 0$$

Summing over windows and normalizing as before, we now obtain:

$$WD = \frac{\sum_{i=1}^{N-k}[|b(i, i+k) - b_R(i, i+k)| > 0]}{(N-k)}$$

Again, WD is a measure of segmentation error–lower scores mean less error, with a perfect segmenter scoring 0. And again, if we want to examine issues of precision and recall independently, we can express it in terms of scores for misses and false alarms:

$$WD = WD_{Miss} + WD_{FalseAlarm}$$

where

$$WD_{Miss} = \frac{\sum_{i=1}^{N-k}[b_H(i, i+k) < b_R(i, i+k)]}{(N-k)}$$

$$WD_{FalseAlarm} = \frac{\sum_{i=1}^{N-k}[b_H(i, i+k) > b_R(i, i+k)]}{(N-k)}$$

11.4.2.3 Pr_{error} (Georgescul *et al.*, 2006a)

While WD does solve many of P_k's problems, it has its own problems; not least of which, it's hard to know exactly what either of them really *mean* intuitively (other than in terms of direct comparison with another system). Most recent work in topic segmentation uses both metrics when reporting performance.

Georgescul *et al.* (2006a) have pointed out another problem with WD: that it effectively assigns a lower penalty to misses than to false alarms. Looking at the formulation for WD_{Miss} and $WD_{FalseAlarm}$ above, we can see that both are normalized by the number of windows $(N - k)$. While this seems correct for false alarms (there are as many opportunities for a false alarm as there are evaluation windows), it doesn't for misses. If we want to evaluate on the basis of the true probability of a miss, we must normalize the number of misses by the number of opportunities for a miss – in other words, the number of windows in which there is a boundary in the reference segmentation. They therefore propose a modified normalization for the *Miss* term:

$$Pr_{Miss} = \frac{\sum_{i=1}^{N-k}[b_H(i, i+k) < b_R(i, i+k)]}{\sum_{i=1}^{N-k}[b_R(i, i+k) > 0]}$$

$$Pr_{FalseAlarm} = \frac{\sum_{i=1}^{N-k}[b_H(i, i+k) > b_R(i, i+k)]}{(N-k)}$$

The two terms can then be combined to give an overall error metric Pr_{error}. Georgescul *et al.* (2006a) propose that this term be weighted to allow a trade-off between the penalties for misses and false alarms, depending on the application being considered:

$$Pr_{error} = C_{Miss} \cdot Pr_{Miss} + C_{FalseAlarm} \cdot Pr_{FalseAlarm}$$

where $0 \leq C_{Miss} \leq 1$ is the cost of a miss, and $0 \leq C_{FalseAlarm} \leq 1$ is the cost of a false alarm. Setting $C_{Miss} = C_{FalseAlarm} = 0.5$ will assign equal costs, and ensure that the trivial no/all boundary baselines both get Pr_{error} around 50%. This proposal hasn't seen much take-up yet, but does seem to promise an improved metric.

11.4.3 Content-based

This directly segmentation-based approach to evaluation has become the accepted standard. It is worth noting here, though, that evaluating purely on the basis of the accuracy of boundary placement may have its drawbacks. First, as ASR and automatic sentence segmentation will be errorful, the exact units (or time periods) over which to calculate the evaluation functions can be unclear.

Second, and perhaps more importantly, this approach takes no notice of the content of the topics themselves. Failure to detect a boundary between two very similar topics should perhaps be penalized less than failure to detect one between two very different topics. It may be, then, that error metrics which combine measures of segmentation accuracy with measures of topic similarity can give us a more useful tool – see Mohri *et al.* (2009) for a suggestion along these lines. However, the suitability of any one method may well depend on the application in mind, and the purpose to which the derived topics are to be put. The next chapter will discuss topic classification, and suitable evaluation methods for that task; we should remember that segmentation and classification are to a large degree joint problems, and that evaluating one alone may not tell the whole story.

11.5 Technical Approaches

11.5.1 Changes in Lexical Similarity

Some of the first successful approaches to segmentation focus on changes in lexical distribution, and this still forms the core of many current algorithms. The essential insight is that topic shifts tend to be marked by a change in the vocabulary used, which can be detected by looking for minima in some lexical cohesion metric.

11.5.1.1 TextTiling (Hearst, 1997)

TextTiling (Hearst, 1994, 1997; Hearst and Plaunt, 1993) was one of the early algorithms to emerge from the TDT Broadcast News effort, and still forms the baseline for many recent improvements; while designed for text documents, it has since been successfully applied to spoken data. The discourse is tokenized, stemmed and divided into windows of a fixed width. Each window is represented by a lexical frequency vector: one row per distinct word type, whose value is the raw frequency of that word type in the window. Moving across the discourse, the lexical similarity is then calculated for each pair of adjacent windows, using the cosine distance between their lexical frequency vectors. The resulting curve is then smoothed, and local

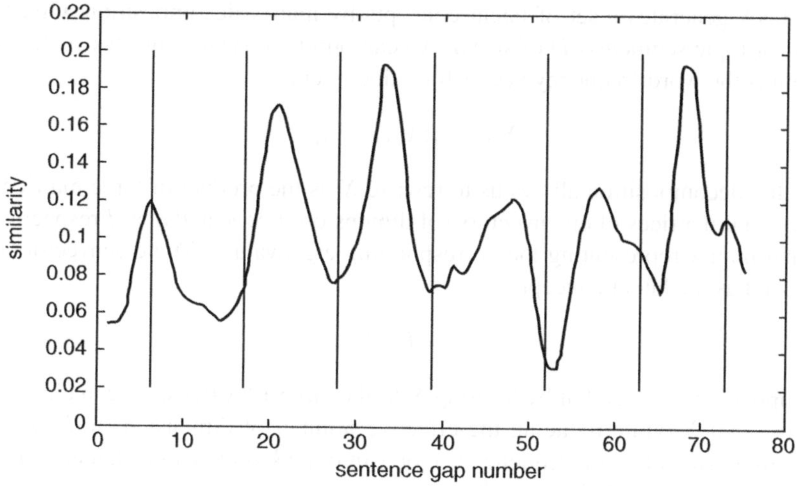

Figure 11.5 True segment boundaries vs. minima in TextTiling's lexical similarity metric (Hearst and Plaunt © 1993 ACM)

minima are found by calculating a *depth score* for each point based on its relative depth below its nearest peaks on either side. Points with the highest depth scores (i.e. the deepest troughs in the smoothed similarity curve) are then taken as the hypothesized boundaries – see Figure 11.5.

Other similarity metrics can be used within the same overall approach: Hearst also proposes an alternative which uses a measure of introduction of new vocabulary within each block (new topics may be expected to introduce new terms); and Reynar (1999) uses the overlap between the two sets of bigrams rather than just unigrams. Whichever exact variant is used, one advantage of this approach is that it is essentially unsupervised – although various parameters do need to be set suitably, such as the window width and the cut-off at which depth scores cause boundaries to be hypothesized.

11.5.1.2 Latent Concept Modelling

Of course, the success of this approach must depend on the suitability of the similarity metric chosen. Using raw lexical frequency vectors as the basis for similarity can cause problems, due to their sparseness and the fact that they necessarily treat words independently, ignoring the real dependencies between related terms. One way to combat this is to project the lexical vectors into some *latent concept* space using methods such as Latent Semantic Analysis (LSA, Landauer *et al.*, 1998).

More details of LSA and related approaches are given in the next chapter, but the main idea is to represent topics using fewer dimensions: characterizing a segment not by counts of each distinct word type, but by weights over a smaller set of latent variables (which can be seen as semantic concepts). The simple lexical frequency approach as used by TextTiling in its original form represents any segment of text (window, topic, document) as a vector x of word frequencies, with one entry for each term in the vocabulary W of size w:

$$x = (f_1, f_2, \ldots, f_w)$$

Instead, LSA generates a set of latent concepts by matrix decomposition. Given a set of documents (or topic segments) D of size d, we can build a lexical frequency matrix X where each column is the word frequency vector for a document:

$$X = (x_1; x_2; \ldots; x_d)$$

Singular value decomposition allows us to rewrite X as the product of three matrices: U and V are orthogonal matrices of eigenvectors (of dimension $w \times w$ and $d \times d$ respectively), and Σ a diagonal matrix representing the corresponding eigenvalues. The eigenvectors of V can now be viewed as the latent concepts:

$$X = U \Sigma V^*$$

This decomposition is exact; but by limiting Σ to the largest k values, we can closely approximate the original X while reducing the effective number of dimensions to k. We can now project a w-dimensional word frequency vector x into the k-dimensional latent concept space using (appropriately truncated) U and Σ:

$$z = \Sigma^{-1} U^* x$$

The vector z is now a representation of a text segment as a set of weights over the k latent concepts. Similarity (or distance) between segments or windows can now be calculated using an appropriate vector distance measure (such as the cosine distance) between these z vectors. This approach does require a dataset on which to learn the concept vectors; but gives a more general, less sparse, and lower-dimensional representation which allows dependencies between words to be expressed (as each concept vector may relate several distinct words).

Olney and Cai (2005) use LSA to provide a similarity metric within a TextTiling-like approach, and show that it can give more accurate segmentation on dialogue data. Their method uses LSA-based distance to compare each utterance with the windows on either side, not only in terms of its similarity (in their terms, its *relevance* to the surrounding topic), but also its difference (its *informativity*, or the amount of new information it may be providing) – and hypothesize boundaries on the basis of a combination of these factors, learnt using a regression model. Other latent concept modelling approaches are also possible – for example, Sun *et al.* (2008) use Latent Dirichlet Allocation (see below) to provide the basis for their similarity metric.

11.5.1.3 LCSeg (Galley *et al.*, 2003)

Another variation of the basic lexical cohesion approach that has been particularly influential in dialogue segmentation is LCSeg (Galley *et al.*, 2003). Here, the similarity metric uses the presence of *lexical chains* (Morris and Hirst, 1991) – implemented here as simple term repetitions – rather than just the presence of words; the insight being that these chains will start and end at topic shifts. Chains are identified for all repeated terms in the text, and weighted according to their term frequency (more frequent terms being weighted higher) and the chain length (shorter chains being weighted higher). The cosine distance between each pair of windows' lexical chain vectors is then used as the key metric, and again the sharpest local minima are taken as the hypothesized boundaries; this simple but robust method has shown good performance on difficult data (multiparty meetings).

11.5.1.4 Supervised Classification (Georgescul *et al.*, 2006b)

If suitable training data is available, the same insight can be given higher accuracy by the use of supervised classification, and Galley *et al.* (2003) showed that this could improve their algorithm's performance. Georgescul *et al.* (2006b) went one step further by characterizing each potential boundary point in the discourse (each utterance boundary) not by a single lexical cohesion score comparing the windows on either side, but an array of lexical similarity features, one for each word in the discourse vocabulary. This results in a very sparse, high-dimensional array of features, but one which contains a large amount of information. By using support vector machines, which can operate with high dimensional feature spaces (Vapnik, 1995), a classifier model can then be learnt which predicts boundaries with high accuracy, outperforming (Galley *et al.*, 2003)'s approach on meeting transcripts. Further performance improvements are also possible by incorporating non-lexical features and latent concept representations – see below. Being a supervised method, though, it does require annotated training data.

11.5.2 Similarity-based Clustering

Alternatively, we can take another viewpoint on the same basic insight: rather than looking for areas of low cohesion (the boundaries), we can look for areas of high cohesion (the topic segments). Clustering together neighbouring areas which are similar to each other leaves us with a segmentation of the discourse. This can be approached using *agglomerative* clustering (growing clusters outwards from peaks in similarity, Yaari (1997)) but *divisive* clustering has proved more effective.

11.5.2.1 Dot-plotting (Reynar, 1994)

Reynar (1994) uses the technique of *dot-plotting*, originally from (Church, 1993), to segment text: the discourse is plotted as a two-dimensional matrix with its words (in linear order) along both axes, and a non-zero entry (a dot) wherever words match (see Figure 11.6). The diagonal is, of course, entirely non-zero, as each word matches itself; but squares can also be seen, corresponding to topics, in areas with more frequent matching between near-neighbours. The boundaries between these squares are the topic boundaries, and the best set of boundaries is that which maximizes the dot density within the squares it delineates, and minimizes the density outside those squares (i.e. finds topics which are maximally similar internally, and maximally different from other topics). This can be performed essentially unsupervised and without any training data, although it needs a search algorithm and some criterion for finishing; Reynar (1994) uses a best-first search algorithm which minimizes the outside density and assumes a known number of boundaries.

This method has been extended and improved since: the *C99* algorithm, of Choi (2000) for example, works on sentences rather than words, with a cosine distance sentence similarity metric and a gradient criterion for finishing. Latent concept modelling may be applied to the similarity metric here too: Choi *et al.* (2001) showed that using a Latent Semantic Analysis-based metric could improve accuracy, although Popescu-Belis *et al.* (2005) found that the benefit was small for meeting dialogue data.

Of course, these techniques were originally developed and evaluated on text, and on corpora created artificially by concatenating distinct text documents; as Figure 11.6 shows, speech data is less cleanly separable, with smoother transitions between topics, and similarities

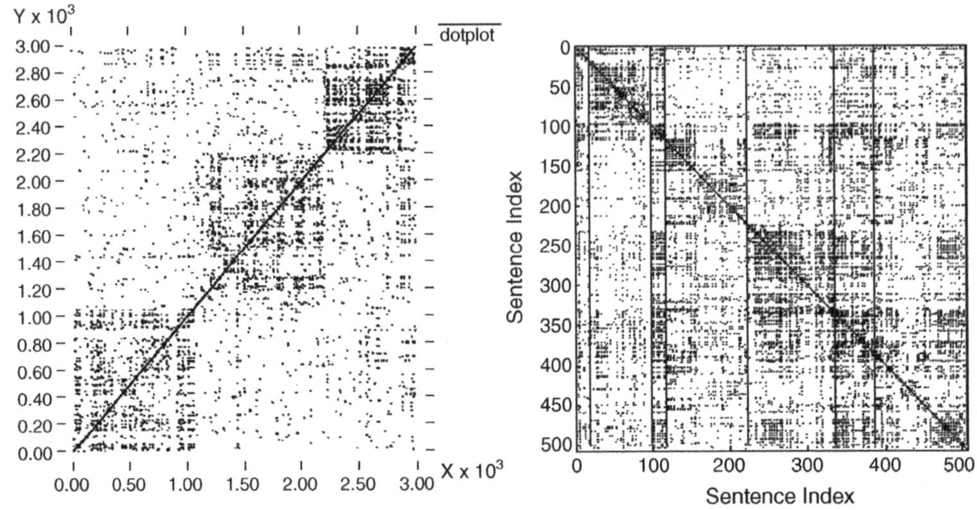

Figure 11.6 Dot-plotting Wall Street Journal articles (Reynar, 1994) and a spoken lecture (Malioutov and Barzilay, 2006)

between temporally distant topics. However, Malioutov and Barzilay (2006) have shown that the approach can be successfully applied to spoken discourse with some modification, by formulating an algorithm to find an exact solution, using a suitable similarity metric, and limiting the long-range distance over which similarity is calculated.

11.5.3 Generative Models

Yet another way of exploiting the same phenomenon is to take a generative perspective. We can model discourse as being generated, via a noisy channel, from some underlying sequence of topics, each of which has its own characteristic word distribution. When the topic changes, the vocabulary used will change; so if we can infer the most likely sequence of topics from the observed words, we can derive the positions of the boundaries between them. Note that this approach does not require us to measure the similarity between utterances or windows directly – rather, the fact that neighbouring utterances within the same topic segment are similar to each other is implicit in the fact that they have been generated from the same topic.

11.5.3.1 Hidden Markov Models (Mulbregt *et al.*, 1999; Yamron *et al.*, 1998)

This is, of course, comparable to the problem of speech recognition (ASR), where the task is to infer the most likely sequence of phonemes from the observed acoustic signal. If we can make similar assumptions about the dependencies between words and topics as ASR does about phonemes and acoustic signals, we can apply similar models, together with their well-researched inference techniques.

The most commonly used generative model in ASR is the hidden Markov model (HMM), and Figure 11.7(a) shows a HMM can be used as a simple topic model. This model assumes

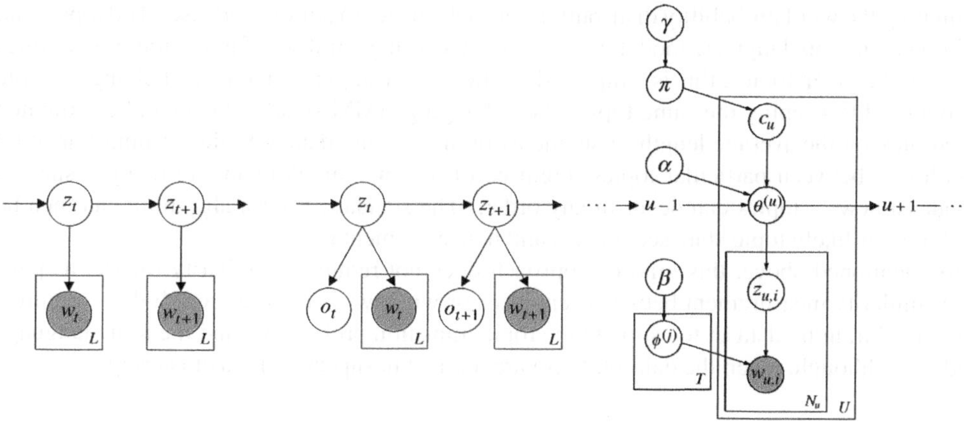

Figure 11.7 From left to right: (a) a simple HMM topic model (Yamron *et al.*, 1998); (b) the aspect model used in (Blei and Moreno, 2001); and (c) the topic mixture model used in (Purver *et al.*, 2006)

that the discourse is composed of a linear sequence of segments of length L words, each of which is associated with a topic state z from which the words w are generated with probability $p(w|z)$. If we can infer the most likely sequence of topic states given the observed words, we can produce a segmentation: if the topic z_t at segment t is different from the topic z_{t+1} at segment $t+1$, we hypothesize a topic boundary between the segments. Performing inference in such a model depends on two major assumptions:

1. the probability of a word being generated depends only on the current topic (the *emission* probability $p(w|z)$);
2. the probability of a topic being discussed depends only on the previous topic (the *transition* probability $p(z_{t+1}|z_t)$).

Given estimates of the emission and transition probabilities, we can calculate the prior probability $p(Z)$ of any topic sequence Z, and the posterior probability $p(W|Z)$ of Z generating an observed word sequence W. Via Bayes' rule, this allows us to calculate the probability of Z given W:

$$p(Z|W) = p(W|Z).p(Z)/p(W)$$

and maximizing this will give us the most likely topic sequence Z (given that W, and thus the prior probability $p(W)$, is fixed). While these assumptions may be good first approximations, note that they do not entirely hold in reality: while some words may be related only to the content of the topic at hand, many are related more to discourse or syntactic function; and the likely sequence of topics may depend on many extra-linguistic factors. However, these models are well understood, and efficient algorithms exist for learning and decoding (see, e.g. Jurafsky and Martin, 2009; Manning and Schütze, 1999, for details).

Yamron *et al.* (1998) were among the first to show that they can be applied to broadcast news segmentation. First, a set of topics z with their associated language models $p(w|z)$ are learnt, by clustering a set of training texts using an appropriate lexical similarity metric, and estimating the word probability distribution for each cluster (Yamron *et al.* used 100 topics and smoothed unigram language models). Rather than learning a full set of transition probabilities between the given topics, this is simplified to allow for a single probability of changing topic (as opposed to keeping the same topic when changing HMM state), which can be estimated based only on the average length of segments in the training data. (While learning transition likelihoods between particular topics might be of use in some domains, in many – such as broadcast news – topics can occur in any order.) The standard Viterbi algorithm can then be used to infer likely topic state sequences, and hence segmentations.

As mentioned above, this kind of approach does not require a similarity metric, as pair-wise similarity measurement between sentences or windows is not required. It does require a segmented training dataset to estimate the topic transition probability, and the topic language models – although, given the dataset, these are learned unsupervised via clustering.

11.5.3.2 Latent Concept Modelling (Blei and Moreno, 2001)

One drawback of this simple approach is that it treats words as being independent of each other, given a topic; as discussed with relation to lexical similarity metrics in the previous sections, this is not a realistic assumption. With probabilistic models, the assumption becomes more accurate as the segment size (L in the model above) increases – but this leads to reduced accuracy as the segmentation granularity necessarily becomes coarser. As above, one way to alleviate this is to use some form of latent concept modelling.

Blei and Moreno (2001) show that a probabilistic form of latent concept model, Probabilistic Latent Semantic Indexing (PLSI, Hofmann, 1999), can be used within a HMM framework to give what they call an *aspect* HMM. PLSI is described in detail in the next chapter, but its essential insight is to associate a document o (in this case, a topic segment) not with one fixed topic z as above, but with a probability distribution over topics $p(z|o)$. The topics can therefore be seen as latent variables, as with LSA, and each topic is associated with a probability distribution over words $p(w|z)$. This allows us to account for segments which may be related to multiple underlying concepts, or which are generated from a "contentful" topic and a "syntactic" topic (see, e.g. Griffiths *et al.*, 2005).

Learning the latent topics, and the word and document distributions, is now performed via expectation-maximization (EM, see, e.g. Manning and Schütze, 1999), rather than matrix decomposition, over a training corpus of segments. Once the topics have been learnt, a HMM can be constructed which uses the learnt latent topics z as the hidden state variables – see Figure 11.7(b). If desired, transition probabilities between the latent topics can also be learnt from the training set, via clustering documents according to their most likely topic. Decoding is less straightforward, as the relevant HMM emission probabilities are no longer just $p(w|z)$ as before, but also $p(o|z)$, which must be estimated during decoding using a version of EM. However, the model can give improved performance (and Blei and Moreno (2001) show this on radio transcripts), especially at lower values of L required for finer segment granularity.

Other forms of latent concept modelling have also been successfully used; one that has recently become more popular is Latent Dirichlet Allocation (LDA, Blei *et al.*, 2003). One advantage of LDA is that it requires less supervision. While PLSI requires a segmented training corpus to provide direct estimates of the probability distributions over topics $p(z)$ and documents $p(o|z)$, LDA takes a fully Bayesian approach: it assumes a range of possible distributions, constrained by being drawn from Dirichlet distributions. This allows a latent topic model to be learnt entirely unsupervised, allowing the model to be maximally relevant to the data being segmented (and less dependent on the domain of the training set and the problems associated with human segmentation annotation). Purver *et al.* (2006) use this approach in an unsupervised generative model applied to meeting dialogues, and show performance competitive with LCSeg's similarity-based approach. As shown in Figure 11.7(c), each utterance u is now associated with a *distribution* θ over possible latent topics z, each of which has its own probability distribution over words ϕ; switching to a new topic segment with probability c means changing the topic distribution θ. Given the assumption that θ, ϕ and c are drawn from Dirichlet distributions (or a Beta distribution in the case of c) with fixed parameters α, β and γ, inference is possible: however, exact solutions are no longer tractable and must be approximated by (computationally intensive) sampling – see Blei *et al.* (2003), Griffiths and Steyvers (2004) and the next chapter for details.

11.5.3.3 Compact Language Modelling (Utiyama and Isahara, 2001)

Another prominent variant of the generative approach that allows essentially unsupervised segmentation is that of *TextSeg* (Utiyama and Isahara, 2001). Here, the underlying assumption is similar: that the discourse is generated from a sequence of topics, each of which is associated with its own language model (a probability distribution over words); and the underlying approach to segmentation also involves placing the boundaries so as to maximize the likelihood of the data given these language models. However, in this approach there is no attempt to learn the most likely set of topic models from a training dataset; rather, the most compact set are chosen given the data being segmented.

This is estimated as part of the segmentation process itself: given any hypothesized segmentation (set of boundaries) S, language models representing each segment can be calculated from the observed words within that segment, given an appropriately smoothed estimation procedure. The likelihood of the data can then be calculated, as above, as the posterior probability of the words given the segmentation $p(W|S)$, and the prior probability of the segmentation itself $p(S)$ – where they assume that $p(S)$ can be calculated from the average length of segments, either known *a priori* or derived from some training set. By comparing the likelihood of the data calculated from different segmentations, the maximum-probability segmentation can be chosen; and this can be performed via an efficient dynamic programming algorithm.

Of course, estimating the language models only from the data being segmented (rather than a large set of possibly clustered training documents) makes the choice of smoothing essential. Utiyama and Isahara (2001) use a form of Laplacian smoothing; but Eisenstein and Barzilay (2008) have since shown that another way to provide this is to generalize the approach into a fully Bayesian version. Rather than estimating one particular smoothed language model, they use an approach similar to LDA to marginalize over all possible language models, and show that this improves segmentation accuracy.

As well as obviating the need for an explicit fixed similarity metric, and being amenable to unsupervised learning, another potential advantage of generative modelling is the acquisition of the topic models themselves: the ability to characterize the topics in terms of their associated language models can be useful for topic summarization, classification or browsing – see later chapters. Depending on the application, approaches which learn models in latent concept spaces, or models which are common across training and/or test datasets, may be more or less advantageous.

11.5.4 Discriminative Boundary Detection

A rather different approach is to look for the characteristic features of the boundaries themselves: the cue phrases people use to signal topic change, the prosodic features often exhibited in speech at the beginnings and ends of topic discussions, or the introduction of new referents.

Passonneau and Litman (1997) showed that all of the above could be useful in segmenting spoken stories. Topic boundaries were correlated with the presence of one of a list of cue phrases from Hirschberg and Litman (1993), such as *So* and *Anyway*, with the presence of significant pauses or sentence-final intonation, and with the absence of noun phrases whose referents were found in, or inferable from, the preceding utterance. These three features seem to be complementary: by combining them in a decision tree, they could produce segmentations with higher accuracy than using any one alone. The intonational information used was hand-coded in that case; but Tür *et al.* (2001) showed that automatically extracted pitch pattern, pause and vowel information could also be used successfully in broadcast news segmentation (again by combining features in a decision tree classifier).

As well as general cues such as *So*, *Anyway*, different domains often have their own specific cue phrases. In broadcast news, phrases such as *Joining us*, *This just in* and *Welcome back* are strongly indicative of topic shifts. Maybury (1998) describes a system which uses these cues in a finite-state automaton to detect and segment news story structure; and Reynar (1999) found that by including cues together with lexical cohesion measures in a maximum entropy model, accuracy could be increased over using lexical cohesion alone.

Of course, as the most useful set of cue phrases will vary between domains, there might be an advantage to learning that set automatically, rather than having to define it manually. Beeferman *et al.* (1999) showed how this can be done using log-linear models which combine many possibly dependent features: by starting with many possible features and using an iterative procedure for selecting the most informative features, a suitable subset can be derived. If the initial features considered consist of each possible word in suitable "cue" positions (immediately before or after a potential boundary, in the next sentence, etc.), this will automatically produce an empirically based cue word set. For their broadcast news dataset, they derive domain-related terms such as *Joins*, *Live* and the letters of *CNN*, as well as those more specific to the content of their data such as *Haiti* and *Clinton*.

Dialogue can bring its own distinctive features to topic shifts. It is often the case that different speakers are more active during the discussion of different topics, resulting in an observable change in relative speaker activity at segment boundaries. The early sections of topic discussions also tend to be more ordered, with less overlap and interruption between speakers, as new subjects are introduced and set out. Galley *et al.* (2003) showed that features based on these observations could be helpful in segmenting ICSI dialogues – see below.

11.5.5 Combined Approaches, and the State of the Art

Of course, given these different approaches with their different insights into the problem, one way towards higher accuracy might be to combine them, and this is the direction that many of the most effective recent systems have taken.

11.5.5.1 Combining Lexical Cohesion and Boundary Detection

The evidence used by lexical cohesion-based approaches (whether from differential, clustering or generative perspectives) seems entirely complementary to the evidence used by the boundary-detection approach. Combining them therefore seems a natural step.

One way to do this is to combine the outputs of the two different approaches via some suitable classifier. Galley *et al.* (2003) tried exactly this, using a decision tree classifier whose input features were taken partly from the output of their LCSeg segmenter (Section 11.5.1.3) – both the raw lexical similarity metric and the smoothed peak hypotheses – and partly from distinctive boundary characteristics. The latter features followed Passonneau and Litman (1997) in including a list of cue phrases, and significant pauses, although they found that pauses should be limited to those which do not occur after a question or in the middle of one participant's speech. They also included measures of *speech overlap* (overlapping utterances tend to be rare at the beginning of topic segments) and *speaker change* (in dialogue, new topics are often associated with changes in the relative activity of the participants), calculating the latter via the change in the distribution across speakers of the number of words uttered immediately before and after a potential boundary. This combination resulted in a large improvement in performance, with P_k improving from 0.32 to 0.23 on the ICSI meeting dialogue data. Arguello and Rosé (2006) used a similar approach within a Naïve Bayes classifier, combining lexical cohesion scores with syntactic features (expressed as part-of-speech bigrams) and information about the identity of the speaker, in two-person tutorial dialogues.

Another way is to include distinctive boundary features directly into the main classifier, alongside the features used to express lexical similarity. For example, in the discriminative approach of Georgescul *et al.* (2006b), lexical similarity is encoded as an array of features in an SVM, one for each distinct word type in the vocabulary; new features related to silence, overlaps or cue phrases can be added directly to the feature vectors, and they found that this gave a small improvement (Georgescul *et al.*, 2007). Within a generative approach, boundary features can be added as new observed variables associated with a special topic-change state; Tür *et al.* (2001) show how to incorporate this within the HMM approach of Yamron *et al.* (1998), Dowman *et al.* (2008) similarly within the LDA-based model of Purver *et al.* (2006) and unsupervised learning procedure, and Eisenstein and Barzilay (2008) show how to treat cue phrases as generated from boundary states in their language modelling approach.

There is some evidence, though, that this combined approach may become less helpful as the desired granularity of topics becomes finer. Hsueh *et al.* (2006) examined segmentation of the AMI corpus at relatively coarse- and fine-grained levels, where the coarse-grained level often corresponded to broad changes in the activity or state of the meeting, such as introductions or closing review, while the fine-grained level corresponded to lower-level changes in subject matter. They found that boundary features such as cue phrases, silence and speaker activity were only helpful for the coarse-grained segmentation.

11.5.5.2 Combining Generative and Discriminative Approaches

Benefits can also be gained by combining some of the benefits of generative approaches, such as the ability to learn models of (latent) topics, with the accuracy of discriminative approaches. Georgescul *et al.* (2008) used generative models similar to those of Blei and Moreno (2001) and Purver *et al.* (2006) described above, to learn topic models in latent concept spaces, via PLSI and LDA respectively. Using these models to provide vector-space representations of windows of discourse, they could then apply the same discriminative SVM classification approach as in Georgescul *et al.* (2006b) to hypothesize boundaries, but with a more compact feature representation; as they show, results on the ICSI dialogue data were improved.

Tür *et al.* (2001) took a slightly different approach, seeking to exploiting the fact that different classification approaches can lend themselves better to different phenomena, with discriminative classifiers often dealing particularly well with prosodic feature data. Their system combined a version of the HMM-based lexical model of Yamron *et al.* (1998) with a decision tree trained on prosodic boundary features, and they experimented with two ways of achieving this: firstly adding the HMM's output posterior boundary probabilities into an overall decision tree, and secondly using the prosodic decision tree to provide emission probabilities for a boundary state in the HMM. On their broadcast news data, the latter approach was more successful.

11.5.5.3 State of the Art Performance

Monologue

The TDT dataset allows us to compare the accuracy of various algorithms on broadcast news data. On manual transcripts, the algorithms developed for general text (and initially evaluated using artificial corpora) perform reasonably well, with C99 (Choi, 2000) achieving $P_k = 0.21$ and TextSeg (Utiyama and Isahara, 2001) achieving 0.14 improving to 0.19 and 0.11 respectively when given knowledge of number of boundaries (see Georgescul *et al.*, 2006a).

The systems which were developed as part of the TDT effort achieve good performance even on ASR output: the supervised maximum entropy classifier of Beeferman *et al.* (1999) achieved P_k of 0.15, with the HMM method of Yamron *et al.* (1998) giving 0.16. Since then, the method of Tür *et al.* (2001) including prosodic features has outperformed those with $P_k = 0.14$; and Beeferman *et al.* (1999) claim $P_k = 0.08$ on a CNN portion of TDT news data.

For spoken lecture segmentation, the divisive clustering method of Malioutov and Barzilay (2006) achieves P_k of 0.30 on manual transcripts, dropping slightly to 0.32 on ASR output. In comparison, C99 and TextSeg give P_k values between 0.31 and 0.37 on the same data.

Dialogue

Multiparty dialogue data is trickier, of course, and accuracies on the ICSI and AMI meeting datasets are correspondingly lower. Approaches developed for text or monologue show only limited accuracy: Georgescul *et al.* (2006a) tested TextTiling, C99 and TextSeg on the ICSI corpus, achieving P_k results ranging between 0.55 and 0.38, although this improved to 0.35 when supplying information about the expected number of segment boundaries.[8]

LCSeg has shown much better accuracy on ICSI, and has become a common baseline to quote: its unsupervised version achieves $P_k = 0.32$, and the supervised version including boundary features achieves $P_k = 0.23$. Higher unsupervised accuracies have now been achieved by the Bayesian generative approaches of Dowman *et al.* (2008) and Eisenstein and Barzilay (2008), with $P_k = 0.26$; and higher supervised accuracies by Georgescul *et al.* (2007) discriminative SVM classifier, with $P_k = 0.21$. Most dialogue segmentation efforts to date have

[8] Note though that Banerjee and Rudnicky (2006) report more success with TextTiling on a different multiparty dataset.

used manual transcripts, but some results using ASR output are now available with little, if any, reduction in segmentation accuracy (Hsueh *et al.*, 2006; Purver *et al.*, 2006).

Comparing system performance on two-person dialogue is difficult, as this area has received less attention (in terms of topic segmentation) and has little in the way of standard datasets for comparison. However, Arguello and Rosé (2006) give results on two corpora of tutorial dialogues: their supervised classifier, with P_k ranging between 0.10 and 0.40, outperforms the lexical cohesion method of Olney and Cai (2005) with P_k of 0.28 to 0.49.

11.6 New Trends and Future Directions

11.6.1 Multi-modality

Including multiple sources of information has become common, as explained above: segmentation accuracy can be improved by including not only lexical information (from lexical cohesion or language model probabilities), but also speech signal information (e.g prosody), discourse information (cue phrases) and pragmatic information (speaker activity). Some recent work has gone beyond this to look at information from streams other than speech; what is available depends, of course, on the data and the application at hand.

Where video is available as well as audio, useful visual features may be extracted and used for segmentation. The task of segmenting TV news broadcasts can be aided if scene changes or commercial breaks can be detected: Maybury (1998) used the presence of black screens and logos to aid segmentation, and since then methods have advanced to include face detection and classification of scenes as reports, single or double anchorperson presentation, outdoor shots and so on (see, e.g. Avrithis *et al.*, 2000; Chaisorn *et al.*, 2003). In face-to-face dialogue, video information on participant pose and gesture can be helpful. Eisenstein *et al.* (2008) investigated the use of hand gesture features: as well as showing cohesion of lexical form, coherent topic segments often show cohesion of gestural form, and they incorporate this to help segment the discourse within a Bayesian model. Other modalities have been used too, for example note-taking in the meeting domain. Banerjee and Rudnicky (2007) provided meeting participants with a note-taking tool, and used their interaction with that tool to constrain and improve the output of their TextTiling-based segmenter.

Information external to the discourse itself may also be available, in particular details of the content of the topics likely to be discussed and/or their likely order. For meeting dialogue, this might take the form of a predefined agenda, something often distributed prior to formal meetings. This can certainly aid segmentation: Banerjee and Rudnicky (2007), for example, also exploit some knowledge of the defined agenda items and their related words. For broadcast monologue, this might take the form of a defined running list, or a model of how content is usually structured in a given domain. Barzilay and Lee (2004) show how to learn such a model, without supervision, for particular text types such as earthquake and accident reports, and use this to segment text for summarization purposes.

11.6.2 Topic Identification and Adaptation

In many applications, topic segmentation is a first step before topic *identification*: classifying or clustering the actual topics discussed within each segment (see the following chapter). As mentioned above, this can be one advantage of the use of generative models, as they effectively treat segmentation and identification as joint problems: as well as producing a segmentation, they derive models of the topics themselves, in terms either of language models (probability distributions over words) or the equivalent in some latent concept space (probability distributions over word vectors). These models can then be used to characterize the topics themselves, extract lists of descriptive keywords or word clouds to present to a user, or cluster related topics in different broadcasts.

However, as discussed at the start of this chapter, the conception of topic – and therefore the segmentation associated with it – can vary depending on the application at hand, the domain and even the interests and intentions of the user. A possible solution to this problem might be to use an *adaptive* approach to segmentation, allowing the segmentation (and the associated topics) to change as indicated by the user's behaviour or the emerging dataset. One way to approach this is via unsupervised methods which learn underlying topic models from entire datasets, such as the Bayesian approaches of Dowman *et al.* (2008) and Eisenstein and Barzilay (2008), for example. As more data is added to a user's personal dataset (as they browse new news broadcasts in which they are interested, or attend new relevant business meetings), the topic models learnt and the corresponding segmentation will change – and this can be achieved online using suitable algorithms (AlSumait *et al.*, 2008).

Another approach might be via supervised methods, using observed user behaviour as direct or indirect supervision. Adaptive topic modelling has been investigated as part of TDT, with models of document topic relevance adjusted according to user feedback as to whether a document is on- or off-topic (see, e.g. Allan *et al.*, 2000; Lo and Gauvain, 2001); but the effect on segmentation has received less attention. However, Banerjee and Rudnicky (2007) show how supervision can be exploited when segmenting meetings, by providing users with a note-taking tool annotated with agenda items: by observing the times when notes are made against particular agenda items, they can improve the accuracy of their agenda item segmenter. By allowing users to define their own topics, a user-specific model could be learnt; one can also imagine this being extended to other domains by observing suitable behaviour such as user interaction with a browser.

References

Allan J, Carbonell J, Doddington G, Yamron J and Yang Y 1998 Topic detection and tracking pilot study: Final report *Proceedings of the 1998 DARPA Broadcast News Transcription and Understanding Workshop*.

Allan J, Lavrenko V, Frey D and Khandelwal V 2000 UMass at TDT 2000 *Proceedings of the Topic Detection and Tracking workshop*, pp 109–115.

AlSumait L, Barbará D and Domeniconi C 2008 On-line LDA: Adaptive topic models for mining text streams with applications to topic detection and tracking *Proceedings of the IEEE International Conference on Data Mining*, Pisa, Italy.

Arguello J and Rosé C 2006 Topic segmentation of dialogue *Proceedings of the HLT-NAACL Workshop on Analyzing Conversations in Text and Speech*, New York, NY.

Asher N and Lascarides A 2003 *Logics of Conversation*. Cambridge University Press.

Avrithis Y, Tsapatsoulis N and Kollias S 2000 Broadcast news parsing using visual cues: A robust face detection approach *IEEE International Conference on Multimedia and Expo*, New York, NY.

Banerjee S and Rudnicky A 2006 Smartnotes: Implicit labeling of meeting data through user note-taking and browsing *Proceedings of the Human Language Techonolgy Conference of the NAACL, Companion Volume*.

Banerjee S and Rudnicky A 2007 Segmenting meetings into agenda items by extracting implicit supervision from human note-taking *Prooceedings of the International Conference on Intelligent User Interfaces (IUI'07)*. ACM, Honolulu, Hawaii.

Banerjee S, Rosé C and Rudnicky A 2005 The necessity of a meeting recording and playback system, and the benefit of topic-level annotations to meeting browsing *Proceedings of the 10th International Conference on Human-Computer Interaction*.

Barzilay R and Lee L 2004 Catching the drift: Probabilistic content models, with applications to generation and summarization *Proceedings of the 2004 Human Language Technology Conference of the North American Chapter of the Association for Computational Linguistics (HLT-NAACL)*, pp. 113–120.

Beeferman D, Berger A and Lafferty JD 1999 Statistical models for text segmentation. *Machine Learning* **34**(1-3), 177–210.

Blei D and Moreno P 2001 Topic segmentation with an aspect hidden Markov model *Proceedings of the 24th Annual International ACM SIGIR Conference on Research and Development in Information Retrieval*, pp. 343–348.

Blei D, Ng A and Jordan M 2003 Latent Dirichlet allocation. *Journal of Machine Learning Research* **3**, 993–1022.

Cassell J, Nakano Y, Bickmore TW, Sidner CL and Rich C 2001 Non-verbal cues for discourse structure *Proceedings of 39th Annual Meeting of the Association for Computational Linguistics*, pp 114–123. Association for Computational Linguistics, Toulouse, France.

Chaisorn L, Chua TS, Koh CK, Zhao Y, Xu H, Feng H and Tian Q 2003 A two-level multi-modal approach for story segmentation of large news video corpus *Proceedings of TRECVID*.

Choi FYY 2000 Advances in domain independent linear text segmentation *Proceedings of the 1st Meeting of the North American Chapter of the Association for Computational Linguistics (NAACL)*.

Choi FYY, Wiemer-Hastings P and Moore J 2001 Latent semantic analysis for text segmentation *Proceedings of EMNLP*.

Church K 1993 Char align: A program for aligning parallel texts at the character level *Proceedings of the 31st Annual Meeting of the Association for Computational Linguistics*, pp. 1–8. Association for Computational Linguistics, Columbus, Ohio, USA.

Doddington G 1998 The topic detection and tracking phase 2 (TDT2) evaluation plan *Proceedings of the DARPA Broadcast News Transcription and Understanding Workshop*, pp. 223–229. Morgan Kaufmann, Lansdowne, VA.

Dowman M, Savova V, Griffiths TL, Körding KP, Tenenbaum JB and Purver M 2008 A probabilistic model of meetings that combines words and discourse features. *IEEE Transactions on Audio, Speech, and Language Processing* **16**(7), 1238–1248.

Eisenstein J and Barzilay R 2008 Bayesian unsupervised topic segmentation *Proceedings of the 2008 Conference on Empirical Methods in Natural Language Processing*, pp. 334–343. Association for Computational Linguistics, Honolulu, Hawaii.

Eisenstein J, Barzilay R and Davis R 2008 Gestural cohesion for topic segmentation *Proceedings of ACL-08: HLT*, pp. 852–860. Association for Computational Linguistics, Columbus, Ohio.

Franz M, Ramabhadran B, Ward T and Picheny M 2003 Automated transcription and topic segmentation of large spoken archives *Proceedings of Eurospeech*, pp. 953–956.

Fügen C, Wölfel M, McDonough J, Ikbal S, Kraft F, Laskowski K, Ostendorf M, Stüker S and Kumatani K 2006 Advances in lecture recognition: The ISL RT-06S evaluation system *Proceedings of Interspeech-ICSLP*.

Galley M, McKeown K, Fosler-Lussier E and Jing H 2003 Discourse segmentation of multiparty conversation *Proceedings of the 41st Annual Meeting of the Association for Computational Linguistics (ACL)*.

Georgescul M, Clark A and Armstrong S 2006a An analysis of quantitative aspects in the evaluation of thematic segmentation algorithms *Proceedings of the 7th SIGdial Workshop on Discourse and Dialogue*, pp. 144–151. Association for Computational Linguistics, Sydney, Australia.

Georgescul M, Clark A and Armstrong S 2006b Word distributions for thematic segmentation in a support vector machine approach *Proceedings of the 10th Conference on Computational Natural Language Learning (CoNLL-X)*, pp. 101–108, New York City, New York.

Georgescul M, Clark A and Armstrong S 2007 Exploiting structural meeting-specific features for topic segmentation *Actes de la 14ème Conférence sur le Traitement Automatique des Langues Naturelles* Association pour le Traitement Automatique des Langues, Toulouse, France.

Georgescul M, Clark A and Armstrong S 2008 A comparative study of mixture models for automatic topic segmentation of multiparty dialogues *The 3rd International Joint Conference on Natural Language Processing (IJCNLP)*, Hyderabad, India.

Ginzburg J 2011 *The Interactive Stance: Meaning for Conversation* Oxford University Press Draft chapters available from: http://www.dcs.kcl.ac.uk/staff/ginzburg.

Glass J, Hazen T, Cypers S, Malioutov I, Huynh D and Barzilay R 2007 Recent progress in the MIT spoken lecture processing project *Proceedings of Interspeech*, Antwerp, Belgium.

Griffiths T and Steyvers M 2004 Finding scientific topics. *Proceedings of the National Academy of Science* **101**, 5228–5235.

Griffiths T, Steyvers M, Blei D and Tenenbaum J 2005 Integrating topics and syntax *Proceedings of NIPS '04, Advances in Neural Information Processing Systems 17*.

Grosz BJ and Sidner CL 1986 Attention, intentions, and the structure of discourse. *Computational Linguistics* **12**(3), 175–204.

Gruenstein A, Niekrasz J and Purver M 2008 Meeting structure annotation: Annotations collected with a general purpose toolkit In *Recent Trends in Discourse and Dialogue* (ed. Dybkjaer L and Minker W) *Text, Speech and Language Technology* vol. 39, pp 247–274, Springer-Verlag Dordrecht.

Hearst M 1997 TextTiling: Segmenting text into multi-paragraph subtopic passages. *Computational Linguistics* **23**(1), 33–64.

Hearst M and Plaunt C 1993 Subtopic structuring for full-length document access *Proceedings of the 16th Annual International ACM SIGIR Conference on Research and Development in Information Retrieval*, pp 59–68, Pittsburgh, PA.

Hearst MA 1994 Multi-paragraph segmentation of expository text *Proceedings of the 32nd Annual Meeting of the Association for Computational Linguistics (ACL)*, Los Cruces, New Mexico.

Hirschberg J and Litman D 1993 Empirical studies on the disambiguation of cue phrases. *Computational Linguistics* **19**(3), 501–530.

Hirschberg J and Nakatani C 1998 Acoustic indicators of topic segmentation *Proceedings of the 5th International Conference on Spoken Language Processing (ICSLP)*.

Hirschberg J and Nakatani CH 1996 A prosodic analysis of discourse segments in direction-giving monologues *Proceedings of the 34th Annual Meeting of the Association for Computational Linguistics*, pp 286–293. Association for Computational Linguistics, Santa Cruz, California, USA.

Hofmann T 1999 Probablistic latent semantic indexing *Proceedings of the 22nd Annual International ACM SIGIR Conference on Research and Development in Information Retrieval*, pp 50–57.

Hsueh PY and Moore J 2006 Automatic topic segmentation and labelling in multiparty dialogue *Proceedings of the 1st IEEE/ACM Workshop on Spoken Language Technology (SLT)*, Palm Beach, Aruba.

Hsueh PY, Moore J and Renals S 2006 Automatic segmentation of multiparty dialogue *Proceedings of the 11th Conference of the European Chapter of the Association for Computational Linguistics (EACL)*.

Janin A, Baron D, Edwards J, Ellis D, Gelbart D, Morgan N, Peskin B, Pfau T, Shriberg E, Stolcke A and Wooters C 2003 The ICSI meeting corpus *Proceedings of the 2003 International Conference on Acoustics, Speech, and Signal Processing (ICASSP)*.

Jurafsky D and Martin J 2009 *Speech and Language Processing* 2nd edn. Pearson Prentice Hall.

Landauer TK, Foltz PW and Laham D 1998 Introduction to latent semantic analysis. *Discourse Processes* **25**, 259–284.

Larsson S 2002 *Issue-based Dialogue Management* PhD Thesis Göteborg University. Also published as *Gothenburg Monographs in Linguistics 21*.

Lisowska A 2003 Multimodal interface design for the multimodal meeting domain: Preliminary indications from a query analysis study. Technical Report IM2.MDM-11, ISSCO, University of Geneva.

Lo Y and Gauvain J 2001 The LIMSI topic tracking system for TDT 2001 *Proceedings of the Topic Detection and Tracking Workshop*.

Malioutov I and Barzilay R 2006 Minimum cut model for spoken lecture segmentation *Proceedings of the 21st International Conference on Computational Linguistics and 44th Annual Meeting of the Association for Computational Linguistics*, pp 25–32. Association for Computational Linguistics, Sydney, Australia.

Mann W and Thompson S 1988 Rhetorical structure theory: Toward a functional theory of text organization. *Text* **8**(3), 243–281.

Manning C and Schütze H 1999 *Foundations of Statistical Natural Language Processing*. MIT Press.

Marcu D 2000 *The Theory and Practice of Discourse Parsing and Summarization*. MIT Press, Cambridge, MA.

Maybury MT 1998 Discourse cues for broadcast news segmentation *Proceedings of the 36th Annual Meeting of the Association for Computational Linguistics and 17th International Conference on Computational Linguistics, Volume 2*, pp 819–822. Association for Computational Linguistics, Montreal, Quebec, Canada.

McCowan I, Carletta J, Kraaij W, Ashby S, Bourban S, Flynn M, Guillemot M, Hain T, Kadlec J, Karaiskos V, Kronenthal M, Lathoud G, Lincoln M, Lisowska A, Post W, Reidsma D and Wellner P 2005 The AMI Meeting Corpus *Proceedings of Measuring Behavior 2005, the 5th International Conference on Methods and Techniques in Behavioral Research*, Wageningen, Netherlands.

Mohri M, Moreno P and Weinstein E 2009 A new quality measure for topic segmentation of text and speech *Conference of the International Speech Communication Association (Interspeech)*, Brighton, UK.

Morris J and Hirst G 1991 Lexical cohesion computed by thesaural relations as an indicator of the structure of text. *Computational Linguistics* **17**(1), 21–48.

Mulbregt PV, Carp I, Gillick L, Lowe S and Yamron J 1999 Segmentation of automatically transcribed broadcast news text *Proceedings of the DARPA Broadcast News Workshop*, pp 77–80. Morgan Kaufmann.

Niekrasz J and Moore J 2009 Participant subjectivity and involvement as a basis for discourse segmentation *Proceedings of the SIGDIAL 2009 Conference*, pp 54–61. Association for Computational Linguistics, London, UK.

Oard DW and Leuski A 2003 Searching recorded speech based on the temporal extent of topic labels *Proceedings of AAAI Spring Symposium on Intelligent Multimedia Knowledge Management*, Palo Alto, CA.

Olney A and Cai Z 2005 An orthonormal basis for topic segmentation in tutorial dialogue *Proceedings of Human Language Technology Conference and Conference on Empirical Methods in Natural Language Processing HLT/EMNLP*, pp 971–978. Association for Computational Linguistics, Vancouver, BC.

Passonneau RJ and Litman DJ 1997 Discourse segmentation by human and automated means. *Computational Linguistics* **23**(1), 103–139.

Passonneau RJ and Litman DJL 1996 Empirical analysis of three dimensions of spoken discourse: Segmentation, coherence and linguistic devices In *Interdisciplinary Perspectives on Discourse* (ed. Hovy E and Scott D) Springer-Verlag.

Pevzner L and Hearst M 2002 A critique and improvement of an evaluation metric for text segmentation. *Computational Linguistics* **28**(1), 19–36.

Polanyi L 1988 A formal model of discourse structure. *Journal of Pragmatics* **12**, 601–638.

Popescu-Belis A, Clark A, Georgescul M, Lalanne D and Zufferey S 2005 Shallow dialogue processing using machine learning algorithms (or not) In *Machine Learning for Multimodal Interaction: First International Workshop, MLMI 2004, Revised Selected Papers* (ed. Bengio S and Bourlard H) vol. 3361 of *Lecture Notes in Computer Science* Springer pp 277–290.

Power R, Scott D and Bouayad-Agha N 2003 Document structure. *Computational Linguistics* **29**, 211–260.

Purver M, Körding K, Griffiths T and Tenenbaum J 2006 Unsupervised topic modelling for multiparty spoken discourse *Proceedings of the 21st International Conference on Computational Linguistics and 44th Annual Meeting of the Association for Computational Linguistics (COLING-ACL)*, pp 17–24. Association for Computational Linguistics, Sydney, Australia.

Reynar J 1994 An automatic method of finding topic boundaries *Proceedings of the 32nd Annual Meeting of the Association for Computational Linguistics (ACL)*, pp 331–333. Association for Computational Linguistics, Las Cruces, NM.

Reynar J 1999 Statistical models for topic segmentation *Proceedings of the 37th Annual Meeting of the Association for Computational Linguistics (ACL)*, pp 357–364.

Sun Q, Li R, Luo D and Wu X 2008 Text segmentation with LDA-based Fisher kernel *Proceedings of ACL-08: HLT, Short Papers*, pp 269–272. Association for Computational Linguistics, Columbus, Ohio.

Trancoso I, Nunes R and Neves L 2006 Recognition of classroom lectures in European Portuguese *Proceedings of Interspeech-ICSLP*.

Tür G, Hakkani-Tür D, Stolcke A and Shriberg E 2001 Integrating prosodic and lexical cues for automatic topic segmentation. *Computational Linguistics* **27**(1), 31–57.

Utiyama M and Isahara H 2001 A statistical model for domain-independent text segmentation *Proceedings of 39th Annual Meeting of the Association for Computational Linguistics*, pp 499–506. Association for Computational Linguistics, Toulouse, France.

Vapnik VN 1995 *The Nature of Statistical Learning Theory*. Springer.

Yaari Y 1997 Segmentation of expository texts by hierarchical agglomerative clustering *Proceedings of RANLP*.

Yamron J, Carp I, Gillick L, Lowe S and van Mulbregt P 1998 A hidden Markov model approach to text segmentation and event tracking *Proceedings of the IEEE Conference on Acoustics, Speech, and Signal Processing*.

Youmans G 1991 A new tool for discourse analysis: The vocabulary-management profile. *Language* **67**(4), 763–789.

12

Topic Identification

Timothy J. Hazen
MIT Lincoln Laboratory, U.S.A.

In this chapter we discuss the problem of identifying the underlying topics beings discussed in spoken audio recordings. We focus primarily on the issues related to supervised topic classification or detection tasks using labeled training data, but we also discuss approaches for other related tasks including novel topic detection and unsupervised topic clustering. The chapter provides an overview of the common tasks and data sets, evaluation metrics, and algorithms most commonly used in this area of study.

12.1 Task Description

12.1.1 What is Topic Identification?

Topic identification is the task of identifying the topic (or topics) that pertain to an audio segment of recorded speech. To be consistent with the nomenclature used in the text-processing community, we will refer to a segment of recorded audio as an *audio document*. In our case we will assume each audio document is topically homogeneous (e.g. a single news story) and we wish to identify the relevant topic(s) pertaining to this document. This problem differs from the topic segmentation problem, in which an audio recording may contain a series of different topically homogeneous segments (e.g. different news stories), and the goal is to segment the full audio recording into these topically coherent segments. Topic segmentation is discussed in Chapter 11. In this chapter we will primarily discuss two general styles of topic identification, which we will refer to as *topic classification* and *topic detection*. As shorthand, we will henceforth refer to the general task of topic identification as *topic ID*.

In topic classification, it is assumed that a predetermined set of topics has been defined and each audio document will be classified as belonging to one and only one topic from this set. This style is sometimes referred to as *single-label categorization*. Topic classification is commonly used in tasks where the speech data must be sorted into unique bins or routed to specific people or applications. For example, the AT&T *How May I Help You?* automated

Spoken Language Understanding: Systems for Extracting Semantic Information from Speech, First Edition.
Edited by Gokhan Tur and Renato De Mori.

customer service system uses topic ID techniques to determine the underlying purpose of a customer's call in order to route the customer's call to an appropriate operator or automated system for handling the customer's question or issue (Gorin *et al.*, 1996).

In topic detection, it is assumed that an audio document can relate to any number of topics and an independent decision is made to detect the presence or absence of each topic of interest. This style is sometimes referred to as *multi-label categorization*. Topic detection is commonly used for tasks where topic labeling will allow for easier filtering, sorting, characterizing, searching, retrieving and consuming of speech data. For example, broadcast news stories could be tagged with one or more topic labels that would allow users to quickly locate and view particular stories about topics of their interest. It could also allow systems to aggregate information about an entire set of data in order to characterize the distribution of topics contained within that data.

Besides traditional classification and detection tasks, the field of topic ID also covers other related problems. In some tasks, new topics may arise over the course of time. For example, in news broadcasts novel events occur regularly requiring the creation of new topic classes for labeling future news stories related to these events. Customer service applications may also need to adapt to new issues or complaints that arise about their products. In these applications, the detection of novel topics or events is important, and this specialized area of the topic ID problem is often referred to as *novelty detection*.

In other tasks, the topics may not be known ahead of time, and the goal is to learn topic classes in an unsupervised fashion. This is generally referred to as the *topic clustering* problem, where individual audio documents are clustered into groups or hierarchical trees based on their similarity.

12.1.2 What are Topics?

In addition to defining the task of topic identification, we must also define what a *topic* is. There are a wide variety of ways in which topics can be defined, and these definitions may be very particular to specific applications and/or users. In many cases the human decisions for defining topic labels and assigning their relevancy to particular pieces of data can be subjective and arbitrary. For example, if we consider the commonly used application of email spam filtering, some people may view certain unsolicited emails (e.g. advertisements for mortgage refinancing services, announcements for scientific conferences, etc.) as useful and hence *not spam*, even though many others may label these emails as *spam*.

In some applications, such as customer service call routing, a specialized ontology containing not only high-level customer care topics but also hierarchical subtopic trees may be required for routing calls to particular customer care specialists or systems. These ontologies tend to be fairly rigid and manually crafted. For the application of news broadcast monitoring, a general purpose topic ontology could be used to help track the topics and sub-topics contained in news broadcasts. In this case the ontology can be fluid and automatically adjusted based on recent news events.

In other situations, an ontological approach is unnecessary. In the area of topic tracking in news broadcasts, the "topics" may be defined to be specific events, people, or entities. Stories are deemed relevant to a topic only if they make reference to the specific events or entities defining that topic. While a hierarchical ontology may well help describe the relationship between the individual entities being tracked, the tracking task may only require detection of references to the specific entities in question and not detection of any higher-level abstract topics.

In this chapter, we will not delve into the complexities of how and why topic labels are created and assigned, but rather we will assume that each task possesses an appropriate set of topic labels, and that each piece of data possesses appropriate truth labels stating which topics are (and are not) relevant to it. We will instead concentrate on describing the various algorithms used for performing topic identification tasks.

12.1.3 How is Topic Relevancy Defined?

In its standard form, topic identification assumes that a binary *relevant* or *not relevant* label for each topic can be placed on each audio document. From a machine learning standpoint, this allows the problem to be cast as a basic classification or detection problem. However, the relevancy of a particular topic to a particular audio document may not be so easily defined. Some documents may only be partially or peripherally related to a particular topic, and hence a more nuanced decision than a simple binary labeling would be appropriate. In other words, the task of topic identification could be viewed as a ranking task in which the goal is to rank documents on a continuous scale of relevancy to a particular topic. In this light, the problem could be cast as a regression task (in which a continuous valued relevancy measure is predicted) instead of a classification task (where a simple *relevant/not relevant* decision is made).

From a computational point of view, it may be just as straightforward to create a relevancy ranking system using standard regression techniques as it is to create a binary classification system. However, from an implementation standpoint, the regression task is typically impractical because it requires continuous valued relevancy values to be defined for each training example. Natural definitions of topic relevancy do not exist and most human-defined measures can be highly subjective, thus resulting in inconsistency across human labelers of a set of data. Even if a continuously scaled measure of relevancy that could be consistently labeled by humans existed, this type of information could still require a substantial amount of human effort to collect for typical speech data sets. For these reasons, this chapter will focus on problems in which topic relevancy for an audio document is simply defined using binary *relevant/not relevant* labels.

12.1.4 Characterizing the Constraints on Topic ID Tasks

There are a variety of constraints that can be used to characterize topic ID tasks. To begin with, there are the standard constraints that apply to all machine learning tasks, e.g. the number of different topic classes that apply to the data, the amount of training data that is available for learning a model, and the amount of test material available for making a decision. Like all machine learning tasks, topic ID performance should improve as more training data becomes available. Likewise, the accuracy in identifying the topic of a test sample should increase as the length of the test sample increases (i.e. the more speech that is heard about a topic, the easier it should be to identify that topic).

Beyond these standard constraints, there are several other important dimensions which can be used to describe topic ID tasks. Figure 12.1 provides a graphical representation of three primary constraints. In the figure, a three dimensional space is shown where each dimension represents a specific constraint, i.e. prepared versus extemporaneous, limited domain versus unlimited domain, and text versus speech. The figure shows where various topic ID tasks fall

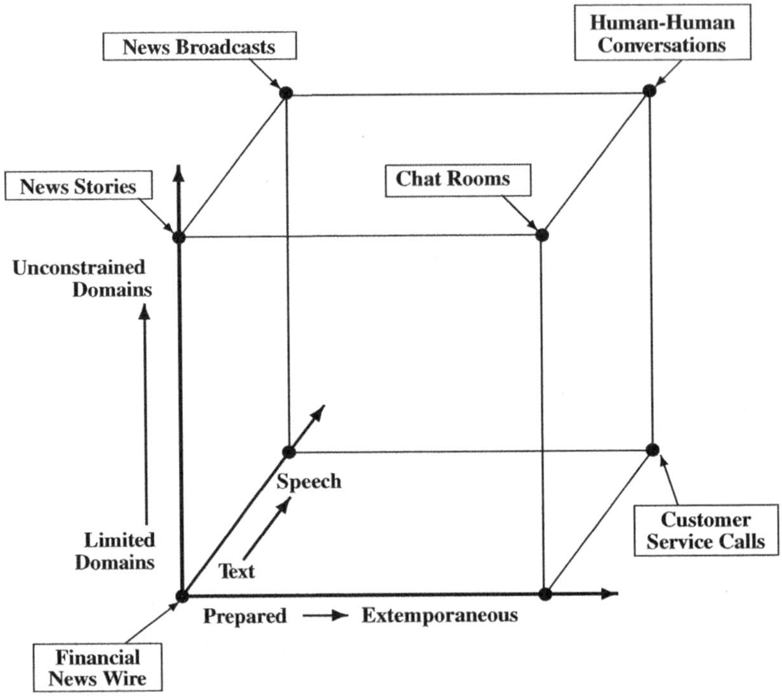

Figure 12.1 Graphical representation of different constraints on the topic ID problem, with example tasks for various combinations of these constraints

within this space. The origin of the space, at the lower-front-left of the figure, represents topic ID tasks that are the most constrained and presumably the easiest. Moving away from the origin, the constraints on the tasks are loosened, and topic ID tasks become more difficult. At the upper-back-right of the figure, the task of topic ID for open domain human/human conversations is the least constrained task and presumably the most difficult.

Along the x-axis of the figure, tasks are characterized by how prepared or extemporaneous their data is. Prepared news stories are general carefully edited and highly structured while extemporaneous telephone conversations or Internet chat room sessions tend to be less structured and more prone to off-topic diversions and communication errors (e.g. typographic errors or speech errors). Thus, the more extemporaneous the data is, the harder the topic ID task is likely to be.

Along the y-axis, tasks are characterized by how constrained or unconstrained the task domain is. News stories on a narrow sector of news (e.g. financial news wire stories, weather reports, etc.) or customer service telephone calls about a particular product or service, tend to be tightly constrained. In these cases the range of topics in the domain is confined, the vocabulary used to discuss the task is limited and focused, and the data is more likely to adhere to a particular structure used to convey information in that domain. As the domain becomes less constrained the topic ID task generally becomes more difficult.

Finally along the z-axis, the figure distinguishes between text-based tasks and speech-based tasks. In general, speech-based tasks are more difficult because the words are not given and must be deciphered from the audio. With the current state of automatic speech recognition (ASR) technology, this can be an errorful process that introduces noise into topic ID tasks. Because the introduction of the ASR process is the primary difference between text-based and speech-based topic ID, the rest of this chapter will focus on the issues related to extracting useful information from the audio signal and predicting the topic(s) discussed in the audio signal from these features.

12.1.5 Text-based Topic Identification

Before discussing speech-based topic ID, it is important to first acknowledge the topic ID research and development work that has been conducted in the text processing research community for many years. In this community topic identification is also commonly referred to as *text classification* or *text categorization*. A wide variety of practical systems have been produced for many text applications including e-mail spam filtering, e-mail sorting, inappropriate material detection, and sentiment classification within customer service surveys. Because of the successes in text classification, many of the common techniques used in speech-based topic identification have been borrowed and adapted from the text processing community. Overviews of common text-based topic identification techniques can be be found in a survey paper by Sebastiani (2002) and in a book chapter by Manning and Schütze (1999). Thus, in this chapter we will not attempt to provide a broad overview of all of the techniques that have been developed in the text processing community, but we will instead focus of those techniques that have been successfully ported from text processing to speech processing.

12.2 Challenges Using Speech Input

12.2.1 The Naive Approach to Speech-based Topic ID

At first glance, the most obvious way to perform speech-based topic ID is to first process the speech data with an automatic speech recognition (ASR) system and then pass the hypothesized transcript from the ASR system directly into standard text-based topic ID system. Unfortunately, this approach would only be guaranteed to work well under the conditions that the speech data is similar in style to text data and the ASR system is capable of producing high-quality transcriptions.

An example of data in which speech-based topic-ID yields comparable results to text-based topic-ID is prepared news broadcasts (Fiscus *et al.*, 1999). This type of data typically contains speech which is read from prepared texts which are similar in style to written news reports. Additionally news broadcasts are spoken by professional speakers who are recorded in pristine acoustic conditions using high-quality recording equipment. Thus, the error rates of state-of-the-art ASR systems on this data tend to be very low (Pallett *et al.*, 1999).

12.2.2 Challenges of Extemporaneous Speech

Unfortunately, not all speech data is as well prepared and pristine as broadcast news data. For many types of data, the style of the speech and the difficulties of the acoustic conditions can cause degradations in the accuracy of ASR generated transcripts. For example, let us consider the human/human conversational telephone speech data contained within the Fisher Corpus (Cieri *et al.*, 2003). Participants in this data collection were randomly paired

Prompt: *Do either of you consider any other countries to be a threat to US safety? If so, which countries and why?*
S1: Hi, my name is Robert.
S2: My name's Kevin, how you doing?
S1: Oh, pretty good. Where are you from?
S2: I'm from New York City.
S1: Oh, really. I'm from Michigan.
S2: Oh wow.
S1: Yeah. So uh - so uh - what do you think about this topic?
S2: Well, you know, I really don't think there's many countries that are, you know, really, could be possible threats. I mean, I think one of the main ones are China. You know, they're supposed to be somewhat of our ally now.
S1: Yeah, but you can never tell, because they're kind of laying low for now.
S2: Yeah. I'm not really worried about North Korea much.
S1: Yeah. That's the one they - they kind of over emphasized on the news.

⋮

Figure 12.2 The initial portion of a human/human conversation extracted from the Fisher Corpus

with other participants and requested to carry on a conversation about a randomly selected topic. To elicit discussion on a particular topic, the two participants were played a recorded prompt at the onset of each call. A typical conversation between two speakers is shown in Figure 12.2.

When examining transcripts such as the one in Figure 12.2, there are several things that are readily observed. First, the extemporaneous nature of speech during human/human conversation yields many spontaneous speech artifacts including filled pauses (e.g. *um* or *uh*), lexically filled pauses (e.g. *you know* or *i mean*), speech errors (e.g. mispronunciations, false starts, etc.), and grammatical errors. Next, human/human conversations often conform to the social norms of interpersonal communication and thus include non topical components such as greetings, introductions, back channel acknowledgments (e.g. *uh-huh* or *i see*), apologies, and good byes. Finally, extemporaneous conversations are often not well-structured and can digress from the primary intended topic of discussion.

The extent to which the various artifacts of extemporaneous speech affect the ability to perform automatic topic ID is unclear at this time as very little research has been conducted on this subject. A study by Boulis (2005) provides some evidence that automatic topic ID performance is not affected dramatically by the presence of speech disfluencies. However, the effect on topic ID performance of other stylistic elements of extemporaneous speech have not been studied.

12.2.3 Challenges of Imperfect Speech Recognition

Dramatically different styles of speech and qualities of acoustic conditions can cause significant reductions in the accuracy of typical ASR systems. For example, speech recognition error rates are typically significantly higher on conversational telephone speech than they are on news broadcasts (Fiscus *et al.*, 2004). Figure 12.3 shows the top-choice transcript generated by an ASR system for the same portion of the Fisher conversation shown in Figure 12.2. In this

Prompt: *Do either of you consider any other countries to be a threat to US safety? If so, which countries and why?*
S1: hi **um but or**
S2: my name's kevin **party don't**
S1: oh pretty good where are you from
S2: **uh have** new york city
S1: oh really i'm from michigan
S2: oh wow
S1: yeah **and also um** uh what do you think about **the** topic
S2: well **it** you know i really don't think there's many countries that are you know really, could be possible threats i mean i think one of the main ones **in** china you know, **older** supposed to be **someone** of our **l. a.** now
S1: yeah, but you can never tell, because they're kind of **a girlfriend** for now
S2: yeah i'm not really worried **and uh** north korea **march**
S1: yeah **and** that's the one they they kind of **for exercise all** the news
⋮

Figure 12.3 The initial portion of the top-choice transcript produced by an ASR engine for the same sample conversation from the Fisher corpus contained in Figure 12.2. Words highlighted in bold-face represent the errors made by the ASR system. Words underlined are important content words for the topic that were correctly recognized by the ASR system

transcript, the bold-face words represent recognition errors made by the ASR system. In this example, there are 28 recognition errors over 119 words spoken by the participants. This corresponds to a speech recognition error rate of 23.5%. Error rates of this magnitude are typical of today's state-of-the-art ASR systems on the Fisher corpus.

In examining the transcript in Figure 12.3 it is easy to see that speech recognition errors can harm the ability of a reader to fully comprehend the underlying passage of speech. Despite imperfect ASR, studies have shown that humans can at least partially comprehend errorful transcripts (Jones *et al.*, 2003; Munteanu *et al.*, 2006) and full comprehension can be achieved when word error rates decrease below 15% (Bain *et al.*, 2005). However, full comprehension of a passage is often not needed to identify the underlying topic. Instead, it is often only necessary to observe particular key words or phrases to determine the topic. This is observed anecdotally in the passage in Figure 12.3 where the correctly recognized content words that are important for identifying the topic of the conversation have been underlined. It has been shown that ASR systems are generally better at recognizing longer content-bearing terms than they are at recognizing shorter function words (Lee, 1990). Thus, it can be expected that topic ID could still be performed reliably, even for speech passages containing high word error rates, provided the recognition system is able to correctly hypothesize many of the important content-bearing words.

12.2.4 Challenges of Unconstrained Domains

As speech-based topic ID moves from tightly constrained domains to more unconstrained domains, the likelihood increases that the data used to train an ASR system may be poorly matched to data observed during the system's actual use. Ideally, both the ASR system and the topic ID system would be trained on data from the same domain. However, the training of an ASR system requires large amounts of accurately transcribed data, and it may not always be feasible to obtain such data for the task at hand.

When using a mismatched ASR system, one potentially serious problem for topic ID is that many of the important content-bearing words in the domain of interest may not be included in the lexicon and language model used by the ASR system. In this case, the ASR system is completely unable to hypothesize these words and will always hypothesize other words from its vocabulary in their place. This problem is typically referred to as the *out-of-vocabulary* (OOV) word problem.

A popular strategy for addressing the OOV problem in many speech understanding applications, such as spoken document retrieval, is to revert to phonetic processing of the speech (Chelba *et al.*, 2008). In these cases, the process of searching for words is replaced by a process which searches for the underlying string of phonetic units (or phones) representing these words. Thus, for the topic ID problem, if the word *cat* was an important word for a particular topic ID task, the system would need to discover that the string of phonetic units [k ae t] carries content-bearing information when observed in an audio document.

12.3 Applications and Benchmark Tasks

While the text-based topic ID community has for many years studied an extremely wide variety of application areas and generated a wide range of benchmark tasks and corpora, the range of tasks and corpora available for speech-based topic ID is considerably smaller. In fact topic identification research on speech data did not begin in earnest until the early 1990s primarily because of a lack of appropriate data. One of the earliest studies into speech-based topic identification was conducted by Rose *et al.* (1991) using only a small collection of 510 30-second descriptive speech monologues covering 6 different scenarios (e.g. toy descriptions, photographic interpretation, map reading, etc.). As larger corpora became available during the 1990s, prominent research efforts began to emerge generally using one of three different types of data classes: (1) broadcast news stories, (2) human/human conversations, and (3) customer service calls. While other speech-based application areas may exist, this chapter will focus its discussion on these three tasks.

12.3.1 The TDT Project

Some of the most widely studied speech-based topic ID benchmark tasks come from the DARPA Topic Detection and Tracking (TDT) project which began in 1998 and continued for several more years into the next decade (Wayne, 2000). This project generated two large corpora, TDT-2 and TDT-3, which support a variety of topic ID oriented tasks (Cieri *et al.*, 2000). TDT-2 contains television and radio broadcast news audio recordings as well as text-based news-wire and web-site stories collected during the first six months of 1998. For speech-based processing the corpus contained over 600 hours of audio containing 53 620 stories in English and 18 721 stories in Chinese. TDT-3 was collected in a similar fashion and contains additional 600 hours of audio containing 31 276 English stories and 12 341 Chinese stories collected during the last three months of 1998. These corpora were organized and annotated to support the following core technical tasks:

1. Topic segmentation (i.e. finding topically homogeneous regions in broadcasts)
2. Topic tracking (i.e. identifying new stories on a given topic)
3. Topic clustering (i.e. unsupervised grouping of stories into topics)
4. New topic detection (i.e. detecting the first story about a new topic)
5. Story linking (i.e. determining if two stories are on the same topic)

In order to support this style of research, stories were annotated with *event* and *topic* labels. An event is defined as "a specific thing that happens at a specific time and place along with its necessary prerequisites and consequences", and a topic is defined as "a collection of related events and activities". A group of senior annotators at the Linguistic Data Consortium were employed to identify events and define the list of topics. Annotators then marked all stories with relevant event and topic labels.

From 1998 to 2004, a series of TDT evaluations were conducted by NIST to benchmark the performance of submitted TDT systems. These evaluations attracted participants from a variety of international laboratories in both industry and academia. Details of these evaluations can be found on the NIST web site (http://www.itl.nist.gov/iaui/894.01/tests/tdt/).

12.3.2 The Switchboard and Fisher Corpora

The Switchboard and Fisher corpora are collections of human-human conversations recorded over the telephone lines (Cieri *et al.*, 2003). These corpora were collected primarily for research into automatic recognition of telephone-based conversational speech. During data collection, two participants were connected over the telephone network and were instructed to carry on a conversation. To ensure that two people who had never spoken before could conduct a meaningful conversation, the participants were played a prompt instructing them to discuss a randomly selected topic. Figure 12.2 provides an example prompt and conversation from the Fisher corpus. The original Switchboard corpus was collected in 1990 and contained 2400 conversations covering 70 different topics. An additional Switchboard data collection known as Switchboard-2 was subsequently collected, though to date it has primarily been used for speaker recognition research. In 2003 a new series of collections using a similar collection paradigm were initiated and named the Fisher corpus. The initial collection, referred to as the Fisher English Phase 1 corpus, contained 5850 conversations covering 40 different prompted topics. Additional collections in Chinese and Arabic were also subsequently collected.

Because all of the Switchboard and Fisher conversations were elicited with a topic-specific prompt, various research projects have utilized these corpora for topic ID investigations (Carlson, 1996; Gish *et al.*, 2009; Hazen *et al.*, 2007; McDonough *et al.*, 1994; Peskin *et al.*, 1996). The corpora are pre-labeled with the topic prompt, but because the data collection was primarily intended for speech recognition work, the recordings were not vetted to ensure the conversations' fidelity to their prompted topics. In fact, it is not uncommon for participants to stray off-topic during a conversation. Researchers who use these corpora typically construct systems to identify the prompted topic and do not attempt to track fidelity to, or divergence from, that topic.

12.3.3 Customer Service/Call Routing Applications

Numerous studies have been conducted in the areas of customer service and call routing. These include studies using calls to AT&T's *How may I help you* system (Gorin *et al.*, 1996), a banking services call center (Chu-Carroll and Carpenter, 1999; Kuo and Lee, 2003), and an IT service center (Tang *et al.*, 2003). Unfortunately, because of proprietary issues and privacy concerns, the corpora used in these studies are not publically available, making open evaluations on these data sets impossible. A more thorough discussion of these applications can be found in Chapter 7.

12.4 Evaluation Metrics

12.4.1 Topic Scoring

To evaluate the performance of a topic ID system, begin by assuming that a mechanism has been created and trained which produces topic relevancy scores for new test documents. Each document will be represented as a vector $\vec{x}$ of features extracted from the document and a set of N_T topic classes of interest is represented as:

$$T = \{t_1, \ldots, t_{N_T}\} \tag{12.1}$$

From these definitions, the scoring function for a document for a particular topic class t is expressed as $S(\vec{x}|t)$. Given the full collection of scores over all text documents and all topics, topic ID performance can thus be evaluated in a variety of ways.

12.4.2 Classification Error Rate

In situations where closed-set classification or single-label categorization is being applied, evaluations are typically conducted using a standard classification error rate measure. The hypothesized class t_h for a document is given as:

$$t_h = \max_{\forall t \in T} S(\vec{x}|t) \tag{12.2}$$

The classification error rate is the percentage of all test documents whose hypothesized topic does not match the true topic. The absolute value of this measure is highly dependent upon the specifics of the task (e.g. the number of classes, the prior likelihoods of each class, etc.), and are thus difficult to compare across tasks. This measure has typically been used to evaluate call routing applications and closed-set classification experiments on the Switchboard and Fisher corpora.

12.4.3 Detection-based Evaluation Metrics

Because many tasks are posed as detection tasks (i.e. detect which topics are present in a document) instead of closed-set classification tasks, evaluation measures of detection performance are required. In detection tasks, individual topic detectors are typically evaluated independently. In these cases, documents are ranked by the score $S(\vec{x}|t)$ for a particular topic class t. A detection threshold can be applied to the ranked list of scores such that all documents with scores larger than the threshold are *accepted* as hypothesized detections of the topic, and all other documents are *rejected*. For each detector there are two different type of errors that can be made: (1) missed detections, or *misses*, of true examples of the topic, and (2) false detections, or *false alarms*, of documents that are not related to the topic. The particular setting of the detection threshold is often referred to as the system's *operating point*.

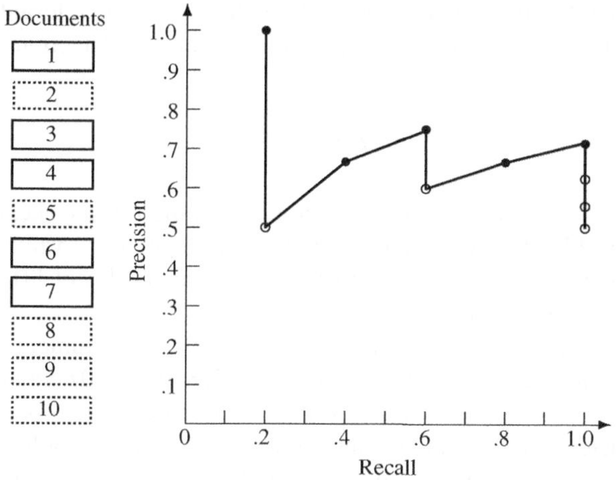

Figure 12.4 On the left is a ranked order list of ten documents with the solid-boxed documents (1, 3, 4, 6 and 7) representing positive example a topic and the dash-boxed documents (2, 5, 8, 9 and 10) representing negative examples of a topic. On the right is the precision/recall curve resulting from the ranked list on the left

The left-hand side of Figure 12.4 shows an example ranked list of 10 documents that could result from a topic detector with document 1 receiving the largest score and document 10 receiving the smallest score. The solid-boxed documents (1, 3, 4, 6 and 7) represent positive examples of the topic and the dash-boxed documents (2, 5, 8, 9 and 10) represent negative examples of the topic. If the detection threshold were set such that the top four documents were hypothesized detections of the topic and the bottom six documents were hypothesized rejections, the system would have made three total detection errors; document 2 would be considered a false alarm and documents 6 and 7 would be considered misses.

There are two widely used approaches for characterizing the relationship between misses and false alarms; (1) the precision/recall curve, (PR) and (2) the detection error trade-off (DET) curve or its close relative, the receiver/operator characteristic (ROC) curve. Details of these two evaluation approaches are discussed in the following subsections. Additionally, there is often a desire to distill the qualitative information in a PR or DET curve down to a single number.

12.4.3.1 Precision/Recall Curves and Measures

The precision/recall (PR) curve is widely used in the information retrieval community for evaluating rank-ordered lists produced by detection systems and has often been applied to the topic detection problem. The PR curve plots the relationship between two detection measures, *precision* and *recall*, as the value of the topic detection threshold is swept through all possible values. For a given detection threshold, precision is defined to be the fraction of all detected documents that actually contain the topic of interest, while recall is defined to be the fraction of all documents containing the topic of interest that are detected.

Mathematically, precision is defined as

$$P = \frac{N_{det}}{N_{hyp}} \tag{12.3}$$

where N_{hyp} is the number documents that are hypothesized to be relevant to the topic while N_{det} is the number of these hypothesized documents that are true detections of the topic. Recall is defined as

$$R = \frac{N_{det}}{N_{pos}} \tag{12.4}$$

where N_{pos} is the total number of *positive* documents in the full list (i.e. documents that are relevant to the topic). Ideally, the system would produce a precision value of 1 (i.e. the list of hypothesized documents contains no false alarms) and a recall value of 1 (i.e. all of the relevant documents for the topic are returned in the list).

Figure 12.4 shows an example PR curve for a ranked list of 10 documents (with documents 1, 3, 4, 6 and 7 being positive examples and documents 2, 5, 8, 9 and 10 being negative examples). Each point on the curve shows the precision and recall values at a particular *operating point* (i.e. at a particular detection threshold setting). As the detection threshold is swept through the ranked list, each new false alarm (i.e. the open circles on the figure) causes the precision to drop. Each new correct detection (i.e. the solid circles on the figure), causes both the precision and the recall to increase. As a result, the PR curve tends to have a non monotonic saw tooth shape when examined at the local data-point level, though curves generated from large amounts of data tend be smooth when viewed at the macro level.

Because researchers often prefer to distill the performance of their system down to single number, PR curves are often reduced to a single value known as *average precision*. Average precision is computed by averaging the precision values from the PR curve at the points where each new correct detection is introduced into the ranked list. Visually, this corresponds to averaging the precision values of all of the solid circle data points in Figure 12.4. Thus the average precision of the PR curve in Figure 12.4 is computed as:

$$P_{avg} = (1 + \frac{2}{3} + \frac{3}{4} + \frac{4}{6} + \frac{5}{7})/5 \approx 0.76 \tag{12.5}$$

The *average precision* measure is used to characterize the performance of a single detection task. In many topic detection evaluations, multiple topic detectors are typically employed. In these cases, an overall performance measure for topic detection can be computed by averaging the average precision measure over all of the individual topic detectors. This measure is commonly referred to as *mean average precision*.

Another commonly used measure is R-precision, which is the precision of the top R items in the ranked list where R refers to the total number of relevant documents (i.e N_{pos}) in the list. R-precision is also the point in the PR curve where precision and recall are equal. The R-precision for the PR curve in Figure 12.4 is 0.6, which is the precision of the top 5 items in the list. Similarly, a group of detectors can be evaluated using the average of the R-precision values over all topic detectors.

The language processing and information retrieval communities have long used precision and recall as evaluation metrics because they offer a natural and easy-to-understand interpretation of system performance. Additionally, for some tasks, precision is the only important and measurable metric. For example, in web-based searches, the full collection of documents may be so large that it is not practically possible to know how many valid documents for a particular topic actually exist. In this case, an evaluation may only focus on the precision of the top N documents returned by the system without ever attempting to estimate a recall value.

The precision and recall measures do have drawbacks however. In particular, precision and recall are sensitive to the prior likelihoods of topics being detected. The less likely a topic is within a data set, the lower the average precision will be for that topic on that data set. Thus, measures such as mean average precision cannot be easy compared across different evaluation sets if the prior likelihoods of topics are dramatically different across these sets. Additionally, the PR curve is not strictly a monotonically decreasing curve (as is observed in the sawtooth shape of the curve in Figure 12.4), though smoothed versions of PR curves for large lists typically show a steadily decreasing precision value as the recall value increases.

12.4.3.2 Detection Error Trade-off Curves and Measures

The traditional evaluation metric in many detection tasks is the receiver operating characteristic (ROC) curve, or its close relative, the detection-error trade-off (DET) curve (Martin *et al.*, 1997). The ROC curve measures the probability of correctly detecting a positive test example against the probability of falsely detecting a negative test example. If the number of positive test examples in a test set is defined as N_{pos} and the number of these test examples that are correctly detected is defined as N_{det}, then the estimated detection probability is defined as:

$$P_{det} = \frac{N_{det}}{N_{pos}} \tag{12.6}$$

Similarly, if the number of negative test examples in a test set is defined as N_{neg} and the number of these test examples that are falsely detected is defined as N_{fa}, then the estimated false alarm rate is expressed as:

$$P_{fa} = \frac{N_{fa}}{N_{neg}} \tag{12.7}$$

The ROC curve plots P_{det} against P_{fa} as the detection threshold is swept.

The DET curve displays the same quantities as the ROC curve, but instead of P_{det} it plots the probability P_{miss} of missing a positive test example where $P_{miss} = 1 - P_{det}$. Figure 12.5 shows the DET curve for the same example data set used for the PR curve in Figure 12.4. As the detection threshold is swept through the ranked list, each new detection (i.e. the solid circles on the DET curve) causes the miss rate to drop. Each new false alarm (i.e. the open circles on the figure), causes the false alarm rate to increase. As a result, the DET curve, when examined at the local data-point level, yields a sequence of decreasing steps. Although the DET curve in Figure 12.5 uses a linear scale between 0 and 1 for the x and y axes, it is common practice to plot DET curves using a log scale for the axes, thus making it easier to distinguish differences in systems with very low miss and false alarm rates.

A variety of techniques for reducing the information in the ROC or DET curves down to a single-valued metric are also available. One common metric applied to the ROC curve is the area under the curve (AUC) measure, which is quite simply the total area under the ROC curve for all false alarm rates between 0 and 1. The AUC measure is also equivalent to the likelihood that a randomly selected positive example of a class will yield a higher topic relevancy score than a randomly selected negative example of that class (Fawcett, 2006).

Another commonly used measure is the equal error rate (EER) of the DET curve. This is the point on the DET curve where the miss rate is equal to the false alarm rate. When examining detection performance over multiple classes, it is common practice for researchers

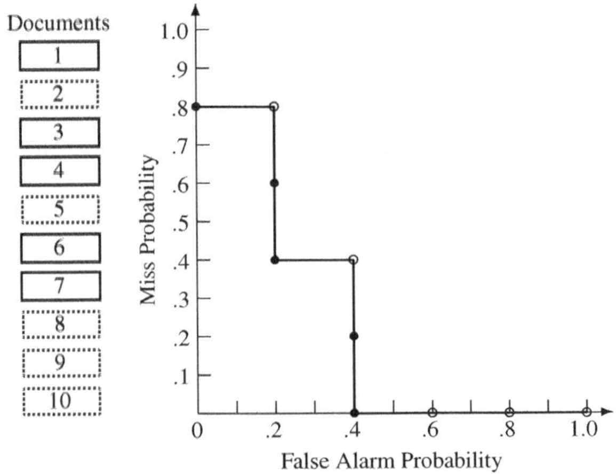

Figure 12.5 On the left is same ranked order list of ten documents observed in Figure 12.4. On the right is the detection error trade-off (DET) curve resulting from the ranked list on the left

to independently compute the EER point for each detector and then report the *average EER* value over all classes.

The average EER is useful for computing the expected EER performance of any given detector, but it assumes that a different detection threshold can be selected for each topic class in order to achieve the EER operating point. In some circumstances, it may be impractical to set the desired detection threshold of each topic detector independently and a metric that employs a single detection threshold over all classes is preferred. In these cases, the scores from all detectors can be first pooled into a single set of scores and then the EER can be computed from the pooled scores. This is sometime referred to as the *pooled EER* value.

DET curves have one major advantage over precision/recall curves; they represent performance in a manner which is independent of the prior probabilities of the classes to be detected. As a result, NIST has used the DET curve as it primary evaluation mechanism for a variety of speech related detection tasks including topic detection, speaker identification, language identification and spoken term detection (Martin *et al.*, 2004).

12.4.3.3 Cost-based Measures

While PR curves and DET curves provide a full characterization of the ranked lists produced by systems, many tasks require the selection of a specific operating point on the curve. Operating points are typically selected to balance the relative deleterious effects of misses and false alarms. Some tasks may require high recall at the expense of reduced precision, while others may sacrifice recall to achieve high precision. In situations such as these, the system may not only be responsible for producing the ranked list of documents, but also for determining a proper decision threshold for achieving an appropriate operating point.

NIST typically uses a detection cost measure to evaluate system performance in such cases (Fiscus, 2004). A typical detection cost measure is expressed as:

$$C_{det} = C_{miss} * P_{miss} * P_{target} + C_{fa} * P_{fa} * (1 - P_{target}) \tag{12.8}$$

Here C_{det} is the total cost associated with the chosen operating point of a detection system where zero is the ideal value. The individual costs incurred by misses and false alarms are controlled by the cost parameters C_{miss} and C_{fa}. The prior likelihood of observing the target topic is represented as P_{target}. The values of P_{miss} and P_{fa} are determined by evaluating the system's performance at a prespecified detection threshold. A related cost measure is C_{min} which is the minimum possible cost for a task if the optimal detection threshold were chosen. If $C_{det} \approx C_{min}$, the selected threshold is said to be well *calibrated* to the cost measure.

12.5 Technical Approaches

12.5.1 Topic ID System Overview

Speech-based topic identification systems generally use four basic steps when converting audio documents into topic ID hypotheses. Figure 12.6 provides a block diagram of a typical topic ID system. The four basic stages of a system are:

1. **Automatic speech recognition:** An audio document d is first processed by an automatic speech recognition (ASR) system which generates a set of ASR hypotheses W. In most systems, W will contain word hypotheses, though subword units such as phones or syllables are also possible outputs of an ASR system.
2. **Feature extraction:** From W, a set of features $\vec{c}$ is extracted describing the content of W. Typically $\vec{c}$ contains the frequency counts of the words observed in W.
3. **Feature transformation:** The feature vector $\vec{c}$ will typically be high in dimension and include many features with limited or no discriminative value for topic ID (e.g. counts of non-content-bearing words such as articles, prepositions, auxiliary verbs, etc.). As such, it is common for the feature space to be transformed in some manner in order to reduce the dimensionality and/or boost the contribution of the important content bearing information contained in $\vec{c}$. Techniques such as feature selection, feature weighting, latent semantic analysis (LSA) or latent Dirichlet allocation (LDA) are often applied to $\vec{c}$ to generate a transformed feature vector $\vec{x}$.
4. **Classification:** Given a feature vector $\vec{x}$ the final step is to generate classification scores and decisions for each topic using a topic ID classifier. Common classifiers applied to the topic ID problem are naive Bayes classifiers, support vector machines (SVMs), and nearest neighbor classifiers, though many other types of classifiers are also possible.

12.5.2 Automatic Speech Recognition

As discussed earlier, the biggest difference between text-based and speech-based topic ID is that the words spoken in an audio document are not known and must be hypothesized from the audio. If ASR technology could produce perfect transcripts, then speech-based topic ID

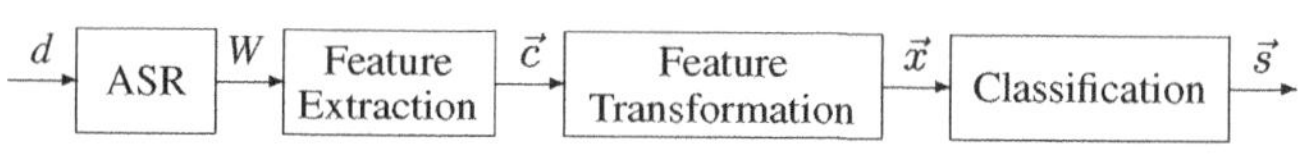

Figure 12.6 Block diagram of the four primary steps taken by a topic ID system during the processing of an audio document

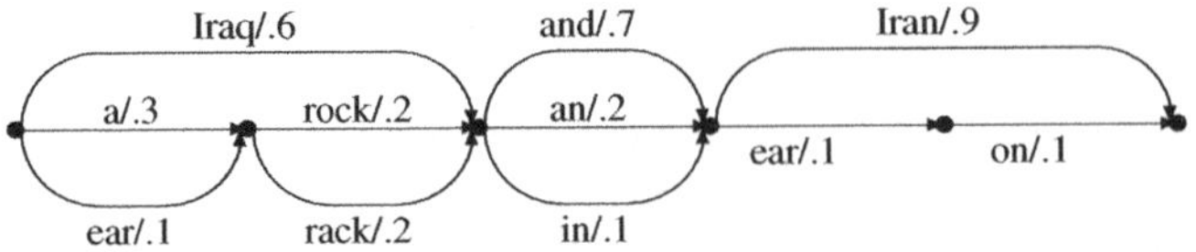

Figure 12.7 Illustration of a possible posterior lattice generated by a word-based ASR system

would simply require passing the output of the ASR system for an audio document to the input of a standard text-based topic ID system. Unfortunately, today's ASR technology is far from perfect and speech recognition errors are commonplace.

Even with errorful processing, the single best ASR hypothesis could be generated for each audio document and the errorful string could still be processed with standard text-processing techniques. However, the use of such hard decisions is typically sub-optimal, and most speech processing applications perform better when the ASR engine produces a collection of alternate hypotheses with associated likelihoods. The most common representation in these cases is the posterior lattice, such as the one shown in Figure 12.7. The posterior lattice provides a graph of alternate hypotheses where the nodes represent potential locations of boundaries between words and the arcs represent alternate word hypotheses with estimated posterior probabilities.

For a variety of reasons, sufficiently accurate word recognition may not be possible for some applications. For example, some application areas may require a specialized vocabulary, but there may be little to no transcribed data from this area available for developing an adequate lexicon and language model for the ASR system. In these cases, the topic ID system may need to rely on phonetic recognition. Numerous studies using phonetic ASR output have shown the feasibility of speech-based topic ID under this challenging condition where the words are unknown (Kuhn *et al.*, 1997; Nöth *et al.*, 1997; Paaß *et al.*, 2002; Wright *et al.*, 1996). In some extreme cases, it is possible that topic identification capability is needed in a new language for which limited or no transcribed data is available to train even a limited phonetic system. In this case it is still possible to perform topic ID using a phonetic recognition system from another language (Hazen *et al.*, 2007) or an in-language phonetic system trained in a completely unsupervised fashion without the use of transcriptions (Gish *et al.*, 2009). In a similar fashion to word recognition, a phonetic ASR system can generate posterior lattices for segments of speech. Figure 12.8 shows an example posterior lattice for a phonetic ASR system.

12.5.3 Feature Extraction

In text-based topic ID the most common approach to feature extraction is known as the *bag of words* approach. In this approach, the features are simply the individual counts reflecting how often each vocabulary item appears in the text. The order of the words and any syntactic or

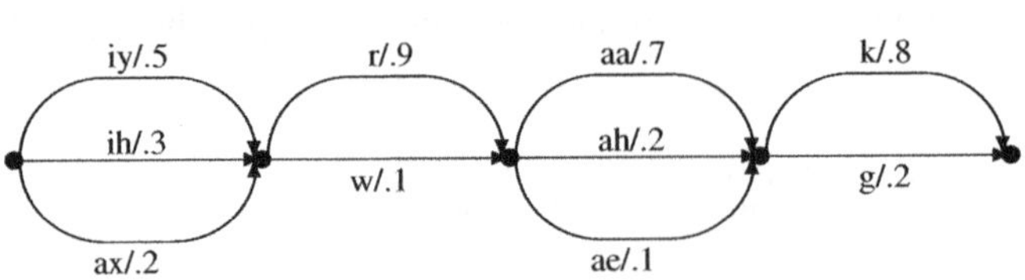

Figure 12.8 Illustration of a possible posterior lattice generated by a phone-based ASR system

Table 12.1 Expected counts derived from lattice posterior probabilities for the words in Figure 12.7 and the triphone sequences in Figure 12.8

Words		Triphones	
Iran	0.9	r:aa:k	0.504
and	0.7	iy:r:aa	0.315
Iraq	0.6	ih:r:aa	0.189
a	0.3	r:ah:k	0.144
an	0.2	ax:r:aa	0.126
ear	0.2	r:aa:g	0.126
rock	0.2	iy:r:ah	0.090
rack	0.2	r:ae:k	0.072
in	0.1	w:aa:k	0.056
on	0.1	ih:r:ah	0.054
		⋮	⋮

semantic relationships between the words are completely ignored in this approach. Despite its relative simplicity, this approach works surprisingly well and does not require any higher-level knowledge. While this chapter will focus its discussion on simple unigram counts, it should be noted that it is also possible to provide a richer, though higher dimensional, representation of a document by counting events such as word n-grams or word co-occurrences within utterances.

In speech-based topic ID, the underlying words are not known *a priori* and the system must rely on posterior estimates of the likelihood of words as generated by an ASR system. Thus, instead of direct counting of words from text, the system must estimate counts for the words in the vocabulary based on the posterior probabilities of the words present in the word lattices generated by the ASR system. For example, the left-hand column of Table 12.1 shows the estimated counts for words present in the word lattice in Figure 12.7. Note that the word *ear* has an estimated count of 0.2, which is the sum of the posterior probabilities from the two arcs on which it appears. For a full audio document, the estimated count for any given word is the sum of the posterior probabilities of all arcs containing that word over all lattices from all speech utterances in the document. The generation and use of lattices has become commonplace in the automatic speech recognition community and useful open source software packages, such as the SRI Language Modeling Toolkit (Stolcke, 2002), provide useful tools for processing such lattices.

12.5.4 Feature Selection and Transformation

Once a raw set of feature counts $\vec{c}$ have been extracted from the ASR hypotheses, it is common practice to apply some form of dimensionality reduction and/or feature space transformation. Common techniques include feature selection, feature weighting, and feature vector normalization. These techniques are discussed in this subsection, while a second class of transformation methods which convert vectors in a term space into vectors in a concept space, such as latent semantic analysis (LSA) and latent Dirichlet allocation (LDA), will be discussed in the next subsection. The basic goal in all cases is to transform the extracted feature counts into a new vectorial representation that is appropriate for the classification method being used.

12.5.4.1 The Cosine Similarity Measure and Unit Length Normalization

In order to understand the need for feature selection and/or feature weighting, let us first discuss the cosine similarity measure for comparing two feature vectors. The cosine similarity measure can be used as the basis for several classification techniques including k-nearest neighbors and support vector machines.

When comparing the feature vectors $\vec{x}_1$ and $\vec{x}_2$ of two documents d_1 and d_2, the cosine similarity measure is defined as:

$$S(\vec{x}_1, \vec{x}_2) = \cos(\theta) = \frac{\vec{x}_1 \cdot \vec{x}_2}{\|\vec{x}_1\| \|\vec{x}_2\|} \tag{12.9}$$

The cosine similarity measure is simply the cosine of the angle θ between vectors $\vec{x}_1$ and $\vec{x}_2$. It is easily computed by normalizing $\vec{x}_1$ and $\vec{x}_2$ to unit length and then computing the dot product between them. Normalization of the vectors to unit length is often referred to as L2 normalization. If $\vec{x}_1$ and $\vec{x}_2$ are derived from feature counts, and hence are only comprised of positive valued features, the similarity measure will only vary between values of 0 (for perfectly orthogonal vectors) and 1 (for vectors that are identical after L2 normalization).

12.5.4.2 Divergence Measures and Relative Frequency Normalization

An alternative to L2 normalization of feature vectors is L1 normalization. Applying L1 normalization to the raw count vector $\vec{c}$ is accomplished as follows:

$$x_i = \frac{c_i}{\sum_{\forall j} c_j} \tag{12.10}$$

In effect this normalization converts the raw counts into relative frequencies such that:

$$\sum_{\forall i} x_i = 1 \tag{12.11}$$

Using this normalization, feature counts are converted into the maximum likelihood estimate of the underlying probability distribution that generated the feature counts. Representing the feature vectors as probability distributions allows them to be compared with information theoretic similarity measures such as Kullback–Leibler divergence or Jeffrey divergence.

12.5.4.3 Feature Selection

Generally, vectors containing the raw counts of all features do not yield useful similarity measures because the count vectors are dominated by the more frequent words (such as function words) which often contain little or no information about the content of the document. Thus, the feature vectors are often adjusted such that the common non-content-bearing words are either completely removed or substantially reduced in weight, while the weights of the important content words are boosted.

Feature selection is a very common technique in which a set of features that are most useful for topic ID are selected, and the remaining features are discarded. An extremely common technique is the use of a *stop list*, i.e. a list of the most commonly occurring function words including articles, auxiliary verbs, prepositions, etc. which should be ignored during topic ID. If is not uncommon for stop lists to be manually crafted.

A wide variety of automatic methods have also been proposed for ranking the usefulness of features for the task of topic ID. In these methods, the features in the system vocabulary are ranked by a feature selection metric with the best scoring features being retained. In prominent work by Yang and Pedersen (1997), numerous feature selection techniques were discussed and evaluated for text-based topic ID. Several of the more promising feature selection methods were later examined for speech-based topic ID on the Fisher Corpus by Hazen *et al.* (2007). In both of these studies, it was found that topic ID performance could be improved when the number of features used by the system was reduced from tens of thousands of features down to only a few thousand of the most relevant features.

Two of the better performing feature selection metrics from the studies above were the χ^2 (chi-square) statistic and the topic posterior estimate. The χ^2 statistic is used for testing the independence of words and topics from their observed co-occurrence counts. It is defined as follows: let A be the number of times word w occurs in documents about topic t, B the number of times w occurs in documents outside of topic t, C the total number of words in topic t that aren't w, and D the total number of words outside of topic t that aren't w. Let N_W be the total number of word occurrences in the training set. Then:

$$\chi^2(t, w) = \frac{N_W(AD - CB)^2}{(A + C)(B + D)(A + B)(C + D)} \tag{12.12}$$

The topic posterior estimate for topic t given word w is learned using maximum *a posteriori* (MAP) probability estimation over a training set as follows:

$$P(t|w) = \frac{N_{w|t} + \alpha N_T P(t)}{N_w + \alpha N_T} \tag{12.13}$$

Here $N_{w|t}$ is the number of times word w appears in documents on topic t, N_w is the total number of times w appears over all documents, N_T is the total number of topics, and α is a smoothing factor which controls the weight of the prior estimate of $P(t)$ in MAP estimate. α is typically set to a value of 1, but larger values can be used to bias the estimate towards the prior $P(t)$ when the occurrence count of a word N_w is small.

When selecting topic indicative words based on their χ^2 or $P(t|w)$ rankings, the ranked list of words can either be computed independently for each topic or globally pooled over all topics. Ranking the words in a global pool can be ineffective in situations where a small number of topics have a large number of very topic specific words thus causing the top of the ranked word list to be dominated by words that are indicative of only a small number of topics. In these cases, it is better to select the top scoring N words from each topic first and then pool these lists.

Table 12.2 shows the top 10 words w for five topics t as ranked by the posterior estimate $P(t|w)$ derived from ASR estimated counts using the Fisher corpus. The words in these lists are clearly indicative of their topics. Table 12.3 shows a same style of feature ranking using the estimated counts of phonetic trigrams derived from phonetic ASR outputs on the same data. In this case, many of the phonetic trigram features correspond directly to portions of topic-indicative words. For example, the "Professional sports on TV" topic contains the trigrams *g:ey:m* from the word *game* and the trigram *w:aa:ch* from the word *watch*. The lists also contain close phonetic confusions for common topic words. For example, for the word *watch* the list also includes the close phonetic confusions *w:ah:ch* and *w:ay:ch*. The presence of such

Table 12.2 Examples of top-10 words w which maximize the posterior probability $P(t|w)$ using ASR lattice output from five specific topics t in the Fisher corpus

Pets	Professional sports on TV	Airport security	Arms inspections in Iraq	U.S. Foreign Relations
dogs	hockey	airport	inspections	Korea
dog	football	security	inspectors	threat
shepherd	basketball	airports	weapons	countries
German	baseball	safer	disarming	nuclear
pets	sports	passengers	destruction	north
goldfish	soccer	airplane	Saddam	weapons
dog's	playoffs	checking	chemical	threats
animals	professional	flights	mass	country's
puppy	sport	airplanes	Iraqi	united
pet	Olympics	heightened	dictators	Arabia

Table 12.3 Examples of top-10 phonetic trigrams w, as recognized by an English phonetic recognizer, which maximize $P(t|w)$ for five specific topics t in the Fisher corpus

Pets	Professional sports on TV	Airport security	Arms inspections in Iraq	U.S. Foreign Relations
p:ae:t	w:ah:ch	r:p:ao	w:eh:p	ch:ay:n
ax:d:ao	s:b:ao	ch:eh:k	hh:ao:s	w:eh:p
d:oh:g	g:ey:m	ey:r:p	w:iy:sh	th:r:eh
d:d:ao	s:p:ao	r:p:w	axr:aa:k	r:eh:t
d:ao:ix	ey:s:b	iy:r:p	axr:dh:ey	th:r:ae
axr:d:ao	ah:ch:s	axr:p:ao	w:ae:p	ay:r:ae
t:d:ao	w:ay:ch	iy:r:dx	ah:m:k	r:ae:k
p:eh:ae	w:aa:ch	ch:ae:k	axr:ae:k	ah:n:ch
d:ow:ao	hh:ao:k	s:ey:f	p:aw:r	n:ch:r
d:oh:ix	ao:k:iy	r:p:l	v:axr:dh	uw:ae:s

confusions will not be harmful as long as these confusions are consistently predicted by the recognizer and do not interfere with trigrams from important words from other topics.

12.5.4.4 IDF Feature Weighting

When using feature selection, a binary choice is made for each potential feature about whether or not it will be used in the modeling process. An alternative approach is to apply continuously valued weights to features based on their relative importance to the topic ID process. It is also possible to perform an initial stage of feature selection and then apply feature weighting to the remaining selected features.

The most commonly used weighting scheme is *inverse document frequency* (IDF) weighting (Jones, 1972). The premise of IDF is that words that occur in many documents in a collection carry little importance and should be deemphasized in the topic ID process, while words that occur in only a small subset of documents are more likely to be topic-indicative content words. In text-based processing the IDF weight for feature w_i is defined as:

$$idf(w_i) = \log \frac{N_D}{N_{D|w_i}} \tag{12.14}$$

Here, N_D is the total number documents in the training set D and $N_{D|w_i}$ is the total number of those documents that contain the word w_i. If $N_{D|w_i} = N_D$ then $idf(w_i) = 0$, and $idf(w_i)$ increases as $N_{D|w_i}$ gets smaller.

In speech-based processing the actual value of $N_{D|w_i}$ is unknown. Wintrode and Kulp (2009) provide an approach for computing an estimated value of the IDF weight as follows:

$$\tilde{N}_{D|w_i} = \sum_{\forall d \in D} \min(1, \max(c_{i,d}, f)) \tag{12.15}$$

Here, $c_{i,d}$ is the estimated count of word w_i occurring in the training document d (as computed from the collection of ASR lattices for d) and f (where $f > 0$) is a floor parameter designed to set an upper bound on the IDF weight by preventing $\tilde{N}_{D|w_i}$ from going to 0.

12.5.4.5 The TF-IDF and TF-LLR Representations

When the estimated IDF is used in conjunction with the estimated counts of the individual features (or *terms*), the features of a document can be represented in *term frequency - inverse document frequency* (TF-IDF) form using this expression:

$$x_i = c_i \log \frac{N_D}{\tilde{N}_{D|w_i}} \tag{12.16}$$

The TF-IDF representation was originally developed for information retrieval tasks, but has also proven effective for topic ID tasks. The TF-IDF measure is also often used in conjunction with L2 or unit-length normalization so that the cosine similarity measure may be applied. When used in this fashion, such as in a linear kernel function of a support vector machine (as will be discussed later), the IDF weight as shown in Equation 12.16 will be applied twice (once within each vector used in the function). In these situations an alternative normalization using the square root of the IDF weight can be applied such that the IDF weight is effectively only applied once within the cosine similarity measure. This is expressed as:

$$x_i = c_i \sqrt{\log \frac{N_D}{\tilde{N}_{D|w_i}}} \tag{12.17}$$

When using L1 normalization of a count vector to yield a relative frequency distribution, probabilistic modeling techniques are enabled. For example, the following normalization has been shown to approximate a log likelihood ratio when applied within a linear kernel function of a support vector machine:

$$x_i = \frac{c_i}{\sum_{\forall j} c_j} \cdot \frac{1}{\sqrt{P(w_i)}} = \frac{P(w_i|d)}{\sqrt{P(w_i)}} \qquad (12.18)$$

Here, $P(w_i|d)$ is a estimated likelihood of observing w_i given the current document d and $P(w_i)$ is the estimated likelihood of observing word w_i across the whole training set. This normalization approach has been referred to as *term frequency - log likelihood ratio* (TF-LLR) normalization (Campbell *et al.*, 2003).

12.5.5 Latent Concept Modeling

An alternative to representing documents using a direct description of the features in a high-dimension feature space is to employ latent variable modeling techniques in which documents are represented using a smaller dimension vector of latent variables. Latent modeling techniques, such as latent semantic analysis (LSA), probabilistic latent semantic analysis (PLSA), and latent Dirichlet allocation (LDA), have proven useful for a variety of text applications including topic ID. The basic premise behind each of these techniques is that the semantic information of documents can be represented in a low-dimension space as weights over a mixture of latent *semantic concepts*. The latent concept models in these approaches are learned from a training corpus in an unsupervised, data-driven manner.

The vector of latent concept mixing weights inferred for a document can be used to represent the document for a variety of tasks including topic identification, topic clustering, and document link detection. Although these techniques have received wide spread recognition in the text processing and information retrieval communities, their use for speech-based tasks has been more limited. LSA has been used for the detection of out-of-domain utterances spoken to limited domain spoken language systems (Lane *et al.*, 2004). PLSA and LDA have both been used to learn topic mixtures for the purpose of topic adaptation of speech recognition language models (Akita and Kawahara, 2004; Gildea and Hoffman, 1999; Hsu and Glass, 2004; Tam and Schultz, 2006). In work by Tur *et al.* (2008), LDA was used to learn topics present in speech data in an unsupervised fashion. In this work the topic labels for describing the underlying latent concepts were also automatically generated using representative words extracted from the latent concept models. The use of PLSA and LDA for speech-based topic ID from predetermined topic labellings has yet to be studied.

12.5.5.1 Latent Semantic Analysis

In latent semantic analysis (LSA), the underlying concept space is learned using singular value decomposition (SVD) of the feature space spanned by the training data (Deerwester *et al.*, 1990). Typically, this feature space is of high dimension. The set of documents can be expressed in this feature space using the following matrix representation:

$$X = \left[\vec{x}_1; \vec{x}_2; \cdots ; \vec{x}_{N_D}\right] \qquad (12.19)$$

Here each $\vec{x}_i$ represents a document from a collection of N_D different documents, where documents are represented in an N_F dimension feature space. The computed SVD decomposition of X has the following form:

$$X = U\Sigma V^T \tag{12.20}$$

Here U is an $N_F \times N_F$ orthogonal matrix containing the eigenvectors of XX^T, V is an $N_D \times N_D$ orthogonal matrix representing the eigenvectors of $X^T X$, and Σ is an $N_F \times N_D$ diagonal matrix whose diagonal elements correspond to the shared non-zero eigenvalues of U and V.

Using this representation, the original N_D documents are represented within the N_D columns of the orthogonal space of V^T, which is often referred to as the *latent concept space*. Mathematically, any document's feature vector $\vec{x}$ is thus converted into a vector $\vec{z}$ in the latent concept space using this matrix operation:

$$\vec{z} = \Sigma^{-1} U^T \vec{x} \tag{12.21}$$

In practice, the eigenvalues of Σ, along with the corresponding eigenvectors of U, are sorted by the relative strength of the eigenvalues. Truncating Σ and U to use only the top k largest eigenvalues allows documents to be represented using a lower dimensional rank k approximation in the latent concept space. In this case, the following notation is used to represent the transformation of the feature vector $\vec{x}$ into a rank k latent concept space:

$$\vec{z}_k = \Sigma_k^{-1} U_k^T \vec{x} \tag{12.22}$$

In general, the LSA approach will yield a latent concept space which is much lower in dimensionality than the original feature space and provides better generalization for describing documents.

12.5.5.2 Probabilistic Latent Semantic Analysis

In probabilistic latent semantic analysis (PLSA), a probabilistic framework is introduced to describe the relationship between the latent concept space and the observed feature space. Using this framework, a probabilistic model must be found which optimally represents a collection of documents $D = \{d_1, \ldots, d_{N_D}\}$ each containing a sequence of word features $d_i = \{w_1, \ldots, w_{N_{d_i}}\}$. The basic probabilistic component for this model is the joint likelihood of observing word w_j within document d_i, as expressed as:

$$P(d_i, w_j) = P(d_i)P(w_j|d_i) = P(d_i) \sum_{\forall z \in Z} P(w_i|z)P(z|d_i) \tag{12.23}$$

In this expression, a latent concept variable $z \in Z$ has been introduced where Z represents a collection of k hidden latent concepts. Note that the variable d_i in this expression only serves as an index into the document collection, with the actual content of each document being represented by the sequence of word variables w_1 through $w_{N_{d_i}}$. The PLSA framework allows documents to be represented as a probabilistic mixture of latent concepts (via $P(z|d_i)$) where each latent concept possess its own generative probability model for producing word features (via $P(w_j|z)$). Bayes' rule can be used to rewrite Equation (12.23) as:

$$P(w_j, d_i) = \sum_{\forall z \in Z} P(w_j|z)P(d_i|z)P(z) \tag{12.24}$$

Using the expression in Equation (12.24), the expectation maximization (EM) algorithm can be used to iteratively estimate the individual likelihood functions, ultimately converging to a set of latent concepts which produce a local maximum for the total likelihood of the collection of training documents. From these learned models, the distribution of latent concepts $P(z|d_i)$ for each document d_i is easily inferred and can be used to represent the document via a feature vector $\vec{z}$ in the latent concept space as follows:

$$\vec{z} = \begin{bmatrix} P(z_1|d_i) \\ \vdots \\ P(z_k|d_i) \end{bmatrix} \tag{12.25}$$

In a similar fashion, the underlying latent concept distribution for a previously unseen document can also be estimated by using the EM algorithm over the new document when keeping the previously learned models $P(w|z)$ and $P(z)$ fixed. In practice, a tempered version of the EM algorithm is typically used. See the work of Hoffman (1999) for full details on the PLSA approach and its EM update equations.

12.5.5.3 Latent Dirichlet Allocation

The latent Dirichlet allocation (LDA[1]) technique, like PLSA, also learns a probabilistic mixture model. However, LDA alters the PLSA formulation by incorporating a Dirichlet prior model to constrain the distribution of the underlying concepts in the mixture model (Blei *et al.*, 2003). By comparison, PLSA relies on point estimates of $P(z)$ and $P(d|z)$ which are derived directly from the training data.

Mathematically, the primary LDA likelihood expression for a document is given as

$$P(w_1, \ldots, w_N|\alpha) = \int p(\theta|\alpha) \left(\prod_i \sum_z P(w_i|z)P(z|\theta) \right) d\theta \tag{12.26}$$

Here, θ represents a probability distribution for the latent concepts and $p(\theta|\alpha)$ represents a Dirichlet density function controlling the prior likelihoods over the concept distribution space. The variable α defines a shared smoothing parameter for the Dirichlet distribution, where $\alpha < 1$ favors concept distributions of θ which are low in entropy (i.e. distributions which are skewed towards a single dominant latent concept per document), while $\alpha > 1$ favors high-entropy distributions (i.e. distributions which are skewed towards a uniform weighting of latent concepts for each document). The use of a Dirichlet prior model in LDA removes the direct dependency in the latent concept mixture model in PLSA between the distribution of latent concepts and the training data, and instead provides a smooth prior distribution over the range of possible mixing distributions.

Because the expression in Equation (12.26) can not be computed analytically, a variational approximation EM method is generally used to estimate the values of α and $P(w_i|z)$. It should be noted that the underlying mixture components specifying each $P(w_i|z)$ distribution are

[1] Please note that the acronym LDA is also commonly used for the process of linear discriminant analysis. Despite the shared acronym, latent Dirichlet allocation is not related to linear discriminant analysis and readers are advised that all references to LDA in this chapter refer specifically to the technique of latent Dirichlet allocation.

typically represented using the variable β in the LDA literature (i.e. as $P(w_i|z, \beta)$), though this convention is not used here in order to provide a clearer comparison of the difference between PLSA and LDA.

Given a set of models estimated using the LDA approach, previously unseen documents can be represented in the same manner as in PLSA, i.e. a distribution of the latent topics can be inferred via the EM algorithm. As in the LDA estimation process, the LDA inference process must also use a variational approximation EM method instead of standard EM. Full details of the LDA method and its variational approximation method are available in Blei *et al.* (2003).

12.5.6 *Topic ID Classification and Detection*

12.5.6.1 Linear Classifiers

For many topic ID tasks, simple linear classifiers have proven to be highly effective. The basic form of a one-class linear detector is:

$$s_t = -b_t + \vec{r}_t \cdot \vec{x} \qquad (12.27)$$

Here, s_t is used as shorthand notation for the scoring function $S(\vec{x}, t)$. The detection score s_t for topic t is generated by taking the dot product of the feature vector $\vec{x}$ with a trained projection vector $\vec{r}_t$. The offset b_t is applied such that detections are triggered for $s_t > 0$. In multi-class classification and detection problems, Equation (12.27) can be expanded into the form:

$$\vec{s} = R\vec{x} - \vec{b} \qquad (12.28)$$

Here, $\vec{s}$ is a vector representing the detection scores for N_T different topics, $\vec{b}$ is a vector containing the detection decision boundaries for the N_T different topics, and R contains the projection vectors for the N_T different topics as follows:

$$R = \begin{bmatrix} \vec{r}_1^{\,T} \\ \vdots \\ \vec{r}_{N_T}^{\,T} \end{bmatrix} \qquad (12.29)$$

R is commonly referred to as the *routing matrix* in the call routing research community, as the top scoring projection vector for a call determines where the call is routed.

The projection vectors in a linear classifier can be trained in a variety of ways. For example, each projection vector could represent an average (or centroid) L2 normalized TF-IDF vector learned from a collection of training vectors for a topic (Schultz and Liberman, 1999). The individual vectors could also be trained using a discriminative training procedure such as minimum classification error training (Kuo and Lee, 2003; Zitouni *et al.*, 2005). Other common classifiers such as naive Bayes classifiers and linear kernel support vector machines are also linear classifiers in their final form, as will be discussed below.

12.5.6.2 Naive Bayes

The naive Bayes approach to topic ID is widely used in the text-processing community and has been applied in speech-based systems as well (Hazen *et al.*, 2007; Lo and Gauvain, 2003; McDonough *et al.*, 1994; Rose *et al.*, 1991). This approach uses probabilistic models to generate log likelihood ratio scores for individual topics. The primary assumption in the modeling process is that all words are statistically independently and are modeled and scored using using the *bag of words* approach. The basic scoring function for an audio document represented by count vector $\vec{c}$ is given as:

$$s_t = -b_t + \sum_{\forall w \in V} c_w \log \frac{P(w|t)}{P(w|\bar{t})} \tag{12.30}$$

Here, V represents the set of selected features (or *vocabulary*) used by the system such that only words present in the selected vocabulary V are scored. Each c_w represents the estimated count of word w in the ASR output W. The probability distribution $P(w|t)$ is learned from training documents from topic t while $P(w|\bar{t})$ is learned from training documents that do not contain topic t. The term b_t represents the decision threshold for the class and can be set based on the prior likelihood of the class and/or the pre-set decision costs. If the prior likelihoods of classes are assumed equal and an equal cost is set for all types of errors then b_t would typically be set to 0.

In order to avoid sparse data problems, maximum *a posteriori* probability estimation of the probability distributions is typically applied as follows:

$$P(w|t) = \frac{N_{w|t} + \alpha N_V P(w)}{N_{W|t} + \alpha N_V} \tag{12.31}$$

Here, $N_{w|t}$ is the estimated count of how often word w appeared in the training data for topic t, $N_{W|t}$ is the total estimated count of all words in the training data for topic t, N_V is number of words in the vocabulary, $P(w)$ is the estimated *a priori* probability for word w across all data, and α is a smoothing factor that is typically set to a value of 1. The distribution for $P(w|\bar{t})$ is generated in the same fashion.

12.5.6.3 Support Vector Machines

Since their introduction, support vector machines (SVMs) have become a prevalent classification technique for many applications. The use of SVMs in text-based topic ID blossomed following early work by Joachims (1998). SVMs have also been applied in numerous speech-based topic ID studies (Gish *et al.*, 2009; Haffner *et al.*, 2003; Hazen and Richardson, 2008).

A standard SVM is a 2-class classifier with the following form:

$$s_t = -b_t + \sum_{\forall i} \alpha_{i,t} K(\vec{v}_i, \vec{x}) \tag{12.32}$$

Here $\vec{x}$ is the test feature vector, the $\vec{v}_i$ vectors are *support vectors* from the training data, and $K(\vec{v}, \vec{x})$ represents the SVM *kernel function* for comparing vectors in the designated vector space. While there are many possible kernel functions, topic ID systems have typical employed a linear kernel function, allowing the basic SVM to be expressed as:

$$s_t = -b_t + \sum_{\forall i} \alpha_{i,t} \vec{v}_i \cdot \vec{x} \tag{12.33}$$

This expression reduces to the linear detector form of Equation (12.27) by noting that:

$$\vec{r}_t = \sum_{\forall i} \alpha_{i,t} \vec{v}_i \tag{12.34}$$

Here, $\vec{r}_t$ can be viewed as a weighted combination of training vectors $\vec{v}_i$ where the $\alpha_{i,t}$ values will be positively weighted when $\vec{v}_i$ is a positive example of topic t and negatively weighted when $\vec{v}_i$ is a negative example of topic t. This SVM apparatus can work with a variety of vector weighting and normalization schemes including TF-IDF and TF-LLR.

12.5.6.4 Other Classification Techniques

While most of the speech-based topic ID work has used either probabilistic naive Bayes classifiers or SVM classifiers, a wide range of other classifiers are also available. Other techniques that have been used are the k-nearest neighbors approach and the decision tree approach (Carbonell *et al.*, 1999). Discriminative feature weight training using minimum classification error (MCE) training has also been explored as a mechanism for improving the traditional naive Bayes (Hazen and Margolis, 2008) and SVM classifiers (Hazen and Richardson, 2008).

In the naive Bayes case, discriminatively trained feature weights can be incorporated into the standard naive Bayes expression from Equation (12.30) as follows:

$$s_t = -b_t + \sum_{\forall w \in V} \lambda_w c_w \log \frac{P(w|t)}{P(w|\bar{t})} \tag{12.35}$$

Here, the set of λ_w represents the feature weights which by default are set to a value of 1 in the standard naive Bayes approach. The feature weights in a SVM classifier can also be adjusted using the MCE training algorithm. It should also be noted that the use of feature selection in a topic ID classifier can also be viewed as a primitive form of feature weighting in which features receive either a weight of 1 for selected features and 0 for discarded features. Feature weighting allows for the importance of each of the features to be learned on a continuous scale, thereby giving the classifier greater flexibility in its learning algorithm.

12.5.6.5 Detection Score Normalization

Closed-set classification problems are often the easiest systems to engineer because the system must only choose the most likely class from a fixed-set of known classes when processing a new document. A more difficult scenario is the open-set detection problem in which the class or classes of interest may be known but knowledge of the set of out-of-class documents is incomplete. In these scenarios the system generally trains an in-class versus out-of-class classifier for each class of interest with the hope that the out-of-class data is sufficiently representative of unseen out-of-class data.

However, in some circumstances the classes of interest may be mutually independent and the quality of the detection score for one particular class should be considered in relation to the detection scores for the other competing classes. In other words the detection scores for a class should be normalized to account for the detection scores of competing classes.

This problem of score normalization has been carefully studied in other speech processing fields such as speaker identification and language identification where the set of classes are mutually independent (e.g. in speaker ID an utterance spoken by a single individual should only be assigned one speaker label). While this constraint is not applicable to the multi-class topic categorization problem, it can be applied to any single-class categorization problem that is cast as a detection problem. For example, in some call routing tasks a caller could be routed to an appropriate automated system based on the description of their problem when there is fair degree of certainty about the automated routing decision, but uncertainty in the routing decision should result in transfer to a human operator. In this case, the confidence in a marginal scoring class could be increased if all other competing classes are receiving far worse detection scores. Similarly, confidence in a high scoring class could be decreased if the other competing classes are also scoring well.

One commonly used score normalization procedure is called test normalization, or *t-norm*, which normalizes class scores as follows:

$$s_t' = \frac{s_t - \mu_{\bar{t}}}{\sigma_{\bar{t}}} \tag{12.36}$$

Here the normalized score for class t is computed by subtracting off the mean score of the competing classes $\mu_{\bar{t}}$ and then dividing by the standard deviation of the scores of the competing classes $\sigma_{\bar{t}}$.

12.5.7 Example Topic ID Results on the Fisher Corpus

12.5.7.1 Experimental Overview

To provide some perspective on the performance of standard topic ID techniques, let us present some example results generated on the Fisher corpus. In these experiments, a collection of 1374 conversations containing 244 hours of speech have been extracted from the Fisher English Phase 1 corpus for training a topic ID system. The number of conversations per topic in this training set varies between 6 and 87 over the 40 different topics. An independent set of 1372 Fisher conversations containing 226 hours of speech are used for evaluation. There are between 5 and 86 conversations per topic in the evaluation set.

Human-generated transcripts are available for all of the training and testing data. These transcripts can be used to generated a text-based baseline level of performance. To examine the degradation in performance when imperfect ASR systems must be used in place of the actual transcripts, three different ASR systems have also been applied to this data:

1. A word-based large vocabulary speech recognition system with a 31 539 word vocabulary trained on an independent set of 553 hours of Fisher English data. The MIT SUMMIT speech recognition systems was used is this experiment (Glass, 2003). This ASR system intentionally did not used any form of speaker normalization or adaptation and its language model was constrained to only contain the transcripts from the training set. As such, the word error rate of this recognizer (typically over 40%) is significantly worse than state-of-the-art performance for this task. This performance level allows us to examine the robustness of topic ID performance under less than ideal conditions.
2. An English phonetic recognition system trained on only 10 hours of human conversations from the Switchboard cellular corpus (Graff *et al.*, 2001). A phonetic recognition system developed at the Brno University of Technology (BUT) was used in this case (Schwarz *et al.*, 2004). The use of this phonetic recognition system allows us to examine topic ID performance when lexical information is not used or is otherwise unavailable.

3. A Hungarian phonetic recognition system trained on 10 hours of read speech collected over the telephone lines in Europe. The BUT phonetic recognition system was again used in this case. By using a phonetic recognition system from another language, the topic ID performance can be assessed under the simulated condition where no language resources are available in the language of interest and a cross-language recognition system must be used instead.

12.5.7.2 Performance of Different Classifiers

To start, the topic ID performance of several different classifiers is examined when using the output of the word-based ASR system. These results are displayed in Figure 12.9. In this figure the performance of the naive Bayes and SVM classifiers are compared, both with and without minimum classification error (MCE) training of the feature weights. In the case of the naive Bayes system, all feature weights are initially set to a value of 1, while the SVM system uses the TF-LLR normalization scheme for initialization of the feature weights. Performance is also examined as the size of the feature set is reduced from the full vocabulary to smaller-sized feature sets using the topic posterior feature selection method described in Section 12.5.4.3.

In Figure 12.9 it is seen that feature selection dramatically improves the performance of the standard naive Bayes system from a classification error rate of 14.1% when using the full vocabulary down to 10.0% when only the top 912 words are used. The basic SVM system outperforms the naive Bayes system when using the full vocabulary achieving an error rate of 12.5%. The SVM also sees improved performance when feature selection is applied, achieving its lowest error rate of 11.0% when using only the top 3151 words in the vocabulary. These

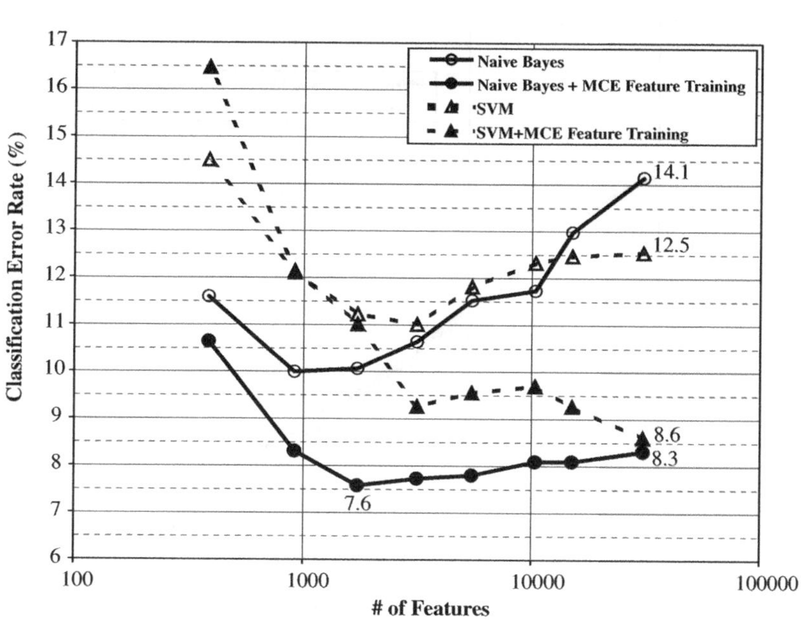

Figure 12.9 Topic classification performance on audio documents from the Fisher corpus processed using a word-based ASR system. Classification error rate is compared for naive Bayes and SVM classifiers, both with and without MCE feature weight training, as the number of features is varied

results demonstrate that the standard SVM mechanism remains robust, even as the dimensionality of the problem increases to large numbers, while the probabilistic naive Bayes approach is a preferred approach for smaller dimension problems where statistical estimation does not suffer from the *curse of dimensionality*.

Figure 12.9 also shows that improvements can also be made in both the naive Bayes and SVM systems when applying the MCE training algorithm to appropriately weight the relative importance of the different features. In fact, when MCE feature weighting in used in this case, the naive Bayes system is preferable to the SVM system at all feature set sizes including the full vocabulary condition. Using the full vocabulary, the naive Bayes achieve an error rate of 8.3% while the SVM achieves an error rate of 8.6%. As feature selection is used to reduce the number of features, the naive Bayes system sees modest improvements down to a 7.6% error rate at a feature set size of 3151 words (or about 10% of the full vocabulary).

Although the naive Bayes classifier outperformed the SVM classifier on this specific task, this has not generally been the case across other studies in the literature where SVM classifiers have generally been found to outperform naive Bayes classifiers. This can also been seen in this chapter in Figures 12.4 and 12.5, where the SVM classifier outperforms the naive Bayes classifier on three out of the four different feature sets.

12.5.7.3 Topic Detection Performance

In Figure 12.10 the detection-error trade-off (DET) curve for a naive Bayes classifier is compared against the DET curve for an SVM classifier when both classifiers use the word-based

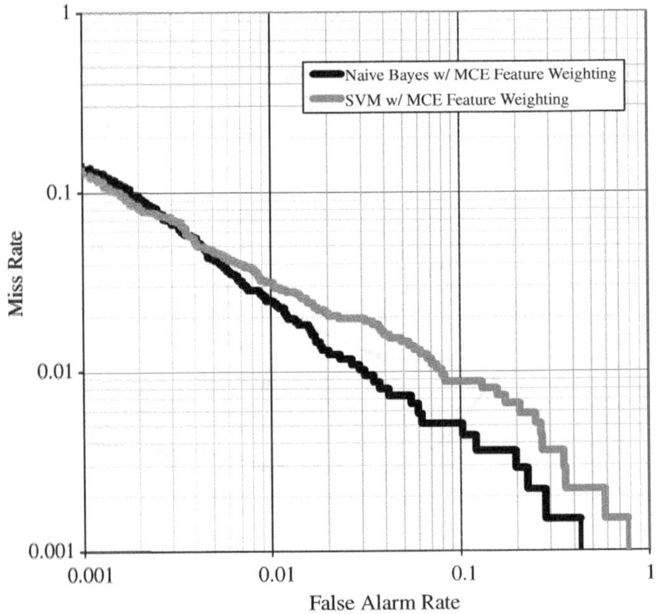

Figure 12.10 Topic detection performance displayed on a detection-error trade-off (DET) curve for audio documents from the Fisher corpus processed using a word-based ASR system. Detection performance for both a naive Bayes and an SVM classifier, with both classifiers using MCE trained feature weights over a feature set containing the full ASR vocabulary

Table 12.4 Topic ID performance on the Fisher Corpus data using a naive Bayes classifier with MCE-trained feature weights for four different sets of features ranging from the words in the manually transcribed text to phonetic triphones generated by a cross-language Hungarian phonetic recognizer

Feature type	Feature source	# of features	Classification error rate (%)	Detection equal error rate (%)
Unigram words	Text transcript	24697	5.17	1.31
Unigram words	Word-based ASR	1727	7.58	1.83
English triphones	Phonetic ASR	6374	20.0	4.52
Hungarian triphones	Phonetic ASR	14413	47.1	14.9

ASR features with MCE feature weight training. This DET curve was generated using a pooling method where each test conversation is used as a positive example for its own topic and as a negative example for the other 39 topics. In total this yields a pool of 1372 scores for positive examples and 53508 scores (i.e. 1372×39) for negative examples. In order to accentuate the differences between the two topic ID systems compared in the plot, the axes are plotted using a log scale. The plot shows that the naive Bayes and SVM systems have similar performance for operating points with a low false alarm rate, but the naive Bayes system outperforms the SVM system at higher false alarm rates.

12.5.7.4 Performance of Different Features

In Tables 12.4 and 12.5 the topic ID performance using different features is displayed. Table 12.4 shows the performance of a naive Bayes classifier with MCE trained feature weights, while Table 12.5 shows the same set of experiments using an SVM classifier with MCE trained feature weights. In both tables, performance is shown for four different sets of derived features: (1) unigram word counts based on the text transcripts of the data, (2) unigram word counts estimated from lattices generated using word-based ASR, (3) phonetic trigram counts estimated from lattices generated using an English phonetic recognizer, and (4) phonetic trigram counts estimated from lattices generated using a Hungarian phonetic recognizer. When examining these results it should be noted the that SVM system outperforms the naive Bayes system in three of the four different conditions.

As would be expected, the best topic ID performance (as measured by both the closed-set classification error rate and by the topic detection equal error rate) is achieved when the known transcripts of the conversations are used. However, it is heartening to observe that only a slight degradation in topic ID performance is observed when the human transcriber is replaced by

Table 12.5 Topic ID performance on the Fisher Corpus data using an SVM classifier with MCE-trained feature weights for four different sets of features ranging from the words in the manually transcribed text to phonetic trigrams generated by a cross language Hungarian phonetic recognizer

Feature type	Feature source	# of features	Classification error rate (%)	Detection equal error rate (%)
Unigram words	Text transcript	24697	5.10	1.17
Unigram words	Word-based ASR	30364	8.60	2.04
English triphones	Phonetic ASR	86407	17.8	4.36
Hungarian triphones	Phonetic ASR	161442	41.0	12.1

an errorful ASR system. In these experiments, the word error rate of the ASR engine was approximately 40%. Despite the high word error rate, the naive Bayes topic ID system saw only a minor degradation in classification performance from 5.2% to 7.6% when moving from text transcripts to ASR output, and the topic detection equal error rate also remained below 2%. This demonstrates that even very errorful speech recognition outputs can provide useful information for topic identification.

The third and fourth lines of Tables 12.4 and 12.5 show the results when the topic ID system uses only phonetic recognition results to perform the task. In the third line the system uses an English phonetic recognizer trained on 10 hours of data similar to the training data. As would be expected, degradations are observed when the lexical information is removed from the ASR process, but despite the loss of lexical knowledge in the feature set, the topic ID system still properly identifies the topic in over 80% of the calls and achieves a topic detection equal error rate under 5% for both the naive Bayes and SVM systems.

In the fourth line of each table, a Hungarian phonetic recognizer trained on read speech collected over the telephone lines is used. This ASR system not only has no knowledge of English words, it also uses a mismatched set of phonetic units from a different language and is trained on a very different style of speech. Despite all of these hindrances the topic ID system is still able to use the estimated Hungarian phonetic trigram counts to identify the topic (out of a set of 40 different topics) over half of the time. The SVM system also achieves a respectable detection equal error rate of just over 12%.

12.5.8 Novel Topic Detection

Traditional topic ID assumes a fixed set of known topics, each of which has available data for training. A more difficult problem is the discovery of a newly introduced topic for which no previous data is available for training a model. In this case the system must determine that a new audio document does not match any of the current models without having an alternative model for new topics available for comparison.

An example of this scenario is first story detection problem in the NIST TDT evaluations in which an audio document must either be (a) linked to a pre-existing stream of documents related to a specific event, or (b) declared the first story about a new event. This problem has proven itself to be quite difficult, largely because stories about two different but similar events (e.g. airplane crashes or car bombings) will use similar semantic concepts and hence similar lexical items (Allan *et al.*, 2000). In this case, an approach based on threshold similarity scores generated from standard *bag of words* topic models may be inadequate.

To compensate for this issue, approaches have been explored in which topic dependent modeling techniques are applied for new story detection. Specifically, these approaches attempt to use important concept words (e.g. "crash" or "bombing") for determining the general topic of a document, but then refocus the final novelty decision on words related to the distinguishing details of the event discussed in the document (e.g. proper names of people or locations, Makkonen *et al.*, 2004; Yang *et al.*, 2002).

12.5.9 Topic Clustering

While most topic ID work is focused on the identification of topics from a predetermined set of topics, topic models can also be learned in a completely unsupervised fashion. This is particularly useful when manual labeling of data is unavailable or otherwise infeasible.

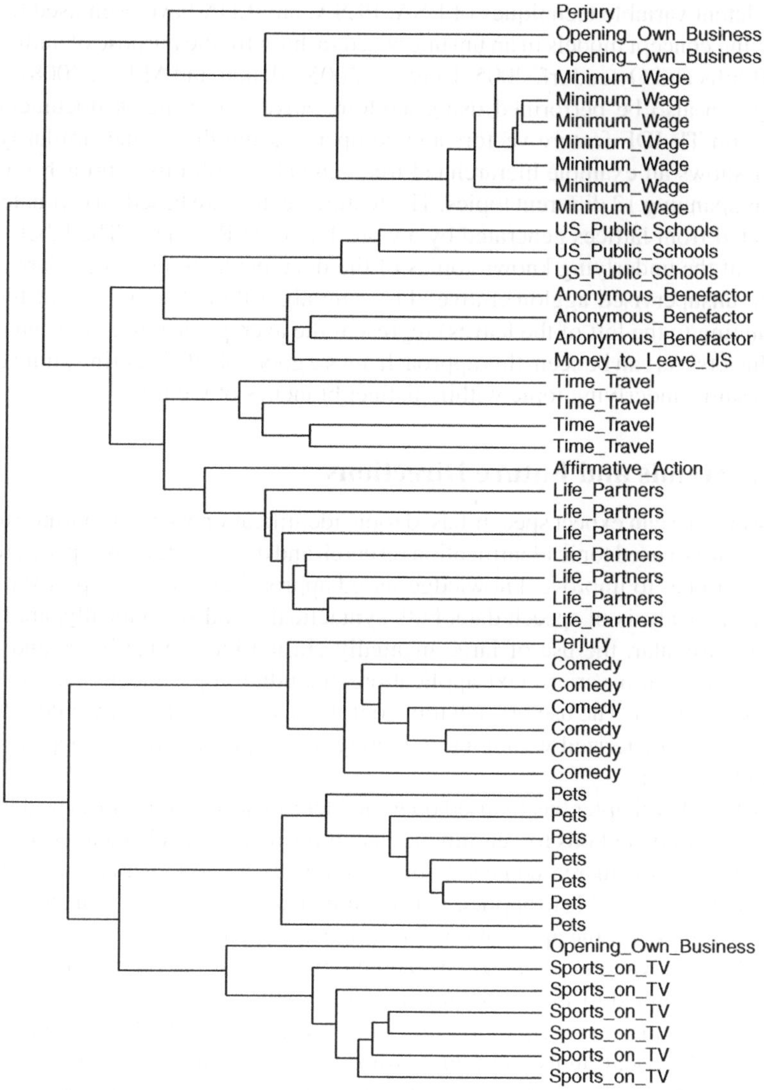

Figure 12.11 Example agglomerative clustering of 50 Fisher conversations based on TF-IDF feature vectors of estimated word counts from ASR lattices compared using the cosine similarity measure

Unsupervised topic clustering has been used in a variety of manners. Perhaps the most common usage is the automatic creation of topic clusters for use in unsupervised language model adaptation within ASR systems (Iyer, 1994; Seymore and Rosenfeld, 1997). Topic clustering has also been used to automatically generate taxonomies describing calls placed to customer service centers (Roy and Subramaniam, 2006).

Early work in topic clustering focused on tree-based agglomerative clustering techniques applied to Bayesian similarity measures between audio documents (Carlson, 1996). More recently, the latent variable techniques of LSA, PLSA, and LDA have been used to implicitly learn underlying concept models in an unsupervised fashion for the purpose of audio document clustering (Boulis and Ostendorf, 2005; Li *et al.*, 2005; Shafiei and Milios, 2008).

Clustering can also be performed using agglomerative clustering of documents that are represented with TF-IDF feature vectors and compared using the cosine similarity measure. Figure 12.11 shows an example hierarchical tree generated with this approach for 50 Fisher conversations spanning 12 different topics. The feature vectors are based on estimated unigram counts extracted from lattices generated by a word-based ASR system. The labels of the leaf nodes represent the underlying known topics of the documents, though these labels were not visible to the unsupervised agglomerative clustering algorithm. The heights of the nodes of the tree (spanning to the left of the leaves) represent the average distance between documents within the clusters. As can be seen, this approach does a good job of clustering audio documents belonging to same underlying topic within distinct branches of the tree.

12.6 New Trends and Future Directions

Moving forward one can expect speech-based topic identification work to continue to follow in the footsteps of text-based topic identification research and development. As speech recognition technology continues to improve, knowledge-based approaches which can perform richer and deeper linguistic analysis of speech data, both syntactically and semantically, are likely to be employed. In particular, the use of large manually crafted knowledge bases and ontologies are now being used in a variety text applications including topic identification (Lin, 1995, 1997; Tiun *et al.*, 2001). The use of such topic ontologies on speech data would allow spoken documents to be characterized within a rich hierarchical topic structure as opposed to simple single-layered class sets.

While much of this chapter has focused on topic identification using supervised training, the need for unsupervised methods for learning topical information and characterizing speech data will likely grow with the increased need to process the larger and larger amounts of unlabeled data that is becoming available to application and human users particularly on the web. Towards this end, one could expect the application of techniques for the automatic discovery of topical n-grams or phrases (Wang *et al.*, 2007) or the automatic construction of ontologies (Fortuna *et al.*, 2005) to be applied to spoken document collections.

Also along these lines, a recent ambitious study by Cerisara (2009) attempted to simultaneously learn both lexical items and topics from raw audio, using only information gleaned from a phonetic ASR system. Fuzzy phonetic string matching is used to find potential common lexical items from documents. Documents are then described by the estimated distances between these discovered lexical items and the best matching segments for these items within an audio document. Topic clustering can be performed on these distance vectors under the presumption that documents with small minimum distances to the same hypothesized lexical items are topically related. One would expect that this area of unsupervised learning research will continue to garner more attention and the level of sophistication in the algorithms will grow.

Another interesting research direction that is likely to attract more attention is the study of on-line learning techniques and adaptation of topic identification systems. Related to this is the longitudinal study of topics present in data and how the characteristic cues of topics change and evolve over time. Studies of this subject on text data have been conducted (Katakis *et al.*, 2005) and it should be expected that similar research on speech data will follow in the future.

The increasing availability of video and multimedia data should also lead to increased efforts into integrating audio and visual information for greater robustness during the processing of this data. Preliminary efforts towards this goal have already been conducted in multimedia research studies into topic segmentation and classification (Jasinschi *et al.*, 2001) and novelty detection (Wu *et al.*, 2007). New research directions examining multi-modal techniques for topic identification can certainly be expected.

Acknowledgment

This work was sponsored by the Air Force Research Laboratory under Air Force Contract FA8721-05-C-0002. Opinions, interpretations, conclusions, and recommendations are those of the authors and are not necessarily endorsed by the United States Government.

References

Akita Y and Kawahara T 2004 Language model adaptation based on PLSA of topics and speakers *Proceedings of Interspeech*. Jeju Island, Korea.

Allan J, Lavrenko V and Jin H 2000 First story detection in TDT is hard *Proceedings of the Ninth International Conference on Information and Knowledge Management (CIKM)*. McLean, VA, USA.

Bain K, Basson S, Faisman A and Kanevsky D 2005 Accessibility, transcription and access everywhere. *IBM Systems Journal* **44**(3), 589–603.

Blei D, Ng A and Jordan M 2003 Latent Dirichlet allocation. *Journal of Machine Learning Research* **3**, 993–1022.

Boulis C 2005 *Topic learning in text and conversational speech* PhD Thesis University of Washington.

Boulis C and Ostendorf M 2005 Using symbolic prominence to help design feature subsets for topic classification and clustering of natural human-human conversations *Proceedings of Interspeech*. Lisbon, Portugal.

Campbell W, Campbell J, Reynolds D, Jones D and Leek T 2003 Phonetic speaker recognition with support vector machines *Proceedings of the Neural Information Processing Systems Conference*. Vancouver, Canada.

Carbonell J, Yang Y, Lafferty J, Brown R, Pierce T and Liu X 1999 CMU report on TDT-2: Segmentation, detection and tracking *Proceedings of DARPA Broadcast News Workshop 1999*. Herndon, VA, USA.

Carlson B 1996 Unsupervised topic clustering of switchboard speech messages *Proceedings of the International Conference on Acoustics, Speech, and Signal Processing*. Atlanta, GA, USA.

Cerisara C 2009 Automatic discovery of topics and acoustic morphemes from speech. *Computer Speech and Language* **23**(2), 220–239.

Chelba C, Hazen T and Saraçlar M 2008 Retrieval and browsing of spoken content. *IEEE Signal Processing Magazine* **24**(3), 39–49.

Chu-Carroll J and Carpenter B 1999 Vector-based natural language call routing. *Computational Linguistics* **25**(3), 361–388.

Cieri C, Graff D, Liberman M, Martey N and Strassel S 2000 Large, multilingual, broadcast news corpora for cooperative research in topic detection and tracking: The TDT-2 and TDT-3 corpus efforts *Proceedings of the 2nd International Conference on Language Resouces and Evaluation (LREC)*. Athens, Greece.

Cieri C, Miller D and Walker K 2003 From Switchboard to Fisher: Telephone collection protocols, their uses and yields *Proceedings of Interspeech*. Geneva, Switzerland.

Deerwester S, Dumais S, Furnas G, Landauer T and Harshman R 1990 Indexing by latent semantic analysis. *Journal of the Society for Information Science* **11**(6), 391–407.

Fawcett T 2006 An introduction to ROC analysis. *Pattern Recognition Letters* **27**, 861–874.

Fiscus J 2004 Results of the 2003 topic detection and tracking evaluation *Proceedings of the 4th International Conference on Language Resouces and Evaluation (LREC)*. Lisbon, Portugal.

Fiscus J, Doddington G, Garofolo J and Martin A 1999 NIST's 1998 topic detection and tracking evaluation (TDT2) *Proceedings of DARPA Broadcast News Workshop 1999*. Herndon, VA, USA.

Fiscus J, Garofolo J, Le A, Martin A, Pallett D, Przybocki M and Sanders G 2004 Results of the fall 2004 STT and MDE evaluation *Proceedings of the Rich Transcription Fall 2004 Evaluation Workshop*. Palisades, NY, USA.

Fortuna B, Mladenič D and Grobelnik M 2005 Semi-automatic construction of topic ontologies *Proceedings of International Workshop on Knowledge Discovery and Ontologies*. Porto, Portugal.

Gildea D and Hoffman T 1999 Topic-based language models using EM *Proceedings of Sixth European Conference on Speech Communication (Eurospeech)*. Budapest, Hungary.

Gish H, Siu MH, Chan A and Belfield W 2009 Unsupervised training of an HMM-based speech recognizer for topic classification *Proceedings of Interspeech*. Brighton, UK.

Glass J 2003 A probabilistic framework for segment-based speech recognition. *Computer Speech and Language* **17**(2-3), 137–152.

Gorin A, Parker B, Sachs R and Wilpon J 1996 How may I help you? *Proceedings of the Third IEEE Workshop on Interactive Voice Technology for Telecommunications Applications*. Basking Ridge, New Jersey, USA.

Graff D, Walker K and Miller D 2001 Switchboard Cellular Part 1. Available from http://www.ldc.upenn.edu.

Haffner P, Tur G and Wright J 2003 Optimizing SVMs for complex call classification *Proceedings of the International Conference on Acoustics, Speech, and Signal Processing*. Hong Kong, China.

Hazen T and Margolis A 2008 Discriminative feature weighting using MCE training for topic identification of spoken audio recordings *Proceedings of the International Conference on Acoustics, Speech, and Signal Processing*. Las Vegas, NV, USA.

Hazen T and Richardson F 2008 A hybrid SVM/MCE training approach for vector space topic identification of spoken audio recordings *Proceedings of Interspeech*. Brisbane, Australia.

Hazen T, Richardson F and Margolis A 2007 Topic identification from audio recordings using word and phone recongition lattices *Proceedings of the IEEE Workshop on Automatic Speech Recognition and Understanding*. Kyoto, Japan.

Hoffman T 1999 Probabilistic latent semantic analysis *Proceedings of the 15th Conference on Uncertainty in Artificial Intelligence*. Stockholm, Sweden.

Hsu BJ and Glass J 2004 Style and topic language model adaptation using HMM-LDA *Proceedings of Interspeech*. Jeju Island, Korea.

Iyer R 1994 *Language modeling with sentence-level mixtures* Master's thesis Boston University.

Jasinschi R, Dimitrova N, McGee T, Agnihotri L, Zimmerman J and Li D 2001 Integrated multimedia processing for topic segmentation and classification *Proceedings of IEEE Internation Conference on Image Processing*. Thessaloniki, Greece.

Joachims T 1998 Text categorization with support vector machines: Learning with many relevant features *Proceedings of the European Conference on Machine Learning*. Chemnitz, Germany.

Jones D, Wolf F, Gibson E, Williams E, Fedorenko E, Reynolds D and Zissman M 2003 Measuring the readability of automatic speech-to-text transcripts *Proceedings of Interspeech*. Geneva, Switzerland.

Jones KS 1972 A statistical interpretation of term specificity and its application in retrieval. *Journal of Documentation* **28**(1), 11–21.

Katakis I, Tsoumakas G and Vlahavas I 2005 On the utility of incremental feature selection for the classification of textual data streams *Proceedings of the Panhellenic Conference on Informatics*. Volas, Greece.

Kuhn R, Nowell P and Drouin C 1997 Approaches to phoneme-based topic spotting: an experimental comparison *Proceedings of the International Conference on Acoustics, Speech, and Signal Processing*. Munich, Germany.

Kuo HK and Lee CH 2003 Discriminative training of natural language call routers. *IEEE Transactions on Speech and Audio Processing* **11**(1), 24–35.

Lane I, Kawahara T, Matsui T and Nakamura S 2004 Out-of-domain detection based on confidence measures from multiple topic classification *Proceedings of the International Conference on Acoustics, Speech, and Signal Processing*. Montreal, Canada.

Lee KF 1990 Context-dependent phonetic hidden Markov models for speaker-independent continuous speech recognition. *IEEE Transactions on Acoustics, Speech, and Signal Processing* **38**(4), 599–609.

Li TH, Lee MH, Chen B and Lee LS 2005 Hierarchical topic organization and visual presentation of spoken documents using probabilistic latent semantic analysis (plsa) for efficient retrieval/browsing applications *Proceedings of Interspeech*. Lisbon, Portugal.

Lin CY 1995 Knowledge-based automatic topic identification *Proceedings of the 33rd Annual Meeting on Association for Computational Linguistics*. Cambridge, Massachusetts, USA.

Lin CY 1997 *Robust Automated Topic Identification* PhD Thesis University of Southern California.

Lo YY and Gauvain JL 2003 Tracking topics in broadcast news data *Proceedings of the ISCA Workshop on Multilingual Spoken Document Retrieval*. Hong Kong.

Makkonen J, Ahonen-Myka H and Salmenkivi M 2004 Simple semantics in topic detection and tracking. *Information Retrieval* **7**, 347–368.

Manning C and Schütze H 1999 *Foundations of Statistical Natural Language Processing* MIT Press Cambridge, MA, USA chapter Text Categorization, pp. 575–608.

Martin A, Doddington G, Kamm T, Ordowski M and Przybocki M 1997 The DET curve in assessment of detection task performance *Proceedings of Fifth European Conference on Speech Communication (Eurospeech)*. Rhodes, Greece.

Martin A, Garofolo J, Fiscus J, Le A, Pallett D, Przybocki M and Sanders G 2004 NIST language technology evaluation cookbook *Proceedings of the 4th International Conference on Language Resouces and Evaluation (LREC)*. Lisbon, Portugal.

McDonough J, Ng K, Jeanrenaud P, Gish H and Rolilicek J 1994 Approaches to topic identification on the switchboard corpus *Proceedings of the International Conference on Acoustics, Speech, and Signal Processing*. Adelaide, Australia.

Munteanu C, Penn G, Baecker R, Toms E and James D 2006 Measuring the acceptable word error rate of machine-generated webcast transcripts *Proceedings of Interspeech*. Pittsburg, PA, USA.

Nöth E, Harbeck S, Niemann H and Warnke V 1997 A frame and segment-based approach for topic spotting *Proceedings of Fifth European Conference on Speech Communication (Eurospeech)*. Rhodes, Greece.

Paaß G, Leopold E, Larson M, Kindermann J and Eickeler S 2002 SVM classification using sequences of phonemes and syllables *Proceedings of the 6th European Conference on Principles of Data Mining and Knowledge Discovery*. Helsinki, Finland.

Pallett D, Fiscus J, Garofolo J, Martin A and Przybocki M 1999 1998 broadcast news benchmark test results: English and non-English word error rate performance measures *Proceedings of DARPA Broadcast News Workshop 1999*. Herndon, VA, USA.

Peskin B, Connolly S, Gillick L, Lowe S, McAllaster D, Nagesha V, van Mulbregt P and Wegmann S 1996 Improvements in Switchboard recognition and topic identification *Proceedings of the International Conference on Acoustics, Speech, and Signal Processing*. Atlanta, GA, USA.

Rose R, Chang E and Lippman R 1991 Techniques for information retrieval from voice messages *Proceedings of the International Conference on Acoustics, Speech, and Signal Processing*. Toronto, Ont., Canada.

Roy S and Subramaniam L 2006 Automatic generation of domain models for call centers from noisy transcriptions *Proceedings of the 21st International Conference on Computational Linguistics and 44th Annual Meeting of the ACL*. Sydney, Australia.

Schultz JM and Liberman M 1999 Topic detection and tracking using idf-weighted cosine coefficient *Proceedings of DARPA Broadcast News Workshop 1999*. Herndon, VA, USA.

Schwarz P, Matějka P and Černocký J 2004 Towards lower error rates in phoneme recognition *Proceedings of International Conference on Text, Speech and Dialogue*. Brno, Czech Republic.

Sebastiani F 2002 Machine learning in automated text categorization. *ACM Computing Surveys* **34**(1), 1–47.

Seymore K and Rosenfeld R 1997 Using story topics for language model adaptation *Proceedings of Fifth European Conference on Speech Communication (Eurospeech)*. Rhodes, Greece.

Shafiei M and Milios E 2008 A statistical model for topic segmentation and clustering *Proceedings of the Canadian Society for Computaional Studies of Intelligence*. Windsor, Canada.

Stolcke A 2002 SRILM - an extensible language modeling toolkit *Proceedings of the International Conference on Spoken Language Processing*. Denver, CO, USA.

Tam YC and Schultz T 2006 Unsupervised language model adaptation using latent semantic marginals *Proceedings of Interspeech*. Pittsburg, PA, USA.

Tang M, Pellom B and Hacioglu K 2003 Call-type classification and unsupervised training for the call center domain *Proceedings of the IEEE Workshop on Automatic Speech Recognition and Understanding*. St. Thomas, Virgin Islands.

Tiun S, Abdullah R and Kong TE 2001 Automatic topic identification using ontology hierarchy *Proceedings of the Second International Conference on Intelligent Processing and Computational Linguistics*. Mexico City, Mexico.

Tur G, Stolcke A, Voss L, Dowding J, Favre B, Fernandez R, Frampton M, Frandsen M, Frederickson C, Graciarena M, Hakkani-Tür D, Kintzing D, Leveque K, Mason S, Niekrasz J, Peters S, Purver M, Riedhammer K, Shriberg E, Tien J, Vergyri D and Yang F 2008 The CALO meeting speech recognition and understanding system *Proceedings of the IEEE Spoken Language Technology Workshop*. Goa, India.

Wang X, McCallum A and Wei X 2007 Topical n-grams: Phrase and topic discovery, with an application to information retrieval *Proceedings of the IEEE Internation Conference on Data Mining*. Omaha, NE, USA.

Wayne C 2000 Multilingual topic detection and tracking: Successful research enabled by corpora and evaluation *Proceedings of the 2nd International Conference on Language Resouces and Evaluation (LREC)*. Athens, Greece.

Wintrode J and Kulp S 2009 Techniques for rapid and robust topic identification of conversational telephone speech *Proceedings of Interspeech*. Brighton, UK.

Wright J, Carey M and Parris E 1996 Statistical models for topic identification using phoneme substrings *Proceedings of the International Conference on Acoustics, Speech, and Signal Processing*. Atlanta, GA, USA.

Wu X, Hauptmann A and Ngo CW 2007 Novelty detection for cross-lingual news stories with visual duplicates and speech transcripts *Proceedings of the International Conference on Multimedia*. Augsburg, Germany.

Yang Y and Pedersen J 1997 A comparative study on feature selection in text categorization *Proceedings of the International Conference of Machine Learning*. Nashville, TN, USA.

Yang Y, Zhang J, Carbonell J and Jin C 2002 Topic-conditioned novelty detection *Proceedings of the International Conference on Knowledge Discovery and Data Mining*. Edmonton, Alberta, Canada.

Zitouni I, Jiang H and Zhou Q 2005 Discriminative training and support vector machine for natural language call routing *Proceedings of Interspeech*. Lisbon, Portugal.

13

Speech Summarization

Yang Liu[1] and Dilek Hakkani-Tür[2]
[1] *University of Texas at Dallas, U.S.A.*
[2] *Microsoft Speech Labs, Microsoft Research, U.S.A.*

The increasing amount of audio recordings (such as broadcast news, talk shows, meetings, lectures, voice mails, podcast, and YouTube videos) has attracted a lot of research interest in speech summarization. This chapter covers some techniques that have been developed for speech summarization. We will also describe task definition, evaluation issues, and some available resources, as well as discussing some issues and future directions.

13.1 Task Description

13.1.1 General Definition of Summarization

Most people agree that there is an information overload in the current world. There is almost an unlimited amount of information on the web and in our everyday life, in various formats, such as news articles, broadcast news, voice mails, videos, meeting recordings, and lecture/presentation recordings. We need techniques that can help effectively digest information. This need has resulted in increasing interest in areas such as automatic summarization – a system takes an input document[1] and returns its summary to the user. This can reduce human effort and help information access. In addition, compared with human effort, automatic summarization is fast, consistent in its selection, and easily scalable to huge amounts of data.

There has been drastic progress in text summarization in the past decades, in summarization approaches, evaluation methods, and development of resources. These have been partly facilitated by benchmark evaluations, such as the ones organized by the Document Understanding Conferences (DUC) (and now the Text Analysis Conferences, TAC). Such evaluations provide

[1] Here we are using *document* in its broad sense. A document can be a written one, transcripts of speech, just the speech recording itself, or a group of these.

Spoken Language Understanding: Systems for Extracting Semantic Information from Speech, First Edition.
Edited by Gokhan Tur and Renato De Mori.

data to the community, help system development, and also foster research on summarization techniques and summarization evaluation.

Recently, in parallel to improvements in automatic speech recognition performance, there is also an increase of efforts on speech summarization. More speech data is available, such as daily meetings, news broadcasts, lectures, political speeches, podcasts, and videos. While it is usually possible to quickly skim through a written document to get an idea on its content, speech data is much harder to browse or navigate than textual documents, because of the cost of hand-indexing and the serial nature of speech itself. Moreover, transcriptions by speech recognizers usually lack style information, such as speaker turns, sentence or paragraph boundaries, and capitalization, that make text easier to read. Rich transcription methods aim to incorporate these. However, automatic speech recognizers and rich transcription systems make mistakes, making it difficult to understand the content when just skimming through automatic transcriptions. Information retrieval (e.g. spoken document retrieval) provides a convenient way to search for useful information; however, it either returns an entire speech document as its output, which is not helpful if the user needs to quickly browse the document; or it returns an excerpt containing the user's query, but this may miss important parts in the speech and fails to provide a picture of the entire document. An effective speech summarization system will allow the users to quickly browse speech for easy information access.

Humans can generally write summaries without much training (of course, quality might be an issue). So what is a summary? In Wikipedia, automatic summarization is defined as: "... the creation of a shortened version of a text by a computer program. The product of this procedure still contains the most important points of the original text."[2] Apparently this definition is restricted to textual input, without taking into consideration speech or other media. Another definition of summarization (Mani, 2001) is: "to take an information source, extract content from it, and present the most important content to the user in a condensed form and in a manner sensitive to the user's application's needs". This definition seems to be not specific to a particular input media, and applies to speech summarization. Note that this definition is also quite general, and does not clearly specify all the factors in automatic summarization, such as summary length (or compression ratio), format, etc.

Summarization can be divided into different categories based on several dimensions, listed below:[3]

- *Extractive versus abstractive*: Extractive summaries are composed of units (typically sentences) selected from the original documents (or recordings) that are concatenated together; abstractive summaries consist of regeneration of sentences, representing often a higher level perspective.
- *Generic versus query or topic oriented*: In the former, summaries are generated without regard to any specific information need, but rather based on the inherent informativeness of the entire original document. For the latter, summaries are generated based on a particular query, therefore, units are selected partly based on their relevance to the provided query or user's information need.
- *Single versus multiple documents*: This is dependent on the number of documents in the input, whether it is just a single document or there are multiple documents. For the latter,

[2] Accessed on March 01, 2010

[3] Some of these are based on (Mani, 2001).

often the collection of documents is around similar topics, and thus identifying redundancy is a critical issue.

- *Input/output media*: Another way to divide summarization is based on the input media, for example, whether it is text or speech based. The same division applies to the output summary: it can be in the format of either text or speech.
- *Other dimensions*: The task of summarization also has other variations. For example, one task in the recent TAC evaluations is update summarization,[4] "the update summarization task is to write a short (about 100 words) summary of a set of newswire articles, under the assumption that the user has already read a given set of earlier articles. The summaries will be evaluated for overall responsiveness and content". Another summarization task is opinion summarization in TAC 2008: "The 2008 Opinion Summarization pilot task is to generate well-organized, fluent summaries of opinions about specified targets, as found in a set of blog documents."

  Another dimension is interactivity. While some systems generate summaries in a single pass, some others allow users to provide further feedback, for example through selecting the most important sentence for each iterative step (Lin *et al.*, 2010a), or selecting key words/phrases or increasing their weight (Mieskes *et al.*, 2007; Riedhammer *et al.*, 2008a).

13.1.2 Speech Summarization

Compared to the various task definition and efforts in text summarization, there is less work on speech summarization and the history is not long. Starting from 1990s, there was some initial work on automatic summarization of audio documents. So far most of the research efforts have focused on extractive generic summarization using a single document (for example, a lecture or a meeting). For this task, systems need to determine the importance of sentences (or other units), "extract" important ones from the original document, and "paste" them to form a summary.

Figures 13.1 and 13.2 show annotated extractive summary examples for two different genres, broadcast news[5] (BN) and meetings,[6] respectively. In both examples, summary sentences are selected from the original transcripts, thus forming extractive summaries. These summary sentences are shown in boldface in the example. We also provide human-written abstractive summaries of these examples.[7]

There is also some investigation of other tasks in speech summarization, for example, query-focused summarization, where a query (or question) is given, and the system needs to return an answer or a summary from a collection of audio recordings (Maskey, 2008); abstractive summarization where the system cannot simply cut and paste to generate a summary, but rather needs to rewrite sentences to form a coherent summary (Kleinbauer *et al.*, 2007; Murray *et al.*, 2010). There are also efforts using multi-documents. Zhu *et al.* (2009) attempted using reoccurrence statistics of acoustic patterns in multiple recordings for acoustic-based summarization, without using transcriptions from speech recognizers. (Banerjee and Rudnicky, 2009) looked into a series of the meetings of the same group to extract noteworthy utterances.

---

[4] http://www.nist.gov/tac/

[5] The broadcast news example is from (Maskey, 2008).

[6] The meeting example is from the ICSI meeting corpus (Janin *et al.*, 2003).

[7] For abstractive summaries, there was no specified targeted length, therefore it was up to the annotators to decide an appropriate length.

Transcripts of an excerpt from a BN document:

s1: california's strained power grid is getting a boost today which might help increasingly taxed power supplies
s2: a unit at diablo canyon nuclear plant is expected to resume production today
s3: it had been shut down for maintenance
s4: coupled with another unit, it can provide enough power for about 2 million people
***** s5: meanwhile, a cold snap in the pacific northwest is putting an added strain on power supplies**
s6: the area shares power across many states
s7: energy officials are offering tips to conserve electricity, they say, to delay holiday lighting until after at night
***** s8: set your thermostat at 68 degrees when you're home, 55 degrees when you're away**
***** s9: try to use electrical appliances before p.m. and after p.m. and turn off computers, copiers and lights when they're not being used**

Abstract:

While California's power grid is getting a boost today, a cold snap in the pacific northwest is putting an added strain on power supplies. Authorities offer tips to conserve electricity, for example, holiday lighting can be delayed, heating can be turned down when houses are vacant, or electrical appliances can be turned off when they are not used.

Figure 13.1 Transcription of an excerpt from a BN document. The symbol s* at the beginning of the sentence is used to represent the sentence ID. The extractive summary sentences are shown with bold-face fonts, and also preceded with "***". The bottom part shows an abstractive summary example for this excerpt

A speech summarization system typically involves addressing the following problems:

- *Speech recognition.* Summarization is typically done at the semantic meaning level, therefore transcribing speech recordings is often a first step, even though there are some attempts to use only audio and features extracted from acoustics for summarization (see Section 13.6).
- *Summarization.* Of course, one can apply existing text summarization techniques to the recognition output from the step above to generate a textual summary. However, as we will see later, there are many challenges arising in this pipeline approach. Furthermore, additional information from audio, such as the prosody of speech, can play a role in summarization.
- *Rendering the output.* A summarization system needs to present the summary to the user in some reasonable fashion, whether it is in text or speech. Other than simply presenting one final output of summary, the system may show highlights of text selected from the original transcripts, allow for different compression ratios, or provide a different granularity for zoom-in. These are also related to human-computer interaction and require some user studies to determine the best rendering strategy.

In this chapter, we attempt to mainly focus on the second item, speech summarization. We describe challenges of summarization (Section 13.2), review data sets that have been used for speech summarization (Section 13.3), discuss evaluation methods used for speech summarization (Section 13.4), and provide a survey of methods (Section 13.5) and trends (Section 13.6).

Transcripts of a meeting excerpt:
***** *me010:* there there are a variety of ways of doing it**
me010: uh let me just mention something that i don't want to pursue today
me010: which is there are technical ways of doing it
me010: uh i- i slipped a paper to bhaskara and about noisy-or's and noisy-maxes
me010: and
me010: there're ways to uh sort of back off on the purity of your bayes-net-edness
me003: mmm
me010: uh so if you co- you could ima- and i-
me010: now i don't know that any of those actually apply in this case
me010: but there is some technology you could try to apply
***** *me003:* so it's possible that we could do something like a summary node of some sort that**
me010: yeah
me003: ok
me010: yeah
me010: and um
me010: so
me003: so in that case the sum- we'd have we
me003: i mean these wouldn't be the summary nodes
me003: we'd have the summary nodes like
me003: where the things were i guess maybe if thi- if things were related to business or some other
me010: yeah
***** *me010:* so what i was gonna say is is maybe a good at this point is to try to informally**
me003: yeah
***** *me010:* i mean not necessarily in th- in this meeting but to try to informally think about what the decision variables are**
me010: so if you have some bottom line uh decision about which mode
me010: you know what are the most relevant things
me003: mmm

Abstract: These can be tackled either with technical adjustments or through careful knowledge engineering.

Figure 13.2 Transcripts of a meeting excerpt. Each sentence has the speaker ID associated with it, included at the beginning of each sentence (for example, me010). The sentences chosen for the extractive summary are shown in bold face, and the bottom part of the figure shows an abstractive summary of this excerpt

13.1.3 Applications

Speech summarization can be a useful tool to handle the overwhelming amount of information available in audio recordings. We know that listening to the entire recording can be time consuming, especially when the information density, that is the ratio of the duration of relevant information to the duration of the overall audio recording, is low. He *et al.* (2000) showed that compared to providing full transcripts, slides, or both to the users, either playing back important audio-video segments or just highlighting the corresponding transcripts is significantly better when browsing presentation recordings. (Tucker and Whittaker, 2008) compared extractive summarization to time compression of speech recordings with different compression rates (used to speed up playback of speech), and showed that summarization is generally preferable to the latter. Murray *et al.* (2009) used a decision audit setup, where the users were asked to browse several meetings to understand how and why a decision was made. They showed that extractive and abstractive summaries are useful to satisfy this information need. These task-based evaluations demonstrate the effectiveness and the usefulness of automatic speech summarization. In the following, we enumerate a few examples where speech summarization can be used.

- A lot of people complain that there are many meetings every day.[8] The information density is quite low in meetings partly due to the conversational style, and many chit-chat and off topic discussions. Meeting summarization is an important component in a meeting browser system. It can be used by both meeting participants and other people who did not attend the meetings, to find and track some action items or other discussions.
- Similar to news articles, broadcast news speech from multiple sources may contain similar content. A multi-document summarization system can be used here to provide users a short summary related to a particular event so that the user does not need to listen to all the news.
- Lectures are being recorded more and more. For example, thousands of lectures and presentations (in video format, sometimes with attached slides) are available online from http://videolectures.net/. Many universities also have their lectures recorded. However, often this good source of education is not well utilized. Lecture summarization will be able to help more effective indexing, search, and information access, resulting in a significant impact on education.
- There are some voice messages left in phones (while the user is not available). Often there is no need to listen to an entire message. Some previous research focused on recording, automatically transcribing, and browsing these messages (Hirschberg *et al.*, 2001). A summarization system for voice mails can generate the important parts of the messages, such as reason for the phone call, information that caller needs, return phone number, etc. This is better than simply removing pauses in voice mails for faster playback. These summaries can be presented to the user in different formats, via email, events in calendar, and so on.
- Speech summarization can also be useful for information analysts working for commercial marketing or government intelligence. A human analyst cannot listen to all the speech recordings, broadcast news, conversational speech, some of which may also be in other languages. Speech summarization can provide a short summary in response to an analyst's query or provide locations for salient segments for humans to listen. For example, the distillation task in the DARPA GALE project aimed to provide excerpts to human analysts from multi-lingual audio and textual information sources (Hakkani-Tür and Tur, 2007), and is similar to query-focused multi-document summarization.

13.2 Challenges when Using Speech Input

Research on text summarization started over 50 years ago, and has seen drastic advances in the past decades. One straightforward approach for speech summarization would be to apply

[8] There are some studies to examine the effect of meetings, on individuals, for example, http://www.guardian.co.uk/education/2006/jan/17/highereducation.research discusses the negative effects of more meetings or more time spent in meetings.

mature text summarization techniques to the speech transcriptions (once an automatic speech recognizer generates them). Indeed, some text summarization techniques (see Section 13.5) have been successfully used or adapted to deal with speech input. However, speech is inherently different from text, which poses challenges to summarization approaches that were originally developed for textual input. This section describes some of the general challenges. More research investigating the effect of these problems on summarization or addressing these challenges will be discussed in Section 13.6.

13.2.1 Automatic Speech Recognition Errors

Dramatic reduction in word error rate (WER) has been achieved in speech recognition during the past decades. Current speech recognition systems generally perform well when dealing with read or clean speech, but degrade significantly for conversational speech, speakers with accents, noisy conditions, overlapped speech, etc. Some of the recognition errors may not affect downstream language processing modules (e.g. deletion of a determiner), but many others will have a negative impact (e.g. incorrect or missing content words). More importantly, a recognizer usually makes errors when coming across out-of-vocabulary words, which in many cases carry important information. For summarization, many techniques rely on the word identity and frequency to determine the importance of words and sentences. Incorrect recognition of important content words changes their identity or frequency, and thus is a potential problem for speech summarization.

Below, we show the recognition output[9] for the meeting transcript example shown in Section 13.1. Some of the recognition errors are highlighted in order to easily see the difference. We can see the problems with out-of-vocabulary and domain specific words. For example, *bhaskara* is recognized as *bust corrupt*, and *noisy-maxes* as *noisy oars*. These errors result in incorrect meanings and may hurt summarization performance.

13.2.2 Speaker Turns

Speech recognizers usually generate only the transcriptions of spoken words. However, when working with conversational speech, who the speaker of the utterance is also carries important information. For example, in Figure 13.2, the identity of the speaker of each utterance is shown. Reading or automatic processing of these transcriptions would be much more difficult if the turn boundaries and speakers were not shown. Automatic diarization methods (Reynolds and Torres-Carrasquillo, 2005) aim to identify who spoke and when in conversations. However, note that even though significant advances have been shown in evaluations organized by NIST (Istrate *et al.*, 2005), this is not yet a fully solved problem, and diarization systems still make mistakes. Such errors cause challenges for further language processing tasks that utilize speaker information.

13.2.3 Sentence Boundaries

Speech recognition output is generally based on acoustic segments, which can contain more than one "sentence" or incomplete sentences, and thus may not be appropriate for some

[9] This is from a state-of-the-art speech recognition system (Stolcke *et al.*, 2006).

s1: they're they're variety of ways of doing it uh let me just mention something that i don't want to pursue today which is there are technical ways of doing it uh i so i slipped the paper to bust corrupt and about noisy oars and always the taxes and their ways to uh sort of back off on the purity of your base net in this uh self if you could do could have matt and no i don't know that any of those actually apply in this case but there is some technology you could try to apply

s2: uhhuh

s3: so it's possible that we could do something like a summary note of some sort that okay

s4: yeah

s5: yeah

s6: and um

s7: so

s8: so in that case the summer we'd have we'd i mean these wouldn't be the summer has we've had some and i was like weather things for i guess maybe taking things were related to business or

s9: that so what i was going to say is is maybe a good idea at this point is to try to in the formally i mean not necessarily in the in this meeting that to try to informally think about what's the decision variables are so if you had some bottom line uh decision about which mode you know what are the most relevant things

s10: some other yeah

s11: uhhuh

Figure 13.3 Speech recognition output for the meeting transcript example in Figure 13.2. We highlight some incorrectly recognized words (underlined)

downstream language processing modules. In contrast, linguistic segments are expected to be more appropriate for summarization. Currently most text-based extractive summarization techniques use sentences as inputs, therefore the lack of proper sentence boundary information is a problem to extractive summarization systems. In addition, sentence length has been shown to be an important cue for summarization, thus incorrect sentence segmentation results in wrong information about sentence length and affects summarization.

In the example shown in Figure 13.3, we can see that the segments in ASR output do not correspond to the sentences shown earlier in the human transcripts. Take the first segment in ASR output as an example. It consists of several sentences. Human-annotated summaries contain one of those sentences. When using ASR output segments as the extractive units for summarization, the system will either select this segment, resulting in low precision (percentage of word matches with reference summaries relative to the system selected summary), or not select this one, hurting recall scores (percentage of word matches with reference summaries relative to the reference summary).

13.2.4 *Disfluencies and Ungrammatical Utterances*

In conversational or spontaneous speech, disfluencies are very common. Here, we loosely use "disfluencies" to mean everything that is not fluent, such as filled pauses (*uh*, *um*), discourse markers (e.g. *you know*), repetitions, corrections, repairs, and incomplete sentences. In the meeting domain, disfluencies are very frequent due to the cognitive load and the planning process during the spontaneous conversations and the frequent floor changes (e.g. yielding a floor in the middle of a sentence or a failed attempt at grabbing a floor can result in incomplete utterances). In broadcast news speech, there are fewer disfluencies or ungrammatical sentences in anchor's speech (as they are often reading news).

In the example shown in Section 13.1, there are some disfluencies in the meeting transcripts. We can also see from the ASR output that there are recognition errors around those regions. Sentences containing disfluencies may also cause problems for summarization. They change the word frequencies (e.g. repeated words) and sentence length information, and make syntactic analysis (e.g. parsing) difficult. One practice to deal with disfluencies in spoken language processing is to identify disfluencies, remove them, and provide the cleaned utterances to subsequent language processing modules.

Note that there may be ungrammatical sentences that do not necessarily contain disfluencies. These may also be problematic for summarization if syntactic analysis is used.

13.2.5 Other Style and Structural Information

There are other structural and style differences between text and speech.

- Written documents are typically well organized into paragraphs and sections; whereas for speech, this kind of information is not readily available. However, in speech, there can be other types of implicit structural information. For example, broadcast news may be segmented into different stories. Furthermore, there may be audio or visual cues for segments, such as music or screen changes at the beginning of advertisements. Meetings are often structured based on meeting agenda, and are composed of sections of discussion, summary, action items, etc. Lecture speech typically consists of introduction, detailed discussion of methods, and conclusions, and is often accompanied by presentation slides. This kind of structural or topic information may be useful for summarization (Xie *et al.*, 2008; Zhang *et al.*, 2007b).
- In written text, an overview generally appears upfront; whereas for speech, information is more distributed. Therefore, features used in text-based summarization may not generalize well to speech summarization. For example, positional information is important for text summarization – the first few lines of a news article provide a good summary; however, this is not always applicable to dialogs or multiparty meetings.
- The output of ASR systems usually lacks capitalization that marks the beginning of sentences and proper names in English. Names are also frequently misrecognized, but they can carry useful information and play an important role in summarization.
- Information density is generally lower in speech than in text. Additionally, spoken dialogues may contain small talk or chit chat that is not related to the topics under discussion.
- Speech data may contain multiple speakers, whereas in text, it is typically just one writer. Speaker changes can provide information about the discourse structure and turn flow. Speaker segmentation and clustering is not an easy task if speech is recorded using a single microphone (i.e. table-mounted microphone in a meeting recording room). In addition, speakers often differ in their speaking style (e.g. verbosity, word usage, prosodic characteristics). Speech summarization systems may need to take into account speaker specific styles by normalizing features used in the system or developing speaker dependent models.
- Overlaps happen when multiple people talk at the same time (often in conversational speech). Overlaps are another factor degrading speech recognition accuracy in conversational speech.

Cetin and Shriberg (2006) examined speech recognition errors during and around overlaps, and showed that recognition errors are highly likely, not just during overlaps, but also around them. Overlaps are also a problem when summaries are presented to the user in the form of audio extracts (which somewhat solves the problem of speech recognition errors in a summary). For example, when multiple speakers are talking at the same time in an excerpt, it may be difficult (if not impossible) for a human to detect which speaker's utterance contains the important information.

- Another difference between ASR output and written text is due to text normalization. Speech recognizers usually perform a form of normalization, partly to account for the difference between written and spoken languages (e.g. handling digits). Sometimes, such re-formatting hides information, for example dates, which makes them easier to be detected visually, or automatically, in text. Such differences, if not de-normalized, also make it difficult to benefit from the abundance of annotated data in text, that can be used for training.
- In addition to the above difficulties, speech also contains information not available in text, such as acoustic and prosodic cues. These are usually lost during the translation from speech to the sequence of words, for example, the fact that a sentence or word is emphasized by the speaker, yet they may provide important information for summarization.

Note that many of the problems above also exist for other spoken language processing systems that use speech input (as described in other chapters in this book). It is known that in general speech recognition errors affect subsequent language processing modules, such as sentence boundary and disfluency detection (Liu *et al.*, 2006), parsing (Harper *et al.*, 2005), audio indexing and retrieval (Makhoul *et al.*, 2000). The impact of sentence boundaries on the subsequent language processing tasks has also been studied recently. Significant negative impact has been observed using system-generated sentence boundaries on parsing (Harper *et al.*, 2005) and machine translation (Zong and Ren, 2003). In addition, the best threshold for the sentence boundary detection task is not the same as that obtained when optimizing performance for downstream processing. Better performance has been shown when sentence segmentation is optimized with the goal of improving parsing (Harper *et al.*, 2005), machine translation (Matusov *et al.*, 2007), and information extraction (Favre *et al.*, 2008). Disfluencies have also been shown to be problematic for many natural language processing tasks, such as parsing (Harper *et al.*, 2005), and machine translation (Wang *et al.*, 2010).

13.3 Data Sets

For text summarization, some benchmark test sets are available, such as DUC or TAC data sets for single-document summarization, multi-document summarization, update summarization, and opinion summarization. In contrast, as yet, there is no widely used benchmark data set for speech summarization. In this section, we describe some of the data resources that have been developed and used in previous work. Such corpora have been developed for several languages. We divide them according to genres, i.e. broadcast news, lectures, and conversational speech including meetings and telephone conversations. In the description below, we focus more on summary annotation, and will only briefly mention other relevant information such as audio recordings, ASR systems, and other annotation. More detailed information can be found in the articles cited.

13.3.1 Broadcast News (BN)

Speech recognition performance in the broadcast news domain is generally quite good (WER is low). In addition, this domain is very similar to news articles in terms of style; therefore it is a good starting point to investigate if text summarization techniques are portable to speech summarization using this genre. Indeed, a lot of the early efforts on speech summarization used broadcast news speech. The following lists a few examples.

- Columbia University created two corpora using a subset of the TDT shows (Maskey, 2008). Their annotation includes summaries and other information related to information extraction, such as named entities, headlines, anchors, reporters, interviewees, soundbites and soundbite-speakers.

  The first corpus consists of 216 stories from 20 CNN Headline News shows (part of the TDT-2 data). The speech data is about 10 hours. Different transcripts were available for this corpus: manual transcription, closed-caption transcripts, as well as some ASR transcripts. The manual transcripts of this data set also include story segment boundaries and topic labels. One annotator created extractive summaries for the stories. The annotator was not given explicit instructions about the desired length of the summaries.

  The second data set consists of 20 CNN Headline News Shows from the TDT4 corpus. The manual transcripts have annotation of turn boundaries, topic labels, and story boundaries. On average, the stories contain less than 10 sentences, but with a large variance. Three native English-speaking annotators created both extractive and abstractive summaries for 447 stories of this data set. The annotators were asked to write a summary with a desired word compression ratio of 30% (i.e. summary length is about 30% of the original length, measured using the number of words) in their own words and whenever possible using the original words in the BN stories. They used a two-step process: first the annotators wrote abstractive summaries, and then extracted sentences from the story that supported their abstract, forming extractive summaries. Of the three annotators who wrote abstracts, two of them also generated extractive summaries. (Maskey, 2008) found that the annotators did not necessarily follow the desired summary length. For example, the compression ratio sometimes is very high, especially for those short stories. The Kappa score (Carletta, 1996) for the extractive summaries is 0.4126, which is considered a reasonable number.
- The University of Sheffield also used part of the TDT2 BN corpus for extractive summarization (Christensen *et al.*, 2003). Their data had closed-caption transcriptions and a set of ASR transcriptions from six different recognition systems (used in the TREC experiment), with WER ranging from 20.5 to 32%. All the transcripts have manually labeled sentence boundaries and story boundaries, and automatically generated speaker turns. They used 114 ABC news broadcasts, consisting of about 43 hours of speech, and 855 stories in total. One human annotator was asked to select one sentence for each story in the corpus, therefore this one-sentence extractive summary is more like a headline. In addition, they randomly selected 44 stories in the corpus, and asked five other annotators to generate summaries for these. The Kappa estimate is 0.56 for the 6 annotators. They did not observe a noticeable difference between native (4 people) and non-native (2 people) human annotators.
- Lin *et al.* (2009b) used a set of 205 Chinese broadcast news documents from the MATBN corpus (Wang *et al.*, 2005). The average Chinese character error rate (CER) of the recognition output for the data was about 30%. Three subjects were asked to create summaries. They first

selected 50% of the most important sentences in the transcript, and then further ranked them by importance. This kind of ranking enables creation of summaries of different compression ratios. On a subset of the data (the test set they used, containing 125 documents), the inter-annotator agreement using ROUGE_2 is about 0.65 for different compression ratios (10 to 30%). This seems a rather high agreement, compared to results reported for other domains in the literature. Another similar data set (consisting of BN shows in Mandarin, and with similar summary annotation method) was used in other studies (e.g. Chen and Chen, 2008; Chen *et al.*, 2006).

- Hori and Furui (2001) and Hori *et al.* (2003) used a set of Japanese TV broadcast news recorded in 1996 for speech summarization. Five news articles, each consisting of 5 sentences, were summarized at 30% summarization ratio. For the evaluation set, they selected 50 utterances with word recognition accuracy above 90%. They used different summarization ratios in different studies, e.g. 70% in Hori and Furui (2001), and 40% in Hori *et al.* (2003). This data set is smaller than most data used in other studies.
- Zhang and Fung (2007) used a subset of the 1997 Hub4 Mandarin corpus. Each broadcast lasted approximately for half an hour. The data has been hand-segmented into speaker turns. They divided these broadcast news stories into three types: one-turn news, weather forecast, and several-turns news. The several-turns news contain more than one reporter, and sometimes interviewees, and were the only type used for summarization. In total, there are 347 stories (4748 sentences). They created three versions of reference summaries based on summarization ratios of 10, 15, and 20%, respectively.
- Ribeiro and de Matos (2007) used a Portuguese broadcast news program in their experiment for extractive summarization. Their data set is segmented into stories. The size of the stories ranged from 10 to 100 sentences. They asked two annotators to create summaries using ASR output, with a compression rate of 10%.

13.3.2 Lectures

- Zhang *et al.* (2007b) used part of a conference presentation corpus. The presentations were from different speakers, and each lasted about 15 minutes on average. 71 lectures together with PowerPoint slides were used in their studies. Their data has both manual transcriptions and recognition results (accuracy is 70.3%). They proposed a method to automatically generate reference summaries using the information on the presentation slides. They argue that this is feasible because the slides are prepared by the authors themselves, and thus represent a good summary of their work. Furthermore, there is a rich rhetorical lecture structure in the slides (e.g. titles, page breaks, bullet points) that can be useful for summarization. A similar idea of using the correlation between the slides and extractive summaries was also investigated in He *et al.* (1999, 2000).

  To automatically generate a reference summary, they proposed a Relaxed Dynamic Time Warping (RDTW) procedure to align sentences from the slides to those in the transcriptions of the lecture. Cosine similarity between sentences in transcriptions and slides was used to find the initial alignment using DTW. Then, considering that speakers may not always follow the slide order strictly, they relaxed the alignment order constraint to allow the matching of sentences close by. Summaries are created in this way for introduction, content, and conclusion in the lectures.

  They compared these reference summaries to human-labeled summaries. They found that the inter-annotator agreement ranged from 30 to 50% when using the original lecture transcripts for sentence selection. However, when the annotators were asked to follow the structure and points in the presentation slides, the inter-annotator agreement increased to 80.2%. In addition, the agreement between automatically generated reference summaries and human summaries also reached 75%. Therefore, they first generated summaries using the RDTW algorithm, and then asked a human to perform manual correction based on the transcription and the corresponding slides.

- Penn and Zhu (2008) used undergraduate Computer Science lectures recorded at the University of Toronto. Each lecture lasts 50 minutes. Three human subjects performed the summary annotation using manual transcripts, aligned audio, and the slides provided by the instructors. They were asked to mark utterances that correspond to the bullets in the slides and also the main utterances that support each bullet. They used an ePresentation interface developed at the University of Toronto for the summary annotation. Results in Penn and Zhu (2008) are based on four different lectures that are from different instructors and different courses. In order to compare with the Switchboard data, they also divided lectures into 8- to 15-minute intervals randomly, and treated each interval as a separate document and summarized them separately. The four lectures yielded 16 Switchboard-sized documents. When comparing to the Switchboard data, they found that the interannotator agreement measured using Kappa statistics is 0.372 on the lecture corpus, slightly lower than 0.383 on the Switchboard data.
- Furui *et al.* (2004) used a part of the Corpus of Spontaneous Japanese (Maekawa *et al.*, 2000) that contains recorded monologues such as lectures, presentations and news commentaries. They excluded the recordings with low spontaneity, such as those from read text. The data was manually transcribed orthographically and phonetically. In Furui *et al.* (2004), three presentations in this corpus were used. They created summaries, with a ratio of 70 and 50% by nine human subjects.

13.3.3 Multi-party Conversational Speech

For conversational speech, we include some resources for both multiparty meeting recordings and two-party conversational telephone speech.

- Meetings

  A. Meeting recordings

  There are several meeting recordings, such as those used in the NIST Rich Transcription evaluations. However, since most of the meeting summarization research used the AMI and ICSI corpora, we mainly describe these two corpora here.

  The AMI corpus consists of about 100 hours of meeting recordings.[10] It is multi-modal, and contains a variety of information such as slides, whiteboard events, and participant notes. There are both scenario and non-scenario meetings in this corpus. In the scenario meetings, four participants play different roles within a fictional company, with a task to design and market a new remote control. The participants' speech and the actions are spontaneous and natural, even though the scenario given to them is artificial. There are 138 such meetings in total. A meeting lasts from 15 to 45 minutes, depending on the function of the meeting and the participants. The non-scenario meetings are real naturally occurring regular meetings. The topics discussed and the number of participants vary across different meetings.

[10] The AMI corpus is freely available from http://www.amiproject.org.

The ICSI meeting corpus contains 75 natural non-scenario meetings recorded at ICSI (Janin *et al.*, 2003). Each meeting is about an hour long. The number of participants in these meetings varies, with an average of six speakers. The topics in the meetings are mainly research discussions, such as on speech processing, computer networks, data recordings, and linguistics. Unlike the multi-modal AMI corpus that also includes video recordings, the ICSI meeting recordings consist of only speech.

B. Annotations

The AMI and ICSI meeting corpora have various annotations, such as dialogue act (DA) units and tags (Shriberg *et al.*, 2004), topic segments (Galley *et al.*, 2004), and subjectivity (Wilson, 2008). Here we only describe summary annotations. Both abstractive and extractive summaries were created for the AMI and ICSI meeting corpora under the AMI/AMIDA project. The annotators were asked to first write an abstractive summary. Four headings for the summary were provided to the annotator for this purpose: general abstract, decision made, actions, and problems. The detailed headings for the AMI and ICSI corpora are different (See Murray (2008) for more information). The maximum length for the abstractive summary is 200 words for each section. After writing an abstractive summary, annotators were asked to create an extractive summary by selecting the DAs that convey the information in the abstractive summary and support the abstract. The number or percentage of DAs for the extractive summaries is not specified. Then in a second-pass annotation, for each selected extractive DA, the annotator was asked to choose the abstract sentences supported by that DA. These steps generate a many-to-many mapping between abstract sentences and extracted DAs.

In Murray *et al.* (2005a) and later research on the meeting summarization task using the ICSI meeting data, 6 meetings were used as test meetings. For these, multiple summaries were available (4 to 5 annotators). For the ICSI test set, the average Kappa value is 0.35. The average Kappa value is 0.45 for the entire AMI data set, and 0.48 for the AMI test set. They attributed the lower agreement on the ICSI data than that on the AMI data to the fact that the ICSI meetings are natural conversations and are less structured compared with the scenario-driven AMI meetings.

There are other smaller scale summary annotations for these meeting corpora. For example, Buist *et al.* (2005) used 6 ICSI meetings, and labeled each pause-based segment for importance on a ternary scale. Segments labeled with a score of 3 form a summary in their experiments. Liu and Liu (2008b) used 27 meetings from the ICSI corpus for a study on human agreement on meeting summary annotation. Three annotators were recruited to extract summary sentences on a topic basis using the topic segments annotated for this corpus. The recommended percentages for the selected summary sentences and words were set to 8.0 and 16.0% respectively. The Kappa score was found to be 0.261 for this data. Further investigation was performed for the impacting factors on agreement. They observed that the topic length does not have an impact on the human agreement, but the number of speakers seems to be correlated with the agreement (lower agreement as the number of speakers increases), suggesting that summary annotation for multiparty conversations is hard.

Banerjee and Rudnicky (2008) also used meeting recordings, but their ultimate goal is note taking, therefore the task is to identify noteworthy utterances. This is quite similar to summarization. They used a sequence of related meetings that are natural weekly project meetings, where participants take notes and share them live (the participants usually take notes to remember some information later on). Both the speech and the notes are recorded. Each meeting is about half an hour long, with 4 or 5 participants. A manual step is used to label utterances that are most closely related to the notes. One line of note can be aligned to multiple utterances. They only used one annotator. Overall, 5% of all the utterances in the meetings are aligned with notes, which corresponds to a quite low compression ratio.

- Conversational telephone speech. Switchboard corpus contains conversational telephone speech where two people talk over the phone about an assigned topic. The conversations average about 6 minutes in length. Penn and Zhu (2008) randomly selected 27 conversations from the Switchboard corpus for summarization. They used pause-based segmentation, resulting in a total of 3,665 utterances. Three human annotators manually labeled each utterance for inclusion in the summary or not. They found it hard to identify important information from this data, mainly because there is no specific goal in these conversations.

  Zechner (2002) also used conversational speech for summarization, including Callhome/callfriend data, newshour TV show, crossfire TV show, as well as some meetings data. 4 to 6 human annotators generated summaries. They first labeled topical boundaries. Then for each topic segment, each annotator identified the most relevant information units (IUs) and somewhat relevant IUs. These units are often equivalent to sentences, but can be longer or shorter, depending on the annotator. Annotators were also asked to mark the most salient words within their annotated IUs, with a defined target length for salient words using 10–20% of all the words in the segment. After each annotator worked independently, two people from the initial group created a common annotation, based on the majority opinion of the whole group. Their results showed low Kappa statistics, ranging from 0.04 to 0.16 for different conversational data. Detailed results can be found in Zechner (2002).

13.3.4 Voice Mail

Koumpis and Renals (2005) used the IBM Voicemail Corpus, with an average of about 90 words per message. They annotated summary words in 1000 messages of the Voicemail corpus. Words that determine the reason for calling were selected as summary words. They also used named entity information (available in the corpus) to help the summary annotation. For example, the first occurrence of the names of the speaker and recipient was selected. No audio was used for annotation. The compression ratio is in the range of 19–31%. They measured human agreement using 16 human annotators on five messages and found that Kappa is 0.48 for summaries with a compression ratio of about 30%. This seems to be a relatively good level of agreement, considering the number of annotators; however, the task may be easier than other generic summarization of longer speech.

13.4 Evaluation Metrics

Evaluation of summarization methods is necessary not only for end-users to decide on the appropriate summarizer to use, but also for researchers and developers to build better summarization algorithms. Evaluation of summarization systems is a challenging task in part due to the difficulty of creating a gold standard that can be considered as the correct summary, because even human-generated summaries are different from each other. For example, Kappa statistics of human agreement is approximately 38%, even for the relatively easy news documents (Mani *et al.*, 2002).

Similar to many other natural language processing tasks, evaluation methods for summarization can be categorized into two: *intrinsic* and *extrinsic* evaluation methods. In intrinsic evaluation of summarization, machine-produced summaries are compared with human-generated summaries with the goal of computing how well the two match. On the other hand, in extrinsic evaluation, the utility of the summarization system for a real-world task is estimated. For example, one can ask human subjects questions after reading the original documents versus the compact summaries, and measure how many of the questions are answered correctly with each type of information sources and how long it takes to write the answers. While intrinsic evaluation methods are usually much easier and cheaper to perform, and hence can help greatly in system development, extrinsic evaluation methods usually are a better way of comparing different approaches to summarization. However, extrinsic evaluation requires a lot of human efforts during the design and employment of the evaluation task. The design of extrinsic tests is usually quite complex, and it may not be so easy to interpret the evaluation results. But once designed, the tests may be used to compare several systems, and may be useful in picking the best system for the final and real task.

Another dimension of summarization evaluation is the performer of the evaluation: Summarization can be evaluated through human assessment or automatic evaluation. Human evaluations can be conducted for the content match, overall quality, grammaticality, coherence, and organization. Tests were performed in SUMMAC for more extrinsic task-oriented evaluations, such as using the summary for categorization and question-answering (Mani *et al.*, 1998). Compared with human evaluation, automated summary evaluation is more objective and can help reduce human efforts and speed up system development.

In the following, we list several evaluation methods that have been used in previous speech summarization research. Many of them were adopted from text summarization, some with variations adapted for evaluating summaries formed from spoken data.

13.4.1 Recall, Precision, and F-measure

For extractive summarization evaluation, the system output can be compared with potentially multiple reference summaries, and precision and recall at the sentence level can be computed. *Precision* is the percentage of the sentences in the system output summary, which are also included in one or more human summaries. *Recall* is the percentage of the human summary sentences (i.e. the sentences that are included in one or more human summaries) that are included in the system output summary. Usually, the harmonic mean of recall and precision, the *F-measure* is also used.

Sentence level recall, precision, and F-measure are easy to implement, and provide developers some information about the content match between the system and human summaries. However, they are very strict (requiring exact sentence matching), and do not model redundancy well. For example, if the original document (or especially multi-documents) contains two sentences with a very similar meaning, and if both sentences are marked by one or more of the human summarizers, these measures will score both sentences when they are included in the summary, and will not punish redundancy. Furthermore, if only one of them is included in the system summary, then the system will be punished for not picking the other sentence.

13.4.2 ROUGE

Similar to the BLEU (bilingual evaluation understudy) scores for machine translation (Papineni *et al.*, 2001), ROUGE scores for summarization evaluation (Lin, 2004) measure the ratio of word n-gram matches between the system-generated candidate summary and a set of human summaries. Among various versions of ROUGE scores, the most commonly used ones are ROUGE-1, ROUGE-2, ROUGE-SU4, and ROUGE-L. ROUGE-1 considers unigrams, ROUGE-2 considers bigrams, ROUGE-SU4 considers unigrams and skip bigrams (i.e. word pairs that are separated by at most 4 words), and ROUGE-L considers the longest common subsequences.

ROUGE scores are used as the automatic evaluation measures in the evaluations performed by the NIST Document Understanding and Text Analysis conferences (DUC and TAC). Though originally developed for text summarization, ROUGE has been used for speech summarization widely. Systems compare their extracted sentences (whether from human transcripts or ASR output) to human-annotated summary sentences and calculate ROUGE scores.

The main advantage of using ROUGE scores is that they are very easy to compute, and they punish redundancy at the word n-gram level. However, since they only work at the n-gram level, they do not capture information spread over sentences. For example, even if a sentence is mistakenly negated in the system summary output, a summary including it may be scored almost as high as the one with the correct version of that sentence, since most n-grams in these summaries would be the same.

While ROUGE scores have been shown to correlate well with human judgments for text summarization, especially when multiple human summaries are used Lin (2004), for speech summarization, there is less correlation between ROUGE and human scores. Murray *et al.* (2005b) reported that ROUGE-1 (unigram match) scores have low correlation with human evaluation for meeting summarization. (Liu and Liu, 2008a) showed similar overall low correlation results, with ROUGE-SU4 yielding better correlation with human scores than ROUGE-1.

13.4.3 The Pyramid Method

Another evaluation measure is the Pyramid evaluation (Nenkova and Passonneau, 2004), which has seen broad acceptance from the research community (especially for text summarization). In this method, summary content is described by summary content units (SCUs), which are units not bigger than a clause and emerge from the annotation of a corpus of summaries. Similar sentences in summaries are identified, and more tightly related parts are extracted. For example, from the analysis of the following sentences presented in (Nenkova and Passonneau, 2004):

- In 1998 two Libyans indicted in 1991 for the Lockerbie bombing were still in Libya.
- Two Libyans were indicted in 1991 for blowing up a Pan Am jumbo jet over Lockerbie, Scotland in 1988.
- Two Libyans, accused by the United States and Britain of bombing a New York bound Pan Am jet over Lockerbie, Scotland in 1988, killing 270 people, for 10 years were harbored by Libya who claimed the suspects could not get a fair trail in America or Britain.
- Two Libyan suspects were indicted in 1991.

two SCUs are obtained:

1. two Libyans were officially accused of the Lockerbie bombing
2. the indictment of the two Lockerbie suspects was in 1991

The frequencies of these SCUs are assigned as their weights. Given a candidate summary for evaluation, first SCUs in it are identified, and then the sum of the weights of the SCUs in each summary is normalized by the total weights of SCUs in an optimal summary (e.g. that is formed by using the highest possible weighted summary for a given summary length).

Longer chunks treated as semantic units, such as SCUs, were also used in factoid analysis (Teufel and Halteren, 2004) and the basic elements (BE) package (Hovy *et al.*, 2005). The BE package is more general and flexible in terms of element selection and scoring.

One disadvantage of the Pyramid, and other similar evaluation measures is the human effort required in performing the evaluation. For example, SCUs must be formed for each document or document set manually, and human annotators must check the system summaries for presence of SCUs in them. Both steps require a very careful examination of meaning similarity and can take a long time.

Galley (2006) used the Pyramid method for meeting summarization evaluation; however, in one single meeting, repetitions and reformulation of the same information are infrequent, and textual units that express the same content among multiple human summaries usually originate from the same sentence. Hence, they defined SCUs for meetings as pairs of words and their positions in the document. This automated formulation of SCUs eliminated human effort necessary for defining them.

13.4.4 Weighted Precision

Similar to the weighting of SCUs in the Pyramid measure, (Murray *et al.*, 2006) have proposed weighting the meeting dialogue act units in proportion to the average number of times they are linked to a human-generated abstractive summary. As described in Section 13.3, in the summary formation for the ICSI and AMI meetings, to generate extractive summaries, annotators were told to extract dialogue acts that would convey the information in the abstractive summary, and could be used to support the correctness of that summary. For each dialogue act unit that the summarizer extracts, the average number of times that each annotator linked that dialogue act unit to a summary sentence was counted, and used as the weight of that dialogue act unit when computing precision. For example, for a given dialogue act unit, it may be that one annotator links it 0 times, one annotator links it 1 time, and the third annotator links it 2 times, resulting in an average score of 1 for that dialogue act unit. Similarly weighted recall and F-measure could also be calculated. Because the summaries created for meetings are short, Murray *et al.* (2006) mainly focused on weighted precision as their central metric. In this way, sentences that are marked by more human annotators are considered as more important in evaluation. However, note that, this measure is very specific to their particular annotation of meeting summaries.

13.4.5 SumACCY and Weighted SumACCY

Hori *et al.* (2003) developed an evaluation method, SumACCY, for speech summarization that tried to value word sequences selected by multiple human summarizers. In their method, a manual summary that is most similar to an automatic summarization result is considered to be the target answer, and word accuracy of the automatic summarization when compared with this target answer is calculated. To find the most similar human summary to the system output, a word network that merges all the manual summaries is formed. Instead of weighting all words equally, weighted SumACCY (WSumACCY) aims to give higher weights to the set of words containing word strings that are selected by many humans, and hence the summarization accuracy is modified to be weighted by a posterior probability based on the manual summarization network. The SumACCY approach is especially suitable for summarization methods that are based on a sentence compaction approach that tries to remove phrases irrelevant for the summary from the original document sentences.

13.4.6 Human Evaluation

Various human evaluation methods have been used for speech summarization evaluation, although compared with text summarization, there has been less effort on conducting human evaluation. Maskey (2008) asked human judges to rate the system output summaries on a scale of 1 to 5 to evaluate its responsiveness to the topic of the story. This is similar to the responsiveness scores in the DUC evaluations. Murray *et al.* (2009) performed an extrinsic meeting summarization evaluation, formulated as a decision audit task, where the aim is to determine how a decision was reached after investigating a set of previously held meetings. They compared extractive and abstractive summaries, and assessed the impact of speech recognition errors on the performance of the user. Liu and Liu (2010) conducted a human evaluation of meeting summarization with the goal of examining the correlation between automatic ROUGE scores and human evaluation. Overall the two are not highly correlated, however, they showed improved correlation when taking into account some meeting characteristics, including disfluencies, speaker information, and domain specific stopwords.

13.4.7 Issues and Discussions

While researchers have converged on the use of ROUGE scores for automatic evaluation of speech summarization during algorithm and system development, as in text summarization, because of the easiness of this measure, one issue that remains to be solved is the baseline used for comparing the new method. Structural cues that have been shown to be useful for forming a baseline for text summarization, such as the position of the sentence in a document, have not been helpful in speech summarization. Therefore, previous work has mainly used random utterance selection and longest utterances for forming the baseline for speech summarization. Another reason for this is due to the lack of commonly used data sets for this task, making it hard to compare one's results with others.

Another issue related to evaluation of speech summarization is the lack of a commonly agreed compression ratio. For example, in DUC multi-document summarization evaluations, summary length is limited to 250 words, or update summarization evaluations, summary length is limited to 100 words for each set. Previous research in speech summarization has used various criteria, such as computing the compression rate in terms of words or sentential units, and often presented results at several word compression rates. Riedhammer *et al.* (2008b) discussed these variations and attempted to form a common ground to compare the previous methods.

Evaluation itself is a research topic of much importance in summarization and studies are currently still ongoing. Given the low correlation between the ROUGE scores and the human evaluation for some speech genres, and the unique characteristics of speech (making it very different from text domains), more studies are needed for appropriate evaluation metrics.

13.5 General Approaches

In this section, we mainly focus on generic extractive summarization, which is a task that has been most extensively studied so far. We will discuss other variations of the task, such as abstractive summarization at the end of this section.

For extractive summarization, the task is to determine the importance of each sentence and select those important ones to form a summary, according to some predefined compression ratio. Note that the extractive summarization units do not necessarily correspond to linguistically meaningful sentences. This is especially true when using conversational speech where sentences are not clearly defined, or speech recognition output where automatic segmentation is performed. Without loss of generality, we use sentences as the extractive summarization units for now. The methods we discuss here apply to other summarization units.

Summarization approaches can be categorized in terms of techniques used, such as rule-based or unsupervised methods, versus supervised classification; or based on the information used, for example, using only lexical or textual information, versus including acoustic or prosodic information. Here we broadly divide approaches into two categories, unsupervised and supervised methods. The latter is a feature-based method that requires a reasonable size of annotated data to train the model. The unsupervised methods may also need some data (size can be much smaller than that required for supervised learning) to tune some parameters and optimize performance.

It is worth pointing out that the methods described below are not meant to be a comprehensive coverage of all the approaches that have been used in prior work, but instead are just some representativė ones. Since these have been used in different data sets, in most cases, their performances are not directly comparable. We will not show all the detailed results when discussing related studies in this section. More details can be found in the referred papers.

13.5.1 Extractive Summarization: Unsupervised Methods

- Maximum Marginal Relevance (MMR)

  MMR (Carbonell and Goldstein, 1998) is a widely used summarization method because of its simplicity and efficacy. It selects the most relevant sentences and at the same time tries to reduce redundancy. In extractive summarization, the score of a sentence S_i in the kth iteration in MMR is calculated as follows:

$$MMR(S_i^k) = \lambda \times Sim_1(S_i, D) - (1 - \lambda) \times Sim_2(S_i, Summ^{k-1}) \tag{13.1}$$

  where D is the document vector, $Summ^{k-1}$ represents the sentences that have been extracted into the summary until the kth iteration, the two similarity functions (Sim_1 and Sim_2) represent the similarity of a sentence to the entire document (salience measure) and to the selected summary (redundancy) respectively, and λ is a parameter that is used to adjust the combined score to emphasize the relevance or to avoid redundancy. The sentences with the highest MMR scores will be iteratively chosen into the summary until the summary reaches a predefined proper size. Note that we use two different similarity functions in Equation 13.1, since they do not necessarily have to be the same.

  One commonly used similarity measure in MMR is the cosine similarity. In this approach, each document (or sentence) is represented using a vector space model. The cosine similarity between two vectors (D_1, D_2) is:

$$sim(D_1, D_2) = \frac{\sum_i t_{1i} t_{2i}}{\sqrt{\sum_i t_{1i}^2} \times \sqrt{\sum_i t_{2i}^2}} \tag{13.2}$$

  where t_i is the term weight for a word w_i, which often is based on the TF-IDF (term frequency, inverse document frequency) value, as widely used in information retrieval. The IDF weighting is used to represent the specificity of a word: a higher weight means a word is specific to a document, and a lower weight means a word is common across many documents.

IDF values are generally obtained from a large corpus. One widely used method for the IDF value for a word w_i is

$$IDF(w_i) = \log(N/N_i) \tag{13.3}$$

where N_i is the number of documents containing w_i in a collection of N documents. Variations of the term weighting methods have been evaluated for many language processing tasks, such as text categorization and information retrieval (Yang and Pedersen, 1997; Salton and Buckley, 1988).

MMR has been widely used as a competitive baseline method in speech summarization. Zechner (2002) built a speech summarization system for conversational speech based on the MMR approach. His system also had the components for sentence boundary detection, disfluency removal, and question and answer link detection. He reported good performance for several different data sets. Murray *et al.* (2005b) compared MMR, latent semantic analysis, and feature-based summarization (the other two methods are discussed below) on the meeting corpus. They showed MMR performed very well when using automatic ROUGE evaluations, and its performance had smaller degradation when using ASR output. Ribeiro and de Matos (2007) also compared these approaches, using Portuguese broadcast news, and showed that MMR achieved the best performance. Penn and Zhu (2008) demonstrated that MMR is a very compelling baseline system for lecture and Switchboard data. Xie and Liu (2008) evaluated different similarity measures in the MMR framework for meeting summarization on the ICSI meeting corpus. They showed that the corpus-based similarity measure (measured using co-occurrence) yielded better performance than the commonly used cosine similarity. They also used some approximations in the iterative MMR process by considering only a subset of the sentence candidates, which helped speed up the system and did not degrade performance.

- Latent semantic analysis (LSA) and topic modeling
In MMR, usually word overlap is used as the similarity measure (or as the salience measure of a sentence). Word overlap literally matches words, without considering any semantic or hidden topic information. Latent semantic analysis (LSA) is a vector-space approach that projects the original term-document matrix to a reduced dimension representation, which is expected to capture hidden semantic information. In an $m \times n$ term-document matrix A, an element A_{ij} represents the weight of term i in document j (e.g. TF-IDF term weighting). LSA is based on the singular value decomposition (SVD) of the term-document matrix A, as follows:

$$A = USV^T \tag{13.4}$$

where U is an $m \times k$ matrix of left-singular vectors, S is an $k \times k$ diagonal matrix of singular values, and V is the $k \times n$ matrix of right-singular vectors. The rows of V^T may be regarded as defining topics, and the columns represent sentences from the document.

Murray *et al.* (2005b) used this method for meeting summarization. They chose sentences with the highest value for each row in V^T, until a desired summary length is reached. For each topic, they extracted the n best sentences. The number of sentences for each topic in the summary is determined by the proportion of the singular values for that corresponding topic. In their comparison of MMR, LSA, and feature-based summarization on the ICSI meeting corpus, they found that LSA performed the best and was not very sensitive to

ASR errors. However, a different observation was shown in Ribeiro and de Matos (2007) in the comparison of these three approaches on Portuguese broadcast news, where MMR outperformed the others.

Another approach along the lines of LSA is probabilistic LSA (PLSA). In this approach, a set of K latent topic variables is defined, T_k ($k = 1, 2, \ldots, K$), to characterize the term-document co-occurrence relationships. Documents and terms are independently conditioned on latent topics. In PLSA, the probability that a document d_i generating a term t_j is calculated using a generative process for each topic, weighted by the probabilities of different topic labels for this document, that is,

$$P(t_j|d_i) = \sum_{k=1}^{K} P(t_j|T_k)P(T_k|d_i) \tag{13.5}$$

All of the model parameters can be estimated using expectation maximization based on the document and term information. This model has been used in information retrieval and other text modeling applications. Another variation is latent Dirichlet allocation (LDA) to model the process of generating words by topics.

Kong and Lee (2006) used the PLSA approach to determine significance of terms for summarization. The significance for a term t_j in a document d_i is computed using its term frequency in the document, weighted by an entropy measure that is defined based on the probabilities of this term belonging to different topics. The sentence score is then calculated using the term significance. Their results showed that the term entropy measure outperformed other existing approaches for term significance measure.

- Language modeling and generative framework
  The problem of summarization can also be tackled using an approach based on a language modeling (LM) or a probabilistic generative framework. Similar methods have been used in information retrieval. In these methods, each sentence has a probability of generating the document D, and the sentences are ranked based on the posterior probabilities $P(S_i|D)$, obtained in a Bayesian framework:

$$P(S_i|D) = \frac{P(D|S_i)P(S_i)}{P(D)} \tag{13.6}$$

The ranking of the sentences is dependent on the prior probability of a sentence, $P(S_i)$, and the probability that the sentence generates the document, $P(D|S_i)$. The key problem is to estimate the probability $P(D|S_i)$, which can be calculated using a statistical LM. Since the LM is trained for each sentence, there is serious data sparsity. Similar problems exist in information retrieval, and various smoothing methods have been proposed and evaluated.

Lin *et al.* (2009b) used this LM framework for Mandarin BN summarization. They ignored the priors and thus only used a LM for $P(D|S_i)$. First they only used unigram LM, i.e. a bag-of-words model. For smoothing, they used an interpolated LM that combined probabilities from the sentence itself with those estimated using the entire data collection. The second model they used is a sentence topic model, where K latent topics are assumed to define the term distribution. The probability $P(D|S_i)$ is thus a mixture of the topic-based models. They compared their proposed approaches with MMR and LSA, and showed a better performance.

- Integer Linear Programming (ILP) based approaches
In this method, summarization is treated as a global optimization problem, where sentences are selected to optimize a defined objective, at the same time satisfying a predefined length constraint. This idea has been used in text summarization (e.g. McDonald, 2007), who proposed formulating MMR with some modifications, as an optimization problem. Gillick *et al.* (2009) instead proposed a concept-based ILP approach and applied this to meeting summarization. In their work, the problem is formulated as aiming to have a maximum coverage of content under the constraint of the summary length:

$$maximize \sum_i w_i c_i \tag{13.7}$$

$$subject\ to \sum_j l_j s_j < L \tag{13.8}$$

where w_i is the weight of concept i, c_i is a binary variable indicating the presence of that concept in the summary, l_j is the length of sentence j, L is the desired summary length, and s_j represents whether a sentence is selected for inclusion in the summary. An off-the-shelf ILP solver was used to solve the optimization problem. To extract concepts, they generated all content word n-grams, and removed those that appeared only once or those embedded in a longer phrase. Then bigram and trigram candidates were re-weighted based on their frequency and the n-gram length. On the AMI data, they showed that this ILP framework performed favorably to the greedy MMR baseline. They also compared their concept extraction method with the use of other resources such as WordNet, and demonstrated better performance with their simple method.

Xie *et al.* (2009a) further extended the above approach to use information based on sentences, in addition to concepts. They evaluated three methods to combine the sentence weights within the concept-based optimization framework: selecting sentences for concept extraction, pruning unlikely candidate summary sentences, and using joint optimization of sentence and concept weights. Their results on the ICSI meeting corpus showed that adding information based on sentences improved summarization compared to only concept-based ILP.

- Graph-based approaches
Graph-based methods originated from information retrieval research, and have been used in text summarization (and other tasks such as keyword extraction). In this approach for summarization, the input document is represented as a highly connected graph. A vertex represents a sentence, and an edge represents similarity between a pair of sentences. Similarity can be defined in various ways, for example, using cosine similarity as shown in Equation 13.2, word overlap, Jaccard similarity (Jaccard, 1912), or other measures. Two sentences that share common words generally will have higher edge weights.

Such a graph represents a Markov chain, where an edge indicates transition probabilities between states (edge scores are normalized to represent probabilities when building a graph). The stationary distribution of the chain is the salience scores of the vertices, which can be used to select important sentences for summarization. The vertex importance in the graph can be computed using an iterative approach, an algorithm similar to Google's PageRank (Brin and Page, 1998) or the HITS algorithm (Kleinberg, 1999). Graph-based methods are able to take into account more global information (connection among all sentences) to determine the importance of a sentence.

Graph-based methods have been shown to work well for text summarization. Unlike structured text, such as news articles, which consist of sentences with meaningful information, spontaneous speech (e.g. meetings) often is not well formed and thus one sentence is often not a meaningful unit. The graph built for this kind of data may have poor connection among sentences. To address this issue, Garg *et al.* (2009) proposed a graph-based method that uses sentence clusters for meeting summarization. For clustering, they used an approach similar to TextTiling (Hearst, 1994) that starts with each sentence in its own cluster and continues to merge two closest clusters with similarity above a predefined threshold. Then a graph is built for the clusters obtained. The standard iterative algorithm is used to find the final score for each node. The sentence score is then obtained by computing its cosine similarity with the centroid of the cluster, and a final greedy approach (similar to MMR) selects a set of sentences to form a summary. They evaluated this approach using the AMI meeting data, and showed significant improvement compared to the baseline graph-based approach that uses cosine similarity (without clustering) and the standard MMR approach.

Lin *et al.* (2009a) proposed to maximize a submodular set function defined on the graph with the constraint that only a certain number of sentences can be selected (similar to the constraint in ILP setup). In such a framework, the optimization is theoretically guaranteed to be near-optimal. They used both cosine similarity (TF-IDF term weighting) and ROUGE scores for edge weighting. Results on the ICSI meeting corpus showed consistent improvement compared to the standard graph-based methods, MMR, and ILP approaches.

- Other methods

Most of the approaches described above try to assign some salience scores to sentences, which is the central goal of extractive summarization. A simple model to determine the sentence scores is the vector space model, where a vector of terms is used to represent a sentence. The significance score for a sentence can be the sum of the weights of all the words in it, similarity score with the entire document, or based on other metrics. Lee and Chen (2005) used this method with TF-IDF as the term weight for a word and cosine similarity with the entire document as the sentence score. This is similar to the first component in MMR. As mentioned earlier, this kind of vector space model performs literal word matching, whereas LSA uses concept matching. Murray and Renals (2007a) evaluated different term weighting approaches for meeting summarization, including residual IDF (R-IDF), and a new surprise score for words from different speakers. These sentence selection methods do not consider redundancy. In contrast, MMR (or ILP) tries to cover more concepts. However, sometimes their advantage is not obvious. For example, in Lin *et al.* (2009b), the authors compared several unsupervised learning methods, but did not find that MMR outperforms simple vector space models that do not consider redundancy.

There are many other unsupervised learning methods that use different information sources to determine sentence importance. Several studies have used a length-based system as a baseline, which selects the longest sentences until the target summary length is reached. This has been shown to be a reasonable baseline (Penn and Zhu, 2008; Xie *et al.*, 2009a). Valenza *et al.* (1999) combined term weighting with acoustic confidence scores. Hori and Furui (2001) and Furui *et al.* (2004) computed sentence significance scores by combining a set of statistical features. The information they used included statistical measures (such as TF-IDF scores), linguistic measures (e.g. name entities and part-of-speech tags), confidence measures of the recognized words, n-gram scores for the words, and the grammatical structure of the sentence. These scores are linearly combined for the final significance of a sentence. Some approaches also utilize more sentence structure or location information. For example, Hirohata *et al.* (2005) selected summary sentences from important parts of the document, such as the introduction or conclusion. However, this may apply only to specific domains.

13.5.2 Extractive Summarization: Supervised Learning Methods

Supervised learning has been widely used in summarization where the task is treated as binary classification that aims to determine whether a sentence is a summary sentence or not. Each sentence (an instance in the classification task) is represented using a set of features. During training, a classifier is trained using the labeled data (speech data, transcripts, and the corresponding summary sentences). Then for each sentence in the test set, the classifier determines its class. Often the classifier can generate posterior probabilities or confidence scores representing the probability of the test sentence being a summary sentence. The summary for the test document is then formed by selecting the sentences with the highest scores until the desired compression ratio is reached. These methods do not have a direct way of modeling redundancy; hence, redundancy is usually modeled separately, or during sentence selection. In this section, we first describe the features used in most speech summarization systems and then discuss various supervised modeling approaches.

13.5.2.1 (A) Features

A variety of features have been investigated for speech summarization. The features are from different knowledge sources, such as lexical, prosodic, structural, discourse, and speaker related information.[11] Here we list some widely used features (or variation of them). Note that this is not a comprehensive list of all the features used in prior work, and not every feature is applicable to all speech genres.

- *Sentence length*: As mentioned before, simply using sentence length has been a very strong baseline for summarization in several different domains. Various normalized length related features have been used in supervised methods.
- *Sentence weight*: This information has been represented using a number of different ways, for example, cosine similarity of the sentence and the entire document, or just the total term weights of all the words in the sentence (e.g. TF-IDF weighting). Similar to the unsupervised methods, in addition to using vector space models, such information can be obtained using LSA approaches at the concept level.
- *Sentence position*: For news articles, sentence position is a very important cue – often selecting the first sentence forms a strong baseline. For the speech domain, this can also represent some structural information. For example, broadcast news stories typically follow a structure of introduction, event description, and conclusion. For lectures and meetings, there is also domain specific structural information conveyed by the position of sentences.
- *Cue words*: Features in this group can include frequent unigrams and bigrams, cue phrases in the document (such as "in summary" or "as a conclusion"), the number of proper nouns

[11] Different terms have been used in the literature for feature categories.

in the sentence, whether the sentence contains long words, words with high TF-IDF values, number of named entities, and first occurrence of named entities.

- *Speaker-related features*: Since often there are more than one speaker in speech genre, information related to speakers can be useful to determine the importance of a sentence. Features that have been used include whether a sentence is said by dominant speakers (this can be decided based on the speaker's role or simply the amount of speech by the speaker), whether there is a speaker change, and frequency of this speaker compared with the other speakers.
- *Discourse related features*: Sentence position mentioned above can be thought of a discourse related feature. Distributions of words can also be put in this category. Zhang *et al.* (2010) used Poisson mixture models to represent nouns. Maskey and Hirschberg (2005) used a measure of "givenness" to represent discourse information – new information included in the sentence. This is similar to the cue word information represented using the first named entity mentioned above in cue words features. Xie *et al.* (2008) used TF-IDF weights calculated using topic information in a meeting, in order to represent how word distribution changes across subtopics in a long document.
- *Prosodic features*: These features make the one important difference between speech summarization and text-based summarization. Many systems have tried to use prosodic information in the classifier. The widely used features include: duration (sentence duration); pitch: various statistics (mean, max, range) of pitch values of the spoken sentence; energy: similar to pitch, statistics (mean, max, range) of energy values of the sentence; speaking rate: how fast/slow the speaker's speech is in the sentence. Note that normalization of prosodic features is quite important. To properly represent prosodic cues and account for speaker or content variability, these features need to be normalized based on speaker's average, or using topic or fixed-length local windows (Xie *et al.*, 2009b).
- *ASR output confidence scores*: This can be the average confidence measure of all the words in a sentence generated by the recognizer. The expectation is that including the estimation of the correctness of the ASR output helps select better sentences (or more correctly recognized sentences) to include in the summaries.
- *Contextual features*: These capture information from the preceding and following sentences. This can be represented by including the contextual features from neighboring sentences in the feature vector for the current sentence, or using the delta features (the difference between the feature values of the current sentence and its neighbors).

In the supervised learning framework, various studies examined the effectiveness of different features. Some work also focused on the differences in feature contributions between text and speech summarization.

Christensen *et al.* (2003) compared the effect of individual features on both text and speech summarization. They showed that classical text summarization features (based on stylistic and content information) are portable to the broadcast news domain, but there is difference in terms of the usability of the individual features. For text, the most informative information is provided by the sentence position feature, but for speech there is no such dominant feature. Sentence length is more discriminative in speech – long sentences from anchors and reporters often contain rich information. Features related to content (e.g. named entity and TF-IDF) are also more important in speech than text. These are all due to the differences in the information structure. Furthermore, because there is no dominant individual feature in speech summarization, the combined features perform significantly better than using one information source alone, unlike in text where the combination of all the features only shows marginal improvement over using only the position information. Note that the summary used in this work (Christensen *et al.*, 2003) is only one sentence long, thus conclusions may not hold for other types of summaries.

Several studies have compared lexical, prosodic, structural and discourse features for speech summarization. Lexical features are often the top-ranked features for different domains, but prosodic features are also useful (Furui *et al.*, 2004; Koumpis and Renals, 2005; Maskey and Hirschberg, 2005; Xie *et al.*, 2008; Zhang *et al.*, 2010). Lin *et al.* (2009b) showed that the prosodic features contribute more than lexical features in Mandarin broadcast news summarization. Zhang *et al.* (2010) found that linguistic features rank higher than prosodic features, but not as high as speaker normalized prosodic features. Xie *et al.* (2009b) demonstrated that using properly normalized prosodic features achieves as good or even better performance than using lexical features, and the difference between the performance of lexical features and prosodic features is even higher on ASR output. Simpson and Gotoh (2005) investigated the use of speaker-independent prosodic features for meeting summarization, and found that pause durations and pitch changes across units were the most consistent features across multiple speakers and multiple meetings. Maskey and Hirschberg (2006) and Zhang and Fung (2007) showed that BN summarization can be done using prosodic and structural features, without even using linguistic features.

It is worth pointing out that, even for speech summarization, there may be some domain differences. For broadcast news, most of the speech is from anchors and reporters, who are professional speakers and are likely to be consistent in terms of using prosody to indicate important sentences. In meetings, speech is usually spontaneous and not well planned, and speakers may not articulate well. In lectures, speech is less spontaneous, since speakers generally plan their speech in advance, and the speaker faces a receptive audience and may sound differently from conversational speech. Even for the same meeting domain, there can be differences. For example, Murray (2008) observed differences between the natural ICSI meetings and scenario-driven AMI meetings.

Zhang *et al.* (2007a) compared the usefulness of feature types on lecture speech and broadcast news speech in Mandarin. They found that prosodic and structural features are more important for broadcast news than for the lecture task, and that ASR has less impact on broadcast news summaries. Not much similar research has been conducted to thoroughly compare the feature differences across speech domains, although we can obtain findings from individual studies for each domain and compare them across genres. Part of the reason for the lack of such studies is due to the limited data available for speech summarization.

13.5.2.2 (B) Modeling Approaches

Different machine learning approaches (classifiers) have been used in the supervised learning framework, such as support vector machines (SVM), Bayesian network, maximum entropy, conditional random fields (CRF), linear regression, multi-layer perceptron (Buist *et al.*, 2005; Kolluru *et al.*, 2003; Maskey and Hirschberg, 2003, 2005; Xie *et al.*, 2008; Zhang *et al.*, 2007a). Galley (2006) proposed using skip-chain CRFs to model non-local pragmatic dependencies between paired utterances (e.g. question-answer pairs) that typically appear together in summaries, and showed that these models outperform linear-chain CRFs and Bayesian models.

Murray *et al.* (2005b) compared MMR, LSA, and feature-based classification approaches (using regression classifier), and showed that when using ROUGE metrics, MMR and LSA had better performance, but it seemed that human judges favor the feature-based approaches. Lin *et al.* (2009b) compared many unsupervised (MMR, LSA, LM approach, topic modeling) and supervised methods (CRF, SVM, and Bayesian classifier), and showed that in general supervised approaches are superior to unsupervised methods. CRF and SVM performed better on human transcripts, with CRF better for low compression ratios; both discriminative approaches suffered more when using ASR output.

In addition to the above standard classification approach for summarization (extracting some features and using a classifier), there have been some new explorations recently that investigate different problems in supervised learning.

Instead of building one single classifier for the entire document, Zhang *et al.* (2010) trained different summarization models for different sections of the lectures, in order to better capture the rhetorical structure of lecture speech. They proposed rhetorical segmental HMMs to find the rhetorical structure, in which state transitions represent rhetorical relations, and the observation probabilities are based on Gaussian mixture models. Then SVM classifiers are used for each rhetorical unit. They showed that the segmental SVMs perform better than a single SVM (8.24% better in ROUGE-L features).

Xie and Liu (2010a) tried to address two problems associated with the supervised classification approach. First is the imbalanced data problem for this task where the summary sentences are the minority class. They used different sampling methods to deal with this problem. Unlike the random upsampling or downsampling methods used in many machine learning problems, they proposed approaches for this task that also partly addressed the human annotation inconsistency problem. The sentences selected for sampling are based on the similarity of non-summary sentences to the annotated summaries. Similarity is measured using cosine similarity or ROUGE scores. For downsampling, they removed the non-summary sentences that are similar to summary; for upsampling, they changed the tag for these non-summary sentences to positive label (meaning summary sentences). Second, they reframed the extractive summarization task using a regression scheme instead of binary classification. The labels (continuous value) are generated based on similarity of the sentence to summaries. They showed performance improvement using these sampling methods and the regression model.

Training a feature-based summarization model usually requires a reasonable size of data (typically high quality). We know that hand labeling is expensive and time consuming. For summaries, it is also inconsistent and unreliable. Research has been conducted to automatically create annotated training data, or select better data for humans to annotate.

Zhang *et al.* (2009) proposed to use active learning to select data for humans to hand correct. The classifier is trained from an initial seed corpus. At each iteration, some unlabeled documents are selected for human labeling based on the criterion that the similarity scores between the extracted summary sentences and the sentences in the lecture slides are top-N highest. Their results showed an increasing learning curve of ROUGE-L F-measure, from 0.44 to 0.514, consistently higher than that of using randomly chosen training samples.

Lin *et al.* (2009c) combined unsupervised and supervised learning. An SVM classifier was used for supervised learning. The training data for the supervised classifier was generated by an unsupervised topic modeling approach that considers the relevance of a sentence to the whole document. They also proposed a training data selection and relabeling approach using two measures: inter-document similarity (measures similarity of the returned relevant documents to a query sentence); and inter-sentence similarity (similarity of a sentence to others in the document). These are used to filter out unreliable labels. The rest is used as automatic labels for training SVM. They observed encouraging results from this combination of supervised and unsupervised summarization methods. Similar approaches to generate labeled data for supervised learning using unsupervised methods have been explored in text summarization, where no extractive summary sentences but only abstractive summaries are provided. Sentences with high similarity to the abstractive summaries are identified to use as summary sentences for training extractive summarizer.

In general the classification approaches used for summarization are optimized for classification accuracy, which may be different from the ultimate summarization performance. Lin *et al.* (2010b) investigated different training criteria for supervised summarization. First, they used a pair-wise ordering of sentences in the document based on their importance. Second, they trained the classifier by directly maximizing the evaluation score using AdaRank (Xu and Li, 2007). They showed improved performance compared to the baseline SVM classifier.

13.5.3 Moving Beyond Generic Extractive Summarization

Most of the approaches above focus on generic extractive summarization. In the past, there have been some attempts to look at other variations of the task. Murray and Renals (2007b) evaluated the possibility of online meeting summarization, without using the global context in the meeting. A new scoring method was used to measure the informativeness of a sentence and reduce redundancy using local context with residual IDF and score-trading. They showed high precision results for the online summarization, compared to using global information.

As described in Section 13.1, summaries can be formed in either an extractive or abstractive fashion. Compared with extractive summarization, abstractive summaries are more human-like, but the task is much harder and posts many challenges to the current language technologies. We describe a few studies on abstractive summarization.

Hori and Furui (2001) extracted a set of words and then connected them to form a summary, which is closer to abstractive summarization compared with sentence-based extractive summarization. Zechner (2002) removed disfluencies and cleaned up the sentences, which can be thought of an initial step towards the goal of abstractive summarization. Liu and Liu (2009) investigated if sentence compression can be applied to extractive summaries to generate abstractive summaries using the meeting corpus. They used different compression algorithms, including integer linear programming with an additional step of filler phrase detection, a noisy-channel approach using Markovization formulation of grammar rules (Galley and McKeown, 2007), as well as human compressed sentences. They showed that, when compared with the abstractive summaries, using sentence compression on the extractive summaries improves their ROUGE scores; however, the best performance is still quite low, suggesting that abstractive summarization is more than extractive summarization plus sentence compression, and that language generation is still needed.

In the VERBMOBIL system (Reithinger *et al.*, 2000) and MIMI dialogue summarizer (Kameyama *et al.*, 1996), an abstractive summarization component was included. However, those were very limited domains (e.g. travel planning, hotel reservation, booking rooms). (Kleinbauer *et al.*, 2007) performed some preliminary studies to generate abstractive summaries using the AMI corpus. They built an ontological representation based on topic structure of the meetings, dialogue act units, and annotations of propositional content. This was then passed to a natural language generation component that first transformed information from the annotation layers of the meeting to a propositional logic-like format, and then used sentence planner followed by a surface realizer implemented using a template-based generator. A one-paragraph summary of the meeting can be generated from their system.

Murray *et al.* (2010) proposed a two-stage method for abstractive meeting summarization. They first mapped meeting conversation to an ontology, based on object properties such as decisions, actions, and opinions. This step used a supervised classification method. The second step is transformation, where a summary is generated by maximizing an objective function represented by sentences and entity weights that are determined from previous sentence-ontology mapping. This global optimization is similar to the ILP approach described in Section 13.5.1. This part is still extractive in nature. The authors suggested that a further language generation component can be applied to the selected sentences. However, they noticed that even without the generation step, their approach could generate more structured extractive summaries since sentences are reorganized. This is expected to be more useful to end users.

13.5.4 Summary

We have briefly described some methods used for extractive summarization, broadly categorized into two groups: unsupervised methods or supervised learning approaches. Since previous studies have been performed using different data sets (different in genre, summary definition, languages, evaluation metrics), it is hard to conclude which method is the best performing one. Because of lack of fair comparisons, we do not fully understand the impacting factors for various methods either. In general, supervised learning methods have been shown to perform favorably compared with unsupervised approaches, but not with a large margin. And of course, this is at the cost of using a large training set, which may not be available.

In terms of efficiency, training in supervised methods takes some time, and usually requires large training data sets. Unsupervised methods are simple, and are likely to be robust to different domains. However, when combining multiple information sources (e.g. lexical, position, ASR confidence, etc.) in unsupervised methods, an ad-hoc way is often used, which also needs some data to optimize, and may also suffer from domain mismatch problems.

There have been a lot of recent research efforts on improving summarization performance for either unsupervised or supervised approaches, as well as exploration of other summarization task variations beyond generic extractive summarization. The text analysis techniques used in speech summarization systems are often simpler than what is used in text summarization, therefore, one future research direction may be to apply more complicated language understanding techniques.

13.6 More Discussions on Speech versus Text Summarization

In this section we will further discuss some research efforts on addressing some of the challenges listed in Section 13.2 when using speech input for summarization.

13.6.1 Speech Recognition Errors

- Effect of recognition errors
  ASR error rate varies for different speech genres. It can be less than 10% for broadcast news, or as high as 40% for meetings. As shown in Section 13.1, recognition errors may affect

summarization. It is not surprising to see that speech summarization performance degrades when using transcripts generated by ASR, compared with using human transcripts, as shown in many previous studies. However, often the degradation is not very large, mainly because some features, such as sentence length, are not very sensitive to speech recognition errors.

There have been several studies that vary the input ASR quality in order to evaluate the effect on speech summarization performance. Christensen *et al.* (2003) used a few different ASR results on broadcast news speech, and showed a relatively little difference of summarization performance due to WER, although there is some degradation for the condition with the highest WER. This is similar to that observed in spoken document retrieval using their data set. They explained that this is partly due to the structure of a typical broadcast news story. The most information-rich parts of a broadcast news story tend to correspond to planned studio speech, whereas there is less information in the spontaneous speech part. The most useful part for summarization is relatively easier for the recognizer. This explanation is consistent with some other experimental results that found better recognition accuracy in summaries than overall recognition results, (e.g. Murray *et al.*, 2005a; Valenza *et al.*, 1999) for meetings and broadcast news, respectively.

Penn and Zhu (2008) created two different WERs (46 and 39%) and found very little impact from WERs on summarization using Switchboard corpus, though the difference of their WERs is rather small. Lin *et al.* (2009b) evaluated the impact of recognition errors on summarization using simulated recognition output with different character error rates (CER), generated by randomly introducing errors in the human transcripts. A supervised method (i.e. CRF) was used for summarization. They observed consistent degradation for different compression ratios when CER increases. Note that there is a caveat – the random errors are different from real ASR output, which may have some effect on the findings.

Since there are not many studies that systematically compare different domains or methods, it is hard to say whether there is a domain difference in terms of ASR effect on summarization, or whether the effect of ASR errors differs for unsupervised or supervised methods. Future research is needed to answer these questions.

- Dealing with errors

  There has been some research that attempts to address the problems resulting from ASR errors. For the speech summarization task using ASR output, the goal of the task can be defined to select sentences that are the most informative (like text summarization), and at the same time have high recognition accuracy. Towards this goal, approaches were developed to leverage the speech recognition confidence scores.

  Zechner (2002) used an MMR framework, and chose words with ASR confidence scores higher than 0.5, together with other importance scores. They showed WER reduction in the selected summary, as well as a better summarization performance. Kikuchi *et al.* (2003) also used recognition confidence scores, together with trigram probabilities, and term weighting for summarization. Maskey (2008) used a word confidence weighted similarity measure and showed slight improvement compared to just using ASR words. As mentioned earlier, confidence score information has also been used in the supervised learning methods.

- Using more hypotheses

  N-best or lattice output has been used in many tasks in order to provide more candidates for the downstream language processing modules to make better decisions (since sometimes the words missing in the 1-best ASR output are included in the n-best list or lattices).

Liu *et al.* (2010) used n-best hypotheses for meeting summarization. They simply extended the MMR approach used for 1-best ASR output to n-best lists. The task now is to determine which segments, as well as which hypotheses, to include in the summary. The entire document is formed using the 1-best hypothesis from each segment. Each hypothesis was treated separately in each segment, that is, each was assigned a salience score. In the iterative selection process, when one hypothesis is selected into the summary, the other hypotheses for that segment will not be considered in the iterative MMR approach. The final summary is composed of all the selected hypotheses. They showed better performance using more hypotheses, with most of the gain coming from the first couple of candidates.

Lin and Chen (2009) investigated using confusion networks and position specific posterior lattices for ASR output for summarization. The posteriors were used to calculate expected word counts. They achieved better summarization performance from using this better representation of ASR output than the 1-best hypothesis. Xie and Liu (2010b) evaluated using word confusion networks (CN) under the MMR framework for meeting summarization. They used a vector representation for the segments by using more word candidates in CNs and their associated posterior probabilities (term weights were computed using posterior probabilities of words). Their experiments on the ICSI meeting corpus showed improved performance when considering the word posterior probabilities, as well as using confusion networks, especially after pruning word candidates with low posterior probabilities.

Finally we want to point out that as mentioned in Section 13.1, speech summarization can use speech output for summaries. Furui *et al.* (2004) and Xie and Liu (2010b) presented results using this kind of output for the ASR condition. This can address some problems related to recognition errors – there are no recognition errors in the output speech, but of course, there are still errors in the selection of summary segments when using ASR output. In fact, Xie and Liu (2010b) showed that using confusion networks achieved similar or even better performance compared to using human transcripts if the goal is to select the right segments.

13.6.2 Sentence Segmentation

Selecting an appropriate unit for extractive summarization (and other summarization tasks as well) is critical to system performance. When using human transcripts, most prior work used reference sentences (or other linguistic units, such as dialogue acts) as the segment units for extractive summarization. Even for the ASR condition, some previous studies did not perform automatic segmentation, but rather mapped the reference sentence information to the ASR words and used that for summarization (Murray *et al.*, 2005a).

Mrozinski *et al.* (2006) have shown that automatically generated sentences degrade summarization system performance compared to using reference sentence segments. Furui *et al.* (2004) compared using sentences, words, and between filler segments for speech summarization, and showed using sentence-based units is generally better.

Liu and Xie (2008) evaluated the impact of sentence segmentation on summarization using the meeting corpus. The decision thresholds from the segmentation system are varied to examine the impact of different segments on summarization. An MMR summarizer was used in that work. They found that using system-generated utterance segments degrades summarization performance compared with using human-annotated sentences; segmentation needs to be optimized for summarization instead of the segmentation task itself, however, the patterns are slightly different from prior work for other tasks such as parsing; and there are effects from different summarization evaluation metrics as well as speech recognition errors.

Maskey (2008) compared different ways of segmentation for speech summarization: using automatic sentence segmentation, pause-based segmentation (250 or 500 ms), and intonational phrases (IP). The IP boundaries were detected using a decision tree classifier. He used a supervised learning approach (Bayesian network) for summarization. He showed that using IPs is better than others (8.2% improvement of F-measure than automatic sentence segmentation, and an even larger improvement when using ROUGE metrics). His analysis showed that there are, on average, 2.75 IPs in a sentence, therefore using IPs as segment units allows the system to extract smaller segments to include in the summaries. The comparison with using short segments generated using pause information also proved that the unit length is not the only reason; rather intonational phrases are more linguistically meaningful units.

In addition to sentence segmentation, some studies also tried to use sentence type information to help summarization. Zechner (2002) identified question and answer pairs explicitly. He used a speech act tagger and a decision tree classifier trained from Switchboard data for question detection, based on words and their part-of-speech tags. Answers were detected using heuristic rules once questions were identified. His results showed that treating question-answer pairs as one unit improved readability of summaries (but not necessarily the ROUGE scores). Penn and Zhu (2008) also adopted a similar approach and incorporated question–answer information in summarization of Switchboard corpus.

13.6.3 Disfluencies

As discussed in Section 13.2, spontaneous speech includes many disfluencies. Research has been conducted to investigate the effect of disfluencies and use information based on disfluencies for summarization.

Hori and Furui (2001) used n-gram LM scores in sentence selection. If there are recognition errors or disfluencies, the expectation is that the n-gram scores will be low, therefore indirectly avoiding the selection of disfluencies in summaries. Zechner (2002) detected disfluencies first and removed them in summarization. He used a part-of-speech tagger to find coordinating conjunctions, filled pauses, and editing phrases; a decision tree classifier to detect false starts; and a rule-based method to detect repeated words (up to four words). He showed that adding disfluency components in the system improves summarization performance, compared with the MMR baseline on different corpora. Penn and Zhu (2008) also adopted a similar approach, which identified repetitions of a sequence of words of length one to four, and used a decision tree classifier to detect false starts based on words and part-of-speech tags. Liu *et al.* (2007) removed disfluencies first (they used manually annotated disfluencies), then used MMR for meeting summarization. However, they found that cleaning up sentences did not improve summarization and gave a few possible reasons. The disfluent words may have a low IDF score (in the similarity calculation) and thus do not have a big negative effect; the sentence length information may not be used properly in the similarity measure; or it may be because of the MMR approach or the ROUGE evaluation metrics.

Maskey (2008) proposed a phrase-level machine translation approach for disfluency detection using weighted finite-state transducers, where the task is to translate a disfluent sentence into a clean one. He removed disfluencies using this method and then used the same features in a supervised setup. On BN summarization, the improvement was small (less than 1%). He explained that this is possibly due to the disfluency detection model that was trained using Switchboard data and the fewer number of disfluencies in the BN corpus.

Zhu and Penn (2006) used disfluency information as features (number of repetitions and filled pauses) in the classification approach, expecting that this information helps to determine the importance of sentences. They obtained small improvement (less than 1%) of ROUGE scores on the Switchboard corpus.

13.6.4 Acoustic/Prosodic and other Speech Features

As mentioned earlier, the features computed from the acoustic signal form one of the important differences between speech and text input for summarization. We described the typical prosodic features used in most speech summarization systems in Section 13.5. Previous work has mostly shown that incorporating this information source generally improves system performance upon using lexical features only. However, the gain from adding these features may not be significant. For example, Penn and Zhu (2008) showed that adding speech features has little impact on performance.

In addition to combining prosodic features with textual sources, several studies have evaluated using only acoustic/prosodic information for speech summarization, and showed promising performance. Maskey and Hirschberg (2006) used an HMM approach for BN summarization, without using transcripts. The states in the HMM represent summary and non-summary sentences, and observations are acoustic or prosodic features. They can generate reasonable summaries, even when using only acoustic prosodic information. Ohtake *et al.* (2003) evaluated using only prosodic features for speech-to-speech summarization on broadcast news. They found that such systems performed similar to that using ASR output. Xie *et al.* (2009b) showed that if prosodic features are properly normalized, using them can achieve similar or even better performance than using lexical information for meeting summarization. They evaluated different normalization methods, based on speaker, topic, or local context information. Note that for these studies using only acoustic/prosodic information, often the assumption is that sentences/segments are generated using transcripts, which is not a very realistic scenario.

Zhu *et al.* (2009) also investigated using acoustic evidence for summarization. Their task is multiple document summarization, thus allowing them to use reoccurrence statistics of acoustic evidence. First, they detected acoustic patterns that reoccur between pairs of utterances in multiple documents that discuss a common topic. This was done using a dynamic programming approach with similarity measure calculated using MFCC features for the audio sequences. Next, they computed similarity score between two sentences based on the match information from the first step. Finally, sentences were selected using the general MMR framework and the similarity matrix calculated from above steps. The overall approach is similar to using textual information, however, the similarity measure is based on acoustic measure, rather than word match. They found that this acoustic-based method achieved similar performance as using ASR output with WER of 33–37%. Their analysis also suggested that the acoustics-based approach is useful when there are frequent out-of-vocabulary errors. The authors pointed out some limitations of this approach – it only uses documents from similar speakers and there may be a generalization problem.

13.7 Conclusions

Speech summarization provides an effective way to access information available in speech recordings. In Section 13.1, we listed a few applications using this technology. Given its potential practical applications and the fundamental scientific problems, this task has attracted a lot of interest from researchers recently. We have discussed methods used for speech summarization, studies with a focus on the difference between text and speech summarization, and evaluation methods in previous sections. Recent efforts on speech summarization have also resulted in some data collection and discussions about possible shared benchmark tests. However, compared with text summarization, especially summarizing news articles, many open problems and issues remain. In the final section of this chapter, we discuss some of these issues.

- *Lack of a public evaluation and data set*: As mentioned earlier, unlike text summarization that has some benchmark tests (e.g. evaluation run at DUC and TAC), there are not standard data sets for speech summarization. Researchers have created their own data sets; however, typically these data sets are rather small, therefore some conclusions in those studies may not hold. The guidelines used in different summary annotations are also different – everyone used their own annotation instructions. The whole process of creating data sets is also expensive. Of course, for speech, there are many different domains, such as meetings, broadcast news, and lecture speech. It is hard to prepare standard data sets for all these domains. Even in text summarization, well-defined data sets are not available for some new genres. The research community may need to discuss data issues, sharing, and annotation standard to help move the research forward.
- *Performance issues*: Different approaches have been developed and evaluated for various speech summarization tasks. Some tried to explore speech specific information, and some tried to address the issues posed by the difference between text and speech (ASR problems, sentence segmentation, disfluencies), as described in the earlier sections. Apparently more research along these directions is still needed for more significant performance improvement and a better understanding of the characteristics of speech summarization.
- *Human-like summarization*: Humans usually form abstractive summaries, which distill information in multiple sentences and formulate them in new sentences that do not necessarily occur in the original transcriptions. However, previous work on speech summarization has mostly focused on extractive methods, which extract utterances to include in a summary, mainly because of the difficulty of abstractive summarization. There have been some efforts to investigate other tasks than generic extractive summarization, such as abstractive summarization or query-based summarization. Future research needs to move more towards those tasks.
- *Evaluation*: Various evaluation measures have been used in previous studies. For speech summarization, evaluation is still an issue (even for text, it is not solved), and new automatic metrics may be needed for this task. Human evaluation is always expensive, and may not be consistent. When done using a small data set, the findings may not be accurate. The research community may need some shared efforts on human evaluation, such as the human judgment experiments done in the TAC community.
- *Task definition*: As discussed in this chapter, various summarization tasks have been studied in the text summarization literature, such as single-document and multi-document

summarization, query-focused summarization, and update summarization. Whereas, on the speech side, mainly generic summarization has been considered. More studies may be needed about the task itself. This is also related to the data and evaluation issues above. What is a proper task definition? How can we address the low inter-annotator agreement problem? How should we define the task to meet user needs for different applications? We may need some utility studies for these and also investigate these questions together with summarization evaluation issues.

- *Human customizability*: Previous work has mainly focused on generating generic summaries. However, different users usually have different needs or interest. Take meetings as an example. One user may be interested in decisions made in the meeting, whereas another user may be interested in the topics discussed. Such information needs can be formulated in terms of user queries, as well as options provided through a user interface. Future summarization research should also allow such variations to better meet user information need.

Given the increasing interest in this task, we believe there will be more studies on the above problems and related issues, advancing the field towards easy-to-use, customizable summarization systems.

References

Banerjee S and Rudnicky A 2008 An extractive-summarization baseline for the automatic detection of noteworthy utterances in multi-party human-human dialogue *Proc. of IEEE SLT*.

Banerjee S and Rudnicky A 2009 Detecting the noteworthiness of utterances in human meetings *Proc. of Sigdial*.

Brin S and Page L 1998 The anatomy of a large-scale hypertextual web search engine. *Computer Networks and ISDN Systems*.

Buist AH, Kraaij W and Raaijmakers S 2005 Automatic summarization of meeting data: A feasibility study *Proc. of CLIN*.

Carbonell J and Goldstein J 1998 The use of MMR, diversity-based reranking for reordering documents and producing summaries *Proc. of ACM SIGIR*.

Carletta J 1996 Assessing agreement on classification tasks: the kappa statistic. *Computational Linguistics* **22**(2), 249–254.

Cetin O and Shriberg E 2006 Analysis of overlaps in meetings by dialogue factors, hot spots, speakers, and collection site: Insights for automatic speech recognition *Proc. of ICSLP*, Pittsburgh, PA.

Chen B and Chen Y 2008 Extractive spoken document summarization for information retrieval. *Pattern Recognition Letter*.

Chen B, Yeh YM, Huang YM and Chen YT 2006 Chinese spoken document summarization using probabilistic latent topical information *Proc. of ICASSP*.

Christensen H, Gotoh Y, Kolluru B and Renals S 2003 Are extractive text summarization techniques portable to broadcast news *Proc. of ASRU*.

Favre B, Grishman R, Hillard D, Ji H, Hakkani-Tür D and Ostendorf M 2008 Punctuating speech for information extraction *Proc. of ICASSP*.

Furui S, Kikuchi T, Shinnaka Y and Hori C 2004 Speech-to-text and speech-to-speech summarization of spontaneous speech. *IEEE Transactions on Audio, Speech & Language Processing* **12**(4), 401–408.

Galley M 2006 A skip-chain conditional random field for ranking meeting utterances by importance *Proc. of EMNLP*.

Galley M and McKeown K 2007 Lexicalized markov grammars for sentence compression *Proc. of NAACL/HLT*.

Galley M, McKeown K, Hirshberg J and Shriberg E 2004 Identifying agreement and disagreement in conversational speech *Proc. of ACL*.

Garg N, Favre B, Reidhammer K and Hakkani-Tür D 2009 Clusterrank: A graph based method for meeting summarization *Proc. of Interspeech*.

Gillick D, Riedhammer K, Favre B and Hakkani-Tür D 2009 A global optimization framework for meeting summarization *Proc. of ICASSP*.

Hakkani-Tür D and Tur G 2007 Statistical sentence extraction for information distillation *Proc. of ICASSP*, Hawaii.

Harper M, Dorr B, Roark B, Hale J, Shafran Z, Liu Y, Lease M, Snover M, Young L, Stewart R and Krasnyanskaya A 2005 Final report: parsing speech and structural event detection http://www.clsp.jhu.edu/ws2005/groups/eventdetect/documents/finalreport.pdf.

He L, Sanocki E, Gupta A and Grudin G 1999 Auto-summarization of audio-video presentation *Proc. of ACM International conference on multimedia*.

He L, Sanocki E, Gupta A and Grudin J 2000 Comparing presentation summaries: Slides vs. reading vs. listening *Proc. of SIGCHI on Human factors in computing systems*.

Hearst M 1994 TextTiling: segmentation text into multi-paragraph subtopic passages. *Computational Linguistics* **25(3)**, 527–571.

Hirohata M, Shinnaka Y, Iwano K and Furui S 2005 Sentence extractive-based presentation summarization techniques and evaluation metrics *Proc. of ICASSP*.

Hirschberg J, Bacchiani M, Hindle D, Isenhour P, Rosenberg A, Stark L, Stead L, Zamchick G and Whittaker S 2001 Scanmail: Browsing and searching speech data by content *Proc. of Eurospeech*.

Hori C, , Hori C and Hori T 2003 Evaluation method for automatic speech summarization *Proc. of Eurospeech*.

Hori C and Furui S 2001 Advances in automatic speech summarization *Proc. of Eurospeech*.

Hovy E, Lin CY and Zhou L 2005 Evaluating DUC 2005 using basic elements *Proc. of DUC*.

Istrate D, Fredouille C, Meignier S, Besacier L and Bonastre JF 2005 NIST RT-05 Evaluation: pre-processing techniques and speaker diarization on multiple microphone meetings *Proc of the 2nd Joint Workshop on Multimodal Interaction and Related Machine Learning Algorithms*.

Jaccard P 1912 The distribution of the flora of the alpine zone. *New Phytologist* **11(2)**, 37–50.

Janin A, Baron D, Edwards J, Ellis D, Gelbart D, Morgan N, Peskin B, Pfau T, Shriberg E, Stolcke A and Wooters C 2003 The ICSI meeting corpus *Proc. of ICASSP*.

Kameyama M, Kawai G and Arima I 1996 A real-time system for summarizing human-human spontaneous spoken dialogues *Proc. of ICSLP*.

Kikuchi T, Furui S and Hori C 2003 Automatic speech summarization based on sentence extraction and compaction *Proc. of ICASSP*.

Kleinbauer T, Becker S and Becker T 2007 Indicative abstractive summaries of meetings *4th Joint Workshop on Multimodal Interaction and Related Machine Learning Algorithms (MLMI), poster*.

Kleinberg J 1999 Authoritative sources in a hyperlinked environment. *Journal of the ACM* **46(5)**, 604–632.

Kolluru B, Christensen H, Gotoh Y and Renals S 2003 Exploring the style-technique interaction in extractive summarization of broadcast news *Proc. of ASRU*.

Kong SY and Lee LS 2006 Improved spoken document summarization using probabilistic latent semantic analysis (plsa) *Proc. of ICASSP*.

Koumpis K and Renals S 2005 Automatic summarization of voicemail messages using lexical and prosodic features. *ACM Transactions on Speech and Language Processing*.

Lee L and Chen B 2005 Spoken document understanding and organization. *IEEE Signal Processing Magazine*.

Lin CY 2004 ROUGE: A package for automatic evaluation of summaries *the Workshop on Text Summarization Branches Out*.

Lin H, Bilmes J and Xie S 2009a Graph-based submodular selection for extractive summarization *Proc. of ASRU*.

Lin J, Madnani N and Dorr B 2010a Putting the user in the loop: Interactive maximal marginal relevance for query-focused summarization *Proc. of NAACL-HLT*.

Lin S and Chen B 2009 Improved speech summarization with multiple-hypothesis representations and Kullback-Leibler divergence measures *Proc. of Interspeech*.

Lin SH, Chang YM, Liu JW and Chen B 2010b Leveraging evaluation metric-related training criteria for speech summarization *Proc. of ICASSP*.

Lin SH, Chen B and min Wang H 2009b A comparative study of probabilistic ranking models for chinese spoken document summarization. *ACM Transactions on Asian Language Information Processing*.

Lin SH, Lo YT, Yeh YM and Chen B 2009c Hybrids of supervised and unsupervised models for extractive speech summarization *Proc. of Interspeech*.

Liu F and Liu Y 2008a Correlation between rouge and human evaluation of extractive meeting summaries *Proc. of ACL-HLT*.

Liu F and Liu Y 2008b What are meeting summaries? An analysis of human extractive summaries *Proc. of SigDial*.

Liu F and Liu Y 2009 From extractive to abstractive meeting summaries: Can it be done by sentence compression? *Proc. of ACL*.

Liu F and Liu Y 2010 Exploring correlation between rouge and human evaluation on meeting summaries. *IEEE Transactions on Audio, Speech and Language Processing*.

Liu Y and Xie S 2008 Impact of automatic sentence segmentation on meeting summarization *Proc. of ICASSP*.

Liu Y, Liu F, Li B and Xie S 2007 Do disfluencies affect meeting summarization: A pilot study on the impact of disfluencies *MLMI, Poster presentation*.

Liu Y, Shriberg E, Stolcke A, Hillard D, Ostendorf M and Harper M 2006 Enriching speech recognition with automatic detection of sentence boundaries and disfluencies. *IEEE Transactions on Speech, Audio, and Language Processing*.

Liu Y, Xie S and Liu F 2010 Using n-best recognition output for extractive summarization and keyword extraction in meeting speech *Proc. of ICASSP*.

Maekawa K, Koiso H, Furui F and Isahara H 2000 Spontaneous speech corpus of japanese *Proc. of LREC*.

Makhoul J, Kubala F, Leek T, Liu D, Nguyen L, Schwartz R and Srivastava A 2000 Speech and language technologies for audio indexing and retrieval. *Proc. of IEEE*.

Mani I 2001 *Automatic Summarization*. John Benjamins.

Mani I, House D, Klein G, Hirshman L, Obrst L, Firmin T, Chrzanowski M and Sundheim B 1998 The TIPSTER SUMMAC text summarization evaluation. Technical report.

Mani I, Klein G, House D, Hirschman L, Firmin T and Sundheim B 2002 Summac: a text summarization evaluation. *Natural Language Engineering* **8**, 43–68.

Maskey S 2008 *Automatic broadcast news speech summarization* PhD Thesis Columbia University.

Maskey S and Hirschberg J 2003 Automatic summarization of broadcast news using structural features *Proc. of Eurospeech*.

Maskey S and Hirschberg J 2005 Comparing lexical, acoustic/prosodic, structural and discourse features for speech summarization *Proc. of Interspeech*.

Maskey S and Hirschberg J 2006 Summarizing speech without text using Hidden Markov Models *Proc. of HLT-NAACL*.

Matusov E, Hillard D, Magimai-Doss M, Hakkani-Tür D, Ostendorf M and Ney H 2007 Improving speech translation with automatic boundary prediction *Proc. of Interspeech*.

McDonald R 2007 A study of global inference algorithm in multi-document summarization *Proc. of European Conference on Information Retrieval*.

Mieskes M, Müller C, and Strube M 2007 Improving extractive dialogue summarization by utilizing human feedback *Proc. of the IASTED Artificial Intelligence and Applications Conference*, Innsbruck, Austria.

Mrozinski J, Whittaker E, Chatain P and Furui S 2006 Automatic sentence segmentation of speech for automatic summarization *Proc. of ICASSP*.

Murray G 2008 *Using speech-specific characteristics for automatic speech summarization* PhD thesis University of Edinburgh.

Murray G and Renals S 2007a Term-weighting for summarization of multi-party spoken dialogues *Proc. of MLMI*.

Murray G and Renals S 2007b Towards online speech summarization *Proc. of Interspeech*.

Murray G, Carenini G and Ng R 2010 Interpretation and transformation for abstracting conversations *Proc. of NAACL-HLT*.

Murray G, Kleinbauer T, Poller P, Becker T, Renals S and Kilgour J 2009 Extrinsic summarization evaluation: A decision audit task. *ACM Transactions on Speech and Language Processing*.

Murray G, Renals S and Carletta J 2005a Extractive summarization of meeting recordings *Proc. of Interspeech*.

Murray G, Renals S, Carletta J and Moore J 2005b Evaluating automatic summaries of meeting recordings *Proc. of the ACL Workshop on Intrinsic and Extrinsic Evaluation Measures for Machine Translation*.

Murray G, Renals S, Carletta J and Moore J 2006 Incorporating speaker and discourse features into speech summarization *Proc. of HLT-NAACL*.

Nenkova A and Passonneau R 2004 Evaluating content selection in summarization: the pyramid method *Proc. of HLT/NAACL*.

Ohtake K, Yamamoto K, Toma Y, Sado S, Masuyama S and Nakagawa S 2003 Newscast speech summarization via sentence shortening based on prosodic features *Proc. of the ISCA and IEEE Worksohp on Spontaneous Speech Processing and Recognition*.

Papineni K, Roukos S, Ward T and Zhu W 2001 Bleu: a method for automatic evaluation of machine translation. Technical report, IBM.

Penn G and Zhu X 2008 A critical reassessment of evaluation baselines for speech summarization *Proc. of ACL-HLT*.

Reithinger N, Kipp M, Engel R and Alexandersson J 2000 Summarizing multilingual spoken negotiation dialogues *Proc. of ACL*.

Reynolds D and Torres-Carrasquillo P 2005 Approaches and applications of audio diarization *Proc. of ICASSP*, Philadelphia.

Ribeiro R and de Matos DM 2007 Extractive summarization of broadcast news: Comparing strategies for european portuguese *Proc. of TSD*, vol. 4629/2007, pp 115–122 Springer Berlin / Heidelberg.

Riedhammer K, Favre B and Hakkani-Tür D 2008a A keyphrase based approach to interactive meeting summarization *Proc. of SLT*.

Riedhammer K, Gillick D, Favre B and Hakkani-Tür" D 2008b Packing the meeting summarization knapsack *Proc. of Interspeech*.

Salton G and Buckley C 1988 Term weighting approaches in automatic text retrieval. *Information Processing and Management* **24**(5), 513–523.

Shriberg E, Dhillon R, Bhagat S, Ang J and Carvey H 2004 The ICSI meeting recorder dialogue act (MRDA) corpus *Proc. of 5th SIGDIAL Workshop*.

Simpson S and Gotoh Y 2005 Towards speaker independent features for information extraction from meeting audio data *Proc. of MLMI, poster*.

Stolcke A, Chen B, Franco H, mana Rao Gadde VR, Graciarena M, Hwang MY, Kirchhoff K, Mandal A, Morgan N, Lei X, Ng T and et al. 2006 Recent innovations in speech-to-text transcription at SRI-ICSI-UW. *IEEE Transactions on Audio, Speech, and Language Processing* **14**(5), 1729–1744.

Teufel S and Halteren H 2004 Evaluating information content by factoid analysis: human annotation a nd stability *Proc. of EMNLP*.

Tucker S and Whittaker S 2008 Temporal compression of speech: an evaluation. *IEEE Transactions on Audio, Speech and Language Processing* pp 790–796.

Valenza R, Robinson T, Hickey M and Tucker R 1999 Summarization of spoken audio through information extraction *Proc. of the ESCA Workshop on Accessing Information in Spoken Audio*, pp 111–116.

Wang H, Chen B, Kuo J and Cheng S 2005 MATBN: A mandarin chinese broadcast news corpus. *International Journal of Computational Linguistics and Chinese Language Processing*.

Wang W, Tur G, Zheng J and Ayan NF 2010 Automatic disfluency removal for improving spoken language translation *Proc. of ICASSP*.

Wilson T 2008 Annotating subjective content in meetings *Proc. of LREC*.

Xie S and Liu Y 2008 Using corpus and knowledge-based similarity measure in maximum marginal relevance for meeting summarization *Proc. of ICASSP*.

Xie S and Liu Y 2010a Improving supervised learning for meeting summarization using sampling and regression. *Computer Speech and Language*.

Xie S and Liu Y 2010b Using confusion networks for speech summarization *Proc. of NAACL-HLT*.

Xie S, Favre B, Hakkani-Tür D and Liu Y 2009a Leveraging sentence weights in concept-based optimization framework for extractive meeting summarization *Proc. of Interspeech*.

Xie S, Hakkani-Tür D, Favre B and Liu Y 2009b Integrating prosodic features in extractive meeting summarization *Proc. of ASRU*.

Xie S, Liu Y and Lin H 2008 Evaluating the effectiveness of features and sampling in extractive meeting summarization *Proc. of IEEE Spoken Language Technology (SLT)*.

Xu J and Li H 2007 Adarank: A boosting algorithm for information retrieval *Proc. of SigIR*.

Yang Y and Pedersen JO 1997 A comparative study on feature selection in text categorization *14th International Conference on Machine Learning*.

Zechner K 2002 Automatic summarization of open-domain multiparty dialogues in diverse genres. *Computational Linguistics* **28**, 447–485.

Zhang J and Fung P 2007 Speech summarization without lexical features for mandarin broadcast news *Proc. of HLT-NAACL*.

Zhang J, Chan HY, Fung P and Cao L 2007a A comparative study on speech summarization of broadcast news and lecture speech *Proc. of Interspeech*.

Zhang JJ, Chan HY and Fung P 2007b Improving lecture speech summarization using rhetorical information *Proc. of ASRU*.

Zhang JJ, Chan R and Fung P 2009 Extractive speech summarization by active learning *Proc. of ASRU*.

Zhang JJ, Chan RHY and Fung P 2010 Extractive speech summarization using shallow rhetorical structure modeling. *IEEE Transaction on Audo, Speech and Language Processing*.

Zhu X and Penn G 2006 Comparing the roles of textual, acoustic and spoken-language features on spontaneous-conversation summarization *Proc. of HLT-NAACL*.
Zhu X, Penn G and Rudzicz F 2009 Summarizing multiple spoken documents: finding evidence from untranscribed audio *Proc. of ACL*.
Zong C and Ren F 2003 Chinese utterance segmentation in spoken language translation *The 4th International Conference on Computational Linguistics and Intelligent Text Processing*, pp 516–525.

14

Speech Analytics

I. Dan Melamed and Mazin Gilbert
AT&T Shannon Laboratory, U.S.A.

Speech analytics refers to the synthesis of actionable information from multiple conversations. The plethora of speech analytics products for sale attests to the enormous economic value of actionable information gleaned from speech data. In this chapter we describe many of the ways that speech analytics can be helpful. We discuss the inherent technical challenges and some of their possible solutions, with reference to the few pieces of relevant research that we have been able to find. We pay particular attention to user interface issues, since a speech analytics system is only as useful as an analyst's ability to understand and control it.

14.1 Introduction

A search of the Web for "speech analytics" turns up a large number of commercial vendors with competing products,[1] but very little published research. The research literature offers no clear definition of speech analytics, and some of the commercial products seem to offer much more functionality than others. The consensus seems to be, however, that speech analytics is a form of speech data mining beyond mere transcription and voice search. Our working definition is that speech analytics refers to the synthesis of actionable information from multiple "conversations." We abuse the term "conversation" to include speech sessions involving only one speaker, such as IVR sessions and lectures.

Speech analytics can be applied to any collection of conversations. By far the most common place to find such collections is in customer service call centers. We shall use this application as a running example in this chapter. Call centers were once owned only by large companies, because it was expensive to maintain the large labor force that they require. As communication technology improved, it became feasible to outsource the labor overseas, bringing costs down, and making call centers affordable to smaller companies. There are also many call centers

[1] For example, Nexidia, Utopy, CallMiner, Nice, and Verint.

Spoken Language Understanding: Systems for Extracting Semantic Information from Speech, First Edition.
Edited by Gokhan Tur and Renato De Mori.

in public service: the U.S. IRS and INS have them, and they are critical in the operation of emergency services (fire, ambulance, etc.) and crisis intervention centers. Organizations that might benefit from speech analytics also include polling organizations that conduct outbound telephone surveys.

What counts as actionable information varies from one application to the next, but the plethora of speech analytics products for sale attests to the enormous economic value of actionable information gleaned from speech data. Examples of how speech analytics in call centers can be valuable include:

- discovering ways to improve customer service based on customer satisfaction surveys, e.g. by coaching service agents;
- discovering ways to reduce average call handling time, thereby reducing labor costs and, in the context of emergency services, possibly saving lives;
- discovering conversation patterns correlated with upselling/cross-selling, or lack thereof;
- predicting product demand for inventory planning, e.g. from calls to a department store asking "Do you carry Product X?";
- discovering problems that many customers are calling about, and reducing call volume and associated labor costs by solving those problems.

The benefits above are in addition to the better-known benefits of systems for speech retrieval and browsing. For example, a speech retrieval system that can help an analyst find conversations where certain words are spoken can save that analyst countless hours of listening to irrelevant conversations. Similarly, a speech browsing system that can play back the particular part of the conversation where those words are spoken can save the analyst many more hours of listening to irrelevant parts of the conversation.

Although a great deal of research has been devoted to analyzing individual conversations (dialogue modeling, speech summarization, etc.), very little has been published on speech analytics, as we have defined it. That is partly because the majority of organizations that own collections of conversations are unable and/or unwilling to release their data, usually due to privacy concerns. Without standard data sets, researchers cannot build on each other's work.

In this chapter we describe many of the ways that speech analytics can be helpful. We discuss the inherent technical challenges and some of their possible solutions, with reference to the few pieces of relevant research that we have been able to find. We begin by describing the architecture of a relatively full-featured speech analytics system. Subsequent sections delve into the details. We pay particular attention to user interface issues, since a speech analytics system is only as useful as an analyst's ability to understand and control it.

14.2 System Architecture

Speech analytics systems vary widely in their level of sophistication. Some offer little more than speech browsing and retrieval. Others present additional layers of functionality, which build one on top of another, as illustrated in Figure 14.1. Before a speech analytics system can do anything with its collection of conversations, it must extract various pieces of information ("features") from each conversation. All speech analytics systems use a variety of features to support one of their most basic functions – retrieving conversations that match certain criteria. A speech analytics system is most useful if it offers analysts a way to see and/or listen to

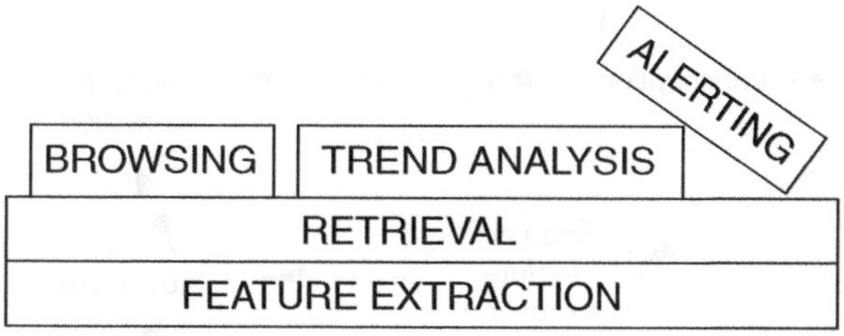

Figure 14.1 Functionality layers of a speech analytics system. Higher layers use the functionality of lower ones

examples of the kinds of data that contributed to salient aspects of its analyses. That is why most speech analytics systems allow their users to browse retrieved conversations. The actual analytics functionality of a speech analytics system begins with the next layer – trend analysis. Finally, an alerting subsystem can be built on top of trend analysis, but it can also work without trend analysis.

A data flow diagram for a relatively full-featured speech analytics system is shown in Figure 14.2.

The browsing and retrieval functionality layer of a speech analytics system is illustrated in the top half of Figure 14.2, above the ANALYST hexagon. Chelba *et al.* (2008) offer an extensive survey of such systems, but in this chapter we shall merely review some of the aspects that are most salient from the analytics point of view. Process modules 1 through 4 in this data flow diagram typically run regardless of whether an analyst is using the system at the time. The original conversation data are converted to a format suitable for streaming through a media player and stored on a media server for subsequent retrieval and play-back. The conversations are also transcribed, resulting in a set of transcripts. Words and various other kinds of information are extracted from the transcripts and added to a database. Non-verbal information can also be extracted from the conversations and used to inform the text feature extraction. Various kinds of metadata, i.e. information about the conversations other than their actual contents, usually play an important role in speech analytics systems. The metadata pertaining to each conversation is extracted and also added to the database.

The operations of modules 5 and 6 are initiated by the analyst. A speech retrieval session starts with the user issuing a query to the database management system (DBMS). The DBMS returns the records that satisfy the query. The records are presented in a user interface that allows the user to "drill down" through the list of records returned to examine individual records and listen to individual conversations. The browsing and play-back functionality is supported by a media server and a media player.

The first layer of analytics functionality can be implemented on top of a speech browsing and retrieval system, merely by exploiting the usual capabilities of a database management system. Most DBMSs support some variant of the ubiquitous SQL relational query language. SQL includes primitives for sorting, grouping, counting, and averaging of fields in database records. The rudimentary analyses supported by SQL enable analysts to ask "what/which" questions about speech data, such as "Which conversations involving customer service agent Jane talked about product XYZ?" and "What was the average length of conversations that discussed issue ABC?" Such questions are typically motivated by a specific business problem that the user is trying to solve, such as agent Jane's understanding of product XYZ or the labor

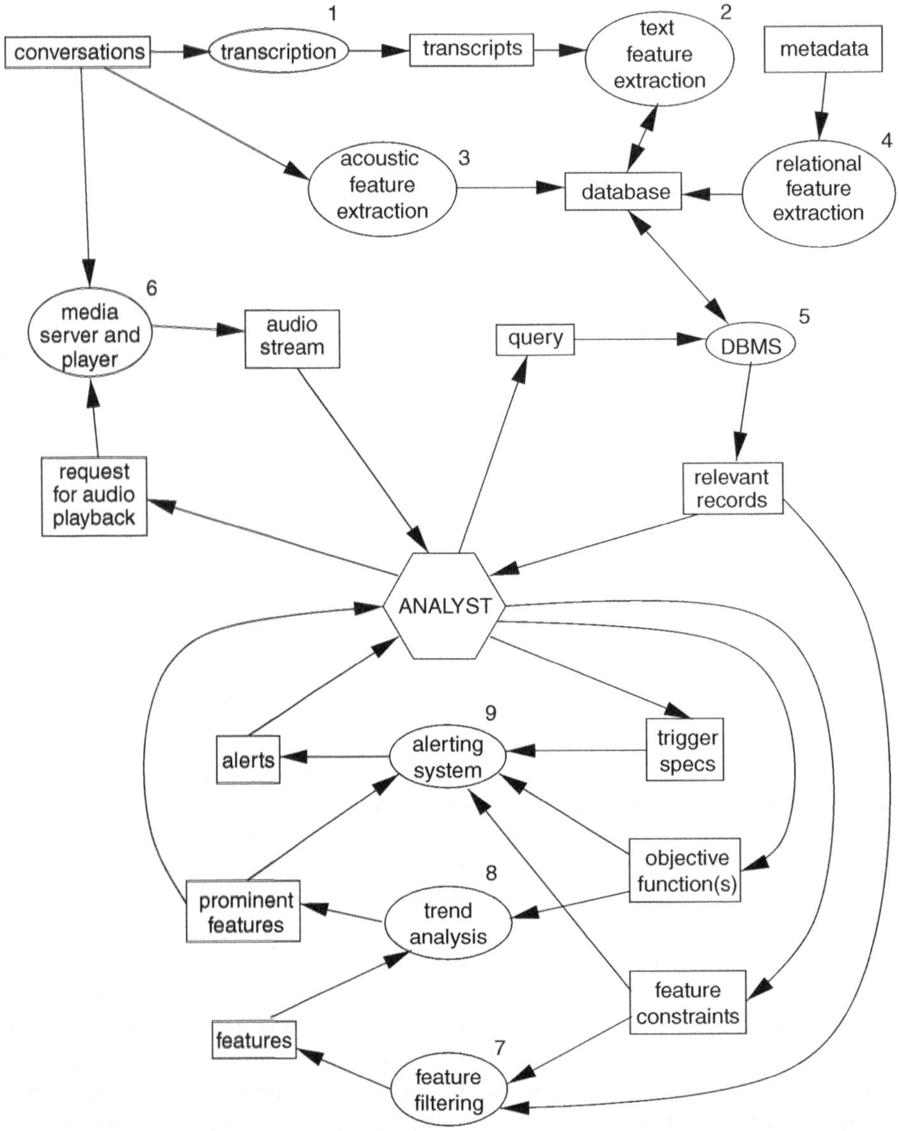

Figure 14.2 Data flow diagram of a speech analytics system. Rectangles are data; ovals are process modules

costs of resolving issue ABC. To ask such questions, then, the user must already know what the problem is.

Yet there are many situations when users know that a problem exists, but don't know exactly what the problem is. They would like to ask the system the more difficult "why" questions, such as "Why were our customers' assessments of our service agents so low last week?" or "Why is the average call duration so high in our Texas call centers?" Such questions can be answered by the next layer of speech analytics functionality, represented by modules 7 and 8 in Figure 14.2. Mathematically, such questions can be formulated as problems of statistical feature selection – essentially, users want to know which "features" of the data best explain one particular statistic of the data, such as call duration. This statistic is often called the objective function. A feature can be any piece of information that the system's database contains about each conversation. The number of potential features can be very large, so an analyst will typically offer some guidance to the system about the kinds of features that might be relevant. Such guidance can be formulated as a set of "feature constraints", which are fed to the feature filtering module. The trend analysis module then induces a model of how the selected features correlate with the objective function, and the most highly correlated features are reported to the analyst. These highly correlated features are often called "drivers" in business contexts. Unfortunately, "drivers" is a misleading misnomer, because correlation is not the same as causation (see Section 14.9). Trend analysis can be generalized from explaining one statistic to explaining how one statistic varies with respect to another, such as time. For example, an analyst might ask which features contribute to the fluctuation of call duration over time, or which features best explain a spike in call volume. In terms of data flow, the only additional information necessary for this generalization is an additional objective function.

All the modules and their functionality that we have described so far either run independently of the user or are initiated by the user. The next layer of functionality, represented by module 9 in Figure 14.2, lets the speech analytics system take the initiative. This module alerts users when the database meets certain conditions that they are interested in. For example, an analyst might want to be alerted whenever the mean call duration increases by 10% from one week to the next. If suitably configured, the speech analytics system can automatically perform the relevant trend analysis every week, and notify the analyst whenever the condition of interest is satisfied.

We now move on to discuss some of the modules in Figure 14.2 in more detail.

14.3 Speech Transcription

In some situations, manual transcription is feasible and preferable, or even mandated by law. For example, the proceedings of many courts and parliaments are manually transcribed, and some of them are also recorded. Usually, however, transcription is done by an automatic speech recognition (ASR) system. In this case, the quality of analyses done by the speech analytics system greatly depends on the quality of its ASR system.

Building accurate ASR systems for call center recordings is often particularly challenging because the vendors of call center recording and archiving equipment aim to minimize storage requirements. They tend to compress the audio to 6000 samples per second or less, which might still be enough for people to understand it. ASR systems are not nearly as good as people at understanding poor quality recordings, but call center recording equipment is typically not designed for ASR. To boost ASR accuracy on such data, some researchers have proposed using word lattices (e.g. Saraclar and Sproat, 2004) or word confusion networks (e.g. Mamou *et al.*, 2006) that can be generated as part of the ASR process.

Another challenge for any large-vocabulary ASR system used in production is that language tends to evolve. For example, a company can introduce new products and services, whose names subsequently come up in call center recordings. So, the accuracy of an ASR system used by a speech analytics system will degrade over time, unless it is regularly updated. Even if an ASR system is updated often, there will usually be a delay between the introduction of an important new term, such as a new product name, and the ASR system's ability to recognize that term. To enable analysts to find those new terms during the delay, some speech retrieval systems employ phonetic indexing and search (e.g. Begeja *et al.*, 2004; Mamou and Ramabhadran, 2008).

An important consideration when building ASR systems is what counts as good ASR. Most ASR systems are built and configured to optimize well-known evaluation measures such as word error rate, but such evaluation measures are not the most relevant for analytics purposes. In particular, for accurate speech retrieval, words that are likely to be used as search terms are more important than other words. Function words are unlikely to be search terms. When tuning the various parameters of an ASR system for use in speech analytics, the ASR system builder should remove function words from consideration by the evaluation measure. For example, the system builder can delete them from the system's hypotheses and from the reference transcriptions. The remaining words, i.e. content words, can be graded by their likelihood of being search terms, and their evaluation can be weighted accordingly. For example, Shichiri *et al.* (2008) use TF/IDF measures for this purpose. More task-specific measures are usually even more relevant. Stark *et al.* (2000) show how measures such as time to task completion and users' perceptions of task difficulty vary with ASR quality.

Another important trade-off in ASR systems is errors of omission versus errors of commission, also known as deletion and insertion errors, respectively. The standard error measures treat the two types of error equally, but insertion errors are much more damaging to most speech retrieval systems than deletion errors. That is because listening to conversations is time-consuming. Analysts usually try to minimize the number of conversations that they listen to for the purpose of any particular analysis. Thus, on the one hand, it is important not to retrieve irrelevant conversations, which would waste the analyst's time. On the other hand, if search terms are obtained from the output of trend analysis (see Section 14.9), then they are likely to appear in many conversations. Therefore, finding a few relevant conversations is typically not difficult, and so deletion errors can be easily tolerated.

The trade-off between insertion and deletion errors can be controlled by the word insertion penalty parameter in most modern speech decoders. This trade-off can be optimized in the usual way given an objective evaluation measure, such as word error rate. However, we are not aware of generally applicable objective evaluation methods for systems with users in the loop, such as speech retrieval and speech analytics systems. We know that insertion errors should be weighted more heavily, but we can only guess how much more heavily, and adjust based on user feedback. Another open research question is how to build acoustic models and language models to maximize the likelihood of a specific ratio of insertion and deletion errors.

14.4 Text Feature Extraction

At a minimum, the text feature extraction module records which words occur in which transcripts. To enable efficient searches for multi-word phrases, the database can use data structures such as suffix trees. The text feature extraction module must then implement the algorithms necessary to populate these data structures (e.g. Ukkonen, 1995). Many other kinds of features can be inferred from the words and phrases in transcripts.

Perhaps the most popular kind of feature inference in the context of speech analytics is classification of each conversation into one or more of a set of predefined classes. For example, each call to a call center might be tagged with one or more reasons for the call; each lecture in a series might be tagged with cross-references to related topics. The classes used can be defined either by the system designer or by the analyst. The classification is then typically performed by automatic classifiers that were built using machine learning techniques, such as boosting (Schapire, 1999).

Like other texts, conversation transcripts exhibit syntactic structure, dialogue structure, and discourse structure. Information about these structures can be very useful for speech retrieval and higher analytics functionality. For example:

- If syntactic dependencies were recorded in the database, then an analyst might be able to search for all records where "widgets" was syntactically associated with "purchase", even if these two words were usually separated by a quantifier like "two boxes of".
- If dialogue structure were recorded in the database, then an analyst might be able to search for all records where the service agent (but not the customer) used profanity.
- If discourse structure were recorded in the database, then an analyst might be able to search for all records where the words "wrong number" occurred in the "Reason for Call" section of the conversation, as opposed to other sections (Park, 2007).

There is a great deal of published research on inferring these structures in written text. The task is more difficult for speech transcripts, because the transcripts usually contain ASR errors, and also because they lack orthographic clues such as case and punctuation. The impoverished orthographic representation necessitates customization of all the basic tools of natural language processing, such as part-of-speech taggers, named-entity taggers, coreference resolvers, and syntactic parsers. On the other hand, speech contains acoustic information that can often be exploited to compensate for the shortcomings of transcripts (see next section). It is an open research question whether the accuracy of the linguistic structures that can be induced in conversation transcripts with today's state of the art is sufficiently high to be useful for analytics purposes.

Another type of language analysis that has recently become popular is opinion extraction. This type of analysis can be particularly relevant for customer service call centers, where tracking and/or improving customers' opinions about a product or its producer is often a large part of a center's *raison d'être*. However, the techniques that are commonly employed for extracting opinions from written text are much less reliable on noisy ASR output. To avoid the compounding of errors from ASR and opinion extraction, Camelin *et al.* (2009a,c) designed a system that transcribes speech directly into opinions without first transcribing into words. In subsequent work, they use the output of this system, together with other clues, to determine which customers are so badly dissatisfied that they merit urgent call-backs from company representatives (Camelin *et al.*, 2009b, 2010).

In addition to serving as search constraints, classification, structural, and opinion features can play an important role in trend analyses (see Section 14.9).

14.5 Acoustic Feature Extraction

Acoustic information is what distinguishes speech analytics from text analytics. Some acoustic features can be used by a speech analytics system by themselves. For example, Lee and Narayanan (2005) and Busso *et al.* (2009) propose methods for classifying speakers into different emotional states. Reliable information about customers' emotional states could greatly help an analyst to focus on problematic calls to a call center. Similarly, Polzehl and Metze (2008) show a correlation between reasons for customers' dissatisfaction and the emotional intensity of their calls, as represented by pitch variance and loudness.

More typically, acoustic features are not stored in the database on their own. Instead, they serve to facilitate various kinds of text feature extraction. Speaker segmentation and classification is perhaps the most common example of where acoustic information is used together with the transcript to infer additional useful features. If the system knows which words were spoken by agents and which words by customers, then it can index the two sources of speech separately. Then, agents can search for calls where certain words were spoken specifically by one source and not the other.

Speaker segmentation and classification is relatively straightforward when customers and agents are recorded on separate channels. Unfortunately, call center equipment often records everything on one channel. So, in most cases, speech analytics systems must rely on automatic segmentation and classification methods. The best of these methods will use information both from the acoustics and from the transcript. The transcript provides some clues about where speaker turns start and end, such as words that are often seen around these transition points. A language model can also help to distinguish word sequences that a customer is more likely to say from word sequences that a service agent is more likely to say. Clues about speaker changes provided by acoustics include:

- sharp changes in mean pitch over adjacent time windows, such as in a typical conversation between a male and a female,
- changes in formant distributions,
- rising pitch contours, which often indicate a question,
- falling pitch and energy near the end of declarative utterances, and
- longer than average silences.

All of the above phenomena are more likely than not to occur between speakers. A few others are described by Cutler and Pearson (1985). We conjecture that the best speaker segmentation and classification methods of the future will take both acoustic and text features into account, though we are not aware of any published attempts to do so yet. Reliable speaker labels can be used to infer other useful features. For example, Park (2007) uses speaker labels to segment calls into Greeting, Question, Refine, Research, Resolution, Closing, and Off-Topic sections.

Beyond speaker segmentation, acoustic and text features can work together for what we might call conversation segmentation. For example, in many call centers, when an agent puts a customer on hold, the customer hears pre-recorded advertisements for one or more of the company's products until the agent comes back on the line. These advertisements are not really part of the conversation between the customer and the agent, but they are nevertheless included in the recording of that conversation. The transcripts of these advertisements can be a problem if an analyst attempts to retrieve calls that mention one of the advertised products. The analyst is typically interested in calls where a product is mentioned by the customer or the agent, not in an ad. Since any given ad usually appears in many calls, the analyst can be swamped with retrieved records where the product was mentioned only in an ad, making it difficult to find what the analyst is really looking for. A good speech analytics system will segment the recording into ad and non-ad segments, and then filter out the ads.

In an ideal world, conversation recordings would be accompanied by information about where ads begin and end. Again, in the real world, this information is rarely available. So, speech analytics systems must find the ads automatically. Melamed and Kim (2009) used both acoustic and transcript information to detect arbitrary ads in call recordings. On the acoustic side, they discovered that the voices in ads tend to vary their pitch much more than the voices of agents or customers. In the transcript, since any given ad appears in many calls, the n-grams that constitute an ad will have much higher frequency, on average, than the n-grams surrounding the ad. Melamed and Kim used these two properties of ads to filter them out with high precision and recall, high enough that they were deployed in a real live speech analytics system.

14.6 Relational Feature Extraction

The job of the relational feature extraction module is to convert metadata into a form suitable for storing in a relational DBMS. Most of the metadata that accompanies conversations in a speech analytics systems is atomic, in the sense that it does not represent anything beyond itself. For example, calls to a call center come with information about who called, who answered, and when the conversation started and ended. Thus, most of the work of the relational feature extraction module entails adding these unstructured pieces of data to separate fields in the relevant database records.

Some metadata is not atomic, however. For example, a customer ID attached to a call might be the key to a great deal of information that a company has about that customer. An agent might well have reason to search for calls from customers of a certain type. For efficiency, the customer information should be added to the call record in advance. To do so, the relational feature extraction module would perform a join[2] operation between the call records and the customer records.

A slightly more difficult task is at hand when some of the metadata is hierarchically structured. The classic example is information about a company's employees, who are usually organized in a hierarchical reporting structure; a customer service agent might report to a supervisor, who reports to a floor manager, who reports to a call center manager, who reports to a VP, who reports to the CEO. An analyst interested in the effectiveness of managers at different levels of the hierarchy might want to analyze calls taken by all the agents that report to a certain supervisor, or all the agents whose supervisors report to a certain manager, etc. To support such queries, the relational feature extraction module must flatten the hierarchy by means of transitive closure. In other words, it must create a separate database table that records every pair of employees that occur on some shortest path from the root to a leaf in the company hierarchy.

14.7 DBMS

The job of the database management system is two-fold. On the server side, the DBMS must efficiently search the database to find records that satisfy the analyst's query. On the client side, the DBMS must make it easy for the analyst to formulate the query, to understand the results, and to iteratively refine the query based on the results.

We assume that the database is relational, except for the text index, since no other kind of database technology is mature and efficient enough for the kind of data in most speech analytics systems. Many volumes have been written on how to configure such databases, so we will not delve into that topic here. Likewise, efficient text search is fairly well understood by now, to the point that standard query languages such as SQL include text search primitives, and

[2] "Join" is a standard technical term in the literature on relational databases (Date, 1989).

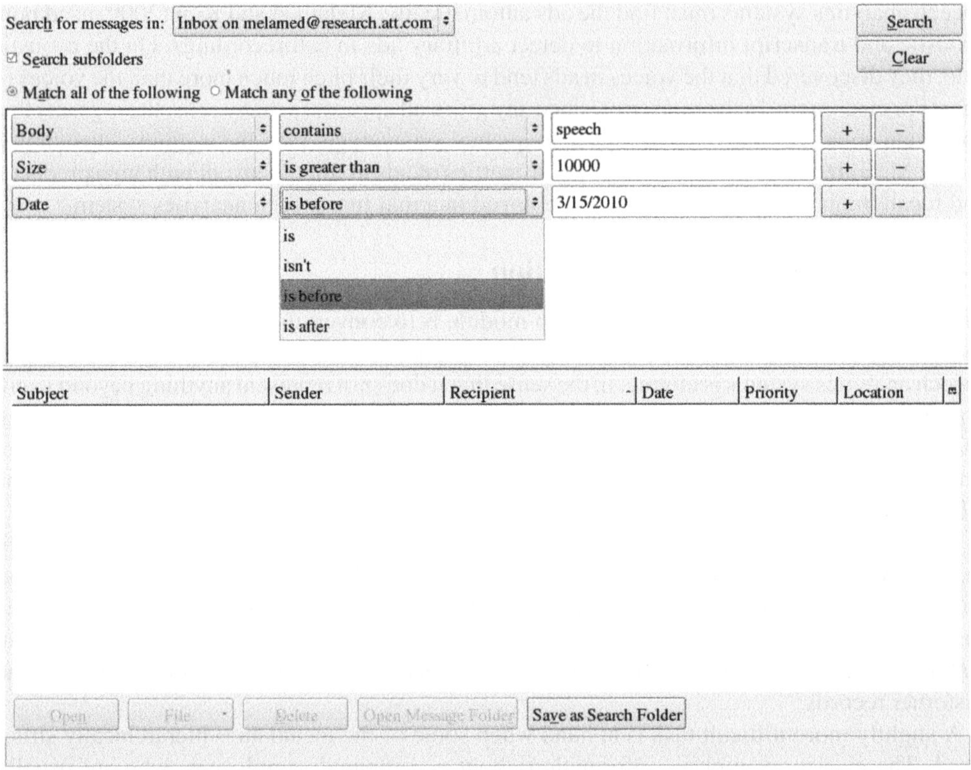

Figure 14.3 The Thunderbird interface for specifying constraints on field values in a database with both relational and text fields

DBMSs such as MySQL provide text indexing facilities. Queries about text fields are routinely combined with queries about other fields in relational DBMSs.

The real challenge here is to design an intuitive user interface, which hides the complexities of the database from the user without limiting its power. Relational query languages usually include syntax for specifying:

- a set of constraints on the values of fields in the database's records
- a set of fields to display from the records that satisfy the constraints,
- a method for ordering those records,

We now translate each of these query components into a component of a graphical user interface (GUI).

Figure 14.3 shows an example of an interface for specifying constraints on field values in a database with both relational and text fields. This UI is part of the Thunderbird email software,[3] but the same kind of search interface can be used in a speech analytics system. The user can

[3] http://www.mozillamessaging.com

increase or decrease the number of field constraints they want by clicking the plus and minus signs. Each constraint is specified in three parts: two pull-down menus and one text box. The first pull-down menu contains the list of fields that the user can constrain. The text box contains a value for the chosen field, and the second pull-down menu contains a list of relations between the field and its value. Different relations are suitable for different fields, so the contents of the second menu depend on the selection in the first. For example, if the `date` field is selected in the first menu, then the list of relations is as shown in the figure, but if the `body` field is selected, then the possible relations are "contains" and "does not contain." When the user clicks `Search`, the results are displayed in a detail report in the bottom half of the UI, one record per row (not shown). The icon to the right of the column headings brings up a menu of field names, each of which can be selected or unselected, to control which fields are displayed. Clicking on a column heading sorts the detail report on the value of the corresponding field. Clicking again sorts in reverse. This kind of UI, when populated with appropriate menus, allows the user to express any constraint that can be expressed by the SELECT, WHERE, and ORDER BY clauses of relational query languages such as SQL. In contrast to using such languages directly, this UI is fairly intuitive even for nonexpert users, does not require them to learn a query language, and is often faster than typing out a SQL query. Having the search constraints above the search results makes it easy for the user to refine the search in an iterative fashion.

As mentioned in Section 14.2, the first layer of functionality that we might call analytics is also provided by standard query languages. For example, using nothing but SQL on the command line, a skilled user can group the records returned by the DBMS on the values of certain fields, count the number of records in each group, sum or average the numeric fields within each group, and then sort on one of those sums or averages, to find the groups with the smallest or largest values in those fields. The basic operations involved in this analysis are grouping, counting, summing, averaging, and sorting. These operations fall under our definition of analytics, because they aggregate information from multiple conversations.

Figure 14.4 shows an example of how this first layer of analytics functionality can be presented in a GUI. This example is a screen shot of the Talkalytics system developed by AT&T Labs. The "Add grouping(s)" box below the search constraints presents check boxes for each field that the system designers allowed grouping on. The user specifies a set of search constraints and a set of fields to display, as before, then selects the fields to group on and clicks `Search`. The result is a summary report over the records that satisfy the search constraints. The first column is a count of the records in each group. The remaining shaded columns correspond to the fields selected for grouping. The unshaded columns show the other fields that the user selected for viewing. Since this is a summary report, the only fields that can be viewed are those for which a sensible summary statistic can be computed. For numeric fields, a sum or average usually makes sense. Summary statistics for other kinds of fields make sense only in relatively rare application-specific circumstances. For example, sometimes it is useful to know the most frequent value of a categorical field, or the most frequent substring of a text field. Thus, the groupings are selected by the user, and then the counting, summing, and averaging is performed automatically. Sorting can also be initiated by the user, as before, by clicking the column headings in the summary report. In Figure 14.4, the report has been sorted by AVG_LGTH (average call length, in seconds). The GUI also makes it easy for the user to "drill down" into a subset of records in the report. If any cell in the shaded columns is clicked, the

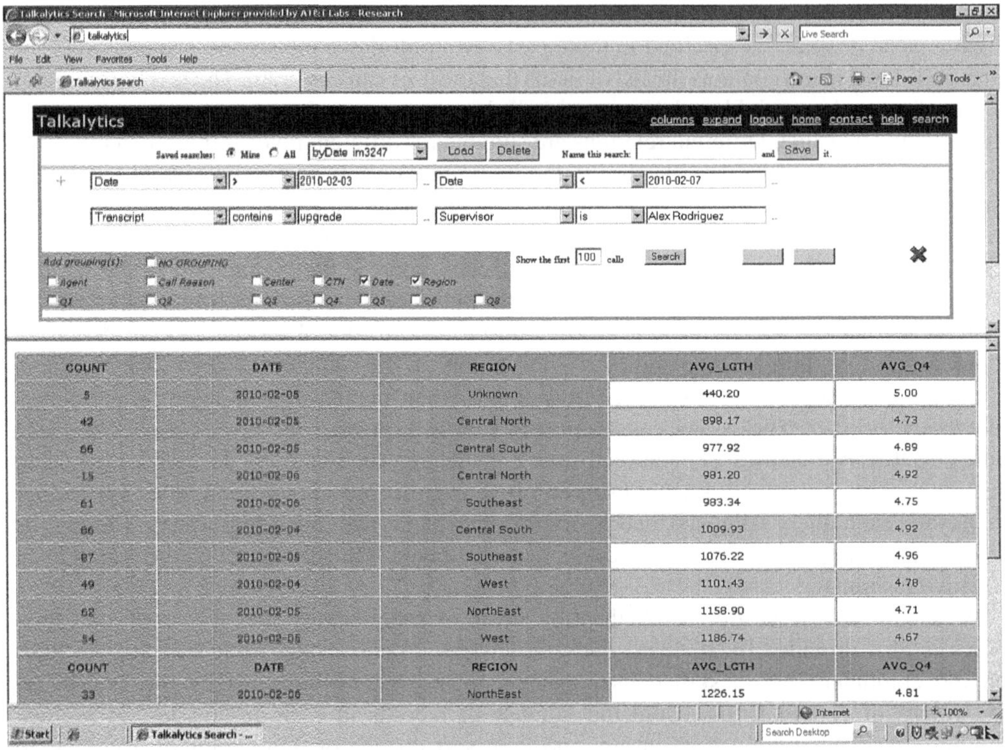

Figure 14.4 A summary report in Talkalytics

value in that cell becomes an equality search constraint on the corresponding field, the field is removed from grouping, and search is repeated. For example, if a user clicked on "Southeast" in the Region column in Figure 14.4, then "Region is Southeast" would become a new search constraint, and the new summary report would be grouped only by Date and not by Region. If a user then clicked on one of the dates in the new summary report, then there would be no more fields to group by, and the result would be a detail report. As before, all the search constraints and grouping fields are displayed above the search results, so that users can easily refine their queries in an iterative manner.

Some speech analytics systems do not allow analysts to formulate queries. Instead, queries are formulated in advance by the designers of the system, based on their understanding of what analysts might need. The system then proactively issues the queries to the DBMS on a recurring basis for trend analysis and alerting (e.g. Douglas *et al.*, 2005).

14.8 Media Server and Player

Once analysts have found a set of conversations that match their search criteria, they will often want to listen to some of them. To support such audio browsing, the detail report can include hyperlinks to the relevant audio files. If an analyst clicks one of these hyperlinks, an audio player is launched to play back the corresponding conversation.

The difficulty with audio browsing is that audio files cannot be skimmed the way that text (or hypertext) files can be. Without special tools, such as the one presented by Cooper *et al.*

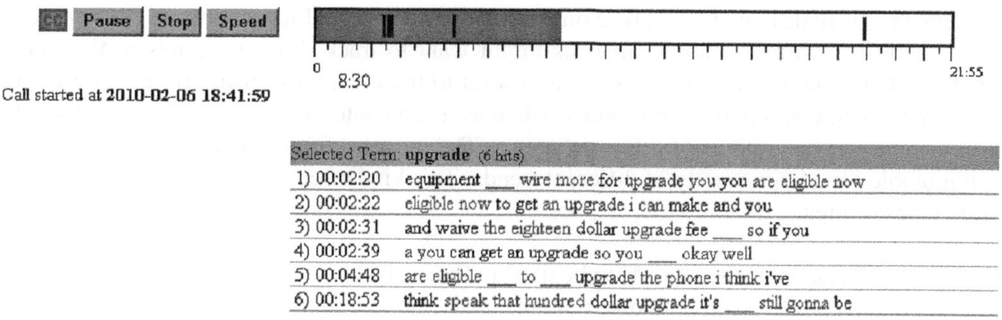

Figure 14.5 The Talkalytics audio player

(2001), analysts have no way to skip to the parts of an audio file that pertain to a certain topic. If they are dealing with long conversations,[4] analysts can waste a great deal of time listening to speech that they are not interested in.

When speech browsing follows speech retrieval, the query used for retrieval, together with the transcripts, can often be used to ameliorate this problem. Specifically, if the query includes one or more search terms, then it is possible to let the analyst skip directly to the part(s) of a conversation where those terms were spoken. Several techniques are required to make this possible. First, the transcripts must include information about the time offset of each word that they contain. Second, the media player must be able to start playing an audio source from a specific time offset. Third, since the audio files that contain long conversations can be very large, they can take a long time to stream from the media server to the media player. So, for optimum effectiveness, the media server must be able to start streaming audio from a specified time offset. This is commonly known as server-side seek.

Figure 14.5 shows the Talkalytics audio player, which is a descendant of the SpeechLogger audio player (Begeja *et al.*, 2004). This audio player makes it easy for an analyst to skip to instances of search terms in a recording. The audio player has some components that exist in many other software audio players, such as a progress bar, a Play/Pause button, and playback speed control. It then adds some features that are specifically designed for audio browsing. For example, the user can click anywhere in the progress bar to play the recording from that point. This feature is particularly useful when the locations of the search terms in the transcript are indicated in the progress bar. As shown in the screen shot, Talkalytics uses vertical tic marks for this purpose. Below the progress bar is a list of word contexts where the search terms are found in the transcript (in Figure 14.5 the search term is "upgrade".). The user can click on any of these contexts to listen to the corresponding audio segment. The player's CC button turns on closed captioning, which displays a moving window of words in the transcript below the progress bar. The window scrolls through the transcript in sync with the audio playback. Many users find closed captioning helpful for following the recording, especially when fast-forwarding.

14.9 Trend Analysis

The ability to perform trend analysis is the main distinction between sophisticated speech analytics systems and simple ones. Most of the published research on this topic pertains to

[4] Calls to call centers can last for hours!

systems that were designed to analyze one particular trend (e.g. Takeuchi *et al.*, 2007; Zweig *et al.*, 2006). However, different analysts might want to track different trends in the same database. For example, a sales analyst might want to track the number of conversations that mention the name of a particular product, whereas a call center manager might want to track the customer service ratings of different agents. The most useful trend analysis modules are configurable for a large variety of different trends. This kind of configurable module requires three kinds of input:

- a set of constraints on the records to be used in the analysis,
- a set of constraints on the candidate features, and
- an objective function with respect to which trends will be analyzed.

Let us consider each of these in turn.

The trend analysis module compiles a query out of the record constraints. It sends this query to the DBMS to obtain a subset of records from the database, just as if the analyst were doing retrieval. However, the set of records returned by the DBMS is then sent to the feature filtering module, instead of being displayed to the analyst (see Figure 14.2).

Almost any aspect of a conversation or its metadata can be a feature, such as the frequency of certain words in the conversation, or whether any part of the conversation was through a cell phone. In the simplest scenario, the set of feature constraints is empty, and all available features of each record in the set are used, including transcript features, acoustic features, metadata features, and higher-order features inferred from them. In this scenario, the feature filtering module filters out nothing. More typically, however, analysts will know in advance that some features or types of features cannot be relevant to the analysis, usually because common sense tells them that those features are not *causally* related to the objective function. In this case, the analyst can remove some features or feature types from consideration.

The objective function can be one of the features, or a mathematical function of one or more features. For example, customer satisfaction is an important objective function for most businesses, and consequently also for their speech analytics systems. That is why call centers sometimes give callers the option to take a survey at the end of their call, in order to gauge the callers' level of satisfaction with their agent, their product, or other aspects of their relationship with the company. The surveys typically elicit scalar responses, using questions such as "How would you rate the agent's courtesy, on a scale from 1 to 5?" The answers to the survey questions then become part of the call's metadata, so they are available for statistical modeling. More generally, an objective function can combine two or more features. For example, a call center analyst might want to analyze the summed frequency of all curse words over some time period.

Given these three kinds of information, the trend analysis module induces a model of how the objective function can be explained by the selected features. The model assigns a weight to each input feature, which represents that feature's correlation with the objective. The features are then ranked on the magnitude of their weights, and the highest-ranked ones are presented to the analyst. We call these "prominent features" in Figure 14.2.

The literature offers many ways to assign weights to features, all of which are beyond the scope of ordinary DBMSs and their query languages. A relatively straightforward method is statistical regression. For a regression problem that includes a large number of features, such as the vocabulary of speech transcripts, it is important to choose a method with built-in regularization, such as the Lasso (Tibshirani, 1994). Note that the purpose of regression here is not the usual one. Usually, when people induce regression models, it is for the purpose of predicting the values of the objective function on future examples. In contrast, here we are interested in the weights of the features, rather than in what they say about any particular examples.

Regardless of how the feature weights are induced, speech analytics system designers must remember that correlation is not the same as causation. High customer satisfaction ratings might correlate highly with the phrase “thank you” in conversation transcripts, but that phrase is probably not the cause of customer satisfaction. More likely, it’s the other way around. Although causal inference is well understood in the setting of a controlled experiment (Pearl, 2009), we are not aware of any reliable and efficient methods for automatic *post hoc* inference of causation among a large number of variables. The leap from correlation to causation is best made by the analyst.

As with the other speech analytics functionalities that have a user in the loop, trend analysis is only as effective as the user interface. A well-designed user interface should offer the analyst an easy way to focus on records with certain highly predictive features. It should also offer an easy way to filter out features and/or feature types in an iterative manner, in order to remove those that the analyst judges as unlikely to be the cause of variance in the objective function.

Figure 14.6 shows a screen shot of the prototype trend analysis interface in the Talkalytics system. To get to this part of the system, users begin by specifying a set of search constraints, via the UI in Figure 14.3. Then, instead of clicking `Search`, users select an objective function from a drop-down menu (not shown), and click a separate `Analyze` button. Currently, the objective functions are limited to individual numeric fields. Figure 14.6 shows the result of a trend analysis with respect to the `Score` field, which in this context represents a measure of customer satisfaction. The display is in two columns. The left column shows the five features that are the most negatively correlated with the objective function, and the right column shows the five features that are the most positively correlated. Both columns are sorted by magnitude from the top down. For each feature, the UI gives a human-readable description, the correlation value, a bar graph to help users visually compare correlation magnitudes, and two check boxes.

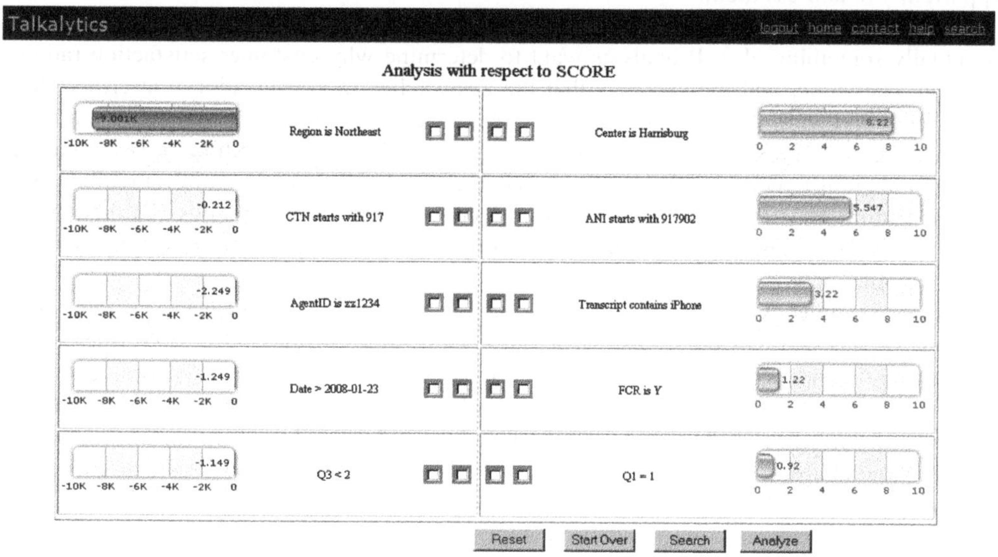

Figure 14.6 Prototype trend analysis GUI in the Talkalytics system

Users use the check boxes, along with the buttons at the bottom of the UI, for iterative refinement of the analysis. One of the check boxes for each feature is the Ignore check box. If a user checks this box for one or more of the displayed features and clicks the Analyze button again, then the analysis is repeated without those features. Thus, other features will make it into the list of top five most highly correlated features, and will be displayed instead of the features that were ignored. The other check box for each feature is the Focus check box. If a user checks this box for one or more of the displayed features and clicks the Analyze button, then the analysis is repeated just for the subset of records whose values on those features contributed to the magnitude of the correlation. For scalar features and positive correlations this means having a value above the mean, and for negative correlations a value below the mean. For Boolean features this means having a value of True for positive correlations and False for negative correlations. Of course, users can also check a combination of Focus and Ignore check boxes, in which case the reanalysis will focus on a subset of the records while ignoring some features. After checking some check boxes, users also have the option to click the Search button instead of the Analyze button. If they do so, then Talkalytics returns them to the search and retrieval interface in Figure 14.3, and immediately executes a search for the records that satisfy the conjunction of the Focus constraints and the originally specified search constraints. In this manner, users can seamlessly switch between the retrieval and trend analysis functionality layers of the system.

A popular way to do trend analysis is with time being the objective function. It is this usage that people usually refer to when they mention trend analysis, although the term can be applied more broadly, since the math is the same with other objective functions. When the analysts choose time as the objective function, they are effectively asking "What features change the most over time?" Examples of possible answers to this question that might interest an analyst include the average customer satisfaction rating, the volume of calls from Kansas, and the frequency of the phrase "cancel my service". When such answers come up, they often reveal problems that were previously unknown, giving analysts or their organization an early opportunity to address them.

The time objective function is sometimes misused when the objective function of interest is actually something else. If analysts want to determine why customer satisfaction ratings fluctuate over time, and they suspect that the answer lies in conversation transcripts, they might run trend analysis with time being the objective function and the features taken from the transcripts, to see what comes out on top. Such an analysis can sometimes reveal valuable clues, but there is a more direct and more reliable way to do it. What the analyst really wants to do is feature selection with respect to two objective functions: the ratings and time. Most speech analytics systems do not offer this functionality, which is a major reason why the time objective function is often misused.

Another example of two objectives that can be usefully analyzed together is customer satisfaction ratings and call durations. Most call centers strive to maximize the former while minimizing the latter. These goals are difficult to achieve simultaneously, because the values of these two statistics tend to rise and fall together. However, the correlation is far from perfect, and there are typically many ways to influence the two statistics disproportionally. An analyst can run trend analysis with these two objective functions to discover features that affect one statistic more than the other.

From a mathematical point of view, feature selection with two objective functions is a straightforward generalization of feature selection with one objective function. Instead of asking which features best explain the variance of one objective, we can ask which features best explain the covariance of two objectives. There is also a well-known generalization of statistical regression for answering such questions, known as multivariate regression. Naturally, these maths can be further generalized to three or more objective functions, but it is more difficult to imagine use cases for such generalizations in a speech analytics system. It is also straightforward to generalize the trend analysis GUI to accommodate two or more objective functions: substitute the pull down menu of objective functions with a set of check boxes, so that any number of functions can be selected.

14.10 Alerting System

Effective alerting systems are the Holy Grail of analytics systems. Most analysts would love a system that automatically alerts them whenever an important change occurs in their data. Broadly speaking, change detection is a very active area of research, with many open problems. The basics of change detection are sufficiently well understood, however, to enable construction of change detection systems with a useful level of functionality (Gustafsson, 2000).

Alerting systems necessarily deal with time series, since their output would always be the same if time was not one of the variables involved. For the purposes of speech analytics, we are concerned with discrete time series, since records in the database are discrete. One of the inputs to the alerting system, then, must be a time interval size. Each element of a time series will represent the records whose timestamps fall into the same interval of the given size. Independent of the interval size is the interval offset, which must be less than or equal to the size. If the interval offset is equal to the interval size, then the intervals are disjoint; otherwise, they overlap.

A typical alerting system will analyze many time series. Any process of analyzing a large number of events for anomalies is susceptible to false alarms. False alarms reduce the effectiveness of alerting systems, because they dilute the attention of the users. Douglas *et al.* (2005) propose the *hbmix* procedure for ameliorating this problem. Regardless of whether sophisticated statistical methods are employed to reduce the false alarm rate, analysts will usually restrict the records that participate in the alerting module using a query, the same way as they would for retrieval or trend analysis. Analysts can also configure an alerting system to analyze time series for a hand-picked set of features, or for all the features of a given type, such as all the customer service agents, or the 1000 most frequent words in the vocabulary.

The numeric value corresponding to each element in a time series is usually derived by summing or averaging the value of one particular feature of the relevant records, such as the frequency of a particular word or call duration. However, it is also possible to derive the time axis tic values from arbitrary mathematical transformations or aggregations of the chosen features. A particularly relevant possibility is to construct a time series of the weights that the trend analysis module assigns to one or more features with respect to an objective function of interest. Such a time series would enable alerts such as "agent ID `abc123` has become highly correlated with customer service ratings." To check for such an alert condition, the alerting module would call the trend analysis module to get feature weights.

Having defined some time series, analysts can choose between alerts about the values of time tics, and alerts about changes in those values over time. In the case of changes over time, a length of time must be specified to compare against. For example, one analyst might want to be notified whenever the mean call duration exceeds 10 minutes; another might want to be notified whenever the mean call duration significantly increases from one day to the next; a third might want to be notified whenever the mean call duration for a given day is significantly higher than the mean for the preceding hundred days. What counts as a significant increase (or decrease) can be expressed in absolute terms, such as 2 minutes, or in relative terms, such as 20%. Of course, after deciding between individual values and changes of values, and, if applicable, between absolute and relative changes, the analyst must also supply the threshold value, such as 10 minutes or 20%.

One more piece of configuration information that an alerting system needs is how often and under what conditions to notify an analyst that an alert was triggered. In the simplest scenario, an analyst gets an email or SMS message whenever one of the alerts is triggered. To prevent a flood of alerts, an analyst might instead request that alerts be sent no more than once per hour, per day, or per week. Or the alerts can appear on a dashboard whenever the analyst logs into the system. Another possible degree of flexibility is to be notified only when some combination of alert conditions is triggered.

To summarize, the specification of a trigger in a fully flexible alerting system includes the following information:

- a time interval size
- a time interval offset
- a set of record constraints
- a set of feature constraints
- an objective function (sum, average, weight, etc.)
- choice between analyzing individual values or changes over time
- if analyzing changes, then a choice between absolute or relative changes
- if analyzing relative changes, then a length of time to compare against
- a threshold of significance
- which alerts or combinations of alerts should generate a notification to the analyst
- the minimum delay between consecutive notifications

It is an open problem to design a flexible and intuitive user interface that allows an analyst to specify all the different kinds of possible alerts. The large variety of possible objective functions is particularly difficult to represent in a GUI. For this and other reasons, most speech analytics systems that offer alerts come preconfigured by their developers to offer only a small subset of the many possible kinds of alerts. Douglas *et al.* (2005) offer examples of a variety of GUIs that can be used in an alerting system for call center data.

14.11 Conclusion

In this chapter we have outlined a vision of a relatively sophisticated speech analytics system, with several layers of functionality. The lowest layer is a system for speech retrieval and browsing. On top of that, a DBMS provides rudimentary relational analytics. Next, a trend analysis layer adds more sophisticated statistical analyses. Finally, an alerting system collects information from the other layers, and takes the initiative to provide actionable information in a timely manner. All of the layers are presented to the user in an intuitive and integrated GUI.

Speech analytics presents a range of research problems in ASR, statistics, system engineering, and human/computer interaction. Very few of these research opportunities have been explored so far. It is our hope that this chapter motivates more researchers to look into this exciting area.

Acknowledgments

Thanks to Taniya Mishra and Bernard Renger for constructive feedback on this chapter. Thanks to the rest of the Talkalytics team for helping to develop Talkalytics: Tirso Alonso, Suhrid Balakrishnan, Yeon-Jun Kim, Valeriy Pogrebitskiy, Bernard Renger, Susanta Routray, Behzad Shahraray, David Smith, Heather Wighton, Wei Yang, and Arthur Zaifman. Thanks also to Laura Labarbera and Jennifer Feay for feedback on the Talkalytics concept and UI.

References

Begeja L, Renger B, Saraclar M, Gibbon D, Liu Z and Shahraray B 2004 A system for searching and browsing spoken communications *HLT/NAACL Workshop on Interdisciplinary Approaches to Speech Indexing and Retrieval.*

Busso C, Lee S and Narayanan S 2009 Analysis of emotionally salient aspects of fundamental frequency for emotion detection. *IEEE Transactions on Audio, Speech and Language Processing* **17**(4), 582–596.

Camelin N, Bechet F, Damnati G and Mori RD 2009a Speech mining in noisy audio message corpus *Proceedings of Interspeech 2007.*

Camelin N, Bechet F, Damnati G and Mori RD 2010 Detection and interpretation of opinion expressions in spoken surveys. *IEEE Transactions on Speech and Audio Processing.*

Camelin N, Damnati G, Bechet F and Mori RD 2009b Automatic customer feedback processing: alarm detection in open question spoken messages *Proceedings of Interspeech 2008.*

Camelin N, Mori RD, Bechet F and Damnati G 2009c Error correction of proportions in spoken opinion surveys *Proceedings of Interspeech 2009.*

Chelba C, Hazen TJ and Saraclar M 2008 Retrieval & browsing of spoken content. *IEEE Signal Processing Magazine* **25**, 39–49.

Cooper JW, Viswanathan M and Kazi Z 2001 Samsa: A speech analysis, mining and summary application for outbound telephone calls *Proceedings of the 34th Hawaii International Conference on System Sciences.*

Cutler A and Pearson M 1985 On the analysis of prosodic turn-taking cues In *Intonation in Discourse* (ed. Johns-Lewis C) Croom Helm pp 139–155.

Date CJ 1989 A note on the relational calculus. *SIGMOD Record* **18**(4), 12–16.

Douglas S, Agarwal D, Alonso T, Bell RM, Gilbert M, Swayne DF and Volinsky C 2005 Mining customer care dialogs for "daily news". *IEEE Transactions on Speech and Audio Processing* **13**(5-1), 652–660.

Gustafsson F 2000 *Adaptive filtering and change detection.* Wiley.

Lee CM and Narayanan SS 2005 Toward detecting emotions in spoken dialogs. *Speech and Audio Processing, IEEE Transactions on* **13**(2), 293–303.

Mamou J and Ramabhadran B 2008 Phonetic query expansion for spoken document retrieval *Proceedings of Interspeech 2008.*

Mamou J, Carmel D and Hoory R 2006 Spoken document retrieval from call-center conversations *Proceedings of SIGIR 2006.*

Melamed ID and Kim YJ 2009 Automatic detection of audio advertisements *Proceedings of Interspeech 2009.*

Park Y 2007 Automatic call section segmentation for contact-center calls In *CIKM* (ed. Silva MJ, Laender AHF, Baeza-Yates RA, McGuinness DL, Olstad B, Olsen ØH and Falcão AO), pp 117–126. ACM.

Pearl J 2009 Causal inference in statistics: An overview. *Statistics Surveys* **3**, 96–146.

Polzehl T and Metze F 2008 using prosodic features to prioritize voice messages *SSCS Workshop at SIGIR 08.*

Saraclar M and Sproat R 2004 Lattice-based search for spoken utterance retrieval *HLT-NAACL*, pp 129–136.

Schapire RE 1999 A brief introduction to boosting *Proceedings of Sixteenth International Joint Conference on Artificial Intelligence 1999.*

Shichiri T, Nanjo H and Yoshimi T 2008 Minimum bayes-risk decoding with presumed word significance for speech based information retrieval *IEEE International Conference on Acoustics, Speech, and Signal Processing (ICASSP 2008)*, pp 1557–1560.

Stark L, Whittaker S and Hirschberg J 2000 ASR satisficing: The effects of ASR accuracy on speech retrieval *ICSLP 2000*.

Takeuchi H, Subramaniam LV, Nasukawa T, Roy S and Balakrishnan S 2007 A conversation-mining system for gathering insights to improve agent productivity *CEC/EEE*, pp 465–468. IEEE Computer Society.

Tibshirani R 1994 Regression shrinkage and selection via the lasso. *Journal of the Royal Statistical Society, Series B* **58**, 267–288.

Ukkonen E 1995 On-line construction of suffix trees. *Algorithmica* **14**(3), 249–260.

Zweig G, Siohan O, Saon G, Ramabhadran B, Povey D, Mangu L and Kingsbury B 2006 Automated quality monitoring for call centers using speech and nlp technologies *Proceedings of the Human Language Technology Conference of the NAACL, Companion Volume: Demonstrations*, pp 292–295. Association for Computational Linguistics, New York City, USA.

15

Speech Retrieval*

Ciprian Chelba[1], Timothy J. Hazen[2], Bhuvana Ramabhadran[3] and Murat Saraçlar[4]
[1]*Google, U.S.A.*
[2]*MIT Lincoln Laboratory, U.S.A.*
[3]*IBM TJ Watson Research Center, U.S.A.*
[4]*Boğaziçi University, Turkey*

In this chapter we discuss the retrieval and browsing of spoken audio documents. We focus primarily on the application of document search where a user provides a query and the system returns a set of audio documents that best match the query. The primary technical challenges of speech retrieval lie in the retrieval system's ability to deal with imperfect speech recognition technology that produces errorful output due to misrecognitions caused by inadequate statistical models or out-of-vocabulary words. This chapter provides an overview of the common tasks and data sets, evaluation metrics, and algorithms most commonly used in this growing area of research.

15.1 Task Description

Speech retrieval refers to the task of retrieving the specific pieces of spoken audio data from a large collection that pertain to a query requested by a user. Before discussing methods for speech retrieval, it is important to define the different types of speech retrieval tasks and the methods in which potential solutions to these tasks will be evaluated.

15.1.1 Spoken Document Retrieval

When discussing speech information retrieval applications, the basic scenario assumes that a user will provide a *query* and the system will return a list of rank-ordered *documents*. The

* Parts of this chapter have been previously published in Chelba *et al.* (2008) [© 2008 IEEE]. The authors thank IEEE for granting permission to reproduce some paragraphs, tables and figures in this chapter.

Spoken Language Understanding: Systems for Extracting Semantic Information from Speech, First Edition.
Edited by Gokhan Tur and Renato De Mori.

query is generally assumed to be in the form of a string of text-based words (though spoken queries may be used instead of text in some applications). The returned documents are audio files purported by the system to be relevant to the query. This scenario is often referred to as spoken document retrieval (SDR).

15.1.2 Spoken Utterance Retrieval

For browsing long spoken documents it becomes important to locate the specific portions of the longer documents that are actually relevant to the query. In some SDR scenarios, this can be achieved by segmenting long documents into smaller segments pertaining to specific topics and then locating these topical segments. Alternatively a system could operate on segments as short as individual spoken utterances (i.e. speech segments roughly equivalent to spoken sentences). When the task requires the retrieval of utterance length segments instead of entire audio documents, the task becomes known as Spoken Utterance Retrieval (SUR). In this case, the purpose of SUR is to find all the utterances related to the query even when multiple utterances related to the query exist within a single longer document. Applications include browsing broadcast news, voice mail, teleconferences and lectures.

15.1.3 Spoken Term Detection

In both SDR and SUR, the goal is to find spoken audio which is *relevant* to the query. In general, it is assumed that documents or utterances containing words in the query will be relevant. However, the perceived relevance of a document is often a subjective notion which is not easily defined or evaluated, as individual users may each have their own opinion about how well a returned list of audio hits match a specific query.

A related application area to spoken document retrieval that provides a more concrete measure of evaluation is spoken term detection (STD). In STD applications, the goal is to find all spoken examples of a specific query word or phrase. In this case, the returned hits are either clearly correct or incorrect and no subjective determination of relevance is needed.

15.1.4 Browsing

For an application to be truly useful, the interface must enable users to search for and browse audio documents quickly and efficiently. One can imagine that an audio document search can be initiated in much the same way as a text search, i.e. the user enters a set of key words in a search field and is returned a set of putative hits. Unfortunately, unlike text, audio is a linear medium which is not easy to browse once the hits are returned, and it would be highly inefficient for a user to listen to each audio hit in order to determine its relevance to his query. Thus, efficient browsing of audio material typically requires visual inspection of returned hits, usually in the form of transcription snippets or video snapshots, in order to assist the user in the determination of which audio hits are relevant and which are not. While the technical challenges of searching for and retrieving audio documents are difficult in their own right, it is vital not to overlook the importance of the user interface and information presentation techniques in the creation of a successful speech retrieval system.

15.2 Applications

Just as information retrieval technology has enabled a wide range of text-based applications, speech retrieval technologies have also begun to enable a variety of speech and multi-media applications. Typically these systems are similar in nature to text-based search and retrieval systems, i.e. users can locate and browse audio or multi-media documents pertaining to text-based queries. With current technological constraints, it is not yet feasible to process and index all audio and multimedia content available on the Web, but applications focusing on constrained sets of data have been successfully introduced and deployed for public use.

15.2.1 Broadcast News

Early speech retrieval systems focused on data sets that existing speech technology could handle robustly, such as the high-quality speech read by professional news anchors in studio news broadcasts. For example, BBN first introduced the Rough 'n Ready system in 1998 to provide retrieval and browsing capability for broadcast news (Makhoul *et al.*, 2007). This research system lead to the development of the PodZinger commercial system for indexing web-based podcasts which debuted in 2005.

15.2.2 Academic Lectures

Though applications based on broadcast news data provided an early success story for the speech technology field, there are many other styles of audio data that are harder to process. For example, academic lectures are generally harder to process than broadcast news because the speech is typically produced in a spontaneous fashion, containing speech artifacts and disfluencies such as filled pauses, false starts, partial words and mispronunciations, which are far rarer in broadcast news. The speech can also exhibit a wider range of speaking rates and emphatic speech which are more difficult for today's automatic speech recognition technology to handle. An example of a system designed to allow searching and browsing of academic lectures is the MIT Lecture Browser (Glass *et al.*, 2007). This system provides users with a range of methods to efficiently search for and browse through lectures recorded at MIT. The system provides the streaming video of each retrieved lecture in addition to a scrolling window displaying the synchronized text transcript. Individual words in the transcript are underlined as they are played, providing easier access for hearing-impaired users.

15.2.3 Sign Language Video

As just mentioned above, an important aspect of speech technology is its ability to enable access to audio material for hearing impaired users. In addition to providing automatic closed-captioning capability, speech technology can also assist in the automatic extraction of sign data from broadcast news recordings for the hearing impaired. In such data, the speaker simultaneously signs with the hands while talking, thus providing an excellent source of annotated sign data. The video of the signer can be segmented via the help of the speech (or both the speech and its accompanying closed-caption text) to generate a corresponding segmented and annotated set of sign videos. From such processing, an application called Signiary has been created which provides a sign dictionary which allows users enter a word as text and retrieve sign videos of the related sign (Aran *et al.*, 2008). This application can also be utilized to automatically create annotated sign databases that can be used for training visual sign recognizers.

15.2.4 Historical Interviews

Even more difficult to process than broadcast news or academic lecture data are human/human conversations such as interviews. For example, the Survivors of the Shoah Visual History Foundation (VHF) was founded to preserve the stories of survivors and witnesses of major, global events such as the Holocaust. Through their efforts, a collection of thousands of hours of audio and video oral history interviews have been recorded across many languages. This collection is unique because of its wide range of diverse, accented, and multi-lingual spontaneous speech. To support access to this collection of data, a five-year, NSF-funded research project entitled Multilingual Access to Large Spoken Archives (MALACH) was initiated. The project resulted in innovations in multilingual speech recognition, spoken term detection and natural language processing technologies that has enabled easier search for the collection's users, who have included historians, educators, anthropologists, psychologists, film producers, and law enforcement officials (Oard *et al.*, 2006).

15.2.5 General Web Video

Moving forward, a challenging goal for speech technology is to be able to process and index the wide and diverse range of multi-media content on the Web. Towards this end goal, Google is developing its own Google Audio Indexing (Gaudi) technology with the goal of providing better search and browsing technology for various YouTube channels. Beyond the difficulties associated with spontaneous speech, accented speech, emphatic or emotional speech, and multi-lingual speech, web-based data may also contain difficult audio conditions including background noise, reverberant speech, variable channel conditions, and poor audio coding. While the range and quality of applications for speech retrieval of multi-media data will continue to grow and improve, there are still many difficult technical challenges to overcome before speech retrieval will reach the level of utility of today's text retrieval systems.

15.3 Challenges Using Speech Input

15.3.1 Overview

When designing a speech indexing and retrieval system, one might initially consider viewing the speech indexing problem as a simple two-stage process where the speech audio is first converted to text using an automatic speech recognition (ASR) system and the resulting text transcript is then indexed using a standard text-based indexing system. In fact, this may be a perfectly reasonable approach in a scenario where the ASR system is capable of producing near-perfect transcriptions. Unfortunately, current ASR technology performance is far from perfect on general audio data and the top-choice recognition result should be expected to be errorful for a variety of reasons.

Typically ASR systems use a probabilistic approach that requires the training of a set of statistical models describing the production of speech. At a high level, the goal of an ASR system is to predict the most likely string of words W given the observed acoustic information A. Mathematically, this requires the system to find the string of words W which maximizes $P(W|A)$.

To model $P(W|A)$, a variety of simplifying assumptions must be made. To begin, words are typically decomposed into sequences of phonetic units (or *phones*) which represent the specific sounds used to distinguish between words (e.g. the word *cat* contains the phones /k/, /ae/, and /t/). By applying Bayes Rule to $P(W|A)$ and decomposing the sequence of words W into a sequence of phonetic units U, the search for the best word hypothesis W given the acoustics A, is typically expressed as follows:

$$\arg\max_{W,U} p(A|U)P(U|W)P(W) \tag{15.1}$$

In this expression, $p(A|U)$ is referred to as the acoustic model, $P(U|W)$ is referred to as the lexical pronunciation model, and $P(W)$ is referred to as the language model. Additionally, the lexical pronunciation model and language model are typically constrained to use only the fixed, predefined set of vocabulary words specified by the system's lexicon. A discussion of basic ASR technology is presented in Chapter 4, so we will not discuss the details of the ASR modeling process here.

In order for a speech recognition engine to produce high-quality transcripts of speech, the system's lexicon needs to cover all of the vocabulary words used in the speech, the language model must accurately predict how these words may be strung together to form sentences, the pronunciation model must accurately predict all of the potential alternate phonetic pronunciations that may be used for these words, and the acoustic model must be able to predict the acoustic realization of the phonetic units used for any speaker, environment or audio condition that may be encountered. Only for the most tightly constrained problems, where each of these ASR models are extremely well matched to the expected speech audio, can near-perfect transcripts be expected. Thus, any indexing and retrieval mechanism that is deployed using current ASR technology must be robust to potential speech recognition errors.

15.3.2 Coping with ASR Errors Using Lattices

There are a variety of ways in which ASR errors can be introduced into a transcript. The most common error is a simple substitution of an acoustically similar word for the actual spoken word. This type of error is common even when the actual spoken word is in the vocabulary of the ASR system, and is typically caused by deficiencies in one of the system's statistical models.

In many cases, the effect of these errors can be mitigated through the examination of the alternate ASR hypotheses considered during the ASR process. Given an audio file and a set of models, an ASR system must apply the model constraints to the acoustic observations, and then search through the vast network of possible word sequences. Because the size of this search space is immense, it is generally pruned on-the-fly during the search to include only the most likely hypotheses. The network of unpruned hypotheses that have been explored can be maintained and saved for future use. These networks, often called speech recognition *lattices*, typically contain all of the word timing information and modeling scores used by the recognizer.

An example speech recognition lattice is shown in Figure 15.1. In this figure each arc in the network contains a word label along with the probability of that arc being taken from the previous state. The single best scoring sequence of words that can be traversed in a lattice is typically called the 1-best result. If desired, secondary searches of this lattice can be made to produce the n-best sentence hypotheses beyond the top scoring hypothesis. Although the best scoring word string hypothesis may be errorful, it is often possible to find the correct word

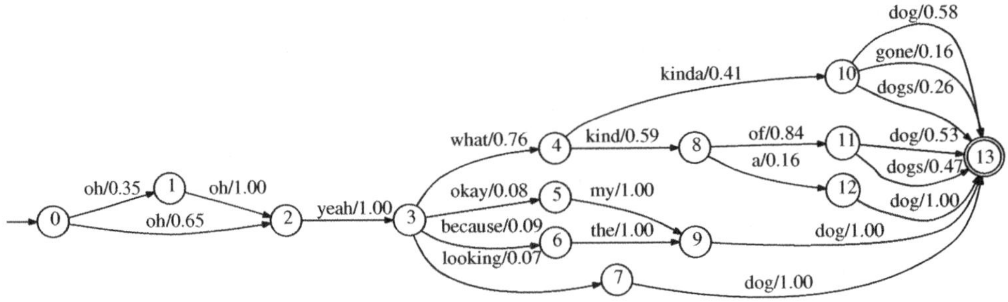

Figure 15.1 Example speech recognition lattice

string embedded with the ASR lattice. Using such lattices allows potential hits of words to be indexed and retrieved even if the words do not appear in the 1-best result returned by the recognizer.

15.3.3 Out-of-vocabulary Words

15.3.3.1 The OOV Problem

When building an ASR system for an information retrieval application, the choice of words used in the system's vocabulary is vital. ASR systems typically employ a closed vocabulary, i.e. the vocabulary is predetermined before the speech is passed to the ASR system for recognition. If a word spoken in the audio is not present in the vocabulary of the recognizer, the recognizer will always misrecognize this word, and requests by users to locate documents containing this spoken word will necessarily fail.

Unfortunately, it is often the less common, topic-specific words which form the basis for information retrieval queries. Studies on a variety of data have shown that out-of-vocabulary (OOV) word rates for previously unseen data are not insubstantial even for large vocabularies (Hetherington, 1995). The introduction of new vocabulary items (e.g. new proper names, scientific jargon, slang, etc.) in new audio data is also unavoidable. Thus, methods for countering the OOV problem in audio information retrieval are needed.

15.3.3.2 Vocabulary and Language Model Adaptation

One potential method for countering the OOV problem is vocabulary adaptation. Commercial dictation software typically addresses this problem by providing the user with a topic-specific vocabulary and language model (e.g. medical transcription), and then allowing the user to add new vocabulary items on-the-fly as needed. In the absence of human supervision, it may still be possible to predetermine a topic-specific vocabulary and language model in some cases. For example, academic lectures could be classified into broad topics based on accompanying metadata such as the title of the academic subject. The vocabulary and language model can then be adapted to match the subject area of the data.

If the topic of the audio content is unknown, an automated solution to determining the topic may be possible. In this scenario, the data is first passed through a topic-independent recognizer. An analysis of the first pass recognition result is conducted to determine the topic, from which a new topic-specific vocabulary and language model is created. The new topic-specific recognizer performs a second recognition pass over the data to formulate a new set of recognition hypotheses. This approach can yield improved recognition accuracies at the computational cost of performing an additional recognition pass.

15.3.3.3 Out-of-vocabulary Word Modeling

Even with topic-specific vocabularies, OOV words are still possible. As a fall back position, an ASR system can attempt to detect when an OOV word occurs then represent the OOV region by a sequence or network of phonetic units. This can be accomplished by building an independent OOV model from sub-word units (e.g. syllables or phones) that is examined in parallel with the existing vocabulary items during the ASR search, and hypothesizing an OOV word when the OOV model scores better than the words in the known vocabulary (Bazzi, 2002). The resulting search lattice can then be post-edited to replace any detected OOV word in the lattice with the underlying phonetic elements that represent it (Hori *et al.*, 2007).

While word-based recognition is generally acknowledged to produce the most accurate information for audio indexing, another school of thought has suggested that the problem can be attacked by ignoring words entirely during the ASR search. Instead the ASR system would only produce a phonetic representation of the speech. Information retrieval of keywords would then be performed by locating audio files containing the phonetic sequences which match the pronunciations of the keywords (Ng, 2000). This approach conceivably eliminates the ASR OOV problem, and the ASR engine can run with far greater efficiency (both in memory and speed) if it only has to produce phonetic hypotheses. However, the post-recognition indexing and retrieval stages necessarily become more complex under this approach.

15.3.4 Morphologically Rich Languages

Morphologically rich languages present many challenges for ASR and retrieval. In particular the OOV problem is more pronounced since these languages require much larger vocabularies to have the same level of coverage. Therefore, techniques to overcome the OOV problem are of special interest for these languages. For these languages, one common approach to overcome the OOV problem is to utilize sub-word units. Both grammatical and statistical methods have been proposed to break down the words into sub-word units. Various sub-word units have been successfully used for retrieval of agglutinative languages such as Finnish (Turunen and Kurimo, 2007) and Turkish (Arisoy *et al.*, 2009).

15.3.5 Resource-limited Languages and Dialects

As the use of technology spreads to increasingly larger portions of the world, speech technology will be introduced to a wide variety of new languages and dialects, posing particular difficulties for the portability of existing technology. There are nearly 7000 known languages around the world (Lewis, 2009), but a vast majority of these languages have little or no transcribed speech data available for training an ASR system. As we move towards the less common languages of the world, the availability of trained linguists or speech technologists capable of transcribing data, developing lexicons, and creating ASR models for these languages decreases. Even worse, for some languages, the written form of the language is not phonetically based and existing standards for specifying phonetic pronunciations do not yet exist. For these languages standard speech processing technology may be incapable of providing a usable solution to the retrieval problem without significant development work, and alternative approaches must be considered in the interim. Towards this end there has been an increased interest in query-by-example speech retrieval systems which are capable of performing speech retrieval based purely on audio examples of a spoken term or phrase without requiring any underlying knowledge of the lexical structure of the spoken language (Hazen *et al.*, 2009; Parada *et al.*, 2009; Shen *et al.*, 2009; Zhang and Glass, 2009).

15.4 Evaluation Metrics

In order to properly evaluate the effectiveness of a spoken document retrieval (SDR) system, it is important to understand the nature of the problem that a system is being asked to solve. In the SDR scenario, it is assumed that a user will provide a *query* and the system will return a list of rank-ordered *documents*. The query could be given in a variety of forms including text-based strings or spoken queries. The system could also perform query-by-example retrieval, in which a user provides a example audio clip or full document as the query. The system then returns audio documents purported to be relevant to the given query.

To ensure that a system developer is making correct design considerations, the evaluation methodology applied to the system must be well calibrated with the system's ability to achieve the user's goals. Thus, the most relevant evaluation metric would presumably be the overall user satisfaction in a deployed system that is being actively used and improved. Unfortunately it is extremely difficult to compare the effect of many different design considerations through such time-consuming user evaluations.

A more common approach is the creation of evaluation data sets that can be easily re-evaluated when system designers wish to examine the effect of changes or improvements to a system. Within this scenario, human judges could be used to annotate the degree of relevance of each document within an evaluation set to a collection of pre-specified queries. The initial collection and annotation of such a data set could be very time-consuming and expensive, but once created the evaluation set could be repeatedly used to assess the effect of new algorithms and processing techniques on system performance.

Given an evaluation data set, appropriate evaluation metrics must be defined which are well correlated with the goals of the system. Since a primary aim in spoken document processing is to bridge the gap between text and speech search technology, one possibility is to compare the results of a fully automatic SDR system against results obtained by a text retrieval system deployed on manually transcribed versions of the same evaluation data. However, using a text-based system's retrieval results as a proxy for the *correct* reference result does not directly address the actual goals of the retrieval system, especially if the text-based system is imperfect in its own right.

In the end, most system developers rely on a variety of clearly defined measures of document retrieval performance. These measures typically assume that the audio documents in the evaluation set have a reference labeling of *relevant* or *not relevant* for each test query. Under these conditions, basic measures of detection performance such precision and recall, or false alarm rate and miss rate, are commonly computed. Performance curves, e.g. precision–recall curves or detection error trade-off curves, derived from these measures are often plotted as the system's detection threshold is swept, thus providing a means of assessing the trade-off between the different types of detection errors. Statistics derived from these performance curves, such as the mean average precision (MAP) or equal error rate, are also often used to characterize a system's performance. A thorough description of these standard detection measures can be found in Baeza-Yates and Ribeiro-Neto (1999).

Because the improvements in the accuracy of the ASR system can lead to improved retrieval performance, metrics for directly evaluating the ASR system are also commonly examined. For example, the out-of-vocabulary (OOV) rate for a recognizer's vocabulary on new previously unseen data is often measured. This helps determine what fraction of words in the document collection can not be properly transcribed using standard word-based ASR. Also of particular interest to spoken retrieval systems is the query-OOV rate, which measures the rate at which query words provided by actual users are not covered by the vocabulary of the ASR system. The ASR system's overall accuracy is also typically monitored using the word error rate (WER) metric, which measures the percentage of errors an ASR system makes relative to the actual number of spoken words. When working with ASR lattices, it is also common to evaluate the lattice-WER – the minimum WER along some path in the lattice, irrespective of its likelihood.

A related application area to spoken document retrieval is spoken term detection (STD). In STD applications, the goal is to find all spoken examples of a specific word or phrase. In this case, specific returned hits are either clearly correct or incorrect and no subjective determination of relevance is needed. An example metric for STD evaluation is the *actual term-weighted value* (ATWV) which is defined in the NIST Spoken Term Detection (STD) 2006 Evaluation Plan (see *http://www.nist.gov/speech/tests/std/*) as:

$$\text{ATWV} = 1 - \frac{1}{Q}\sum_{q=1}^{Q}\{P_{miss}(q) + \beta P_{FA}(q)\} \tag{15.2}$$

where β is a user defined parameter (set to 1000 in the 2006 NIST STD evaluation), and where

$$\text{P}_{\text{miss}}(q) = 1 - \frac{C(q)}{R(q)} \qquad \text{P}_{\text{FA}}(\text{q}) = \frac{A(q) - C(q)}{T_{speech} - C(q)} \tag{15.3}$$

with T_{speech} being the total duration of the speech in the collection. Here the definitions of $R(q)$, $C(q)$, and $A(q)$ refer to the specific individual examples of the query phrase q in the audio data and not to whole documents, i.e. $R(q)$ is the total number of times the specific query phrase q actually appears (word for word) in the audio collection, $A(q)$ is the number of purported examples of q returned by the system, and $C(q)$ is the number of these purported examples of q that are actually correct. This metric specifically measures the system's ability to locate query keywords within audio files relative to perfect audio transcriptions.

15.5 Benchmark Data Sets

15.5.1 TREC

Many of the prominent research efforts aimed at spoken document retrieval (SDR) have been centered around the SDR portion of the TREC evaluations conducted in 1999 and 2000 – a.k.a. TREC-8 and TREC-9 (Garofolo *et al.*, 2000). While the TREC-SDR evaluations mark a significant milestone in the speech retrieval field, a large body of SDR research existed previously, including notable contributions of Brown *et al.* (1996) and James (1995), and significant recent contributions have also been made (Glass *et al.*, 2007; Hansen *et al.*, 2005; Oard *et al.*, 2004; Van Thong *et al.*, 2002; Whittaker *et al.*, 2002).

One problem encountered in work published prior or outside the TREC-SDR community is that it does not always evaluate performance from a document retrieval point of view – using a metric like MAP or similar – but rather uses word-spotting measures, which are more technology-centric rather than user-centric. Depending on the application, the document retrieval performance may be more important, whereas the word-spotting accuracy is an excellent indicator for how an SDR system might be improved.

The TREC-SDR evaluations focused on a corpus of broadcast news speech from various sources: CNN, ABC, PRI, Voice of America. About 550 hours of speech were segmented manually into 21 574 stories each comprising about 250 words on the average. The pre-existing approximate manual transcriptions (or closed captions for the video case) used for the SDR system comparison with text-only retrieval performance had fairly high WER: 14.5% for video and 7.5% for radio broadcasts. ASR systems tuned to the broadcast news domain were evaluated on accurate manual transcriptions at 15–20% WER, not far from the accuracy of the approximate manual transcriptions.[1]

In order to evaluate the accuracy of retrieval systems, search queries (created based on general "topics") along with binary relevance judgments were compiled by human assessors for each of the 21 574 retrieval documents. SDR systems indexed the ASR 1-best output and their retrieval performance (measured in terms of MAP) was found to be flat with respect to ASR WER variations in the range of 15–30%. The most significant finding was that no severe degradation in retrieval performance was observed when evaluating with the ASR outputs in comparison with the approximate manual transcriptions. As a result NIST's final report on the TREC-SDR evaluations declared the research effort "a success story" (Garofolo *et al.*, 2000).

15.5.2 NIST STD

More recently, the NIST Spoken Term Detection (STD) 2006 Evaluation (NIST, 2006) introduced the task of locating the exact occurrence of a query in large heterogeneous speech archives – broadcast news, telephone conversations and roundtable meetings. The corpus used for the evaluation also included Arabic and Mandarin in addition to English and attracted many sites (Mamou *et al.*, 2007; Miller *et al.*, 2007; Vergyri *et al.*, 2007).

15.6 Approaches

15.6.1 Basic SDR Approaches

Before discussing various design decisions related to spoken document search, it is useful to give a brief presentation of state-of-the-art text document retrieval algorithms.

15.6.1.1 Vector Space Models for Information Retrieval

Probably the most widespread model for text retrieval is the TF-IDF vector model (Baeza-Yates and Ribeiro-Neto, 1999). For a given query $\mathcal{Q} = q_1 \dots q_i \dots q_Q$ and document D_j one

[1] The distribution of errors in manual transcriptions or closed captions can be very different from the ASR errors, and may have a very different impact on retrieval performance.

calculates a similarity measure by accumulating the TF-IDF score $w_{i,j}$ for each query term q_i:

$$S(D_j, Q) = \sum_{i=1}^{Q} w_{i,j}, \quad w_{i,j} = f_{i,j} \cdot idf_i \tag{15.4}$$

where $f_{i,j}$ is the term frequency (TF) of word q_i in document D_j, and $idf_i = \log N/n_i$ is the inverse document frequency (IDF), n_i/N being the fraction of documents containing q_i.

The main criticism to the TF-IDF algorithm is that the query terms are assumed to be independent. *Proximity information* is not taken into account at all. For example, the fact that the words LANGUAGE and MODELING occur next to each other in a given document is not used for relevance scoring, although the occurrence of the bigram LANGUAGE MODELING is more relevant than the combined occurrences of LANGUAGE and MODELING as unigrams. Moreover, the ability to evaluate proximity of query terms in the document becomes critical if one wishes to enhance the query language such that it allows phrase matching functionality, e.g. returning only documents that contain "LANGUAGE MODELING".

Another issue is that query terms may be encountered in different *contexts* in a given document: title, abstract, author name, font size, etc. For hypertext document collections even more context information is available: anchor text,[2] various HTML sections of a given document being just a few examples. The TF-IDF algorithm completely discards such information although it is clearly important in practice.

15.6.1.2 Language Modeling Approach

One can rank using the "point-wise mutual information" between the query and some document:

$$S(D_j, Q) = \log \frac{P(Q, D_j)}{P(Q)P(D_j)} \propto \log P(Q|D_j) \tag{15.5}$$

This amounts to building a language model $P(W|D_j)$ from each document, and then using it to score the query, $P(Q|D_j)$, see Ponte and Croft (1998). If the language model is an n-gram with order higher than 1, then this solution will indeed take into account word adjacency, or even more general proximity features depending on the language modeling approach being used.

15.6.1.3 Early Google Approach

Aside from the use of PageRank which is query independent and derived from the WWW connectivity graph, the early Google approach also uses both word *proximity* and *context* information heavily when assigning a relevance score to a given document.

In order to compute the PageRank for a given web page D_j, one builds the citation graph of web pages: for each page, it lists the pages it points to. To make sure the transition matrix that describes it is full rank stochastic, one smooths the transition probabilities by assuming that with a very small probability we can visit any other page from a given one. PageRank

[2] Text describing the hypertext link pointing to the given document/web page.

is the probability of each page under the stationary distribution of this ergodic Markov chain $PR(D_j)$.

Each web page also receives a score $R(D_j, \mathcal{Q})$ that describes how relevant it is to a given query $\mathcal{Q}$, so one uses an overall score that is loosely described as:

$$S(D_j, \mathcal{Q}) = \log PR(D_j) + R(D_j, \mathcal{Q}) \tag{15.6}$$

For a detailed description of $R(D_j, \mathcal{Q})$ the reader is referred to Brin and Page (1998), Section 4.5.1. As a high-level description, for each given query term q_i one retrieves the list of *hits* in document D; hits can be of various types depending on the *context* in which they occurred: title, anchor text, etc.; each type of hit has its own *type-weight*. For a single word query, the ranking algorithm takes the inner-product between the type-weight vector and a vector consisting of count-weights (tapered counts that discount the effect of large counts) and combines the resulting score with PageRank in a final relevance score. For multiple word queries, terms co-occurring in a given document are considered as forming different *proximity-types* based on how close the hits are, from adjacent to "not even close". Each proximity type comes with a proximity-weight and the relevance score includes the contribution of proximity information by taking the inner product over all types.

15.6.1.4 Inverted Index

Of essence to fast retrieval on static document collections of medium to large size is the use of an *inverted index*. The inverted index stores a list of hits for each word in a given vocabulary–the indexing terms.

For the TF-IDF model, the inverted index is the term-document co-occurrence matrix itself

$$(w_{ij})_{\substack{i=1,V \\ j=1,D}} .$$

In the "early Google" approach, the hits are grouped by document; the list of hits for a given index term must include position–needed to evaluate counts of proximity types–as well as all the context information needed to calculate the relevance score of a given document using the scheme outlined previously; for details, the reader is referred to Brin and Page (1998), Section 4.

The language modeling approach does not immediately lend itself to inverted indexing, and storing an n-gram language model for each document becomes prohibitively expensive for large collections of documents. However, the advantage over TF-IDF and other vector space retrieval techniques due to better use of proximity may become very important when sequencing of index terms is critical to good retrieval performance, such as when using sub-word indexing units for being able to deal with OOV words. A good solution for storing a very large set of small n-gram models–one per document–would make this approach very appealing for many problems.

15.6.2 Basic STD Approaches

Today, most systems perform speech retrieval tasks using large-vocabulary continuous speech recognition (LVCSR) to transcribe audio samples, after which the transcripts are indexed at the word or sub-word level, and the index is subsequently searched. Query terms that are not in the lexicon of the speech recognition system, called out-of-vocabulary (OOV) terms, can be retrieved using phonetic queries against phonetic indexes. Pure phonetic decoding systems allow for rapid indexing of audio, but the indexes they produce can suffer from poor accuracy and may not provide a good alternative to word or sub-word indexes. The requirement for high-quality indexes has spawned research in using both word and sub-word information to find in-vocabulary and OOV query terms, and trade-offs between search accuracy and the speed of audio transcription (transcription speeds from several times slower than real time up to 30 times faster than real time). A vocabulary independent, hybrid LVCSR approach to audio indexing and search shows that using phonetic confusions derived from posterior probabilities estimated by a neural network in the retrieval of OOV queries can help in reducing misses in spoken term detection tasks (Ramabhadran *et al.*, 2009). These methods are evaluated on data sets from the NIST 2006 spoken term detection task.

The classical approach in STD consists of converting the speech to word transcripts using LVCSR tools and extending classical information retrieval (IR) techniques to word transcripts. The drawback of such an approach is that search on queries containing out-of-vocabulary (OOV) terms will not return any result. The effects of OOV query terms in spoken data retrieval are discussed in Woodland *et al.* (2000). An approach for solving the OOV issue consists of converting speech to phonetic, syllabic or word-fragment transcripts and representing the query as a sequence of phones, syllables or word-fragments respectively. Popular approaches are based on search on subword decoding (Clements *et al.*, 2002; Mamou *et al.*, 2007; Seide *et al.*, 2004; Siohan and Bacchiani, 2005) or search on the subword representation of word decoding enhanced with phone confusion probabilities and approximate similarity measures for search (Chaudhari and Picheny, 2007). Named entities or foreign language query terms are frequently OOV terms with respect to the underlying ASR system vocabulary. Although these terms might occur infrequently in the index, they are often rich in information and are of great interest in most retrieval tasks.

The main difficulty with retrieving information from spoken data is the low accuracy of the transcription, particularly on terms of interest such as named entities and content words. Generally, the accuracy of a transcript is measured by its word error rate (WER), which is characterized by the number of substitutions, deletions, and insertions with respect to the correct audio transcript. Substitutions and deletions reflect that an occurrence of a term in the speech signal has not been recognized. These misses reduce the recall of the search. Substitutions and insertions reflect that a term that is not part of the speech signal has appeared in the transcript. These misses reduce the precision of the search.

Search recall can be enhanced by expanding the transcript with extra words. These words can be taken from the other alternatives provided within an ASR lattice; these alternatives may have been spoken, but were not the top choice of the ASR. Such an expansion might be expected to correct the substitutions and deletions and consequently improves recall, but at the expense of reduced precision. However, when using an appropriate ranking model, it has been found that both recall and precision can be improved when searching over lattices instead of considering only the 1-best path word transcript (Mamou *et al.*, 2008). The use of lattice-based indexing in search is generally used when the query terms are all in the vocabulary of the ASR system.

In word transcripts, OOV terms are deleted or substituted; therefore, the usage of word-fragment and phonetic transcripts for locating OOV query terms is desirable. A possible combination of word and phonetic search was presented by Mamou *et al.* (2007) in the context of

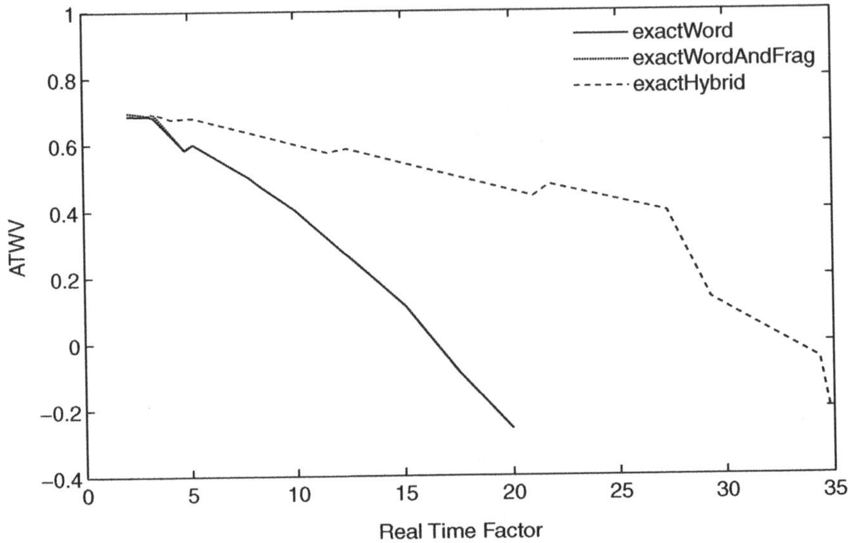

Figure 15.2 Effect of indexing speed on ATWV for a STD task

spoken term detection with fuzzy phonetic search extending Lucene,[3] an Apache open source search library written in Java, for indexing and search (Ramabhadran *et al.*, 2009).

The performance of a spoken term detection system is measured using DET curves that plot the trade-off between false alarms (FAs) and misses. This NIST STD 2006 evaluation used the Actual Term Weighted Value (ATWV) metric that allows one to weight false alarms and misses per the needs of the task at hand (NIST, 2006). Figure 15.2 illustrates the effect of indexing speed on ATWV on the NIST STD 2006 Dev06 data set using 1107 query terms. As the speed of indexing is increased to many times faster than real time (by introducing lossy approximations into the ASR process), the ASR word error rate increases, which in turn decreases the ATWV measure. In this case, it can be seen that the use of word fragments yields less loss in accuracy on OOV queries thus making the hybrid word and word fragment search better than the basic word search. The primary advantage of using a hybrid decoding scheme over a separate word and fragment based decoding scheme is the speed of transforming the audio into indexable units. The dashed line in the figure illustrates that when using a hybrid setup, the same performance can be achieved at speeds twice as fast.

15.6.3 Using Sub-word Units

Words are the most natural and most common units used for ASR and retrieval. However certain limitations of word based systems have forced many researchers to investigate sub-word units, both for recognition and retrieval. Although very large vocabulary ASR systems are becoming more common, typically the vocabulary is limited for practical reasons, as well as due to limited amount of training data. Since query words are chosen to be discriminative,

[3] http://lucene.apache.org/

they tend to be low frequency words. This means that a typical query word is likely to be either an OOV word or a word for which the language model probability has not been well estimated due to data sparseness. Morphologically rich languages pose related challenges for ASR systems. For agglutinative languages such as Finnish and Turkish, it has been shown that sub-word based language models yield better accuracies than word-based language models. In addition, sub-words obtained by morphological analysis or simply by stemming improve retrieval performance.

A wide range of sub-word units for language modeling and retrieval have been proposed, including linguistically motivated units such as phones, syllables and morphemes, as well as data-driven units called multigrams, particles and morphs. For retrieval, indexing fixed length sequences of these sub-word units (typically phones) has also been proposed.

The smallest typical linguistic units are phonetic. These are the counterpart of using letters in text retrieval. Letters or *graphemes* have also been proposed as sub-word units for speech retrieval. Although using phones completely solves the OOV problem, the performance of phone recognition is inferior to word recognition, even when the OOV rates are very high. This can be explained by the short acoustic duration of these units as well as by poor language model predictability. Syllables have been proposed since they are considered to be stable acoustically, but they still yield poor language models. Morphemes, being the smallest meaningful units, provide better language modeling, but can be hard to distinguish acoustically. An alternative which proved successful in agglutinative languages groups all the suffixes in a word together to yield a stem-ending decomposition of a word. Stem-endings result in acceptable OOV rates while keeping acoustically long and distinguishable segments.

Linguistically motivated units require knowledge about specific languages and may be costly to extract, especially in the case of morphological analysis. Data driven units are derived by utilizing statistical and information theoretic principles. Phone *multigrams* (Ng, 2000) are nonoverlapping, variable-length, phone subsequences with some predefined maximum length. These are found using an unsupervised iterative algorithm maximizing the likelihood of the training data under the multigram language models. Similarly, *particles* (Logan *et al.*, 2005) are selected in a greedy fashion so as to maximize the leave-one-out likelihood of a bigram language model. Statistical *morphs* (Turunen and Kurimo, 2007) are based on the Minimum Description Length (MDL) principle, which means that in addition to the corpus representation given by the data likelihood, the lexicon representation is also taken into account.

15.6.3.1 Sub-word Units for Recognition, Indexing and Retrieval

Depending on the structure of the language, the amount of OOV words, and language model mismatches, ASR systems based on sub-word units may improve the recognition accuracy. In addition to improving ASR performance by decreasing or eliminating OOVs, in certain cases sub-word units can also be used solely at the indexing and search stage. Even when there is no improvement in accuracy, the additional information provided by the sub-word units is often beneficial for retrieval. In fact, in those cases where word-based ASR is more accurate than sub-word based ASR, converting the output of word based ASR into sub-words improves the retrieval performance on OOV terms. This technique was shown to be effective for phone based indexing (Logan *et al.*, 2005), where the phone index is obtained by converting the words in the lattice into phone sequences. At retrieval time, when an OOV query is encountered, the query is converted into a phone sequence and the phone index is used for retrieval. The conversion is performed using a grapheme-to-phoneme mapping module typically found in text-to-speech systems. This step can be bypassed by using graphemes as the sub-word units. The ASR system substitutes OOV words with similar sounding words, which means that the phonetic sequence corresponding to the query may be present in the phone lattice used for indexing. In languages where homophones (words that sound the same but are written differently) or homophonic word sequences (as in the classical example: recognize speech versus wreck a nice beach) are common, using phonetic units in retrieval makes it possible to retrieve OOV words.

Using sub-words for indexing requires efficient methods for indexing and retrieving sequences. Proposed methods range from indexing fixed-length subsequences such as triphones (Dharanipragada and Roukos, 2002) to full indexing of lattices represented as weighted automata (Allauzen *et al.*, 2004).

15.6.4 Using Lattices

15.6.4.1 Lattice Indexing Approaches: CN, PSPL, WFST

As highlighted in the previous section, position information is taken into account when assigning relevance score to a given document. In the spoken document case however, we are faced with a dilemma. On one hand, using 1-best ASR output as the transcription to be indexed is suboptimal due to high WER, which is likely to lead to low recall–query terms that were in fact spoken are wrongly recognized and thus not retrieved. On the other hand, ASR lattices (Fig. 15.1) do have much better WER – Chelba *et al.* (2007) report 1-best WER of 55% whereas the lattice WER was 30% – but the position information is not readily available: it is easy to evaluate whether two words are adjacent, but questions about the distance in number of links between the occurrences of two query words in the lattice are hard to answer.

To simplify the discussion let us consider that a text-document hit for some word consists of (document id, position) – a pair of integers identifying the document and the position of the index term in the document, respectively. For speech content, the occurrence of a word in the lattice is uncertain and so is the position at which it occurs. However, the ASR lattice does contain the information needed to evaluate proximity information, since on a given path through the lattice we can easily assign a position index to each link/word. Each path occurs with some posterior probability, easily computable from the lattice, so in principle one could index *soft-hits* which specify the (document id, position, posterior probability) for each word in the lattice. A simple dynamic programming algorithm which is a variation on the standard forward-backward algorithm can be employed for performing this computation. The computation for the backward pass stays unchanged, whereas during the forward pass one needs to split the forward probability α_n arriving at a given node n according to the length l of the partial paths that start at the start node of the lattice and end at node n. For details on the algorithm and the resulting position specific posterior probability lattices (PSPL, see Figure 15.3) the reader is referred to Chelba *et al.* (2007).

Soft-indexing for speech content could easily use other representations of the ASR lattices such as confusion networks (CN, see Fig. 15.4) developed by Mangu *et al.* (2000), where lattice links are approximately binned based on the time span of the link. Both approaches result in approximate word proximity and adjacency representations of the original lattice but have the advantage of compressing it. The PSPL representation guarantees that all n-grams present in the original lattice (with arbitrarily large n as allowed by the lattice) will also be present in the PSPL lattice; it is unclear whether this is true for the CN. Non emitting ϵ arcs

0	1	2	3	4	5	6	7
oh 1.0	**yeah** .65	**what** .46	**kind** .27	dog .26	EOS .34	**EOS** .44	EOS .16
—	oh .35	yeah .35	what .27	**of** .23	**dog** .29	dog .09	—
	—	because .06	kinda .19	kind .16	dogs .13	dogs .06	
		okay .05	the .06	kinda .11	of .13	—	
		looking .05	my .05	dogs .05	a .03		
		—	dog .05	EOS .05	gone .02		
			... ...	... ...	—		

Figure 15.3 Position-specific posterior probability lattice derived from ASR lattice; similar to a text document, each "soft-token" (list of words with associated probability) occurs at some integer position in the document (Chelba *et al.*, © 2008 IEEE)

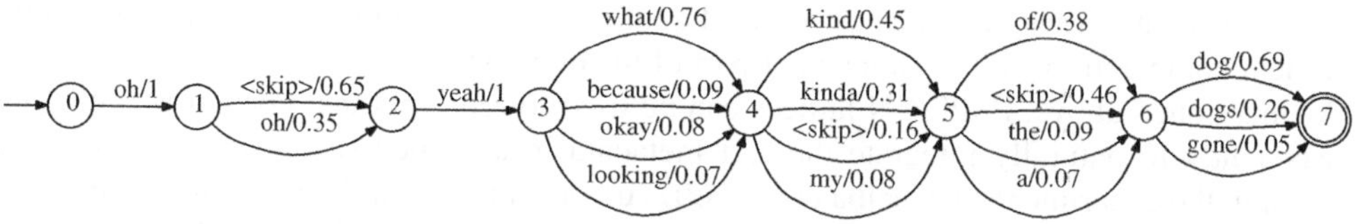

Figure 15.4 Confusion network derived from ASR lattice (Chelba *et al.*, © 2008 IEEE)

may complicate the evaluation of proximity and adjacency features in a CN, in particular when using sub-word units such as phones. It is important to note that the manual transcription for the spoken content, as well as any text metadata available can be represented as a lattice with a single path or equivalently a PSPL/CN with exactly one word per position bin and posterior probability 1.0.

Also noteworthy is that the PSPL/CN representation enables porting of any text information retrieval algorithm to the spoken document retrieval case: instead of simply counting the number of occurrences of various features in a given document, one now has to calculate expected counts according to the posterior probability distribution $P(W|A)$ as approximated by the PSPL/CN.

The effects of various approximations of hit proximity information – PSPL, CN, or other methods – deserve a more careful evaluation and comparison. The experiments in Chelba *et al.* (2007) show a 15–25% gain in MAP when indexing ASR lattices instead of 1-best output; similar results were reported in Siegler (1999) and Saraclar and Sproat (2004).

One aspect specific to soft-indexing – whether 1-best hypothesis with word-level confidence scores, or word alternates with posterior probabilities – is the ability to allow for different precision – recall operating points of the spoken document retrieval system, a feature that is not available when indexing only the 1-best word sequence. Indexing word alternates as opposed to 1-best increases the support of the posterior probability distribution and may be valuable in scenarios where recall is at a premium.

15.6.4.2 Indexing of Weighted Automata

Soft-indexing can also be implemented by representing lattices as weighted automata and building an index of all (or a restricted subset) of the possible substrings (called factors) contained in the automata (Allauzen *et al.*, 2004). Under this general framework, the index itself is a weighted automaton which allows efficient retrieval using string, and even regular expression queries. The procedure consists of turning each automaton into a transducer where the inputs are the original labels (e.g. words) and the outputs are the index labels (e.g. utterance number or position in an archive). Next, these transducers are combined by taking their union. The final transducer is determinized, resulting in optimal search complexity – linear in the length of the query string. The weights in the index transducer correspond to expected counts that are used for ranking.

15.6.4.3 Spoken Document Ranking in the Presence of Text Metadata

Spoken documents rarely contain only speech. Often they have a title, author and creation date. There might also be a text abstract associated with the speech, video or even slides in some standard format. Saving hit context information (type of content where the hit occurred) emerges as a natural way to enhance retrieval quality: e.g. a hit in the title deserves different treatment compared to a hit in some other part of the document.

As mentioned above, PSPL/CN lattices can be used to represent text content as well, and consequently to naturally integrate the text metadata in a unified search framework. As a data point, the experiments in Chelba *et al.* (2007) use a simple linear interpolation scheme for combining text metadata and speech relevance scores. When placing all the weight on metadata segments and ignoring the speech content, there is a significant drop in MAP performance; looking at it the other way, the performance gain obtained by adding speech content instead of only indexing text metadata is 302% relative, despite the fact that the ASR system operates at about 50% WER. This dramatic improvement can be easily explained by the fact that the meta-data constitutes only about 1% of the amount of words in the transcription of speech content, a situation representative for many other scenarios.

In Alberti *et al.* (2009) the authors conclude that large document collection search is truly about the precision of the top 10–20 returned results, and as such, there is seldom a good reason to replace a result in the top-10 that is based on solid keyword hits in text metadata accompanying an audio signal with one whose keyword hits are based on the (usually noisy) ASR transcript. While core ASR technology continues to improve allowing for increasing coverage over the wide variety of spoken content available on the web, scenarios where search is likely to benefit from ASR are those that emphasize recall, e.g. for queries which return none or very few documents when indexing only the text metadata.

15.6.5 Hybrid and Combination Methods

In many scenarios it is necessary to use both word and sub-word units for speech retrieval. The combination can be done at different stages of the process and using different strategies. Hybrid models with both words and sub-words have been utilized with success for different tasks. These models can be structured or flat. In the structured case, the sub-word model – used to model OOV words – is embedded in the word model. In flat models, there is no embedding and the recognition units can be mixed arbitrarily. In both cases, the recognition output contains both words and sub-words.

Word based indexing and sub-word-based indexing have different strengths and weaknesses. Word-based approaches suffer from OOV words and as a result have lower recall. Sub-word-based approaches result in higher recall at the potential expense of lower precision. Hence a combination of both methods yields the best performance. One way to achieve this is combined indexing, resulting in a joint index (Hori *et al.*, 2007; Yu *et al.*, 2005). Other strategies keep the

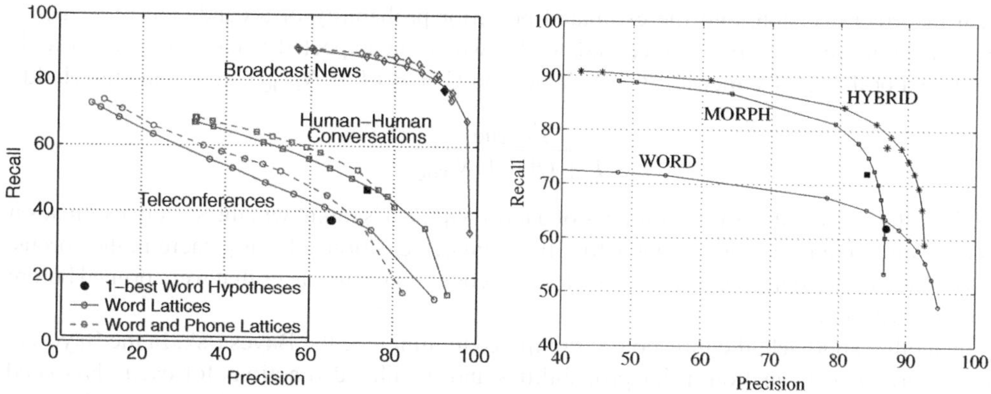

Figure 15.5 Effects of using lattices, sub-word units, and hybrid (cascade) methods on various tasks. On the left is a precision–recall curve on three English tasks with varying ASR accuracies showing the effectiveness of lattices and word/phone hybrids (Saraclar and Sproat, 2004). On the right is a precision–recall curve on Turkish Broadcast News illustrating the use of words and sub-words as well as their combinations (Arisoy *et al.*, 2009; Chelba *et al.*, © 2008 IEEE)

word and sub-word indexes separate and use both for retrieval. When each index has a score associated with each entry, it is possible combine the results returned via score combination. However, this approach requires determining some parameters such as interpolation weights or normalization constants. A simpler and more effective approach is using word-based and sub-word-based retrieval in cascade. Since the word-based retrieval is more accurate, the word index is the default. One cascade alternative (vocabulary cascade) uses the sub-word index only for OOV words, while another (search cascade) uses the sub-word index whenever word retrieval returns no answers. The latter was shown to be slightly better (Saraclar and Sproat, 2004). Figure 15.5 illustrates the effects of using lattices, sub-word units, and hybrid methods on various tasks.

15.6.6 Determining Thresholds

A speech retrieval system using lattices can also return the posterior probability of a query as a detection score. It is possible to obtain precision–recall (PR) or DET curves by changing the parameter controlling the trade-off between precision and recall (or misses and false alarms). Various operating points can be obtained by comparing the detection scores to a threshold. Using the same global threshold for all terms corresponds to moving on the PR or DET curves. In addition to using a global detection threshold (GT), choosing term specific thresholds has been shown to be beneficial. A term-specific thresholding method that optimizes the STD evaluation metric known as the Actual Term-Weighted Value (ATWV) was proposed by Miller *et al.* (2007). A similar approach which trains a neural network mapping various features to the target classes was used in Vergyri *et al.* (2007). More recently, a method for choosing term specific thresholds to minimize the Bayes risk has been proposed by Can and Saraclar (2009).

The STD task scores systems based on a binary decision of which candidate detections to return and which not, and the performance is measured using ATWV. In general, if an evaluation metric assigns marginal benefit B to each correct decision and marginal cost C to each incorrect decision, and the estimated posterior probability of a candidate is p, then a system should return only those candidates for which the expected value $pB - (1 - p)C$ is positive. For the ATWV metric, $B = 1/N_{\text{true}}$ and $C = \beta/(T - N_{\text{true}})$, giving the threshold

$$\frac{\beta N_{\text{true}}}{T + (\beta - 1)N_{\text{true}}}.$$

Since the true number of occurrences of a term $N_{\text{true}}(s)$ is unknown, the system estimates it as the sum of the posterior estimates for all candidate detections of s anywhere in the corpus, scaled by a term-independent learned factor to account for occurrences that were pruned before lattice generation.

In another approach, the threshold is computed to minimize the Bayes risk. In the Bayesian framework, a cost function, prior probabilities and likelihood functions for each class need to be specified. The cost of a miss is taken to be 1 and the cost of a false alarm is left as a free parameter, α. The prior probabilities and the likelihood functions are estimated from the posterior scores of the candidate results for each query. The likelihood functions are found by fitting parametric models to the score distributions (Manmatha *et al.*, 2001).

In Can and Saraclar (2009), the score distributions are modeled by exponential distributions. When the system returns a score, it is not known whether it belongs to the correct or incorrect group, so a mixture of two exponential distributions are used to model the posterior scores returned by the system. The exponential mixture model (EMM) parameters are determined via unsupervised estimation using the Expectation-Maximization (EM) algorithm.

If the posterior score of each candidate is denoted by x, incorrect class by c_0 and correct class by c_1, then

$$p(x) = P(c_0)p(x|c_0) + P(c_1)p(x|c_1)$$

where the incorrect class likelihood $p(x|c_0) = \lambda_0 e^{-\lambda_0 x}$ and correct class likelihood $p(x|c_1) = \lambda_1 e^{-\lambda_1(1-x)}$. The model parameters λ_0, λ_1, $P(c_0)$, $P(c_1)$ are estimated using the EM algorithm given the scores x_i for $i = 1, \ldots, N$. Each iteration consists of first computing $P(c_j|x_i) = P(c_j)p(x_i|c_j)/p(x_i)$ for $j = 0, 1$ and then updating

$$P(c_j) = \frac{1}{N}\sum_i P(c_j|x_i),$$

$$\lambda_0 = \frac{\sum_i P(c_0|x_i)}{\sum_i P(c_0|x_i)x_i},$$

$$\lambda_1 = \frac{\sum_i P(c_1|x_i)}{\sum_i P(c_1|x_i)(1 - x_i)}.$$

After the mixture parameters are estimated, it is assumed that each mixture represents a class and mixture weights correspond to class priors. Then, the Minimum Bayes Risk (MBR) detection threshold for x is given as:

$$\frac{\lambda_1 + \log(\lambda_0/\lambda_1) + \log(P(c_0)/P(c_1)) + \log\alpha}{\lambda_0 + \lambda_1}.$$

Another strategy builds a regression to predict the correctness from a set of features (GT-REMAP). The input consists of features related to the retrieved term and the predictor, for example, a neural network, predicts the correctness which is then converted into a hard decision (YES/NO) using a global threshold. The optimal global threshold was found to be at 0.5, which is an indication that the predicted values are better tuned to the detection task.

15.6.7 Presentation and Browsing

While this chapter has largely focused on the technology required to index, search, and retrieve audio documents, it is important not to overlook the final utility to the end user. For an application to be truly useful, the interface must enable users to search for and browse audio documents quickly and efficiently. In practice, an audio document search can be initiated in much the same way as a text search, i.e. the user enters a set of key words in a search field and is returned a set of putative *hits*. Unfortunately, unlike text, audio is a linear medium which is not easy to browse once the hits are returned. It would be highly inefficient for a user to listen to every hit in order to determine its relevance to his query.

To allow visual browsing, the interface could approximate text-based browsing by providing a snippet of the automatically transcribed speech produced by the ASR system. Even if ASR errors corrupt the transcription, users should be able to determine the relevance of the hit as long as the error rate of the transcription is not excessively high. Human comprehension of errorful transcripts is generally not degraded for lower error rates (i.e. $\leq$15%, Bain *et al.*, 2005), and identification of the general topic is generally possible even for higher error rates. Comprehension can be aided by incorporating ASR word confidence information into the interface, i.e. highlighting confident words and graying out words with low confidence.

Once a relevant document is identified, it is important to provide the user with the capability to easily traverse the audio file in order to listen to the specific regions which are of interest. The ability to speed up or slow down an audio recording during playback can be helpful toward this end. At the very least the browser should allow the user to listen to the audio region immediately surrounding keywords hits.

For long audio files, it is also desirable to segment the file into shorter segments that represent specific topics of discussion within the file (e.g. different stories in a news broadcast). This would allow users to jump to the start of relevant audio segments and not just to the points where specific keywords occur. The task of segmentation of spoken audio files is discussed in more detail in Chapter 11.

As an example interface, Figure 15.6 shows a screen shot of the MIT Lecture Browser, a system designed to allow searching and browsing of academic lectures recorded at MIT (Glass *et al.*, 2007). This browser was designed to provide users with a range of methods to efficiently search for and browse through lectures. The browser enables the user to type a text query and receive a list of hits contained within the indexed lectures. Queries can be constrained by allowing users to specify a topic category from a pull-down menu before searching. An automatically derived segment structure for each lecture is displayed graphically as a series of *Play* buttons along a time line, with segments containing query word hits highlighted in yellow. The individual query word hits within each segment can be displayed together with their surrounding context in the transcript. The user can play the video starting at any displayed word, utterance, segment, or lecture that is shown on the screen. Accompanying the streaming video is a scrolling window displaying the synchronized text transcript. Individual words in

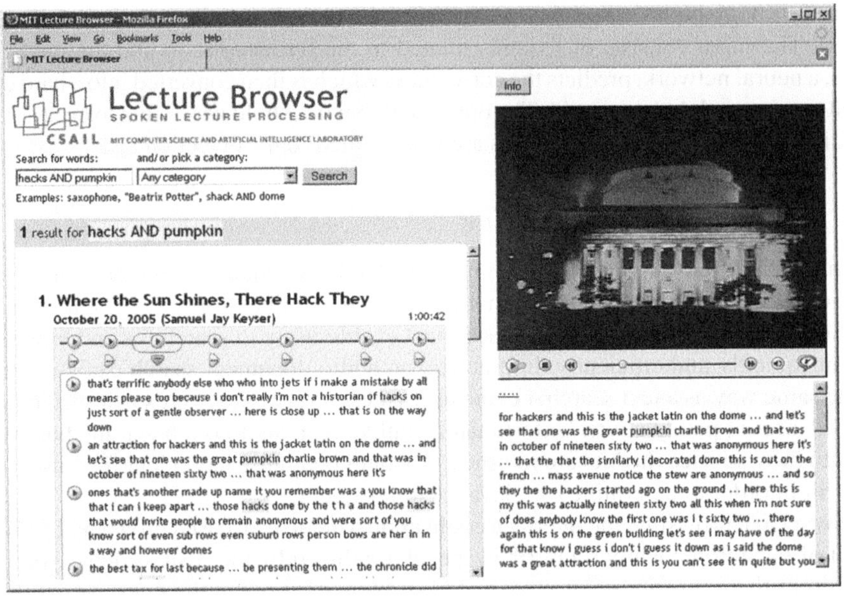

Figure 15.6 A screen shot of the MIT Lecture Browser (Chelba *et al.*, © 2008 IEEE)

the transcript are underlined as they are played, providing easier access for hearing-impaired users. The user can also scroll the text transcript window and begin playing the video starting from any specific word.

15.6.8 Other Previous Work

Having a common task and an evaluation-driven collaborative research effort represents a huge gain for the community, but there are shortcomings to the TREC-SDR framework: the speech recognizers were heavily tuned for the domain, leading to very good ASR performance. In general it is unrealistic to expect error rates in the 10–15% range, especially when decoding speech is mismatched to the training data. It is not uncommon to observe WER values of 30% or higher on data that is not well matched to the training conditions of the ASR system. To mitigate the effect of ASR errors, the work in Siegler (1999), Saraclar and Sproat (2004) and Chelba *et al.* (2007) have demontrated that making use of more than just the 1-best information–N-best lists or ASR lattices–improves retrieval accuracy significantly.

The large-vocabulary ASR systems used in the TREC studies had very low OOV rates, typically below 1%. Since the queries were long and stated in plain English rather than using the keyword search scenario, the query-side OOV (Q-OOV) was very low as well, an unrealistic situation in practice. A study in Woodland *et al.* (2000) evaluates the effect of Q-OOV rate on retrieval performance by reducing the ASR vocabulary size so that the Q-OOV rate comes closer to 15%, a much more realistic figure since search keywords are typically rare words. The study showed severe degradation in MAP performance–50% relative, from 44 to 22.

The ability to effectively deal with OOV query words is an important issue. The most common approach is to represent both the query and the spoken document using sub-word units – typically phones or phone n-grams – and then match sequences of such units. The work in Ng (2000) shows the feasibility of sub-word SDR and advocates for tighter integration between ASR and IR technology. This approach was to index phone n-grams appearing in ASR n-best lists. This work also focused on Broadcast News speech, thus benefiting from good ASR performance. Similar conclusions are drawn by the work in Siegler (1999).

As pointed out in Logan *et al.* (2005), word level indexing and querying is still more accurate and thus more desirable, were it not for the OOV problem. The authors argue in favor of a combination of word and sub-word level indexing. Another problem pointed out by the paper is the abundance of word-spotting false-positives in the sub-word retrieval case, somewhat masked by the MAP measure. Similar approaches are taken by Yu *et al.* (2005); one interesting feature of this work is a two-pass system whereby an approximate match is carried out on the entire set of documents after which the costly detailed phonetic match is carried out on only 15% of the documents in the collection.

Saraclar and Sproat (2004) proposed an approach that builds an inverted index from ASR lattices–word or phone (sub-word) level – by storing the full connectivity information in the lattice; retrieval is performed by looking up strings of units. This approach allows for exact calculation of n-gram expected counts but more general proximity information (distance-k skip n-gram, $k > 0$) is hard to calculate.

For browsing long spoken communications it becomes important to locate the portion that is actually relevant to the query. From the SDR point of view, this can be achieved by segmenting the documents into topics and locating topics. When dealing with spoken communications where these segments are short or when they consist of short utterances, the task becomes that of Spoken Utterance Retrieval (SUR, Saraclar and Sproat 2004). The purpose of SUR is to find all the utterances containing the query. Systems of this type have been developed for a variety of data types including broadcast news (Makhoul *et al.*, 2007), voice mail (Whittaker *et al.*, 2002), teleconferences (Saraclar and Sproat, 2004) and lectures (Hori *et al.*, 2007).

15.7 New Trends

15.7.1 Indexing and Retrieval for very Large Corpora

In a recent report, an international digital library working group called for the creation of systems capable of providing access to an estimated 100 million hours of culturally significant spoken word collections (Goldman *et al.*, 2005). Achieving that vision requires two fundamental advances over the present state of the art: (1) a robust ability to identify spoken words and other useful features in many types of collections, and (2) development of systems that can leverage those features to meet the real needs of real searchers. Recent work on searching collections of broadcast news indicates that these goals are now within the reach of our technology (e.g. Allan 2002).

Research challenges in recognizing a phrase in an audio stream to provide effective audio information retrieval are addressed in the National Gallery of Spoken Word project (NGSW, Hansen *et al.*, 2005). Key component technologies to do audio segmentation, speaker and channel adaptation metadata construction and digital water marking become essential. NGSW was the first large-scale repository of speeches, radio broadcasts, TV broadcasts and public hearings of significant historical content that covered a broad variety of audio recordings, speaking styles and formats. One approach to retrieval of query terms presented uses classic IR techniques, such as document expansion, which identifies other documents closely related to the one in question that contains *trigger* words (using blind relevance feedback), or query expansion to handle missing query terms including OOV terms.

Classical audio mining has focused on keyword spotting techniques that can look for topics or specific phrases in the audio (Hansen *et al.*, 2005). However in digital libraries such as this, advanced audio segmentation, speech recognition model adaptation for acoustic background noise and speaker variability, and information retrieval using natural language processing for text query requests that include document and query expansion play a critical role to make phrase search in unrestricted audio streams more robust.

The MALACH (Multilingual Access to Large Spoken Archives) project developed the technologies needed to facilitate access to large collections of spontaneous speech (Byrne *et al.*, 2004). The project leveraged a unique collection of oral history interviews with survivors of the Holocaust that has been assembled and extensively annotated by the Survivors of the Shoah Visual History Foundation. MALACH fundamentally focused on supporting information access to portions of that collection based on recognition of spontaneous speech. The largest such collection of digitized oral history interviews ever created on a single topic: almost 52 000 interviews in 32 languages; a total of 116,000 hours of audio and video formed the core of this project. Collection of the interviews required an enormous effort by an international team of interviewers, historians, archivists and computer scientists over ten years.

For each of these interviews, human catalogers identified boundaries between topically coherent segments (with a typical duration of 1–5 minutes), prepared three-sentence structured summaries of each segment, and annotated each segment with multiple descriptors from a large thesaurus and the names of all persons mentioned in that segment. The descriptors vary from entities such as locations, personal names and dates (typically at one-year granularity) to broader categories, such as political, psychological and religious concepts. This unprecedented annotation (cataloging) effort represents an enormous investment, accomplished by a team of human catalogers working at a rate of fifteen times real time.

The terms searched for in this collection were obtained from a wide variety of users with interests in anthropology, material and non material culture, linguistics, psychology, human rights advocacy, and law enforcement, among others. Two-thirds of the requests specified named entities (places, persons, and/or events), the remainder asked about more abstract concepts. Many of the ASR errors are due to OOVs, a good number of these are foreign words, names, places and sequences of words uttered in a foreign language (such as, German, Yiddish or Hebrew). This is where one expects the maximum impact to from OOV detection schemes as the speech recognizer cannot be expected to cover all possible search terms. Examples include *The liberation of Buchenwald and Dachau concentration camps*, *Sarah Ehrenhalt-Israel's life*, and *Motivational strengths that sustained survivors through the Holocaust*. While some search requests require access to concepts that are not present in the spoken audio or thesaurus, these can be determined using subsequent NLP techniques that operate on the output of speech recognition.

Figure 15.7 explains how the various component technologies come together in MALACH. Term-based searching, content annotation techniques such as text classification and named entity recognition provide alternative ways to convey information about the data being searched searched (Merlino and Maybury, 1999).

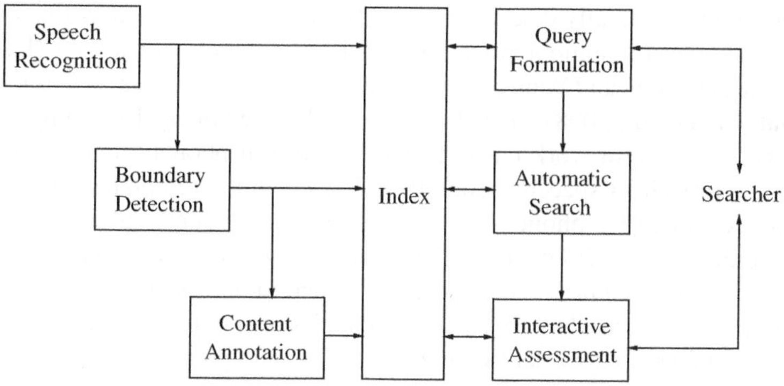

Figure 15.7 The MALACH search system architecture

15.7.2 Query by Example

As has been discussed already, there can be many instances in which standard techniques for document retrieval are not adequate. While phonetic approaches can be employed in cases where word-based retrieval fails, phonetic approaches generally assume that an accurate mapping between words and phones can be obtained. This is only possible if a pronunciation dictionary mapping words to phone strings is available, or if the user of the system is linguistically knowledgeable in the phonetics of the language of interest. In some scenarios, this phonetic knowledge may not be available. In other situations, the resources may not exist to even train a phonetic recognition model for the language or dialect of interest.

To combat the issues raised above, a *query-by-example* approach may be a reasonable alternative. In this case, the user does not provide a query based on written words or phone strings, but instead provides one or more audio examples of the word or phrase of interest. These audio examples could have been found by the user in their data pool through initial browsing, or could potentially be directly spoken by the user. Within query-by-example retrieval the user is, in essence, asking the system to "find me more items like this one". *Query-by-example* search for Out of Vocabulary (OOV) terms (not in the speech recognizer's lexicon) can be considered as an extension to the well-known query expansion method proposed in text-based information retrieval (IR) methods. In classical IR, query expansion is based on expanding the query with additional words using relevance feedback methods, synonyms of query terms, various morphological forms of the query terms and spelling corrections. In *Query-by-example*, the rich representation of the query as the phonetic lattice from the output of an LVCSR system, provides additional information over a textual representation of the query.

Although query-by-example has become a topic of recent interest, it has its roots in the early template-based approaches to speech recognition (Ney, 1984; Rabiner *et al.*, 1978). Before statistical methods became the predominant approach to speech recognition, early speech recognizers often employed dynamic time-warping search mechanisms which relied on direct acoustic similarity measures between stored templates and test data. Unfortunately, acoustic similarity measures can often suffer from mismatches due to speaker, channel or environment, and statistical methods eventually proved superior in their robustness to these variations. Nevertheless, direct acoustic similarity measures were recently used with some success by Park and Glass (2008) who used segmental dynamic time warping, without the use of any statistical speech models, to automatically discover segments within long audio files that contained the same lexical items. Several audio applications, such as sound classification (Zhang and Kuo, 1999), music retrieval (Tsai and Wang, 2004; Tzanetakis *et al.*, 2002), as well as in spoken document retrieval (Chia *et al.*, 2008) have also successfully used query-by-example approaches.

Alternatively, some recent work has examined the use of phonetic features within a template matching approach to speech recognition. For example, templates based on phonetic posteriorgrams generated by phonetic ASR systems were recently used for isolated word recognition (Aradilla *et al.*, 2006) and digit string recognition (Aradilla *et al.*, 2009). The template-matching approach has recently been extended to the task of spoken term detection. A variety of template structures have been explored including phonetic lattice cuts (Parada *et al.*, 2009), phonetic confusion networks (Shen *et al.*, 2009), and phonetic posteriorgrams (Hazen *et al.*, 2009; Zhang and Glass, 2009).

In each case above, instead of modeling the true phonetic string of the query, the templates incorporate information about the phonetic uncertainty of the phonetic recognition process within the template. In fact, in these systems the phonetic recognition itself need not be performed with a well-matched phonetic model making query-by-example retrieval based on cross-dialect or even cross-language phonetic templates possible, albeit with reduced accuracy.

Additional constraints to further refine the retrieved results either during retrieval itself or as a post-filtering method have been proposed recently (Jelinek *et al.*, 1991; Parada *et al.*, 2010). Methods such as, incorporation of phonetic confusability and boosting the probability of a hit based on the number of neighboring hits for the same query, have specifically aimed at either boosting the probability of a hit, while others such as, automated out-of-vocabulary (OOV) tagging and query length normalization reduce the false alarms and misses. Overall, these methods provide up to 20% relative improvement in performance of a query-by-example based spoken term detection system.

A novel application of the query-by-example approach, to serve as a *query expansion* technique that improves performance for textual query retrieval was proposed recently (Parada *et al.*, 2009). Here, a two-pass approach which combines a search using textual queries and a query-by-example searching approach is used. Specifically, given a textual query, relevant instances using a baseline spoken term detection system are retrieved and the highest scoring hit for each query serves as input to the query-by-example system. The second pass serves as a means to identify richer representations of query terms incorporating phonetic confusions. This approach demonstrates how the performance of text-based queries can be enhanced when using a two-pass approach to refine search results from a first pass based on textual queries.

15.7.3 Optimizing Evaluation Performance

One recent trend in spoken term detection has focused on efforts to directly optimize systems to their evaluation metrics. In Wallace *et al.* (2010), a simple linear model is introduced to transform the phone log-posterior probabilities output by a phone classifier to produce log-posterior features that are more suitable for the STD task. Direct maximization of the figure of merit, which is defined as the expected rate of detected search term occurrences over operating regions with a low false alarm rate is performed by training the parameters of this model using a nonlinear gradient descent algorithm. STD evaluation metrics have also been used recently to optimize the weights on the indexing features (terms in a query) to reflect their importance for different contexts in which the query term may occur (Chen *et al.*, 2010). In Lee and

Lee (2010) user feedback is also integrated into a discriminative training learning process in order to optimize retrieval performance. Specifically, the posterior probabilities in a lattice are enhanced to minimize a loss function that boosts the weight of the correctly retrieved answer over the competing incorrect ones as specified via user feedback obtained from the initial set of retrieved results.

15.7.4 Multilingual Speech Retrieval

Multilingual speech retrieval has also received increased interest recently, specifically, in searching through multilingual lectures and in enhancing retrieval through incorporation of translated corpora (foreign language to English) in projects such as GALE. In an open-ended distillation task such as GALE, summarization techniques such as, Maximum Marginal Relevance (MMR) which reflects the similarity between the given query term and the unit (document, utterance or phrase) being retrieved, and Support Vector Machines (SVMs) have been used for STD (Toth *et al.*, 2010). It was also demonstrated here that the well-known text summarization metric, ROUGE can be used to evaluate distillation systems, particularly to measure STD on ASR generated portions of the corpora which tend to be noisy and introduce robustness into distillation systems.

15.8 Discussion and Conclusions

In this chapter we have examined approaches to spoken document processing for retrieval and browsing. While there is a great deal of similarity between spoken document retrieval and text retrieval, this chapter has highlighted the unique and challenging aspects of speech retrieval that make it different, and in many ways more difficult, than text retrieval.

SDR poses new challenges for the core ASR technology, in particular for large and nonhomogeneous document collections where training an ASR system to narrow domains, such as broadcast news, is not a scalable approach; universal ASR technology that is able to perform robustly over many domains is desirable in this context, though not yet a technical reality. Thus current approaches to SDR often put a focus on mitigating today's ASR limitations by a variety of means.

To compensate for ASR errors, soft-indexing provides better retrieval performance than using the 1-best ASR output, particularly in scenarios with high word error rates. In such cases the reliability of 1-best document representation is highly suspect, but by taking into account the confidence of the ASR system in its output, as well as the possible alternatives, the ASR lattice better represents the document content. Soft hits also allow the precision–recall operating point to be adjusted to the needs of a given application or user.

Next, a variety of methods for handling the OOV word problem using subword units have demonstrated improved retrieval performance, in particular when they are used in conjunction with existing word-based methods. These remain active areas of research, and new techniques will hopefully continue to surface.

Finally, though system developers often focus on the technical issues of performing accurate search and retrieval, it is vital not to overlook the importance of the user interface. Audio is not an easy medium to browse efficiently and techniques for converting information contained in audio files into visual representations are desirable. Only through a careful integration of speech search technology with user-friendly visualization tools and interface design will end-to-end systems actually allow users to efficiently search for, retrieve and browse audio content.

References

Alberti C, Bacchiani M, Chelba ABC, Drofa A, Liao H, Moreno P, Power T, Sahuguet A, Shugrina M and Siohan O 2009 An audio indexing system for election video material *Proceedings of ICASSP*, pp 4873–4876.

Allauzen C, Mohri M and Saraclar M 2004 General indexation of weighted automata - application to spoken utterance retrieval *Proceedings of HLT-NAACL 2004 Workshop on Interdiciplinary Approaches to Speech Indexing and Retrieval*.

Allan J (ed.) 2002 *Topic Detection and Tracking: Event-based Information Organization*. Kluwer Academic Publishers, Boston.

Aradilla G, Bourlard H and Magimai-Doss M 2009 Posterior features applied to speech recognition tasks with user-defined vocabulary *Proceedings of ICASSP*. Taipei, Taiwan.

Aradilla G, Vepa J and Bourlard H 2006 Using posterior-based features in template matching for speech recognition *Proceedings of Interspeech*. Pittsburgh, PA, USA.

Aran O, Ari I, Akarun L, Dikici E, Parlak S, Saraclar M, Campr P and Hruz M 2008 Speech and sliding text aided sign retrieval from hearing impaired sign news videos. *Journal on Multimodal User Interfaces* **2**(2), 117–131.

Arisoy E, Can D, Parlak S, Sak H and Saraclar M 2009 Turkish broadcast news transcription and retrieval. *IEEE Transactions on Audio, Speech, and Language Processing* **17**(5), 874–883.

Baeza-Yates R and Ribeiro-Neto B 1999 *Modern Information Retrieval* Addison Wesley New York chapter 2, pp 27–30.

Bain K, Basson S, Faisman A and Kanevsky D 2005 Accessibility, transcription and access everywhere. *IBM Systems Journal* **44**(3), 589–603.

Bazzi I 2002 *Modelling Out-of-Vocabulary Words for Robust Speech Recognition* PhD thesis Massachusetts Institute of Technology.

Brin S and Page L 1998 The anatomy of a large-scale hypertextual Web search engine. *Computer Networks and ISDN Systems* **30**(1–7), 107–117.

Brown M, Foote J, Jones G, Jones K and Young S 1996 Open-vocabulary speech indexing for voice and video mail retrieval *Proceedings of ACM Multimedia*, pp 307–316.

Byrne W, Doermann D, Franz M, Gustman S, Hajic J, Oard D, Picheny M, Psutka J, Ramabhadran B, Soergel D and Ward TWJZ 2004 Automatic recognition of spontaneous speech for access to multilingual oral history archives *IEEE Transactions on Speech and Audio*, vol. 12, pp 420–435.

Can D and Saraclar M 2009 Score distribution based term specific thresholding for spoken term detection *Proceedings of North American Chapter of the Association for Computational Linguistics - Human Language Technologies Conference (NAACL-HLT)*.

Chaudhari UV and Picheny M 2007 Improvements in phone based audio search via constrained match with high order confusion estimates *Proceedings of ASRU*.

Chelba C, Hazen T and Saraçlar M 2008 Retrieval and browsing of spoken content. *IEEE Signal Processing Magazine* **25**(3), 39–49.

Chelba C, Silva J and Acero A 2007 Soft indexing of speech content for search in spoken documents. *Computer Speech and Language* **21**(3), 458–478.

Chen YH, Chou CC, Lee HY and Lee LS 2010 An initial attempt to improve spoken term detection by learning optimal weights for different indexing features *Proceedings of ICASSP*.

Chia TK, Sim KC, Li H and Ng HT 2008 A lattice-based approach to query-by-example spoken document retrieval *Proceedings of SIGIR*, pp 363–370. ACM, New York, NY, USA.

Clements M, Robertson S and Miller MS 2002 Phonetic searching applied to on-line distance learning modules *Proceedings of IEEE Digital Signal Processing Workshop*.

Dharanipragada S and Roukos S 2002 A multistage algorithm for spotting new words in speech. *IEEE Trans. on Speech and Audio Processing* **10**(8), 542–550.

Garofolo J, Auzanne G and Voorhees E 2000 The TREC spoken document retrieval track: A success story *Proceedings of the Recherche d'Informations Assiste par Ordinateur: Content Based Multimedia Information Access Conference*.

Glass J, Hazen T, Cyphers S, Malioutov I, Huynh D and Barzilay R 2007 Recent progress in the MIT spoken lecture processing project *Proceedings of Interspeech*, pp 2553–2556.

Goldman J, Renals S, Bird S, de Jong F, Federico M, Fleischhauer C, Kornbluh M, Lamel L, Oard DW, Stewart C and Wright R 2005 Accessing the spoken word. *International Journal on Digital Libraries* **5**, 287–298.

Hansen J, Huang R, Zhou B, Seadle M, Deller J, Gurijala A, Kurimo M and Angkititrakul P 2005 SpeechFind: Advances in spoken document retrieval for a national gallery of the spoken word. *IEEE Trans. on Speech and Audio Processing* **13**(5), 712–730.

Hazen T, Shen W and White C 2009 Query-by-example spoken term detection using phonetic posteriogram templates *Proceedings of the IEEE Workshop on Automatic Speech Recognition and Understanding*. Merano, Italy.

Hetherington I 1995 *A Characterization of the Problem of New, Out-Of-Vocabulary Words in Continuous-Speech Recognition and Understanding* PhD Thesis Massachusetts Institute of Technology.

Hori T, Hetherington I, Hazen T and Glass J 2007 Open-vocabulary spoken utterance retrieval using confusion networks *Proc. ICASSP*, pp 73–76.

James D 1995 *The application of classical information retrieval techniques to spoken documents* PhD Thesis University of Cambridge, Downing College.

Jelinek F, Merialdo B, Roukos S and Strauss M 1991 A dynamic language model for speech recognition *Proceedings of HLT*.

Lee HY and Lee LS 2010 Integrating recognition and retrieval with user feedback: a new framework for spoken term detection *Proceedings of ICASSP*.

Lewis M (ed.) 2009 *Ethnologue: Languages of the world* sixteenth edition edn. SIL International, Dallas, TX, USA.

Logan B, Van Thong JM and Moreno P 2005 Approaches to reduce the effects of OOV queries on indexed spoken audio. *IEEE Trans. on Multimedia* **7**(5), 899–906.

Makhoul J, Kubala F, Leek T, Liu D, Nguyen L, Schwartz R and Srivastave A 2007 Speech and language technologies for audio indexing and retrieval. *Proceedings of the IEEE* **88**(8), 1338–1353.

Mamou J, Ramabhadran B and Siohan O 2007 Vocabulary independent spoken term detection *Proceedings of ACM SIGIR*.

Mamou J, Ramabhadran B and Siohan O 2008 Phonetic query expansion for spoken term detection *Proceedings of Interspeech*.

Mangu L, Brill E and Stolcke A 2000 Finding consensus in speech recognition: Word error minimization and other applications of confusion networks. *Computer Speech and Language* **14**(4), 373–400.

Manmatha R, Rath T and Feng F 2001 Modeling score distributions for combining the outputs of search engines *Proceedings of ACM SIGIR*. New York, NY, USA.

Merlino A and Maybury M 1999 An empirical study of the optimal presentation of multimedia summaries of broadcast news In *Automated Text Summarization* (ed. Mani I and Maybury M).

Miller DRH, Kleber M, Kao C, Kimball O, Colthurst T, Lowe S, Schwartz R and Gish H 2007 Rapid and accurate spoken term detection *Proceedings of Interspeech*.

Ney H 1984 The use of a one-stage dynamic programming algorithm for connected word recognition. *IEEE Transactions on Acoustics, Speech and Signal Processing* **32**(2), 263–271.

Ng K 2000 *Subword-based approaches for spoken document retrieval* PhD Thesis Massachusetts Institute of Technology.

NIST 2006 The spoken term detection (STD) 2006 evaluation plan.

Oard DW, Demner-Fushman D, Hajic J, Ramabhadran B, Gustman S, Byrne WJ, Soergel D, Dorr B, Resnik P and Picheny M 2006 Cross-language access to recorded speech in the malach project *Text, Speech and Dialogue, Lecture Notes in Computer Science*, vol. 2448/2006, pp 197–212.

Oard DW, Soergel D, Doermann D, Huang X, Murray GC, Wang J, Ramabhadran B, Franz M, Gustman S, Mayfield J, Kharevych L and Strassel S 2004 Building an information retrieval test collection for spontaneous conversational speech *Proceedings of ACM SIGIR*, pp 41–48.

Parada C, Sethy A and Ramabhadran B 2009 Query-by-example spoken term detection for OOV terms *Proceedings of the IEEE Workshop on Automatic Speech Recognition and Understanding*. Merano, Italy.

Parada C, Sethy A and Ramabhadran B 2010 Balancing false alarms and hits in spoken term detection *Proceedings of ICASSP*.

Park A and Glass J 2008 Unsupervised pattern discovery in speech. *IEEE Transactions on Audio, Speech, and Language Processing* **16**(1), 186–197.

Ponte JM and Croft WB 1998 A language modeling approach to information retrieval *Research and Development in Information Retrieval*, pp 275–281.

Rabiner L, Rosenberg A and S.Levinson 1978 Considerations in dynamic time warping algorithms for discrete word recognition. *IEEE Transactions on Acoustics, Speech and Signal Processing* **26**(6), 575–582.

Ramabhadran B, Sethy A, Mamou J, Kingsbury B and Chaudhari U 2009 Fast decoding for open vocabulary spoken term detection *Proceedings of NAACL-HLT*, pp 277–280. Association for Computational Linguistics, Morristown, NJ, USA.

Saraclar M and Sproat R 2004 Lattice-based search for spoken utterance retrieval *Proceedings of HLT-NAACL*, pp 129–136.

Seide F, Yu P, Ma C and Chang E 2004 Vocabulary-independent search in spontaneous speech *Proceedings of ICASSP*.

Shen W, White C and Hazen T 2009 A comparison of query-by-example methods for spoken term detection *Proceedings of Interspeech*. Brighton, England.

Siegler M 1999 *Integration of continuous speech recognition and information retrieval for mutually optimal performance* PhD Thesis Carnegie Mellon University.

Siohan O and Bacchiani M 2005 Fast vocabulary independent audio search using path based graph indexing *Proceedings of Interspeech*.

Toth B, Hakkani-Tur D and Yaman S 2010 Summarization and learning based approaches to information distillation *Proceedings of ICASSP*.

Tsai WH and Wang HM 2004 A query-by-example framework to retrieval music documents by singer *Proceedings of the IEEE International Conference on Multimedia and Expo (ICME)*, pp 1863–1866.

Turunen V and Kurimo M 2007 Indexing confusion networks for morph-based spoken document retrieval *Proceedings of ACM SIGIR*.

Tzanetakis G, Ermolinskiy A and Cook P 2002 Pitch histograms in audio and symbolic music information retrieval *Proceedings of the 3rd International Conference on Music Information Retrieval (ISMIR)*, pp 31–38.

Van Thong VM, Moreno P, Logan B, Fidler B, Maffey K and Moores M 2002 SpeechBot: An experimental speech-based search engine for multimedia content on the web. *IEEE Trans. on Multimedia* **4**(1), 88–96.

Vergyri D, Shafran I, Stolcke A, Gadde R, Akbacak M, Roark B and Wang W 2007 The SRI/OGI 2006 Spoken Term Detection System *Proceedings of Interspeech*, pp 2393–2396.

Wallace R, Vogt RJ, Baker BJ and Sridharan S 2010 Optimising figure of merit for phonetic spoken term detection *Proceedings of ICASSP*.

Whittaker S, Hirschberg J, Amento B, Stark L, Bacchiani M, Isenhour P, Stead L, Zamchick G and Rosenberg A 2002 SCANMail: A voicemail interface that makes speech browsable, readable and searchable *Proceedings of SIGCHI Conference on Human Factors in Computing Systems*, pp 275–282.

Woodland P, Johnson S, Jourlin P and Jones K 2000 Effects of out of vocabulary words in spoken document retrieval *Proceedings of ACM SIGIR*, pp 372–374.

Yu P, Chen K, Ma C and Seide F 2005 Vocabulary-independent indexing of spontaneous speech. *IEEE Trans. on Speech and Audio Processing* **13**(5), 635–643.

Zhang T and Kuo CCJ 1999 Hierarchical classification of audio data for archiving and retrieving *Proceedings of ICASSP*, pp 3001–3004. IEEE Computer Society, Washington, DC, USA.

Zhang Y and Glass J 2009 Unsupervised spoken keyword spotting via segmental DTW on Gaussian posteriorgrams *Proceedings of the IEEE Workshop on Automatic Speech Recognition and Understanding*. Merano, Italy.

Index

Spoken Language Understanding: Systems for Extracting Semantic Information from Speech, First Edition.
Edited by Gokhan Tur and Renato De Mori.

Printed and bound by CPI Group (UK) Ltd, Croydon, CR0 4YY
16/09/2026
14963473-0006